THE
CLEVELAND
ORCHESTRA
STORY

THE
CLEVELAND
ORCHESTRA
STORY

"Second to None"

Donald Rosenberg

GRAY & COMPANY, PUBLISHERS
CLEVELAND

Photo credits are located on page 553.

GRAY & COMPANY, PUBLISHERS
1588 E. 40th St.
Cleveland, Ohio 44103
www.grayco.com

Library of Congress Cataloging-in-Publication Data
Rosenberg, Donald.
The Cleveland Orchestra Story / Donald Rosenberg.
Includes bibliographical references and index.
1. Cleveland Orchestra. 2. Music—Ohio—Cleveland—History and criticism.
2. I. Title.
ML200.8.C7 R67 2000
784.2'06'077132—dc21   00-009951

ISBN 1-886228-24-8

Printed in the United States of America
10 9 8 7 6 5 4 3 2 1
First Edition

To my loving domestic symphony—
Kathy, Seth, and Emily

Contents

Introduction

*J*anuary 8, 2000. Few dates in the life of the Cleveland Orchestra can have aroused as much anticipation and anxiety. It was on this unseasonably mild, clear night that Severance Hall, the orchestra's 69-year-old home in University Circle, reopened after a $36.7 million renovation, restoration, and expansion. Over the previous nine months, the ensemble had performed at the restored Allen Theatre in downtown Cleveland and at Blossom Music Center, its alfresco summer home north of Akron. By the first week of 2000, feelings of hope were running sky high. Severance had long been a beloved destination for thousands of concertgoers, who had shown little concern that amenities were limited or that the modernist stage shell—installed at the behest of George Szell in 1958—had been entirely out of sync with the rest of the concert hall's Art Deco architecture. Audiences in the last four decades of the 20th century revered Severance Hall and its crisp (if unforgiving) acoustics for enabling the Cleveland Orchestra to make music with the refinement, clarity, and precision that had come to define its personality.

Now, with the gala reopening concert at hand, audience members kept their collective fingers crossed as they marveled at the gleaming building's smooth melding of traditional and contemporary elements and awaited the first public sounds from the luxurious new stage, finally a seamless architectural fit with the rest of the auditorium. Listeners around the world have learned that even the most extravagant concert hall construction and renovation projects can end in acoustic disaster. Many Clevelanders, starting with the orchestra's musicians, had been aghast when plans to redo the Severance stage were announced. But as the orchestra and music director Christoph von Dohnányi made their elegant way through a varied and eclectic reopening program, anxiety about the hall diminished with each passing moment. By evening's end, musicians, orchestra staff, and concertgoers knew they could look forward to a new century, and a new millennium, confident that their concert hall's unique qualities had been preserved and even enhanced.

The loving renewal of Severance Hall was accompanied by another remarkable accomplishment. Just as the edifice was reintroduced to the public, the orchestra's board of trustees was preparing to announce, with customary restraint, that its five-year, $100 million "Campaign for the Twenty-First Century" had gone over the top. The orchestra had raised $115.9 million to renovate the hall, increase the endowment (up to a healthy $155 million), and provide operating support. For the city to succeed in such a formidable financial endeavor, even as it reinvented its august concert hall, was a testament to the men and women who cherished their orchestra with a fervor bordering on obsession.

It was also part of a long and remarkable tradition. The orchestra that played its inaugural concert one month to the day after the end of World War I has been blessed with an astonishing level of local support. The devotion emanated first from the industrial giants, enterprising lawyers, and political movers of post–Gilded Age Cleveland; the general public deemed the orchestra an essential element in the region's quality of life but wasn't encouraged to do much more than attend concerts in the early decades. Crucially, financial support was complemented by artistic vision, especially from the conductors who insisted that Cleveland continue to improve standards and increase national and international awareness of its orchestra's artistry. For a symphony orchestra of international stature to have emerged from a midsized, Midwestern industrial city was an extraordinary achievement. Even today, people around the globe continue to marvel at Cleveland's ability to sustain such a jewel.

It could not have happened without an undercurrent of struggle. There would always be conflict, uncertainty, and anxiety involved in the process of nurturing Cleveland's orchestral tradition. Amid the virtually unparalleled musical stimulation of the symphonic repertoire, every major American orchestra has endured traumas of its own in the not-for-profit world that is the glory and the bane of our nation's arts institutions. But not every city views its orchestra as its cultural heart. More than any other institution in town, even the resplendent Cleveland Museum of Art, the Cleveland Orchestra, through its tours, broadcasts, and recordings, has served as the city's domestic and foreign goodwill ambassador. It has been an incalculable source of self-esteem, especially during times when Cleveland has been battered by Rust Belt financial woes, embarrassed by a burning river, and bombarded by stinging jokes.

Clevelanders are hardy folks: they have to be to endure unwarranted condescension and unforgiving winter weather. And they are demanding. The moguls and society matrons who helped found the Cleveland Orchestra—and the conductors they hired—wouldn't settle for less than the best in personnel, programming, or soloists. In this respect, nothing has changed. The musicians who make up the orchestra, the powers that keep the machinery running, and the patrons who remain faithful at the dawn of the 21st century are as uncompromising as ever. Except for a pronounced dip during World War II, when a large number of orchestra members were away in the armed forces—including its conductor, a youthful Erich Leinsdorf, who held the post for the briefest of tenures—the orchestra has experienced uninterrupted artistic growth. While there have been ongoing debates about the orchestra's achievements under its various conductors, the high standards that have made Cleveland a major force in the world of music have been maintained throughout the orchestra's history and can be heard in the large body of recordings the ensemble has made since 1924.

Other books have explored the symphony orchestra largely from an institutional perspective. Howard Shanet's *Philharmonic: A History of New York's Orchestra* is the unsurpassed virtuoso in this respect. Cleveland received less persuasive treatment in Robert C. Marsh's *The Cleveland Orchestra*, a "birthday present" commissioned by the Musical Arts Association in 1967 to mark the ensemble's 50th anniversary. It abandoned history and dissolved into idol worshipping when it arrived at the Szell era. The Cleveland Orchestra deserves a more balanced approach. This book, an independent and unofficial account of the orchestra's history, takes a different route. It aims to weave a sweeping yet detailed narrative of the people and events that have shaped the orchestra, recounting a tale full of both inspiration and intrigue. Rising to the top, and staying there, demands talent, perseverance, and even guile, and all three can be found in the drama that is the story of the Cleveland Orchestra.

And what a cast of characters, notably on the podium: Nikolai Sokoloff, with his imperious manner and penchant for innovative (and controversial) programming; Artur Rodzinski, the gun-toting maestro whose unpredictability was matched by his musical brilliance; Leinsdorf, a promising conductor who found himself in the wrong place at the wrong time; Szell, an orchestral alchemist of commanding ability and impeccable taste, and an intimidating presence; Lorin Maazel, a virtuoso baton technician of towering gifts and often questionable taste; and Dohnányi, a conductor of intellectual integrity and musical imagination whose full legacy has yet to be assessed. These leaders spent their early careers in opera houses as players, coaches, or full-fledged conductors. They learned the inner workings of their craft backstage, in rehearsal rooms, and in the orchestra pit. But like many of their colleagues, they gravitated away from the complexities of operatic production and the politics of singers, stage directors, designers, and managers, and opted for the (supposedly) calmer realm of the symphony orchestra. In most cases, they experienced the greatest satisfaction of their professional lives standing onstage before an ensemble of superbly trained musicians.

One imposing figure of the late 19th and early 20th centuries emphasized the impact such an ensemble could have. It is the symphony orchestra, not opera, that "shows the culture of a community," wrote Theodore Thomas, the late-19th-century dean of American conductors, who had ample experience in both musical endeavors. "The man who does not know Shakespeare is to be pitied; and the man who does not understand Beethoven and has not been under his spell has not half lived his life. The master works of instrumental music are the language of the soul."

Judged by Thomas's—or any other—criteria, culture is thriving in Cleveland. For more than three-quarters of a century, its orchestra has spoken the "language of the soul" with a combination of interpretive insight and technical mastery that is the envy of major cities both at home and abroad. And just as the diverse musicians attracted by its renowned orchestra have brought the world to Cleveland over the decades, the orchestra's recordings, broadcasts, tours, and special events such as the reopening of Severance Hall have taken Cleveland to the world.

THE
CLEVELAND
ORCHESTRA
STORY

– PART ONE –
SHOWING PROMISE
1842–1933

— 1 —

Overtures

In 1842, two of the world's great orchestras came to life. In Austria, the Vienna Philharmonic played its first notes at the city's Imperial Palace on March 28. In Manhattan, nine months later, the New York Philharmonic gave its first perfomance at the Apollo Rooms.

In Cleveland that year, cows still grazed peacefully on downtown's Public Square.

Europe already had a long orchestral heritage. The Dresden State Orchestra had been performing since the early 17th century; the Leipzig Gewandhaus Orchestra since 1781. The comparatively youthful United States now was launching its own rich tradition with the New York Philharmonic.

The small town on the southern shore of Lake Erie, however, was only beginning to show an interest in the arts, fine or otherwise. Cleveland would, in fact, be one of the new nation's last cities—the 17th—to boast of a major orchestra.

Founded in 1796 by Moses Cleaveland and a party from the Connecticut Land Company, Cleveland was in no position to compete with more populous and accessible American cities that had developed their resources to the point where they could nurture artists and artistic institutions. The small metropolis's ruggedly wooded terrain (the source of its nickname, the Forest City), elusive location, and challenging climate conspired to keep its growth on a slow track. Only after the Ohio and Erie Canal was completed in 1832 and roads later began to lead to the area was the city's life transformed through shipping and trade, the creation of jobs, and a steady influx of European immigrants.

By the time Cleveland's permanent orchestra made its debut in December 1918, American orchestras had established themselves, with varying success, in New York (Philharmonic and Symphony), St. Louis, Boston, Chicago, Cincinnati, Pittsburgh, Dallas, Philadelphia, Minneapolis, Seattle, San Francisco, Denver, Houston, Detroit, and Baltimore.

In the decades leading up to Cleveland's orchestral coming of age, music was already providing a way for immigrants drawn by the city's burgeoning industries to maintain their cultural identities far from home. The earliest music-making in Cleveland, aside from church choirs, revolved around amateur singing societies, bands, and small ensembles (two dozen or so players) that today would be called chamber orchestras. One group that had an impact on the town was the Cleveland Grays Band, an ensemble of the military unit known as the Cleveland Grays, whose director brought with him an imposing European pedigree: Balthasar B. Schubert was a nephew of the late Austrian composer Franz Schubert. The younger Schubert evidently was a talented bandsman. In 1840, he formed an 11-member group comprising seven brass, two wind, and two percussion players.

Within a few years, Clevelanders had heard not only band concerts but also occasional performances featuring operatic music. Whether the repertoire was performed with piano or orchestra isn't clear. Most orchestras that appeared in Cleveland during this period were local amateur groups that accompanied choruses or played in the pit for opera productions—many of them heard but not seen. Ensembles that did perform onstage or in ballrooms presented light fare, such as waltzes and overtures.

In 1842, local industry was beginning to flourish. Mills, tanneries, and cheese and flour factories opened their doors. Sandstone quarrying started in Berea. The region welcomed its first shipment of fruit. In the decade that followed, the railroad boom stimulated manufacturing and the mining of iron ore and coal that would be so crucial to the city's future. These industries attracted a multitude of workers, especially German and Irish immigrants who began pouring into Cleveland in 1848. By 1850, the city's population had jumped to 17,034, slightly behind Detroit, Milwaukee, and Chicago, but well behind Cincinnati, whose economic development had brought its population to 115,435.

Of the ethnic groups that left their homelands for better lives, the Germans were to become Cleveland's largest and most influential. They exhibited a rigorous work ethic but also found time to maintain their strong cultural tradition. They established singing societies and instrumental ensembles, including the Germania Orchestra, which performed with choral groups and played for social functions. Among the German arrivals in 1853 was Baptiste Dreher, founder of the Dreher Piano Company. His grandfather, Meinhard, was an organ builder near Ulm who had known Johann Sebastian Bach.

Pianos, mostly by the Boston firm Chickering, were already being sold in Cleveland by S. Brainard's Sons, an instrument dealer and music publishing

house founded by Silas Brainard in 1836. Brainard built a small musical empire, managing Brainard's Opera House (later the Globe Theater) and publishing a monthly journal, *Brainard's Musical World*, before moving to
Chicago in 1889. Along with sheet music for the general public, the firm
supplied musical materials for the local orchestras of the Cleveland Mozart
Society, St. Cecilia Society, Cleveland Musical Society, and Cleveland
Mendelssohn Society, as well as the Germania Orchestra. These ensembles
occasionally played major choral works—Handel's *Messiah*, Rossini's *Stabat
Mater*—and short orchestral pieces, but they mostly served in accompany-
ing capacities.

Opera brought orchestral sounds to local audiences, though most ensembles of the day tended to employ reduced rosters to fit the pit and the
budget. Cleveland began to import opera in 1849, when a troupe known as
the Manvers Operatic Company performed Bellini's *La Sonnambula* and
Donizetti's *Daughter of the Regiment*, works hardly renowned for their use
of the orchestra. As travel to Cleveland became easier and new theaters
opened in the 1850s and 1860s, opera companies from New Orleans, New
York, Boston, and Chicago made their way to the city to present pieces that
were richer from an orchestral point of view, among them Verdi's *Un Ballo
in Maschera*, Weber's *Der Freischütz*, and Gounod's *Faust* (just five years
after its 1859 Paris premiere). These productions raised the sophistication
level of audiences that had been used to hit-and-miss playing by local amateur ensembles.

Another troupe that came to Cleveland, in 1866, was the American Opera
Company, which performed works by Gluck, Delibes, Massenet, and
Wagner (the last three were living at the time) in English with American
singers. The conductor of these productions, Theodore Thomas, would
have a lasting impact on orchestral life in the United States. Thomas had created his own symphony orchestra, the Theodore Thomas Orchestra, which
began touring in 1869, when Cleveland became part of his "great musical
highway," as his wife, Rose, called the orchestra's itinerary through
America's larger cities. After performances in Cleveland in November 1869,
the *Musical World* reported that Thomas's orchestra was "the finest we have
ever heard in the city, and the concerts [were] successful in every way."
Thomas, who would make frequent appearances in Cleveland for the rest
of his life, went on to serve as conductor of the New York Philharmonic
(1877–78 and 1879–91) and as founding conductor of what later would become known as the Chicago Symphony Orchestra.

Local conductors were attempting to give the city's own musicians opportunities to pursue their art, too. Austrian-born Ferdinand Puehringer, a

student of Franz von Suppé, arrived in 1872. He worked with the Germania Orchestra, began a singing and instrumental school, and, in 1881, created the Philharmonic Orchestra. Puehringer's ensemble initially had 30 amateur musicians; professional players eventually joined. Rehearsing at the YMCA building, they made their debut on October 31, 1881, with a program of music by Verdi, Chopin, Brahms, Mendelssohn, and Ole Bull, the extraordinary Norwegian violinist.

In 1873, Alfred Arthur founded the Cleveland Vocal Society. A year before, he had led a series of orchestra concerts—some with as few as 16 players—at Brainard's Piano Rooms, though these performances evidently couldn't approach the quality of the music that Thomas was bringing to the city. "The orchestral numbers at both concerts were wretchedly given," reported *Musical World* in May 1872. "Mr. Arthur either has no control over his orchestra or does not understand his business." He apparently began to understand his business in following years, as he not only developed his orchestra but also imported ensembles from Cincinnati and Boston to collaborate with the Cleveland Vocal Society.

❖   ❖   ❖

By the 1870s, Cleveland was on the verge of major postwar industrial and commercial expansion. Eugene Grasselli, whose company had made chloroform for Union forces, founded the Grasselli Chemical Company. Theodore H. White transported his sewing-machine enterprise from Massachusetts. Shipyards owned by Captain Alva Bradley opened in Cleveland. Perhaps most significantly, an ambitious young entrepreneur named John D. Rockefeller organized the Standard Oil Company, which would make Cleveland the oil capital of the world in little more than a decade. Euclid Avenue, lined with mansions of the city's nouveaux riches, was considered one of the most beautiful streets in the country. The city's population rose to 92,828 (15th largest in the U.S.) in 1870 and 160,146 (12th largest) in 1880.

As Cleveland grew, its residents sought greater artistic stimulation, including a broader range of musical events. Clevelanders had heard soprano Jenny Lind, the "Swedish nightingale," in 1851. The Thomas Orchestra, featuring pianist Anton Rubinstein and violinist Henri Wieniawski, gave a concert in May 1873 introducing "the most supreme organization of musical talent that has ever performed in one evening before a Cleveland audience," according to the *Leader*, a daily newspaper. Recitals followed by violinist Pablo de Sarasate and pianist Hans von Bülow (soloist in the world premiere of Tchaikovsky's First Piano Concerto in Boston during the 1875–76 season). In 1889, 14-year-old Austrian violinist Fritz Kreisler made his Cleveland debut with pianist Moritz Rosenthal.

Audiences also enjoyed opera performances featuring richly colored orchestration (if reduced instrumental forces). Maurice Grau brought the Metropolitan Grand Opera Company to the Euclid Avenue Opera House in 1886, offering Carl Goldmark's *Queen of Sheba*, and Wagner's *Rienzi*, *Lohengrin*, and *Tannhäuser* with "150 performers, an orchestra of fifty-five, a chorus of fifty, and a ballet." The 1890s held a panoply of performances by great singers (Adelina Patti, Nellie Melba). Walter Damrosch presented his opera company and the New York Symphony Orchestra in Wagner's *Lohengrin*, *Siegfried*, and *Tannhäuser* in 1897, the same year that Victor Herbert's operetta, *The Serenade*, received its world premiere at Grays Armory, home of the Cleveland Grays, on Bolivar Road. Grau inaugurated the Metropolitan Opera's long relationship with Cleveland with the 1899 spring tour, which included *The Barber of Seville*, *Carmen*, *La Traviata*, and *Faust* starring Emma Calvé, Marcella Sembrich, and Édouard de Reske.

Before the turn of the century, the city heard a generous sampling of noteworthy orchestral ensembles. The Boston Symphony Orchestra, founded in 1881, came to town in 1886 and 1887 with Wilhelm Gericke. In 1889, the ensemble returned under one of the commanding figures in orchestral history, Arthur Nikisch, who was later described by George Szell as "in the best sense hypnotic and magic . . . You could not extricate yourself from his spell." Cleveland also heard performances led by Anton Seidl, head of German repertoire at the Metropolitan Opera, who had assisted Wagner at the inaugural Bayreuth Festival in Germany in 1876. Seidl provoked an outpouring of American affection for Wagner, especially among women. In Cleveland, Seidl conducted his so-called Wagner Orchestra (actually the Met orchestra) in 1893 and 1897.

Starting in the early 1890s, prominent American orchestras came to Cleveland at the invitation of N. Coe Stewart, a conductor and composer who had guided music curriculum in the city's public schools since 1869. He expanded his reach as director of the Star Course concert series, which presented solo artists and orchestras. His roster included the New York Symphony Orchestra (with Damrosch) and the Pittsburgh Orchestra, then in its infancy under cellist-composer-conductor Victor Herbert.

❀   ❀   ❀

While all of these visitors were making welcome appearances, Cleveland's resident musicians were trying to establish a homegrown orchestral tradition, without much success. The conductorship of the Philharmonic

Orchestra had passed from Puehringer to Müller Neuhoff to Franz X. Arens. In 1888, the post went to Emil Ring, a Czech-born oboist, pianist, composer, and conductor who had arrived in the United States the previous year to play principal oboe in the Boston Symphony under Gericke. Ring, who was born in 1863, would become a key figure in Cleveland's musical community as conductor and teacher. His vast experience made him well suited to conduct the Philharmonic Orchestra, which now had 60 players. Ring expanded the repertoire and the concert schedule, collaborating with the Cleveland Gesangverein, a German chorus, and, in the summer, taking the orchestra to Haltnorth's Gardens, a former beer hall at Woodland and Willson avenues that had thrown off its erstwhile reputation as a den of iniquity. (The *Leader* once reported that "scenes are enacted there every Sabbath that should excite a blaze of indignation in the breast of every respectable citizen.")

By 1893, Ring had honed the Philharmonic Orchestra so impressively that he was chosen to be musical director for the 27th Saengerfest, a national festival of amateur singing societies. Even so, the orchestra couldn't sustain itself, especially after the festival's expenses placed a crushing burden on its guarantors. Although Ring offered to work without pay, the orchestra was doomed. It reorganized in 1894 but finally went out of existence in 1899.

❉   ❉   ❉

The big problem with the local orchestral scene in Cleveland wasn't necessarily lack of talent. Local managers simply could make more money importing an orchestra than organizing one of their own, for they had to pay musicians' salaries and music costs, as well as other expenses. And audiences would rather hear renowned orchestras than a fledgling local ensemble. Still, Clevelanders in the early decades of the 20th century listened hopefully to three local ensembles that set out to give the city a permanent orchestra. The time was ripe for such an enterprise. With industry booming, the population in 1900 had leaped to 381,768, putting Cleveland seventh among U.S. cities.

The first entirely professional ensemble that attempted to put down roots in the city was the Cleveland Symphony Orchestra, which was conceived in part as a new incarnation of the defunct Philharmonic Orchestra. The conductor was Johann Beck, who, with Emil Ring, would become one of Cleveland's most visionary and influential musicians of the period. Born in Cleveland in 1856, Beck pursued part of his education at the Leipzig Conservatory. As composer, conductor, and violinist, he returned home in

1882 in triumph. He formed the Beck String Quartet and conducted numerous American orchestras in his own compositions, and also taught.

The Cleveland Symphony Orchestra, with Ernest Farmer as manager, played its first concert on January 16, 1900, at Grays Armory. Beck conducted Beethoven's *Leonore* Overture No. 3, the second and fourth movements of Beethoven's Fourth Symphony, Borodin's *In the Steppes of Central Asia*, arias and songs by Mozart and Schubert, an excerpt from Wagner's *Lohengrin*, and Beck's overture, *Lara*, based on the poem by Lord Byron. Among the soloists were violinist Sol Marcosson, the orchestra's concertmaster, and cellist Elsa Ruegger. *Cleveland Town Topics*, a weekly journal devoted to the arts and social events, was impressed: "Beck produced unexpectedly good results with a new body of players and demonstrated himself to be a musician of scholarly endowment, a conductor of authority, judgment, progressiveness and spirit, and a composer of high ability." The orchestra of 50 musicians played three concerts in its first season.

The second season began on a high note on November 5, 1900, with a program that included Beethoven's First Symphony and excerpts from Mendelssohn's incidental music to *A Midsummer Night's Dream*. Once again, *Town Topics* chimed in with encouraging words, stating that the "experimental Cleveland Symphony Orchestra season of last year has given way to the substantial and assured one of this season." *The Plain Dealer*, the Cleveland newspaper published since 1842, proclaimed, "success had come and come to stay." Both views were premature, though the season's remaining four concerts must have proved intriguing. The soloists included violinist Fritz Kreisler (in the Bruch G minor Concerto) and pianist Ossip Gabrilowitsch (in the Schumann Piano Concerto). Beck programmed more of his own music, as well as works by colleagues from Cleveland and Pittsburgh. When pianists were needed to accompany, Beck turned to two prominent local musicians—James H. Rogers, a composer who later would serve as longtime music critic of *The Plain Dealer*, and Adella Prentiss, a fledgling impresario whose true impact on Cleveland's musical life was still decades away.

Unfortunately, the audacious Farmer tried to run the Cleveland Symphony Orchestra entirely by himself, and his management skills were questionable. Believing that ticket sales would take care of funding, he didn't seek donations from the public, including the wealthiest audience members, until it was too late. Rather than admit he had blundered, Farmer lashed out at the city's inability to support its own, saying that Cleveland's musical community reminded him "of the story of a Mississippi river steamboat that had a bigger whistle than a boiler. When the whistle blew they had to stop the boat."

Aside from his mishandling of money matters, Farmer was inept at scheduling. When he noticed that the fourth concert of his orchestra's second season, on February 5, 1901, would compete with local performances the same week by Eduard Strauss and his Viennese orchestra and by soprano Marcella Sembrich, he only changed the program, convincing Beck to add Johann Strauss II's *Tales from the Vienna Woods*. But ticket sales went nowhere for the Cleveland Symphony Orchestra concert, and Farmer was forced to cancel. The situation drew protests from both Farmer and local journalists. The manager fumed that "a permanent local orchestra has to postpone its concert (because it is dependent on public support) so that more showy and transient concerts may whistle merrily and successfully." As *Town Topics* observed, "knocking [down] has always been a favorite diversion in Cleveland musical circles. An undercurrent of it has existed contemporaneously with the establishment of the local orchestra."

True as these statements may have been, they did nothing to help the new orchestra. Farmer attempted to reschedule the February program for the following month, to virtually no response from the public. Lack of confidence in the local product and in Farmer's business methods led to bankruptcy in the spring of 1901, though the orchestra showed its appreciation to the manager by offering a benefit concert on May 28, 1901, to help him reduce his debts.

❁   ❁   ❁

Cleveland was once again without a local orchestra. Soon to come to the rescue was Conrad "Coonie" Mizer, a Cleveland tailor and music lover who had instituted seasons of Sunday afternoon summer band concerts in public parks in 1898 with funds from the city. Now he envisioned a similar scenario to bring the Cleveland Symphony Orchestra back to life. He called on some of the town's heaviest political and industrial hitters—including future Cleveland mayor and U.S. secretary of war Newton D. Baker and chemical magnate Eugene Grasselli—to provide support for an orchestra that would play Sunday afternoon concerts at Grays Armory. Beck and Ring were invited to alternate as conductors.

The new institution was dubbed the Cleveland Grand Orchestra, though it was advertised for the 1904–05 season as the Cleveland Orchestra, probably the first time a local ensemble used this name. The orchestra comprised 45 players (all men, according to *Town Topics*) who were paid the paltry sum of $30 each for the entire season. Ticket prices were low, too: most cost 10, 15, or 25 cents. The orchestra made its debut on January 4, 1903, when pianist William Sherwood performed Liszt's E-flat major Piano Concerto on a program that included Weber's *Euryanthe* overture, Borodin's *In the Steppes of Central Asia*, an excerpt from Bizet's *Carmen*, and the "Wedding March" from Mendelssohn's *A Midsummer Night's Dream*. Throughout their dual tenures with the orchestra, Beck and Ring paid generous attention to local soloists and composers, and they led standard classical fare.

The orchestra encountered the problem faced by every local symphonic organization—it was compared, fairly or not, with visiting orchestras, which were now being brought to town by concert manager Adella Prentiss in her highly successful Symphony Orchestra Concerts series. The Cleveland Grand Orchestra came to be regarded as a "pop orchestra," or, by implication, a lowbrow ensemble.

Many, though, considered its existence a positive sign. Prentiss was enthusiastic about the new venture, telling Mizer that he was "not only a 'pop' but a 'prop' because he is giving the people a taste of orchestral music which will bring them to a better plane of musical appreciation." *Town Topics* noted in 1905 that "if these same guarantors and lovers of music would rally and come to the aid of Cleveland musical talent, the day might not be so far distant when we could hope to compare with other symphony orchestras. Pittsburgh capitalists have made it possible for the famous Pittsburgh Orchestra to live and thrive. New York, Boston, Chicago, and Cincinnati have done the same, and why, with all the wealth in this city, we should be a back number in the greatest of arts has always been a mystery. Can it be a lack of civic pride?"

It could have been, but it is more likely that the Cleveland Grand Orchestra simply was not good enough to convince citizens that they should support the local product over fine visiting orchestras. Tensions within the orchestra itself also seemed to be taking a toll on the musicians, who had difficulty coming to terms with two leaders with highly different personalities: Beck was perceived as a much more authoritative conductor than Ring. In 1910, the orchestra changed its name to the Cleveland Symphony Orchestra and performed for two more years under Beck and Ring. Then waning financial support and attendance, as well as brickbats from the press, darkened the orchestra's horizon. The biggest blow came from Wilson G. Smith, a local composer and pianist who had become the music critic of the *Cleveland Press,* which would cover the orchestra's high-profile successor for decades. Smith blamed the ensemble's erratic quality on "inadequate rehearsals, and absence from the ranks of some of our best orchestra talent, and the fact that two directors of divergent temperament and qualifications have been in control." The solution: better musicians and one charismatic conductor who could attract financial support and raise the orchestra's standing in the community. Adella Prentiss Hughes (she had married vocal instructor Felix Hughes in 1904) offered a typically forthright reason for the waning popularity of the Cleveland Symphony Orchestra in 1912: "The Sunday pops had begun to be monotonous."

❊   ❊   ❊

The conductor chosen to ward off the monotony was Christiaan Timmner, former concertmaster of the Concertgebouw Orchestra of Amsterdam under Willem Mengelberg and most recently concertmaster of the St. Paul Symphony Orchestra. The Dutch violinist and his wife, Anna, a cellist, had arrived suddenly in Cleveland in the spring of 1912. The Timmners quickly established themselves in the musical community by joining forces with pianist Betsy Wyers for a series of public and private recitals managed by Adella Prentiss Hughes. The public concerts drew a favorable response from the press.

To bolster Timmner's reputation locally, the savvy Hughes printed a formidable testimonial, from no less a figure than the noted German composer Richard Strauss, on a recital advertisement: "Mr. Timmner is well remembered by me from the performances of the Concertgebouw Orchestra as a superior violinist, a distinguished musician and an amiable artist, and it gives me particular pleasure to recommend him most warmly to concert associations as soloist as well as concertmeister."

With the Cleveland Symphony Orchestra on the edge of extinction, Hughes and others, including *Press* critic Smith, pianist Wyers, and Alice Bradley of *Town Topics*, lobbied for Timmner to replace Beck and Ring. Smith would refer to the Cleveland conductors in his column as "old brooms" and call Timmner the "new broom who can sweep clean all the accumulated rubbish." In December 1912, the management brought in the "new broom" for a clean sweep. Timmner was appointed sole conductor of the Cleveland Symphony Orchestra. In addition, an executive committee (comprising musicians' union representatives Walter Logan and Robert Brew, managers Adella Prentiss Hughes and Victor Sincere, lumber magnate Archibald Klumpf, and architect Frank Meade) was formed to bring responsible business practices to the organization and to appeal to wealthy donors.

Timmner led his first concert on January 19, 1913, at Engineers Hall. It was followed by eight more Sunday afternoon concerts that generally sold out (tickets cost 25 to 50 cents). To rid the orchestra of its reputation as a pops ensemble, Timmner programmed beloved and substantial European works, and drew accolades from critics. Smith raved about the results and denigrated Beck and Ring in the process.

The previous conductors weren't about to let the success of the new man in town overshadow their achievements or ambitions. Two months after Timmner's inaugural concert with the orchestra, Beck—keenly aware that the Dutch violinist had no conducting credentials—began a petition drive to oust him. Writing to Newton D. Baker, who had become Cleveland's mayor in 1912, Beck stated, "we have local men who are unquestionably better musicians and who are far more capable as Orchestral Directors, to occupy this position, which should be open to competition, and secured on merit alone, and not upon the suggestion or recommendation of a few individuals." His words were to fall on deaf ears, at least for the time being.

In April 1913, a month after the mayor received Beck's petition, Baker appointed Timmner as Municipal Director of Music for the city of Cleveland and named Smith as advisor to the superintendent of parks. Timmner was to lead the orchestra—renamed the Cleveland Municipal Orchestra—in Sunday afternoon concerts in city parks throughout the summer and in winter concerts at the 4,000-seat Hippodrome Theatre.

Dubbed the "anti-ragtime director" for his aversion to the popular syncopated music ("It is too rotten. Until I have to play it, I won't play it"), Timmner began his tenure by firing almost half of the former Cleveland Symphony Orchestra. The *Cleveland News* listed some of his reasons:

They practice with a long stogie or a black cigar in their mouths.

They cross their legs.

They slouch down in their seats and rest their elbows on the arms of the chairs.

They yawn audibly and without attempting to conceal their mouths with their hands.

They ignore his appeals for them to come to rehearsal and became peeved when he corrected their technique.

With the players he had chosen, Timmner set out to provide summer audiences with music they could simply sit back and enjoy (even though this sounded, oddly, like a pops approach). "People in general like music according to the ease with which they can remember the melody," he told the *Cleveland Press*. "That is the reason ragtime is so popular and everyone whistles it. They would whistle the 'Blue Danube' or the intermezzo from 'Cavalleria Rusticana' if they heard them often enough." But listeners wouldn't be hearing serious classics, at least during the summer. "The heavier music will be all right later on, perhaps, but if you play it at the start people will say, 'I know it's very good, but I don't like it,' and so they won't come again," Timmner said.

By the first summer concert on June 15, when the orchestra played music by Bizet, Delibes, Saint-Saëns, Wagner, and others, Timmner had an ensemble of 46 musicians. Attending a rehearsal before this performance, the *Press* noted that the bass players wore blue suspenders, and that although the cymbal player had the least to do he had to be "on the job all the time. If he is the fiftieth part of a second late with his crashes, Timmner begins to roar." The story also depicted the orchestra's work as far from glamorous: "Rehearsals are held each day on the fourth floor of the old gas company building adjoining city hall. The highbrow organization is buttressed on one side by the street cleaning department and on the other by the smoke inspector's office."

But the first concert elicited a glowing review from Smith: "If any doubt existed concerning the practicality of a symphony orchestra for Sunday park concerts, it was dissipated at Edgewater park Sunday afternoon by the municipal orchestra under Muny Director Christiaan Timmner."

The success of the summer concerts led to hope that the new orchestra might become a fixture in Cleveland. "I cannot possibly see failure for the project," said James D. Johnston, a viola player in the orchestra and also its personnel manager. "I know that no man leading an orchestra, big or little, in Cleveland or in any other city can hope to do his work without having opposition. He is bound to have trouble, prompted, generally, by jealousy. But the more opposition there is the more backbone it will take to fight it and to bring the project to a successful conclusion. Successful conclusion it must be and nothing else, for a Cleveland symphony orchestra will mean wonderful things for the musicians and the music lovers of Cleveland alike."

However visionary Johnston may have been about the place of such an ensemble in the city's life, he was hasty in assuming that the Municipal Orchestra could be the group that would succeed. In early 1914, at the suggestion of critic Smith, Mayor Baker made the orchestra a project of the city. It was to be funded through taxes, with the city taking full responsibility for the budget. The deal meant additional work for Timmner, whose obligations included starting amateur orchestras at social centers. He would be paid $2,400 a year. Baker, a staunch supporter of the arts, didn't appear concerned that the venture might affect the city's deficit, and he shared

Johnston's optimism. "There is no question in my mind that the orchestra should be continued," Baker told members of the City Club. "The esthetic development of the city is just as important in my mind as are paved roads and other physical improvements."

As admirable as Baker's view may have been, it was misguided in two ways. The city's funding of the orchestra didn't pay Timmner enough to make a living, so he augmented his income by giving high-priced lessons. This may have seemed innocent enough, but the conductor was soon accused of using his teaching to "sell" jobs in his orchestra to his students. Musicians complained, and the charges led to a court case against Timmner in March 1915. With Baker and others defending him, Timmner prevailed in court, but his reputation was forever tainted in Cleveland.

The last straw for the orchestra came in May 1915, when city officials realized that Cleveland's deficit of $52 million would mean the end of funds for the orchestra (and thus the end of the orchestra itself). Timmner's power base had eroded. His only recourse was to seek employment out of the region, armed with recommendations from Baker and Smith.

It was during Timmner's court case in March that the public learned why he had arrived so suddenly from Minnesota in 1912. He had been let go as concertmaster of the St. Paul Symphony Orchestra after behaving badly toward conductor Walter Rothwell, fellow musicians, and students whom he had overcharged and promised seats in the orchestra. Adella Prentiss Hughes later suggested that the period under Timmner had tried everyone's nerves: "Years later, with a twinkle in his eye, Mr. Baker told me that he had more trouble handling the Municipal Orchestra than all the affairs of the city of Cleveland put together!"

By 1915, Hughes had been a hardy survivor of Cleveland's symphony wars for almost two decades. The indomitable woman who so zealously spread appreciation for great music—in an environment dominated by high-powered men—was about to lead the city to a cultural milestone.

Adella

*I*n November 1897, Adella Prentiss attended an event that became the catalyst in her transformation from a fine accompanist into a bona fide impresario. At a concert presented by the Fortnightly Musical Club of Cleveland, she heard a quartet of local singers perform Liza Lehmann's song cycle *In a Persian Garden,* set to words from the *Rubáiyát of Omar Khayyám.* When Prentiss mentioned to a friend that she would like to hear the cycle sung in Cleveland by top-notch artists, he asked, "Why don't you bring them here?" Prentiss thought about it overnight and wrote a letter to Estelle Ford, the soprano who had sung at the inaugural concert of the Philharmonic Orchestra in Cleveland six years earlier.

Ford had been performing Lehmann's work on tour; Prentiss wondered if the soprano could help her schedule a concert in Cleveland. She could. The performance took place in March 1898, and was a success. Prentiss's managerial career was off and running, though she was not without trepidation. "My personal bank account at that time was fifteen dollars," she recounted in her charming (and highly selective) autobiography, *Music Is My Life.* "I had signed contracts for $750. My mother was alarmed. My father, a clear-sighted lawyer, looked at me gravely and then said, 'I think you can do it, daughter.'" Never was a parent more accurate about a child's abilities. "The aftermath of this concert was a surprise to me," Prentiss recalled. "I had not been aware of the fact that the management of a concert was anything to be labeled or taken into consideration, for it had been handled in a way that was natural to me." It would turn out to be a good thing for Cleveland that management suited her.

Adella Prentiss can be considered *the* galvanizing force behind the city's immersion in great music—even long before she helped found the Cleveland Orchestra. Many presenters had brought major artists and ensembles to town over the previous half-century. But Prentiss possessed something her predecessors lacked, a rare combination of intelligence, taste, foresight, and confidence that enabled her to lure America's finest orchestras to town. That, and a heritage that helped prepare her for the job. A descendant of the pioneering Rouse and Long families, she grew up in a social and intellectual environment that allowed her to move easily among the city's power brokers. A resourceful and enterprising woman, Prentiss developed the artistic instincts and the business acumen to master the complexities of arts management, and she did so at a time when few women of social standing pursued careers.

Like her Grandmother Rouse, a descendant of Oliver Cromwell who had led the Northern Ohio Sanitary Commission during the Civil War and founded a Protestant orphan asylum, Prentiss was a high achiever. Born on November 29, 1869, Prentiss developed an early interest in music and literature and began playing piano at the age of six. As a teenager, she showed a knack for speaking her mind. The principal at Miss Fisher's School for Girls, upon receiving a photograph of a serene Adella from the subject, deemed the likeness inaccurate: "It's good enough, but you know you never do look natural with your mouth shut!"

Prentiss certainly didn't remain quiet at Vassar College, which she entered in 1886 with the intention of becoming a teacher. She appeared as the soprano lead in an operetta, *The Doctor of Alcantara*, opposite "a tall and handsome blonde upper-class girl, Tessie Wooster, '88, [who] was the [mustachioed] hero. My one solo was very nearly wrecked by the laughter of the audience when I, the heroine, sang with much feeling: 'His eyes are like the shining stars, that nightly deck the sombre skies . . .' Tessie had chosen that week to have a terrible sty on her eye!" Aside from operettas, Prentiss sang in the glee club and choir, but when these activities alone didn't satisfy her artistic cravings in her senior year, she founded the college's banjo club— and the seeds of her future as an impresario were sown. Invited to take the ensemble on tour, Prentiss made all of the plans and even conducted the performances. She also persuaded classmates to write songs for the glee club. "And there began my life-long occupation of trying to stimulate the American musician," she recalled.

Upon graduating Phi Beta Kappa in 1890, Prentiss set off with her mother for a winter abroad. Basing themselves in Berlin, they toured Germany, France, Belgium, Switzerland, Italy, and England. Prentiss's musical education was furthered at weekly Tuesday night concerts of the Berlin Philharmonic, conducted by Hans von Bülow. On one occasion, Prentiss sat behind the percussion section and faced von Bülow in action with the Berliners: "The noise was overwhelming, but I learned that night what the conductor of a symphony orchestra has the power to do with his players. I became fairly hypnotized in following the music through my eyes, in watching the conductor, thereby almost losing consciousness of the sound. When the end came it was a shock to come back to my surroundings."

She heard the Joachim String Quartet and Polish pianist Jan Paderewski in his first Berlin concert. Prentiss met violinist Sol Marcosson, an American who was studying with the great Joseph Joachim (and who would be the first concertmaster of the Cleveland Orchestra in 1918). Adella and her mother also encountered two Cleveland friends, Elisabeth Huntington DeWitt Severance (wife of industrialist John Long Severance) and her cousin, Julia Severance.

Prentiss had no career plans upon her return to Cleveland in 1891, but several events pointed her toward her life's work. A gifted pianist, she was encouraged by Johanna Hess-Burr, a highly regarded accompanist, to perform with singers and instrumentalists, which she did successfully during the following years. Then, when a group of wealthy Cleveland women who wanted to promote music in the community got together in February 1894 to create the Fortnightly Musical Club, Prentiss joined as a charter member. Marcosson, who had recently moved to town, was among those hired to form the Cleveland Philharmonic String Quartet and play concerts under the club's auspices. The organization also offered performances by visiting ensembles, including the Theodore Thomas Orchestra. Finally, in 1897, Prentiss heard Lehmann's *In a Persian Garden*, and her direction was decided.

❉   ❉   ❉

Prentiss found working with artists, negotiating contracts, and mixing with Cleveland society so natural that she quickly gained a reputation as a superb booking agent. After the *Persian Garden* performance and a second U.S. tour of the song cycle with the vocal quartet, including a stop at Prentiss's alma mater, Vassar, Fortnightly appointed her to manage solo and ensemble concerts that they were presenting in Cleveland.

The impresario's upbringing had given her advantages that would serve her well in her newly chosen field. At Vassar, she had met Bessie Rockefeller, oldest daughter of oil industry mogul John D. Rockefeller. Prentiss and her parents were invited to Forest Hill—the Rockefellers' second Cleveland residence, four miles east of their downtown mansion on Euclid Avenue—in 1886. It was the start of an important family relationship based on a love of music (the Rockefeller children all played instruments) and mutual admiration. The death of Prentiss's mother in 1908 brought the young manager even closer to Mrs. Rockefeller.

By this time, Prentiss had come in contact with more than a few of the world's best musicians. Her promotion of symphonic music in Cleveland had begun in 1900, when the Fortnightly club agreed to host the second biennial festival of the National Federation of Music Clubs in May 1901. The festival would need an orchestra, and Prentiss knew which ensemble would not be invited—the fledgling Cleveland Symphony Orchestra, which she and others had come to look down upon.

After using her considerable powers of persuasion on the board of the Fortnightly club, Prentiss booked the Pittsburgh Orchestra and Victor Herbert for three concerts at the festival. Among the soloists was the ebullient Bohemian-born contralto, Ernestine Schumann-Heink, who became a lifelong Prentiss friend. The performances, held at Grays Armory, were so successful (and profitable) that the National Federation quickly hired Prentiss to manage a new series featuring visiting orchestras and solo artists at the armory starting in the fall of 1901. The Pittsburgh Orchestra returned during the first subscription season for three concerts, one featuring the celebrated American soprano Lillian Nordica. The following year, the orchestra again played three programs, and the Cincinnati Symphony offered two.

Thus began 19 years of top-notch, imported orchestral performances in Cleveland as part of the Symphony Orchestra Concerts, the first such series in the United States. "My first interest was orchestral music," Prentiss wrote in her memoirs. From 1901 until 1920, mostly at Grays Armory, she managed 162 concerts by 11 orchestras under 21 conductors, including some of the most renowned maestros of the era: Karl Muck, Theodore Thomas, Frederick Stock, Leopold Stokowski, Eugene Ysaye, Ossip Gabrilowitsch, and Walter Damrosch. Two other figures who stepped onto the podium in the Cleveland series rose above even that formidable assemblage—Richard Strauss and Gustav Mahler, who would become better known as transcendent composers.

One of the visits by the Pittsburgh Orchestra changed Prentiss's life in a crucial way. In 1903, the ensemble arrived with its new conductor, Emil Paur, for a concert performance of Gounod's *Faust* featuring bass Herbert Witherspoon as Mephistopheles and baritone Felix Hughes, Witherspoon's brother-in-law, as Valentin. The engagement led to summer teaching stints in Cleveland for Witherspoon (who would become the Met's general manager in 1935, but die two months later) and, as his assistant, Hughes. When Witherspoon had to leave, Hughes took over. Prentiss became his accompanist and soon made music with him in more ways than one. Their relationship deepened swiftly, and they were wed in 1904.

It was also in 1904 that Prentiss, forever thereafter to be known as Adella

Prentiss Hughes, introduced German composer-conductor Richard Strauss to Cleveland with the Pittsburgh Orchestra. The performance, on March 10, was part of Strauss's first North American tour. Before Strauss's Cleveland concert, Hughes went to New York to hear his Carnegie Hall debut. Then she promoted his appearance by visiting local German groups and talking him up in the press. "He is all that they have said of him; he has succeeded Richard Wagner as the storm center of musical discussion the world over," Hughes told *The Plain Dealer*. Strauss was "the most interesting figure in the domain of composition today, and a great conductor. We are very proud of having secured him for a Cleveland appearance, for his coming to this country is one of the most important musical events of the decade."

Hughes's lobbying did the trick: Grays Armory was filled for the concert. Strauss conducted Beethoven's Seventh Symphony, accompanied his wife, Pauline, on the piano in three of his songs, and led the first Cleveland performances of his tone poems *Till Eulenspiegel* and *Tod und Verklärung (Death and Transfiguration)*. The Strausses were feted afterwards at the Hollenden Hotel, on Superior Avenue, with an impromptu concert by 300 singers from local German societies who performed, among other pieces, "My Old Kentucky Home" in German. Hughes couldn't have hoped for a better event for her series or her city: "Cleveland knew its Richard Strauss from then on."

One conductor disrupted Hughes's customary concert format. Until March 9, 1910, when Leopold Stokowski came to town with the Cincinnati Orchestra, the Symphony Orchestra Concerts had lumped together the soloists and the major symphonic work in the first half of the program and presented the less challenging music after intermission. Hughes, perhaps rightly, believed that the wooden seats in Grays Armory took their toll on her listeners after an hour or so and that the audience needed to be soothed. The 24-year-old Stokowski would hear nothing of the policy. If he had, his soloist, soprano Marcella Sembrich, might have upstaged him. Instead, according to Hughes, Stokowski conducted a very short first half: Beethoven's *Leonore* Overture No. 3 and "Ah, fors'è lui" (from Verdi's *La Traviata*, with Sembrich). To open the second half, the soprano sang German lieder (with a pianist) and encores (with the orchestra). Then Stokowski galvanized the Cleveland audience with his account of Tchaikovsky's "Pathétique" Symphony. Sol Marcosson, substituting as a music critic for the *Cleveland News*, dubbed Stokowski a "young Jupiter of a conductor."

Critics also raved when Gustav Mahler arrived in Cleveland on December 6, 1910, with the New York Philharmonic for their joint local debut. After a triumphant and turbulent decade (1897–1907) as director of the Vienna Court Opera, Mahler had come to the United States for the first time to conduct at the Metropolitan Opera, where he had a short, triumphant, and turbulent tenure. He soon moved his base of musical operations uptown to Carnegie Hall to become conductor of the New York Philharmonic. There, he instituted a new tour policy that made use of the orchestra's full complement of 92 players, instead of reducing the ensemble for traveling purposes.

Cleveland must have learned a stunning lesson from Mahler and the New Yorkers. For the first five seasons of the Symphony Orchestra Concerts, audiences had heard ensembles of little more than 50 players—not an adequate number for many pieces from the late 19th century. Beginning with the 1906–07 season, the Boston Symphony brought 75 musicians, inspiring the orchestras of Chicago, Cincinnati, and Pittsburgh to travel with 65 players. But this still would have paled in comparison with the Philharmonic's 92 musicians, at least for several of the program's Wagner pieces: the Prelude and "Liebestod" from *Tristan und Isolde* and the Act I prelude from *Die Meistersinger*.

Mahler certainly created a stir. In her review of the concert, *Plain Dealer* critic Miriam Russell didn't restrain herself:

> Little Mahler with the big brain.
> Little Mahler with the mighty force.
> Little Mahler with the great musical imagination.
> Little Mahler, whose gigantic power makes other conductors look like pygmies.

❉   ❉   ❉

Though busy with preparation, promotion, and presentation of her Symphony Orchestra Concerts series, the inexhaustible Hughes found time to support other aspects of Cleveland's musical life. In 1912, she helped Almeda Adams, a blind singing teacher, found the Cleveland Music School Settlement. The school was to be modeled after a New York school where children of immigrants had successfully been taught music. Lessons were given for a small fee or for free. Adams envisioned a similar school in Cleveland, serving immigrants and anyone else who wanted to study music, regardless of their ability to pay. Hughes introduced the idea to the Fortnightly Musical Club, which made the first donation, of $1,000, to get the Music School Settlement started. It would remain a thriving institution into the 21st century, serving thousands of residents in the areas of music, dance, and childhood development.

By 1913, Hughes had been a concert manager for 15 years, and her reputation had spread throughout the country. At home, critic Archie Bell acknowledged her contribution in the *Cleveland News*. "Now Cleveland is recognized as one of the half dozen musical centers of America," wrote Bell. "It is easy to argue that the city has grown by leaps and bounds and demanded better music, even that someone else might have assumed the reins if she had not done so. But the fact is that she did things, not waiting to see if anyone else would undertake them. When a celebrated artist reaches New York one of the first points considered for an American tour is Cleveland, and Cleveland in most of the managerial offices of New York where music is dispensed means Mrs. Hughes as the local manager."

She had grown more daring and imaginative as a manager over those 15 years. In 1913, she presented a mammoth event in her series—a Wagner festival of three concerts in two days, featuring Frederick Stock and the Chicago Symphony, to mark the 100th anniversary of the composer's birth. The programs included vocal and orchestral excerpts from Wagner's major music dramas performed with a stellar group of international soloists—soprano Olive Fremstadt, tenor Karl Jörn, and bass Herbert Witherspoon— and two local choruses, the Singers' Club and the German Club. The critics and the public were ecstatic.

Hughes's resourcefulness saw her through managerial crises of all kinds. After booking the New York Symphony Orchestra, with conductor Walter Damrosch and pianist Josef Hofmann, for a program at Grays Armory in January 1914, she discovered that a poultry show was scheduled there for the same date. (At least one concert had been cancelled in the past for this reason.) Hughes tried to get the armory to postpone the odiferous extravaganza, but it was too late: the chickens were on their way and "the poor things would freeze to death" if they didn't arrive at the armory as scheduled. A lawyer helped Hughes work out a deal with the armory, which was forced to rent the nearby Miles Theatre for the orchestra concert at $1,100 for the night. Hughes had been paying $150 at the armory.

The manager was undaunted when the outbreak of World War I in August 1914 threatened the continuation of her series. She quickly traveled to New York and Boston to make sure that the artists she had booked for the 1914–15 season would honor their commitments. Her determination to go forward was announced in *Musical America* several weeks after Austria declared war on Serbia. "A very successful season here seems assured," Hughes wrote. "More season tickets have been ordered for the Symphony

Orchestra Concerts than at the same time last year, with orders coming in daily. The possible changes of a few men among the artists and soloists of the orchestras will not disturb the season in my opinion."

In fact, the season would prove to be a turning point for Hughes, her series, and Cleveland's cultural life. A proposal by the Metropolitan Opera that Hughes present Diaghilev's Ballets Russes in Cleveland during its first American tour "fired my imagination at once." And the fire didn't simply concern ballet. Hughes had long been contemplating the creation of an association that would support many types of musical events in Cleveland. With her contacts in the city's business and philanthropic worlds, she was confident that she could count on a visionary board of trustees to assist her. The list of men she had assembled over the years as major contributors and advisors to her orchestra series was formidable indeed: John L. Severance, the industrialist with ties to Hughes's maternal family; David Z. Norton, a partner in the iron ore and shipping firm Oglebay Norton Company; iron ore and steel magnate Samuel Mather; William Gwinn Mather, his half-brother, a pioneer in iron ore, steel, and banking; banker Howard P. Eells; and Frank Hadley Ginn, a corporate lawyer.

Discussions during the summer of 1915 led to the formation of the Musical Arts Association, a for-profit corporation to further "the interests of music in the community, accepting and administering trust funds and guaranty funds for musical purposes, and acquiring, holding and operating property to promote the efficiency of musical enterprises." Upon the signing of articles of incorporation on October 5, the funds Hughes had raised for her Symphony Orchestra Concerts were turned over to the association, and she was hired as manager. Norton was appointed president.

The first presentation of the Musical Arts Association featured the Ballets Russes at the Hippodrome Theatre on March 16, 17, and 18, 1916. Serge Diaghilev's Paris-based company performed 11 works, including two, *The Firebird* and *Petrouchka*, with music by Igor Stravinsky, whom many believed to be the most radical composer of the era. The conductor was Ernest Ansermet. If the eyes of Cleveland critics were entranced by *Petrouchka*, their ears generally were not. "But the music—ah, there's the rub," wrote Wilson G. Smith, a composer himself, in the *Press*. "Such a compendium of atrocious dissonances and unrelated thematic material the ear of normal man never heard—to say nothing of imagining. If such be music, Horatio, I would have but little of it!" Alice Bradley, in *Town Topics*, was more graceful: "Shut your eyes and listen for a moment to the music alone, and its eccentricities are almost unbearable . . . yet so perfect is the accord between the action and the music, that in watching *Petrouchka* you are hardly ever conscious of the orchestral turmoil and hear the music only as an element underlying and punctuating the doings of the characters. Then again there are some moments of positive genius, and at all times the orchestration is masterly."

The success of the Ballets Russes encouraged Hughes to continue her adventures on behalf of the Musical Arts Association. Three months later, Hughes imported a production of Wagner's *Siegfried* for an open-air performance at League Park, home of the Cleveland Indians. The event, on June 19, featured a massive orchestra, conducted by the Metropolitan Opera's Artur Bodanzky, and a cast of seasoned Wagnerian singers, including Hughes's friend, the exuberant contralto Ernestine Schumann-Heink, as Erda. The papers played the event up big, and with no shortage of whimsy. "SIEGFRIED IN BOX, WAGNER AT BAT — PLAY BALL! How operatic fans will yell when the fiery dragon dies on first!" roared the *Sunday Leader*. Hughes had worried that rain might postpone the performance, but the weather behaved and between 10,000 and 15,000 people showed up to hear Siegfried slay Fafner.

As Hughes had predicted, the war hadn't had much of an effect on her Symphony Orchestra Concerts, although some major ensembles were beginning to find touring difficult. Hughes had done so much good work on behalf of Cleveland's musical life that critic Archie Bell appeared ready to declare her an institution. "Sometimes a prophet has more honor just a little beyond the borders of his bailiwick," he wrote in the fall of 1917. "That's the case with this local manager. I don't mean to insinuate that her efforts have not been appreciated by music-lovers in Cleveland; but I do mean to say that several big cities in the United States wish they had an Adella Prentiss Hughes. If you consider it rightly, such a person is a part of the great machinery of a municipality, like the president of a university, the librarian, the director of the art museum, looking to the development of something that is not reckoned in dollars."

Within a year, Hughes would begin to develop something that the city thus far had been unable to sustain, and that would transform Cleveland's cultural life: the belated, but swift, birth of its own permanent orchestra.

– 3 –
Big Noise and an Orchestra

T he church needed roof work and the mortgage was coming due. How, the priest wondered, could he raise enough money to cover these expenses? The previous year, Father John Powers had helped reduce the mortgage on St. Ann's Parish in Cleveland Heights by holding a benefit concert at the Hippodrome Theatre in downtown Cleveland. An accomplished tenor, he had even sung several solos during the performance, which featured the Singers' Club, a local amateur male chorus. Now he had to come up with another exciting, and lucrative, event.

Archie Bell, the dapper drama and music critic of the *Cleveland News*, suggested that the priest contact Adella Prentiss Hughes, manager of the nationally admired Symphony Orchestra Concerts series. Surely she would be able to provide advice. As the force behind the Musical Arts Association, Hughes was said to be forming a symphony orchestra to help the city board of education improve instrumental music programs in the schools and spread the gospel of good music. For this, she had arranged for the association to hire a passionate, Russian-born American conductor and violinist, Nikolai Sokoloff. He was "the big noise now," Bell told Powers. The priest didn't need any more convincing. He headed straight for Hughes's office in the Caxton Building, where the imposing impresario and Sokoloff were already waiting for him after being tipped off by a phone call from Bell. "Is there to be an orchestra?" the priest inquired. "Yes," Hughes replied. "When can I buy a concert?" asked Powers.

Most accounts of the Cleveland Orchestra's birth begin with a scenario involving Bell, Powers, Hughes, Sokoloff, and a contract for the inaugural concert on Wednesday, December 11, 1918, at Grays Armory on Bolivar Road. The exception is Sokoloff's recollection of this seminal incident in his memoirs, a colorful, partly revisionist narrative written almost a half-century later. According to the conductor, Powers was already conferring with Hughes when Sokoloff arrived to inform her that he had found 50 local musicians for the educational program's orchestra. Waiting in the anteroom, Sokoloff listened to Hughes tell Powers that a concert by a vocal quartet from the Metropolitan Opera might raise the requisite funds. The conductor quickly seized the opportunity and rushed into the office to make his pitch. "I'm sorry, but I could not help overhearing a little of your conversation. You seem to be having trouble finding exactly the thing to bring you in some money. Now I have a wonderful idea for you," Sokoloff said to the priest. "How would you like to have the honor—the great honor—of presenting the first concert of Cleveland's Symphony Orchestra?" Mrs. Hughes, aghast, "seemed to be struck speechless by all this, but her eyes were blazing and she looked daggers at me." When the impresario asked where he would find such an orchestra, Sokoloff said he had been scouting around for musicians for the past month and was ready to begin rehearsing. Contemporary accounts of this story may diverge—as they often would where Sokoloff's memory was concerned—but there is little doubt that the meeting in early November 1918 precipitated what may have been the fastest creation of an orchestra in the annals of American history.

Two months earlier, Cleveland's board of education and the Musical Arts Association had requested that Sokoloff make a survey of music education in the city and eventually lay the foundation for a permanent orchestra. No one had a specific description of what Sokoloff's mission would be, as the vague language in his first contract with the Musical Arts Association reveals: "We recognize the difficulty of defining in any accurate way the work which you are to do, but in a general way, our understanding is that you are to cooperate with the Association in its general plans to further the interests of music in Cleveland through existing associations and communities and such as may be hereafter organized or encouraged by you or by the Association."

Nor could Sokoloff have anticipated that his dream of leading his own orchestra would become a reality so quickly. In one of his first Cleveland interviews, he said the Musical Arts Association had hired him "to stimulate music in the community—and, as I have said, I shall make use of every force already active, with the ultimate hope, of course, of forming the symphony orchestra, which, at a long guess, I may place at five years from the present."

Forming the ensemble would take little more than a month. Ten rehearsals would follow. An orchestra would come to life before the year was out.

❈   ❈   ❈

Sokoloff was no stranger to Cleveland when he arrived in town in September 1918. He had performed several times in the Symphony Orchestra Concerts series, starting with a concert during the 1906–07 season with Karl Muck and the Boston Symphony Orchestra, whose first violin section he had joined when he was 17. He was concertmaster of the Russian Symphony Orchestra under Modest Altschuler when he appeared as soloist in short works by Massenet and Saint-Saëns with the ensemble in Cleveland in March 1910. Reports from the time suggest that Sokoloff played the violin superlatively, though it was not the musical endeavor to which he ultimately wished to devote himself.

Born in Kiev, Russia, on May 26, 1886, he started violin at a young age and played alto tuba at 9. His involvement with music can be traced to his father, who "supplied and conducted various orchestras, and when I was about ten years old, he was engaged to conduct the orchestra at the municipal theater." At 11, Sokoloff was appointed concertmaster in a Kiev theater where operas by Verdi and other Italian composers were the main fare. After the family emigrated to the United States in 1900, the 13-year-old violinist studied at the Yale University School of Music and then in Boston with Charles Martin Loeffler, an eminent American composer. Sokoloff couldn't believe his good fortune when he won a post in the Boston Symphony, but after three years of rehearsals and performances under numerous conductors he was ready to try his own hand at conducting.

His first stop was New York, where he became concertmaster of the Russian Symphony Orchestra and served as its assistant conductor, without ever stepping onto the podium. This was followed by studies in Paris with Vincent d'Indy and in Belgium with Eugene Ysaye. Sokoloff's period in Europe coincided with the beginning of World War I. Rejected for military duty, for unspecified reasons, he was hired to conduct incidental music at a repertory theater in Manchester, England, where two renowned playwrights, George Bernard Shaw and John Galsworthy, attended rehearsals of their works. Sokoloff was in raptures: "Finally, and for the first time, I was able to earn money not by playing or teaching the violin, but by *conducting*."

The rapture didn't last long, as Sokoloff soon decided it was time to return to the United States. In New York, he met Cecelia Casserly, a wealthy woman who invited him to form a string quartet in San Mateo, California. Sokoloff agreed to be first violinist under one condition: he would leave the quartet if offered a conducting post. After his move to California in April 1915, Sokoloff attended a concert by the Boston Symphony in San Francisco, where he was reunited with an orchestra colleague, Rudolph Ringwall, whom he persuaded to join his string quartet as second violinist.

(Ringwall would be reunited with Sokoloff again a decade later in Cleveland.)

Finally, a conducting job materialized. Sokoloff was hired to lead the People's Philharmonic Orchestra in San Francisco, an ensemble that supplemented the work of the San Francisco Symphony. Sokoloff went about his business with alacrity, programming adventurously and discovering that the life of the maestro held built-in challenges. Alfred Hertz, conductor of the San Francisco Symphony, felt so threatened by Sokoloff's presence that he removed all of his ensemble's music from the San Francisco Library, depriving the other orchestra of the works its conductor wanted to play.

The last straw came when Sokoloff was ordered by board members to program more Russian and French music and ignore German repertoire, a reaction against the culture that had drawn the world into the current conflagration. After one season, Sokoloff packed away his baton, picked up his violin, became a YMCA volunteer, and played recitals throughout Europe for American troops. His war effort was to bring about a fateful encounter that would lead him to Cleveland.

❁   ❁   ❁

In January 1918, Adella Prentiss Hughes attended a party in Manhattan held by a friend, Lillie Lawler, who introduced her to one of her guests, a young violinist-conductor: Sokoloff. He had just returned from France after giving 60 recitals for military personnel. "Sokoloff was a vivid, interesting person," Hughes later wrote. "His accounts of the suffering among French musicians and their families resulted in the formation of the Friends of Musicians in France. This had been the purpose of his return to America."

It was also the purpose of his trip to Cleveland on February 26, 1918, when Sokoloff and Hughes next met. Hughes was busy that day presenting a recital by the American pianist Mischa Levitzki. Sokoloff was a guest at the recital and at a dinner the following night at Hughes's Cleveland Heights home, where he and Levitzki decided to play chamber music. Hughes rustled up a pile of music and an instrument for Sokoloff from Walter Logan, a well-known local violinist who often contracted musicians for theater and concert engagements. Sokoloff's sublime artistry and riveting stories about his war experiences made an indelible impression on Hughes.

True to form, Sokoloff proffers another version of this trip in his memoirs. Gone is any mention of French suffering. In its place is an ambitious conductor determined to find a city in desperate need of a local orchestra. At the top of his list is Cleveland, where he has been invited to talk with a manager, Hughes, whom he gives no indication of having met before.

Sokoloff mentions the Levitzki recital and ensuing chamber music session, but adds a dramatic coda, telling Hughes that American cities deserve their own orchestras, which should be entrusted to American conductors. A skeptical Hughes counters that her visiting orchestra series has raised the sophistication level in Cleveland to the point where a local orchestra would never satisfy. Not only that, she says, it is less expensive to import an orchestra than to fund a local entity. "So you see," Hughes tells Sokoloff, "it would be utterly useless for me to start an orchestra which wouldn't play well for years and years and, in the meantime, see the chance of losing our public for these magnificent concerts. In fact, I don't think we could get support for your idea."

Sokoloff berates Hughes, telling her that "Cleveland is sponging on the cities which have the obligation and responsibility to maintain their orchestras . . . you do not have fine musicians living among you—these orchestras come and play and leave the next morning. Where is your musical life? Where is the musical education of your children? Where [are] the artists to train whatever real talent your children may possess? Where [is] the contribution musicians make to every city in which they live? You have nothing but a concert."

Fanciful or accurate? Whatever transpired in his discussion with Hughes, Sokoloff left town without any prospect of a conducting job.

✧   ✧   ✧

Two attractive engagements did emerge for Sokoloff in the ensuing months. In the spring of 1918, he formed an orchestra of 40 musicians from the New York Symphony and 48 members of the New York Philharmonic and conducted a concert of French music at Carnegie Hall. Praised by New York critics, Sokoloff soon was asked by the Cincinnati Symphony to conduct a series of popular concerts during the summer.

One of the concerts was scheduled for the Cincinnati Zoo as part of the Ohio Music Teachers' Association annual meeting in June. Sokoloff agreed to speak to the teachers about the need for orchestras to be connected to public schools and universities. Orchestral musicians could help train young people, Sokoloff told the teachers, and make them aware that music is a vital factor in forming well-rounded individuals. Another speaker at the meeting was none other than Hughes, who focused on the necessity "to promote pupil attendance at concerts of great music."

Hughes had two revelations during the meeting. Upon hearing a high school chorus and orchestra perform a cantata by a local composer, with a 13-year-old oboe virtuoso as soloist, she later recounted, "I realized that our visiting orchestra concerts could never accomplish that for Cleveland. I lay awake hours that night pondering what we could do about it." The next day, she heard Sokoloff speak, listening as he raised the possibility that American conductors might never have their own ensembles if no one gave them the chance. Hughes found Sokoloff disarming, especially the way he talked to children during a concert he conducted that afternoon: "I began to realize that all of us in Cleveland had been doing the same thing for twenty years—fine things, if you like—but the germ of future growth was missing. I had been warned, both by Philadelphia and Chicago, that with large increases in local consumption of orchestral music, they would have to reduce their touring. The Visiting Orchestra series had arrived at a climax."

Hughes wasted no time in formulating and moving ahead with a new plan. She told Frank E. Spaulding, Cleveland's superintendent of schools, that the city needed to improve instrumental music programs. Her solution: let the Musical Arts Association hire an orchestral conductor to survey the state of music education and suggest ways to bring fine music to citizens of all ages. To bolster her plan, Hughes turned to an old friend, business magnate and arts lover John Long Severance, whom she sensed would be responsive. In early August 1918, Severance informed Hughes that he was a bit unclear about the proposition, but that he would be willing to discuss the matter with Sokoloff. Hughes's salary figure of $15,000 for Sokoloff was unrealistic, however, Severance noted with the graciousness that marked all of his letters.

Hughes followed through by meeting Sokoloff several weeks later in New York and laying out her plan. The conductor told her he would consider taking the job only if given the go-ahead to form an orchestra and conduct it. "I was equally frank with him," Hughes says in her autobiography. "Our Visiting Orchestra Series had not been nearly as expensive to carry on, and up to this time had completely satisfied our directors. I assured him that I would gladly cooperate with him in an endeavor to convince them that the time had come to go forward into the larger field. That satisfied him."

The meeting between Severance and Sokoloff took place in late August at New York's Waldorf-Astoria Hotel (not the Plaza, as Sokoloff claims in his memoirs), and the two hit it off immediately. The conductor impressed upon Severance what he had made clear to Hughes: "No matter how many glorious orchestras visited Cleveland, the city must have at least a small orchestra of its own to implement the educational part of my program. There had to be resident musicians to promote really good music education. And furthermore, that if there were no orchestra, I was not interested. I wanted to be a conductor—not a teacher." Convinced the plan could work,

Severance set things in motion, agreeing to personally pay Sokoloff $6,000 for the nine-month period starting September 1.

Before Sokoloff could begin work, the Musical Arts Association had to agree to the project, which it did at the board meeting of September 10. Trustees voted to donate Sokoloff's services to the public schools with the ultimate goal of developing "a fine local orchestra with adequate audiences for its support . . . altho' it was pointed out that this could not be expected to actually materialize for a number of years." Sokoloff signed his contract two days later, and the appointment hit the newspapers the following day. Hughes let Severance know that events were moving more swiftly than anyone had anticipated. She told him that the Fortnightly Musical Club and the Cleveland Music School Settlement were delighted to hear about the appointment and that Sokoloff and Walter Logan were already studying the feasibility of a professional orchestra.

Sokoloff wasn't exactly pleased with the conditions he encountered in his new job with the board of education. He was stationed "in a cubbyhole in a horrible old building." He discovered that music education in the schools was also "horrible" and that training in instrumental music was virtually nonexistent. "I interviewed many teachers and potential music students and made an outline of needs and suggestions for meeting them." Even so, the press, which had been covering the ups and downs of Cleveland orchestras for decades, heralded Sokoloff's arrival with bursts of optimism, however premature. *The Plain Dealer* proclaimed: "Cleveland is to have a symphony orchestra that will rank with similar orchestras in such cities as Boston, New York, Cincinnati and San Francisco." Archie Bell was no less giddy in the *Cleveland News*: "Nikolai Sokoloff! Get used to pronouncing it, because it's a name you're likely to see and hear a good deal in the future."

Bell provided Cleveland with a thorough account of Sokoloff and his mission, which would not include teaching or directing choirs. Instead, the conductor would be the "central pivot from which all of these musical activities will radiate, community singing in the schools, settlement orchestras and the various clubs." Sokoloff told Bell he was impressed with the numerous adequate auditoriums around town and that he intended to bring good music to factory workers. Then Sokoloff began dropping tantalizing hints about an orchestra: "I find that Cleveland is full of musical talent. There will be no question about that. What we must do is to bring it together. Why, in the past week I have been making a sort of preliminary survey and I have been delighted to find that this city has many very talented musicians who have played with some of the biggest orchestras in the country." In five years, Sokoloff predicted, the city would have an orchestra comparable to the best in America, if it could tap the "appreciation of the big public" and "the contributions of men who can afford to give sums of money."

Meanwhile, Hughes was using her considerable powers of persuasion on the men with the money. On September 28, she told trustees of the Musical Arts Association that Cleveland had become an important city for orchestral music, despite the fact that it had been depending on major ensembles from out of town. Now, in the midst of a war, it was time for the association to help further "Americanization" by giving Clevelanders—three-fourths of them foreign born—concerts of great music performed by a local professional ensemble. (The fact that most of the music would be by European composers didn't seem to matter.)

✽   ✽   ✽

Being foreign born had proved detrimental recently to the career of Frederick Stock, the revered conductor of the Chicago Symphony Orchestra, and a favorite presence at concerts in Cleveland. Having failed to take out naturalization papers, the German-born Stock was forced to resign temporarily from his post in late August 1918. The situation left Cleveland in a bind: Stock and his Chicago musicians were scheduled to open the Symphony Orchestra Concerts on October 29 with a program featuring the young Brazilian pianist, Guiomar Novaes. With Stock relegated to the sidelines after 13 years at the helm of the Chicago Symphony, his ensemble was trying to substitute a new assistant conductor, Eric DeLamarter, on tour engagements. Hughes nixed the idea for Cleveland. She wouldn't think of allowing an unknown conductor to appear in her series, so she told Fred Wessels, Chicago's manager, that he should hire Sokoloff to appear with the orchestra in Chicago and then in Cleveland as the opening event in the season's Symphony Orchestra Concerts. Fine, Wessels replied, but only if Sokoloff would conduct the scheduled program—Sibelius's Symphony No. 1, the Saint-Saëns Piano Concerto in G minor, and Richard Strauss's *Death and Transfiguration*. An agreement was reached. Less than a month after arriving in Cleveland, Sokoloff had his first big chance to prove himself. The Chicago engagement was announced in Cleveland in early October, and the conductor was soon on his way to the Windy City to firm up plans for his concerts.

Meanwhile, excitement was mounting in the Forest City. Hughes told the trustees that Sokoloff hoped "to assemble fifty men and have five rehearsals for each of three programs" that would be repeated around Cleveland. The orchestra would receive something that was to be rare for many decades—enthusiastic cooperation from the musicians' union. If things turned out well, the orchestra could engage 50 players for up to 20 weeks for the 1919–20 season. "This gradual development of local musicians into good orchestral players would mean the ultimate importation of but few men when the orchestra grows from a popular into an artistic organization," Hughes said. Having thus far called the musicians "men," Hughes then stated that Sokoloff intended "to have both men and women" in his professional orchestra. Unlike most European and American orchestras of the period, Cleveland's ensemble would have female musicians from the start.

❂   ❂   ❂

By mid-October 1918, musical plans in Cleveland, as elsewhere, were on the verge of collapse. Adding to the anguish caused by the war in Europe, an epidemic of Spanish influenza had been sweeping the world in recent months. It began to take on massive proportions in Ohio by autumn. The flu, which would eventually kill 51 million people around the globe and 550,000 in the United States, closed Cleveland schools and colleges in October; on the 19th all concerts and public gatherings were banned until further notice. Sokoloff traveled westward that week to begin rehearsing with the Chicago Symphony, unaware that his concert in Cleveland on October 29 was about to be postponed. The day the ban went into effect, an interview with Sokoloff appeared in *Cleveland Town Topics* stating that the conductor hoped "to provide music, in the leisure time of people, that will not only entertain them, but inspire them and warm up their emotions so that they shall become united in emotional feeling." Sokoloff said, "I would like to make the city scream with delight and joy and bring up children to do the same. Such an emotional expression would be cheap at any price. We must have the most magnificent band and orchestra."

The public had yet to see any signs of such an orchestra. Upon introducing Sokoloff to his readers, the genial *Plain Dealer* music critic, James Rogers, tiptoed gracefully around the subject. "Mr. Sokoloff comes to us, then, as an orchestral conductor, and it is not to be denied that a query as to the whereabouts of the orchestra he is to conduct would be a pertinent one," he wrote. "It cannot be said that the orchestra is ready and waiting for its leader."

It also couldn't be said that Sokoloff was sitting around and waiting for a local engagement to crop up before beginning to seek out competent musicians, either. He had already claimed that there were enough fine players in town to create an ensemble of about 50 members. He discovered them when he started hitting the pavement with Walter Logan, whom he dubbed "my Man Friday." Logan took the conductor to hear theater orchestras around the city. They went to hotels to listen to small ensembles that played during lunch. They contacted musicians who had been members of Cleveland's previous orchestras.

They found their first trombone at the Elysium ice-skating rink. Logan noted a decade later: "Sokoloff and I went to the Elysium, climbed a ladder into the orchestra perch and begged the leader to release the trombone player long enough to play our first symphony concert."

Logan could be as expansive, and unreliable, as Sokoloff in recounting his musical endeavors in Cleveland, though he may not have been off the mark when he said that the musicians in the inaugural concert came from many walks of life. But it is not true that "the first bass was an undertaker [who] had to figure his dates pretty closely to keep up both connections," as Logan claimed. The founding principal bass of Cleveland's Symphony Orchestra was Gerald Fiore, a native of Calabria, Italy. Fiore was one of a healthy number of musicians who made the early Cleveland Orchestra a family affair. One brother, Salvatore, played violin in the orchestra from the first season until 1958. Another, Joseph, was a member of the flute section during the early seasons. Yet another brood that had deep roots in the orchestra's annals and the city's musical history was the Hruby family, which supplied no fewer than five brothers and a sister, out of a total of eight siblings, to the Cleveland Orchestra's violin, cello, clarinet, trumpet, and percussion sections over the decades. Clarinetist Frank, violinist John, and cellist Mamie (the last listed incorrectly in the program as S. Hruby) played in the inaugural concert.

Cleveland was a melting pot of musical dynasties. "I found another family of musicians whose business it was to supply small orchestras for hotels," Sokoloff wrote in his memoirs. "Their name was Spitalny. One son, named Phil, was a clarinet player who afterwards organized the 'All Girls Orchestra' and toured the country. Another brother, Maurice, was a gifted violinist, and there was an elder brother [H. Leopold] who had charge of all the music in the Cleveland theaters. This brother eventually became the music contractor for NBC." Maurice was assistant concertmaster in Sokoloff's orchestra for two years and then became conductor of the orchestra that played during silent movies at the Knickerbocker Theater at Euclid Avenue and East 83rd Street. Another Spitalny, identified only by the first initial "J," was in Sokoloff's viola section during the first season.

Perhaps the most intriguing musician Sokoloff hired was Charles Rychlik (1875–1962), who played in the first violin section during the inaugural season. Rychlik had studied with Johann Beck and, at 12, had become the youngest member ever accepted into the Cleveland musicians' union. He began teaching as a youngster but left for the Prague Conservatory at 16. He was serving as assistant concertmaster of an opera orchestra in Prague when he was asked to join the Bohemian String Quartet and tour Europe. On one extraordinary day, March 27, 1896, the quartet met with three great composers in Vienna: Anton Bruckner in the morning, Johannes Brahms at lunch, and, accompanying Brahms in the evening, his friend, Antonin Dvořák. Several years earlier in Prague, Rychlik had boarded at the home of Dvořák and coached him in English to help him prepare for his historic trip to the New World. Rychlik returned to Cleveland in late 1896 and joined the Chicago Orchestra under Theodore Thomas. Back in Cleveland in 1901, he was a member of the Cleveland Philharmonic String Quartet for 18 years and participated in Timmner's failed orchestra. Rychlik left Cleveland's Symphony Orchestra after one season to concentrate on composition and teaching, in which he distinguished himself by counting as pupils more than 40 musicians who played in the Cleveland Orchestra. Sokoloff programmed a number of Rychlik's works during the orchestra's early seasons.

✻   ✻   ✻

These musicians and several dozen colleagues were not quite ready to be called to rehearsal in early November 1918. The flu continued to keep arts organizations "relegated to the limbo of unessential industries," as music critic Rogers put it. A recital by the great Spanish cellist Pablo Casals was postponed from November 12 to November 26, and Sokoloff's Cleveland engagement with the Chicago Symphony was put off until mid-December. There was still hope that Symphony Orchestra Concerts performances by the New York Symphony Orchestra under Walter Damrosch on November 22 and the Philadelphia Orchestra under Leopold Stokowski on December 5 could go on as planned.

Hope also remained that Sokoloff would proceed with the educational mission that had brought him to town, even if the situation was becoming mired in confusion. An item in the *Musical Leader* on October 31 stated that Sokoloff would organize "whatever of latent talent there may be here in orchestra material for the ultimate realization of a sure-enough Cleveland Symphony Orchestra. Meantime, there will be organized community groups of those amateurs ambitious to become performers and out of these district bands will eventually come the nucleus of the wished-for rival to Boston—and Detroit!"

On November 1, 1918, at least three people were confident that the ban on public performances soon would end. With Sokoloff looking on, Hughes and Father Powers signed a contract stating that the Musical Arts Association would agree "to furnish the services of Cleveland's Symphony Orchestra"—the first such reference to the ensemble—"consisting of not less than fifty (50) musicians under the direction Mr. Nikolai Sokoloff, for one evening concert to be given in Cleveland on Wednesday evening, Dec. 11, 1918." Powers agreed to pay the association $600 the day after the concert.

The absence of performances due to the flu ban clearly was having an impact on the public, especially audiences hungry for good music. On November 3, Rogers sounded an impassioned lament in his Sunday column. "In the desert waste of things musical we thought, a few days ago, to discern a more hopeful outlook. Rumor had it that today would see the lifting of the ban. Now we perceive that the pleasing prospect is a little farther away and that we still, for a season, must possess our souls in patience," he wrote. "When the season finally does get under way, it will be a sadly dislocated affair, with dates confused in a general mix-up of postponements and conflicting engagements."

The clouds soon would lift, in more ways than one. The world had been waiting for Germany to accept the inevitable reality that it could not win the war. Kaiser Wilhelm finally abdicated the throne on November 9. Two days later, the guns went silent in Europe, and President Woodrow Wilson informed Congress that German delegates had signed the armistice agreement.

Sandwiched between these events was an important announcement of a more local nature. On November 10, the Cleveland public read an item in *The Plain Dealer* that appeared in the middle of Rogers's column—and didn't get to the crucial news until the third paragraph: ". . . a notable attraction will be offered in the new Cleveland symphony orchestra, which will be heard for the first time in public" on December 11. Sol Marcosson, a well-known Cleveland violinist, would be concertmaster. Walter Logan was announced as orchestra manager. Oscar Eiler would head the cello section. "The complete roster is not yet available," wrote Rogers, "but the names we have given are a guarantee of the quality of the orchestra, which is rapidly approaching a state of complete organization."

The *Cleveland News* had more to report a few days later. The orchestra would probably begin rehearsals during the coming week. "Most of the members this year will be Cleveland musicians—the picked best of them—with the possible addition of bassoons and oboes from out of town." Sokoloff was to have ten rehearsals before the December 11 debut. As per the contract with Hughes, Father Powers would pay the union rate of $600 for one rehearsal and one performance. Hughes claims that her board approved another $600 for extra rehearsals. Sokoloff says he told Severance "it would be impossible to groom an untried group into a respectable orchestra in three rehearsals" and that Severance agreed to pay for seven extra rehearsals to "waterproof the padre's roof." Women at Father Powers's parish sold tickets to the concert.

The joy generated by word of the armistice grew even greater in Cleveland's cultural community when the flu ban was lifted on November 19. By this time, Sokoloff and his orchestra had completed their first rehearsal, which was reported to have gone beautifully, reported the *News*: "A profitable and most agreeable time 'was had by all present,' [according to Sokoloff] and it is the opinion of the musicians that even this year, with opportunity for only a comparatively few rehearsals and entirely with local talent, the orchestra will make a record for itself, looking forward to enlargements in the personnel and programs of wider scope next season." The first piece the orchestra rehearsed was the exuberant last movement from Tchaikovsky's Symphony No. 4.

To the enormous relief of Hughes and her audience, the six-month hiatus in Cleveland's musical life came to an end on November 22, when Damrosch led the New York Symphony Orchestra in the opening event in the Symphony Orchestra Concerts series at Grays Armory. In a format that had become traditional, the evening's major work, Beethoven's Seventh Symphony, was performed on the first half, followed after intermission by arias by Meyerbeer and Bemberg, lighter works, and excerpts from Delibes's ballet, *Sylvia*.

Rogers reported two days later that Sokoloff had held two rehearsals with his new orchestra "with highly promising results. Forty-eight musicians were present at these rehearsals and the membership goal of fifty, as previously announced in this place, has been moved forward to sixty. Mr. Sokoloff is greatly pleased with the work so far done and expects to have his forces in fine fettle for their debut."

Sokoloff had more than Cleveland rehearsals and school duties to keep him occupied. In late November, he became the first of eight guest conductors to lead the Chicago Symphony that season. His concerts on November 29 and 30 at Chicago's Orchestra Hall were praised, adding to his stature in Cleveland. Not surprisingly, he gets the dates of his Chicago Symphony concerts in Chicago and Cleveland mixed up in his memoirs, but he remembers precisely their effect on his career: "The concert at once established me as a young (I was thirty-two) but serious and talented musician."

Before Cleveland audiences heard Sokoloff with his own new orchestra, or even Chicago's ensemble, they were provided a rather daunting means of comparison, as a wave of genuine symphonic greatness surged into town. Stokowski, in his seventh season at the helm of the Philadelphia Orchestra, arrived for an all-Tchaikovsky program with his musicians on December 5 at Grays Armory.

If anyone was intimidated by the presence of the fabulous Philadelphians under Stokowski, it wasn't Sokoloff. "You'll be surprised," he told *The Plain Dealer*'s Rogers. "I have had a good deal of experience with new orchestras, as well as with old ones, and the Cleveland players have surprised me. They do fine work for a beginning." Sokoloff chose his words carefully for several reasons. He must have realized immediately that Cleveland could not field the level of players he would demand in every instrumental section. And by concert time, in any case, he would have only 54 musicians, fewer than any of the orchestras that had visited Cleveland in recent years.

Cleveland was so hungry for an ensemble to call its own that it didn't seem to care that Sokoloff wouldn't have quite enough players to do complete justice to the music on the inaugural program. None of the critics would mention the absence of a second oboe or second bassoon, though the shortages in these departments had been noted a month earlier in the *Cleveland News*.

✵   ✵   ✵

The week Cleveland's Symphony Orchestra was to make its debut, theaters in town were bustling with activity, thanks in part to the lifting of the flu ban. Virtually every type of entertainment, high and low, could be enjoyed within blocks of Grays Armory. Henry Miller and Ruth Chatterton were starring in a revival of Alexander Dumas's play, *A Marriage of Convenience*, at the Opera House. The New York cast of the Jerome Kern-P. G. Wodehouse-Guy Bolton musical, *Oh, Boy*, with Ann Wheaton in a leading role, had arrived at the Schubert-Colonial. Representing burlesque were *The Innocent Maids* at the Empire and Fred Irwin's Big Show ("with a list of burlesque offerings of unusual merit") at the Star. In vaudeville, the Liberty was headlining Lottie Mayher and her diving girls, while the comic team of Blossom Seeley and Lew Dockstader was onstage at the Hippodrome.

A few days before 1918's big orchestral event, its sponsor, Father Powers, was hailed by Rogers as "not only a faithful shepherd of his flock, but an enterprising citizen, a lover of music, and the possessor of a pleasing tenor voice. When he heard of the formation of our new symphony orchestra, he at once offered to engage it for the benefit concert for St. Ann's that he proposed to give. So it is to Father Powers that we are indebted for this opportunity."

Hughes—who had witnessed the demise of three local orchestras over the past two decades—was taking a wait-and-see attitude on the future of her new venture. The day of the inaugural concert, she wrote to Winston & Livingston, an artist management firm in New York, that the orchestra was not going to consider out-of-town soloists this season. But she said major artists might be considered for the second season.

Sokoloff's program for the first concert appears to have been devised to charm the audience and provide a hint of the orchestra's potential. With anti-German feeling still in the air, the conductor steered clear of anything remotely Teutonic. Instead, he concentrated on the music he loved best (and would conduct often in Cleveland)—Russian, French, and American repertoire. Following a rendition of "The Star-Spangled Banner," Victor Herbert, the Irish-born American operetta master and a close friend of Logan's, became the first composer to have a work performed by Cleveland's Symphony Orchestra—his *American Fantasy*. This gave way to Anatol Liadov's *The Enchanted Lake* (its premiere in Cleveland) and Armas Järnefeldt's *Berceuse*, with concertmaster Marcosson and principal cellist Eiler as soloists.

Father Powers never actually sang a note with the orchestra. He performed three sacred selections with pianist George Gale Emerson, after which Sokoloff and his musicians performed the slow movement and finale from Tchaikovsky's Fourth Symphony to end the first half. Following intermission, Bizet's *Carmen* Suite No. 1 and sentimental songs—the latter performed by Father Powers and Emerson—preceded the finale, Liszt's tone poem, *Les Préludes*. In a program note to the audience, Father Powers lobbied for support of the new ensemble: "By securing the Orchestra, and [by] our presence at this, its initial concert, may we not hope to assist in stimulating the interest of music lovers of Cleveland, to the end that Cleveland's Symphony Orchestra may soon march with the leading Symphony Orchestras of our great cities?" The possessive title, Cleveland's Symphony Orchestra, could be construed as a sign of Hughes's long-standing desire to end the city's reliance on visiting orchestras.

In his review, proudly headlined "Our Symphony Orchestra" in the *Cleveland Press* the morning after the concert, Wilson G. Smith got straight to the point:

I presume that what I am about to say will greatly please some while undoubtedly surprise others. Here it is without fear or favor: Cleveland has at last a symphony orchestra. I know whereof I speak, for I heard it with no little astonishment Wednesday night when it debutized at St. Ann's Church benefit concert at Grays Armory. We have in the past heard much of our orchestra nucleus and its possibilities under favorable circumstances. Those favorable circumstances seem to have arrived in the person of Nicolai [sic] Sokoloff, who, I sincerely believe, is destined to lead our ever existing nucleus out of the house of bondage and into the land of honey and pleasant pastures.

Smith enthused about Sokoloff's "highly intelligent musicianship allied to a fine discrimination in climaxes and a refined sense of tonal nuances" in the Tchaikovsky and "the manner in which his players responded to his dynamic and temperamental suggestions . . . we have an orchestra in the making and a director who evidently knows his business."

Rogers was no less glowing in his *Plain Dealer* review the same day, and he earmarked certain characteristics of the maestro's style—clarity and precision—that were destined to become hallmarks of the orchestra. "Conductor Nikolai Sokoloff has succeeded in getting together an orchestra of adequate size and excellent quality," he wrote. "A musician of fine attainments, he is also a leader of capacity and resource. There is no wavering or uncertainty either in his beat, which is a model of clarity and precision, or in his conception of the work in hand. Which is to say that Mr. Sokoloff knows what he wants, and how to get it, and Cleveland's new conductor is not content with lesser things. He hitches his chariot to a star."

The music critics weren't the only audience members who felt something special had occurred. Hughes had invited the Reverend A. B. Stuber, of St. Peter's Rectory in Canton, to the concert. He sat with Frank Ginn for the first half, after which the priest had to leave. "I can honestly say that I don't think I shall have to look elsewhere in need of a large orchestra as Cleveland's Symphony will answer my purposes," Father Stuber wrote to Hughes the next day. "Admittedly they are going to increase and improve and will soon be the equal of our best."

Taking advantage of the critical and public response, as well as the prospect of Sokoloff's success with the Chicago Symphony in Cleveland on December 19, Hughes quickly announced a repeat of the inaugural program for December 22 at popular prices (25 cents, 50 cents, and $1)—and without Father Powers. Weber's *Der Freischütz* overture, the first Germanic piece played by the ensemble, helped to fill out the repertoire. Rogers, again enthusiastic in a follow-up review, captured the excitement of the orchestra's birth best in a column the morning of the second concert, saving his highest accolades for Sokoloff: "His fifty-four players are with him to a man—and woman. If this were not so his labors would be in vain. He has gained the confidence and respect of his musicians—and trust an orchestral player to know whether a conductor is on the job!—and he has fired them with his own zeal."

— 4 —

The Lusty Infant

N ikolai Sokoloff and Adella Prentiss Hughes knew they had to maintain momentum and proceed quickly with their plans to develop the
orchestra. Their first concern was personnel. An ensemble of 54 players was
too small to perform much of the music Sokoloff wanted to conduct, and
which local audiences had heard played by the country's great orchestras.
Key positions needed to be filled immediately to strengthen the ensemble.
Aware that there weren't enough orchestral musicians, seasoned or not, currently living in Cleveland, Sokoloff traveled to New York in late December
to audition players. Hughes, who would become known as "the mother of
the Cleveland Orchestra," already sounded a bit overbearing when she
wired Sokoloff at the Hotel Richmond in New York soon after his departure:
"ENGAGE OBOE BASSOON VIOLA SEVENTY FIVE WEEKLY GOOD PLAY-
ERS ESSENTIAL. HAPPY NEW YEAR." While Sokoloff continued searching
for new players in New York over the next months, Hughes dealt with unhappy musicians in Cleveland: they hadn't been paid for the second concert
in December. They hadn't been paid for the rehearsals that preceded the
inaugural concert, either, but that issue wouldn't come up for several
months.

Sokoloff's auditions led to the hiring of two players—a principal bassoon
and a principal oboe/English hornist. The conductor was back in New York
in March for two trips, the first with Hughes in tow (or vice versa), to hear
more candidates. This 10-day trip resulted in the hiring of principal viola,
horn, and trumpet players. During the second journey, Hughes wired
Sokoloff: "We can afford two horns, one trumpet one trombone eight weeks
beginning March twenty-fourth."

Other musicians, including principal violist Herman Kolodkin, arrived in
Cleveland in mid-March, just in time to play an important event, the first orchestra concert sponsored by the American Steel & Wire Company. Back in
the fall, Sokoloff had stated publicly his desire to bring good music to factory workers through concerts with his new ensemble, whenever it got

started. Then, on a train trip to New York in early 1919 to audition players, Sokoloff had met William P. Palmer, president of American Steel & Wire. Palmer became intrigued with the conductor's ideas about concerts for workers. Although he had no love for fine music himself, Palmer appreciated the value of serving his employees. Sokoloff was persuasive. He told Palmer "most of the people in our mills and plants are Middle Europeans, all of whom instinctively respond to music. I'm sure that if the plants gave the concerts advance publicity, they could be sold outright at each plant at twenty-five cents a ticket." The conversation led to Palmer's donation of $5,000 for five concerts in March at Grays Armory for 12,500 workers, the first industrial concerts at Sokoloff's suggested price of 25 cents per ticket.

Forbes magazine was so struck by the idea that it assigned a reporter to cover the orchestra's project. "It may be shown that the future patrons of music, painting, sculpture, etc., must be the people at large," wrote the reporter. "Most business men have not yet caught the big-gauged call of art. From a business, money-making aspect, they do not give a continental for art. It makes no difference whether we have concerts, opera, sculpture, art museums, beautiful parks. But this is all wrong. *It does make a big difference, and in a business, dollars-and-cents way, too.*"

Sokoloff was helping to raise dollars and cents not only through crusading but through concertizing—and not only on the podium. On January 30, 1919, at Grays Armory, he made his first appearance as soloist with his orchestra in the Vieuxtemps Violin Concerto No. 4, with Logan conducting. "He revealed attainments of a high order," Rogers wrote of Sokoloff, who conducted the rest of the program.

✿   ✿   ✿

Nearby communities began clamoring to hear Sokoloff and his ensemble. Oberlin College had intended to hire the Chicago Symphony for its annual May Festival, but organizers decided instead to make a goodwill gesture by inviting the new group in the neighborhood. Akron became one of the first cities to present the orchestra, in the series offered by the Tuesday Musical Club, which was run for many years by Hughes's close friend, Gertrude Seiberling.

Hughes and Sokoloff became nonstop advocates for their orchestra, working with the local publicity firm Henderson & Jappe to generate newspaper coverage in Cleveland and elsewhere. The outcome of their initial efforts was an impressive first season of 27 concerts: three evening, four popular Sunday, four community, six industrial, two benefit, one choral, and seven out-of-town performances.

Sokoloff had not intended to perform an entire symphony during the first season. "He will select movements and give parts of symphonies as a very wise means of making programs perhaps more popular with audiences unused to the long drawn-out measures of a single composition," the *News* reported. But when he saw the orchestra becoming more capable, Sokoloff changed his mind and programmed one complete masterpiece, Beethoven's Fifth, toward the end of the season.

More new players arrived before the season was out. Sokoloff had decided to remove concertmaster Sol Marcosson (who would return a decade later as a violist), and Hughes called on conductor Josef Stransky, who had appeared often in the Symphony Orchestra Concerts series with the New York Philharmonic Society, to proffer a candidate. Stransky suggested a member of the Philharmonic, Louis Edlin, and released him for the rest of the season to play concertmaster in Cleveland. By April, Hughes had imported eight players, and this began to get the attention of Local 4, the musicians' union. It would not be inclined to approve of more non-Clevelanders being hired.

Edlin's arrival not only buoyed the violin section, but also planted the seeds for the first chamber ensemble drawn from the orchestra. As a welcoming gesture to Edlin at Frank Ginn's house in early April, Sokoloff put together a string quartet composed of himself (first violin), Edlin (second violin), Kolodkin (viola), and Otto Eiler (cello). Hughes found the session enthralling: "Never have three [sic] people played together for the first time with such absolute unity of spirit and tone—even their vibrato is the same." Sokoloff's love for chamber music would find expression not only in the quartet, but in the orchestra he was developing with such zeal.

Eiler would not remain in his important posts. In June, he was replaced in the quartet and as principal cello by Victor de Gomez, whom Leopold Stokowski had released from the Philadelphia Orchestra at Sokoloff's request. De Gomez would remain Cleveland's principal cellist for two decades.

Another important addition to the orchestra at this time was Philip Kirchner, who became principal oboe at the end of May. Born in 1892 in Lithuania, Kirchner came to the United States in 1906 and studied with Marcel Tabuteau of the Philadelphia Orchestra and Bruno Labate of the New York Philharmonic. He played in the Russian Symphony Orchestra, possibly while Sokoloff was concertmaster, and as a member of the New York Philharmonic from 1915 until he came to Cleveland. Kirchner had one more interesting credit: he had performed with John Philip Sousa's band.

❄   ❄   ❄

In order to attract such distinguished musicians as de Gomez and Kirchner, Hughes had to offer them a minimum of 20 weeks for the 1919–20 season, and the Musical Arts Association had to begin a massive fund-raising effort. The orchestra would need about $100,000 for its second season. Hughes advertised that supporters would be listed in the program if they donated at least $25.

The mounting admiration for the orchestra led to heartwarming encounters. A salesman from a jewelry store on Woodland Avenue, who had been helping Hughes sell tickets in the Italian community, visited her in March 1919. At first, he told her he couldn't afford the $25 pledge. Two weeks later, he returned and signed the card, praising the orchestra, as Hughes recounted in a letter to Severance: "This orchestra a greata thing. I want to be a supporter. Mr. Sokoloff, he a greata Conductor, just like the man with the big orchestra from Philadelphia."

Yet many of the concerts during the first season weren't coming close to selling out at Grays Armory, which could seat 3,500. Sokoloff theorized that the city's wealthy people tended to look down on a local ensemble, "though how the marvel of hearing a great orchestra of their own develop and improve could be anything but a thrilling experience, I'll never know."

Concert receipts and the association's fund-raising efforts weren't always enough to pay the musicians with regularity during the first season, leading to the first clashes between players and management. Hughes complained to Sokoloff, once again in New York auditioning players, that principal bassist Gerald Fiore had brought up the matter of payment for the orchestra's original rehearsals at a meeting with the musicians' union—which in those days had little power to discuss salary matters with orchestra management. The association agreed to come up with the $400 to pay the players, leading Hughes to decide that Fiore shouldn't be offered a contract for the second season. In the end, she changed her mind, and Fiore stayed until 1936.

For its performances, the fledgling orchestra was starting to gain a reputation as a phenomenon in the music world. As Hughes told *Cleveland News* critic Archie Bell in an interview toward the end of the first season, "why, you ought to go to New York to hear about our lusty Cleveland infant, the orchestra, which we all know has made such a record for itself within one year. Everywhere I went the first word I heard was one of compliment in regard to this organization."

The infant was proving true to form in one particularly inconvenient way:

it was expensive. Sokoloff expected to have at least seventy-five players for his second season. The board acknowledged that deficits would be inevitable, since there was no way to earn enough income from ticket sales to cover overall expenses. As the inaugural season came to a close, the association decided that annual gifts of $100 or $250 from trustees were inadequate to meet growing financial needs. Guarantors were asked to contribute large sums annually to a general maintenance fund. The donors who had been most generous in supporting the Symphony Orchestra Concerts and the early endeavors of the Musical Arts Association once again stepped forward to keep the orchestra on a firm financial foundation. More than half of the anticipated $100,000 budget for the second season was supplied by John L. Severance ($20,000), Samuel Mather ($10,000), William G. Mather ($5,000), David Z. Norton ($5,000), Mrs. F. F. Prentiss ($5,000), H. G. Dalton ($2,500), Frank Ginn ($2,000), and F. F. Prentiss ($1,000). For decades, deficits would be wiped out with personal checks from one or two or more of these guarantors.

Severance's handsome donation reflected his devotion not only to Cleveland, but also to the conductor he had met less than a year earlier at the Waldorf-Astoria. "You have accomplished marvels far beyond even the brilliant vision of Mrs. Hughes and I deem it a privilege to have been associated with such an enterprise as has produced the Cleveland Symphony Orchestra," he wrote to Sokoloff. "We are under great obligation to you and this but faintly expresses my own sense of our debt, and [I] wish you even greater success in the future."

❀   ❀   ❀

Their future might have changed swiftly. Plans for the orchestra's second season were moving along when Sokoloff, vacationing in California for the summer, was asked to become conductor of the soon-to-be-organized Los Angeles Symphony Orchestra by its principal sponsor, William Andrews Clark, Jr. But Sokoloff, elated by his experience in Cleveland, turned down the offer.

To lure more concertgoers for the second season, Hughes and Sokoloff engaged renowned soloists, some of whom had appeared in the Symphony Orchestra Concerts series. The roster included violinist Toscha Seidel, soprano Frances Alda, and contralto Gabriella Besanzoni from the Metropolitan Opera, tenor Edward Johnson from the Chicago Opera, pianist Mischa Levitzki, and cellist Pablo Casals. The concerts no longer were to be performed in Grays Armory, home of orchestral performances in

Cleveland for almost three decades. Hughes was invited to present her orchestra at Masonic Hall, a new, $1.2 million building on East 36th Street between Euclid and Chester avenues (later renamed Masonic Auditorium). She booked 36 dates for the 1919–20 season.

Bell provided a glimpse into Sokoloff's rehearsal methods at the beginning of the second season, calling the conductor "an excellent drill master, not in the old-fashioned Prussian military manner, but in the 'now-altogether-boys' way that brings results." Rehearsing Debussy's *Prelude to the Afternoon of a Faun*, and not getting what he wanted, Sokoloff "seemed like a stern father rebuking naughty children whom he loved so well that he wanted them to be perfect in all good works. His tongue was in his cheek— and the men knew it."

Maybe. But they may not have felt this way when Sokoloff chastised them for playing wrong notes and going through the motions. "What are you? Are you musicians?" he was reported as saying. "Can you tell beautiful music when you see it on the printed page, or when you hear it? That's Debussy, gentlemen, Debussy. Do you realize that fact, or are you sitting here unmoved and merely playing the notes that you see before you? Do you realize that this is as beautiful music as you are likely to hear this side of Paradise? Now come on, try again; realize what you are doing and don't let me hear what I have just heard."

By this time, audiences at home and around the country were beginning to hear about the Cleveland Orchestra, as the ensemble was now officially dubbed (although "Cleveland Symphony" would be a long-lived misnomer). When Sokoloff took his musicians to Chicago in January 1920 to make their debut together in the Windy City, critics got the name right—and they liked what they heard. "Nikolai Sokoloff's Cleveland Orchestra that came to Orchestra Hall last evening deserved the hearty welcome it received," wrote Herman Devries in the *Chicago Evening American*. "A Chicago audience is not slow to appreciate sincerity and achievement and these two admirable qualities are outstanding in this year old and precocious neighbor of ours."

Upon the group's return to Cleveland, Sokoloff welcomed Pablo Casals to Masonic Hall for his debut with the orchestra in the Schumann Cello Concerto. The conductor had been entranced when he first encountered Casals in Paris in 1913. On the same trip, he heard violinist Jacques Thibaud, whom he invited to make his debut with the Cleveland ensemble a few weeks before Casals in the Symphony Orchestra Concerts series.

Rogers hailed Thibaud for his playing of the Mozart E-flat major Violin Concerto and Chausson *Poème*, but Sokoloff remembers the concert dif-

ferently, and amusingly, in his memoirs. Rehearsal the morning of the concert went fine. Then Sokoloff made the mistake of taking Thibaud to lunch
at the Statler Hotel. During the meal, a waiter handed Sokoloff a note from
one of the orchestra's female volunteers, who was dining with a friend, a
blonde who appeared to be quite taken with Thibaud. The women invited
the musicians to their table, and the blonde invited them to her home for
cognac, despite Prohibition. Sokoloff and the other woman declined, but
not Thibaud, who said he hated to be alone. At the concert that night,
Sokoloff says, the violinist "had nothing to give and gave nothing. Or worse
than nothing, rather, for he gave me cold chills and sinking nausea as I realized what had happened—he had spent the afternoon with the blonde, and
not just chatting, either."

Although Thibaud had let him down, Sokoloff reengaged him as soloist
in 1923 for Lalo's *Symphonie espagnole*. Again, the rehearsal was magical.
And again, Sokoloff took Thibaud to lunch. "I looked him straight in the eye
and said, 'Monsieur Thibaud, this time after lunch, you are going to your
room and to bed *alone*!' He looked at me in surprise for a moment, and then
he started to laugh. 'You knew, eh? And you are so right,' he said. 'I never
met her again—and I hope I never do—at least *before* a concert!' He played
superbly that night, and he had rave reviews."

Sokoloff's own exhaustion began to plague him in the middle of the second season. He had conducted every concert since the orchestra's inaugural benefit, expanded the ensemble to 72 players, and helped Hughes establish a 28-week season. During the second year, he was scheduled to conduct 61 concerts—44 in Cleveland and 17 on tour. "We have run a very grave
risk this season in having no assistant conductor, there being literally not one
person in Cleveland who could carry through a concert should [Sokoloff] be
suddenly indisposed," Hughes wrote to Severance. "I have dared to do this
because of his splendid physique and spirit. It is however something that
cannot be continued another season when the responsibility will be much
heavier through the larger number of concerts scheduled."

The conductor chosen to be Sokoloff's assistant was Arthur Shepherd,
then living in Boston, who was also an accomplished composer. In 1906,
Shepherd had won the $500 prize in a Boston competition for American
composers created with trust funds donated by Polish pianist Jan Paderewski. Hughes told Severance that Shepherd's duties would be numerous.
He would rehearse and conduct the orchestra whenever needed, "organize
and rehearse the Cleveland Orchestra Chorus, which we must have to produce important works, notably Beethoven's Ninth Symphony, . . . lecture on

our programs, occasionally in places like Youngstown when we have a series and in public schools in Cleveland, . . . write all our program notes" and eventually conduct summer concerts. Severance gave his blessing, and Shepherd was engaged to arrive in October 1920.

Sokoloff's assistant conductor would also be responsible for one of the principal missions that had brought the ensemble to life: educational concerts. Upon Shepherd's arrival, the Cleveland Orchestra began to leave the concert hall to perform for children in school buildings. The new conductor planned the programs and spoke about the music during the concerts.

Along with these performances, many of the orchestra's musicians were hired—at $5 to $10 a week for up to eight hours of work—to teach instrumental music in high schools, starting a shift from the existing emphasis on choral music. Central High School became ground zero for the instrumental music experiment. Eleven orchestra musicians taught more than 100 students the first year. Harry Clarke, a bass player in the orchestra and former leader of the 135th Artillery Band, supervised the program. "As a result of this teaching, a band was organized, which has had a direct influence upon the moral and social work of the school, according to the testimony of its Principal, Mr. Edward L. Harris," Hughes told her board.

In addition to Clarke, Russell J. Morgan, a faculty member at Northwestern University, was hired to oversee the instrumental music program and make Cleveland a leader in band and orchestra training programs. Morgan and Osbourne McConathy, later a horn player in the Boston Symphony, developed class methods for band students that became standard around the country. These projects were models for educational programs that would later bring the orchestra the highest national acclaim in this field.

*   *   *

The orchestra in its second season had grown, but had it improved? Pianist Mischa Levitzki seemed to think so after he appeared as soloist under Sokoloff. "It is most astonishing that an orchestra of one year's existence should give such beautiful performances," Levitzki wrote to Hughes in March 1920 from New York. "To have attained such an ensemble in such a short space of time is indeed a remarkable achievement which speaks most eloquently for Mr. Sokoloff and his men."

Another measure of the orchestra's growth came from the other end of the country. The new orchestra in Los Angeles had made its debut in the fall of 1919. One of its frequent concertgoers was Severance, who mailed a few lines of partisan music criticism back to Hughes from his second home in

Pasadena: "I again heard the Lost Angeles Symphony Orchestra last week and am sending you one of their programs but it doesn't compare with our own Cleveland Orchestra. The Wagner Symphony I did not care for at all."

Along with improvement in personnel, the season's seven pairs of concerts were stronger in programming than the preceding ones. Sokoloff threw off the caution he had displayed during the first season and began to luxuriate in performances of complete symphonies. Among the repertoire were Brahms's Symphony No. 2, Mozart's Symphony No. 40, and Tchaikovsky's Symphony No. 5. Sokoloff continued to reveal his leaning toward French and American composers, including local composers, by programming them generously. Johann Beck became the orchestra's first guest conductor when he led the ensemble in a performance of his own overture *Lara*. Charles Rychlik, a member of the violin section the first season, had been honored with inaugural-year performances of his Caprice, Op. 2, and Elegy, Op. 7, under Sokoloff. The conductor presented Rychlik's Overture, Op. 16, during the second season and his *Dramatic Overture* during the third.

Paying tribute to his mentors quickly became a Sokoloff tradition in Cleveland. Eight works by Vincent d'Indy, the conductor's teacher in Paris a decade earlier, were performed during the Sokoloff years, beginning in 1920 with the orchestral legend *Saugefleure*. The first of eight works by Charles Martin Loeffler, Sokoloff's violin teacher in Boston, was performed during the second season. *A Pagan Poem*, for orchestra with piano (and three prominent trumpets), showed up in no fewer than seven Sokoloff seasons, the first performance featuring pianist Beryl Rubinstein.

One of the most intriguing appearances of the second season was made by a disembodied soloist. The orchestra had been offered a handsome fee by the Aeolian Piano Company to perform with one of its newest products— a player piano propelled by a Harold Bauer recording of the Saint-Saëns Second Piano Concerto. Sokoloff found the experience "unnerving" but evidently managed to keep the orchestra synchronized with the phantom soloist.

New works and experiments fit the conductor's orchestral philosophy. "I want to give people, if possible, something more than musical prettiness," Sokoloff told *Musical America*. "In some of our great orchestras I have been impressed over and over by the technical perfection, the sheer loveliness of sound. But I have not gotten that which thrilled me. I have not heard a genuine message, a momentous outpouring. I want my men to give that. I want them to provide something which indisputably makes the listener feel spiritually richer for the experience."

Sokoloff's vision couldn't have been timelier. Now that World War I was over, the visiting orchestras that had been performing in Cleveland for 19 years were discovering that their communities needed them at home. After 162 concerts by 11 orchestras under 21 conductors, Hughes quietly disbanded the Symphony Orchestra Concerts at the end of the 1919–20 season. She would present four orchestras the following season (Detroit with Ossip Gabrilowitsch, New York Symphony with Walter Damrosch, La Scala Orchestra with Arturo Toscanini, New York Philharmonic with Stransky) under the auspices of the Musical Arts Association, and a final visiting ensemble, the New York Symphony led by Albert Coates, during the 1921–22 season. "Cleveland may well congratulate itself that our own orchestra is here ready to fill the vacancy and develop our musical life as it should be," Hughes wrote to Severance. Hughes also made more plans to take her own ensemble on the road, adding tour dates for the third season (1920–21). The orchestra would play 104 concerts this season, including 47 on tour.

Sokoloff expanded the personnel to 86 players with "better instruments than before." This expansion brought to Cleveland two musicians who would make lasting contributions: Frank Sholle, who joined the percussion section in the fall of 1920 and would remain until 1960, serving as a principal player for many years; and Carlton Cooley, a violinist from the Philadelphia Orchestra who came to Cleveland to succeed Kolodkin as principal viola (and as violist in the Cleveland String Quartet). After his first year, Cooley switched back to violin to play assistant concertmaster for two seasons. He later distinguished himself as the orchestra's solo violist until his departure in 1937.

Archie Bell preceded the third season with a glowing preview in the *Cleveland News* detailing the orchestra's expansion in personnel and activity. "As a matter of unadulterated fact," he wrote, "we are in for a veritable orgy of music, a sort of Niagara of tone, compared to which all previous seasons were drops of water over the Chinese chair of torture."

When the season finally got under way in late October 1920, Bell let the superlatives soar, proclaiming that the city finally could claim to have "a truly great symphony orchestra all our own, a Cleveland institution, one that must carry us over that humiliating border of 'commercialism,' where Cleveland has heretofore had the reputation of lingering . . . we have not only crossed the border . . . we have taken a hurdle, and not a citizen of Cleveland henceforth has cause to hesitate in comparing our orchestra to any in the country, with perhaps two exceptions, Chicago and Philadelphia."

The Bell euphoria was only getting started. Early in 1921, the critic had even better reason to go overboard: Toscanini, who hadn't been to Cleveland since making his local debut conducting Metropolitan Opera performances of *Otello* and *Aida* in 1911, came to town to lead the La Scala Orchestra on February 2 and 3. His programs included such works as Beethoven's Symphony No. 7, Brahms's Variations on a Theme by Haydn and Symphony No. 2, Rossini's *William Tell* overture, Respighi's *Fountains of Rome* (only six years old at the time), and Strauss's *Don Juan*.

The headline on Bell's review of Toscanini's second performance read "Best Concert Ever," and the critic waxed grandiose: "When Cleveland is exhumed about 5,000 or 6,000 A.D. I would like to have the excavators find a little clay brick on which I had scribbled that in my opinion the best symphony concert to the year of grace 1921 was that by La Scala orchestra of Milan, Maestro Arturo Toscanini directing, Thursday evening. From the first phrase to the final drop of the conductor's baton, it was a superb achievement on the part of the 100 talented Italians . . ."

After the first concert, Toscanini attended a supper party at the home of Felix and Adella Prentiss Hughes. It may have been one of the last times the couple was seen together at a public gathering. Sometime in 1921, Felix Hughes—who had closed his Euclid Avenue voice studio in the fall of 1918 to take a government job in Washington, D.C.—packed his bags again and left, for good, for New York, where he opened a studio. The marriage would end in divorce in 1923, with Adella charging gross neglect of duty. "Our marriage resulted in discord instead of harmony," she told the press. "Felix called my artist friends 'highbrows.' He preferred the white lights of Broadway."

❖   ❖   ❖

New York in 1921 was also an exciting destination for the Cleveland Orchestra, which made its debut there on February 13 under Sokoloff at the 5,000-seat Hippodrome Theatre, on Sixth Avenue and 43rd Street, as part of its first eastern tour. (The ensemble also played in Boston and Washington, D.C.) The cavernous Hippodrome had not been built with symphony orchestras in mind—not onstage, at least. But that wasn't the only problem with Cleveland's debut at this extravagant theater. There was also the soloist, Italian baritone Titta Ruffo. The day before the concert, Sokoloff began the rehearsal with Ruffo nowhere to be found. Soon, a man approached Hughes and told her that he was Ruffo's secretary, Paul Longone. "Oh, do you sing?" Hughes asked. "No," said Longone, "I will tell the conductor how Mr. Ruffo desires the accompaniment played." Sokoloff kept his cool. When Ruffo made his entrance at the concert, the audience responded with loud applause. What followed was worthy of comic opera. Ruffo ignored the orchestra and began singing before his cue in the serenade from Mozart's *Don Giovanni*. Sokoloff got the orchestra back on track, and everyone wound up together at the end. "I was wild," Hughes recalled, "and met Sokoloff as he came offstage, expecting to find him furiously angry. His sense of humor had come to his rescue, however, and he didn't 'emote.' "

The New York critics didn't emote much, either. The erudite Henry Krehbiel wrote in the *Tribune* that "the string band of the visitors seemed to lack sap and fiber; the woodwinds without homogeneity or charm. How much of merit all these factors may possess cannot be said after such a hearing; nor would it be fair to attempt to assign a rank to the band among those of New York and other cities which Cleveland has emulated in sending its organization to us for a metropolitan hearing." Equally blasé was the *Herald*'s William J. Henderson: "As far as could be judged last evening the orchestra is one of respectable merits. Its ensemble tone is good; the strings, though somewhat rough, have spirit; the wood is passable, and the brass acceptable. Nikolai Sokoloff, the conductor, has apparently labored hard to bring about good attack, precision and unanimity. In another place the orchestra might sound better. It was kindly received last evening."

It was more kindly received by the critic of the *Times*, too, who wrote, "the quality of the band in its brief history reflects credit upon the Lake Erie city." An unsigned review in the *Evening World* also contained praise, however roundabout, noting that "with all the crudities of youth it made a brave display of precosity and virtuosity that upset nobody's digestion." The critic of the *World* identified Sokoloff as a former resident of Manhattan who had done much in a short time. "In the Tschaikowsky sixth symphony," the reviewer stated, "it was evident that the musicians were well drilled, could provide a good tone and perform well together."

✿   ✿   ✿

Sokoloff, the "excellent drill master," was getting his orchestra in shape by establishing a disciplined working environment. He would tolerate no lapses of concentration or decorum during rehearsals. One day, according to Musical Arts Association board minutes, the strict regimen led to an altercation between Sokoloff and bassoonist R. J. Griffith. As Sokoloff was trying to convey an interpretive detail to his musicians, Griffith ignored the explanation and continued conversing with another musician. When Sokoloff asked him to refrain from gabbing, Griffith refused.

"One of these days I am going to send you home," the conductor said.

"I don't care," answered Griffith.

"Is that all you care about your work?" asked Sokoloff. "It would be better that you study your parts."

"I play as well as you conduct," came the retort.

Sokoloff told Griffith to leave immediately. The bassoonist would never return.

The incident led to a meeting between Hughes and the orchestra committee—four musicians chosen by their colleagues to represent them in labor matters—about grievance procedures. Their discussions resulted in an agreement allowing musicians and management to circumvent the union and decide how most orchestra matters should be settled. When rulings were required from the union, they would have to be made in writing to avoid "misunderstanding and discontent."

Nevertheless, discontent was surfacing within the orchestra. The season was only 28 weeks, which meant playing in the Cleveland Orchestra was a part-time job—as it would remain to varying degrees until 1968. And the musicians would always be paid widely differing salaries. Principal players negotiated higher salaries based on their responsibilities and stature, a situation evident in the figures for the 1920–21 season. Minimum weekly salaries for first violins ranged from $45 for section players to $125 for the concertmaster. Second violins were paid $45 to $75. Also receiving the top amount of $125 were the principal cello and principal oboe, while the lowest fee, $30, went to third clarinet. The total for weekly salaries of 81 musicians this season was $5,225. Even in 1920 dollars, this was not much.

In 1921, orchestra players in Cleveland had few musical ways to supplement their incomes during the season, aside from teaching. They could work at nonmusical jobs when they weren't rehearsing or performing under Sokoloff, but taking another *musical* job was forbidden, especially when the conductor perceived a threat to his orchestra's discipline and, indeed, survival. The principal threat at that time was jazz. "A player cannot do his most beautiful work if he has misused his talent by playing ragtime," Sokoloff remarked. "The life of a musician has become so strenuous he cannot waste his time and energy on jazz. But who would want to make ugly sounds, when he knew how to make beautiful ones? And that's what jazz is, ugly sounds." Sokoloff and Hughes became so spooked about jazz—in its seemingly radical way the rock or rap music of its day—that they slipped a rule into the orchestra's contract: "No member of the orchestra shall play at a dance or in a parade."

The issue became heated, prompting reporters to elicit views from prominent musicians on the merits, or lack thereof, of jazz. Swiss composer

Ernest Bloch, who had become the first director of the Cleveland Institute of Music when the school opened its doors in December 1920, shared his open mind on the subject. "I adore jazz," said Bloch. "Because one loves the classical master in music is no reason why one should not be receptive to anything so entertaining as jazz." Hughes showed her conservative inclinations when she said that she loved "the rhythm of jazz, but I must add that I abominate the noise that seems to go with it."

Jazz may have been perceived as pernicious, but it did not appear to affect the artistic growth Sokoloff was achieving with the Cleveland Orchestra. (The conductor even stepped back from his position about musical jobs outside the orchestra on occasion if a player pleaded convincingly that he couldn't make ends meet without the extra work.) By 1921, Cleveland had gained in national stature. Though there was no objective way to measure such an ascent, Hughes had proclaimed at the end of its first season that her orchestra had taken a place among the country's top 12 symphonic organizations. A year later, she assigned it to the eighth position. Sokoloff, at the start of the fourth season, believed his musicians comprised "a good orchestra of the second class. It did not rank with the Boston, Philadelphia, Chicago and the two New York orchestras, of course, but it was a fine orchestra in a class just below them."

Sokoloff was beginning to instill in the Cleveland Orchestra a quality of togetherness—of chamber music–style finesse and intimacy—that would, eventually, become synonymous with the institution. "I believe in ensemble, naturally," Sokoloff wrote. "When a phrase was given from one instrument to another, or a phrase was imitated by another instrument, I wanted them to be more or less alike because of the ensemble, but at the same time, I wanted every instrumentalist to have a sense that he was saying something from his own musical feeling. I wanted them all to be completely free when they played, to be without tension; never to play as a sort of duty, or as a part of a mechanical precision instrument, but always feeling, with a sense of joy." (Considering that these words were written in the mid-1960s, the references to "tension" and "duty" and "a mechanical precision instrument" sound like not-so-veiled criticisms of George Szell, the orchestra's taskmaster at the time.)

❖   ❖   ❖

Cleveland's critics supported the development of the orchestra almost without reservation until the fourth season, when debates arose regarding the level to which some observers were claiming the ensemble had risen. Board member Newton D. Baker, the prominent lawyer and former Cleveland mayor and U.S. secretary of war, announced on opening night of the 1921–22 season that the orchestra already was one of the world's greats. *The Plain Dealer's* Rogers, ever supportive, gentle, and provincial, echoed Baker's remarks by making the outlandish suggestion that the orchestra needed no further improvement: "The building process has been completed; and the architects have done their work well. We have now an orchestra that can hold its own anywhere, and we have in Mr. Sokoloff one of America's most gifted directors."

The *Press's* Smith begged to differ. In his assessment of the opening program of the season, he did what no critic had yet done in Cleveland—he took Sokoloff to task, citing his performance of Beethoven's Fifth as willful and messy. "In my humble opinion, Sokoloff lacks the poise and self-restraint necessary to an exact and fully balanced interpretation of Beethoven's master work," wrote Smith, who would become more disenchanted with the conductor as the years passed. "We have in its adolescence a fine orchestra even tho [*sic*] one may not presume to classify it as one of the world's greatest."

If a recalcitrant critic wasn't enough, the orchestra was also facing a pressing financial challenge: how to raise more money from the community. The Musical Arts Association was kept afloat by a small group of generous citizens—volunteers who provided the cash and brainpower to develop and sustain a growing arts institution. Many of these donors were civic leaders with a true appreciation for music; others had little interest in artistic endeavors beyond their beneficial effect on business and social standing. The fact that most association trustees had (and always would have) little knowledge of music was both a positive and a negative. Positive, because they knew that they had to leave the artistic decisions to the artists (largely meaning the conductors). Negative, because trustees would have little contact with the artists they employed (meaning the orchestra's musicians).

In the early 1920s, the Musical Arts Association could not count on a single wealthy benefactor to fund the operation, as was true of the Los Angeles and New York symphony orchestras. On the West Coast, William Andrews Clark, Jr., picked up the entire tab for the young ensemble in the early decades; Harry Harkness Flagler did largely the same for the New York Symphony. The Philadelphia Orchestra had amassed an endowment of $1.8 million, and in Chicago the orchestra owned $2 million worth of property, which provided income. As a young organization, Cleveland also trailed far behind other orchestras in contributors. In Detroit, the number was 700; in Minneapolis, 360. In Cleveland in 1921, only 135 contributors supported the orchestra.

The Musical Arts Association's top donors faced the challenge by recruiting 200 citizens to raise the $200,000 needed to pay the orchestra's bills for the 1921–22 season. Almost all of the donors, and those who helped solicit contributions, were businessmen who had no personal interest in the music but realized that a symphony orchestra provided the community with a valuable cultural benefit. These volunteers "are strongly endowed with sentiment and they will get behind civic projects and work with unlimited zeal," reported the *Cleveland Commercial News*. "They think not only of money, but also of the good they can do in bringing satisfaction and happiness to the lives of others." Board member Dudley S. Blossom spearheaded the campaign, as he would many times in the future, with assistance from as far away as California. Severance and other Clevelanders who owned residences on the West Coast sent $52,000 back home.

In the midst of the campaign, on April 15, 1922, the orchestra and Sokoloff reached out to a far larger audience than usual—13,000, among whom there must have been more than a few potential donors—when they performed at the opening of Cleveland's massive Public Auditorium. Their portion of the program included Wagner's *Die Meistersinger* prelude, Elgar's *Pomp and Circumstance* march, Berlioz's *Rakoczy March*, and, from their inaugural concert in 1918, Liszt's *Les Préludes*.

The campaign was going well. By early summer, Blossom was urging committee members to get out and collect pledges, even if it meant defying Prohibition: "The bars are down. Ask your Aunt, your Doctor, your Bootlegger—everybody to contribute, whether you hold his card or not." In July, Blossom could report that 500 new contributors had brought the total of maintenance-fund donors to 675, "over five times the number contributing a year ago!" he crowed. "But we must have 1,000!" The campaign ended in triumph, if slightly below Blossom's goal: the final tally was 803 donors, who gave gifts ranging from $5 to $30,000.

The campaign wiped out the deficit for the previous season and placed the orchestra, at least temporarily, on solid financial ground for the 1922–23 season. Now the board, Hughes, and Sokoloff turned their attention to other important matters. Hughes and Sokoloff were becoming concerned that so many players, especially those from out of town, were leaving the orchestra. Many musicians who were imported from New York and other cities didn't even bother to bring their families with them. Why should they? They knew they would only have employment in Cleveland for little more than half a year. Salaries were higher in the big eastern orchestras (Boston, New York, Philadelphia), and, besides, those ensembles were still more prestigious.

Cleveland was to suffer from a revolving-door personnel situation for decades.

Hughes tried to reverse the trend. Most players had one-year contracts, but in an effort to retain key musicians, the manager now offered some three-year contracts. Still, many of these players left immediately after their long-term contracts expired. Hughes also told her board that the musicians were clamoring for a summer season, which had become a regular part of the operations of other orchestras. "Under the present condition in Cleveland," Hughes reported to the board in January 1923, "a living for thirty weeks only is furnished by the Musical Arts Association contract, and a large number of players are forced to go east and find work to carry them through the other twenty-two weeks." She suggested forming a citizens' group to organize a summer season, saying the project would help the orchestra keep its musicians—and also possibly earn a profit from concerts of popular symphonic music. The idea would take several years to come to fruition.

Several other Hughes ideas already had taken hold to splendid effect. In 1921, she realized that she needed something other than male-dominated, money-oriented assistance to convince the public that the Cleveland Orchestra was worth hearing and supporting. She turned to a group of women who had volunteered for charitable organizations during the war and were now available to employ their considerable energies elsewhere. The Women's Committee of the Cleveland Orchestra was formed, and its original 30 members—donors or season subscribers who were invited to join—were charged with helping at children's concerts, talking up the orchestra, and selling tickets.

Among their most meaningful contributions on behalf of children was the orchestra's Music Memory Contest, which was inaugurated on March 12, 1921, at Masonic Hall. Hughes was galvanized into action after Anne Faulkner Oberndorffer told her about the contests the National Music League in New York had started for solo instrumental and vocal repertoire. Oberndorffer had failed to convince Frederick Stock, the newly reinstalled conductor of the Chicago Symphony, to transfer the concept to orchestral music. Hughes needed no prodding. She told her Women's Committee that the contest would fit in beautifully with the orchestra's school program as a heightened form of music appreciation.

The contest was designed to make youngsters aware of the richness of the symphonic literature. Before attending the event, students were introduced to 26 major works and given information about the composers. They had to be able to recognize each piece and composer and spell everything correctly. At the inaugural contest, attended by 2,000 students, Sokoloff and the orchestra performed 10 selections for teams of 30 students from 33 public, parochial, and private schools. The audience heard a full concert while the cards were being scored. The first contest was so successful that it became a model for similar projects around the country. "The important thing in all this is that the child is getting knowledge of the beauty of music at the time when it sinks into its mind to remain as leaven throughout its life," Sokoloff told music teachers in 1923. "Grown up, that child will be a splendid citizen supporting a great orchestra."

The emphasis was placed on music that was deemed beautiful, as opposed to the popular forms the general public was beginning to devour. The Music Memory Contest (later renamed the Music Memory and Appreciation Contest) fulfilled the need "to cultivate a distaste for jazz and other lower forms, and a mind for the great compositions," reported a local magazine. "Lovers of good music, who have decried the modern tendency toward jazz, ultra-syncopation, and the poorly written popular songs, welcome the movement as having great promise of developing in the community a finer appreciation of music, with all that it means in a cultural sense."

Children weren't the only members of the community who were to benefit from the contest. Mothers who had become intrigued with the music their progeny were discovering led the way to the creation of adult music-appreciation classes that sprang up in private homes, clubs, libraries, and churches. Experienced music instructors or amateurs who knew the subject were hired as teachers. (The adult classes would outlive the Music Memory Contest: the Music Study Groups, as they came to be called, still exist.)

✤   ✤   ✤

"By the orchestra's fifth season, I felt I had a responsive instrument of real beauty and one with which I could creditably present new and technically difficult works," Sokoloff wrote in his memoirs. To stretch the repertoire and challenge his orchestra, Sokoloff continued programming works by d'Indy (Symphony No. 2), added music by Stravinsky (*Firebird* suite), and conducted tone poems by Richard Strauss (*Death and Transfiguration* and *Don Juan*). The orchestra was now at the point where it could play such scores with finesse and accuracy.

During the fifth season, Sokoloff introduced the orchestra to one of the greatest pianists and composers of the era, Sergei Rachmaninoff. Three years earlier, on March 13, 1920, the orchestra had given the premiere of Rachmaninoff's Symphony No. 2 in a version the composer had revised at

Sokoloff's request. "You know I was much younger and more voluble when I wrote that symphony," Rachmaninoff once told Sokoloff. "I believe we can revise it, and make it shorter." The new version—about 10 minutes shorter than the original—was a big success, and it became one of the most frequently performed works in the Sokoloff-Cleveland repertoire. After further performances at home and on tour, they gave the revised symphony's New York premiere at Carnegie Hall on January 23, 1923, a concert that was considered the orchestra's first national triumph.

Rachmaninoff himself made his debut with the orchestra during its fifth season, as soloist in his Piano Concerto No. 2, on March 29 and 31, 1923. The morning after the first concert, which honored Hughes on her 25th anniversary as Cleveland's impresario of fine music, Rachmaninoff accepted Sokoloff's invitation to hear the revised version of the Second Symphony for the first time. Only four people were in the audience at Masonic Hall when conductor and orchestra played the work—Rachmaninoff, his wife, Hughes, and Sokoloff's wife, Lyda. Following this special performance, the composer ran onstage to thank Sokoloff and was greeted by a roaring ovation from the orchestra. "It was a regular love feast," Sokoloff recalled. "I never saw so much emotion turned loose all at once."

Another composer conveyed his appreciation to the orchestra in 1923. Alfredo Casella was bowled over by the ensemble when he appeared as guest conductor in a program of his music in March. Publicist Henry L. Hewes reported to Severance that the Italian composer said "the Cleveland Orchestra was the only symphonic organization except one that had been able to play his 'Pupazzetti' suite on first reading. The other was the Vienna Philharmonic, admittedly the greatest orchestra in the world." The composer gave much of the credit to Sokoloff, whom he hoped would travel to Rome to conduct. "Casella himself has conducted practically every great Orchestra in Europe as a guest, which does not detract from his estimate of the men trained by Sokoloff," Hewes wrote to Severance. "No orchestra, he says, can be larger than its conductor."

Despite the reputation that Sokoloff was building, many members of the orchestra weren't willing to continue performing under him unless they were paid better. At the end of the 1922–23 season, Hughes raised the salaries of 35 valued members who were threatening to leave for other orchestras.

The orchestra, nevertheless, would add some important musicians. Arthur Beckwith, a British musician Sokoloff had heard on tour as a member of the London String Quartet, replaced Edlin as concertmaster. Beckwith was also coming to play first violin in the Cleveland String Quartet.

First, he had to get past Ellis Island, where he and his family were detained briefly when immigrant officials initially told them the British quota for July had been filled. Beckwith was cheerful upon his arrival in Cleveland a few days later. "All the musicians of importance in Europe are coming to America," he said. "You give us financial support, and you give us the courage of your genuine enthusiasm. The musical development of the country is just beginning. With the impetus it has in every section of the country, you should produce some very remarkable musicians of your own. I should like to see more musical conductors developed here."

Circumstances financial and otherwise had reduced the size of the ensemble slightly during the fifth season. Money was saved by putting Frank Hruby on a part-time contract as bass clarinetist and having Ernest K. Janovsky double on viola and contrabassoon. (He also played bassoon and percussion from 1921–23.) When Janovsky died in midseason, the orchestra had to hire two players to replace him. An improved fiscal forecast allowed Hughes to expand the cello section back to 10 players, making a total of 87 musicians for the coming season.

Those musicians included women, as would always be the case in Cleveland. The subject prompted attention in 1923, when female musicians first won acceptance into the Royal Philharmonic Society in London. Aside from harpists, few women were playing in orchestras in the United States at the time. When the Cleveland ensemble performed its annual concert in New York during its fifth season, several prominent (male) figures in the orchestra business commented on the orchestra's female phenomenon. Conductor Walter Damrosch stated that women didn't have the physical strength to withstand the strain of rehearsals, concerts, and touring. A similar view came from the manager of the Chicago Symphony, who expressed the belief that women couldn't handle the rigors of orchestral life.

He must have forgotten who was managing the Cleveland Orchestra.

— 5 —

For Posterity

*A*della Prentiss Hughes was at the top of her game at the start of the orchestra's sixth season, despite (or, perhaps, because of) the finalization of her divorce from Felix Hughes. She began delegating some of the trickiest matters, such as touring, to Carl Vosburgh, a former bank teller she had met through orchestra business. Vosburgh knew little about music, but he had superb organizational skills that would come in handy in the near future and for the next three decades. He joined the orchestra as one of two assistant managers (the other was A. A. Brewster, who handled finances).

Hughes negotiated contracts, developed the orchestra's radio broadcasts, and bragged about the achievements of her young orchestra. "The only woman manager in America," as the press called Hughes, relished her position at the forefront of the Musical Arts Association, which was starting to build public support for the orchestra. As Hughes told a reporter:

> My great idea was to have not one man, but hundreds of men and women, interested in the orchestra in a financial way, for where the money is there is the heart also. This would be the right kind of foundation, for everyone would be interested in its welfare. Of course, it wasn't the easiest thing in the world to get backers for an orchestra among hard-headed business men, but I finally did, and I am proud to say that many of the original backers are still with us as directors of the orchestra. It is such an institution now that everyone says it wouldn't be Cleveland without it. But I am proudest of all of the fact that I am the mother of ninety musicians.

Hughes was padding the personnel number—by including assistant conductor Arthur Shepherd and baggage master George Higgins—almost to the proportions of the Szell era, more than two decades later.

By the 1923–24 season, the roster of musicians had shifted dramatically away from native Clevelanders. The orchestra comprised 16 nationalities, including 30 Americans and 24 Russian-born players. From wherever they hailed, however, the musicians were subjected to autocratic treatment by Sokoloff, who tended to badger his players when things weren't going as he wished. At the first rehearsal of the sixth season at Masonic Hall, he delivered three commandments: "Be on time. Love your work. Look at me." Also included in Sokoloff's speech were several basic tenets that would forever take hold in Cleveland: "Conduct yourself in accordance with the dignity of the profession. Play all the notes, no matter how few or soft, and play them in tune and in time. Remember that one instrument which is out of tune may spoil the whole orchestra."

These proclamations came just as the orchestra was evaluating the quality and focus of its weekly one-hour radio broadcasts, which had begun on November 16, 1922, on Cleveland station WJAX. Radio had become the quickest way for an orchestra to reach an audience, infiltrating living rooms, stores, hospitals, and automobiles locally, around the country, and in Canada. But along with these benefits, orchestras were noticing a worrisome trend: the public was starting to stay home to get its arts and entertainment fix.

Hughes regarded radio highly. It afforded people who were unable to attend concerts for physical or financial reasons the pleasure of experiencing orchestral performances without leaving their homes. And even more important, it was helping the orchestra's reputation grow outside of Cleveland. Many listeners throughout the United States and Canada who heard the orchestra on radio bought tickets to concerts when the ensemble toured to their communities. Back in Cleveland, however, the reverse appeared to be true. Salesmen in piano stores where orchestra tickets were sold didn't take up the offer of free concert tickets because they said they could hear the programs on radio.

In an attempt to remedy the attendance decline, Hughes devised a clever plan. Only the first half of Thursday night programs would be broadcast, generally the portion containing a symphony. "This will deprive the radio people of hearing all soloists and the lighter numbers of the program, so that we feel we are reserving something that they would have to pay money to hear," she wrote.

✣   ✣   ✣

Another young medium was beginning to win the attention of the Cleveland Orchestra: recording. Thomas Edison's remarkable talking machine was changing the way people listened to music. Early recording had served mostly to preserve music and spoken-word performances by celebrated artists. Singers and solo instrumentalists were most commonly recorded because the primitive technology could capture only a small number of musicians adequately. Symphony orchestras didn't record until recording companies addressed the problem of capturing large complements of instruments. And even so, compromises had to be made. A single microphone, or recording horn, was set up in a studio or concert hall, making it necessary for players to be stationed in odd setups so that their sounds were directed toward the recording source. Some musicians, such as French horn players, might not be able to see the conductor, because their bells had to be pointed at the microphone. The sound inevitably was narrow and favorable to higher frequencies.

In 1918, the 76-year-old New York Philharmonic had already begun to make recordings in the 78 rpm format of the day. Josef Stransky recorded two dozen works on 30 phonographic sides with the orchestra from January 1917 to October 1919 for Columbia Records. The Philharmonic and Willem Mengelberg moved over to the Victor Talking Machine Company in 1922, producing uncut versions—rather than the abridged performances many recording companies released—of Beethoven's *Coriolanus* overture, Liszt's *Les Préludes*, Wagner's *The Flying Dutchman* overture, and Joseph Schelling's *A Victory Ball*.

For three years, Hughes tried to negotiate a contract between her ensemble and the Brunswick-Balke Collender Company, which initially told her they weren't ready to enter the orchestra field. The company answered a second Hughes request by saying that the Cleveland Orchestra's reputation wasn't big enough to warrant recording. Even when Sokoloff and his orchestra began to develop a reputation (especially after their Carnegie Hall debut on January 24, 1922), Brunswick put Cleveland off further, saying the company had to record an East Coast ensemble first. Brunswick officials were finally ready for the Cleveland Orchestra when Mengelberg and the Philharmonic turned down Brunswick and made a deal with Victor. Then, Brunswick signed Sokoloff and Cleveland.

The Brunswick agreement, negotiated in December 1923, called for Sokoloff to receive $500 for each double-faced record. Four records were to be made each year for a period of two years. The Musical Arts Association was to receive a 10 percent royalty on the records, which sold at $1.08 for 12-inch records and 81 cents for 10-inch records. Sokoloff pointed out that Leopold Stokowski had made an arrangement with the Philadelphia Orchestra giving him 50 percent of royalties earned from their Victor recordings. Cleveland's conductor believed he deserved the same. Philadelphia had earned $12,000 from recordings the first year, though record sales had declined with the spread of radio. The Musical Arts Association agreed to pay Sokoloff the same percentage that Philadelphia paid Stokowski.

The first composer Brunswick chose for the Cleveland Orchestra to record was an old friend, Tchaikovsky—movements from whose Symphony No. 4 Sokoloff had led throughout the ensemble's inaugural season. This time, the Russian composer's *1812 Overture* would occupy the Clevelanders—half of the overture, actually, played by little more than half of the orchestra. Twelve-inch recordings made in the 78 rpm format had space for about four and a half minutes of music per side. Brunswick intended to fit the recording onto two sides, so the *1812 Overture* had to go under the knife. The record company requested that the piece be edited down to eight minutes and 55 seconds, an assignment that Sokoloff quickly—and deftly— undertook.

Sokoloff conducted the first recording session in New York on January 23, 1924, the day after he and the orchestra gave a concert at Carnegie Hall. Only 47 of the ensemble's 87 musicians were hired to play the Tchaikovsky—13 violins, four violas, four cellos, two basses, two flutes, two oboes, one clarinet, two bassoons, four horns, four trumpets, three trombones, two tubas, timpani, two percussion, and one other player (maybe second clarinet, maybe percussion). Fifteen principal players received $25 each for the session; the remaining musicians, and the orchestra contractor, were paid $15 apiece, for a total of $870. Brunswick had agreed to pay union wage scale for recordings, plus railroad and hotel expenses for sessions in New York.

✿   ✿   ✿

Sokoloff recalls the first session in vivid detail in his memoirs, though he gets the site of the recording wrong, claiming it occurred in the boardroom at Cleveland's Masonic Hall. "Why we ever had the courage to continue after our first recording session, I'll never know," he wrote. "We were made of stern stuff in those days, I imagine." Sokoloff goes on to paint a comical scene, describing how the musicians were placed in groups "on tables, risers, packing boxes, books, even two stepladders, in addition to tall stools" in front of three microphones. The session, he says, took three hours due to numerous errors, retakes, and mishaps, including a packing case falling on the first trumpet—"unhurt, thank heavens"—10 seconds before the end of the piece.

Originally released on two sides as Brunswick 50047, the maiden-voyage recording of the Cleveland Orchestra is a performance that flies like the wind to cram itself into less than nine minutes. The bass response is thin, a victim of the recording process, and the lower brasses aren't always clearly defined. Yet the recording reveals some specifics about the orchestra and Sokoloff. The strings are firm and sweet, the winds adequate, the horns crisp, the trumpets not always in tune. Sokoloff emerges as a conductor very much of the romantic Russian school—generous with string portamento (sliding between notes) and viscerally exciting. The playing has enormous energy, as if the musicians were aware that this was a historic moment. Sokoloff and company's rendition of Tchaikovsky's fanciful battle between French and Russian forces may be one of the least heroic on record: the performance has no cannons and a dearth of majesty at this speed, but the chimes peal nicely. It is an impressive recording debut by a five-year-old orchestra.

Sokoloff made 10 other recordings with his ensemble in October of the same year (1924) that are generally less effective than the *1812 Overture*. Considering that all of these short pieces were recorded in one month— probably over several sessions in one week, and compromised by time limitations—it may be no wonder that the performances of works by Johann Strauss II, Brahms, Wagner, and Sibelius sound hurried and somewhat graceless. The finest of these recordings are readings of the Sibelius *Valse triste* (rich in string vibrato, full of temperament) and the Brahms Hungarian Dance No. 5 (exuberant, nimble, and warm).

❈   ❈   ❈

The same season, Sokoloff and the orchestra had their first joint encounter with one of the towering works of the symphonic repertoire: Beethoven's Symphony No. 9. In November 1923, Hughes and Sokoloff began planning for the ensemble's first performances of the Beethoven Ninth on April 24 and 26, 1924. The board authorized Hughes to spend $2,500 to engage soloists and the 200-voice Oberlin Musical Union, and to precede the Masonic Hall concerts with a performance in Oberlin.

Sokoloff, however, wasn't destined to conduct the Ninth on these occasions. The week of the performances, after having rehearsed the work, he was stricken with tonsillitis and replaced at the concerts by Arthur Shepherd. Sokoloff listened to one of the Masonic Hall performances in bed by telephone. Wilson G. Smith had praise for Shepherd in the *Cleveland Press*: "In fact, one can say with assurance that it was the best demonstration he has given us of batonic manipulation."

Aside from Sokoloff and Shepherd, few other conductors had been given the opportunity to lead the Cleveland Orchestra. Those selected were part of a plan Sokoloff and Hughes devised to give Sokoloff a week off now and then. In place of guest conductors, they invited composers to conduct their own music—and sometimes also perform it. In the second season, Johann Beck led several of his works. Ernest Bloch, the most renowned composer in town (and the founding director of the Cleveland Institute of Music), conducted during three consecutive seasons starting in 1920.

The sixth season included four distinguished composers as conductors—an American (Douglas Moore), an Englishman (Frank Bridge), a Romanian (Georges Enesco), and a Hungarian (Ernst von Dohnányi). Aside from his stature as a composer of richly conceived music blending elements of Liszt and Brahms, Dohnányi (1877–1960) was a virtuosic pianist, vibrant conductor, and superb teacher who stood with Zoltán Kodály, Béla Bartók, and Leo Weiner as Hungary's leading musical figures. He came to Cleveland a few weeks after the orchestra's first recording session to appear as conductor, composer, and pianist. He was soloist in Beethoven's "Emperor" Concerto and his own *Variations on a Nursery Song*, both conducted by Shepherd, and he mounted the podium for his Suite in F-sharp minor. Archie Bell called the opening concert "a grand musical love-feast." Of Dohnányi, Smith wrote, "He wields the baton with infectious persuasion, and imparts to the players the spirit of interpretation with which he is possessed. His beat is incisive and compelling and full of the ardor of a musician who feels what he interprets." While in Cleveland, Dohnányi told an interviewer that Western European art was essentially dead and that America—"You have no cultural roots that go deep in your own soil"—probably would not be contributing much creatively for a long while.

Writing to Sokoloff in New York, Hughes remarked that Dohnányi demanded the highest standards and rehearsed his suite scrupulously. At the first rehearsal, principal violist Carlton Cooley had to be absent due to another engagement, and the viola section "fell down completely," noted Hughes. "Dohnányi required each desk to play separately." But the concerts were lauded, and the week with Enesco soon afterward "went even better." Enesco also appeared with the orchestra in three capacities—violinist, composer, and conductor. After serving as soloist in the Brahms Violin Concerto, he conducted his own Symphony in E-flat and Rumanian Rhapsody No. 1. Sokoloff deemed him the most successful of the conductors invited to Cleveland. "He was a dear and charming man and both the audience and the orchestra loved him," Sokoloff remembered. "His control and technique were so splendid that, after the first rehearsal, I could go off without a qualm and be sure that the orchestra would give a fine performance and that everyone would have a good time."

A composer-conductor who appeared the same month (February 1924) but didn't make much of an impression was Siegfried Wagner, son of the titanic German composer of music dramas. The younger Wagner had embarked on an American tour to raise money for the beleaguered Bayreuth Festival, which his father had created in the 1870s exclusively for performances of his stage works. Siegfried's tour program was titled *Music of Three Generations*. In one of his rare negative reviews, Rogers noted that Wagner's son did not possess his father's "gift of summoning orchestral sonorities. He may console himself with the fact that nobody else has it either."

Sokoloff wasn't much taken with the conducting abilities of perhaps the most acclaimed and controversial composer of the era, Igor Stravinsky, who made his debut with the orchestra on February 12, 1925. Sokoloff opened the program, conducting Tchaikovsky's "Pathétique" Symphony, after which Stravinsky took to the podium to lead three of his scores: *Fireworks, Chant du Rossignol,* and the *Firebird* suite—the last of which the orchestra had played on two subscription programs under Sokoloff. Although he revered Stravinsky as "a splendid musician and a great composer," Sokoloff also found him to be "something of a showman and not entirely endearing." When the short Russian genius began rehearsing his works, his conducting "did little or nothing to make them easier to comprehend. He was terribly stiff—you know how a metronome goes, tick–tick–tick, with nothing in between—well that was Stravinsky. There was no flow between one beat and the next, his hand moved like an automaton, which made it all dreadfully difficult for the players." Stravinsky added to the difficulty by rehearsing in Russian or French, but not English. "He was, in short, a pain in the neck, and the concerts were far from successful," Sokoloff says. "He appealed no more to the audience than he did to the men in the orchestra, and his music, as he conducted it, appealed to no one, save possibly himself."

Smith went out of his way to condemn Stravinsky in his review, piling up the syllables to do so. "We found him an anarchist of iconoclastic tendencies, the foremost exponent of ultraism, urged thereunto by the strength of his convictions and his transcendent ability for conceiving and concocting sounds discordant and inharmonious."

At least one person appeared to enjoy himself the week Stravinsky was in town: the composer himself. In apparently adequate English, he told an interviewer that he had heard or conducted many of the world's great orchestras. "But, I assure you," Stravinsky remarked, "I have never seen an orchestra in which there was finer discipline and a greater responsiveness than right here in your Cleveland orchestra. I despise compliments and I say nothing that is insincere, so you must realize that I mean this with all my heart. I had heard many fine things about the Cleveland orchestra and Nikolai Sokoloff, of course—but I was not prepared to find them as truly great as they have proved themselves to be."

In 1925, Sokoloff wasn't ready to budge from his composer-conductor plan, even when Leopold Stokowski wrote to him asking if the Cleveland Orchestra could provide an engagement for a splendid Polish conductor he had just heard leading Wagner's *Die Meistersinger von Nürnberg* at the Warsaw Opera. This was Artur Rodzinski, whom Stokowski was about to bring to the United States to become his assistant at the Philadelphia Orchestra. "Alas, all of our engagements are filled and I am not going away this coming season," Sokoloff wrote back. "We are doing only twenty Symphony Pairs, and I am conducting all of them. I am so sorry I am unable to have Dr. Rodzinski with us."

Several other admired composers conducted the Cleveland Orchestra in the following years, including Howard Hanson, Beryl Rubinstein, and Carlos Salzedo. Ottorino Respighi, whose scintillating orchestral gifts had catapulted some of his works to world popularity, came to Cleveland in February 1927, repeating the feat performed by Dohnányi and Enesco by filling the roles of composer, conductor, and soloist. He conducted two of his finest scores, *Ancient Airs and Dances* Suite No. 2 and *The Pines of Rome* and appeared as soloist in his piano concerto (*Concerto in modo misolidio*) under the orchestra's new assistant conductor, Rudolph Ringwall.

Sokoloff enjoyed Respighi's visit enormously and was surprised that he could speak perfect Russian. The Italian composer reminded the Russian-born conductor that he had lived in Russia while studying with Rimsky-Korsakov. Respighi "loved the orchestra and the way we played his compositions," said Sokoloff. "Nothing could have been happier than his visits to Cleveland." Wilson G. Smith confirmed this happiness in his review of the concert in the *Cleveland Press*, at the same time revealing his growing disenchantment with Sokoloff: "Respighi got more from the players, in delicate shading and nuances entailing the tonal blend in the several choirs, than has ever been realized before."

No one could have been more of a contrast to the larger-than-life Respighi than Maurice Ravel, the diminutive legend of French music, who was the orchestra's guest composer-conductor in January 1928. Ravel, in the United States for a four-month tour, gave a lecture about his music at the Cleveland Museum of Art and led the orchestra at Masonic Hall on January 26 and 27 in some of his greatest scores: *Le tombeau de Couperin, Valses nobles et sentimentales, Rapsodie espagnole, Shéhérazade, Ma mère l'oye*, and *La valse*.

The events leading up to the concerts evidently wouldn't have been out of place in a French farce, according to Sokoloff. The morning of the first rehearsal, Sokoloff asked principal violist Carlton Cooley to pick Ravel up at the Statler Hotel. By 10 o'clock, neither Ravel nor Cooley had entered Masonic Hall. When they finally arrived 10 minutes later, Ravel registered surprise that a rehearsal would begin on time. "In France we are not so particular," he told Sokoloff. "I shall try to be prompt tomorrow." He wasn't. Cooley again was dispatched to drive Ravel to the rehearsal, and again they were late. The violist told Sokoloff "that the reason they had been late was because Ravel had become entangled in a hair net which he wore at night to keep his hair in place. When Cooley arrived at the hotel and had sent his name up, Ravel had asked that he come to his room. There Cooley found him in front of the mirror, completely entangled in the hair net from which his nearsightedness made disentanglement impossible. Even Cooley had had difficulty getting him out of it!"

Sokoloff hints that the rehearsals and concerts were also a tangle: "I saw immediately that his technique was simply abominable, the musicians couldn't understand a thing he did." Ravel was so short that the players had difficulty seeing him, and he bunched up his fingers, without baton, into a configuration that resembled "the head of a snake." To make matters worse, Ravel tended to cue the wrong instruments. By performance time, Sokoloff was apoplectic: "The whole concert was terribly shaky and I almost had a nervous breakdown. The audience, appreciating his greatness as a composer, was polite, so he had a certain success. But that was his first and last appearance with us as a conductor. I, for one, couldn't have lived through a return engagement."

Sergei Prokofiev, who had been recommended by Serge Koussevitzky, conductor of the Boston Symphony, was signed for his Cleveland Orchestra debut after much wrangling between Hughes and the composer's concert management in New York. Like other composer-conductors who had collaborated with the orchestra, Prokofiev was engaged both as soloist and conductor in a number of his works. But the Russian composer "falls down dead at the idea of conducting more than one piece," Hughes informed Sokoloff in September 1929. "Archie Bell gave me an imitation of the way he came on the stage on the occasion of his appearance in a piano recital several years ago and it was a scream. He evidently is a shrinking violet!" She would soon discover otherwise.

The Prokofiev program that Sokoloff originally envisioned comprised the "Classical" Symphony, Piano Concerto No. 1, *Love for Three Oranges* suite, and *Scythian Suite*. The composer wrote to his manager that he was astonished to be asked to undertake an entire program. He proposed playing the concerto, conducting the suite from his ballet *Le Pas d'Acier*, and leaving the rest to the assistant conductor. Not long before concert week, Prokofiev's manager told Cleveland that the composer would be in town long enough for only two rehearsals, compelling Hughes to provide a revised train schedule that would get the orchestra's guest to Cleveland for at least three rehearsals. (Ironically, the first movement of *Le Pas d'Acier* is titled "Arrival of the train.")

Prokofiev ultimately had his way in terms of repertoire. On January 9 and 11, 1930, he appeared with the orchestra in the pieces he had proposed. A program that was supposed to be a salute to the purported "strong man of Russia" wound up being a mishmash that included an Italian work (Leone Sinigaglia's overture to *Le Barouffe Chiozzotte*), an Irish piece (Charles Villiers Stanford's *Irish Rhapsody No. 1*), and a Russian score more famous than any the orchestra's guest had composed to this time: Rimsky-Korsakov's colorful *Capriccio Espagnol*. Assistant conductor Rudolph Ringwall did most of the conducting.

The day of the first concert, Prokofiev was depicted by Archie Bell in the *Cleveland News* as an "enfant terrible" and "the naughty boy of Russia." "But, it should be known at the start," wrote Bell, that "the bad boy is trying to be good." The composer spoke to Bell in "excellent English" and stated, "melody is everything." Prokofiev then noted that much nonsense had been written about his music: "I don't want to think that I am indifferent to such things; but I must say that I toss these things aside, unless I believe that they are genuine opinions, carefully arrived at, after my pieces have been heard intelligently played and intelligently considered by the ones who write of them. Adverse criticisms do not deter me in my onward march; I have my own work to do and I shall do it, irrespective of what they say."

The Cleveland critics had plenty to say, all of them praising Prokofiev's pianism, many contributing adverse opinions about his music. Arthur Shepherd, a composer himself, said in the *Press*, "There is something baffling in the art of this young Russian, with its hard brilliance, its precocious efficiency, its nonchalant disregard for emotional appeal." It wouldn't be the last time one of Cleveland's composer-critics missed the point.

Prokofiev, on the other hand, found much to admire during his only visit to the city. He called the Cleveland Orchestra "quite respectable and large—of course there are Russians among the musicians. Cleveland is a most colossal city, sown with skyscrapers: thirty-three kilometers along the shores of Lake Erie! America is, after all, an incredible country."

– 6 –

Upbeats and Downbeats

*N*ikolai Sokoloff does not stand alongside giants like Toscanini or Stokowski in the annals of conducting. But he brought crucial gifts to Cleveland as an orchestra builder and an imaginative (too imaginative, some would say) programmer. Striking evidence of artistic growth can be heard in the eight pieces Sokoloff and his orchestra recorded in May 1927. These recordings find the Cleveland Orchestra emerging as a very different ensemble from the Cleveland Orchestra of 1924 in terms of cohesion, refinement, and personality. The performances reveal strings with far more tonal depth, winds that are bright and confident, bold and balanced brasses, and percussion finely placed in context. In them, a Cleveland tradition is beginning to take hold.

In the three years since the initial Brunswick session in New York, many changes in recording methods had occurred. Recording companies had abandoned the acoustical process and adopted the electrical method, using a multidirectional microphone instead of a recording horn to imprint the music on 10- or 12-inch shellac platters. Lengthy works were still marred by numerous side changes required by the speed (78 revolutions per minute). But remarkable technical advances enhanced clarity, bass response, and tonal breadth. Even so, cumbersome and limited editing processes could not remove every blemish or mask instrumental (or vocal) weaknesses.

The Cleveland Orchestra's rapid evolution from 1924 to 1927 can be confirmed by a direct comparison: Sokoloff and the orchestra rerecorded the *1812 Overture* in 1927, partly to take advantage of the new electrical recording method. The new performance, 20 seconds longer than the breathless battle of 1924, has a sense of drama and ensemble unity not present in the earlier version. Sokoloff fills out the space with tautly controlled yet flexible phrasing, and the orchestra has thrown off the frenzied quality apparent in the 1924 recording. The 1927 performance also goes 1924 one better by including cannon shots, of sorts, produced on what sound like bass drums. Tchaikovsky's scoring doesn't quite get its due here, however: the shots rarely hit the target, rhythmically.

The 1927 recordings include new versions of the two excerpts from Wagner's *Lohengrin* (Act III prelude; Wedding March). Again, the new versions are slightly slower than the 1924 performances. More importantly, both selections show an orchestra that has gained in nuance, energy, and elegance. As he would state years later, Sokoloff encouraged his musicians to bring a lyrical quality to their playing, and he clearly achieved his goal. The waltz from Tchaikovsky's *The Sleeping Beauty* may be brisk by choreographic standards and Nicolai's overture to *The Merry Wives of Windsor* jolted by cuts, but both works receive vital and affectionate treatment. The violin solos in the Saint-Saëns *Danse macabre* are played with enormous élan by Josef Fuchs, who joined the orchestra as concertmaster at the start of the 1926–27 season, succeeding Arthur Beckwith.

Sokoloff not only had the ability to train an ensemble and stretch his musicians with challenging repertoire, he also brought much-needed experience and skill to the orchestra through his hiring of Fuchs and other players. Throughout the 1920s (and continuing well into the 1960s), an almost bewildering number of musicians left Cleveland for orchestras that paid higher salaries or provided longer seasons. But aside from such departures, Sokoloff was constantly tweaking his lineup of players—as his successors would, sometimes to painful effect—to bolster the quality of the ensemble.

Personnel changes came fast and furious in Cleveland in the mid-1920s. At the start of the 1925–26 season, 17 players succeeded musicians who had been let go or who had departed (most contracts, aside from those for principals, were still for one year). The turnover was far more dramatic during the 1926–27 season, when the orchestra had an influx of 29 new members, including an unusually large number in principal positions—concertmaster (Fuchs), principal clarinet (Louis de Santis), principal horn (Walter G. McDonald), principal trombone (Simone Belgiorgno), and principal harp (Edward Vito)—as well as Rudolph Ringwall, who became assistant conductor when Arthur Shepherd stepped down to pursue his composing career and duties as head of Western Reserve University's Graduate School of Music. The total turnover of 46 players over two seasons accounted for more than half of the orchestra.

In most cases, the musicians who joined at this time were hired after private auditions in New York or elsewhere with Sokoloff—or with the assistant conductor or even key principal players if the boss wasn't available to hear candidates. That practice was beginning to get on the nerves of

Cleveland's Local 4 of the American Federation of Musicians, which was determined to give local musicians the first opportunity to land jobs in the orchestra. The union tried to flex its muscles by stubbornly adding a clause to contracts: "Before importing or endeavoring to import musicians for the Symphony Orchestra, the manager or conductor must first apply to the organization for permission to import, and file a list of the instruments desired with the organization." If these rules weren't followed, a musician could be barred from playing with the orchestra or the conductor or manager could be fined from $50 to $500 for each case. The union was to fight this battle numerous times over the decades and lose more often than not: the orchestra could easily point out that quality had to come before chauvinism.

The orchestra's quality certainly rose with the hiring of Fuchs, who would have a striking impact on the ensemble in general and the violin section in particular. Born in New York City in 1900, he studied at the Institute of Musical Art (now the Juilliard School) and in 1919 traveled to Europe, where he met composer-pianist Ferruccio Busoni, who asked Fuchs to appear as soloist in his concerto with the Berlin Symphony. Busoni's untimely death, before the concerto engagement, ended Fuchs's European journey. Upon his return to the United States, Fuchs won a post in the music department of Teachers College at Columbia University and the concertmaster chair at New York's Capitol Theater. Maurice Van Praag, personnel manager of the New York Philharmonic, brought the violinist to Sokoloff's attention. Fuchs was prone to unpleasant relations with colleagues, but he was also a violinist of sublime ability. Tidbits of his artistry can be heard on the Sokoloff recordings, and his solo playing on Artur Rodzinski's Cleveland recordings of Strauss's *Ein Heldenleben (A Hero's Life)* and *Till Eulenspiegel's Merry Pranks* has perhaps not been surpassed.

❊   ❊   ❊

By the mid-1920s, wages for musicians and other costs had multiplied the orchestra's budget to almost eight times the figure for the first season. In 1918–19, expenses amounted to $31,876. By the 1924–25 season, the budget had reached $223,409. Controlling expenses, as the orchestra did in 1924–25, didn't mean trustees were being less aggressive about fund-raising. Led again in this realm by Dudley S. Blossom, the board had succeeded in securing $200,000 for the maintenance fund, slightly short of its goal. Frank Ginn, always scrutinizing the efficiency of the organization, suggested at the end of the 1924–25 season that contributors whose checks hadn't arrived should be sent an urgent letter stating that their support was necessary or the orchestra would have to be disbanded. Blossom calmed Ginn down and nixed the letter, pointing out that the orchestra had shown appreciable gains in attendance, ticket sales, and touring business.

The orchestra—at least the rank-and-file players—helped the bottom line by continuing to play for meager wages. As would always be true, salaries were widely disparate for the 30-week season. Principal oboist Philip Kirchner was paid the top salary of $5,750 for the 1924–25 season, far more than concertmaster Beckwith ($2,900), even with the latter's participation in the Cleveland String Quartet. Among principals receiving large salaries were cellist Victor de Gomez ($5,120), hornist Louis Dufrasne ($4,960), and violist Carlton Cooley ($4,070), while many musicians received the minimum of $1,080.

Whatever their salaries, the players seem to have appreciated the precarious nature of running a young arts organization. The musicians agreed with the board's belt tightening and made few demands in union negotiations during this period. Trustees exulted in the situation: "This will make six years without change or raise of wage scale—a remarkable record." It was also a time when the trustees could still wipe out season deficits by asking the most well-heeled board members once again to come to the aid of the orchestra. At the end of the 1926–27 season, the orchestra showed a loss of $25,619—a deficit that was retired instantly through gifts from Blossom ($14,619), Severance ($10,000), and Mrs. Coburn Haskell ($1,000).

❊   ❊   ❊

Apart from finances, there were moments when the board was called upon to throw its unqualified support behind Sokoloff, whose relationship with his orchestra was becoming increasingly stormy. During a tour to Dayton in spring 1926, a concert was delayed 25 minutes while Adella Prentiss Hughes tried to bring about a reconciliation between Sokoloff and the orchestra. The rift had occurred during the afternoon rehearsal, when the conductor treated several musicians in a manner that was deemed "unbecoming a gentleman." The musicians vowed to file a grievance with the board and the musicians' union. The incident involved principal trumpet Frank Venezie, viewed by Sokoloff as an agitator who "played three times louder" when told to reduce the volume, and principal bassoonist Morris Kirchner, brother of principal oboist Philip Kirchner. The bassoonist claimed Sokoloff referred to him during the rehearsal as "a dummy." Venezie was dismissed and replaced by Alois Hruby. Morris Kirchner, an orchestra member for seven years, played the Dayton concert and remained as principal bassoon until 1933. Sokoloff told the board he had merely corrected Venezie and Kirchner and reserved the right to do so. The orchestra responded with a petition, signed by 69 of the 87 members, decrying the conductor's behavior. The board concluded that there was no reason to take the complaint seriously.

✿   ✿   ✿

Sokoloff, displaying the mercurial personality so prevalent among conductors, could be volatile and imperious. But he had a generous side not often seen by his players. In late 1925, he sent one of his violins, a French instrument by an unknown maker, to Mrs. Marutha Mnuchin in New York for use by her son. The boy, known by the family's Anglicized surname, was Yehudi Menuhin, a nine-year-old prodigy whose sensational gifts were becoming widely known. Sokoloff wrote to Mrs. Mnuchin (misspelling the name) saying that he believed the instrument would be ideal for the young violinist, though he regretted he had no bow to send along.

Sokoloff also had an adventurous musical spirit that brought much excitement and admiration, and no small amount of controversy, to his orchestra's activities. During the 1925–26 season, he masterminded a concert series, Music of Many Lands, whose programs represented various nationalities and thus drew listeners who may have never heard the orchestra before. The concerts were presented at the new Music Hall in Public Auditorium. Sokoloff championed living composers, including Americans, and long-deceased European composers whose works had been lost or neglected. In March 1926, he led the orchestra in a program of American works, including Carlton Cooley's *Song and Dance* (with the composer as viola soloist), Howard Hanson's symphonic poem *Lux Aeterna*, Henry Hadley's tone poem *Lucifer*, and Emerson Whitorne's *The Aeroplane*. During other seasons, he programmed pieces by William Berwald, Howard Brockaway, Henry F. Gilbert, Edward MacDowell, Douglas Moore, Leo Sowerby, and Deems Taylor.

One of Sokoloff's most curious endeavors was a program he and the orchestra gave in Cleveland and at Carnegie Hall late in 1929 that included the premiere of Joseph Schillinger's First Airphonic Suite, Op. 21. Schillinger (1895–1943) was a Ukrainian-born composer and theorist who developed a system of music theory based on mathematics. (In the early 1930s, he taught the system to George Gershwin, who used it in creating his opera, *Porgy and Bess*.) The Schillinger work Sokoloff presented is scored for orchestra and an unconventional solo instrument, the theremin. Named for its Russian inventor, Leon Theremin, the device is made of radio tubes and antennas. It produces sound by electrical means, without actual human touch. A musician "played" the theremin by standing in front of the instrument and moving his right hand in the air to control pitch and his other to control volume. The resulting series of eerie tones and effects seemed to emanate from outer space. (Indeed, Hollywood soon adopted the theremin to help scare the wits out of lovers of horror, science fiction, and mystery films.)

Going out of his way to be radical, Sokoloff filled out the theremin program with obscure fare: Chabrier's *Marche joyeuse*, d'Indy's *Jour d'été à la montagne*, Rivier's *Overture to a Don Quixote*, and Werner Janssen's *New Year's Eve in New York*. The New York critics didn't like much of what they heard on December 3, 1929, but they truly hated the theremin, which was waved at by its creator. The *Herald Tribune's* distinguished critic, Lawrence Gilman, said the instrument "scoops and wobbles like a bad singer. Moreover, the tone quality is often disagreeable—like that of a slightly adenoidal saxophone."

Oscar Thompson, of the *New York Evening Post*, described what he heard as "colossal outwellings of sound such as all but baffle description— at times suggesting a balalaika orchestra multiplied by ten, a regiment of children singing through combs and tissue paper, a musical saw once heard above the roar of heavy traffic on the streets of London, and what might result if all the neighbors' radios were tuned in on the same station." To add a touch of insult, he noted that "the new music of the evening was played with precision, spirit and enthusiasm, and the old with clarity and structural good qualities, if in tonal glow (particularly with respect to the strings) somewhat below the standards of excellence that Carnegie Hall audiences have come to batten on in these days of technical virtuosity."

❖   ❖   ❖

Carnegie continued to be the scene of important Sokoloff-Cleveland recording sessions for the Brunswick company. The major work preserved in May 1928 was the revised version of the Rachmaninoff Second Symphony, which Sokoloff and the orchestra had performed almost three dozen times around the country. The recording was released the following September on six 12-inch records at a cost of $6, or $7 with an explanatory booklet. The performance, warmly expressive and urgent, represents Sokoloff and the Cleveland Orchestra at their estimable best.

Critical response was enthusiastic. Along with a cover photo of Sokoloff and an extensive article about his work in Cleveland, *Music Lovers' Phonograph Monthly Review* contained a review that led the field in praise:

Altogether apart from their musical and intellectual interest, these records are a balm to the ear and the mind solely by virtue of their tonal beauty. The strings are predominant; the brass and woodwind augment or darken its mass, or mark out details. One might almost say there are no solos—but at times the entire fabric of the work has suddenly been concentrated into a single strand! The performance is as fine an example of orchestral team-work as is available on records.

The Rachmaninoff symphony was one of eight works Sokoloff and the orchestra recorded in 1928, their final year of recordings together. During the three days of sessions in May 1928 at Carnegie Hall, they also recorded Schubert's "Unfinished" Symphony, an admirably refined account emphasizing the first movement's stormy aspects and the second movement's tender profile.

Sokoloff was in a Schubertian mood throughout the second half of 1928, for he was planning to give the first U.S. performances of the composer's other "unfinished" symphony, the Symphony in E major, with his orchestra. The conductor, who had been alerted to the existence of the symphony by New York music critic Herbert Peyser, regarded the Schubert project as a top priority for the 1928–29 season, as he wrote to Hughes from New York in September 1928: "I have decided *not* to announce the 'New Schubert' Symphony till November because some one else may also order it copied! Please *keep very still* on the subject!" She did. Sokoloff and the orchestra gave the work's first U.S. performances on November 22 at Masonic Hall and on December 4 at Carnegie Hall. No one, aside from Sokoloff, was overly thrilled. "The whole symphony is richly melodious, albeit some of the thematic ideas are, for Schubert, unusually short breathed and sketchy," wrote W. J. Henderson in the *Evening Sun* the day after the Carnegie performance. "But such a symphony in these days of musical aridity is a gift from the gods and music lovers owe Mr. Peyser a debt of gratitude for his suggestion to Mr. Sokoloff and [a similar debt to] the latter for his care in preparing an excellent performance."

— 7 —

Home, Sweet Severance

O nly four people knew in advance just how important an event the
Cleveland Orchestra concert on December 11, 1928, would be for
the ensemble: Mr. and Mrs. John L. Severance and Mr. and Mrs. Dudley S.
Blossom. The concert had been planned as a gala affair for the orchestra's
10th anniversary. Adella Prentiss Hughes had booked the six-year-old
Public Hall, whose 10,000 seats could easily accommodate all of the listen-
ers who regularly attended the orchestra's Thursday night and Saturday af-
ternoon Masonic Hall performances. Nikolai Sokoloff planned a festive program: three works from the orchestra's inaugural concert (Herbert's
American Fantasy, Liadov's *The Enchanted Lake*, and Bizet's *Carmen* Suite
No. 1) and a Strauss score they were performing for the first time, *Ein
Heldenleben*.

Things were going smoothly during the first half of the concert when
Blossom approached Hughes and told her that he wanted to speak to the orchestra and audience before intermission. Hughes had no idea what he was
going to say, but she made arrangements for the musicians to stay in place.
Blossom walked onstage and announced that the Severances had pledged
$1 million to build a new hall, if at least $2 million were raised for an endowment fund. The place went wild.

Hughes and the public received more good news the next day, when
Blossom and his wife, Elizabeth, announced that they were kicking off the
endowment fund with a pledge of $750,000.

Hughes had been lobbying for a first-class concert hall in town for almost
three decades, well before the earliest attempts at establishing a permanent
orchestra. Grays Armory, where she presented her visiting orchestra concerts, had proved inadequate in acoustics and ambience. Guarantors of the
concert series suggested buying the facility and converting it into a concert
hall, but Hughes talked them out of it, despite the fact that she had no other
solutions at the time. Grays Armory had become a nuisance for another reason—chickens. When planning the 1907–08 season of her Symphony Orch-

estra Concerts, Hughes was jolted by a "fowl reality": "Grand Orchestra Ousted by Hens, Poultry Show Is Bar to the Visit of the Boston Symphony, Only One Hall in Cleveland," read the headlines in the *Cleveland Leader*. (The Boston Symphony, which had played in the series the previous year with a fellow named Sokoloff in the violin section, nevertheless would be back many times.) And another poultry show would cause the relocation of a concert in 1914.

Even before chickens reared their heads, Hughes had pushed for an alternative to Grays. In 1905, Andrew Carnegie, the steel magnate and philanthropist, came to Cleveland on business and met Hughes at one of her concerts. Carnegie's generosity was well known. He had invested millions in libraries and other projects in Pittsburgh, where he had made his fortune, and elsewhere. The glittering hall he funded on the corner of 57th Street and Seventh Avenue in New York City, and which still bears his name, had become the country's major magnet for the world's great artists.

Hughes discussed her work with Carnegie and followed up a few days later with a letter detailing her struggles to interest locals in a hall project. She told him that a concert facility would cost about $500,000, of which $400,000 could be raised in Cleveland for land and endowment. Moreover, David Z. Norton, a generous donor to the Symphony Orchestra Concerts, had offered an initial gift of $25,000, and could be counted on to gather even more support through his own fund-raising efforts. And, noted Hughes, "I have personally raised all the guarantee funds for our Symphony Concerts, so that I am not lacking in experience or understanding of the task I am asking you to allot to me." Carnegie quickly turned down the request, the first in a series of similar rejections from him and others.

Two years later, Hughes made her plea to Cleveland native John D. Rockefeller, Jr., whom she had known since childhood, and who had played violin in his youth. Rockefeller had moved to New York City but maintained ties to his hometown. Hughes talked Harvey D. Goulder, president of the Cleveland Chamber of Commerce and a donor to the Symphony Orchestra Concerts, into discussing the issue with Rockefeller advisors in New York. The situation looked promising until news reached Rockefeller that a Hippodrome Theatre (like the famous one in Manhattan) was about to be built in Cleveland to serve multiple artistic purposes. Why did the city need yet another hall?

The matter remained in limbo for the next dozen years. When the Cleveland Orchestra abandoned Grays Armory in the fall of 1919 for Masonic Hall, Hughes hoped that the problem of a musical residence with adequate acoustics, space, and amenities would be solved. But the Masons often scheduled events that conflicted with the orchestra's practical needs, sending Sokoloff and his musicians elsewhere to rehearse. They practiced at the Ohio and Hanna theaters and the Euclid Avenue Baptist Church. Hughes "was never driven to occupy the East 9th Street pier or the Public Square," a reporter noted, "but she had a lively run about the city." Then, Hughes recalled, "John Royal made us welcome in the magnificent new Keith's Palace Theatre one morning. The only drawback there was the buzzing of vacuum cleaners, upstairs and down—the house had to be in order for the afternoon show. Would music never be given the first consideration anywhere!"

Not quite yet. Aware of the vacant house on Euclid Avenue and 40th Street where the Rockefellers had lived before moving to New York, Hughes contemplated turning again to her old chum, John D. Rockefeller, Jr. In early 1920, orchestra board directors Norton and Severance gave her permission to ask Rockefeller if he might convince his father to donate the land for a hall. She would raise the $500,000 for construction and possibly persuade J. H. Wade to donate his property across the street for a park. The younger Rockefeller wrote back: "When the time comes that you will undertake the building of a music hall definitely, regardless of whether we make a contribution or not, you may write to me again." He even refused to see Hughes about the matter, a callous response from a lifelong friend. At this point, many would have abandoned the idea. Hughes remained committed. She even commissioned drawings for a possible concert hall on the Rockefeller property from a local architect.

❋ ❋ ❋

By the late 1920s, Hughes was promoting the project with greater urgency. She had convinced the Women's Committee to study the issue and put together a subcommittee to don research hats. After much discussion, they decided that the orchestra would indeed benefit from its own permanent home. The orchestra's Executive Committee, except for Frank Ginn, who took a typically cautious position, hailed the women's work, and granted them permission to study such specifics as funding and location.

In gathering data about a hall, Hughes and her committee came to the conclusion that the orchestra's home shouldn't necessarily be located in Public Square or even downtown. Their research pointed out that only a small percentage of orchestra subscribers lived close to Masonic Hall. Most concertgoers and donors lived near the area known as University Circle, an oasis of parks and cultural and educational institutions four miles east of downtown, the land for which been donated to the city in 1882 by Jeptha

Wade. Among the institutions in University Circle was Western Reserve University, which had bought the Wade property at the corner of Euclid Avenue and East Boulevard for campus use. Along with the nearby Cleveland Museum of Art on East Boulevard north of Wade Lagoon, the Wade property was the most important piece of land in the area, a commanding point of entry into University Circle. Hughes initially met with resistance from Musical Arts Association members who insisted that the orchestra would lose its audience if the concerts were not held downtown. She countered that land near Public Square was unreasonably expensive. When Robert E. Vinson, president of Western Reserve University, declared that the university would donate its new property if the association would build a hall and create an endowment, a collaboration was forged.

As early as 1924, the university—like the orchestra—had identified a need for a sizable auditorium. In 1928, both institutions realized that this was perhaps the ideal time to consider a joint venture, since Cleveland was enjoying prosperity from its shipping, manufacturing, and iron-ore mining industries. Still, whether trustees of the Musical Arts Association would take their orchestra to University Circle anytime soon was a question that loomed throughout the year. In February, board members received preliminary sketches for a hall from Walter McCornack, a Hughes friend who had been the official architect for the Cleveland Board of Education from 1914 to 1925. Hughes and McCornack had begun discussing the challenge of taking orchestra concerts into city schools with Frank Spaulding, superintendent of the school system, in 1919.

To understand the architectural and acoustical properties needed for a fine auditorium, McCornack spent much of his time visiting important American concert and opera facilities. In New York, he explored Carnegie Hall and the Metropolitan Opera House; in Boston, Symphony Hall and the Opera House; in Rochester, the auditorium at the Eastman School of Music; in Philadelphia, the Academy of Music; in Chicago, Orchestra Hall and the Auditorium Theatre; in Detroit, Orchestra Hall; and in Ann Arbor, the University of Michigan's Hill Auditorium. "During the period from 1921 when the first sketches were made (plans of which I have) until 1927, I worked in my own studio at home, developing all manner of sketches based on rooms of varying sizes and forms, in order to determine the proper form for a hall for orchestral music," McCornack wrote several years later.

After the Musical Arts Association received McCornack's preliminary drawings in February 1928, John L. Severance ran hot and cold on the plans, as did his wife, Elisabeth, who suggested crucial design changes that would make the hall capable of accommodating theatrical productions. "Will there not be occasion when light plays or even operettas might be given requiring a stage and its equipment?" the industrialist wrote to Hughes.

Now that the design phase was moving ahead, Hughes and board colleagues turned their attentions to identifying the main source of funding for the project. Although one benefactor seemed like a sure thing, he was at first reluctant. In March 1928, Western Reserve University's Vinson visited the ever-benevolent John L. Severance, now president of the Musical Arts Association, and asked him to donate $1 million for the hall. Shocked by such a large request, Severance told Vinson "that he was not willing to make any change in his method of living or in any way [reduce] his usual expenditure, nor did he wish Mrs. Severance to be penalized in any way." Severance reiterated his support for the orchestra, especially in retiring annual deficits up to $50,000, and said he might be able to afford $500,000 for the hall.

In June 1928, the board of Western Reserve University approved Vinson's proposal to offer the university property, valued at $600,000, to the Musical Arts Association. By October, Severance still had not agreed to sign on as the major donor. Hughes and McCornack kept chipping away at his reservations. Severance began to respond favorably when the architect submitted more detailed drawings and provided a specific dollar figure for construction ($949,600). One afternoon in early December, Hughes and McCornack went to Longwood, the 161-acre Severance estate in Cleveland Heights, to show the hall plans to Mrs. Severance, who told them that the audience's comfort was paramount. "The two butlers were directed to bring chairs and place them in double rows, concert hall fashion; width and space were measured, Mrs. Severance testing the arrangement by walking in and sitting down," recalled Hughes.

When the Blossoms told Severance that they were thinking of donating $750,000 for endowments ($600,000 for the hall; $150,000 for orchestra maintenance), the board president needed no further prodding. As the orchestra's 10th-anniversary concert approached, he let the Blossoms—and only the Blossoms—know that he was leaning toward making the biggest monetary contribution of his life.

❈   ❈   ❈

The euphoria surrounding the announcement of the Severances' $1 million gift and the Blossoms' endowment donations was followed by intrigue and tragedy.

Within weeks of the anniversary concert, the board carried a motion to engage Walter McCornack as the hall's architect once the additional endowment funds were raised. There is no evidence that a contract with McCornack was ever drafted. Frank Ginn was asked to negotiate the land deal with Western Reserve University, resulting in a 99-year lease (expiring in 2029) that called upon the Musical Arts Association to pay an annual rental fee of one dollar. Ginn was also appointed chairman of the building committee, which was to include William G. Mather, H. G. Dalton, W. M. Clapp, Severance Millikin, Robert Vinson, and, in *ex officio* capacities, Severance, Blossom, Hughes, and A. A. Brewster. Blossom was named chairman of the endowment fund committee, and trustees agreed that "a personally conducted quiet campaign without publicity be made" for the $2.5 million the Severances wished to secure for the endowment. The general public would be invited to send gifts later.

Several days into 1929, Ginn telegrammed Severance in California that he had received from Dudley Blossom "important and reliable information" that led them to become skeptical of McCornack's abilities. Severance would come to agree with Ginn, especially after he learned that McCornack had suddenly, and mysteriously, resigned from his architectural firm (Warner, McCornack and Mitchell) the previous October. The information about McCornack's qualifications had come from one of his former partners, who accused McCornack of submitting sloppy reports on construction projects. McCornack wasn't oblivious to the apparent change in the wind. "I have a very distinct feeling that my ability to carry on an important project is being questioned," he wrote to Hughes in late January. "After all the time I have spent on this plan, I do not feel like allowing any thoughts to gain headway which might injure me professionally, especially in view of the fact the plan seems to have met with universal approval."

Whatever his view, another event put off any action regarding McCornack's fate on the project. On January 25, a day before her 64th birthday, Elisabeth Severance died suddenly of a stroke at the couple's winter home in Pasadena. Although she had been in ill health for several years, which limited her participation in social and philanthropic projects, she had been an enthusiastic supporter of the hall project. Mrs. Severance's death dramatically altered her husband's concept of the hall. It was no longer merely to be his gift to the orchestra and to Cleveland. The hall would become a lasting monument to his beloved wife. To achieve this end, Severance would supply whatever amount was needed to complete the hall—though he asked Ginn to keep this information confidential.

Severance was from the start a hands-on benefactor. Less than a month after his wife's death, he again was corresponding with Ginn—on black-edged paper—about the McCornack situation. Both trustees were thoroughly disenchanted with the architect by this time, believing that his plans contained wasted space. Severance was content to let Ginn hammer out details of a proposed contract with the prestigious Cleveland architectural firm Walker and Weeks. "I hope that by the time this reaches you [McCornack] will be practically out of the picture so far as the architect is concerned," Severance wrote to Ginn. The board president proposed that certain facets of McCornack's internal design be retained but that Frank Walker, a partner from Walker and Weeks, be hired to design the exterior. After being paid $6,500 for the work he had done, McCornack was removed from the project on May 18, 1929, when the Musical Arts Association signed a contract with Walker and Weeks, who were to serve as the hall's principal architects.

Actually, hiring the architects couldn't be done without the endowment funds in hand, as Severance had dictated. Blossom and his committee were swift. Within two months of the initial Severance announcement, they solicited (quietly, as planned) almost $2 million from 28 donors. Blossom's "ever-ready wit and unfaltering belief in the outcome inspired every worker," according to Hughes.

The public became involved in April 1929, when Blossom guided more than 500 volunteers in a nine-day campaign to raise endowment funds. Upwards of 3,000 people raised or donated money. Columnists and reporters helped the drive by urging the community to do its share in making the hall a reality. A headline in the Cleveland News suggested that the new facility promised to provide a level of concertgoing dignity that the town had lacked: "Cleveland Habit of Mixing Music With Poultry Shows, Tractors and Trained Seals Will Come to an End With Completion of the Orchestra's New Home."

Buoyed by the public's response, Severance supplemented his original $1 million gift by wiring an additional $250,000 donation for the endowment fund from California. Another philanthropist on the board, mining magnate Samuel Mather, wrote a check for $400,000. For Hughes, the most heartwarming donation arrived in late April from the man who had rejected several requests. It was from John D. Rockefeller, Jr., who wrote: "While my active interest in general Cleveland enterprises has for some years been practically terminated, as a tribute to what you have done in building up and centralizing in so marvelous a way the musical values of the city, I shall be happy to contribute two hundred and fifty thousand dollars to the music hall endowment campaign."

During the same period, a very different contribution demonstrated both the breadth of support for the orchestra and the extent to which it had taken root in Northeast Ohio. In mid-April, Blossom received a letter from the

Cleveland Boy's Farm—a school for juvenile delinquents—thanking him and Mrs. Blossom for their kindness in allowing boys from the Hudson facility to attend orchestra concerts. They wanted to do something in return, so they had appointed a committee of four boys to raise money for the endowment campaign. "Of course," their letter said, "we have not lots of ready cash out here but we felt that each boy could afford to give about 7 (seven) cents. So we tried to collect that amount from the 139 boys present Tuesday. We got a grand total of $9.68 (nine dollars and sixty eight cents)." The letter was signed, "Very respectfully yours," by Steve Kosa, Earl White, Wm. Hess and Homer Fleming, and was followed by an endearingly streetwise postscript: "It really should have been $9.73 instead of only $9.68—but one nickle [sic] turned out to be bad. We don't know the scum who passed the bad nickle on us. When are you coming to Hudson again? Come soon."

Blossom and his associates finished their work toward the end of April, when the endowment fund reached a total of $2.36 million. In addition, the children of David Z. Norton contributed $60,000 for a pipe organ (a feature of the hall that would prove frustrating for seven decades). *Time* magazine marked the end of the campaign with a chipper, if exaggerated, article headlined "Solvent Symphony." The story profiled the four principal figures behind the hall—Severance, Blossom, Hughes, and Sokoloff—who were depicted having dinner together to celebrate "the financial emancipation of Cleveland's orchestra, the casting out of an old theme which one can nearly always hear booming from the tympanum of any U.S. symphony—the theme of debt."

❧   ❧   ❧

The design for the hall wasn't nearly as complete as the fund-raising, though McCornack's initial studies were proving helpful. The plans he had submitted in February 1928 included a main concert hall, foyer, and small concert hall. It would be the job of Walker and Weeks to refine the designs, provide sufficient space for the orchestra and administration, and make the auditorium suitable for radio broadcasting and many types of events (lectures, movies, stage productions), as well as fit everything onto the wedge-shaped piece of land donated by Western Reserve University. One other thing was essential: Walker and Weeks had to satisfy John L. Severance, who had definite ideas about how he wanted the memorial to his wife to be designed and used.

An early matter of concern was the pipe organ. Severance was delighted that Norton's children wanted to salute their father by donating an imposing instrument, but he was determined that it shouldn't divert attention from the main point of the facility. "I do not wish to interfere in this matter, and am anxious to have as fine an organ installed in the building as possible," Severance wrote to Ginn. "To do so it is desirable to have the organ builders advise with the architects. Nevertheless, the Hall is being built primarily for orchestral purposes and the installation of the organ should be a secondary consideration." This view, while reasonable at the time, would have unhappy consequences for the organ and for the hall's acoustics.

Word of the pipe organ spread quickly. Organ-playing maestro Leopold Stokowski, elated that Cleveland was planning to incorporate a mighty instrument into its new auditorium, wrote to Sokoloff from Paris that he recommended installing an organ built by the Aeolian Company "because I know, from personal experience, of the high quality and honesty of the work done in their factory." Despite the advice, orchestra officials eventually chose a magnificent E. M. Skinner organ—and then virtually hid it away in a loft high above the stage, the only space left in the final design.

Severance and his late wife were not inexperienced in matters of design. The spacious mansion on their estate, Longwood, reflected their love for architecture and the fine arts, as well as the influence of homes and other buildings they had viewed during extensive travels throughout Europe. When Mrs. Severance died, her husband vowed to carry out her wishes regarding the hall's comfort, beauty, and usage (she was partial to stage works). "Please see that the seats in the balcony are just as comfortable as those on the floor," Mrs. Severance had said. But John L. Severance concurred with Walker and Weeks that the prime consideration in the main auditorium was acoustical. They consulted with Dayton C. Miller, a physics professor at the Case School of Applied Sciences, who suggested certain materials and shapes, only to see various details of his plan discarded as the building was transformed into a multipurpose hall.

Acoustics would have to wait. Severance wanted his monument to be monumental, and he had chosen the right firm to provide the splendor. Walker and Weeks had designed a multitude of superb structures in the Midwest, including many in Cleveland. In selecting Walker and Weeks, Severance sought a guarantee that the hall would possess the same grandeur the firm had lavished on such local buildings as the Cleveland Public Library and the Federal Reserve Bank, as well as two edifices near the site of the new concert hall, the Allen Memorial Medical Library and Epworth-Euclid United Methodist Church (later affectionately known as the Holy Oil Can Church for its octagonal metal roof topped with a thin spire). The architects were renowned for an eclectic style that melded such elements as frescoes, murals, sculptures, marble, bronze, and granite.

All of these elements would find a home at Severance Hall, though Hughes—perhaps miffed about the treatment of McCornack—didn't always agree with design decisions made by Walker and Weeks. "The architects have much improved the exterior but I do not care for the suggestive sketches for interior treatment of the hall. Much too fancy," she wrote to Sokoloff in the summer of 1929. "The statuary has been completely eliminated." Hughes may have been onto something. The building was becoming more luxurious than anyone had imagined. Some of the rich materials used in the main auditorium would work against sonic clarity for many years. But what Walker and Weeks achieved must be considered remarkable, especially because they had so many constraints. They had to fit the size and configuration of the land. They had to fashion the hall to conform to the architectural scheme of the nearby Cleveland Museum of Art and Allen Memorial Medical Library. They had to provide a proscenium and an orchestra pit for stage productions, and they had to fit an organ into a space that, unfortunately, was destined to draw sound upward from the stage and away from the musicians and audience.

The size of the main auditorium was determined by Ginn's building committee, which voted to have 800 seats on the main floor, 900 in the uppermost sections (dress circle and balcony), and 25 boxes—arranged in a horseshoe—seating about 200. If the total of almost 1,900 seats (later increased to 2,000) was considered small by concert-hall standards in the United States (Carnegie Hall has 2,800), the intimacy was seen as beneficial to the public. "Even the fifty-cent seat holders will be able to see and hear as well as the soloists," Hughes noted.

For the front facade, Walker and Weeks designed a series of terraced steps leading up to a grand portico in Georgian style. The principal materials are Indiana limestone and Ohio sandstone. The majesty of the exterior does not prepare the observer for the explosion of eclectic elements inside the main entrance. Art Deco meets Egypt in the grand foyer. Red marble and gilded details rub shoulders with striking murals, by Cleveland Institute of Art faculty member Elsa Vick Shaw, of ancient Egyptian, Greek, and Middle Eastern figures with instruments, illustrating the story of music.

To fit the building onto the property and achieve the requisite elegance, Walker and Weeks designed the hall so that the grand foyer would serve as a central rotunda from which two wings would flank the main auditorium. Just as the contrast from exterior to grand foyer is surprising, the stylistic distance from the grand foyer to the main auditorium is enormous. The grand foyer's glitter gives way to muted blues and tans in the hall itself. The silvery lines on the ceiling, according to legend, are based on lace from Mrs.

Severance's wedding dress. She also appears to have been the inspiration for the lotus blossoms (her favorite flower) that adorn many surfaces throughout the hall, including the grand foyer's magnificent terrazzo floor.

The remainder of the building is a lovely mix of styles. The boardroom on the box level and the 424-seat chamber hall on the ground floor have an aristocratic, 18th-century ambience. The green room, on the main floor near East Boulevard, is a quietly refined space for exhibits that was used as a recording booth during the Szell era. One of the most unusual innovations of the original building was the motor driveway, between Euclid Avenue and East Boulevard, where patrons could be dropped off to enter the hall. A broadcasting studio on the fourth floor, overlooking Euclid Avenue, could hold a 125-piece orchestra.

As originally envisioned, the building was to have five floors, not including the basement. But in conferences with Severance and orchestra associates, assistant manager Carl Vosburgh—who would become hall manager upon the facility's opening—learned that the engineers had run up against a problem in the construction of the top of the hall. "Mr. Severance called me in to look over the office space in a new design which they have prepared," Vosburgh wrote to Hughes. "This design cuts out the fifth floor and puts our offices on the fourth floor but don't be alarmed as everything you desired is still included in the hall. The offices on the fourth floor will be as formerly, overlooking the park."

Several of the building's other original features were doomed to failure. One of these was the cyclorama, also known as the sky dome, which Severance thought would be a fine backdrop for stage productions. There was one problem: the massive structure tended to devour sound. A related oddity that quickly became extinct was a spotlight system that altered the color of lights to enhance stage productions or even symphonic works. At first, Severance, Sokoloff, and the architects were enthusiastic about this lighting method, which was devised by S. R. McCandless of the Yale School of Drama and controlled by a "color organ," with a console similar to that of a pipe organ. "I must say I never imagined that such a remarkable magic could be produced by lights," Sokoloff wrote to Severance. "I feel completely inspired because [of] the possibilities of doing fascinating performances of the kind of music which is decorative in character and also [because] certain excerpts or parts of Wagnerian or other masterpieces in opera can now be done in Cleveland with lights rather than static scenery."

Sokoloff's enthusiasm wouldn't last. "This was the most ghastly thing imaginable, throwing a red light on us when we played Brahms, a blue light when we played Debussy, and so on," he later wrote in his memoirs. "A third-rate movie house couldn't have devised a more vulgar effect. Fortunately, the public felt as I did and the light organ was abandoned."

✳   ✳   ✳

It must have taken remarkable courage and devotion for Severance to follow through on his financial commitment to the new hall. On October 29, 1929—"Black Tuesday"—the stock market crash plunged the United States into a quick, downward economic spiral. Severance would lose a large portion of his fortune and remain heavily in debt until 1935, in part because of Severance Hall. But the industrialist was determined to see his monument rise. Soon after the crash, he officially informed the orchestra's board that he intended to pledge "any and all funds which may be required in excess of funds to the amount of $1,000,000 which Mrs. Severance and I pledged" to build the hall. His total contribution would be more than $2.6 million.

On November 14, 1929, only two weeks after "Black Tuesday," Severance—still wearing a black armband to mourn the death of his wife—pushed a shovel into the dirt at the corner of Euclid Avenue and East Boulevard to break ground for the hall. Surrounding him were associates from the orchestra and representatives from the Crowell and Little Company, the Cleveland construction firm hired for the project. A light rain fell, but it didn't stop trumpeter Alois Hruby from playing the solo from Beethoven's *Leonore* Overture No. 3 to symbolize the heroic act of creation that was to follow. The orchestra hoped to inhabit its new home by the start of the 1930–31 season.

Though known for his patience, Severance often registered mild displeasure at the slow progress of construction. He maintained a lively correspondence with Ginn from California on issues ranging from hangings and furniture to the numbering of boxes and air-conditioning. "I think we would regret it if we did not make this installation," Severance wrote to Ginn. "I am not at all interested in the phase of cooled air which many movie houses advertise, but I do think there is considerable interest in a system that will take out of the air excess moisture, especially under certain atmospheric conditions that may arise."

On January 20, 1930, Ginn sent a happy message to Severance: "ERECT- ING STEEL SEVERANCE HALL COMMENCED THIS MORNING AND BY NINE O'CLOCK TEN COLUMNS IN PLACE AND WORK PROCEEDING." Two months later, Ginn reported that "the steel work is all in place, only a few more rivets here and there to be driven. The setting of stone will start in a few days, sufficient of the sandstone being ready for setting." On May 2, Severance presided at the cornerstone-laying ceremony, smoothing the mortar as orchestra trumpeters Alois Hruby, William Hruby, and Max Woodbury played an excerpt from Strauss's *Ein Heldenleben.*

As chairman of the building committee, Ginn was partly responsible for planning the hall's gala opening, whenever it would happen. Sokoloff wanted to commission his old teacher, Charles Martin Loeffler, for a composition for the program, and Severance had approved the idea. Ginn took a gentle approach when writing to Loeffler at his home in Medfield, Massachusetts: "We do not want to make this a burden or an obligation in any way but only place the matter before you so that if the inclination and inspiration comes you may know that we will be most grateful and appreciative." The inclination and inspiration came, and Loeffler composed *Evocation* for the opening concert.

❖　　❖　　❖

Throughout his tenure, Sokoloff had spent summers away from Cleveland vacationing or conducting. In June 1930, he traveled to Russia to guest conduct, attend performances at the Bolshoi in Moscow, and become better acquainted with his homeland. "I am feeling very fit, and blowing Cleveland's horn to beat the band," he wrote to Hughes from Leningrad.

By the fall of 1930, it was clear that Severance Hall wouldn't be ready for Sokoloff and his orchestra until after the New Year. Despite the delay, excitement about the hall was growing. Arthur Shepherd, the former assistant conductor who was now music critic of the *Cleveland Press*, even wrote optimistically about the hall's 6,025-pipe, 94-rank Skinner organ, whose placement he termed, perhaps diplomatically, "unique." The organ, Shepherd reported three months before the instrument's installation was to begin in December, "will be directly over the orchestra and the tone will reach the auditors thru a grill placed over the front of the stage. Sound reflectors will be used for the purpose of co-ordinating the sonorities of organ and orchestra. The purpose of these reflectors is to give the hearer the impression of immediacy as tho the organ were being heard from within the body of the auditorium." This turned out to be wishful thinking.

Sokoloff, meanwhile, exulted that after 12 years in Cleveland, he was finally happy with the ensemble's standards. "The orchestra this year has given me the greatest joy for I think at last I have an instrument which is sensitive and beautiful in quality and on a very high musical level," he wrote to music critic Lawrence Gilman in New York. "Every program has been a delight to prepare because of the ease with which I can now work, having an instrument to do it with."

Toward the end of December, Sokoloff led one of the orchestra's final concerts at Masonic Hall, a program of Mozart's Symphony in D major, K. 504, Bloch's *Schelomo* (with Victor de Gomez as cello soloist), and Strauss's *Death and Transfiguration*. Archie Bell sounded a discordant note in the *Cleveland News* by taking exception to the conductor's "increasing tendency to speechify" during concerts: "A conductor's business is to conduct; nobody cares much whether the performers like a selection of music, that being a matter for the people on the other side of the footlights to decide for themselves."

❉   ❉   ❉

Finally, after years of struggle and planning, the grand moment was about to arrive. To test out the new hall's acoustics, Sokoloff plinked out several notes on the celesta and Hughes did the same, on the celesta and a new vibraharp, before the first rehearsal on Sunday, February 1. The orchestra got in on the act soon afterward, when they opened their inaugural rehearsal in their luxurious home with a Severance request, the Prelude and "Liebestod" from Wagner's *Tristan und Isolde*, an opera that would figure prominently in the orchestra's history in just a few years. The musicians also presented Severance with a tribute scroll.

On Thursday, February 5, 1931, a cold and rainy night, there were no objections to speeches as the hall opened to elated response from the press and public. Sokoloff and the orchestra began with Goedicke's arrangement of J. S. Bach's Passacaglia in C minor, continued with Loeffler's *Evocation*, and ended, once again in C minor, with the Brahms First Symphony. The evening's most poignant moment was provided by Severance, who told the capacity crowd that the hall had been built as the orchestra's home, but also to serve Western Reserve University "for congregations, commencements, lectures and various other activities" that wouldn't conflict with the needs of the hall's resident ensemble. Then he came to what he must have considered the heart of the matter. "When the pledge of this building was made, Mrs. Severance was by my side," he said. "She has since passed away and it has been my task to carry on alone the completion of this hall; and now, Mr. Blossom, in turning it over to the Musical Arts Association as the owner, and Dr. Vinson as representing Western Reserve University, which is to share in its use, I wish to give it as a memorial in memory of my beloved wife, Elisabeth DeWitt Severance."

The hall's benefactor was followed by Blossom, who hailed his colleague and then placed the hall's inauguration in a broader perspective. Severance Hall, Blossom said, "is in the last analysis a gift to all of the people of Cleveland. It is they who are the real beneficiary; it is they who are going to come here day after day and year after year to enjoy the comfort, the charm, and the loveliness of this beautiful hall." Vinson told the audience that the hall would serve as an ideal location to "contribute to the organized life of the university in many ways."

Among the opening-night audience—a mixture of high society and orchestra mavens—sat Sergei Rachmaninoff, who had given a piano recital the night before at Public Hall. The great composer-pianist joined Severance in his box (dead center in the horseshoe of boxes) with several other special guests, including the Loefflers. Forty-five minutes of the concert, including the speeches by Severance, Blossom, and Vinson, were broadcast live on WTAM.

All of Cleveland's newspapers ran extensive stories the next day, starting on their front pages and filling many columns inside. *The Plain Dealer*'s banner headline read, "SEVERANCE HALL OPENS IN SPLENDOR," with smaller headlines proclaiming, "Brilliance of Gathering is Unsurpassed; Architecturally, Musically and Socially Dedication Is Acclaimed Event Triumphal; Richness And Beauty Like Giant Jewel Box; Capacity Audience Kindles Atmosphere With Civic Spirit." William F. McDermott's story echoed the general sentiment. "One sees many premieres in the course of writing about the theaters over a period of years," he wrote. "I never saw one like this, nothing so genuinely splendid as a spectacle, nothing so brilliant from the viewpoint of social display, nothing so impressive in combination of architectural beauty harmoniously adapted to serve the ends for which it was created." McDermott also suggested that Cleveland could now take a place in the international pantheon of the world's artistic capitals: "The great opera houses of Paris, Vienna, Berlin and Moscow are larger and perhaps outwardly more imposing. But there is nothing in them to compare with the intimate jeweled richness of the foyer of Severance Hall, nor anything approaching the serene, chaste, quiet loveliness of the auditorium."

At the same time, an editorial in the *Press* mirrored Blossom's opening-night words, asking the city to concentrate on music, rather than mere status: "We hope that 'society' in the society page sense is not going to take possession of the city's principal musical activity, at the expense of Society in the Sociological sense. We do not believe it is the wish of Mr. Severance, Mr. Blossom, and other generous patrons of the institution, that this should happen. We believe that Mr. Severance intended to build a temple to music, and not a temple to wealth; and we believe it is his intention that all music lovers should be welcome there."

The hall's festivities continued the night after the inaugural when Sokoloff and chamber ensembles from the orchestra christened the

Chamber Hall, which possessed a small stage suitable for recitals and intimate theatrical productions, as well as a tiny orchestra pit. The program included works by Haydn, d'Indy, and British composer Robin Milford, and a performance of Wagner's *Siegfried Idyll* played by 25 orchestra members under Sokoloff's baton.

Hughes expressed her gratitude to the orchestra in a note the day after the Chamber Hall inauguration: "My heart is full of joy—joy for the wonderful home we have been given—for the friendships, kindness, and the generosity of the many people who have contributed to bringing this wonderful thing to pass. To you, who have played music in a manner that was worthy of this great moment in our history, I send my heartfelt appreciation, and for the beautiful roses and the message they brought to me from each of the eighty-six my warmest thanks."

Cleveland, along with Boston and Chicago, now was one of the few cities in the country whose orchestra claimed its own concert hall. The New York Philharmonic, which was 89 years old in 1931, had played in eight different halls before taking up residence in 1892 at the newly completed Carnegie Hall, where it remained—sharing the busy facility—until finally finding a permanent home at Philharmonic (later Avery Fisher) Hall in 1962.

Not everything was perfect at the new Severance Hall, however. The building's wonders were accompanied by shortcomings that wouldn't be addressed for decades, including a paucity of women's restrooms and no locker room for female musicians (of which the orchestra had only one, harpist Alice Chalifoux, in 1931). The principal defect, however, was acoustical, and this was no fluke. Mrs. Severance's desire for patron comfort, management's interest in recordings and radio broadcasts, and the planned need for the hall to accommodate music, theater, and lectures had led the architects to decorate the hall with fabrics that kept the reverberation time low—and the sound dry. The floor of the main auditorium was covered with blue carpet. The boxes had heavy blue drapes. The stage was framed in contour curtains. These materials had a muffling effect on the strings, though brasses and percussion had no trouble being heard (particularly in the dress circle and balcony). A further acoustical hindrance was the orchestra shell, a flimsy stage set with no true reflective surfaces that was open at the sides and top, allowing sound to escape backstage. The acoustics, in short, were miserable. "When we held our first rehearsal there, we could have wept," Sokoloff recalled years later. "We sounded as though we were in a recording studio— the hall, in fact, is excellent for recording." (Sokoloff never made a recording in Severance Hall.)

For the opening concert, Sokoloff had placed most of the orchestra on risers to achieve the balance he desired. But the acoustical dilemma forced him to change his mind. Writing to Severance in California at the end of February, Ginn noted that for the second program, Sokoloff had taken three-fourths of the orchestra off the platforms, which made the sound even worse. Ginn noted that the predominance of cloth onstage might be fine for theatrical productions, but not for orchestral performances. E. M. Skinner, in town soon afterward to attend the dedication of his hidden organ, gave Ginn the impression that he, too, was not pleased with what he heard.

The most pointed, and probably most accurate, assessment came from Alice C. Hickox, an orchestra subscriber from Euclid Heights, who was distressed by the volume of brass and percussion sound that reached the balcony. She complained to Hughes at the end of March:

> If the audience, in the upper part of the hall, has not *anacoustic ears*, it will demand that something be done or that part of the auditorium will be an empty wilderness, leaving the rails to flourish in loneliness. The *noise* (there is no other word) on Thursday night during the last half of the program was *deafening*—much worse than the first concert on the opening night . . . If 'La Mer' could produce such an effect of sound, how would one suffer when Mr. Sokoloff embarks on one of his modernistic programs? I shudder to think of it. It would be a tragedy, certainly, to spend so vast a sum of money on *magnificence* only and fail in the *one important* requirement of a concert hall! . . . I hope I am not doomed to leaving town to hear symphonic music!

Hughes, delighted with the hall she had helped bring to life, pooh-poohed the criticism a few days later in a letter to Ginn: "Mrs. Hickox's is the only complaint that we have received of the acoustics from the dress circle and balcony subscribers. So far, universal praise has been coming in generous volume."

In any case, Hughes had other concerns at the moment. There was continued unease about Sokoloff, both professionally and personally, within the orchestra and the community. And she remained committed to fulfilling the mission that had brought Sokoloff to town in the first place, even before an orchestra existed—educating young people about symphonic music.

– 8 –

Education and
Transition

The articles of incorporation bringing the Musical Arts Association into existence on October 5, 1915, state nothing about a symphony orchestra. Nor is there mention of educational activities. The phrase "for the purpose of furthering the interests of music in the community" leaves room for many interpretations. But it is not surprising that education would be high on the agenda of Adella Prentiss Hughes. Her entire career could be summed up as an effort to educate the public about good music, especially the symphonic repertoire. She had been involved in projects of the Fortnightly Musical Club since the 1890s. In 1912, she helped Almeda Adams, a blind voice teacher, find funding to establish the Cleveland Music School Settlement, whose original objective was to bring music to the lives of immigrants and their children. The school later broadened its programs to provide instruction and performance opportunities for all segments of the community at affordable prices.

Then Hughes met Nikolai Sokoloff. Here was the opportunity for music education through first-hand exposure to great music: a real conductor; training on orchestral and band instruments; and attendance at live concerts by a local, professional symphony orchestra. The orchestra would become the principal focus of the association, but education would remain an integral part of the orchestra's mission. "The heart of the matter is what we do for the children," Sokoloff told music teachers in 1923. His orchestra was just shaping up during its first season, when Sokoloff began taking the ensemble into school buildings to give students and their families a taste of symphonic richness. But by 1921, the concerts had generated so much interest that the orchestra needed more space to accommodate students and their teachers at its one-hour educational programs, which were moved to Masonic Hall.

With children's concerts came a clearly visible sign of educational progress—school buses, dozens of them. The long lines of yellow vehicles parked in front of Masonic Hall, and later Severance Hall, would signify the orchestra's belief that music is no luxury but an essential part of the human experience. Hughes understood this well before she met Sokoloff, but the conductor added his own impassioned take on the educational process even as he molded his orchestra. "Our children are learning not only what the instruments are but what is the meaning of great music," said Sokoloff in the 1923 speech. "That brings a great thing into one's life. Supposing a child is made conscious of the marvelous sound of a great orchestra or the wonderful design of a great civic center, or sees a splendid building and knows what it is. When he grows up, and opportunity comes, this child will be a fine citizen, the kind of citizen that will make a new life in this country."

As part of its goal to point youngsters to such a new life, the orchestra inaugurated the Music Memory Contest in 1921, involving several thousand children a year. Hughes formed the Women's Committee the same year to organize the children's concerts, which were conducted by Arthur Shepherd until Rudolph Ringwall succeeded him. The first official education concerts were presented on November 18, 1921, at Masonic Hall with a program especially designed for children. Members of the Women's Committee sold tickets to local schools. The education program grew quickly and expanded well beyond the concert hall. By the end of the 1922–23 academic year, 33 members of the orchestra were teaching 800 students at two Cleveland public schools (East Technical High and West Technical High) in instrumental classes on Saturdays. Music appreciation received another boost in the fall of 1926, when five children's concerts were broadcast on the radio from Masonic Hall to classrooms throughout the city.

Other than these activities, however, preparation of children for orchestra concerts generally was negligible during the 1920s. Someone—aside from the tireless Hughes—was needed to tie all of the loose music-education strands together. Just as plans for Severance Hall were being finalized in the fall of 1929, that someone appeared. Her name was Lillian Baldwin.

A native of Marion, Indiana, Baldwin was born in 1887 into a family with Quaker roots. Her musical education began at home, where the family joined voices in singing sessions on Sunday nights. After voice and piano studies in Cincinnati, she left for Europe to study to be a concert singer. A stint in Berlin in 1912–13 was followed by a period as a music teacher in Gambier, Ohio. Eventually, she came into contact with the great educator Daniel Gregory Mason, whose renowned courses in music appreciation inspired her future programs. Baldwin's interest in literature complemented her musical studies. By the time she was contacted about the Cleveland position, she had earned a bachelor's degree in music education and a master of arts degree from Columbia University.

It was during her years in New York that Baldwin was introduced to children's concerts. By the mid-1920s, the idea wasn't new. Theodore Thomas had started educational concerts in the 1880s with the Philharmonic Society of New York. The New York Symphony Orchestra began presenting children's concerts soon afterward, first under Leopold Damrosch and then under his son, Walter. Josef Stransky's programs for young people, which started in 1914 with the New York Philharmonic, were admired far more, it turns out, than his concerts for adults. Soon thereafter, the Philharmonic presented programs for youngsters in Cleveland under the auspices of Hughes's Symphony Orchestra Concerts series. Frederick Stock began educational concerts in Chicago in 1919.

Baldwin intended to surpass all previous models. "The idea of musical literacy has given new significance to concerts for children," she wrote. "They can no longer be considered mere hopeful entertainment. We have come a long way from Walter Damrosch's grandfatherly 'Good morning, dear children' and Ernest Schelling's rhymes and lantern slides."

Hughes believed that Baldwin's ideas were just what she had long envisioned for Cleveland, and she saw Baldwin as the ideal music education liaison between the orchestra and the board of education. Baldwin had reservations about accepting the post until she concluded that the orchestra would be central to the success of her educational principles. She received the cumbersome title "Consultant in Music Education for the Cleveland Orchestra" and, in 1931, her own office in Severance Hall.

Baldwin's programs would help revolutionize music education in America and become known as "the Cleveland Plan." This plan called for thorough student involvement in educational concerts through careful reading, listening, and postconcert discussion. And the program wasn't reserved for children with musical talent: it was aimed at all students, partly as a means of putting them in touch with feelings that could be expressed in no other way. Baldwin believed that "audience appreciation" had to go beyond the concert itself. "For learning that lasts," she wrote, "nothing has yet taken the place of the good old preparation and follow-up. An isolated event, however delightful, adds little continuity."

Baldwin focused on pieces the youngsters were to hear at orchestra concerts. In addition to listening skills, they were taught to read musical symbols. Baldwin devised the materials with assistant conductor Ringwall, who reveled in the contact with young people and proved a genial host during performances. As "the Cleveland Plan" evolved, Baldwin created programs for specific age levels: Little Folks' Programs, for fourth graders; Children's Concerts, for fifth- and sixth-graders; and Young People's Concerts, for junior and senior high-school students.

"Musicianly listeners discover that music is more than pretty sound," Baldwin wrote. "They learn to recognize and enjoy the many fine details of music's workmanship—details the untrained listener misses. They learn that music may be the voice of a nation speaking; it may be the emotional record of a period of world history; the reflection of a famous story or the portrait of a great man done in tone."

Within a few years of her arrival, Baldwin succeeded in making Cleveland known for its educational concerts. Thousands of children—sometimes up to 40,000 or 50,000—were immersed in symphonic repertoire each year. The interest spilled over to their parents, many of whom enrolled in adult music-appreciation courses.

Even citizens without much inclination toward classical music approved of these goings-on at Severance Hall. One day during an educational concert, Baldwin was approached by a streetcar dispatcher who, not knowing who she was, proceeded to list the benefits of the program: "And I said to my wife, 'Look at the kids lined up in front of these cheap movie shows—what do they see? Why just some fella pullin' a gun or runnin' off with some other fella's wife. Fine notions that gives 'em! Naw, they oughta all be out there at Severance Hall — it's a decent place. That's where our kids oughta be.'" The fellow must have been surprised when Baldwin told him how much his support meant to her: "For these are all *my* children."

❊   ❊   ❊

By the mid-1920s, expansion of the children's concerts, growth of the orchestra's concert schedule, and the promising start of its recording activity appeared to be giving Nikolai Sokoloff the stature he sought in the musical world. But clouds were gathering over Cleveland. Sokoloff's behavior on the podium during both rehearsals and performances had begun to alienate the musicians and was getting under the skin of at least one of the city's music critics, Wilson G. Smith, of the *Press*. The conductor continued to be an adventurous and imaginative programmer—too much so for subscribers who couldn't tolerate his penchant for modern music.

There is no evidence that Sokoloff wasn't doing a top-notch job. He was hiring better players, expanding the orchestra's repertoire, and receiving the unqualified support of the board. Sokoloff had no closer ally than Adella Prentiss Hughes, who was completely devoted to her orchestra and its conductor. Whether she and Sokoloff—a married man with three sons—went beyond mere friendship is unclear. Several letters between the divorced manager and the conductor suggest more than just a professional relationship, possibly of a mother-son nature (she was almost 20 years his senior), possibly something else. A missive Sokoloff wrote to Hughes in May 1930 begins, "My dear Adella" and ends, "Yours sincerely, Nikolai," which appears tame enough. But the letter's post-postscript alters the tone: "should be—love." (Hughes would later step down as the orchestra's manager when Sokoloff left as conductor in 1933, which could be viewed as an acknowledgment that more than 30 years as a manager was enough—or that she couldn't continue without the man she had brought to town.)

No matter what his relationship with Hughes may have been, Sokoloff's music-making was straining his relations with a sizable portion of the public. Smith considered his performance of Tchaikovsky's "Pathétique" Symphony in March 1927 far too flamboyant: "There were moments of a fine realization of tonal finesse, but they were sporadic, lost in the unrestrained frenzy of emotionalism of the director. He has yet to learn that restrained and repressed emotional utterance is more effective than blatancy." Smith appreciated the conductor's rapturous handling of the oft-performed Rachmaninoff Symphony No. 2, but about the account of Beethoven's *Fidelio* overture that opened the 1927–28 season, the critic didn't hold back. "Its reading was sadly lacking the Beethoven nobility and dignity of spirit, moreover it was not played with any degree of certainty and ensemble nuance," he wrote.

If some of Sokoloff's performances were considered undisciplined, his choice of repertoire occasionally was deemed strange, such as Joseph Schillinger's First Airphonic Suite with its electronic theremin solos. Among other unusual projects during his tenure were collaborations with the Neighborhood Playhouse of New York. Their first joint effort was a series of staged symphonic works in April 1929 that featured distinguished modern dancers (Martha Graham, Charles Weidman, Doris Humphrey, Anna Sokolow) and actors. Directed by sisters Alice and Irene Lewisohn, the opening program consisted of Strauss's *Ein Heldenleben* (advertised as "first time given in a stage presentation"), *The White Peacock* by Griffes, and Enesco's Rumanian Rhapsody No. 1.

Sokoloff and the orchestra traveled eastward to perform the Neighborhood Playhouse programs at the Manhattan Opera House on West 34th Street. The *New York Telegram* was distinctly unimpressed, especially with the treatment given *Ein Heldenleben*. "Musically, the occasion did scant honor to Strauss," its critic wrote. "Mr. Sokoloff and his men, strung along the orchestra pit and running up into two stage boxes, were disadvantageously placed, and even had such not been the case the tone poem would inevitably have sunk at times to a mere accompaniment to miming."

In February 1930, the Clevelanders were back in Manhattan to team with the Neighborhood Playhouse in a program comprising Loeffler's *A Pagan Poem*, Henri Ribaud's *La Procession Nocturne*, and Werner Janssen's *New Year's Eve in New York*. Graham and Weidman again were soloists. One of the actor-dancers was a newcomer named Henry Fonda. Both music and theater critics reviewed the 1930 Neighborhood Playhouse production. Among them was J. Brooks Atkinson, who would reign as the gentlemanly chief drama critic at the *New York Times* for more than three decades. "No matter how kindly you may feel disposed toward the principle of experimentation toward a more universal form of drama, you cannot avoid the impression that, in the last analysis, this is not drama but elaboration of music," said Atkinson. "For the most part these pieces of music seem to be self-contained; the dance designs grow out of no need the music may have for them." One performance, attended by Leopold Stokowski, elicited a positive response from Richard L. Stokes in the *New York Evening World*: "The playing of the Cleveland Orchestra was, with minor exceptions, admirable; for this chronicler it had never before seemed quite so opulent and harmonious an instrument."

His sometimes odd choice of projects notwithstanding, Sokoloff clearly was gifted as an orchestra builder. "Rehearsal drill in The Cleveland Orchestra is stiff and steady," wrote a reporter in 1931. "Young himself, Sokoloff likes young players, with keen and flexible minds, like his own. It is said among orchestra players that one can play anywhere after a season under Sokoloff." A season is all some players lasted. During the latter half of the 1920s and early years of the 1930s, dozens of musicians left for other jobs or were replaced by players who helped the conductor solidify and refine his instrument. Maurice "Mo" Sharp, who began a 50-year tenure as principal flute in 1931, recalled that the refining process could be tense. "Sokoloff would sometimes give a cue to his fledgling orchestra in a difficult new work and would almost literally wince as he anticipated the results," he observed half a century later.

❀   ❀   ❀

Many musicians stuck it out in Cleveland during these early decades despite the virtual absence of work from late May until early October. In 1927, the situation improved for the players when the ensemble was hired for the first season of "Open Air Concerts" during June and July at Edgewater and Gordon parks. The programs of short classics were conducted by Rudolph

Ringwall and presented by the city of Cleveland. The crowds were enormous. Dudley Blossom, who returned from a vacation in Wyoming in time to hear the final Gordon Park concert, gave the best description of the orchestra's impact during its first series of summer concerts:

> That crowd, that throng of people, sitting all over the benches, all over the place, on automobiles, in automobiles, anywhere they could, to hear the music! They were poor people most of them, some perhaps not so poor, but many of them with their families, even with their babies, sitting there silently drinking in that music. It was really a thrilling experience. It made one's heart throb; and I want to make arrangements so that never again will I take a vacation when the summer concerts are going on, and I think you all feel the same way and that you all enjoyed the concerts last year. Those summer concerts, it seemed to me, meant more to the appreciation of the Orchestra in this town and more for the love of the Orchestra throughout the community than anything that has happened.

It would happen only once more in the next decade—the following year, when Ringwall led the "Cleveland Civic Summer Concerts," as they were now called, a 31-concert series that included seven Nationality Night programs. Almost a dozen ethnic groups were represented in these programs, which were presented with the partnership of the city of Cleveland. The concerts, plus popular programs played by Maurice Spitalny's Orchestra, were budgeted at $25,000. Plans for the construction of Severance Hall in 1929 may have kept the Musical Arts Association too busy to try to organize a summer season that year.

As the nation's economy weakened and the stock market plunged in October 1929, the Cleveland Orchestra was left without summer activity. Blossom, the city's director of Public Health and Welfare, tried to lobby for the musicians. In May 1930, he received word that City Council had appropriated $11,000 for parks concerts that summer. Donning his hat as vice president of the Musical Arts Association, he asked city officials to give consideration to the members of the orchestra, or they would be without work. Nothing came of his efforts.

The times were not good for expansion, aside from the bold and much needed construction of Severance Hall. The Musical Arts Association addressed financial instability in the early 1930s by keeping personnel down to 83 or 84 players and cutting salaries across the board. The musicians' wish for a pension could not be granted. Frank Ginn, hard-nosed as ever, told trustees that the players were lucky to be employed at all in light of the economic situation. "If the wage which we pay as our minimum is not gratefully received by the players, there are very many who would be glad to take their places," said Ginn. "It is unfortunate that we have to put it this way, but the facts are not to be denied."

The players were employed for shorter seasons. By 1931–32, the season was reduced from 28 weeks to 27 weeks. Alice Chalifoux, who joined that year as principal harpist, took a 10 percent pay cut (from her original salary of $100 a week) after six weeks and another 15 percent cut the following January. A season later, principal oboist Philip Kirchner protested that his annual salary—still the highest in the orchestra—was being sliced from $7,500 to $4,300. The situation was so drastic at the end of 1931 that Sokoloff offered to do without his midwinter vacation the next season in order to eliminate the need for a guest conductor.

Little did he know that the Musical Arts Association was thinking about eliminating *him*.

On April 16, 1932, when the orchestra's board met to discuss the 15th season, Sokoloff backed down from his offer to give up his vacation. He suggested that he leave for eight weeks instead of four and that Pierre Monteux be engaged for four weeks at $4,000. The board said, in essence, "No. Take four weeks and we will not engage Monteux." Then the trustees dropped a bomb, as board minutes for the meeting recount: "It was the sense of all directors present that the manager be instructed to advise Mr. Sokoloff that they do not care to consider a renewal of his contract at its expiration."

Public rumblings about his possible departure began immediately, though confirmation wouldn't come for three months. On July 27, the board issued a resolution saluting "the devoted and skillful guidance of its conductor" but also saying that "future development for the Orchestra can be better planned if this Company is free to investigate and experiment without the restrictions implied by a fixed contract with a single conductor." They were to change their minds on the last item, but not on Sokoloff's contract, which would expire as planned on May 31, 1933. Despite the convoluted language of the board resolution, it was clear that the orchestra was headed for a totally new experience: the replacement of its conductor. Sokoloff had brought the institution far, making it a real player on the national scene. Yet there can be little dispute that "the orchestra had sort of outgrown him," as Chalifoux put it.

A week after the July 1932 board meeting, Sokoloff told the press he "agreed with the management that too long a stretch with one conductor is likely to hide the orchestra beneath his personality." His emphasis is slightly different in his memoirs, in which he says that he had begun to feel drained and unable to communicate by this time. He claims that he asked the board for more time to rest or to guest conduct. Whatever Sokoloff's suggestions, the board went for none of them.

✼   ✼   ✼

The press didn't spend much time wallowing in nostalgia when news of the board decision was released. An editorial in the *Press* on July 28, 1932, the day after the board's announcement, expressed gratitude for the conductor's hard work, while being realistic about his accomplishments. "Public attitude toward Director Sokoloff has long been mixed," the editorial stated. "Due to a certain ungraciousness in dealing with his men and a stiffness and seeming lack of cordiality toward the public, his critics have been more numerous and vigorous than should have been set against as able a musician as is Dr. Sokoloff. His musicianship has been very little criticized at any time." Pitts Sanborn, in the *New York Telegram*, commented that Sokoloff's friends "have excused shortness of temper and a seeming contempt for people as merely the 'crankiness found in all geniuses.' " Another article claimed that the conductor had no friends at all. He was depicted as a "lonely figure" who "did not mingle with other musicians," but this was a pointless complaint, considering that few conductors ever keep close company with their players.

Most of the press reports concentrated not on the past, but on speculation about Sokoloff's successor. The *Press* quickly threw the names of Rudolph Ringwall, Eugene Ormandy, and Sir Hamilton Harty (who had been engaged for the coming season as guest conductor) into the hat. Blossom and Hughes were keeping mum on the subject, though they said a season of guest conductors might be possible for 1933–34.

The orchestra received a mountain of recommendations and inquiries about the conducting position. In retrospect, the most intriguing is the August 1932 letter from William E. Walter, manager of the St. Louis Symphony, who had engaged a gifted Hungarian-born conductor in 1930 and 1931 for his U.S. debut. His name, in the German spelling of the day, was Georg Szell. If French-born Vladimir Golschmann had not "caused a veritable riot amongst the women" in St. Louis, Szell might have been named that orchestra's conductor instead of Golschmann. Walter hired Szell as a guest in St. Louis after hearing him conduct *Boris Godunov* and *The Marriage of Figaro* at the Berlin Opera.

His letter on behalf of Szell is a remarkable document, even if it appears to smack of anti-Semitism—"Racially he is a Hungarian (not Jew)"—and he calls the conductor's knowledge of music "appalling," when he really means astonishing:

> Szell is now in his mid-thirties, a big, good looking fellow, cultured, speaking a half-dozen languages including excellent English—a man with a fine mind. He is one of the finest musicians it has been my fortune to know. He was a wunderkind (he says he started out to beat Korngold at being a second Mozart but somehow both of them missed out), a more than excellent pianist, a first-class horn player and has been conducting seriously since he was eighteen . . . There seems to be nothing he can not play from memory, from the latest jazz to the latest Berg and Hindemith. I'm told his "Wozzeck" in Prague was masterly. I myself can testify to his soundness in Beethoven, Brahms, etc . . . I am tremendously interested in the boy and in his future. I should like to see him back in America where I think he would become a power for the good of the art.

Walter's testimonial basically fell on deaf ears. Hughes wrote back a non-committal note asking if Szell was still represented by Arthur Judson, the top New York manager. (He wasn't.) "I happened to have heard that his name appeared on a list of conductors submitted by Mr. Judson to Seattle which they disregarded and took Basil Cameron for the concerts they are giving this season," Hughes wrote. "I will be glad to have you consider this inquiry a confidential one if you please." Szell's name wouldn't surface again in Cleveland until 1936, when he was proposed as a guest conductor.

But another important name did surface a few days after Walter wrote his letter. Along with Ringwall, Ormandy, and the Russian-born Norwegian conductor Issay Alexandrovich Dobrowen as possible candidates, the press mentioned Artur Rodzinski, the 40-year-old conductor of the Los Angeles Philharmonic. Sokoloff had rejected a request by Leopold Stokowski, conductor of the Philadelphia Orchestra, to hire the Polish conductor as a guest in Cleveland in 1925. Now Rodzinski (pronounced ruh-JIN-skee) appeared to have an edge. He had been conductor in Los Angeles since 1929, and his concerts had been attended by Severance when he wintered in Pasadena. Severance told colleagues on the Cleveland board about Rodzinski, and an invitation to conduct (and talk) was made.

News leaked out to this effect, and by late September 1932, Rodzinski was being touted in Cleveland newspapers as Sokoloff's successor, especially after he was engaged to be guest conductor for concerts on January 26 and 28, 1933, at Severance Hall. "The Cleveland Orchestra management refuses to say anything beyond the announcement that Rodzinski is being brought here as a guest conductor, but it is generally believed in musical circles that he is to be offered a permanent post if he can arrange to leave Los Angeles," wrote David Dietz in the *Press*. "A number of the trustees of the Cleveland Orchestra have heard him conduct during the last three years while visiting in Los Angeles and Pasadena." Stokowski notified Rodzinski in early October that he would be happy to go to bat for him: "Do not think that your future is in my hands because everybody's future is in their own hands. If I can do anything to help you with the Cleveland Board, please let me know."

Sokoloff wasn't gone yet. He opened his final season October 10, 1932, with a program of old and more recent favorites: Beethoven's "Eroica," Debussy's *La Mer* and Ravel's *Bolero*. Archie Bell paid him high tribute in the *Cleveland News* by saying, in his inimitably flamboyant fashion, "Cleveland has one of the magnificent orchestras of the country and anyone who ventures an opinion to the contrary, puts himself down as a nit-wit."

The trustees believed the orchestra would become even more magnificent under Rodzinski. They were so eager to hear the conductor in Cleveland that Hughes managed to advance his guest dates to December 29 and 31, 1932, giving him a jump on the season's other guest, Harty, who was scheduled for the following two weeks. One person prominent in the music business didn't like the prospective pairing of Rodzinski and Cleveland—his own agent, Arthur Judson. A brilliant but devious man, Judson told Hughes that Rodzinski wasn't the right man for the job. But the matter wasn't in Hughes's hands.

Rodzinski arrived in Cleveland in an expansive mood. Speaking to the press, he made statements that may not have been entirely sincere, but would be certain to impress trustees, musicians, and the public. "Severance Hall is the most beautiful hall in the world," he told Denoe Leedy, who had succeeded Arthur Shepherd as music critic of the *Press*. "The acoustics are perfect. One could not wish for anything better. And the orchestra—magnificent, unusually responsive." Rodzinski already sounded like the orchestra's next conductor as he praised the musical atmosphere in Cleveland and suggested programming ideas. "What a fine orchestra! What a place for symphony concerts and what a place for opera!" he told the *Cleveland News*. "Why, in addition to the concerts, Cleveland should have a month of opera . . . Audiences must hear something in addition to a few old Italian operas like 'Lucia,' 'Cavalleria' and 'Pagliacci' or 'Rigoletto.' Strauss's 'Salome,' for example, 'Rosenkavalier' and Russian operas that are totally unfamiliar to our audiences."

Rodzinski had devised an eclectic program for his debut concerts that week: Bach's Toccata and Fugue in D minor (arranged by Julius Wertheim), Beethoven's Fifth Symphony, Tchaikovsky's *Romeo and Juliet* fantasy-overture, Stravinsky's *Petrouchka* suite, and Johann Strauss II's *Tales from the Vienna Woods* waltz. The Bach and Stravinsky works were firsts for Cleveland Orchestra audiences.

Bell, writing in the *News*, led the pack in praising Rodzinski the day after the first concert. "My private tip to the powers that be (and it will be echoed by the vast majority in last night's big audience) is—grab him, steal him if necessary, tempt him with a salary that's handsome, because that's one of the things that all men work for, beg, negotiate and all the rest—but land him for the permanent post to be left vacant at the end of the season by Nikolai Sokoloff," the critic rhapsodized.

Rodzinski had conquered Cleveland even before the public got a glimpse of him. After observing the conductor in rehearsal with the orchestra, the trustees voted to hold an informal conference with him within a day or two "to outline an agreement which might be satisfactory to both the Board of Directors and Mr. Rodzinski."

The conference with Rodzinski was held on Saturday, December 31, when the executive committee offered him a three-year contract—with an option of two further years—to begin with the 1933–34 season. Rodzinski's initial salary was set at $27,000, with the stipulation that it would be upped to $30,000 when finances improved. Along with symphony concerts, Rodzinski would prepare and conduct operas and broadcasts with no additional compensation. One important clause would have crucial implications for the conductor's future: "It is understood that you will be accorded the privilege of occasional appearances as guest conductor elsewhere during the season at dates mutually arranged not to exceed three weeks in any season." Announcement of the appointment was set for January 14.

One orchestra official wasn't thrilled. Adella Prentiss Hughes didn't let on that the choice had been made when she wrote to a friend on January 3, but her feelings were evident:

> The world has been too much for me these last six months. I have managed to keep on getting a little bit better all the time and to do a really very good job here at the office. For myself, I have digested the difficult experience of the uprooting of fifteen years' association with Sokoloff and am valiantly going forward cooperating with the desire of the Committee for a new conductor. Things are not yet settled with us but I hope they will be before long.

She informed another friend that it "is definitely settled that Mr. Sokoloff goes . . . I have managed to bow to the inevitable with grace and am rather full of new ideas."

In a letter to Sokoloff in New York a few days later, Hughes was more up-beat, though she said that she, like the orchestra, had taken a large pay cut: "We had a very exciting week with Rodzinski and he made a very fine impression. The last six days with Sir Hamilton [Harty] have been entirely different and yet delightful for he is an entrancing person with a gentle flow of Irish wit that has delighted us all. The Orchestra has played well and both conductors are full of praise for your creation."

Now the press and the public began to hunger for any morsel of information about the new conductor. Rodzinski's ability to memorize scores and rehearse quickly was pointed out in many articles. Stokowski suggested that Clevelanders stop referring to Rodzinski as his assistant, for he surely "can stand on his own merits as an artist and conductor." Within weeks of the announcement, Hughes began to thaw. She even employed a bit of revisionist history to demonstrate her enthusiasm for the new conductor. Writing to a friend in Washington, D.C., she claimed that she and the board had been studying Rodzinski for seven months with the hope he would impress Cleveland and could be signed as the next conductor. The letter includes the first signs that Hughes, too, had grown disenchanted with the orchestra's lame duck conductor. "In many ways [Rodzinski] is an entirely different person from Nikolai and that is from my point of view desirable," she wrote. "I do not expect to enjoy everything he does as much as I have Nikolai's music but I may tell you privately that he will be a far easier person to work with in his handling of musicians and people than Nikolai has been."

Sokoloff's stature as a conductor couldn't be termed lofty at this point. With his flamboyance on the podium and his penchant for high collars, he had come to be regarded as a bizarre figure. Nor was his behavior offstage always considered admirable. When he took the orchestra on tour weeks after the Rodzinski announcement, he spent an inordinate amount of time openly trying to land another job. Hall manager Carl Vosburgh wrote to Hughes that Sokoloff was "losing dignity fast" through his pursuit of other orchestras. "In fact, I know several managers who formerly had the highest regard for him but are now quite disgusted."

There were moments on the tour when Sokoloff was as charming as ever. Discussing his trip to Russia in the summer of 1930, he recounted his attempt to rid himself of 8,000 rubles that he had earned in conducting fees and couldn't take out of the country. One reporter noted that while in Russia Sokoloff "gave parties mornings, noons and nights. He flabbergasted the retinue at his hotel by buying peaches at $3.50 each. He bought $1,000 worth of tunes to take home to the boys in Cleveland. What he paid for a glass of milk, he could buy the cow for here. But he had a grand time and so did everyone else he met in Russia."

Despite periods of frustration and impatience, Sokoloff had done grand work in Cleveland for 15 years. "His work is so well known here that comment seems superfluous," wrote Herbert Elwell, successor to James H. Rogers as music critic of *The Plain Dealer*, a few days before Sokoloff's final concerts. "But the fact that we have come to take it so much for granted tends to obscure the significance of his achievement. His parting should remind us that he has built an orchestra. Out of crude beginnings, he has shaped one of the finest instrumental organizations in the country. If we cannot subscribe to every phase of his art, we should not fail to credit him with the superior qualities he possesses."

Sokoloff, of course, had received help from an inexhaustible manager, a dedicated board, an enthusiastic body of musicians, and a public eager to hear symphonic music played on a high professional level. But he had established an orchestra that was moving swiftly upward in the national consciousness. It had become good enough to attract a successor of internationally recognized gifts.

By the end of Sokoloff's tenure, the orchestra had given 1,608 concerts—934 in Cleveland, 674 on tour. Any recriminations that may have existed between the conductor and forces in Cleveland were set aside when he led his last performances as boss on April 7 and 8, 1933. The centenary of Johannes Brahms's birth was only a month away, which gave him an opportunity to end his tenure with a majestic salute to a composer whose music would become prime Cleveland repertoire: the *Academic Festival Overture*, Piano Concerto No. 1 (with Severin Eisenberger as soloist), and Symphony No. 1. The critics waxed eloquent, and Sokoloff accepted a gift of orchestral scores from his friend Dayton C. Miller, the physics professor at Western Reserve University who had served as acoustical consultant on Severance Hall. "Tell them good luck, and that I've had a good time," Sokoloff answered when a reporter asked if he had anything to say to Cleveland before leaving for his home in Westport, Connecticut.

Little more than a month after Sokoloff's departure, Hughes wrote to Blossom asking to be relieved of her managerial duties. Still, the "mother of the Cleveland Orchestra" had no intention of giving up her children: she would continue to be active—some would say *too* active—on the board for a dozen more years.

PART TWO

EARNING A REPUTATION

1933–1946

— 9 —
A New Level

"*H*e came out of the West (Los Angeles) in 1933, wearing the shining armor of a conductorial Lochinvar to rescue the orchestra from the symphonic doldrums and a drab artistic existence." This affectionate, if melodramatic tribute, written by Milton Widder soon after Artur Rodzinski's death in 1958, portrays not only a musical hero but also an orchestra in distress. Cleveland had certainly needed a change from Nikolai Sokoloff, but were things so bleak in 1933, when the "conductorial Lochinvar" arrived to take over at Severance Hall?

In many ways, they were. The Great Depression had forced the reduction of the orchestra to 80 players. The season had been scaled back to 24 weeks. Salaries were cut deeply. Musicians were leaving for other ensembles or to pursue more lucrative lines of work. Contributions were down and deficits were up. The orchestra had no recording contract. Months before Rodzinski was scheduled to assume leadership, trustees were uncertain about the orchestra's future.

Dudley Blossom, as always a calming influence, told the board in June 1933 that this was no time to consider abandonment. In fact, the city's cultural health depended upon the orchestra's continuation. The compassionate former welfare director was aware that "people might think it a great extravagant project calling for the money which perhaps should be spent feeding the poor. I think the answer to it is that not only would we lose everything that we have gained in the last fifteen years by so doing but a great deal more. It seems just too bad when 80 musicians need that work that we should even think of stopping the Orchestra."

Rodzinski gave no mind to such thoughts. He was deliriously happy to have landed a post closer to the East Coast and to the four orchestras that were now perceived to be on a higher level than Cleveland—Boston, Chicago, New York, and Philadelphia. These were the ensembles Rodzinski secretly coveted. Cleveland would serve as a fine stepping-stone until one of those orchestras knocked on his door.

At 41, Rodzinski had come far in a short period, especially considering that he had arrived in the United States just seven years before. Born in Split, Dalmatia, of Polish parentage on January 1, 1892, he had gone to Vienna as a teenager to study law at the behest of his father, a general in the Austro-Hungarian army. Rodzinski was more interested in music, but he dutifully earned a doctor of law degree, playing piano in clubs and theaters to pay his tuition. These musical experiences couldn't have been called fulfilling. Rodzinski's penchant for inventing tricky rhythms won the wrath of one female dancer who told him he was "a lousy pianist." He was wounded in World War I while serving in the Austro-Hungarian army and returned to Vienna for a second doctorate, this time in music, earning money by inspecting meat markets. A job as chorus and opera conductor in the provincial Polish city of Lvov led to his appointment to orchestra and opera posts in Warsaw. Sometime in 1924, Rodzinski met Leopold Stokowski, conductor of the Philadelphia Orchestra. The formidable British-born maestro heard him conduct Wagner's *Die Meistersinger* in Warsaw and began lobbying for the young musician to come to the United States.

In May 1926, Stokowski invited Rodzinski to be his assistant at the Philadelphia Orchestra for a salary of $100 a week. In addition, Rodzinski was hired to head the orchestral department at the city's distinguished Curtis Institute of Music. After three years of assisting Stokowski, he was ready for his own American orchestra, the Los Angeles Philharmonic, which claimed as one of its subscribers the man who would be the prime force in stealing the new conductor away for Cleveland, John L. Severance.

Cleveland didn't know quite what it was in for. From Rodzinski's guest stint in December 1932, the orchestra was aware that its new boss was a powerful and authoritative podium figure who often used neither music nor baton in performance. His eclectic programming in Los Angeles, including works of recent vintage, piqued interest, as did his hint that he would bring opera to Severance Hall. His new town would become acquainted with a man who dreamed big, pushed hard, and created enormous excitement whenever he stepped onstage or into the pit. Cleveland would also encounter eccentricities and bursts of temperament.

Chief among Rodzinski's quirks was the gun. Late in life he told his son, Richard, that he once had fallen deeply in love with a woman whose husband was a fireman. Rodzinski decided to kill the husband, so he obtained a revolver and put it in his right back pocket. Just as he was planning to carry out the deed, the regular conductor at the Lvov Opera fell ill, and Rodzinski was called in at the last minute to preside over a performance of Verdi's *Ernani*. Only after the performance, which was a triumph, did he realize that the gun was still in his back pocket. He evidently never fired a shot in his life, but his success with *Ernani* convinced him that the gun was a good-luck charm he couldn't do without. The revolver was loaded at all times, even during concerts. Contrary to some claims, Rodzinski never used it to intimidate orchestra players. (He did that in other ways.) He needed the gun to quell his nerves, just as he needed to kiss a photo of his father and have the stage manager—or, in Cleveland, baggage master George Higgins—pinch his left arm forcefully before he conducted a performance.

Rodzinski was all enthusiasm when he arrived in Cleveland in September 1933 to begin his first season. He had already filled key positions in his new orchestra. For the post of principal clarinet, he hired Daniel Bonade, a Swiss-born musician from the Philadelphia Orchestra who would be a superb presence in Cleveland until 1941. Rodzinski's new assistant concertmaster was a fellow Pole, Felix Eyle, who had played in the Vienna Philharmonic and Vienna State Opera Orchestra before becoming head of the violin department at the Cleveland Music School Settlement in 1927.

A number of Cleveland players were already familiar with Rodzinski, having been trained by him in orchestral repertoire at the Curtis Institute of Music. Two musicians who were appointed to principal positions in 1933 would not work out—Harry Miller on timpani and Theodore Seder on horn. Nor would literally dozens of others. Rodzinski had a tendency to hire and fire impulsively or to test string players individually in front of the entire orchestra, a nerve-wracking practice that prompted musicians to dub the first rehearsal day of the week "Black Monday."

❧ ❧ ❧

The charismatic conductor turned on his considerable charm when he made his first public appearance, addressing the Cleveland Orchestra Women's Committee a month before the opening of the 1933–34 season. "The orchestra is a splendid one," Rodzinski said. "I am very happy and I hope it is going to be better yet." The speech sounded like a politician making campaign promises, except that this conductor would deliver. He talked of giving concerts devoted to music of various ethnic groups in town, "not cheap dance folk music" but "the highest class music."

His biggest project was to be a series of staged operas to complement the orchestral fare. Rodzinski told the women that his first production, scheduled for November, would be Wagner's *Tristan und Isolde* (given the Anglicized title of *Tristan and Isolde*, although it was to be sung in German). It would make use of Severance Hall's sky dome for lighting and be performed with simplified staging, with the emphasis placed on the music.

Other plans included an expanded and varied repertoire featuring modern music and the first Cleveland performances of Stravinsky's *Le Sacre du Printemps*. Rodzinski would also offer concerts for workers, as did Sokoloff in his early years. It would be up to the Women's Committee, he remarked, in his most seductive manner, to see that concerts at Severance Hall were sold out. "I believe that George Bernard Shaw once said, 'I can resist everything but temptation.' I believe that nobody is going to be able to resist you because you are going to do your best with what nature has endowed your beautiful sex."

Even without hearing a note from Rodzinski as the orchestra's conductor, the Cleveland public was smitten. And why not? He was making the city sound as if it would soon be one of the world's great music centers. "With all the rich offerings of Cleveland in music, sculpture, painting, theatre, and the splendid cosmopolitan variety of its people, it seems to me there is everything here to make possible a union of all the arts," Rodzinski said in a radio interview. "Is the time not coming when, like Salzburg, Florence, and Rome, we in Cleveland can produce great festivals for all the world to attend?" Rodzinski even went so far as to claim that he liked the weather in Cleveland. "You've got the best climate in the world here. . . . In California there is too much sun."

The orchestra's musicians may have been less enamored. By the first week of October, Rodzinski had announced only his first program of the season, which was just three weeks away. Players who wanted to get a head start on preparing the season's repertoire were out of luck. (Rodzinski would replay this scenario many times during his tenure, to the frustration of Carl Vosburgh, Adella Prentiss Hughes's successor as manager.)

For his opening program, Rodzinski chose an orchestral smorgasbord consisting of Weber's *Oberon* overture, Brahms's Symphony No. 1 (the same work, oddly, with which Sokoloff had ended his final season just six months before), Mussorgsky's prelude to *Khovantchina*, and Respighi's *The Pines of Rome*. The orchestra had seven rehearsals—an unusually large number—for its first pair of concerts under Rodzinski.

On October 26, when the new era began, it was immediately clear that something extraordinary was happening. Herbert Elwell, reviewing the opening concert in *The Plain Dealer*, wrote that Rodzinski "in three days of rehearsing with the Cleveland Orchestra has improved it almost beyond recognition. Though a few changes in personnel have contributed to the orchestra's new luster, it is rather the unassuming but commanding personality of the conductor which is chiefly responsible for the marvels that filled last night's program." Elwell appeared to take a parting shot at Sokoloff in assessing Rodzinski's performance of the Brahms First. "Nowhere was it marred by inflating details with unrelated 'significance,' nor undue emotionalizing of portions, whose beauty lies in pure line and form." John L. Severance sent his new conductor red roses the night of his inaugural concert. Rodzinski was touched by the gesture. "I am very happy over the way the orchestra played and over the reception the Cleveland people have given me," he wrote to Severance the next day.

The public also noticed the new level of artistic achievement. "You are a blessing to us all!" wrote Joel B. Hayden, headmaster of Western Reserve Academy in Hudson, after hearing Rodzinski's first program at Severance and again in Oberlin. "I have seen the Cleveland Orchestra build up over the years. You are transmuting its metal into fine gold. There is something so direct, straightforward and essentially right in your leadership and interpretation. The score you take unto yourself, you incarnate its genius, and then you go forth and lead—what an experience for us all!"

If Cleveland was beginning to know Rodzinski the conductor, it was also learning interesting tidbits about Rodzinski the man. The News's Archie Bell told readers that Freddie, "his sepia valet-chauffeur-butler and general factotum," always called the new boss "Mister Doctor." The conductor ate little meat, enjoyed all kinds of fruits, smoked only on occasion, and never drank alcoholic beverages. "He is very fond of dogs, likes the radio and motion pictures and is interested in all kinds of music. He speaks as many languages as a good dragoman and reads some that he does not speak."Another story revealed that Rodzinski's hobby was photography. Local newspapers won his appreciation by printing his pictures.

One aspect of the new maestro's life that wasn't publicized in the fall of 1933 was his family situation. His wife, Ilse, and son, Witold, were not with him when he arrived in Cleveland. Rodzinski had already begun divorce proceedings against Ilse, a pianist who had been on the faculty at the Curtis Institute of Music, and quietly brought to town the woman who would become his second wife, Halina Lilpop, a grandniece of the great Polish composer-violinist Henri Wieniawski. Lilpop received moral support in Cleveland from violinist Eyle and another Polish-born musician, pianist Severin Eisenberger, who was teaching at the Cleveland Music School Settlement. While Rodzinski lived in an apartment on Cedar Road in Cleveland Heights, Lilpop was nearby at the Alcazar Hotel. Eventually, Lilpop emerged from her seclusion and discovered that all the secrecy was for naught. "I found that Clevelanders were like humanity anywhere else, that we had been excessively cautious," she wrote years later in her touching memoirs, Our Two Lives. "Cleveland friends would have been quite understanding of our situation had they known all the facts. I could agree with Artur, however, that gossip based on half-truths or less would have been disastrous at the outset of this new phase of his career, and so I took part in the conspiracy to be a nonexistent person."

Rodzinski was not allowing personal matters to get in the way of his new job. He was too occupied with orchestra concerts and plans for the first operatic production at Severance Hall, *Tristan und Isolde*, performed with the traditional cuts. This was not going to be Wagner with all the ostentatious trimmings. Rodzinski had done a thorough study of the theatrical possibilities at Severance, whose stage possessed little wing or fly space for sets. Rather than concentrate on realistic scenery, he opted to employ the hall's color organ (3,600 combinations of colors) to suggest the locales and atmosphere in Wagner's music drama. Frederick McConnell, from the Cleveland Play House, was hired to direct.

For the initial plunge into opera at Severance Hall, Rodzinski and Vosburgh succeeded in lining up a cast of seasoned Wagnerian singers that many opera houses would have envied. From the Metropolitan Opera, they engaged Cleveland-born contralto Rose Bampton to sing Brangäne and tenor Paul Althouse to portray Tristan. Two principals were coming from the Chicago Civic Opera: Elsa Alsen, as Isolde, and Chase Baromeo, as Kurwenal. Baromeo would become a regular in Rodzinski's Cleveland opera productions. Smaller roles were filled with local singers, as was the chorus.

By the time the curtain rose on November 30 for the first of three *Tristan* performances, Rodzinski had immersed his orchestra in the score. At his very first rehearsal as boss on October 23, he had begun with portions from the Wagner opera. Throughout the ensuing weeks, he juxtaposed preparation for each week's subscription programs with sections from *Tristan*. By November 30, the orchestra had had 20 rehearsals on the score, an amount of preparation no opera house in America could approach (or afford, even today). The principal singers, however, arrived the weekend before the performances, which gave them only three full days of rehearsal.

The press helped to create momentum in preview articles, some of which are colorful relics of the time. Rodney C. Sutton's article on *Tristan* in *The Plain Dealer* was headlined "Real Love and Tragedy Behind Grand Opera's Fantastic Scenes—A study of their life stories shows that famous composers often had real inspiration behind their themes and that this was—Woman!" Denoe Leedy, in the *Press*, praised the simplified staging even before he had seen it.

Tickets—$1 to $5—for the November 30 and December 2 performances sold so quickly that orchestra officials scheduled a third performance for

December 4. The public and critics were not disappointed. "Musical History was made last night at Severance Hall," read the opening sentence of a three-paragraph review squeezed into the *News* the morning after the first five-hour performance. "Had Wagner himself sat in the audience, he would have been as enthusiastic as the audience which fairly lifted the roof with its ovation of applause for Conductor Artur Rodzinski. Here was the ideal performance of 'Tristan and Isolde.' Everything in it was subjugated to the music itself. Playing with a skill and precision far beyond that of the average opera house orchestra, Cleveland's symphony orchestra brought out every beauty of the magnificent score." The ovations on opening night went on for 47 minutes.

Frederic C. Lake, a Cleveland Heights baritone who sang the short role of the Steersman in the *Tristan* performances, praised Rodzinski for serving the music, "one of the things for which people love you and respect you," he wrote in a letter soon after the production. One member of the audience who could claim objectivity was the celebrated American soprano Emma Eames, a resident of Paris who was in Cleveland visiting family. The long-retired Eames attended the first two performances of *Tristan* at Severance Hall and told a reporter, "Rodzinski is a great conductor, one of the few great conductors. His subdued and blended interpretation of the score gives the singers support, yet opportunity for the voices to be fully heard. Then he brings out the orchestra in a great climax. He must be inspired for such a performance."

✿   ✿   ✿

Rodzinski remained inspired throughout his first season. Following a concert several weeks after the conductor's debut, Dudley Blossom received a letter from George B. Sowers, a prominent Cleveland engineer, who said he liked everything about Rodzinski, including the manner in which he had been treating the orchestra during this honeymoon period. "Mr. Rodzinski's programs are wonderfully fine and well balanced," wrote Sowers. "He always ends the evening with something beautiful which clings in your memory. His conducting without a score adds so much to the finish and perfection of the numbers. We like his conducting without a baton—he seems to mold the orchestra in his hands. One hears much favorable comment upon [the] very gracious way in which he gives credit to his men for their good work." Sowers appreciated one more thing: "I am so glad to have him maintain the continuity of the symphonies by eliminating the applause between movements as you promised that he would."

Rodzinski came through on his promise to present new pieces in January, when he brought John Alden Carpenter's *Skyscrapers* to Severance Hall. The work included blues singers and factory whistles in its depiction of contemporary life in a metropolis. Nothing of the sort could have happened under Sokoloff, who detested the type of music Carpenter employed in his score. One headline told the story: "Jazz Invades Sacred Precincts of Symphony."

Other highlights of the season included March performances of Ermanno Wolf-Ferrari's one-act comic opera *The Secret of Suzanne*, about a woman whose husband suspects her of infidelity, only to learn that her surreptitious vice is smoking. The opera shared a bill with modern dance works, including Ravel's *Bolero*, performed by Ruth Page and Harald Kreutzberg. Rodzinski conducted the opera, which starred the admired Cleveland soprano Eleanor Painter Strong (also a trustee of the Musical Arts Association), while Rudolph Ringwall did honors during the dance portion.

Reaction to Rodzinski's performance this season of Honegger's oratorio *King David*, in its Cleveland debut, was especially positive, from both press and audience. One letter of gratitude to Rodzinski came from Arthur W. Quimby, head of the music department at Western Reserve University, who took the opportunity to urge the conductor to extend his courage to areas beyond programming. "I realize also that you do not have as yet the personnel in the orchestra you would like," Quimby wrote. "Your woodwind section is remarkable, but there are other weak spots in the orchestra, and I would like you to have the knowledge that there are a great many of us who will be backing you in making the difficult but necessary changes which will have to be made before the Cleveland Orchestra is capable of becoming a first rank orchestra."

Along with the necessary changes he was already making, Rodzinski was advocating a federal arts agency in Washington, D.C., to raise money through a tax on radio sets. "There should be a department of fine arts in the national government, just as there is one for agriculture," Rodzinski told a reporter. "At least, there should be a bureau. Even the fish have a bureau to themselves." He proposed an annual tax of $1 on each of the country's 20 million radio sets. The funds would pay the annual deficits of America's major orchestras, averaging $150,000 per ensemble. Rodzinski based his high-minded idea on practices in Europe, where governments began supporting the arts after aristocratic and wealthy families could no longer pick up the tab. The issue of radio was important beyond the tax, as Dudley Blossom wrote to Rodzinski: "There is a great deal of truth in the idea that unless radio comes to the rescue, radio will find that there are no decent symphony orchestras left with which radio can entertain its listeners."

Rodzinski was positively loquacious his first season in Cleveland. He pushed his views of eclectic programming by pointing out the difference between good music and good wine. "There are no vintage years in music and contrary to popular belief, it does not improve with age. Good wine is good when it is made and it is still good a hundred years later. Bad wine is bad when it is made and it is nothing more than vinegar after it has been aged. Music that is written by an inspired composer may gain with the years because the taste of the musical public has been educated to appreciate it, but it was good when it was written. The date on music means nothing." Of his scant attention to American music so far in Cleveland, he was equally forthright: "I am much more concerned about music in America than I am about American music."

He also wasn't inclined to subject his audiences to what he considered reactionary programming. For his second season, "it had been suggested that we give a Beethoven cycle; but that appears to me just now as though we were copying others," Rodzinski said at the end of his first year. "Cleveland must not copy; Cleveland sets a precedent, as observe how other orchestras are now giving operas as well as symphonies." A Beethoven cycle would have to wait until the 1938–39 season. Rodzinski conducted only one Beethoven symphony (the seventh) during his inaugural season; in his second year, he led the third, fifth, and ninth symphonies.

Works from the late 18th and early 19th centuries, while not neglected, were not to be Rodzinski's focus in Cleveland. Critics were delighted with the clarity, precision, and rhythmic crispness—ideal qualities in the classical repertoire—that he was instilling in the orchestra. But he was always more at home with Romantic and 20th-century scores, as the Cleveland recordings he soon would begin making would reveal. In addition to the Honegger and Carpenter works in 1933–34, Rodzinski led the orchestra's first performances of Prokofiev's "Classical" Symphony, Kodály's *Hary János* suite, and Bartók's First Rhapsody for Violin and Orchestra, with Joseph Szigeti as soloist. He would have programmed even more 20th-century music if Cleveland audiences hadn't clamored for their favorites (a reality in every age). "Why not let him play for us the music he desires to play?" asked Leedy in the *Press*. "It might not be entirely to our liking. But he should have complete freedom in his choice of material . . . Let the Severance Hall audience hiss if it wants—throw cabbages at the conductor and fight up and down the aisles. This is the sort of thing which has happened on certain exciting occasions in Europe. At least, it proves that the audience is alive and given to reactions. As history proves, more than one masterpiece has first seen the light under such circumstances."

Despite the occasional grumbling, trustees were thrilled with the rapid improvement Rodzinski was making in the orchestra and the excitement his performances were generating. Soon after the success of the *Tristan* production, the board forged ahead, even in the face of mammoth expenses, with ambitious plans for Rodzinski's second season. Along with the reinstatement of a 28-week season and 18 pairs of concerts, the board agreed to present six operas. The first list of possibilities comprised *Madame Butterfly, Die Meistersinger, Otello, Die Walküre, Pelléas et Mélisande*, and "a Russian opera." Vosburgh, doing his homework as usual, learned that he might be able to engage the great Russian basso, Feodor Chaliapin, for a week at $2,000 for *Boris Godunov* or another Russian opera. Leedy told readers the Russian opera would be a new work by Shostakovich that Rodzinski hoped to secure for its American premiere in Cleveland. Bell wrote in the *News* that the title role in *Otello* probably would be sung by Lauritz Melchior, the reigning heroic tenor of the day. Interest in the new opera season was running high long before definitive plans were in place.

Rodzinski's inaugural year was a happy one, and not only for the new maestro: At the end of the season, assistant conductor Rudolph Ringwall was rewarded for his efforts with a promotion to associate conductor. Ringwall had teamed with Lillian Baldwin to present stimulating educational concerts to upwards of 30,000 children. He had no idea quite how busy he would be during the Rodzinski era. In coming seasons, he would have to be ready to step in when more Rodzinski quirks surfaced, such as his penchant for not showing up on time for morning rehearsals (he had trouble getting out of bed and finishing his ablutions) or feigning illness when he didn't feel like conducting at Severance or on tour. Vosburgh would tell Ringwall to leave Severance Hall "just before intermission and go walk somewhere, because if Rodzinski saw me I might have to conduct the rest of the concert," Ringwall recalled years later. "Once I had to conduct 'Petrouchka' and I hadn't even seen the score until 7 o'clock that night. But the men were with me all the way."

Ringwall presided over the orchestra's most unusual activity of the 1933–34 season—concerts of light classics on Sundays at 8:45 p.m. between movies at the Allen Theatre downtown (admission: 40 cents). The goal was to broaden the orchestra's audience, even if some observers found the endeavor odd. "Probably the only thing to evoke greater surprise would be the thought of one of the burlesque shows moving up to Severance Hall," Elwell wrote in *The Plain Dealer* before the first Allen concert in late December 1933. "A movie audience is not musically the dumbest in the world, nor yet by any means the most highly cultivated. It seems reasonable to suppose, therefore, that the orchestra will stand a greater chance of success at the Allen if it puts on a high grade of popular music and plays it with all the vim and vigor that goes into a Beethoven symphony, rather than to regard the whole affair as a slumming expedition or an uplift party." Ringwall and the orchestra played to a standing-room-only crowd the first week and then to rapidly diminishing audiences on four successive Sundays, after which the board accepted the request of the Allen directors to cancel the sixth and final concert.

During his first season at Severance Hall, Rodzinski also led four popular concerts—"An Hour of Music"—on Tuesday nights at 50 cents per ticket. The program featured overtures, movements from symphonies, waltzes, polkas, and tone poems. The concerts, also broadcast on WHK, were so well received that they were moved to Music Hall the following season on Sunday afternoons, with tickets ranging from 25 cents to $1.50.

✿   ✿   ✿

His first Cleveland season a triumph, Rodzinski left in April to spend the summer in Europe conducting, studying, and checking out the latest music. And procrastinating. Vosburgh could not get the conductor to devise programs for the coming season. The situation was making it difficult for Vosburgh to promote the new season or let the musicians know what they would be playing. The manager had to tiptoe lightly. "Now, for my usual plea!" Vosburgh wrote to Rodzinski in Vienna. "Will you please be a very nice conductor and take a little time and answer some of the questions I have sent in all my letters? Also, please do not forget your promise to send us a tentative list of programs or the works you are considering for this next season."

A few weeks earlier, in Warsaw, the conductor had talked about the possibility of presenting concerts of American music in major European halls. "Not Indian tomtom beating or jazz, but the genuine work of talented and ambitious young American composers," Rodzinski told a reporter. "It need not be only music; we should exchange all artistic products. Europe is altogether misinformed about our music, our poetry, our paintings, our theaters. Here they know what they see in the movies, and America is far from a combination of Ziegfeld Follies girls and racketeers."

Vosburgh was beginning to reveal his real strengths as a manager. While his conductor was away, he negotiated a deal with the National Broadcasting Company to present the Cleveland Orchestra and Rodzinski in 10 one-hour broadcasts during the 1934–35 season. The orchestra would be paid $500 per broadcast. More importantly, the combination of Rodzinski and Cleveland would be heard around the country on a regular basis, cementing them as a team and enhancing their reputation nationally.

What they would be playing during the broadcasts was anybody's guess. By late summer, Rodzinski still had not supplied Vosburgh with a single completed program for the 1934–35 season, telling his manager he probably would make many changes throughout the season. He sent along a list of possible works, but nothing specific. Vosburgh would never get used to Rodzinski's telegram-style letters, which were filled with dashes, underlined words, abbreviations, exclamation points, tantrums, and stream-of-consciousness ramblings. "So Dear Mr. Vosburgh," Rodzinski wrote in mid-August, "don't hurry my return—if it is not absolutely necessary—I have to attend so many things here—and I need a perfect—long rest to be in A.1 shape for my work in Clevel. But if my earlier return would seem to be 'indicated' I can be at Cleveland disposal—at any time."

Rodzinski perhaps could be forgiven for being distracted during the summer of 1934. On July 19, he quietly married Halina Lilpop in Warsaw. He was also flying high for another reason. He had succeeded in nabbing a work for Cleveland that would put the city and its orchestra on the international map—Shostakovich's opera *Lady Macbeth of Mzensk*, sometimes referred to as *Katerina Ismailova*, the name of its lead character. Rodzinski's excitement can be felt in his letter to Vosburgh in late June:

> I spent nearly three weeks in Russia to get the opera by a 26 years old genius—Shostakovich the opera—which I saw 6 times—is called Kateryna Ismailova—In my estimation the best opera written in this century—Sensational—I am still negotiating with the Soviet government, to obtain the material—which has to be copied specially for us—(translated—because they don't want us to do it in Russian only in English)—Most complicated—and difficult opera—but would cause much more sensation than WOZZECK in Phila—Still we have to wait—till I hear more positive from them—I hope to have some news in the next few days.

Rodzinski would have plenty of news for Cleveland in the coming years. Along with stimulating and provocative symphonic programs, Severance Hall, less than three years after opening, was about to become the scene of an adventurous musical endeavor that would bring the city national attention.

Nights at the Opera

*C*leveland was starved for opera in 1933, and Artur Rodzinski knew it. The Metropolitan Opera, which had first offered full-scale productions in 1899 at Grays Armory, had been presenting an annual week of performances at the massive Public Auditorium since 1927, as part of its spring tour. After the 1932 season, though, the Met put the tour on hold (the Depression forced the travel budget to be sliced), leaving Cleveland, like many sponsoring cities, without opera of professional caliber. Rodzinski deftly exploited the Met's absence by persuading the board of the Musical Arts Association to include a stipulation in his first contract—"your service would include preparing and conducting opera"—that was not standard in symphony conductor contracts. His landmark production of *Tristan und Isolde* in the fall of 1933 quickly established his authority in the medium and prompted the board to bless his plan to present 6 operas during the 1934–35 season.

Rodzinski had hoped to produce 10 operas per season in Cleveland. He never reached that goal, but during the four seasons he conducted full-scale productions at Severance Hall, he led 14 works that became highlights of the city's cultural calendar. (Albert Stoessel conducted a 15th, Beryl Rubinstein's *The Sleeping Beauty*.) The casts contained some of the world's finest singers, including many who performed on Metropolitan Opera radio broadcasts, and the performances were on a level few opera houses could match. Many orchestras presented operas in concert versions. But in terms of staged opera, Rodzinski put Cleveland ahead of every other major American symphony orchestra of the day.

Wagner would be a constant companion during the conductor's operatic excursions in Cleveland. Rodzinski chose *Die Walküre*, the second music drama in the *Ring* cycle, as the opening stage production of his second season. He was so confident about his project that he not only opened with Wagner, but also closed the opera season with perhaps even more formidable Wagner, *Die Meistersinger*.

Between these majestic productions, he scheduled two beloved works, Verdi's *Otello* and Puccini's *Tosca*, as well as the sensational new Shostakovich opera, *Lady Macbeth of Mzensk*.

Putting the season together was largely the responsibility of Vosburgh, who proved to be diligent and enthusiastic, if exhausted, by the new project. "Believe me, this opera business is some job," he wrote to Rodzinski in Vienna. For instance, Rodzinski wanted to engage the heralded Danish Heldentenor Lauritz Melchior to sing Otello. Vosburgh offered him $1,500 for three rehearsals and two performances. Melchior insisted that Cleveland match the Met's fee of $1,500 *per performance*. His request was "an absolute impossibility," Vosburgh declared. He signed Aroldo Lindi instead.

One great singer who slipped through the cracks was the Italian bass-baritone Ezio Pinza, the reigning Don Giovanni of the era (and later Mary Martin's enchanted co-star in *South Pacific*). Rodzinski had the interesting notion of casting Pinza as Wotan, the chief god in *Walküre*, whose lyrical music and temperamental orations might have suited the singer perfectly. If that weren't possible, the conductor hoped to secure him for one of the bass roles in *Meistersinger*. Pinza informed his agent that he wouldn't have time to study Wotan—he read music poorly, anyway—and, of the roles in *Meistersinger*, had only Pogner in his repertoire. Vosburgh spent months trying to track down the right singers for many roles.

Another learning experience that took Vosburgh by surprise was the negotiating process with the Metropolitan Opera, from which the orchestra was drawing many of its principal singers. Edward Ziegler, the company's assistant manager, informed him that the Met would grant the Cleveland Orchestra no permissions to hire its artists unless Vosburgh helped to pay part of the steamship fare for the singers from abroad. Cleveland's manager shot back a letter, and one to artist manager Arthur Judson, saying there was no way he would agree to such a swindle. Of the performers hired, all but one were American.

Orchestra patrons and critics in Cleveland had no hint of the hair pulling—normal where this intricate art form is concerned—that was involved in bringing great opera to Severance Hall. They were excited at the prospect of spending so many nights at the opera with their orchestra in the pit. Announcing that *Die Walküre* and *Otello* were set to open the opera season and the Shostakovich was a strong possibility, Denoe Leedy speculated in the *Press* that *Walküre* could lead to a complete performance of the *Ring* cycle. "We might just as well have our Bayreuth up on the corner of University Circle and Euclid Avenue," he wrote in late July 1934. "Dr.

Rodzinski has literally thrown a bomb into the musical life of this city. He has ambitions for us as a wide-awake, up-to-the-minute musical public. Such painstaking care as he lavished on the production of 'Tristan and Isolde' last year is something we must conjure with. He is insatiable for perfection—insatiable in his desire to produce nothing but the best."

To do so with *Die Walküre* on November 1 and 3, 1934, Rodzinski collaborated with a cast of veteran Wagnerian singers. In Friedrich Schorr, he had the finest Wotan of the generation. Bringing the Hungarian-born bass-baritone to Cleveland twice in one season was a double coup. Dorothee Manski, a European-based American singer, excelled in dramatic-soprano roles, having sung Brünnhilde with many opera companies. Siegmund was sung by Paul Althouse, no match for Melchior, but a reliable tenor who would participate in most of Rodzinski's Wagner productions in Cleveland. Anne Rosell, a Hungarian-born, American-trained soprano who had been nurtured by the great baritone Antonio Scotti, sang Sieglinde at Severance Hall in November and returned as Tosca in January. Rodzinski regular Chase Baromeo provided the menace as Hunding, and Edwina Eustis sang Fricka.

Along with imported artists, the production featured eight Ohio singers as the Valkyries, who didn't ride horses but relied on the hall's sky dome and lighting effects to achieve the requisite magic. "These young Ohio artists have fine voices," Rodzinski said of his Valkyrie octet. "That is one of the things about our opera I am so much interested in—that our young Cleveland people, who have the ability, can have good training and become always better artists." Tickets to the performances ranged from $1.50 to $5.

Rodzinski's "fiery zeal" as conductor of *Walküre* was noted in *Musical America*, which also hailed Richard Rychtarik's "striking yet relatively simple sets" and the "expert stage management" of director Wilhelm von Wymetal, Jr. Most of the praise was reserved for the orchestra, which "seemed tipped in flame, from the opening measures of the storm prelude to the concluding chord of the fire music." Leedy, perhaps, went slightly overboard in the *Press*: "I defy anyone to suggest a performance anywhere that ever came closer to the majesty and splendor inherent in this miraculous creation for the lyric stage." Hazel B. King, curator at the Allen Memorial Art Museum in Oberlin, wrote to Rodzinski, saying she had seen *Walküre* in Freiburg, Frankfurt, Berlin, New York, and Munich, but no production had touched her like the Cleveland staging. "The dignity and sincerity of the singers, the restraint and beauty of the stage setting and lighting combined with the incredibly superb orchestra made this one of the greatest experiences of my life."

The energy that went into mounting *Walküre* would have been impressive enough in itself. But Rodzinski also had symphonic programs to prepare and perform. He had begun the season on October 11 with a coupling of heroic proportions—Strauss's *Ein Heldenleben* and Beethoven's "Eroica" Symphony. "Somehow, the conceit of Strauss, the occasion, and Artur's mood were all in perfect accord," his wife, Halina, wrote in her memoirs. "I was later to hear him conduct the work many times when its details were better articulated, and with orchestras that yielded richer sounds, but his flair that night was so extraordinary he could possibly have drawn the music from a stone."

Elwell wrote of this concert in *The Plain Dealer* that Rodzinski "achieved a degree of perfection in ensemble that puts our orchestra in the front rank. Other cities might sit up and take notice—*Cleveland has a great conductor.*" Rodzinski continued to luxuriate in symphonic works even as he prepared the orchestra for *Walküre*. In the two weeks preceding the opera, he led works by Bach, Beethoven ("Emperor" Concerto, with Severin Eisenberger as soloist), Sibelius, Debussy, Albeniz, Mendelssohn, Schumann, Rachmaninoff, and Ravel. A week after *Walküre*, Elwell told the public that the operatic demands had done nothing to throw the orchestra off kilter in a Rodzinski program comprising Handel's Concerto Grosso No. 10, Stravinsky's *Petrouchka* suite, and Brahms's Second Symphony: "They seemed, on the contrary, more intent than usual on careful study of details and on rounding out their work with exceptional finish."

These were heady times. A week after the Handel-Stravinsky-Brahms concerts, Rodzinski welcomed renowned violinist Bronislaw Huberman to Severance Hall as he made his debut with the orchestra in the Brahms Violin Concerto. Less than a month later, in mid-December, the second opera of the season, *Otello*, was staged featuring Aroldo Lindi in the title role, Rosa Tentoni as Desdemona, and Richard Bonelli as Iago. Coming so soon after *Walküre*, the production inspired Denoe Leedy to put Rodzinski's Verdian triumph in perspective: "That its conductor can turn with such ease from the thick, heavy emotionalism of the Teuton to this clear, vividly stroked creation of the 19th Century Italian is magnificent proof of his ability to cope with anything the operatic stage might offer."

Rodzinski seemed to be on a mission to show Cleveland that it had hired a great conductor. Before 1934 was out, he led an all-American program of music by David Stanley Smith, Emerson Whithorne, Werner Josten, and Deems Taylor, as well as the orchestra's first performances of Strauss's *Also sprach Zarathustra*. The first week of 1935, he was in the pit once again to conduct the season's third opera, *Tosca*, with Anne Roselle in the title role, Mario Chamlee as Cavaradossi, and Carlo Morelli as Scarpia. Herbert Elwell wrote that Rodzinski "is as much at home with Italians as with Wagner."

❊   ❊   ❊

Rodzinski's next production, the American premiere of *Lady Macbeth of Mzensk*, was preceded by an unusual amount of intrigue. The conductor had gone to Russia in late spring of 1934 to conduct at the Borodin Festival in Leningrad. On a trip to Moscow, he attended the premiere of Dmitri Shostakovich's controversial opera (with its violence and overtly sexual situations) and was astonished by what he heard and saw. Shostakovich enjoyed Rodzinski's concerts at the Borodin Festival, and the composer agreed that the conductor could give his opera's U.S. premiere, if he could secure the rights from the Russian government.

Rodzinski's adventures in Russia sound preposterous—part comedy, part spy story. In Moscow, he approached officials who kept him waiting for weeks. The opera that Stalin would condemn a year later already had earned a reputation for its scenes of moral corruption and a biting score. Rodzinski, deeming it "the best opera written in this century," was determined that no other conductor would gain the rights to present it first in America. But he had competition. He found out that his mentor, Leopold Stokowski, was trying to secure it for Philadelphia. One day in Moscow, Rodzinski ran into Vladimir "Vlady" Drucker, who had played principal trumpet in his former orchestra, the Los Angeles Philharmonic, and whom he had just hired for Cleveland. The Russian-born Drucker agreed to assist Rodzinski as translator. More help came from another chum, pianist Artur Rubinstein, who was in Moscow on a concert tour. Rubinstein had connections that allowed Rodzinski to meet with the famous directors of Moscow's theater and opera, Konstantin Stanislavsky and Vladimir Nemirovich-Danchenko. The directors listened sympathetically and moved things along. Eventually, Rodzinski received the go-ahead to give the American premiere.

Upon his return to Cleveland, the conductor gave a colorful account of the difficulties that ensued. "It was fortunate I could speak some Russian!" Rodzinski told a reporter. "At Leningrad I was ready to board the plane for Danzig with part of Shostakovich's precious manuscript and some drawings for stage settings—with crosses, circles and dotted lines on them. The big customs officer found them in my luggage. He looked ominous and sternly said, 'We will keep these. For all we know, these may be drawings of fortifications, the placement of guns and guards.' Such a business! Here was the work of my whole six weeks to be snatched away! My heart stopped beating! It took me more than one hour to persuade and explain—and finally he let me take them!"

Rodzinski was bringing *Lady Macbeth* to America with several goals in mind. He wanted to shower attention on his orchestra in Cleveland. But he was also determined to do so in the city whose venerable orchestra he harbored dreams of leading someday. Rodzinski was already set to make his debut with the New York Philharmonic on November 22 at Carnegie Hall, followed by three more concerts over the next 10 days. Early in October, he urged the Cleveland board to make a performance of *Lady Macbeth* possible in Manhattan. The trustees voted to send Vosburgh to New York to find an appropriate theater and an organization to sponsor the event. Rodzinski announced that the cast would consist of principal singers and chorus from the Musical Art of Russia, an opera company of Russian émigrés in New York.

The League of Composers, an organization promoting music by living composers, agreed to sponsor a New York performance. Claire Reis, chairman of the league's board, was so taken with Rodzinski's idea that she offered to present the production to benefit the Composers' Fund. She helped convince Giulio Gatti-Casazza, manager of the Metropolitan Opera, to let the league rent the Met for a *Lady Macbeth* performance on Monday, February 5, 1935. It didn't hurt that Rodzinski's mentor, Arturo Toscanini, was a close friend of Gatti-Casazza. The two Cleveland performances (January 31, February 2) were budgeted at $8,100. The New York performance cost $5,800, including $1,100 for rental of the Met.

Most of Rodzinski's opera productions in Cleveland, including *Lady Macbeth*, were directed by Wilhelm von Wymetal, Jr., an assistant stage director at the Met who also kept himself busy in Hollywood staging operetta sequences in Metro-Goldwyn-Mayer movies. Rodzinski called him "Wymie." Another important contributor to *Lady Macbeth* was pianist Severin Eisenberger, who helped the conductor and the orchestra's librarian remove a multitude of errors from the opera's score and recopied orchestral parts. Rodzinski was a stickler for fidelity to the score. "Shostakovich's patterns and tempi would be followed to the letter with only one innovation, Scene VII, the second scene of Act Three, which takes place in a police station," Mrs. Rodzinski recalled. "The stage set, which had to afford quick scene changes (there were nine in four acts in Shostakovich's first score), covered by a minimum of between-scene music, was designed to Artur's satisfaction by Richard Rychtarik. It conveyed the milieu of Russia circa 1840, but was spare and modern, and most importantly, functioned like an integral piece of a mechanism."

In Cleveland, the public needed assurance they weren't going to be subjected to a contemporary work that would offend their conservative Midwestern sensibilities. It would be difficult to soothe them on this issue. *Lady Macbeth* had already raised eyebrows in Leningrad with its blatant portrayal of Katerina Ismailova, a married woman who has an affair, kills her husband, and commits suicide by tossing herself into a river. The opera includes a scene during which the stage is empty but a trombone glissando graphically depicts the union of Katerina and her lover. The effect came to be known as "pornophony."

No less a figure than Shostakovich contributed tantalizing words about his opera to a Cleveland publication the month of the premiere. "When you see the Cleveland Orchestra's presentation of the American premiere of my opera in Severance Hall the last day of January, you will see no traditional opera," the composer wrote. "I have repudiated all old forms of opera. I do not consider Wagner a genius. I do not like his operas. He does not understand the passions and interests of the people in his operas. I have tried to make my music as simple and as expressive as possible."

Herbert Elwell also helped to dispel the general belief that the audience would have to cover its ears. Conjecture about the score, he wrote in *The Plain Dealer*, "has led to the erroneous assumption that it is one of those dissonant, cacophonous, incomprehensible scores with which the ultra-modernists love to bewilder the uninitiated. It is dissonant, all right—in spots. But even more frequently it jumps into a simple, direct folk-song idiom and with its lively hopaks and satirical waltzes, it hits you between the eyes with tunes as garish as the Russian equivalent of 'Hail, Hail, the Gang's All Here.'"

To do justice to Shostakovich's score, Rodzinski engaged Russian singers who could handle the original Russian text—not translated into English, as Russian officials had wanted—and convey its stark nuances. As Katerina, Anna Leskaya was hailed for her beauty and towering personality. Her lover was portrayed by Ivan Ivantzoff, whom Mrs. Rodzinski said "could have been younger, but he was such a good actor and singer that it scarcely mattered." The two Cleveland performances were completely sold out and attended by critics and music lovers from near and far. Among the VIPs sitting in Mrs. Rodzinski's box at Severance Hall on opening night were Chicago composer John Alden Carpenter (whose *Skyscrapers* Rodzinski had conducted the previous year) and Ossip Gabrilowitsch, conductor of the Detroit Symphony. In another box sat American soprano Grace Moore, the piano duo Fray and Bragiotti, and George Gershwin, who was working on an opera of his own, *Porgy and Bess*. (Gershwin had become friendly with Rodzinski while the conductor headed the Los Angeles Philharmonic.)

Elwell's review was headlined "Shocked, Amused, Gasping Audience Roars Acclaim to Rodzinski at Soviet Opera." Arthur Loesser wrote one of the most sensitive reviews as guest critic for the *Cleveland News*. "The Lady Macbeth premiere is a sign of Cleveland's cultural maturity; but it is the creation of Dr. Rodzinski," he wrote. "Ergo, if we value our maturity, we will value Dr. Rodzinski. Among conductors at present in America he is the man of the hour. We may be able to keep him if we deserve to have him."

In the *Press,* Denoe Leedy evoked the opera's sensational aspects in no uncertain terms, hinting at the sexy trombone glissando and celebrating Rodzinski's achievement. "Young Shostakovich leaves little to the imagination, and when the dramatic action arrives at the point where a Hollywood censor might be needed the music does the rest," he wrote. "The sheer technical difficulties involved in performing such a work are hair-raising. The accomplishment of Dr. Rodzinski in holding the forces together makes one want to shout bravos to the house-top. Under his fiery baton the orchestra tossed off the score with the most miraculous virtuosity. The effect at times left one a little dizzy." Rodzinski was so buoyed by the reception for Shostakovich's opera that he sent a telegram to the composer in Leningrad the day of the second Cleveland performance: "Packed House Tremendous Enthusiasm About Lady Macbeth Criticisms Excellent."

A few days later, Rodzinski and the orchestra presented the New York premiere at the Met. *Lady Macbeth*—with tickets priced at $75 and $50 for boxes and $1 to $7 for the rest of house—attracted the cream of New York society and top luminaries of the musical world. From the former were members of the Rockefeller, Belmont, and Vanderbilt families. As for the latter, the Met probably never had so many eminent conductors, composers, and soloists in the house at one time. The audience included Toscanini, Otto Klemperer, Serge Koussevitzky, Fritz Reiner, Bruno Walter, Leopold Stokowski, Walter Damrosch, Igor Stravinsky, Jascha Heifetz, George Gershwin, Artur Schnabel, Lawrence Tibbett, and Mischa Elman.

Among those in the New York audience on Tuesday, February 5, was Olin Downes, music critic of the *Times*, who had consulted with Rodzinski on his Cleveland opera series. After stating that the work was "performed magnificently," Downes essentially proceeded to tear the piece itself to shreds:

 . . . an opera with a musical score flimsily put together, full of reminiscences and obvious and shallow tricks, with almost no originality or creative quality, attached to a libretto of communistic hue, lurid, overdrawn, naive and sensational . . . the performance . . . reflected the highest honor upon Mr. Rodzinski, born, one would say, to conduct opera, and perhaps especially this opera. The principal singers acquitted themselves in very difficult parts with marked success. The acting was vivid, eloquent, excellent in character parts as in larger roles. It was well to present this formative work of a young composer—Shostakovich is 29—so sympathetically and so brilliantly. And who knows—some day Mr. Shostakovich may write a real opera!

Rodzinski was particularly touched by the response of the maestro he admired above all others. After the Met performance, Toscanini heaped praise on Cleveland's conductor, telling him over and over, "Bravo, bravo, Rodzinski, magnifico lavoro, bravo, bravo." The sold-out performance netted the orchestra a profit of $1,900, which was applied to the tour fund.

Originally, Rodzinski had planned to follow Shostakovich's melodrama six weeks later with Debussy's *Pelléas et Mélisande*—which would have given Cleveland audiences two gloomy operas in a row. But problems with materials and casting had forced the Debussy to be scrapped and replaced by Rossini's merry *Barber of Seville*. Earlier in the season, Vosburgh had informed Rodzinski that he had signed three principals for *Barber*—tenor Charles Hackett as Almaviva, mezzo-soprano Eva Bandrowska as Rosina, and baritone Nelson Eddy as Figaro. Eddy wouldn't wind up fulfilling his contract: In March, he would be in Hollywood filming his first leading role opposite Jeanette MacDonald in Victor Herbert's *Naughty Marietta* for MGM. Carlo Morelli replaced him as Figaro.

Aside from Wolf-Ferrari's short *The Secret of Suzanne* the previous season, Cleveland hadn't heard Rodzinski conduct a vivacious stage work like *Barber*, so the March 7 and 9 performances were eagerly awaited. Though far removed from the impassioned worlds of Wagner, Puccini, and Shostakovich, Rossini suited the conductor just fine. "Dr. Rodzinski, following tradition, conducted from his harpsichord bench. (It made little difference that the harpsichord was not a genuine one, but a piano with the necessary gadgets for producing a harpsichord tone)," wrote Leedy in the *Press*. "As before, he held everything together with a masterful hand, making every phrase sparkle with musical distinction."

A week after *Barber* came a totally different work in its first Cleveland Orchestra performance, Stravinsky's *Le Sacre du Printemps (The Rite of Spring)*. Rodzinski had triumphed with this revolutionary score during his tenure in Los Angeles, where Gershwin heard the piece on the same program with his *An American in Paris*. Oscar Levant, the pianist and Gersh-win's friend and champion, called *Sacre* the conductor's "most accomplished performance," a work that "he performed with magical ease. This complex modern score was the kind of thing Rodzinski enjoyed." Not everyone in Cleveland did. A few days before the performances, Vosburgh informed Severance that he had printed program notes about the work in the previ-ous week's program book to prepare audiences for the volcanic score. "From what I have heard in rehearsal, they are going to need it," Vosburgh wrote to the board president. Even so, both Leedy and Elwell hailed the score's arrival 22 years after its clamorous Paris premiere, though the latter opined that the work probably would function better as a ballet than as a symphonic work. Leedy didn't hold back: "It remains an incomparable masterpiece—one of the most thrilling original works in all music."

The climax of the 1934–35 opera season was Rodzinski's production of *Die Meistersinger*, which was given with cuts. The first two performances, on April 11 and 13, sold so briskly that the board decided to add a third per-formance on April 15. It was the largest production of the year, requiring al-most 250 principals, choristers, orchestra players, dancers, and stage crew, with a cast headed by Friedrich Schorr, a transcendent Hans Sachs. Elwell noted that Rodzinski's "management of the orchestra as well as the vocal en-sembles was marked by that calm concentrated mastery, that forceful inci-siveness and those flashes of intuition characteristic of the very best that is in him."

During this period, buoyed by the success of *Lady Macbeth*, Rodzinski tried to secure another high-profile premiere for his ensemble. While on a trip to New York in the spring of 1935, according to Mrs. Rodzinski, her hus-band made an attempt to duplicate the coup he had scored with Shostakovich's opera. Visiting Gershwin, the conductor took a look at the score of the composer's soon-to-be-completed opera, *Porgy and Bess*, and turned on the charm. "Porgy and Bess will be a fantastic hit, George," he said. "You are creating a true American folk opera! Give it to me for a Cleveland premiere, then New York. We'll create a sensation every bit as great as Lady Macbeth did." Gershwin told him the rights had already been bought, but that he would see what he could do. A letter from Gershwin to Rodzinski in early March 1935 presents a slightly different scenario. "Received word from our friend Kay [Halle], stating that you would like to do the premiere of my opera 'Porgy' in Cleveland," the composer wrote. "Of course you realize that the Theatre Guild of New York commissioned the work + are planning to produce it early next season, going into rehearsal in August. Smallens is to be the conductor. I needn't tell you how much I admire your conducting + how I'd love to have you wield the baton over my opus but at the moment I don't see how it is possible." Rodzinski wasn't easily put off. "It would give me the greatest pleasure not only to conduct your opera here in Cleveland next season but also to present it at the Metropolitan Opera House in New York," he wrote back immediately. History had other intentions. How the work would have been perceived if it had been produced first as an opera—and in Cleveland under Rodzinski—rather than on Broadway, where it was misunderstood, makes for interesting speculation.

✿   ✿   ✿

Even before the end of the 1934–35 season, Rodzinski was juggling ideas for his next season of opera at Severance Hall. He requested that the board consider producing Alban Berg's new opera, *Lulu*, which was finished except for the orchestration (but would be left incomplete upon the composer's death in December 1935). When *Lulu* didn't strike the board's fancy, Rodzinski became interested in securing the rights to another new piece, Lodovico Rocca's *Il Dibuk (The Dybbuk)*, for its American premiere. That wouldn't work out, either. By the end of 1934–35, Vosburgh was estimating a budget of $47,500 for the coming opera season, which tentatively was scheduled to include *Il Dibuk, Carmen, Parsifal*, and Strauss's *Der Rosenkavalier*. More juggling was inevitable. Rodzinski didn't like the idea of casting the unknown Margaret Codd, wife of newly hired chorus master Boris Goldovsky, to sing Sophie in *Der Rosenkavalier*. He preferred Susanne Fisher, who eventually got the part. Soon thereafter, the 1935–36 opera season was set: *Rosenkavalier, Carmen, Fledermaus*, and *Parsifal*.

Along with Schorr's Wotan and Hans Sachs, Lotte Lehmann's Marschallin in *Der Rosenkavalier* in the fall of 1935 must be considered a highlight of Rodzinski's opera seasons in Cleveland. The German soprano's creamy soprano and noble stage presence were legendary through appearances in Europe under the greatest conductors of the day, including Strauss (who coached her as the Marschallin and many of his other heroines) and Toscanini. How she sounded at Severance Hall in 1935 can be surmised from her historic recording the same year as Sieglinde in Act I of *Die Walküre* with Melchior as Siegmund and Bruno Walter conducting the Vienna Philharmonic.

Lehmann had distinguished company in the *Rosenkavalier* performances at Severance Hall on October 31 and November 2 and 4. Viennese bass Emanuel List, the top interpreter of Baron Ochs in the 1930s, came to Cleveland to repeat one of his signature roles. Grete Stueckgold, another admired German soprano, wore the pants as the libidinous teenager, Octavian. Lehmann held everyone in thrall at Severance Hall, and she in turn was highly impressed with the music-making around her. "During the second act, when the Marschallin has nothing to do but repair her makeup and change costumes, Mme. Lehmann stayed in the wings listening to the orchestra," Mrs. Rodzinski recalled. "She told Artur that she had never heard the music played so beautifully—a rare compliment, considering that she knew the score as well as most conductors and had often sung it under the composer's own skilled baton." Elwell was a bit more reserved in his assessment, though he acknowledged that Rodzinski once again had proved a commanding motivator: "This reviewer has seen more sumptuous and dazzling performances of 'The Rose Bearer' in Vienna and Paris, but in none was the collaboration between soloists and orchestra more efficient or spontaneous. And in none was Strauss's music more faithfully or ardently set forth."

Rodzinski's ardor extended offstage. It was during this *Rosenkavalier* that Halina Rodzinski observed her husband's eye for the ladies. His "flirtation" with Stueckgold wasn't the first, nor would it be the last. Mrs. Rodzinski had been warned "that conquering women was something of a sport for him, that his ego frankly and crudely fed on women throwing themselves at him. He went so far as to say that for an artist an occasional affair is stimulating, even necessary." And *Rosenkavalier* had always been a piece that had an "aphrodisiac effect."

Matters of sex remained purely artistic less than a month later when Rodzinski led one of the most ardent operas of them all, *Carmen*, with Bruna Castagna as the lusty gypsy, Armand Tokatyan as Don Jose, Carlo Morelli as Escamillo, and Margaret Codd as Micaela. Having rejected Codd as Sophie, Rodzinski agreed to cast her as the shy peasant girl in Bizet's opera. It may have been a mistake: all of the critics made note of her poor pitch.

✻   ✻   ✻

The season's zaniest opera wasn't open to the public. On December 1, between *Carmen* performances, the Rodzinskis held a party at their Cleveland home, centered around a parody of all the operas the conductor had brought to Severance Hall thus far. *The Secret of Lady Carmen of Seville, or The Tragic Adventure of La Tosca and Barber Tristan, The Mastersinger of Nürnberg with the Silver Rose* was presented by the Barnstorming Opera Company of Buckeye State "with world famous cast and bloodcurdling effects." The three-act opera had music by "Boris Goldunoff, Inc. (disapproved by the Ohio Board of Censors)." The unofficial piano was "Upright." Goldovsky wrote the nonsensical libretto and rehearsed the cast, which comprised singers from the *Carmen* production and others, including Stueckgold, dressed not as a teenaged male, as in *Rosenkavalier*, but as a fetching lady. Another participant was a familiar bearded figure, John L. Severance, in the role Lehmann had inhabited so sublimely weeks before in the hall bearing his name. "The performance was a sensation," Mrs. Rodzinski noted, "but the success of the evening belonged to Mr. Severance—dressed in the full hoop skirts of the Marschallin, his white hair hidden by the towering silvered assemblage of curls of the Fürstin von Werdenberg's traditional wig, his own goatee disguised by a pink scarf." Even Rodzinski got in on the act and won a few new friends. "People who had always regarded Artur as a bit of a terror or someone too Olympian to be approached discovered how essentially simple, outgoing and hospitable he was," his wife wrote.

Midway through the three-month gap between *Carmen* and the next opera, *Die Fledermaus*, Cleveland lost the man who had given the city so many artistic riches. Severance died of a heart attack on January 16, 1936, at his estate, Longwood, at the age of 72. His death hit the community hard, but it was an especially enormous blow to Rodzinski, who had come to consider Severance more than his boss. "I have once again lost my father," he said. The two had met in Los Angeles and developed a close relationship based on mutual respect. "Mr. Severance provided Artur the appreciation on which he thrived and guaranteed him the freedom to pursue his work as a sensitive craftsman," wrote Halina Rodzinski. "Artur's part of the compact was to work as best he could." *The Plain Dealer* captured the pervasive sentiment about Severance's death in an editorial: "In a thousand ways Cleveland music will inevitably feel the loss of this American Esterhazy, who, as devoted to the arts as any European aristocrat, was as democratic and friendly a man as any of us has ever known." Severance's successor as president of the Musical Arts Association was Dudley Blossom.

✿   ✿   ✿

The next opera, an English-language production of *Fledermaus* on February 27 and 29 and March 2 with Stueckgold as Rosalinda, ended up being more of a Goldovsky-Wymetal production than a Rodzinski production. Many of the orchestra's players had caught colds during a February tour, and Rodzinski's fever was so high that he was sent to bed. He could lead only one of the five *Fledermaus* rehearsals, which didn't stop Vosburgh from figuring out a way for Rodzinski to have input. The clever manager "placed a microphone in front of the Orchestra, ran a line back to the ticket office in the main foyer, and put a loud speaker at the end of the line; then, [he] laid the telephone receiver in front of the loud speaker and Rodzinski listened to the opera rehearsals over the telephone," he wrote to Blossom in Florida. "In this way he could acquaint himself with the tempos Goldovsky was taking. I am happy to say his temperature and fever abated so that he was able to come down and do the first two acts Thursday evening (opening night) and then turned over the baton to Goldovsky to finish the third act." Goldovsky conducted the entire second performance before handing the baton to, of all people, stage director Wymetal, who flew back from Hollywood to conduct the final performance.

His health restored, Rodzinski proceeded from the merry to the majestic on April 9, 11, and 13, when he conducted the last opera of the season, *Parsifal.* The critics were mesmerized by Rodzinski and the cast, which included Althouse as Parsifal, Gertrude Kappel as Kundry, Julius Huehn as Amfortas, Ludwig Hofmann as Gurnemanz, Alfredo Gandolfi as Klingsor, and Eugene Loewenthal as Titurel.

Rodzinski was intent upon conducting more Wagner at Severance Hall during the 1936–37 season. Initially, he envisioned a season opening with *Götterdämmerung*, featuring Kirsten Flagstad as Brünnhilde, and continuing with Mozart's *Don Giovanni* (with Ezio Pinza or Mariano Stabile in the title role). Then he received a welcome, if inconvenient, invitation from New York. The Philharmonic called to see if he was interested in an extended stint as guest conductor for the 1936–37 season. Rodzinski, a possible candidate to succeed Toscanini at the Philharmonic, told the Cleveland board "that he was 100% for the Cleveland Orchestra, and this opportunity, should it come, would in no way interfere with his responsibility for, and his interest in, the affairs of the Cleveland Orchestra."

But opera at Severance Hall was on the wane. The Metropolitan Opera probably would resume its spring tour in 1937, reducing the need for the Cleveland Orchestra to continue its productions at Severance Hall. The orchestra's opera deficits were rising, and officials were receiving complaints from subscribers who believed opera was too prevalent in the programming. There was talk of abandoning the opera season entirely, until it was pointed out that this would disappoint many patrons who loved opera, as well as young local artists who had gained valuable experience by participating in the productions as secondary characters, choristers, and dancers.

The end of the orchestra's opera endeavors became almost a foregone conclusion in April, when Rodzinski formally accepted the New York Philharmonic's invitation to split the coming season with Wilhelm

Furtwängler (who later withdrew due to political pressures about his relationship with the Nazis). Rodzinski's absence for the second half of the
Cleveland season would leave room for only two operatic productions in the
fall. The conductor chose works by composers closest to his heart—
Wagner's *Tannhäuser* and Strauss's *Elektra*.

Cleveland almost heard Maria Jeritza, the great Moravian soprano, as
Elisabeth in *Tannhäuser* and Nelson Eddy as Wolfram. When they weren't
available, Stueckgold was hired as Elisabeth and Richard Bonelli as
Wolfram. Paul Althouse sang the title role. The *New York Times's* Olin
Downes, still a champion of Rodzinski's opera ventures, came to Cleveland
and was swept away by his *Tannhäuser*. "The performance was exhilarating
and it was illuminative of the position that an orchestra and its various agen-
cies can hold in a community of which it is genuinely a part and a musical
center," he wrote.

Downes mentioned that a few more violins wouldn't have hurt. The issue
of sufficient strings would plague Rodzinski throughout his tenure. How
could the Cleveland Orchestra, with 80 or so players during the 1930s and
early 1940s, hope to compete soundwise with the orchestras of Boston, New
York, and Philadelphia, which had 100 or more musicians? Vosburgh told
the board in March 1936 that "on the present basis, the national reputation
and standing of the Cleveland Orchestra could never equal these orchestras." Financial concerns continuously prompted the board to put off any action on increasing personnel, leading to a widening rift with Rodzinski.

Whether 100 or more players could have squeezed into the pit at
Severance is another matter. Alice Chalifoux, who played all of the
Rodzinski operas requiring harp, said fitting the entire orchestra into the pit
was no problem. Nor is it unreasonable to assume that Rodzinski drew
sufficient sound from the orchestra for the work that was to prove his operatic swan song at Severance, Strauss's *Elektra*. Though the orchestra in
Strauss's ultra-violent opera is massive, the composer said he preferred textures closer to Mendelssohn than Wagner in this score. With the lighter approach, the singers wouldn't have to force their voices to be heard over the
orchestra.

With Rodzinski in charge, it is probable that the singers could be heard
even over the occasional Straussian din. The first Cleveland performances
of the opera on December 3 and 5, 1936, featured Gertrude Kappel as
Elektra, Enid Szantho as Klytämnestra, Julius Huehn as Orestes, Charlotte
Boerner as Chrysothemis, and Marek Windheim as Aegisthus. At least one
prominent member of the community was overwhelmed by the production
and Rodzinski's "incomparably magnificent" conducting—lecturer/journal-

ist Dorothy Fuldheim, who interviewed everyone from Hitler to rock stars. "I am grateful to you not only for your contribution to life's beauties but because your courage in including Elektra made it possible for me and many others to hear this rarely performed work," Fuldheim wrote to Rodzinski. "Even in Vienna I never heard it."

The Plain Dealer's Elwell, a composer of conservative leanings, had another view of the work. There is no mention in his review of Rodzinski's conducting or of the orchestra's playing. Mostly, Elwell just ranted about the piece. "Though it makes extraordinary demands on the singers, there is little in it that could be called singing. It is rather an exaggerated declamation, or a continued soaring on high notes. The principals were equal to the task, and some of them made stunning effects."

Rodzinski's series of operas with his orchestra had had a similar effect on Cleveland. It had brought some of the era's great singers to Severance Hall and demonstrated how imaginative artists could succeed in a theater without optimum stage machinery. Rodzinski had triumphed in a medium—full-scale opera—virtually untouched by other American symphony orchestras (up to that time and for the rest of the century). Many orchestras offer concert versions of operas, with singers standing onstage in gowns or tuxedos, minus scenery or theatrical effects. In at least one way during the 1930s, Rodzinski saw to it that the Cleveland Orchestra was unique.

1. Adella Prentiss plays a maiden opposite a mustachioed Tessie Wooster in *The Doctor of Alcantara* at Vassar College in 1888.

2. Thirteen-year-old Nikolai Sokoloff, left, in April 1900, shortly before he moved from Russia to the United States with his family. He is pictured with two brothers believed to be Joel and Samuel Belov, later string players with the Philadelphia Orchestra.

3. Adella Prentiss, center, poses with the singers who performed Liza Lehmann's song cycle, *In a Persian Garden*, in March 1898, the first concert she managed professionally: David Bispham, Marguerite Hall, Estelle Ford, and Mackenzie Gordon.

4. Adella Prentiss Hughes thrives as manager of the Symphony Orchestra Concerts series, which brings the finest American orchestras to Cleveland for two decades starting in 1901.

5. The earliest known photograph of the Cleveland Orchestra and conductor Nikolai Sokoloff on November 13, 1919, at Grays Armory.

6. Of eight siblings in the Hruby family, six played in the Cleveland Orchestra. Shown here are Mamie, Frank, Fred (never an orchestra member), John, William, Charles, and Alois.

7. Sokoloff, left, plays first violin in the Cleveland String Quartet during the 1919–20 season with violist Herman Kolodkin, cellist Victor de Gomez, and violinist Louis Edlin.

8. David Z. Norton, the orchestra's first board president, and his wife on their 50th anniversary in 1926.

9. Sokoloff and Hughes inspect the orchestra's first recording, an abridged version of Tchaikovsky's *1812 Overture*, in 1924.

10. The Cleveland Orchestra and Sokoloff make their New York debut on February 13, 1921, at the 5,000-seat Hippodrome Theatre.

11. Nikolai Sokoloff and the orchestra perform at Public Auditorium on October 11, 1925, for 10,000 concertgoers.

12. Students outside Masonic Hall before one of the orchestra's education concerts in the 1920s.

13. Rudolph Ringwall and the orchestra perform at Edgewater Park in Cleveland in July 1927.

14. Sokoloff in the late 1920s.

15. John and Elisabeth Severance in the late 1920s.

16. Cleveland string students participate in the Saturday-morning orchestra class at East Tech High School in April 1929.

17. Dudley S. Blossom, an orchestra trustee who later served as board president, announces the results of the campaign to endow Severance Hall in 1929.

18. Frank Hadley Ginn, a lawyer and longtime trustee of the Musical Arts Association, headed the Severance Hall building committee.

19. Musical Arts Association board president John Long Severance, still wearing the black armband to commemorate the death of his wife, breaks ground for Severance Hall on November 14, 1929.

20. The exterior of Severance Hall begins to take shape in May 1930.

21. The stage at Severance Hall during the inaugural season in 1931.

22. Artur Rodzinski charms members of the Women's Committee during his first season, 1933–34.

23. Rodzinski at Severance Hall in October 1933 with nine orchestra members who had been part of the orchestra department he founded at the Curtis Institute of Music in Philadelphia. Seated, left to right: Theodore Seder, Alice Chalifoux, and William Polisi. Standing: Samuel Goldblum, George Drexler, Fred Rosenberg, Paul Gershman, Rodzinski, Guy Boswell, and Maurice Sharp.

24. The first scene of Act III (the "Ride of the Valkyries") from the Cleveland Orchestra's production of Wagner's *Die Walküre* at Severance Hall in November 1934.

25. Adella Prentiss Hughes, center, is flanked by John Long Severance and Cleveland Orchestra colleagues outside her Cleveland Heights home. Halina Rodzinski, wife of conductor Artur Rodzinski, is seated in the front row, second from left.

26. Rodzinski in the pit at Severance Hall in 1935 during rehearsals for *Der Rosenkavalier*.

27. Lotte Lehmann, Rodzinski, Grete Stueckgold, and Emanuel List in the Green Room at Severance Hall after a performance of *Der Rosenkavalier* in 1935.

28. The cast of the Rodzinskis' opera parody, including John L. Severance dressed up as the Marschallin in *Der Rosenkavalier*, at their Cleveland home in 1935.

29. Arturo Toscanini and Rodzinski discuss Bartok's Music for Strings, Percussion, and Celesta in Salzburg, Austria, in 1936.

30. A scene from the Cleveland Orchestra's American premiere of *Lady Macbeth of Mzensk* at Severance Hall in January 1935. Rodzinski and his Cleveland forces repeated the production at New York's Metropolitan Opera House in early February.

31. Rodzinski in concert at Severance Hall in 1938.

32. Columbia Records producer Moses Smith and Rodzinski listen to a playback during the orchestra's first recording session in 1939 at Severance Hall.

33. Rodzinski and orchestra members with the conductor's goats at his farm in western Massachusetts in the early 1940s.

Amazed by Artur

Artur Rodzinski was the first conductor to build a great orchestra in Cleveland. The decade he spent at Severance Hall was one of the most productive and turbulent periods in the ensemble's history. Rodzinski brought to his post electrifying artistry, along with a charismatic and explosive personality. He arrived at a low point in American life, the Depression, and departed during another cataclysmic event, World War II. Rodzinski never hid his ambitions. He was always looking elsewhere in the United States—and toward Europe—to fulfill his personal musical goals, yet he was devoted to his orchestra. And he raised the sophistication of Cleveland's cultural scene—by prodding the Musical Arts Association to think in less provincial terms.

Onstage, Rodzinski rarely failed to excite audiences. Offstage (and sometimes during rehearsals), he showed signs of paranoia. He could be highly mercurial, even in the eyes of those closest to him. Rodzinski was churlish about complimenting his musicians, an issue brought up by a friend, assistant concertmaster Felix Eyle. "We only hear your criticism and your grumbling, and think we never satisfy you," Eyle told him. "If we do meet with your approval, why not show us a pretty smile now and then?" It didn't happen often. A *New York Post* reporter observed that Rodzinski "[is] a bundle of contradictions, and a hot bundle at that," and then quoted the conductor's wife. "Artur," she said, "is completely unpredictable. I've learned not to pay the slightest attention to his changes in mood. One moment he's furious at nothing. The next—here comes the sun! When he gets temperamental I just say, 'Woof, woof!' Then he giggles like a little boy and forgets he ever was angry."

Gianfranco Scarlini, a doctor in Cassino, Italy, who treated Rodzinski in the mid-1950s and became a close friend, theorized that the conductor's complex personality placed him in a special category inhabited by a select group of musicians of genius:

Perhaps he landed in music because more than any other art form, it allowed him to stimulate this need of his to experience the most fantastic and intense sensations and to communicate them to others. And in music, always dissatisfied, he would wear himself out always seeking something more, something deeply concealed, something transcendent. . . He could not feel himself limited to the role of a reader, music is [something] he would recreate, would relive. Hence, his torment as an artist, in fact, as a man: the tension of the search for an impossible way to live and to feel above the usual human capacity. Hence, the instability of his moods, hence his furious rages when he could not succeed in attaining his dreams, and his radiant happiness when his dream was attained.

Like other imposing conductors, Rodzinski was determined to attain those dreams solely in the service of the composer. Personal relations didn't matter if musical justice wasn't being done. The large turnover in personnel during Rodzinski's tenure—upwards of 120—was only partly due to economic conditions and natural attrition. Clearly, it also reflected the conductor's intolerance toward musicians he deemed weren't up to snuff.

In the name of quality, Rodzinski fought publicly with the musicians' union, which insisted that he hire local players instead of out-of-town candidates. When management tried to engage five imported string players at the beginning of the 1937–38 season, the union threatened to halt the season if local musicians weren't considered. General manager Carl Vosburgh accused union president Milton W. Krasny of trying to dictate which players the orchestra could hire. Krasny shot back that the orchestra was discriminating against Cleveland musicians.

The season began with the imported musicians barred from playing for the first eight weeks, at a savings to the Musical Arts Association of $2,864 in salaries. The impasse dragged on until December, when orchestra and union jointly chose an arbitrator to compare the five imported players with local candidates. The orchestra had the potential to be expanded by up to 10 musicians. Albert Stoessel, a composer and conductor from the Juilliard School of Music in New York, listened to 13 candidates and proclaimed that only the five imported players were suitable. These were the same players Rodzinski had hired in the first place. An editorial in *The Plain Dealer* already had put the subject in sane perspective the day the season opened: "There may be a hundred unemployed local violinists, but if a first-class player is needed it might be found that none of them would fill the role. Artur Rodzinski is the proper judge of an orchestra member's ability."

And he was a keen judge. "Artur had an uncanny feel for musicians," noted his wife. "He once said that he could tell if a player was an artist by the way he entered a room." Rodzinski hired dozens of splendid musicians for the Cleveland Orchestra, some so splendid that he later whisked them away for the NBC Symphony or the New York Philharmonic.

Until World War II made a deep dent in the orchestra's personnel, the biggest turnover during Rodzinski's tenure occurred at the start of the 1937–38 season, when there were 16 changes (three of them principals—viola, bassoon, and horn—that Rodzinski recruited from his own orchestra while creating the NBC Symphony for Arturo Toscanini). Nine players left Cleveland that season "of their own accord" for other orchestral jobs, three departed because they couldn't agree on financial terms, and four were either discharged or not renewed.

Alice Chalifoux, who served as principal harpist from 1931 to 1974, praised Rodzinski as "a great guy" who would "go to a bar with us after a concert occasionally and have a great time." Even so, neither the musicians nor the public much appreciated the way Rodzinski often handled personnel issues, terrorizing players and raiding orchestras at will. A sense of his rehearsal technique can be gleaned from a colorful account of a New York Philharmonic session provided by cellist Leonard Rose, whom Rodzinski hired for the NBC Symphony, then hired away from that orchestra to become principal in Cleveland, and then hired away from Cleveland for the Philharmonic. According to Rose, "Let's say the strings botched some difficult passage in a Strauss composition—he would stop everything and demand: 'First violins alone!' They would play it. 'Phooie!' Rodzinski would growl. 'That was bad. Spell it out.' He would begin to conduct again, slowly. If things still didn't sound good, he would stop and say: 'Terrible! Outside players alone.' They would play it. 'Awful! Inside alone. Dreadful! Last three stands alone. Terrible, terrible!' Then he would put down his baton and glare at the strings and say: 'Gentlemen, if it's not better tomorrow, you'll each play it solo!' By God, the next day it would sound better."

Rodzinski put the Cleveland Orchestra's string players through a similar ordeal. "At the beginning of next season," he stated in a 1941 memo, "each string musician will be asked to play a concerto or sonata before the members of his section in addition to myself. The members of each section will then, through a secret ballot, intimate his idea as to the seating of his particular section. I, of course, reserve the right to make the final decision."

Less than three years into Rodzinski's tenure, word had spread through the musical community that the orchestra was demoralized by the conductor's intimidating treatment. "Good orchestras are not made by wholesale dismissals and a constant turnover each year," wrote one subscriber, "and it is possible for Dr. Rodzinski to lose his prestige in the same manner that his predecessor did." The woman threatened to withdraw her support of the orchestra if matters didn't improve. They did get better, at least temporarily. For the next three seasons, the orchestra had fewer than 10 personnel changes per season. But with U.S. involvement in World War II, the situation worsened considerably. In 1941, Rodzinski again had to fill 16 spots. The following year, the number rose to 22.

Adding to this dilemma was the board's unyielding stance on enlarging the orchestra. During most of the Rodzinski decade, the ensemble had only 80 to 82 players, causing much resentment on the conductor's part. By comparison, the New York Philharmonic was an immense orchestra—upwards of 100 players. A Boston critic noted Cleveland's thinness when reviewing a tour concert in 1937. "With an orchestra of eighty, even after allowance has been made for musicians occasionally engaged for thickly-scored romantic and modern works, it would seem impossible to achieve the sonority of the Eastern orchestras," read the otherwise laudatory review. "Necessarily the string section will want fullness and accompanying richness."

Rodzinski and Vosburgh were constantly struggling—with both the board and one another—to maintain the orchestra at a high artistic level. Even before the conductor came to town, the musicians' salaries had been slashed because of the Depression. In some cases, the board had to consider offering better salaries and longer contracts to keep key players. Vosburgh, always the voice of conscience during these years, frequently engaged in battle with Rodzinski over the practice of raising salaries for principals but providing no increases for section players.

The wage freeze occasionally affected longtime principals as well. The orchestra's loquacious principal bass, Gerald Fiore, a member since the first season, finally had enough after he again tried to convince Rodzinski to restore some of his lost salary. "Why I should be expected to continue at my present salary of $3360 is to me unreasonable," he wrote in April 1936. Fiore had made $3,750 in 1923, $4,050 in 1928, and $4,500 from 1929 to 1932. "Surely I am no less valuable now than in 1923, still I receive less in proportion to my colleagues of the old days. In those days I was a single man and now I have a family." Rodzinski was never squeamish about asking the board to raise his own salary (and the board was never reluctant to put him off), but he didn't budge on Fiore, who left soon after writing his letter to become principal bass of the Metropolitan Opera Orchestra.

✿   ✿   ✿

Rodzinski also never held back from telling Vosburgh what was on his mind. In 1936, he urged the manager to make sure that Chicago would be a stop on one of his tours with his Cleveland musicians. Chicago was important to him because he coveted the top post of the Windy City's orchestra. When Vosburgh wasn't quick enough to do his boss's bidding, Rodzinski shot off a 12-page, handwritten letter from Italy starting "Dear Mr. Manager!" and continuing with a slew of emotional eruptions (and exclamation points): "How can I trust such a manager—!!!!!!!!!!!!!!!! Better yourself . . . You will have surprise of your life to get all of my programs very soon—They are actually ready!!!—but as I said in the beginning it all depends on a 'beautiful Middle West City also located in a Lake Region'—in which every conductor (imaginable) conducted—except myself." Rodzinski went on to ask Vosburgh about a recent Cleveland concert by the Philadelphia Orchestra under his mentor, Leopold Stokowski. "I understand—you all including Mr. Blossom and yourself—overcome by the blond Apollo—forget that I gave Cleveland and still am giving and will give always—the best I can. But this cursed artist!!" The letter is signed, curiously, "With love to all!! Artur."

Vosburgh's response gives a vivid indication of the firm hand and humor (and exclamation points) he had to use in dealing with his mercurial maestro. "I am amazed, astonished, and completely flabbergasted! Four cables, a twelve page letter from you, as well as one from Mrs. Rodzinski! Surely something has gone wrong. Are you ill, or what? Never before have I been so swamped with correspondence from you in connection with the Cleveland Orchestra!" He also wasn't above stroking Rodzinski's ego in an effort to bring him back to earth—and Ohio. "I can assure you that practically all of Cleveland, as well as myself, has forgotten that the 'blond Apollo' was even here. There is much more interest in the return of the 'graying Adonis,' and what he will have to offer for another exciting and inspirational winter here in Cleveland."

✽　　✽　　✽

Of inspiration, there was no dearth: Rodzinski's programming could be so adventurous (and was so often decided at the last minute) that Cleveland's conservative cravings often forced him to switch pieces shortly before a series of concerts. Along with traditional works, he conducted the local premieres of such pieces as Bruckner's Eighth Symphony, Hindemith's *Mathis der Maler* symphony, Sibelius's Fourth Symphony, Mahler's second and fourth symphonies and *Das Lied von der Erde*, the Vaughan Williams

Symphony in F minor, Strauss's *Sinfonia domestica*, and Piston's *The Incredible Flutist* suite. He also conducted the world premiere of Sir William Walton's Violin Concerto, with Jascha Heifetz as soloist.

Many works that would eventually come to be adored sounded alien to Cleveland audiences of the 1930s and '40s. Mahler's Symphony No. 2 ("Resurrection") was considered especially novel in 1936 for the massive performing forces it required. Rodzinski didn't stint, cramming the 300-member Cleveland Philharmonic Chorus onto the Severance stage (forcing the front sections of the orchestra onto an apron above the pit). In his review in the *Cleveland Press*, Denoe Leedy noted that "the volume of sound at times was close to deafening. But you cannot perform Mahler without making noise."

Orchestra trustee Frances Payne Bolton was full of praise, encouragement, and metaphysical ecstasy in a letter to Rodzinski about the Mahler: "It took courage to present such a work—and I can imagine that perhaps you felt a certain disappointment that Cleveland is still slow to seize its opportunities. Ah—do not feel so—it was so indescribably beautiful that I feel sure that whatever empty chairs may have looked bleak to you, they were filled by those we cannot see who came to share the magnificent majesty."

A work that completely perplexed audiences and critics at its Cleveland premiere in December 1940 under Rodzinski was Alban Berg's Violin Concerto, which was played by Louis Krasner, who had commissioned the score from the late composer in 1935. Herbert Elwell, once again showing his old-fashioned stripes as a composer, attacked the piece with his sharpest rapier. "This being Cleveland's first exposure to the virus of atonality, the atmosphere was about as opaque as the peasoup fog outside," he wrote in *The Plain Dealer*. "The soloist appeared as a true hero in service of what, I fear, is already a lost cause . . . It is all too precious, too personal, too esoteric, too restless and morbid in its introspective probing." (Berg's concerto has proved to be no such lost cause: it is standard repertoire for the world's major orchestras, and has had many performances at Severance Hall.)

Another 20th-century Viennese composer introduced to Cleveland during this time was Arnold Schoenberg, creator of the revolutionary and complex 12-tone system. Schoenberg gave a lecture on the problems of harmony at the Cleveland Museum of Art on January 27, 1935. Announcing the event, Leedy presented the German composer as a "crazy radical" who is "canonized by some and damned by others, at present attempting to establish himself in an America happily free from the social mess which rages in middle Europe, all in all a genius of the first rank—we can well sit at his feet and absorb what he has to say." Rodzinski took up the radical's cause in 1938 by

programming one of Schoenberg's less rigorous pieces, his flavorful orchestration of Brahms's Quartet for Piano and Strings in G minor, Op. 25. The
composer didn't make the process easy for Vosburgh, whom he bombarded
with insistent letters about musical matters and money. Schoenberg, who
was making a modest living teaching in Los Angeles, clearly needed cash:
"Would you be so kind to send me a list of the places in which you performed
the piece, and in case the number of performances [agreed to] was surpassed, may I ask for an additional check?"

Rodzinski later commissioned a work for the Cleveland Orchestra from
a very different contemporary composer. Broadway's Jerome Kern agreed
to devise a symphonic transcription based on themes from his score to *Show
Boat*, a task he initially found daunting. "The plain truth of the matter is that
my activity in music over a longish period of years has been in a field far removed from the distinguished precincts of the concert hall," Kern told
Rodzinski, "and I find myself unequipped with sufficient skill, technique or
experience to create a symphonic arrangement of the melodies of 'Show
Boat' worthy of your baton." Rodzinski actually had to be sold on the Kern
idea by Moses Smith of the Columbia Recording Corporation. Smith
proved a fine salesman in this respect. "Maybe European audiences
wouldn't be thrilled. And I say, to Hell with them," he wrote to Rodzinski.
"This score was and is for Americans, and it's an exciting musical document."
Olin Downes, music critic of the *New York Times*, picked up on the same
theme, telling Kern to "discover your own form and not an over-worked
European formula." Similarly, Rodzinski maintained a gently constructive
correspondence with Kern during the process of transforming a Broadway
vehicle into a symphonic piece, which the composer vowed would "not add
a single note of new material not contained in the original work."

It was an entirely new experience that the gifted Kern quickly found exhilarating. "The panicky apprehension of being a cobbler half-soling and
heeling a comfortable old pair of shoes has been superseded by a genuine
enthusiasm," he related to Rodzinski in August 1941. "Of course, the actual
scoring may present hurdles, giving me headaches and jim-jams aplenty.
But I have no doubt I can be helped over the former." He *did* receive help
on the orchestration—some claim from Robert Russell Bennett or Emil
Gerstenberger, others say from Morton Gould—and produced a "Scenario
for Orchestra" that Rodzinski and his musicians performed often, mostly on
tour. Their recording of the work for Columbia became the orchestra's
biggest seller to that time. The piece netted the composer the very humble
sum of $940.

Cleveland was a natural for the premiere of Kern's adaptation. The original production of *Show Boat* had played the Ohio Theatre on Euclid Avenue in November 1927 as part of its pre-Broadway tryout (the other cities were Washington, D.C., Pittsburgh, and Philadelphia) before opening at New York's Ziegfeld Theatre on December 27 and proceeding to make history. Fourteen years later, on October 23 and 25, 1941, Rodzinski and the Cleveland Orchestra gave the premiere of the *Show Boat* compilation four miles east of the Ohio Theatre, at Severance Hall. Kern, grieving over the death of a friend on the West Coast, didn't attend the premiere, but he heard a broadcast of the performance and sent a congratulatory telegram.

Elwell's review of the piece in *The Plain Dealer* was appreciative, if mildly condescending: "They used to call it a medley. Jerome Kern calls it 'scenario for orchestra.' Whatever you call it, it made some members of last night's symphony audience in Severance Hall think for a moment they were in the wrong place and reach for their hats. But they didn't leave. They stayed and liked it . . . Comparing this with the Strauss waltzes that sometimes find their way into symphony programs, one can honestly say that Kern's contribution is just as good if not better." A month later, Kern was able to attend the work's Carnegie Hall premiere, which was scorched by Virgil Thomson in the *Herald Tribune*: "If your sister came out on a concert stage got up like that you would tell her she looked like a Christmas tree or ask her if she hadn't forgot the kitchen stove." But Rodzinski adored the piece. And Kern was overwhelmed with the reception his score received.

❊   ❊   ❊

Although opera had been out of the picture since 1936 for economic reasons and because of the Metropolitan Opera's return to Public Auditorium, Rodzinski made two attempts to bring it back. In 1938, he asked the board to fund a performance of *Tristan und Isolde*, this time at Public Auditorium with Lauritz Melchior and Kirsten Flagstad in the title roles and Cleveland's Rose Bampton again as Brangäne. The board opted not to take the risk. Two years later, Rodzinski asked to present Strauss's *Salome*, which Columbia Records was showing interest in recording, until he and the board agreed that the cost would be prohibitive. One opera that did make it to Severance Hall in January 1938 with the Cleveland Orchestra in the pit was the local premiere of *The Sleeping Beauty*, with music by Beryl Rubinstein, now director of the Cleveland Institute of Music, and libretto by John Erskine. The production was conducted by Albert Stoessel, staged by Alfredo Valenti, and designed by Richard Rychtarik. The Juilliard School of Music, which had already presented the production in New York, funded the performances.

Despite their reluctance to spend money on opera, the trustees didn't object to the pricey list of guest artists proposed for the 1938–39 season. Vosburgh received the go-ahead to sign Sergei Rachmaninoff, Artur Rubinstein, Myra Hess, Walter Gieseking, Jascha Heifetz, Nathan Milstein, Joseph Szigeti, Erica Morini, Emanuel Feuermann, Gregor Piatigorsky, Sergei Prokofiev, and Georges Enesco.

Rodzinski accepted a new five-year contract with the orchestra in February 1938, though his relations with the board were now often strained. Ever determined to enlarge the orchestra, he proclaimed that he would personally raise the money to hire up to eight string players, an interesting offer that the trustees couldn't refuse. But Rodzinski later rescinded the offer and asked the board to find the funds, which didn't happen.

✽   ✽   ✽

In May 1938, Rodzinski bought a farm near Tanglewood, the Boston Symphony's summer home in the Berkshires of western Massachusetts, as a summer getaway. The 232-acre property, just outside Stockbridge, had horses, chickens, ducks, and cows. Rodzinski became "a full-fledged member of the landed gentry" and bought a herd of registered Swiss goats, which produced 20 quarts of milk a day—some of which the Rodzinskis intended to sell, some of which the conductor (a health nut and hypochondriac) intended to drink. "Would like to have photos of yourself milking cows—feeding chickens—pitching hay or anything," Vosburgh wrote to Rodzinski. "I don't know how to milk the cows yet," the conductor-farmer answered from his Berkshire abode, which was dubbed White Goat Farm.

The first summer Rodzinski spent on his Massachusetts farm, members of the orchestra engaged in various activities outside of Cleveland to make money or get some rest. Principal cellist Victor de Gomez, for his second summer in a row, played in the orchestra at Paramount Studios in Hollywood. He returned his new Cleveland Orchestra contract to Vosburgh by quipping, "All along I've known that I would eventually sign a contract in Hollywood!!! Since the news leaked out, Clark Gable and Robert Taylor have left town and even Jack Benny is looking nervous." Oboists Philip Kirchner and Bert Gassman and hornists Rudolph Puletz and William Namen played in the Mexico City Symphony Orchestra under Carlos Chávez. Concertmaster Josef Fuchs was in California, and principal bassist Michael Lamagna was in Italy. Alice Chalifoux spent the summer in Maine running the harp colony she would inherit from her mentor, Carlos Salzedo.

The musicians, eager to be employed in Cleveland throughout the year, had been urging management to find them summer work for more than a decade. Aside from the summers of 1927 and 1928, when they played at

Edgewater and Gordon parks under Rudolph Ringwall, the orchestra generally was idle from May to October. In 1932, a summer season of operas was held at Cleveland Municipal Stadium for the second consecutive year, with 17 members of the orchestra playing productions of *Aida, Carmen,* and *Die Walküre* and the premiere of a "Negro opera" titled *Tom-Tom* by "a young Negro woman student at Oberlin College." Sixty members of the orchestra organized the Promenade Concerts in May and June of 1932 and 1933 at "ice-cooled" Severance Hall. The concerts had half-hour intermissions to allow audience members to buy ice cream and lemonade, but not beer or wine—leading to complaints.

In 1936, members of the orchestra received summer employment when Edgar A. Hahn, a local businessman and orchestra trustee, hired them to play in the Great Lakes Symphony Orchestra as part of the Great Lakes Exposition, the regional festival chaired by Dudley Blossom. The concerts were held at the Aquacade, a wooden shed on the East Ninth Street pier built by the Sherwin Williams paint company. Guest conductors for these programs were Frank Black, Hans Kindler, Erno Rapee, and Jose Iturbi. There was no musical activity the second year of the Exposition, but in 1938 the Shubert brothers, the well-known producers of lavish Broadway shows and touring productions, offered such a generous fee that Hahn handed management of the rebuilt and renamed Aquastage over to them to present such light operas as *Rose Marie* and *Rio Rita*, with orchestra members providing accompaniment. One season, however, was enough for the Shuberts.

The Aquastage was scheduled to present 12 summer orchestra concerts in 1939, but in early June the Cleveland Summer Music Society—with Hahn again at the helm—moved the events to a garden setting inside Public Auditorium. The *Press* reported "the Aquastage was abandoned as a locale for the concerts because arrangements for the World Poultry Congress made the parking facilities and driveways to the lakefront spot difficult." Rodzinski agreed to help the summer cause by conducting one of the 12 inaugural-season summer concerts, on July 15, for which he was paid $75 to cover expenses.

Programs featuring overtures and single movements of major works were instituted during the regular season in 1932–33, when 25 Twilight Concerts—so-called for their starting time of 6 p.m. on Sundays—were presented at Severance Hall. Pops concerts began the next year, when Vosburgh received permission from the board to present the orchestra in programs of light music under Ringwall at popular prices—25, 50, and 75 cents the first season. Rodzinski had given his blessing to these programs, especially the Twilight concerts, since they contained music he didn't conduct. Or so he thought. In 1939, when NBC offered to broadcast five one-hour concerts—at $500 per concert—of music played at children's and Twilight concerts, Rodzinski noticed that the programs contained serious fare. The repertoire, in fact, duplicated works he had led in Cleveland during the previous five years on the same network. In a memo to Vosburgh, Rodzinski protested that the concerts—"entirely un-rehearsed"—were a disgrace to the orchestra's reputation: "I have given more than five years of hard and most devoted labor to molding this Orchestra which is today regarded as one of the finest in the United States and I regret greatly that this reputation is now being endangered by unfavorable representation of our Orchestra to the public at large. To anyone who has a feeling of musical values this Orchestra, on these Sunday broadcasts, sounds like a third-rate, provincial band. The repercussions of these broadcasts will certainly be felt in many places, and might hurt our business." Despite his objections, these programs continued.

❋   ❋   ❋

Rodzinski was delighted to lead the orchestra at Public Auditorium in music with which he was identified. The gargantuan building, used more often for conventions, wrestling, and boxing matches than for concerts, was packed with 10,000 people on November 22, 1936, when Rodzinski shared a program with Erno Rapee, the Hungarian-born conductor of the orchestra at New York's Radio City Music Hall, in a General Motors Hour broadcast heard on 60 NBC stations. Only 15 minutes of the concert were broadcast in Cleveland on WTAM, which miffed local citizens and critics.

Another Public Auditorium concert under Rodzinski, on January 8, 1939, featured Kirsten Flagstad, who sang arias by Wagner. The concert had been scheduled for the previous November, but the revered Norwegian soprano had come down with a cold and the event had been postponed. She told the *Cleveland News* that she was thrilled at the prospect of singing for 10,000 at Public Auditorium. "Such a great audience is in itself an inspiration to great song," said the soprano, who had sung in the auditorium with the Metropolitan Opera. "Dr. Rodzinski and the Cleveland Orchestra have an international reputation as great exponents of Wagner." Rodzinski continued to participate on occasion in "All-Star Popular Concerts" at Public Auditorium the following season, welcoming such artists as Lauritz Melchior, Fritz Kreisler, Giovanni Martinelli, Marjorie Lawrence, Lily Pons, and André Kostelanetz.

At Severance Hall, the autocratic hand of Rodzinski tended to have a decisive effect on musical standards, as well as a significant impact on the repertoire. During the 1938–39 season, Cleveland heard him conduct six of Beethoven's nine symphonies (Ringwall, Enesco, and Dimitri Mitropoulos conducted the others). The programming that season contained yet more Beethoven, including several of the piano concertos with Schnabel as soloist. For conducting the first Cleveland performance of Bruckner's Symphony No. 8, Rodzinski was awarded a medal from the Bruckner Society of America.

Rodzinski maintained the high level of artistry in part by strengthening the list of guest soloists and conductors and inviting prominent figures to return. Igor Stravinsky was back at Severance Hall in February 1937 for the first time since his debut in 1925 to conduct music by Weber, Bach, and Mozart, as well as his own *Fireworks*, Violin Concerto (with Samuel Dushkin), and *Petrouchka* suite. The composer gave an interview to Milton Widder in the *Press* that was headlined "Igor Stravinsky—Small Body but a Giant Brain," along with the subhead "Composer Abhors Communism, 'Interpretive' Conductors; Likes Poker, Wine." Widder invoked Stravinsky's ire by asking whether the work he was in the midst of composing, the ballet *Jeu de cartes*, would be modern. "What do you mean 'modern?'—I don't like the word," the composer answered. "If you mean, is the composition contemporary, of course. If you mean is it tomorrow's, then I don't know and there is no soul in the world who does know. I write what I feel or what I think is right—there is nothing 'modern' about that. All I can hope for is that some of the things I write will live."

Neither the *Press*'s Leedy nor *The Plain Dealer*'s Elwell was convinced that the Stravinsky works on his program would endure. "This reviewer begs liberty to throw in a personal note," wrote Leedy. "Present at the first performance in this country of *Le Sacre du Printemps*, he rose up out of his chair and cheered until hoarse. Last night he alternately stifled yawns and the desire to throw something." Elwell was more favorable, but also more patronizing: "Let it be 'Hats Off' to Igor Stravinsky, the most commanding presence in contemporary music, but at the same time an earnest prayer that he ponder some more on the aesthetic significance of music."

Rodzinski also introduced to Cleveland the one-handed Austrian pianist Paul Wittgenstein, who came to Severance Hall in February 1939 to play Ravel's Concerto for the Left Hand, which the composer had written for him. Wittgenstein's right arm had been amputated after he was wounded in World War I near the Russian front. "At first I was not interested in what amputation may have done to my career," he told the *Cleveland News*. "I was too much interested in whether I would live or die to care about playing the piano. Later, when the problem of health had gone, I felt that I had lost everything. Then I decided to take up the piano again and see how far I could go with only a left hand." He went far, commissioning important left-hand piano works by such composers as Prokofiev and Britten.

Yet another superb pianist who made his debut with the orchestra during Rodzinski's tenure was Arthur Loesser, who was serving as music critic of the *Cleveland Press* (as successor to Denoe Leedy) when he played Brahms's Piano Concerto No. 1 in March 1938 under the conductor's baton. Loesser didn't review this particular concert, of course, but he did receive enthusiastic notices from colleagues Elwell, Widder (subbing for him in the *Press*), and Elmore Bacon in the *News*. Journalistic ethics were relatively loose at the time: Both Loesser and Elwell served as program annotators for the Cleveland Orchestra while they were music critics in town, and both performed with the orchestra (Elwell as conductor); Elwell had his compositions played by the orchestra, too. Adella Prentiss Hughes approved of the situation: "It means a great deal to the quality of our institution to have a person of Elwell's reputation as program editor and I think it is good to have the close connection with the Plain Dealer," she wrote to Vosburgh in 1935.

One pianist who made a big impression at Severance Hall was Béla Bartók, who was also represented in his capacity as one of the most audacious composers of the day. Rodzinski was on the podium on December 5 and 7, 1940, when the composer made his debut as soloist in his Second Piano Concerto. The week of his Severance Hall concerts, an unsettled Bartók told *The Plain Dealer* that the weather in Cleveland was "nasty" and "uninspiring." He continued, "Still, you are lucky. You have plenty of fuel and good lodgings. That is more than we have in Europe. I like it here. I am happy." He told the *Cleveland News* that he enjoyed playing jazz with clarinetist Benny Goodman as much as he liked playing classical music.

The critics largely admired Bartók's playing, though they were divided about the concerto, which the *News*'s Bacon called "modern music of the mathematical sort, rather empty," and the *Press*'s Loesser characterized as combining an "elemental, barbaric, almost brutal rhythmic dynamism with an intellectual approach to thematic development, and some occasionally rather remarkable sophistications of tone color."

❖   ❖   ❖

Bartók's journey to the United States in the fall of 1940 was not fated to be a short concert tour. Nazi Germany had been threatening Hungary for some time, as it had neighboring countries. By the time Bartók left Budapest in October 1940 for America, Hitler was on the verge of bringing Hungary into the Axis alliance, a process that was finalized in November. The alarming events already had touched Rodzinski: Poland had been invaded by the Nazis in September 1939, plunging Europe into World War II. Rodzinski worried about his 69-year-old mother, who was still in Warsaw. When asked about the conflict, he saluted his country and defended his right to program repertoire that might be construed as controversial in light of the war. "Poland's music springs from its soil, but its existence as a nation goes even deeper," he told a reporter. "We have Chopin, Szymanowski, Moniuszko. But then, German music is the finest in the world—gorgeous. A nation's music is entirely distinct from its politics."

The hearts of friends, associates, and strangers went out to the Rodzinskis when news of Hitler's atrocities in Poland reached Cleveland. "I cannot tell you how often I have thought of you during these tragic days and weeks, when Poland was being so shattered and torn by the hostile foe that was invading her borders," Elisabeth Prentiss, sister of John L. Severance, wrote the Rodzinskis in late September 1939. "Please know that, even though we do not speak of it, your many friends are sympathetic and feel sadly for you, and wish they might do something for you. The fact that this country is entirely in sympathy with the democracies of Europe must be a satisfaction."

Rodzinski and the Cleveland Orchestra struck a symbolic blow against Hitler by programming Wagner's *Rule Britannia* overture on a worldwide radio broadcast in April 1942. Referring to the "Nazi gang," the conductor told the audience he believed Hitler's actions to be on the same level as the "murders, robberies, forgeries and adultery" in Wagner's *Ring* cycle. But Elwell judged the piece on a purely artistic level. The overture, he wrote in *The Plain Dealer*, "proved to be such abominable music that it left one wondering whether Wagner might not have been trying to insult the English by writing it. Even Rodzinski's drastic cuts in the work did not raise it above a level of hopeless mediocrity."

Like European colleagues whose countries were being ravaged by Hitler, Rodzinski felt enormous pain as the war continued to unfold. He had the strange distinction of being guest conductor with the New York Philharmonic at Carnegie Hall on the afternoon of December 7, 1941, when news arrived that the Japanese had attacked Pearl Harbor. Some sources claim that Rodzinski made the announcement to the radio audience. Halina Rodzinski says, correctly, that her husband declined when Warren Sweeney, the broadcast announcer, asked him to read the news. Rodzinski immediately led the Philharmonic and the audience in "The Star-Spangled Banner" (for the second time that afternoon).

As the United States entered the war, orchestras quickly realized that

they would face the departure of many players for the armed forces. Thomas
L. Sidlo, who had succeeded the late Dudley Blossom as president of the
Musical Arts Association, had already begun to battle another threat to orchestral health by this time: a bill passed by Congress in the summer of 1940
had added a stiff 15 percent tax to all tickets sold for artistic events. His comments to the board on this subject display an almost Wagnerian sense of
foreboding. "Expense we shall be able to control, but income will be in the
lap of the gods," he said.

Later, when the United States had become immersed in the war, Sidlo
employed all of his formidable gifts of oratory to keep the board on a forward track. "Despite the general uncertainty that overhangs everything we
hold precious, we face the coming year with determination and confidence,"
said Sidlo. "Our Orchestra was born during the First World War. It has just
come through the first year of another, grimmer war, with greater success
and, I believe with greater public support than in any year in its entire existence." It was the board's job, he continued, "to keep the good ship
Cleveland Orchestra sailing, to bring it over its course, and to land it tri-
umphantly back in port."

Doing so would be difficult, financially and artistically. Almost a dozen
members of the orchestra left to join the military in 1942. Rodzinski faced
the challenge of replacing these players, at least temporarily, with musicians
of equal ability. He probably raised a few eyebrows that fall by stating that
the war could force American orchestras to hire female musicians to replace
men who had gone into the service. "I don't look for it this year in
Cleveland," he told a reporter, "but we have about the youngest orchestra
in the country and when they begin cutting deep into Class 3-A for draftees
we are liable to be hit hard." Rodzinski considered the employment of
women in an orchestra a "rather revolutionary innovation," though he believed "they would make an excellent addition to any first class symphony
orchestra."

For audiences and performers alike, the realities of war made the spiritual uplift of artistic endeavors more important than ever. Adella Prentiss
Hughes touched upon the issue in a letter to Halina Rodzinski soon after
Hitler invaded Poland. "It is a blessing that we all have work to do," she
wrote. "That way lies healing and the strength to carry on."

A big boost for the orchestra came in January 1942, when Morris Markey,
announcer for the Metropolitan Opera's radio broadcasts, paid tribute to
Rodzinski and his musicians during an intermission feature. "It is one of the
very great symphony orchestras playing in the world today," Markey told in-

ternational listeners. "All praise to Cleveland—which does not linger over
tradition but, instead, goes out to make music now—for living, hungry ears
to hear."

Rodzinski planned a promising series of concerts for the orchestra's 25th-
anniversary season, including appearances by pianist Claudio Arrau and cellist Raya Garbousova. He didn't neglect local composers, including the local
composer-critic. In late October, he conducted Herbert Elwell's
Introduction and Allegro and received a letter from the composer thanking
him for his "insight and skill" and admitting that, as critic, "I realize I must
often be as irksome to you as ants in the pants." Rodzinski wrote back that
he hoped "you could give some anesthetic to your ants and fill your column
with lots of bees, which are also stinging sometimes, but still produce wonderful honey."

Two significant events in Cleveland's musical history soon followed. On
November 15, Rodzinski and the orchestra welcomed Marian Anderson,
the pioneering black alto, to Public Hall to sing operatic arias by Handel,
Verdi, and Massenet, songs by Brahms, and spirituals. The other event was
the debut, on December 3, of 21-year-old pianist Eunice Podis, who, replacing indisposed violinist Ruth Posselt, played the Tchaikovsky First Piano
Concerto under Ringwall. Podis, one of the few musicians invited to study
with renowned concert pianist Artur Rubinstein, "presented a skillful, vigorous and brilliant performance," said Elmore Bacon in his review the next
day in the *News*.

Then, in December 1942, an old acquaintance returned to Severance
Hall for the first time in almost a decade. Rodzinski had invited Nikolai
Sokoloff back to conduct an anniversary subscription program that included
Beethoven's "Eroica," Holst's *St. Paul* suite, Bloch's *Winter-Spring*, and
Strauss's *Don Juan*. "I used to feel that Sokoloff's interest in expressive detail sometimes blurred his architectural perspective," wrote Elwell. "But, although in his molding of the great 'Eroica' of Beethoven there was no less
attention than usual to its expressive features, there was also a sturdy and
honest wielding of its form, and I was deeply impressed to hear again how
completely and conclusively the emotional intention is revealed by
Sokoloff's deliberate kind of emphasis."

Sokoloff encountered a much finer instrument in 1942 than the one he
had left in 1933. Rodzinski had brought the ensemble to a level of technical
accomplishment that few American orchestras could match, even with the
continued shortage of strings. The proof of this accomplishment is not just
anecdotal. It can be heard on the recordings Rodzinski made in Cleveland
from 1939 until 1942.

Recording with Rodzinski

Nikolai Sokoloff and the Cleveland Orchestra had no idea that their recording sessions for Brunswick in May 1928 would be their last together. Nor did the orchestra expect to wait 11 years before making another recording. The aftershocks of the stock market crash brought production of phonograph records to a virtual halt for several years, after which companies began mustering their courage and signing up ensembles and artists. Most classical recordings were still being made in Europe, where such venerable companies as Deutsche Grammophon, Decca, Telefunken, and EMI braved the political instability brought on by Hitler's rise to power. In the United States, the leading record companies for classical music were RCA and Decca, although Columbia was trying to seize part of the market.

The recording drought in Cleveland had almost ended in 1935, when the Columbia Phonograph Company approached the orchestra with an offer to hold one five-hour session, during which two or three recordings would be made. Costs for the musicians' services were estimated at between $3,000 and $3,300. But nothing came of the proposition.

The next firm to negotiate with Severance Hall was the RCA Manufacturing Company, which offered $10,000 for three recording sessions before the end of the 1935–36 season. These sessions, which didn't happen either, would have provided documentation of the orchestra during the period Artur Rodzinski conducted *Der Rosenkavalier, Parsifal,* Hindemith's *Mathis der Maler,* Sibelius's Fourth Symphony, and Mahler's "Resurrection" Symphony. A year later, after Rodzinski led a superlative Carnegie Hall concert performance of Strauss's *Elektra* with the New York Philharmonic and Rose Pauly in the title role, RCA again came knocking at Cleveland's door. RCA's Charles O'Connell this time requested that the Cleveland Orchestra and Rodzinski repeat their production of *Elektra,* which they had performed to acclaim in December 1936, for purposes of recording. O'Connell proposed that the orchestra put up the expense ($4,000, not including Rodzinski's fee) for two of the three three-hour sessions. The board voted to make no recordings unless the recording company paid all costs.

Despite the enormous advances the orchestra had made under Rodzinski, Cleveland remained an underdog in attracting broadcast and recording contracts. The big reason was personnel, which hovered around 80 musicians—small compared with the 100 or more players in the orchestras of Boston, Philadelphia, and New York. Cleveland had insufficient strings for certain scores. Another disadvantage was reputation. The major orchestras on the East Coast were not only larger but also older; they had had years to develop identities on the national scene. Cleveland was only a teenager.

Even so, the orchestra under Rodzinski was growing quickly to adulthood, and one recording company was taking notice. In 1938, William S. Paley, president of the Columbia Broadcasting System, paid $700,000 for beleaguered Columbia Records and began beefing up its roster with American orchestras that weren't recording for rival RCA. Along with the Chicago Symphony (led by Frederick Stock), the San Francisco Symphony (Pierre Monteux), the Minneapolis Symphony (Dimitri Mitropoulos), and the All American Youth Orchestra (Leopold Stokowski), the Cleveland Orchestra and Rodzinski were signed. The terms called for the Musical Arts Association to receive a ten-percent royalty, half then going to Rodzinski.

The first three days of sessions were held at Severance Hall on December 11, 12 and 13, 1939, when Rodzinski recorded Sibelius's *Finlandia*, the prelude to Mussorgsky's *Khovantchina* (which wasn't released, though a later version was), "the high spots" (only a test) from Strauss's *Ein Heldenleben*, Rimsky-Korsakov's *Scheherazade*, and portions of Tchaikovsky's Fifth Symphony (completed the following month). Milton Widder observed the trial recording of *Heldenleben* and described it in the *Cleveland Press*: "After some suggested changes on performance, the first wax master-disc was cut. It lasted 4 minutes and 17 seconds—and the maximum a 12-inch recording takes is 4 minutes and 40 seconds."

Timing these pieces to fit the limited recording space, wrote Halina Rodzinski in her memoirs, posed challenges that intrigued her husband, who was making his first recordings for Columbia. "The line of a piece had now to be broken into three-, four-, and four-and-a-half-minute segments (all that could fit on a shellac disk's side) without destroying the shape of the composition," she noted. "The problems were ticklish, but Artur enjoyed solving them." Rodzinski also savored his new relationship with Goddard

Lieberson, a British-born composer and recording engineer who had been assigned to produce the Cleveland recordings.

A few weeks after his first Cleveland recording sessions, Rodzinski was ecstatic, as he made clear in a telegram to Vosburgh:

HAVE JUST HEARD SHEHERAZADE AND FINLANDIA RECORDS. STOP. ALL
I CAN SAY IS THEY ARE MARVELOUS. ENSEMBLE PERFECTION. SPLENDID
BALANCE SOLO WIND INSTRUMENTS WOOD AND BRASS GORGEOUS.
FUCHS SOLOS JUST A DREAM. STOP. PLEASE SEND THIS TELEGRAM TO
THE GENTLEMEN OF THE BAND WISHING THEM A HAPPY NEW YEAR AND
ASK THE WORRIED STRING PLAYERS TO CHEER UP. EVERYONE HERE IN
COLUMBIA CRAZY ABOUT OUR RECORDS. ONE HARDBOILED ENGINEER
HAD EVEN TEARS IN HIS EYES.

These recordings reveal, for the first time, how responsive, disciplined, and cohesive the orchestra had become under Rodzinski. The ensemble heard here bears little resemblance to the Cleveland Orchestra of 1928 in terms of confidence or character. Rodzinski comes across as a no-nonsense conductor who favors generally brisk tempos (perhaps required by recording length limits, yet not sounding rushed) and animated playing. Even without enough strings, the performances are penetrating and clear.

Rodzinski's account of *Scheherazade* (included on the orchestra's 75th-anniversary compact-disc set) compares favorably with later versions that have better recorded sound. Even as heard in mono, the performance possesses a wonderful sense of romantic sweep and dramatic flair. In his telegram, Rodzinski was correct about Josef Fuchs: the concertmaster's violin solos are silvery and seductive. But this *Scheherazade* has so much more. Its sound is luxuriant (the strings, though limited in number, are close to the microphone) and shaped with a keen ear for detail. Throughout the recording, the pictorial elements in Rimsky-Korsakov's score are depicted with swashbuckling and alluring personality.

Rodzinski's Cleveland recordings tend to be much faster—startlingly so, in some cases—than more recent performances, but they don't lack depth. In *Finlandia*, he builds a reading of immense pride and lyrical finesse. Rodzinski's Tchaikovsky Fifth doesn't brood or wallow, as it can under some conductors, but instead sounds buoyant and confident. The horn solo in the second movement, played by Rudolph Puletz, is so poetic that one can understand why Rodzinski once stopped a performance of the Fifth Symphony featuring Puletz, turned to his listeners, asked if they'd ever heard anything more beautiful—and then repeated the movement from the top.

❋   ❋   ❋

Early in January 1940, Columbia producers and engineers returned to Severance Hall for more recording sessions. During five days, they completed the Tchaikovsky Fifth, continued *Heldenleben* (two sections of which were rejected and redone later in the year), and set down performances of Debussy's *La Mer* (not released, but recorded again in December 1941) and Jaromir Weinberger's *Under the Spreading Chestnut Tree*, with chorus director Boris Goldovsky as pianist.

The Weinberger, a series of variations on the old English song, was the first Rodzinski-Cleveland recording to be released, just a month after the January sessions, at $4.50 for the two-disk album. "The performance leaves nothing to be desired," wrote Arthur Loesser in the *Press*, "and is fully worthy of the very high standards that the Cleveland Orchestra has set." The review makes no mention of Rodzinski, who deserves credit for recording a work that was new in 1939. He emphasizes the festive and dreamy writing, which sometimes sounds like a Bohemian version of "Over the Rainbow" (coincidentally, *The Wizard of Oz* was released the same year). There is even Munchkin-like music, to which Rodzinski gives delicious treatment, as he does the exuberant fugue that comes near the work's end.

The second release was *Scheherazade*, which would prove to be one of Rodzinski's finest Cleveland recordings, though the conductor was not entirely satisfied when it was released soon after the Weinberger. Detecting a tonal flaw in the recording, he asked Columbia producer Moses Smith to investigate why this would happen if the company, as they claimed, had the best equipment. "The play-backs on this were so extraordinarily fine that it is extremely disappointing to me to note this defect in the commercial releases," he wrote to Smith. Rodzinski wasn't pleased with something else: Vosburgh told Smith that the conductor was unhappy about the company's catalogue of recordings. "You tout Barbirolli and Mitropoulos to the skies and practically give nothing on Rodzinski outside his life history," wrote Vosburgh in November 1940. "You will also hear more of this in Cleveland, I am sure."

Smith likely did hear more from Rodzinski in person two weeks later. The second series of Columbia sessions was held in December 1940, when the orchestra and Rodzinski entered into a flurry of activity. In three days of sessions over a 12-day period, they finished *Ein Heldenleben*, redid Mussorgsky's *Khovantchina* prelude, began Ravel's *Rapsodie espagnole* (completed the following April), and recorded the Berg Violin Concerto (with Louis Krasner as soloist), Strauss's *Till Eulenspiegel's Merry Pranks* and *Der*

Rosenkavalier waltzes, and Tchaikovsky's *Romeo and Juliet* fantasy-overture and *Marche slav*. The label on the *Marche slav* disks lists Rodzinski as conductor, as does a later performance of the *1812 Overture*, though associate conductor Rudolph Ringwall claimed he conducted both recordings.

Why *Heldenleben* proved such a trial is not clear from the recording, a bold performance propelled by Rodzinski's fastidious attention to motion and nuance. The account possesses equal amounts of warmth and swagger, with a fierce battle section and lyrical final pages (hornist Puletz and violinist Fuchs caress Strauss's tender phrases). This recording, as well as his *Till Eulenspiegel* and *Rosenkavalier* waltz disks, shows Rodzinski to be a first-rate Strauss conductor. His *Till Eulenspiegel* is extremely merry, a bit untidy in the brass, yet full of character. The *Rosenkavalier* waltzes avoid piling up the schmaltz.

Columbia at first balked at recording the Berg concerto, a work that features 12-tone music (however poetic). But the sympathetic reading of the solo part by Krasner (who commissioned the score) justifies Rodzinski's advocacy of the work. It is detailed and impassioned, with a striking air of desperation in the second movement. The final section, in which Berg harmonizes a Bach chorale to convey his grief over the death of young Manon Gropius, sounds like a benediction. The orchestra handles the intricate writing securely.

While longtime principal oboist Philip Kirchner sometimes produced a squeezed tone on Rodzinski's recordings, he sounds noble in Mussorgsky's *Khovantchina* prelude, which is lovely. The conductor's performance of Tchaikovsky's *Romeo and Juliet* captures the score's mystery, ardor, and tragedy without letting the intensity flag. Whether conducted by Rodzinski or Ringwall, *Marche slav* is vividly defined and no mere showpiece, though it probably would sound even more smashing in stereophonic sound.

The next four recordings were made (and, in the case of *Rapsodie espagnole*, completed) in mid-April 1941. Rodzinski's limber rhythmic approach and his attention to balances and tuning are ideal for the two French scores. Berlioz's *Symphonie fantastique* is enchanting. There are letdowns caused by the recording process (boomy timpani, distant harp and wind lines), but the drug-induced scenarios are vibrantly propelled by the conductor's judicious, and never hectic, pacing, and his masterful way of relaxing when the landscapes needs space.

A hint of how *Lady Macbeth of Mzensk* must have sounded at its American premiere can be gleaned from Rodzinski's recording of Shostakovich's Symphony No. 1. Quicker than most accounts (except Toscanini's), the performance bursts with brilliance. Finally, on its third try, the

Cleveland Orchestra recorded a complete performance of the *1812 Overture*. But again, the musicians and recording engineers didn't get it quite right. The orchestra is alert, occasionally imprecise. It is much larger than the ensembles on the 1924 and 1927 recordings and therefore juicier. But this doesn't sound like Rodzinski at the helm. Everything is competent, a bit ordinary, lacking Rodzinski's pervasive zeal. The cannon shots are haphazard and some brass bloopers, as well as an exposed cough, can be heard along the battle route. Ringwall would have done himself no favor by taking credit for this recording.

❊   ❊   ❊

Between these recordings and the next sessions, at the end of December 1941, Columbia's Smith asked Rodzinski if he would be willing to make recordings with the New York Philharmonic while serving as guest conductor. "I think that your conducting a session with the Philharmonic for us would be not only a good thing for the Columbia Recording Corporation and a good thing for you, but also for the Cleveland Orchestra," wrote Smith. The board of the Musical Arts Association at first looked skeptically at the proposal, but voted that it had no legal means to stand in Rodzinski's way. What's more, Smith was right: Cleveland stood to benefit from the recordings through the extra publicity garnered by its conductor. The following season was to be the Philharmonic's 100th, when Rodzinski would share the podium—and possible recording dates—with such distinguished colleagues as Dimitri Mitropoulos, the Boston Symphony's Serge Koussevitzky, and the Cincinnati Symphony's Eugene Goossens.

Rodzinski's final 1941 sessions in Cleveland took place on December 28 and 29. These recordings feature a richly varied repertoire, from Beethoven's Symphony No. 1 and Sibelius's Symphony No. 5 to two French scores (Debussy's *La Mer* and Ravel's *Daphnis et Chloé* Suite No. 2) to Kern's *Show Boat* synthesis and Armas Järnefelt's brief *Praeludium*. Rodzinski began recording Mendelssohn's incidental music to *A Midsummer Night's Dream* at these sessions and completed it two months later during his final sessions with the orchestra.

The Beethoven recording provides a portrait of the ensemble that so impressed Szell—a commanding interpreter of Beethoven symphonies—when he heard it for the first time during a concert under Rodzinski at Carnegie Hall on February 6, 1940. The program included *Scheherazade*, *Till Eulenspiegel*, and the Sibelius Fifth. "There was discipline and cleanliness in its playing," Szell said later. He probably would have admired only some of the Beethoven First recording. Rodzinski infuses the opening movement with enormous energy but slows down markedly at certain points, something Szell would avoid. Yet the ensemble playing is first rate and Rodzinski is meticulous in bringing out contrasting dynamics and articulations. It is the only work from the Classical era he recorded in Cleveland.

Rodzinski's recording of the Sibelius Fifth, made the same day, is one of his grandest Cleveland performances. There are moments of golden sonority amid the basically brisk pacing. The orchestral cleanliness that Szell noted can be discerned in this proud reading, from the sun-drenched horn opening to the quickly dispatched final chords. Only a few too many breaths in the trumpet in the last movement distract from the overall excellence.

Rodzinski again proves his mettle as a man of the theater in his recording of the Kern *Show Boat* synthesis. The piece, a symphonic narrative woven from the work's famous tunes, abounds in Kern's inimitable melodic genius. Rodzinski and the orchestra play it with great warmth and vitality, revealing why the score was so popular in its day. Moving later in this recording session to the Ravel and Debussy pieces, Rodzinski deftly evokes the composers' individual sound worlds. The Ravel is notable for Maurice Sharp's flute solo, George Rowe's spunky E-flat clarinet, and the ensemble's unbuttoned revelry in the final 5/4 dance. *La Mer* is restrained and majestic, benefiting from the orchestra's corporate precision (a few brass inaccuracies aside) and vivid sense of detail.

One more session wrapped up the recording relationship between Rodzinski and the orchestra. It was the last, in part, because James C. Petrillo, president of the American Federation of Musicians, placed a ban on all recording activity in the United States starting August 1, 1942, believing that commercial recordings were taking performance jobs away from union members. In one day (February 22, 1942), Rodzinski and his ensemble completed *A Midsummer Night's Dream* (Scherzo) and recorded four demanding scores: Ravel's *Alborado del gracioso*, Shostakovich's Symphony No. 5, Weber's *Der Freischütz* overture, and the "Dance of the Seven Veils" from Strauss's *Salome*.

The most impressive selections are the Shostakovich and Strauss, which suit the conductor's artistic temperament to a remarkable degree. The Shostakovich Fifth has towering climaxes within vividly defined structures. Rodzinski neither overplays the bombast nor neglects the poetry. Strauss's libidinous teenager, on the other hand, is a wild child—vehement, sensual, and glittering. The Weber, Ravel, and Mendelssohn are vibrant performances with fine solo playing and solid ensemble work.

Regarded as a whole, Rodzinski's recordings summarize his Cleveland legacy. They debunk the idea that an orchestra of distinction sprang only later from the baton of Szell. Rodzinski set standards that established Cleveland as a center of symphonic (and, for a short period, operatic) performance, even though other cities had longer histories of musical achievement and Cleveland's size and location didn't always benefit the orchestra's position in the hierarchy of national ensembles. Rodzinski may have been looking for ultimate artistic fulfillment elsewhere throughout much of his tenure, but his recordings with the Cleveland Orchestra provide forceful evidence that his commitment to the ensemble never flagged, and they document his lasting impact on it.

New York Beckons

Artur Rodzinski's accomplishments in Cleveland were accompanied by achievements elsewhere. Almost from the moment he took over the orchestra, he was in demand for engagements in Europe and, especially, in New York, where the Philharmonic showed increasing interest in his presence as a guest. No one doubted Rodzinski's devotion to Cleveland; the product spoke for itself. But musicians, board members, and the public often wondered whether their conductor really intended to make Severance Hall his home or whether he was only passing through.

Clevelanders actually were flattered when Rodzinski was invited to make his debut with the New York Philharmonic, the nation's most venerable orchestra, in November and December 1934. His Cleveland players even rallied around him, sending a telegram the day of his first Philharmonic concert (November 22) expressing confidence that he would succeed. The telegram was signed, "Eighty of Us." Rodzinski bowled everyone over at Carnegie Hall, including the Philharmonic's tough musicians. Days later, Maurice van Praag, the orchestra's personnel manager, dispatched a congratulatory telegram to Cleveland's general manager, Carl Vosburgh:

WE THE PHILHARMONIC SYMPHONY ORCHESTRA OF NEW YORK WISH TO THANK YOU AND THE DIRECTORS FOR SENDING US DOCTORE RODZINSKI HE HAS INSPIRED US WITH HIS WONDERFUL CONDUCTING AND OUR ORCHESTRA FEEL THAT THE MEMBERS OF YOUR ORCHESTRA ARE INDEED FORTUNATE IN HAVING RODZINSKI AS THEIR MAESTRO REGARDS.

Vosburgh, writing to Rodzinski that Cleveland was thinking about him, sounded an early signal of hometown anxiety: "Cheerio for now and do not become too enamoured with the big city and the musical life there. 'We miss you very much in Cleveland.'"

Neither Rodzinski, nor his orchestra—nor the Philharmonic—knew that events soon would raise him to an even more prominent place in the musical world. Among his major advocates was the conductor who was esteemed above all others of the period—Arturo Toscanini. The maestro had come to admire Rodzinski, welcoming him to his homes in the United States and Europe to discuss music and life. He once helped Rodzinski with shoulder pains by sending him to a doctor in Italy who had treated Toscanini for similar problems. He was happy to secure the Cleveland Orchestra's conductor an engagement at the Salzburg Festival, one the world's most prestigious summer music festivals, in 1936.

At Salzburg, Rodzinski was in towering company, sharing the Vienna Philharmonic's podium with Toscanini (who attended Rodzinski's rehearsals and concert), Bruno Walter, and Felix Weingartner. After conducting Shostakovich's First Symphony, Wilhelm Jerger's Partita, and Franz Schmidt's Concertante, with Paul Wittgenstein as piano soloist, Rodzinski was compared with Toscanini by the critic of the *Salzburger Volksblatt*. The critic wrote that Rodzinski is "a master of economy in the moving of his hands, except for the individual fingers of his left hand which are a little more lively than with Toscanini. For the rest, he is the same type, a man who knows his business, conducting from memory, obtaining clarity of real artistic purity in the orchestra crescendos. Being younger, he is still softer, still a little less inexorable than his model, but the command of the subject as well as of the orchestra is already of distinguished quality." Seated in the audience was Musical Arts Association president Dudley Blossom, who sent a cable back to Cleveland celebrating its conductor's triumph.

Even before Salzburg, Rodzinski had received an encouraging sign of Toscanini's approval. Upon announcing that he would step down as conductor of the New York Philharmonic at the end of the 1936–37 season and return to Europe, Toscanini encouraged the Philharmonic to engage Rodzinski as a guest conductor.

Many people in Cleveland and elsewhere misconstrued the Philharmonic's invitation to Rodzinski to lead 12 weeks of concerts during 1936–37 as an outright invitation to become principal conductor. The rumors hit Cleveland like a thunderbolt. "I have heard nothing of any such move," Adella Prentiss Hughes told the *Cleveland News*. Rodzinski, answering a testy group of trustees in Cleveland, said he indeed had been contacted about a prolonged guest stint in New York, but that no offer had been made. The offer soon was tendered, and the Cleveland trustees agreed to let Rodzinski accept eight weeks of concerts with the Philharmonic. Harriet C. Waltz, secretary to headmaster Joel B. Hayden at Western Reserve Academy in Hudson, let Rodzinski know that she was happy about the

Philharmonic invitation, adding, "but may we insert this little ever-so-earnest hope that you won't desert us?"

News of the Philharmonic engagements brought conductors in Cleveland and abroad out of the woodwork. Among the musicians who desired to fill Rodzinski's shoes temporarily (or longer) were associate conductor Rudolph Ringwall and choral director Boris Goldovsky. Another hopeful was composer, annotator, and *Plain Dealer* critic Herbert Elwell, who, according to board minutes, "formally requested that he be engaged for a pair of symphony concerts." Vosburgh received one telegram containing a suggestion, from the agent Eric Simon in Paris, that proved to be a decade early: PLEASE URGE POSSIBLY [*sic*] ENGAGEMENT CONDUCTOR GEORG SZELL REPLACING RODZINSKI.

✿　　✿　　✿

The Cleveland trustees braced themselves for what they believed would be the inevitable—Rodzinski's departure at the end of the 1937–38 season. They sanctioned two weeks of concerts to be led by Mexican conductor-composer Carlos Chávez, who had just had a big success at Severance Hall. Chávez was "a distinctly likely successor," Vosburgh told the board.

Toscanini's third choice to be his successor (after Furtwängler and Fritz Busch) was Rodzinski, though his advocacy came to nothing. In a strange power play that would have ramifications for years, Arthur Judson, manager of the Philharmonic and also Rodzinski's personal manager, talked his board into hiring John Barbirolli, the gifted but inexperienced British conductor, as Toscanini's successor. Rodzinski was shocked. "Plot!" he exclaimed when he heard of the Barbirolli appointment. Toscanini thickened the plot with a stunning decision. He announced that he would return to New York and accept a proposal by the National Broadcasting Company to conduct a newly formed symphony orchestra in weekly radio broadcasts. Among the more startling aspects was his suggestion—translation: demand—that Rodzinski be hired to form, train, and co-conduct the orchestra. "Thus, in accepting an offer from NBC, Judson's and the Philharmonic's Columbia Network competitor, Maestro could show his pique," wrote Halina Rodzinski. "His point: if the Philharmonic had no faith in Rodzinski's talents, let that august body see what Rodzinski can do by making an orchestra that will satisfy Toscanini. Nothing could have given Artur a sweeter taste of artistic revenge."

For Cleveland, these fractious New York doings were starting to leave a bittersweet taste, though the Musical Arts Association put a happy face on the NBC situation, saying it was an honor (which it was) for Rodzinski and (less so) for Cleveland. But not only would Rodzinski be splitting his time between the two cities; he would be creating an orchestra that he, Toscanini, and others would conduct on the same radio network that broadcast Cleveland Orchestra concerts.

Rodzinski did his utmost to prove that he wasn't on the way out. "I am thoroughly convinced after our talk and after reading your letter," board president Blossom wrote to Rodzinski, "that you are for Cleveland first and foremost, and that you will continue to be an enthusiastic Cleveland musician as long as Cleveland evidences a desire to have you here—which I am sure will be for many years." Rodzinski protested publicly when rumors about his supposed departure continued to spread. "My work in Cleveland never will be finished musically and Cleveland is my love," he said. "Why do people always want to make trouble for me and spread the reports that I am going elsewhere?"

Reports of Cleveland Orchestra players going elsewhere turned out to be true. NBC contractor H. Leopold Spitalny, a former Clevelander, had approached several musicians in his hometown with offers to join the new NBC Symphony. Rodzinski didn't put a halt to a raid on his own orchestra. Principal oboist Philip Kirchner turned down Spitalny, but principal violist Carlton Cooley, principal bassoonist William Polisi, and principal hornist Albert Stagliano evidently decided they couldn't pass up the chance to play for Toscanini—or secure 52 weeks of employment at salaries far higher than their Cleveland fees.

The new orchestra promised to be a dazzling conglomeration of talent. Rodzinski had persuaded RCA president David Sarnoff, the brains behind the NBC Symphony, to create a 92-member ensemble made up of the best players from NBC's staff orchestra augmented by superb musicians from other orchestras. Attending NBC auditions in New York, Norman Siegel, radio editor of the *Cleveland Press*, reported that Rodzinski "hears about 60 or 70 applicants a day. And, he estimates that before he's through he will have listened to between 400 and 500 musicians." Yet when NBC officials didn't appreciate Rodzinski's harsh treatment of the musicians in early rehearsals, they entrusted the orchestra's two opening broadcasts in November 1937 to Pierre Monteux. Rodzinski, who had done virtually all of the preliminary work, was left to conduct three broadcasts in December prior to Toscanini's first, historic concert on Christmas Day.

Despite the frustrations that must have surrounded his work with the NBC Symphony, helping to create an ensemble for Toscanini provided a much-needed morale boost for Rodzinski at this time. Not only had the Philharmonic hired Barbirolli over him, but the Cleveland Orchestra's board had discontinued his operatic productions at Severance Hall and continued to resist his call for expanding the orchestra. The death of John L. Severance in early 1936 deprived him of the father figure who had responded to his artistic needs and temperament.

Institutional uncertainty was magnified by the deaths in 1938 of trustee Frank Ginn and board president Dudley Blossom. Ginn, who had watched orchestra budgets vigilantly and overseen the triumphant completion of Severance Hall, died in February. Blossom's death in October ended a distinguished chapter in the orchestra's and the city's history.

❖   ❖   ❖

Rodzinski could have withdrawn completely from his Philharmonic engagements after Barbirolli's appointment, but he chose to continue as a guest, perhaps hoping the top job might some day still be his. In the meantime, he immersed himself in his Cleveland duties, making his series of excellent recordings and dealing boldly—if sometimes eccentrically—with challenges presented by the board and the war. At one point, members of the board decided they had to resolve certain touchy issues, including Rodzinski's impatience with his musicians, and so scheduled a meeting with their conductor. Rodzinski wasn't about to be browbeaten. He called chief stagehand Bill Ables (or possibly, according to others, baggage master George Higgins) and asked him to place a stepladder at the far end of the boardroom. When the trustees arrived, Rodzinski was sitting atop the ladder, looking imperiously down on them. Nothing was resolved that day.

Important personnel matters were at times decided by Uncle Sam, and at other times by the orchestra's lean checkbook. As players were called to military service, Rodzinski had to fill positions, including principal chairs, without being able to promise that these jobs would be there once the war was over. Ethics, and humanity, demanded that players who had gone to war be employed when they returned. For Hugo Kolberg, the ensemble's concertmaster for one season, the problem was money. The orchestra said farewell to him in the spring of 1942 (soon after he participated in Rodzinski's final Cleveland recordings) and hired Tossy Spivakovsky, a former concertmaster of the Berlin Philharmonic.

Spivakovsky was only two months into his tenure as concertmaster when a stunning announcement, appearing in newspapers on December 29, 1942, put an end to all conjecture about Rodzinski's plans for the future. The maestro had accepted the New York Philharmonic's offer to become musical director and conductor starting with the 1943–44 season. Barbirolli had failed to excite New York audiences or critics. Arthur Judson, who had worked hard to foil Rodzinski's ascension to Cleveland in 1933 (and failed) and New York in 1936 (and succeeded), switched gears in 1943 and opened his arms to the conductor at the Philharmonic—for the time being, anyway.

One conductor who admired Rodzinski's work with the Cleveland Orchestra sent him a note the day of the announcement. "Although we don't really know each other personally . . . may I take the liberty of congratulating you and specially the 'Philharmonic' on to-day's good news," wrote George Szell. "It is gratifying to see that somehow, sometimes—of late—the right thing happens to the right person and I feel confident that my impulse as a concertgoer to hear more of the Philharmonic concerts next year than in the past few years will be shared by many thousands of music lovers."

To say that the Rodzinski news surprised Cleveland would be a vast understatement. "When the New York Philharmonic announced his becoming their conductor, that was the first anyone in the Cleveland Orchestra management knew about it," recalled Vosburgh's widow, more than half a century later. "Carl was so shocked!" If so, Vosburgh didn't let on to the public. Nor did he suggest that life with Rodzinski had been anything less than rosy. "I think he did a swell job here," Vosburgh told a reporter the day of the announcement.

Rodzinski was instantly transformed into the orchestra's lame-duck conductor. The media lost no time speculating on successors. The day news of Rodzinski's appointment broke, Milton Widder suggested in the *Press* that Cleveland had the options of hiring a well-known conductor or an unknown—"as they did in the case of Rodzinski 10 years ago"—or presenting a season of guest conductors, with Ringwall heading the roster. Then Widder provided a lengthy list of possibilities for the post, including two conductors who recently had appeared as guests—Herman Adler, from Prague, and Efrem Kurtz, former conductor of the Monte Carlo Ballet Russe. His list bulged with intriguing names, some of which would be considered seriously by the orchestra's board: Howard Barlow, Sir Thomas Beecham, Frank Black, Vladimir Golschmann, Edwin McArthur, Dimitri Mitropoulos, Erno Rapee, Fritz Reiner, William Steinberg, George Szell, and Alfred Wallenstein.

As always with conductor searches, the president of the orchestra's board had principal input in the process. In 1943, the president was Thomas L. Sidlo, who had succeeded Blossom in 1939. Sidlo had tried, in vain, to forge a fruitful relationship with Rodzinski. A Cleveland native whose parents were Czech immigrants, Sidlo was already a formidable presence in the city's cultural and social circles. In 1916, he had been invited by former Cleveland mayor (and soon-to-be U.S. secretary of war) Newton D. Baker to be a founding partner in his law firm, which became Baker, Hostetler, Sidlo & Patterson (today known as Baker & Hostetler). Sidlo's biggest assignment was as general counselor and controller of the Scripps-Howard newspaper empire. By the age of 50, Sidlo had made enough money to retire from business and devote himself to his interests, including music. As chairman of the Northern Ohio Opera Association, which sponsored the Metropolitan Opera's annual spring visits to Public Auditorium, and president of the Musical Arts Association, he was dubbed "Mr. Music." Sidlo was generous and eloquent. He donated abundant time and money but also lived the high life.

Relations between Sidlo and Rodzinski deteriorated rapidly in the final months of the conductor's tenure. News that the Philharmonic might hire Cleveland players made the papers, prompting Rodzinski to deny allegations of "labor-pirating" and exclaim, disingenuously, that he was "very happy to leave [the orchestra] untouched, just the way it is." He didn't, and Sidlo sparred with him over the resignations of two key Cleveland musicians, principal cellist Leonard Rose and principal violist William Lincer, who had decided to join the conductor in New York.

It is no wonder, therefore, that the board president would ignore Rodzinski's advice to hire Golschmann, Reiner, Szell, or Wallenstein as his successor. Sidlo had another candidate in mind—Erich Leinsdorf, the Viennese-born conductor and former Toscanini assistant who had succeeded Artur Bodanzky as head of German repertoire at the Met. Sidlo had become impressed with Leinsdorf during the Metropolitan Opera's performances in Cleveland, starting in 1939, but particularly in the spring of 1941, when he led *Die Walküre* featuring Kirsten Flagstad, Rose Bampton, Kerstin Thorborg, Lauritz Melchior, Emanuel List, and Julius Huehn.

While Cleveland waited to learn about its new conductor, however, three months of unprecedented intrigue ensued. On December 30, 1942, the day after the announcement of Rodzinski's appointment to the Philharmonic, Nikolai Sokoloff, who had returned to Severance Hall three weeks previously to lead concerts, contacted trustee Grover Higgins with an offer. "I know that it is not without precedent that a conductor returns to an orchestra after an absence of some years," wrote Sokoloff. "Gericke, for instance, was the conductor of the Boston Symphony for some years, left for a period of years and returned to conduct it again. I was very pleased to find that I still have a strong following in Cleveland." Sokoloff proposed a salary of $15,000 for a full season or $8,000 for half a season, leaving the orchestra the option to engage guest conductors for the remaining concerts. There is no indication that Sokoloff's proposal was ever considered.

Possibly feeling the need to calm his Cleveland players, Rodzinski made a suggestion regarding his successor that must have seemed radical at the time (and, to some extent, still seems so today). "I would take the choice of the orchestra men above anyone else's," he told a reporter. "After the four or five guest conductors are heard next season, the men should be polled by secret ballot and their choice should have a paramount voice in the selection."

Sidlo and the board were impatient, however. They clearly wanted a new conductor in place for the 1943–44 season, though the president made noises about a season of guest conductors. He also admitted that the possibility of hiring an American was remote, as "the number of available American conductors with the proper experience is very low." In any case, Sidlo told the board, Cleveland would expect the Musical Arts Association to continue the policies of "one of the great Orchestras of the world—easily in the first six, perhaps the fourth in quality." Some writers immediately speculated that the top contenders were two conductors active on the New York scene—Reiner, a frequent guest of the Philharmonic, and Szell, who "even takes fire in such a drab war-horse as *Tannhäuser*" at the Met.

By February 19, 1943, an 11-trustee "conductorship committee" had decided that the orchestra needed Rodzinski's successor to be in place soon in order to firm up concert and tour plans for the coming season. They submitted to the board a list of 10 candidates, which included many names mentioned in speculative articles:

Howard Barlow, Musical Director of Columbia Broadcasting Company
Vladimir Golschmann, Conductor of the St. Louis Symphony Orchestra
Eugene Goossens, Conductor of the Cincinnati Symphony Orchestra
Erich Leinsdorf, Conductor of the Metropolitan Opera Company
Dimitri Mitropoulos, Conductor of the Minneapolis Symphony
Fritz Reiner, Conductor of the Pittsburgh Symphony Orchestra
Rudolph Ringwall, Associate Conductor of the Cleveland Orchestra
Albert Stoessel, Head [*sic*] of the Juilliard School, and Conductor of the
    New York Oratorio Society, the Worcester Festival and the Chautauqua
    Symphony Orchestra
George Szell, Conductor of the Metropolitan Opera Company
Alfred Wallenstein, Conductor of the *Firestone Hour* and other radio programs

This board meeting may have been Sidlo's finest hour. An impassioned speaker, he let flow the words in a big way to persuade the board that great things lay ahead, despite budgetary constraints. The climax of the speech was a stream of oratory worthy of an expert lawyer:

> Do we wish to be Little Clevelanders, with our outlook envisaging no more than the limits of our own community, satisfied with a mediocre orchestra and indifferent to what other communities think of it or us, and surrendering every claim to greatness that we have earned by dint of so much toil and sacrifice; or do we want to be Great Clevelanders, men and women who take pride in their city and in the esteem and regard of the outside world, who want our Orchestra to continue to be one of our chief instruments and symbols of community achievement and civic worth, who get real inspiration and have justifiable pride in hearing our orchestra on the air waves of the world, its recordings played in thousands of homes throughout the land, and giving concerts in scores of American cities that tell in their way the kind of city that Cleveland is?

Trustees on the board of the Musical Arts Association—charged with all sorts of institutional decisions, including choosing the chief conductor—were hardly unanimous in their views of the search process. Elizabeth Blossom, widow of Dudley Blossom, suggested that a season of guest conductors would provide a better means of assessing candidates. Victor B. Phillips stated that making a selection too quickly could hurt the orchestra. Others urged that a young conductor be engaged. Russell Morgan, longtime director of music of the Cleveland Public Schools, appeared to criticize Rodzinski when he said that the orchestra should engage "a normal human being, not exotic, remote and shut-off." The trustees got things off their chests and then, pressured by Sidlo and others, voted to engage a permanent conductor as quickly as possible. The five-member committee charged with choosing the final candidate included Sidlo, Percy W. Brown, Edgar A. Hahn, Charles B. Merrill, and Lewis B. Williams.

The day after this meeting, news arrived that Rodzinski, with the blessing of manager Judson, was firing 14 members of the Philharmonic—including concertmaster Mishel Piastro—whom he had been observing closely during rehearsals and concerts. The action provoked an "open civil war," with the Philharmonic players enlisting the services of the musicians' union and even receiving a message of sympathy from Cleveland's orchestra committee (Warren Burkhart, LeRoy Collins, Philip Farkas, Fred Rosenberg, and Leonard Rose). Rodzinski took the barrage of criticism, even answering a gentle rebuke from First Lady Eleanor Roosevelt, but prevailed. "I had plenty of troubles with the 'sweet' boys of the Philharmonic," he wrote to Cleveland Orchestra violinist Jac Gorodetsky , who then was playing in the 3rd Army Air Force Band in Boca Raton, Florida. "Everything looks much better right now, and I hope that everything will be settled satisfactorily very soon." Satisfactorily for Rodzinski, that is: the 14 fired Philharmonic musicians were put in the uncomfortable position of having to play the remainder of the season knowing they soon would be out of jobs.

News about the search for Rodzinski's successor was beginning to leak out in Cleveland. In the *Cleveland News*, Elmore Bacon proclaimed six conductors to be possible finalists, hitting the target with the names Golschmann, Leinsdorf, Mitropoulos, Ringwall, and Szell, but making the erroneous assumption that German conductor Erich Kleiber—who had been on the search list in 1932—was also being considered. In March 1943, the trustees quietly brought Leinsdorf, Szell, and Stoessel to town for interviews. With Rodzinski conducting concerts, Leinsdorf and Szell being sized up as his successor, and a young maestro named Lorin Maazel making his debut with the orchestra, a total of four Cleveland Orchestra music directors, present and future, were in town in a single month.

Maazel, then only 13, had been called "the prodigy of the century" by Leopold Stokowski and "the second Mozart" by others for his concerts with the NBC Symphony, Los Angeles Philharmonic, New York Philharmonic, and, most recently, his hometown orchestra, the Pittsburgh Symphony. Rodzinski took a moment before conducting the last piece on his March 11 concert to defend himself for deciding to leave for New York. He also introduced Maazel to the audience: "The Cleveland Orchestra will have a new conductor at the Pension Fund concert Sunday. Look him over carefully and use your own judgment concerning him. He wouldn't fit in as a conductor to go around to cocktail parties. A nursing bottle of milk would be more appropriate as he's a mere child. Look him over, he may be your next conductor."

Appearing with the Cleveland Orchestra on March 14 at Public Music Hall in its third annual Pension Fund concert, Maazel (dressed in short pants) and 14-year-old violinist Patricia Travers delighted listeners and critics. The miniature maestro led Wagner's *Rienzi* overture, Schubert's "Unfinished" Symphony, Mussorgsky's *A Night on Bald Mountain*, and Liszt's *Les Préludes*. "The orchestra played well for this young man, who made a pleasant appearance, free from any trace of affectation," Herbert Elwell wrote in *The Plain Dealer*. "Far from showing any signs of exhibitionism, he appeared to be honestly engrossed in the music, at least to the full extent that his present emotional equipment is able to carry him. Although there is still something calf-like about his muscular co-ordination, his work is already mature enough to claim serious attention and it has many signs of great promise." The orchestra's guest is "a real conductor," wrote Arthur Loesser in the *Press*. "Master Maazel is extraordinarily gifted and has studied well. We look forward to his progress with great interest."

Maazel's debut was followed two weeks later by another milestone, the 45th anniversary of the start of Adella Prentiss Hughes's career as the city's top impresario. At a party given by friends on March 29, 1943, Hughes received a three-week-old puppy and other tokens of affection. "Before the Adelian era," Edgar A. Hahn told *The Plain Dealer*, "Cleveland was almost a musical desert, whereas it is now a garden spot, thanks largely to the indomitable zeal of this intrepid woman." Spirits probably weren't as high at Hughes's party as they might have been, for Sergei Rachmaninoff, whose relationship with the Cleveland Orchestra as both composer and pianist had spanned two decades, had died the day before at his home in Beverly Hills.

Two days after the Hughes party, the full board of the Musical Arts Association gathered for what must have been one of the most dissonant meetings in its history. Sidlo prefaced his recommendation of Leinsdorf as the next conductor with a long speech defending the choice. No, he said, Leinsdorf didn't have a large symphonic repertoire or vast experience conducting symphony orchestras. No, he didn't have the credits in touring, broadcasting, or recording that might be desired. But these were disadvantages that could be turned into advantages, Sidlo suggested, in fluent lawyerese: "He has given such outstanding proof of capacity for rapid, continued and sustained growth, and his record along this line has been so unique among all living American conductors, that we feel we are not speculating with uncertainty but are rather availing ourselves of one of the most promising opportunities that any orchestral board has ever been presented with."

Describing the search process, Sidlo revealed that Dimitri Mitropoulos and Alfred Wallenstein had withdrawn their candidacies. Columbia Records, with which the orchestra still had a contract, had lobbied for Fritz Reiner, conductor of the Pittsburgh Symphony. The list of candidates had been whittled down to four candidates—Golschmann, Leinsdorf, Stoessel, and Szell—after which Szell had been dropped, for no clear reason.

Sidlo employed some careful editing to push his case for Leinsdorf, quoting favorable reviews but not damaging ones, such as a notice Olin Downes had given the conductor several months before in the *New York Times* after a Met performance of *Tristan und Isolde* featuring Melchior, Helen Traubel, and Alexander Kipnis: "The principal defect in the performance was the headlong pace and the poorly controlled orchestra of Mr. Leinsdorf.

A born musician, and on occasions eloquently lyrical and communicative, he seems not always to realize what he intends when he leads. No doubt this is partly due to his relative inexperience, for Mr. Leinsdorf, still a young man, has learned most of his Wagnerian conducting at the Met. His short-comings may be his immaturity in practice rather than any deeper fault."

Was this the type of conductor the Cleveland Orchestra needed after Rodzinski? Board member Percy W. Brown didn't think so, and he cast the lone dissenting vote of the five-man search committee. Brown, who had been involved in orchestra affairs for more than a decade, especially in rais-ing maintenance funds, objected to Leinsdorf on several counts. "Our Orchestra is now mature and needs a mature conductor with wide experi-ence, which Mr. Leinsdorf lacks," said Brown in his minority report before coming to his main point. "But my primary objection is his draftability. Not only is he subject to the draft, but were he to escape it, the effect of his ex-emption on others who have entered the armed services and on civilians who have close relatives in the armed services would be such that I believe our orchestra board would be subject to criticism."

Brown initially had been taken with Szell, but when this conductor's name was dropped he instead recommended that the board hire Stoessel, who had conducted the orchestra several times—Leinsdorf never had—and whose proven abilities promised to make Cleveland "a greater center of music than it has ever been." According to Leinsdorf's memoirs, "the Dudley Blossoms" favored Golschmann, which although possible, is not ev-ident in the minutes of the March 31 meeting (and Dudley Blossom, in any case, had died in 1938). After much discussion, pro and con, about Leinsdorf, Sidlo took a vote of the board—20 in favor of the committee's recommendation, 5 opposed. Leinsdorf had the job.

He won it partly for a reason Sidlo had mentioned only fleetingly in his speech. Bluntly put, Leinsdorf was a bargain. He agreed to accept the post at a fee far below what Rodzinski had made—and even below Sokoloff's compensation for most of his tenure. Sokoloff's salary began at $6,000 in 1918 and rose to $30,000 for his last five seasons. Rodzinski, arriving in the midst of the Depression, started at $27,000, received $28,500 for his second season, and $30,000 for the next eight seasons (with some deductions for weeks he was out of town guest conducting the New York Philharmonic). In contrast, Leinsdorf accepted a three-year contract at 40 percent below Rodzinski's salary—$18,000 per season—along with a clause stating that the board could terminate the agreement after one or two seasons if things weren't working out.

Leinsorf clearly was exhilarated upon learning that he was Cleveland's new maestro. "A musician's job today is more than just going to rehearsals and conducting concerts," he said in Chicago, where he was conducting *Tristan*. "A conductor must become an integral part of the community where he works in order to make his instrument—the orchestra—speak not only for the great music it produces, but reflect the life and culture of the community."

An editorial in the *Cleveland Press* hailed the appointment: "In choosing Erich Leinsdorf as the future conductor of the Cleveland Orchestra, the orchestra board of trustees has speculated on talent, intelligence and youth rather than on established symphonic experience and achievement. In all probability it will turn out to be a wise speculation." A story in the *Press* the same day mentioned Leinsdorf's draft status as 3-A, though "trustees pointed out that he has a wife [an American, Ann Frohnknecht], son [David, nine months old] and two aged dependents."

Another story, in the *Cleveland News*, quoted Leinsdorf as saying that he had no intention of making personnel changes in Cleveland, a comfort, no doubt, to all who knew about the Rodzinski-Philharmonic brouhaha. "You have to know your orchestra before you can take the responsibility for any changes," Leinsdorf said. "The orchestra is new to me. I'll take over the baton with an open mind." Adella Prentiss Hughes, extremely pleased, found a fresh way to answer the experience issue. "I never heard him conduct a symphony," she remarked, "but I've heard him conduct Wagner, and what symphony is greater than that?"

Hughes's role in the Leinsdorf appointment was more cunning than board documents or newspaper stories could impart. As honorary vice president and secretary of the Musical Arts Association, she had lobbied heavily for Leinsdorf and instigated smear campaigns against Golschmann, Stoessel, and Szell, to the dismay of Percy W. Brown, who poured out his feelings in a poem, "To Adella Prentiss Hughes," in his personal notebook the day after the appointment:

Adella, friend of music, patroness
Of Cleveland's orchestra thro' many wars,
Defending you, my friend, I did profess
To all, your true devotion to its cause.
A new conductor, then, we had to choose,
We talked and parted, each to go each way,
Each honoring the other, win or lose,
I trusting in you in the coming affray.
But I fought fairly, you with poison gas

To choke opponents who might try to rise
And give supporting votes to mine—alas
Your rotten smear-campaign gave you the prize.
Although you think that you have gained your end,
My self-respect is won, you lose a friend.

Brown's lyrical diatribe wasn't the only condemnation of Hughes, nor the only opposition to the Leinsdorf appointment. Six of the 11 female trustees who attended the March 31 board meeting wrote a letter to Sidlo deploring the methods used during the meeting. They believed the vote had been pushed through too quickly, without providing adequate room for discussion. Unlike board minutes, in which they customarily used their husbands' first names, the letter was signed, "Florence Raymond Clark, Clara G. Bickford, Lucia McBride, Alice W. Teagle, Marion Halle Strauss, and Jane M. Bourne."

Ironically, Leinsdorf, though favored by Hughes, found her insufferable: "She acted as if she *were* the Cleveland Orchestra. There were some who not only disliked Mrs. Hughes with great passion but who would almost automatically vote against anything and anyone she promoted. She was, like many domineering women, truly formidable, full of vitality, peremptorily decisive, musically knowledgeable—which made her part of a minority on the board—and so direct as to be considered by softer and less-outspoken people rather tactless. At first it was considered a boon, then a drawback, that she became leader of the Leinsdorf faction."

Leinsdorf would have his chance to win over the community and at least part of the board. First, Cleveland had other business to complete— Rodzinski's tenure. He led his final concert as the orchestra's conductor on April 17, when he repeated much of the program with which he had made his debut more than a decade before: J. S. Bach's Toccata and Fugue in D minor (Wertheim transcription), Beethoven's Fifth, Richard Strauss's *Death and Transfiguration* (replacing Tchaikovsky's *Romeo and Juliet* and Stravinsky's *Petrouchka* suite), and Johann Strauss II's *Tales from the Vienna Woods* waltz. Sidlo, who came onstage at intermission to present the conductor with the gift of a silver tray, was "downright drunk," remembered Halina Rodzinski, "which became apparent as soon as he began a speech of presentation and farewell." The orchestra with which Rodzinski had collaborated so vibrantly (and so contentiously) was more than willing to celebrate his remarkable contribution. At the concert's end, the ensemble played the scherzo from Tchaikovsky's Fourth Symphony, unconducted, as a tribute. "My husband was spoiled by his decade in Cleveland," his wife would later

NEW YORK BECKONS   199

write, after Rodzinski had suffered torturous times in New York and Chicago and died in 1958, still artistically commanding but physically a shell of his former self.

Loesser summed up the departing maestro's tenure with a forthright and honest assessment. "Dr. Rodzinski's sojourn here was not a perpetual idyll of unclouded geniality," he wrote in the *Press*. "During his 10 years reports of numerous frictions of a personal and professional nature occurred between him and his associates. There were dismissals, resignations, recriminations, unfulfilled promises, frustrations and lacerated feelings. But none of these incidents could ever seriously impugn the general acceptance of his quality as a great musician and great conductor. The sincere and unprompted applause of the orchestra after the last two concerts is evidence of it. He is indeed one of a tiny handful of masters at the pinnacle of his profession."

No one yet knew if Leinsdorf could come close to being considered such a master. But Cleveland was about to find out.

− 14 −

Luckless Leinsdorf

*L*ife seemed to be going Erich Leinsdorf's way in the spring and summer of 1943. He had landed one of the top orchestra jobs in the country. He had fled the Metropolitan Opera, where an inadequate rehearsal policy and uncooperative singers had driven him to seek a less troubled existence in the realm of the symphony orchestra. Eager and resolute, Leinsdorf plunged into his Cleveland duties with the alacrity of a young man ready to conquer the musical world.

He had achieved much by the time he arrived at Severance Hall at the age of 31. Born in Vienna in February 1912, Leinsdorf was a fine pianist and accompanist by the age of 14. His ability to absorb orchestral scores quickly and play them at the piano led to appointments as conductor in small Italian cities. His engagement as conducting assistant to Bruno Walter at the Salzburg Festival in 1934 had a profound effect on his future: There, he met Arturo Toscanini, who hired him to play piano in Zoltán Kodály's *Psalmus Hungaricus* in Vienna. Toscanini became his mentor.

Leinsdorf continued to work at Salzburg with Toscanini and Walter until 1937, when Lotte Lehmann recommended him to another Viennese native, Artur Bodanzky, at the Met. Bodanzky had been looking for an assistant to relieve him of his heavy workload. Two previous young conductors, Karl Riedel and Maurice Abravanel, had not lived up to his expectations. But Leinsdorf did. Bodanzky "would sneak Leinsdorf in for an act at a time, to take over the conducting," recalled pianist Oscar Levant, who became a Leinsdorf friend. The young conductor got his big chance to lead a full performance on January 21, 1938, when he made his official debut conducting *Die Walküre* with a remarkable cast—Kirsten Flagstad, Paul Althouse, Elisabeth Rethberg, Kerstin Thorborg, Ludwig Hofmann, and Emanuel List. He followed up soon with *Elektra* and *Parsifal*, assignments that tested the budding conductor's mettle. He generally received little or no rehearsal before the curtain rose. Critics admired Leinsdorf's confidence and straightforward style, if not his flaccid way with rhythm and tendency to let the orchestra overwhelm the singers.

But his stock rose with a jolt when the 61-year-old Bodanzky died suddenly on November 23, 1939, as the Met season was about to open. Promoted to head of German repertoire, Leinsdorf conducted 55 performances his first season. He scuffled publicly with Danish Heldentenor Lauritz Melchior over issues of preparation and musical accuracy. But he won the respect of (most) Met artists and audiences. His appearances with the Met in Cleveland, starting in 1939, came to the attention of Adella Prentiss Hughes and Cleveland Orchestra board president Thomas L. Sidlo, who then became his champions in the search to replace the departing Artur Rodzinski.

Had his destiny been different, Leinsdorf might have effected a revolution in Cleveland. Speaking at the board's annual meeting in June 1943, he urged the trustees to consider a full-year schedule for the orchestra. "The highest excellence in quality can be achieved only if the orchestra will eventually develop from a seasonal institution to an institution which functions actively throughout the entire year," Leinsdorf said. "Only through permanence can music develop from a fine entertainment to become part of our spiritual life. Carnival is a short season. Church is open all year long. Music has such a range that it expresses with equal eloquence Carnival and Religion." He was aware that the times weren't quite ripe for expanding the orchestra, but they eventually would be—when the war was over: "Then will be the moment because we can not let down those who come back, and we can not dismiss those who have taken their places and who have proven their value."

His first order of business would be the daunting task of replacing musicians. At the end of the 1942–43 season, in the midst of World War II, the orchestra lost 22 musicians—more than a quarter of its players. Some went into military service; some joined other orchestras (such as principal cellist Leonard Rose and principal violist William Lincer, who went to Rodzinski's New York Philharmonic); others left the field to pursue new careers. Cleveland still couldn't muster salaries to compete with eastern orchestras; half of the 82 musicians received minimum scale, now $72 per week, for the 28-week season. Even so, Leinsdorf had no difficulty attracting musicians to auditions in New York in May 1943. He heard 125 players, occasionally serving as accompanist during the auditions (usually without using any printed music). Among the players he hired in New York and back in Cleveland were the orchestra's first female violinists, Madeleine Carabo and Evelyn

Botnick, and first female bass player, Nathalie Claire. His new principal bassoon was George Goslee; his new principal viola, Marcel Dick.

❁ ❁ ❁

Leinsdorf had to vie for attention with what many people considered Cleveland's biggest musical event of the year—the local debut of Frank Sinatra, with the Cleveland Summer Orchestra under Rudolph Ringwall on July 14 at Public Hall, performing favorites by Kern, Gershwin, and Porter. The media added to the frenzy. "Better get a tight rein on your libidos, girls. Frank Sinatra, America's latest heart crusher, is coming to town," began a *Cleveland News* story. Referring to Sinatra as the "No. 1 boudoir voice of the nation" in another story, the *News*'s Marjorie Western interviewed the singer and put a lackadaisical spin on the phenomenon. "Frank Sinatra is not the heart crusher I expected," she wrote. "He does not have the devastating charm of a Rudolph Valentino or Clark Gable. He is just a slender boy with an unruly head of black curls and a frightened smile." The heartthrob didn't exactly enthrall music critic Arthur Loesser. "As a mere musician, neither young nor female, I confess that the agitation in the audience seemed way out of proportion to what was taking place on the stage," he wrote in the *Press*. "Last night's Public Hall audience seemed a little overwrought, something like a bargain-counter rush at Woolworth's . . . Perhaps the orchestra made some new friends. Anyway, it made some money."

Once Sinatra left town, the orchestra could begin promoting Leinsdorf's first season. Among the soloists engaged were Yehudi Menuhin, Artur Rubinstein, Efrem Zimbalist, Josef Hofmann, Rudolf Serkin, and Helen Traubel. Leinsdorf was to have 16 weeks of subscription concerts and Ringwall two. Sir Thomas Beecham was coming as a guest conductor for one week. Yet another conductor promised to eclipse everyone: Toscanini, mentor to both Rodzinski and Leinsdorf. The previous December, Sidlo had telegrammed the maestro at NBC telling him that the Cleveland Orchestra would celebrate the 25th anniversary of its first concert in December 1943. "No greater honor could be ours than if we might have the privilege of your appearing in Cleveland that week conducting the Cleveland Orchestra," Sidlo wrote. In February, Toscanini's son, Walter, informed general manager Carl Vosburgh that December 16 and 18 would be suitable dates, and the engagement was set.

Another development would add prestige to Leinsdorf's first season: Vosburgh successfully negotiated a contract with the Mutual Broadcasting System and the United Broadcasting Company to air 28 live weekly radio

broadcasts on Sundays from 8 to 9 p.m. Not only would the orchestra receive handsome fees for the programs, it would also be heard with its new
conductor and guests on 209 stations in the United States, by wire direct to
33 stations in Mexico, and by short-wave transmissions to Europe, South
America, and the South Pacific. The concerts were also to be recorded for
rebroadcast to military zones overseas. Leinsdorf encouraged the orchestra
to reach out to local audiences by making program notes for each week's
concerts available a week in advance to prepare them for the Severance Hall
performance.

The Plain Dealer's Herbert Elwell was amazed that Leinsdorf managed
to do at least one other thing his predecessors couldn't. "Neither of the former conductors of the Cleveland Orchestra seems to have been able to plan
an entire season in advance," he wrote in September. "Hence, the fact that
Leinsdorf has already announced all his programs has been advertised as a
remarkable accomplishment. To persons who are attracted to the concert
by the music that is to be played, rather than the names of the soloists who
are to play it, the advance announcement of the season's repertoire will be
gratifying." Leinsdorf's first season would include a mix of traditional and
contemporary fare. There was to be plenty of Mozart, Beethoven, and
Brahms, as well as music by Wagner, Barber, and Gould, and the world premiere of Bohuslav Martinů's Symphony No. 2.

Personnel, however, were proving slightly less easy to manage than programming. The season hadn't even begun and Leinsdorf's concertmaster,
Tossy Spivakovsky, was already giving him headaches. The violinist, who had
played the world premiere of Béla Bartók's Second Violin Concerto the previous season in Cleveland under Rodzinski, was invited to repeat the piece
with Rodzinski and the New York Philharmonic in November. On the phone
from Maine, Spivakovsky painted a dire picture of Bartók's health and asked
that Leinsdorf make it possible for the composer to hear the work played by
him and the Philharmonic. Leinsdorf refused to let his concertmaster out of
his Cleveland responsibilities in November, but, oddly, agreed to release
him in mid-October, despite a conflict between the performances at
Carnegie Hall and Leinsdorf's second pair of subscription concerts.

In September, Leinsdorf and his family moved into a spacious brick
house on Larchmere Boulevard in Shaker Heights (directly next door to the
house where George Szell would later reside for most of his Cleveland
tenure.) The Leinsdorfs felt immediately at home. "The neighbors on both
sides of us have been splendid," the conductor told a reporter. "They always
want to help and are doing so many things. For example, when I drive to re-

hearsals at Severance Hall, they are only too glad to give my wife, Anna, a lift to the store, and we appreciate such little things."

Mostly, Leinsdorf appreciated that he had an orchestra to call his own. Unlike at the Met, he could rehearse thoroughly (though he would do so perhaps too thoroughly, according to musicians who were at Severance Hall at the time). He reseated the orchestra, moving the second violins across from the first violins, as Rodzinski had positioned them several times. On opening night, October 7, 1943, Leinsdorf led a new arrangement of "The Star-Spangled Banner." Eclecticism reigned during the program, which consisted of Haydn's Symphony No. 97, Franck's Prelude, Chorale and Fugue (orchestrated by Gabriel Pierné), Gould's *American Salute* ("When Johnny Comes Marching Home"), and Brahms's Symphony No. 1. "If there were any doubts about Mr. Leinsdorf's great resources of musicianship and leadership they were certainly dispelled by listening to him conduct the Brahms First Symphony," wrote Loesser. "It was as sound, full-bodied, authentic a performance as one could wish." Loesser's colleagues also were positive. (And Elwell noted in the final paragraph of his review: "There are 15 new members in the orchestra this season, some of them girls.")

The orchestra and its new boss played an hour's worth of the program for the first live radio broadcast the following Sunday. New York was listening. Goddard Lieberson, director of the Masterworks Department at Columbia Records, wrote Leinsdorf praising his conducting but decrying the poor microphone pick-up, especially of the strings. He may have been reacting to the old Cleveland story—too few players in the string sections. The Met's assistant general manager, Edward Ziegler, wrote to congratulate his former conductor, saying that Toscanini had heard the broadcast "and murmured 'bravo' on a number of occasions."

Days before his second subscription concerts, Leinsdorf sent a letter to George Brown, personnel manager of the Met orchestra, asking him to recommend possible replacements for timpanist Cloyd Duff, who was up for induction in the army. The situation soon proved ironic. On October 15, the morning after he welcomed pianist Rudolf Serkin to Severance Hall for his debut with the orchestra during an all-Beethoven program, Leinsdorf received a letter himself "bringing me 'Greetings from the President,'" he wrote in his memoirs. He had been reclassified from deferred status to 1-A. Eleven months before, Leinsdorf had become a U.S. citizen at the suggestion of a friend, Charles Marsh, who also helped him win the job in Cleveland. The conductor never expected his adopted country's armed forces to take a serious interest in him: "All my life I have had a curvature in the lower spine, a weak back, and not very excellent feet—the classic case of a body that is generally not considered ideal for marching or crawling or firing from the prone position, the curricula of basic military training."

Leinsdorf didn't panic. Believing he would still be rejected by the draft board, he forged ahead with orchestra business with an enthusiasm bordering on compulsion. He rehearsed with an intensity that began to elicit the displeasure of his musicians, who found his booming voice unnerving and his penchant for favoritism unsettling. "When he came here he was an eager beaver," said harpist Alice Chalifoux. "He wanted everything perfect. He kept the winds after rehearsal. They took it for two weeks and went to the union. 'If we do this, we have to be paid!' "

The new maestro programmed an imaginative quartet of works for his third week. He welcomed back concertmaster Spivakovsky, who had been gone the previous week playing Bartók in New York, and introduced his new principal viola, Marcel Dick, in Mozart's Sinfonia Concertante for Violin and Viola. Along with this sublime work, he led Mozart's *Don Giovanni* overture, Samuel Barber's *Music for a Scene from Shelley*, and Franck's Symphony in D minor. Elwell's review the next day revealed his increasingly critical view of Leinsdorf's conducting. The Franck was a "laudable effort" that unfolded at a "somewhat pedestrian pace." The overture was "very adequate." Not exactly high praise.

Leinsdorf may have sensed the need to reach out to the critics, or to give them what he considered help, as the world premiere of Martinů's Second Symphony approached the following week. "I feel that it is almost an impossible task for a critic to review such a work properly after one hearing," he wrote to Elwell, Elmore Bacon (*News*), Walter Blodgett (*Press*), and Oscar Smith (*Akron Beacon Journal*). He invited them to attend the final rehearsal, look at the score, and discuss the work with the composer—a practice he hoped would continue whenever a new piece was presented. The day of the premiere, Leinsdorf contacted Elwell again, asking his help in making "real propaganda for the music of the living" and, perhaps unwittingly (or not), putting critics in their place. "We shall, therefore, not lose sight of the ultimate goal of getting contemporary music, or better, the contemporary public to a point where there will be again a consummate ability to appreciate and evaluate works at a first hearing." Elwell seems not to have taken these words as an insult. He praised the Martinů, but showed guarded admiration in his assessment of Leinsdorf's performance of the Schubert C major Symphony: "Much of his interpretation was highly commendable, and the conception made up in warmth and dramatic vigor for what it missed in the way of quiet and effortless lyricism."

On October 29, the day this review appeared, the public finally was informed that Leinsdorf had received a draft notice, which might mean induction into the army in December. The conductor told the *Cleveland News* that there would be no appeal. "I intend to abide by the orders of my government," he said. This was hardly ingenuous of Leinsdorf: Mary Vosburgh Bohannon, widow of manager Vosburgh, later claimed that the conductor pushed her husband and Sidlo to keep him out of the army by impressing upon the Selective Service Board his importance to the orchestra. In other words, there *would* be an appeal.

✳ ✳ ✳

Leinsdorf probably believed in early November that something could be done to keep him in Cleveland. He continued to concentrate on his concerts and his correspondence on behalf of the orchestra. He devoted his first subscription program in November to music of Wagner, with soprano Helen Traubel as soloist. *The Plain Dealer*'s Elwell called Leinsdorf's conducting his "best work" since arriving in Cleveland. Soon thereafter, Leinsdorf led the season's first all-star concert—a program of lighter music featuring a celebrity soloist—at Public Hall, with Oscar Levant performing Gershwin's Concerto in F. The engagement with Levant provided the conductor with an opportunity to encourage the famously neurotic pianist to break away from his identity as a Gershwin champion and consider performing concertos by Prokofiev and Beethoven, as well as recitals. Leinsdorf understood Levant's predicament all too well. "I had, as you probably know, the greatest difficulty of getting the 'Wagner specialist' tag off my back," he wrote tartly to Levant the day after the Public Hall concert, "and I realize that I still have to go quite a few years until the experts and morons (which is about the same thing), will have realized that I am not a specialist."

Leinsdorf was also spending time lobbying prominent politicians on behalf of arts organizations. The U.S. House Ways and Means Committee was about to recommend that a 20 percent admission tax be imposed on all performances given by nonprofit organizations, a new way to raise money for the war effort. The tax, Leinsdorf believed, would place an unreasonable burden on American arts groups, which received most of their support from the public. He wrote to friends in Washington, D.C., who he hoped would have some clout on the issue, including Lyndon Baines Johnson, the U.S. representative from Texas. After making his plea to "Lyndon," as he addressed Johnson in the letter, he sent greetings to Lady Bird and noted, "it would undoubtedly please you to hear that so far my season has been full of work and has brought me good success and acknowledgement all around."

Johnson wrote back a few days later, saying he would look into the admission-tax matter.

One letter Leinsdorf appreciated greatly during this period came from Julius Korngold, the formerly prominent Viennese music critic, whose son, Erich Wolfgang, had become a successful movie composer in the United States. The elder Korngold had heard Leinsdorf's Cleveland broadcast of the Mozart Sinfonia Concertante for Violin and Viola. "I praise without further analysis the performance of the glorious double concerto," Korngold wrote. "I praise the first rate soloists and the excellent orchestra and last, but not least, the outstanding conductor. Such a thing rehabilitates the radio!" Leinsdorf responded that he had read the critic's columns regularly in the *Neue Freie Presse* while growing up in Vienna, and that he was gratified to receive comments "from such an authoritative source."

One authority Leinsdorf had expected to bolster his first season in Cleveland was Toscanini, who was scheduled to conduct in December. But in September, the maestro's son, Walter, informed Vosburgh that his 76-year-old father probably would cancel because of ill health and depression over the war situation in Italy. Vosburgh pleaded with Walter Toscanini to convince his father to honor the engagement. "Not only does it promise to be the greatest musical event in our history, but the expected appearance of your father as Guest Conductor has been one of the greatest factors in increasing our season ticket sale," wrote Vosburgh. Even requests for help from David Sarnoff, president of RCA, would be of no avail. In mid-November, the orchestra announced Toscanini's cancellation, the substitution of Leinsdorf as conductor, and the debut of Dorothy Maynor, "the distinguished Negro soprano," as soloist. Toscanini never would conduct the Cleveland Orchestra.

❉   ❉   ❉

Leinsdorf sensed that efforts to keep him out of the army would fail. "I have always been eager to enter the service," he told *The Plain Dealer* on December 15. "In the summer of 1942, I applied for admittance into the School of Military Government at Charlottesville, Va., on the theory that my knowledge of Austria and Europe could be best utilized in that branch. I was considered too young and was not accepted." Two days later, Leinsdorf informed Constance Hope, his New York agent, that Sidlo and Vosburgh had been unable to convince the Selective Service Board to defer his induction, which was set for December 31, even though two Cleveland orthopedists had deemed him unsuited for the military. He asked Hope to cancel his Met commitments and told her he probably would conduct his last concert in

Cleveland on January 16 at Public Hall, provided that he received the customary three-week furlough before entering the army.

Resigned to his fate, Leinsdorf was trying to put the best face on the situation even as he maneuvered to reduce the pain. To a concerned concertgoer who hoped he would be rejected for the army, he sent a consoling letter. "The trouble with our modern life is that it is so highly specialized and sometimes even limited in tracks which can keep people from broadening," wrote Leinsdorf, "and I don't see any reason why a musician should not go to war and thereby broaden his experience in the same way as the people of the Renaissance period tried to grasp the world and the secret of life from all different angles and aspects." He had no intention of going to war, however. He appealed to Harold Spivacke, head of the Music Division of the Library of Congress, to let him know if there was "anything around your working orbit where I might fit if I am accepted and, if such is the case, if you could request me for any special purpose which you might have in mind." Leinsdorf would be assigned to Camp Lee in Virginia, near his principal residence, and not far from Washington, D.C.

A headline in the *Cleveland News* on December 31 announced the end of the drama while indulging in speculation: "Leinsdorf Is Accepted, Enters Army Jan. 21; Ringwall May Take Orchestra's Baton." Leinsdorf rallied high spirits after undergoing his physical exam and being informed that he had been accepted into the army. "I like the atmosphere already," he told the *News.* "Here I found many men who are symphony fans and they came up and told me how much they enjoy our concerts. It is good that they found nothing wrong with me." In his memoirs, Leinsdorf took a different view, blaming Hughes and Elwell for courting disaster by spreading the word around town that he could never be drafted. This couldn't have been a conspiracy on Hughes's part: she had lobbied heavily to hire Leinsdorf. Elwell, on the other hand, may have realized quickly that Leinsdorf was not a conductor near Rodzinski's, or the Cleveland Orchestra's, artistic level.

The Musical Arts Association now faced a dual dilemma—how to fill out the weeks left vacant by Leinsdorf for the current season and what to do about the 1944–45 season. Vosburgh had done his homework for the most immediate needs. He told the board that he could secure Frank Black, general music director at NBC in New York, for upcoming tours and three weeks of subscription concerts. Sir Thomas Beecham was already signed for one week and Ringwall could conduct another. This left two weeks, which could be assigned to Eugene Goossens, conductor of the Cincinnati Symphony, and Vladimir Golschmann, conductor of the St. Louis Symphony. A slight problem had arisen, however: Ringwall, upset that he wasn't going to be made chief conductor, had submitted his resignation. The board was able to placate Ringwall by raising his salary slightly and commending him for his contribution to the orchestra. Ringwall stayed (for another 12 years), and the changes in the 1943–44 season soon were announced.

Word that Leinsdorf was about to enter the army brought him letters from musicians offering help—and asking favors. Among the latter was Otto Klemperer, conductor of the Los Angeles Philharmonic at the time, who wired Leinsdorf requesting that he be recommended to replace the departing maestro at the Met and in Cleveland. Leinsdorf replied that all slots for the current season were filled, but that he would let Vosburgh know of Klemperer's possible availability for the 1944–45 season. More helpful to Leinsdorf was John R. Barrows, conductor of the Army Air Forces Band and one of America's great horn players, who wrote to Leinsdorf praising his radio broadcasts with the Cleveland Orchestra—"the most vital artistic manifestations on the air by any symphony"—and telling the conductor he would be happy to assist him once he was in the army. Leinsdorf would, in fact, eventually be assigned to band duties, keeping him out of combat but still away from the type of ensemble for which he felt most qualified.

Leinsdorf first had to fulfill his obligation to conduct the Cleveland Orchestra's pension-fund benefit concert at Public Hall on the afternoon of January 16. The concert, featuring Metropolitan Opera soprano Helen Jepson and tenor Charles Kullman, included arias, duets, and symphonic excerpts from famous operas. An audience of 6,000 gave Leinsdorf a "rousing farewell," Bacon wrote in the News, and violinist Paul Gershman presented Leinsdorf with a silver cigarette case on behalf of the orchestra. Leinsdorf's satisfaction with the results of the pension-fund concert was not matched by his view of the musicians' attitude toward the benefit. Many orchestra members had not shown up to play the concert, or they had played in only part of the performance in order to fulfill other commitments. Writing to the chairman of the Pension Fund Committee, Leinsdorf said that the musicians had to put "selfish considerations behind the interests of a larger group."

Leinsdorf and the orchestra put such considerations aside two days later for a Severance Hall concert in memory of Elisabeth Severance Allen Prentiss, a charter member of the Musical Arts Association, a board member since 1925, and sister of the late John L. Severance. She had died on January 4 at the age of 78. The main work on the January 18 program was Brahms's A German Requiem, in English, a suitably dignified performance that was broadcast live and later made available on a recording. Several months later, the orchestra received $869,938 from Mrs. Prentiss's estate. (Money from this bequest would have far-reaching ramifications, later providing support for the 1957 and 1967 European tours, the 1958 acoustical renovation of Severance Hall, and the construction of Blossom Music Center.)

✿   ✿   ✿

Unable to gaze into a crystal ball and predict the length of his army career, Leinsdorf agreed that plans for the orchestra's 1944–45 season had to be concluded, even if this meant scheduling most of the subscription and tour weeks with Ringwall and guest conductors. Golschmann, who had impressed some board members as a candidate for conductor the previous year, inherited the majority of weeks (12) for the following season. Ringwall apparently was satisfied to be given five weeks. Reiner was set to lead three weeks, while Black and Goossens would conduct three apiece. Two weeks were entrusted to another conductor who had been in competition with Leinsdorf to succeed Rodzinski: George Szell was engaged to make his debut with the orchestra in November 1944. One week of concerts at the end of the season was left without a conductor, possibly to keep a spot open for Leinsdorf, should he be discharged from the army by then. The list of guest soloists once again was formidable, including pianists Claudio Arrau, Alexander Brailowsky, Artur Rubinstein, and Rudolf Serkin; violinists Jascha Heifetz and Tossy Spivakovsky; cellist Gregor Piatigorsky; and soprano Helen Traubel.

By March, Leinsdorf was serving at Camp Lee in Virginia though still very much preoccupied with matters in Cleveland. He had heard that 25 members of the Metropolitan Opera orchestra, mostly winds and brasses, were being fired (by Szell, who, now charged with conducting most of the company's German repertoire, had been given the go-ahead to clean house). "Since replacements are hard to find, I expect that some raiding is to be expected," Leinsdorf wrote to Vosburgh. "In this connection it will be advisable to watch Beecham and Szell and also to inform Tom [Sidlo], who can settle with Mr. [Edward] Johnson that they don't take our men." Szell's potential as a raider would not blossom until several years later in Cleveland, but Vosburgh wasn't taking any chances in 1944. He told Sidlo that the danger of losing musicians was great, especially with the war continuing and guest conductors leading the orchestra the following season. The only solution for keeping key players, especially principals, was to raise salaries, Vosburgh advised.

Leinsdorf was trying to keep his spirits up despite conditions in the army.

"I am always very elated when I hear good news about our concerts and the attendance figures," he wrote to Vosburgh. "I wish I could say that from the 'inside' this looked like a short war; but the opposite is true. After basic I am supposed to go through some 'technical training' which in my case would mean 8 weeks of learning the basic elements of music. What good that period of my life will do to the Army, is beyond me."

While Leinsdorf was brooding in Virginia, the board in Cleveland was considering the delicate issue of players—and now conductor—who would be returning from the service. Sidlo believed the trustees had to treat everyone equally, "from top to bottom, from conductor to call-boy." The result was a resolution stating that the association would not reinstate musicians who had left for military service if this meant losing money or canceling the contracts of players who had been hired as replacements. The ramifications seemed harsh for some players. And they would be for Leinsdorf.

Vosburgh now had to deal with difficult personnel issues without a chief conductor around to oversee the situation. Signing players had become unusually complex, what with musicians being drafted or leaving for other jobs. From the tone of his letters, Leinsdorf was hardly in the mood to show much enthusiasm for Vosburgh's moaning—or the manager's attempts at humor: "How are you getting along with your scales in the Band Training Course?" Vosburgh asked in a letter.

As the months passed and the war continued without an end in sight, Sidlo began to rethink the association's stance on key issues. He now concluded that the orchestra soon would have to be enlarged to accommodate musicians returning from the service and to take advantage of the touring and radio business, in which Cleveland was invariably beaten due to its inadequate string complement. "I am certain that if we had an orchestra of eight to ten additional players we would go a long way toward overcoming this obstacle," Sidlo told trustees. "For the larger the Orchestra becomes and the finer artistically, the more will our services be in demand and the more we can charge for them."

Leinsdorf, meanwhile, remained at Camp Lee, performing humiliating band duties and musing on the war in dispirited letters to Vosburgh. He was also keeping in touch with the music world, having spent part of a furlough in New York signing a new contract with artist manager Arthur Judson and hearing about problems at the Met. "Otherwise I avoided the live gossip-columns, sticking close to the family. When one is active, all that dirty linen talk is silly, but when one is somewhat detached, as I am now, it all sounds plainly idiotic."

Leinsdorf was discharged honorably from the army in early September 1944—for flat feet—and he began the arduous task of putting his career back together. The prospects in Cleveland didn't look good. Sidlo told the press about the association's position regarding the 1944–45 season, which had been booked with guest conductors, and reiterated that Leinsdorf would only be on the podium for the final concerts in April 1945. An editorial in the *Cleveland Press* attempted to put the circumstances in context. "If the army had got its flat-foot detector working last winter on the feet of Erich Leinsdorf, it would have been more convenient for the management of the Cleveland Orchestra," the editorial stated. "We don't know whether it applies in a sphere covered by all these special contracts or not, but we seem to recall there is supposed to be a law. It says servicemen are supposed to get their jobs back when they are discharged from the Army."

※   ※   ※

The 1944–45 season began on October 12 as planned, with Vladimir Golschmann on the podium, facing a much-changed Cleveland Orchestra. Elwell gave the guest the benefit of the doubt, considering the atmosphere, with a rave review the next day. "With only the courtesy authority of a guest conductor, Golschmann had the task of whipping together in about a week an orchestra in which there have been 18 replacements since last season," Elwell wrote. "The result was amazing and could have been achieved only by the most arduous and honest workmanship of a long-experienced craftsman. For here was a finished, authoritative performance by an orchestra which has already assimilated its new elements and sounds in top form."

The day after opening night, Sidlo presided over a board meeting that explored, but didn't solve, the Leinsdorf matter. In his finest speechifying, the president laid out the complexities of the situation and described how he had gone to bat for the conductor to find him employment during the period when Cleveland was unable to use his services. Sidlo had put in a telephone call to Edward Johnson at the Met just in time to secure for Leinsdorf a healthy series of performances (including several broadcasts) from which Sir Thomas Beecham had withdrawn. Leinsdorf would return to the Met to conduct *Tristan, The Marriage of Figaro, Lohengrin,* and *Parsifal,* the latter two possibly coming to Cleveland during the company's spring tour. Johnson also had landed Leinsdorf two concerts with the Rochester Philharmonic (instrumental in his later appointment there as music director). In addition, Leinsdorf's agent booked him for concerts with the Havana Orchestra. So he wasn't going to be idle. "Under the circumstances, therefore, I think it is not unfair to say that a very great deal has been done to meet the problem presented by Mr. Leinsdorf's return to civilian life," Sidlo told the trustees.

He wasn't finished, however. Sidlo made it fairly clear that despite these efforts, Leinsdorf's future as conductor of the Cleveland Orchestra was not assured, noting that his contract gave the association the option of canceling at the end of any season "if by chance we made a mistake," the first hint that the board knew it needed an out if Leinsdorf proved to be the wrong conductor to lead the orchestra.

Then, to reconcile the trustees to the prospect of hiring a second chief conductor within the space of three years, Sidlo said, "We are the custodians of an enviable artistic reputation and standing which it has also taken years to acquire and which is now, by virtue of our Orchestra being one of the four or five leading orchestras in the world, and the most precious single asset we could possibly have." The Cleveland Orchestra hadn't fallen to pieces when Sokoloff left, Sidlo pointed out, nor had the artistic level dropped after Rodzinski's departure (a statement that would prove to be untrue). "As you may recall," he added, "we had the largest advance sale last year in years and the largest earned income in the entire history of the Orchestra."

The writing appeared to be on the wall for Leinsdorf. And his prospects would soon decline further, when a conductor who had been impressing audiences at the Met made his debut at Severance Hall. George Szell stepped onto the stage on November 2, 1944, to begin a two-week stint that effectively changed the course of the Cleveland Orchestra's history. Szell (correctly pronounced "sell," not "zell") had arrived in town on October 29, telling *The Plain Dealer* that he was "looking forward to working with the Cleveland Orchestra, which Artur Rodzinski has brought to such a high standard of excellence." The statement implied that Leinsdorf had had no impact on Cleveland.

For his first week of concerts, Szell chose an all-orchestral program comprising Beethoven's Sixth Symphony, his own arrangement of Smetana's String Quartet No. 1 in E minor ("From My Life"), and Strauss's *Till Eulenspiegel*. The results were electric, according to critics and musicians who were there. "In his debut as guest conductor with the Cleveland Orchestra at Severance Hall last night, George Szell had a brilliant artistic and personal success. The audience lost no time in recognizing his natural virtuosic talent and gave him a resounding ovation. Obviously, he is a conductor whose musicianship commands the highest respect and admiration," wrote Elwell in *The Plain Dealer*. "He conducts without score and without eccentricities, and there is something warm and friendly, as well as authoritative, in his approach to the music and to the orchestra, a fact which seemed to cause the musicians to work as they have not worked for some time." The phrase "warm and friendly" is curious in retrospect; the term "authoritative" would never be refuted.

Milton Widder went even more directly to the point in a review full of insights. "George Szell is a great conductor," he wrote in the *Press*.

> He is great in every connotation of the word. It has been a long time—
> if ever—[since] Cleveland has heard a Sixth Symphony of Beethoven as it
> was conducted by Mr. Szell last night. There were things in the sympho
> ny never before revealed, there were songs in it that were never so joyous
> and there was a new vigor in it that brought the old master out among the
> living again . . . This conductor creates his orchestral effects not with Gallic
> impetuosity or saccharine posing, but with a direct, natural beat that is nei
> ther metric, nor studied. And the responses by the choirs of the orchestra
> were definitely the best this season.

An idea of what Widder and Elwell raved about can be gathered from a broadcast tape of the one-hour WHK radio concert Szell led the Sunday after his debut. He repeated the Smetana quartet and Strauss tone poem and opened with a work he had already prepared for his second program, Smetana's *The Bartered Bride* overture. The performances reveal a Cleveland Orchestra in transition—one that isn't accustomed to Szell's taut sense of rhythm or obsession with clarity of balance and texture. The ensemble doesn't crackle the way it did under Rodzinski at its best (or would under Szell in later years). But the performances suggest a special relationship in the making. And one thing is quite likely: the orchestra probably never sounded as motivated under Leinsdorf.

Between the two concerts his second week, Szell attended a party at the home of Percy and Helen Brown, where the guests also included, violinist Joseph Knitzer and his wife, Mary, and pianist Beryl Rubinstein and his wife, Elsa. The Browns, who would become Szell's most ardent champions in Cleveland, succeeded in convincing the conductor to demonstrate another aspect of his art that night: pianist Szell played chamber music with Knitzer and Rubinstein. "Perfect party," Brown wrote in his notebook.

The excitement may partly have spilled over from the previous night, when Szell had conducted the *Bartered Bride* overture; Mozart's Piano Concerto in A major, K. 488; Hindemith's *Symphonic Metamorphosis on Themes by Weber*; and Rachmaninoff's Rhapsody on a Theme of Paganini.

The soloist, for the first of numerous times with Szell in Cleveland, was Artur Rubinstein. "Unprecedented interest in Szell's work combined with the enthusiasm always evoked by the distinguished soloist made the hall ring with hearty plaudits," noted Elwell in *The Plain Dealer*. "One can feel with assurance that in the two short weeks he has been here he has brought our orchestra to a most complete and illuminating realization of its splendid potentialities." Brown made note of the phenomenon more succinctly: "Thrilling."

Elmore Bacon, writing a provocative article the same day in the *News*, speculated that Szell might once again be a candidate for the conductor's post in Cleveland. "We join in the opinion of many that the Cleveland Orchestra in all its history has not had such vitalizing, fervent and virtuosic leadership as under the magic baton of Director Szell. Sir Thomas Beecham, Dr. Artur Rodzinski, at times, and one or two other guest conductors have come close to matching the Szell artistry. But none has excelled it." He reported that ticket sales were up, reflecting the interest Szell had aroused, and that the orchestra was playing as it never had before. "Rehearsals reveal a tenseness and devotion heretofore lacking. That the symphonists were thrilled by the Szell direction has been apparent from the first beat of his baton." The following two nights, Szell and Golschmann led the orchestra in back-to-back concerts in Ann Arbor and Saginaw, Michigan.

While Cleveland concertgoers were discussing Szell's debut, the ban on recording implemented in August 1942 by American Federation of Musicians president James C. Petrillo was lifted. The situation prompted agent Arthur Judson to begin lobbying for Leinsdorf to record with the orchestra that was still his by contract. The Judson request spurred Vosburgh and Sidlo to action. Talk around town and in musical circles elsewhere was suggesting that Leinsdorf's status in Cleveland had weakened. Sidlo decided to put the gossip to rest by bringing up the subject of the 1945–46 season and Leinsdorf's right to be conductor of the orchestra for the third year of his contract. He was doing so in part to silence criticism that the association hadn't acted quickly enough to reinstate Leinsdorf after his discharge from the Army. "If a poll of the Board were taken at this time," Sidlo insisted, "it would show that a majority felt that as a matter of simple justice Mr. Leinsdorf should be given the opportunity of a further hearing since he had been deprived of that opportunity by reason of the draft."

Justice was to come in what Leinsdorf may well have regarded as a series of massive compromises. In fulfilling the terms of their conductor's three-year contract, the association now decided to give a number of weeks during the first half of the 1945–46 season to Golschmann and Szell, "it being the opinion of those present that these two gentlemen with Mr. Leinsdorf would in all likelihood constitute the field from which we would wish to make our choice." Sidlo further stated that it was the board's "paramount duty to find and to choose the best man the world has to offer for our permanent conductor, regardless of what we do about the coming season." In other words, Leinsdorf was to be placed in a three-way race to retain his post.

Columbia Records was extending the orchestra's recording contract to January 1946, which meant Cleveland could begin making records early in 1945. But now along with Leinsdorf, Columbia wanted the orchestra to record with Szell and Bruno Walter. Leinsdorf gave no public indication that the situation was fraught with tension. "I am delighted that after unavoidable complications my return as conductor of the Cleveland Orchestra has been arranged," he told *The Plain Dealer*. "I am looking forward with pleasure to seeing Mr. Vosburgh here in New York to discuss details."

Golschmann and Szell weren't the only conductors who provided competition for Leinsdorf. The formidable Hungarian-born Fritz Reiner, music director of the Pittsburgh Symphony, made his debut with the orchestra in December 1944 and January 1945, leading three weeks of concerts that were hailed almost as fervently as Szell's recent performances. Reiner's repertoire for these programs was vast, including the Cleveland debut of Shostakovich's Sixth Symphony, as well as smatterings of Mozart, Brahms, Wagner, Weber, Bach, Kodály, Johann Strauss II, Rossini, Mendelssohn, William Schuman (*Side Show*), Kabalevsky, Prokofiev, and Stravinsky.

Reiner's debut was used by Elwell in *The Plain Dealer* as the springboard for a weak defense of the Cleveland Orchestra's quality, which some observers believed had dropped since Rodzinski's departure. He refuted the idea that the orchestra was greatly weakened by the musicians replacing players who had gone into military service. "Had it degenerated as some persons seem to think, it would not be playing to capacity audiences as it has all this season." Tapes of performances from this period suggest that the quality indeed varied greatly, depending upon who was on the podium and what players, including replacements, were onstage. Elwell unwittingly admitted how erratic the orchestra had become by stating that "if [the Boston Symphony's Serge] Koussevitzky could conduct our orchestra today, I believe you would find that, given a reasonable amount of time, he would have little difficulty in molding it into the superior instrument which his orchestra seems to be. All the potentialities are there."

Although Leinsdorf was busy elsewhere during most of this period, he was in constant touch with Vosburgh and Sidlo, as well as with members of the community interested in orchestra affairs. Also staying in touch with high-powered Clevelanders at this time was George Szell. Percy and Helen Brown, smitten with the conductor, traveled to New York in January 1945 to sit with Helene Szell in a box at the Met while her husband conducted *Die Meistersinger.* "Great triumph," was Brown's assessment. A week later, Szell, serving as guest conductor of the Boston Symphony, informed Vosburgh that he had reserved the materials for Bartók's Concerto for Orchestra (which had received its world premiere the previous month by the Boston Symphony under Koussevitzky) from the publishing company Boosey & Hawkes for one of his Cleveland programs the following season. "I am very happy about this as I consider that work one of the most important compositions written during the past 25 years," wrote Szell. "I should like to think that you will welcome my introducing it to the Cleveland public." Typically, Szell was thinking far ahead.

That Szell appreciated the Cleveland Orchestra—and may already have been coveting the top spot—is apparent in a letter to Rodzinski, who had established himself at the New York Philharmonic. Szell, who conducted the Philharmonic soon after he first appeared with the Cleveland Orchestra, told Rodzinski that his Philharmonic engagement had been glorious. "I enjoyed every split-second of it," wrote Szell. "It was the same combination of the finest virtues of orchestral playing and the right spirit and artistic approach which I could admire already in Cleveland earlier this season."

Szell had already made such an impact on Cleveland that the Musical Arts Association didn't hesitate when his manager asked for an increase in his fee for the following season. The board voted to pay him $4,000 for three weeks; Golschmann, by comparison, would receive $3,300 for his three. The presence of Szell was beginning to be a nuisance for Leinsdorf. Columbia Records now suggested that the orchestra make recordings with Leinsdorf, Szell, and perhaps André Kostelanetz. When Leinsdorf demanded that he be given more than one recording session, the board decided that he should have two and Szell one. This proposition also proved unacceptable to Leinsdorf, who realized that the guest conductors, who were taking over concerts that rightly belonged to him, were eroding his power in Cleveland. In an impassioned letter to Vosburgh in January 1945, he decried the recording situation and the board's attitude toward him. "Since it is not customary and would be a serious decrease of both my prestige as a conductor and of my potential income from the recordings to be made, I can interpret this proposal only as a vote of limited confidence," he wrote to Vosburgh. Leinsdorf may have come to the conclusion that the events of the previous year had ruined whatever options remained for him in Cleveland: "I had little time to prove what kind of a job I could do in Cleveland, and as of to-day it seems to me that I shall not get the opportunity to do so."

As Leinsdorf was pondering his Cleveland fate, various factions on the board were staking out positions for and against him. Sidlo, who initially had championed Leinsdorf, was showing increased signs of uncertainty about his appointee, agreeing to the split recording deal (which, in any case, would never happen because of concerns over the exorbitant national musicians' union scale) and speaking in general terms that appeared to point the orchestra in a different direction. "Let's work toward the goal of a great orchestra, adequate numerically—90 to 100, and superlative artistically," Sidlo told the board. "Let's never forget there is no substitute for the actual business of making music, that is the first and indispensable function of an orchestra—great music, greatly played."

At least one board member, Adella Prentiss Hughes, was maneuvering to keep Leinsdorf on the podium, and Percy Brown wasn't about to let her do so. "I gave her a complete bawling out," he wrote in his notebook at the end of January 1945. "Unholy alliance with [New York agent] Constance Hope. Leinsdorf a great mistake. She must stop her smear campaigns of Szell and Golschmann as with Stoessel, and stop interviewing trustees secretly. Orchestra no longer her baby."

By contract, the orchestra still belonged to Leinsdorf, and he was fulfilling his responsibilities. He urged Vosburgh to try to forestall the departure of musicians for "the big money" in New York by extending the Cleveland season to 32 weeks and incorporating into all contracts a summer pops season of seven weeks. Despite Leinsdorf's hopes of retaining musicians, however, 15 players had decided to seek greener pastures, musical and otherwise, at the end of the 1944–45 season. In addition to concertmaster Tossy Spivakovsky and assistant concermaster Felix Eyle (who left in a huff when he wasn't tapped to be Spivakovsky's successor), the orchestra was about to lose five violins, one viola, one cello, its second oboe and third horn, and no fewer than four principal winds—flute (Maurice Sharp, who was moving to New York), clarinet (Emerson Both, who had been hired by the Chicago National Broadcasting Company), bassoon (George Goslee, new principal of the Philadelphia Orchestra), and horn (Philip Farkas, who was becoming principal of the Boston Symphony).

Leinsdorf continued to lobby for a year-round season for the orchestra, though he knew this wouldn't happen soon. "As far as maintenance and improvement of our musical personnel is concerned, we are at present at a disadvantage compared to other cities which offer more outside work and more income to residing musicians," Leinsdorf wrote in a memo. "But, I believe that the economic trend of future years will develop in most people a strong preference for security instead of continued struggles of so-called 'free lance' work."

By April 1945, the three recording sessions planned by Columbia for the end of the season were postponed to November as the result of high musicians' costs. The board explored another benefit for the musicians (one that hadn't gained much ground among trustees)—pensions. From 1918 until 1940, the Cleveland Orchestra had no pension plan, one of many reasons players sought jobs elsewhere. The Cleveland Orchestra Pension Institute, begun in 1940, was intended to provide musicians who had completed 25 consecutive years of service in the orchestra with full pensions of $500 a year, starting at age 55. No pensions were to be paid for the first five years of the plan. Now, in 1945, the plan didn't have enough funds from dues ($75 per year) to pay out pensions. The board had to find a way to finance the plan or the current policy would have to be dissolved.

✻   ✻   ✻

In April, finally, Leinsdorf returned to Severance Hall to conduct the closing program of the 1944–45 season—his first concerts with his ensemble in 15 months. He chose what he believed would be a well-rounded program: Bruckner's Fourth Symphony, Schubert's Grand Rondo (transcribed for orchestra by Leo Weiner), Copland's *El salón México,* and Beethoven's *Leonore* Overture No. 2. But between the final rehearsal and first performance on April 12, tragedy befell the country when President Franklin Delano Roosevelt died of a stroke in Warm Springs, Georgia. "As it was, the constellation of all my Cleveland enterprises seemed poor," Leinsdorf said dryly in his memoirs of the circumstances surrounding his return.

In tribute to the late president, Leinsdorf added a work to the beginning of the second half of the program, a chorale from Bach's *St. Matthew Passion*. Widder, writing of the Bach in the *Press*, said, "As the broad lines of this beautiful and inspiring music unfolded slowly, members of the audience started to rise and by the time the music was finished everyone had risen, and men and women with bowed heads stood for a minute more, deeply affected."

The zesty Copland score, in its first Cleveland Orchestra performance, was not especially appropriate for the day of a national tragedy ("somewhat blatant and coarse, but nevertheless entertaining and sprightly," Widder called it), but Leinsdorf went through with the performance. "I am afraid that the reception of the piece was not quite what I hoped for," he related to Hans Heinsheimer at the publishing firm Boosey & Hawkes, before the second concert, "and this I do not attribute to any fault of the work nor resistance on the part of the public, but rather to the unfortunate and tragic coincidence which put our program on the night of the President's death and I can quite understand the mood of the public was not too receptive to the popular dance hall in Mexico City." At the program's end, Leinsdorf and the orchestra followed the heroic *Leonore* overture with the national anthem, restoring the proper atmosphere. It had in it "a note of farewell to a nation's valiant leader," wrote Bacon in the *News*.

Cleveland would soon be saying farewell to a leader of its own. Adella Prentiss Hughes, the founding manager of the orchestra and current secretary of the Musical Arts Association, resigned on July 6. The board voted to continue paying her full annual salary as pension compensation (even though the trustees couldn't come up with an adequate pension plan for the musicians) and to give her the title of Honorary Vice President. "I am asking today to be relieved of the responsibilities of the Secretaryship," Hughes wrote in a statement. "Music for Cleveland has dominated my life for more than fifty years and will continue to do so. I have an abiding satisfaction in the knowledge we are firmly established and that the ideals of the founders are so well advanced."

Behind the scenes, the story was very different. "It took 5 or 6 big strong men to oust one lone woman, aged 75, but we did it and a great victory was the result," Percy Brown wrote in his notebook. "Now if she behaves I shall be friendly, maybe renew old affections, despite her selfishness, fabrications and general busybodiness. It may dissolve some of the cliques."

Yet even Brown would have agreed that, however much of a busybody Hughes may have been, she had made a profound contribution to Cleveland. She had nurtured symphonic music and worked tirelessly for an orchestra that now was on the verge of achievements neither she—nor anyone else in the music world—could have imagined.

– 15 –

*Something Fine
and Beautiful*

The ensemble that participated in the great Cleveland Orchestra conductor sweepstakes of 1945–46 reflected the instability that war had
brought to Severance Hall. Of the orchestra's 84 musicians that season, 22
players were new or returning from the armed forces. The previous year,
there had been 18 personnel changes. The total of 40 changes in two seasons meant that almost half the orchestra members had joined the group
since Erich Leinsdorf's Cleveland conducting debut in October 1943. Of
the 21 musicians who had gone into the service, only 10 would return.

While peace had been restored to most of the world in September 1945,
it was not to be a frequent visitor at Severance Hall in the coming months.
Leinsdorf had to contend with two guest conductors, the St. Louis
Symphony's Vladimir Golschmann and the Metropolitan Opera's George
Szell, whom he knew to be vying for his post. The insecurity of the situation
had led him to move to an apartment in Cleveland and leave his family—his
wife was expecting their third child—back East. Along with these anxiety-
inducing conditions, he was starting the season with an ensemble he could-
n't possibly know on intimate terms, even though he believed he had the
right musicians in place. "I couldn't find a weak spot," Leinsdorf said after
the season's first rehearsal.

Among the gifted musicians facing Leinsdorf this season were principal
bassoonist Frank Ruggieri, returning from the service, and principal hornist
James Stagliano, whose uncle, Albert, had held the position during the
1936–37 season. Although Ruggieri and Stagliano would be gone after the
1945–46 season when former principals were lured back to their posts, they
must have been valuable to the ensemble. Stagliano had been principal in
the Detroit Symphony before spending seven years as an orchestra player
in Hollywood. (He can be heard swooping up that famous tomorrow-is-an-
other-day octave as first horn on the soundtrack of *Gone With the Wind*.)

Cleveland's 1945–46 season was to hold ample intrigue. The roster of soloists, as always, was on the highest level, including such eminent artists as soprano Rose Bampton; violinists Yehudi Menuhin, Zino Francescatti, and Mischa Elman; and pianists William Kapell and Rudolf Serkin. Possibly hoping to focus attention on the level of orchestral playing—especially considering the situation that was brewing—Leinsdorf chose a program for opening night that had no soloists: three sinfonias from Bach cantatas, Copland's suite from *Appalachian Spring*, Strauss's *Don Juan*, and Beethoven's Fifth. Herbert Elwell put a generally positive spin on the occasion, "the first postwar symphony concert of the Cleveland Orchestra," and called the musicians' efforts admirable. But none of Leinsdorf's interpretations was much to the critic's liking, and he noted that there was much room for technical improvement. "The strings have developed some nice uniform bowings, but I would like to hear more color and authority from the first violins," wrote Elwell in *The Plain Dealer*. "The horns were guilty of a little bleating, and in general there could be more assurance and a better singing tone. There was a tenseness in the playing that was only natural on opening night, and will likely give way to freer production."

Over the next four weeks, Leinsdorf had the orchestra to himself. He led an all-Brahms program the second week, with Beryl Rubinstein as soloist in the First Piano Concerto, and again went Austro-Germanic for his third week, starting with Bruckner's Seventh Symphony and ending with the third scene from Act III of Wagner's *Siegfried*, with Rose Bampton as Brünnhilde and Arthur Carron in the title role. Handel, Haydn, Walton, George Antheil, and Ravel kept Leinsdorf and the orchestra busy the fourth week, while his fifth program comprised Mozart's Symphony No. 39, his own arrangement of preludes and interludes from Debussy's *Pelléas et Mélisande*, and Shostakovich's Fifth Symphony.

Leinsdorf was making plans to enter the recording studio with a number of these works. He discussed with Columbia's Goddard Lieberson a proposal to record Antheil's Fourth Symphony. The Antheil symphony wasn't greeted with much enthusiasm when Leinsdorf conducted it on November 1 and 3. Elwell wrote of the composer "this 'enfant terrible' of the '20s cannot seem to outgrow the childish impulse to be simply rowdy in his music. In this and other respects he is like Shostakovich, whom he antedates, but on whose bandwagon he has climbed with a valise full of Hollywood buildups and tongue-in-cheek, tear-jerking cantilenas." The Antheil recording was scrapped. General manager Carl Vosburgh told Leinsdorf it simply wouldn't sell.

The conductor spent part of the opening month of the season outlining a master plan to nurture the city's cultural personality. Now that the orchestra, supported by some 5,000 residents, had become "this city's Number One civic asset," according to Milton Widder in the *Press*, through national attention from tours, recordings, and radio broadcasts, it had the responsibility to give the players year-round employment and become a musical mecca, especially for the area's music students. Widder said the orchestra needed "a young and ambitious conductor" to carry out the plan. "In Erich Leinsdorf Cleveland has such a man," he wrote. "That he is a musical talent far above average is an established fact. He is, I think, devoted to the cause outlined. And also he is willing and able to dedicate himself to the placing of Cleveland among the first cities in America in musical accomplishment."

❧   ❧   ❧

No matter how dedicated Leinsdorf may have been, he couldn't control the forces that were moving in to thwart his ambitions for Cleveland. In late November, Vladimir Golschmann arrived for three weeks of concerts. The dashing conductor was admired by some for his flamboyant performances of colorful works, especially those from the French and Russian repertoire. His programming in Cleveland included both well-known and obscure music by Berlioz, Khrennikov, Antheil, Sibelius, Vivaldi, Khachaturian, Schoenberg, Tchaikovsky, Mozart, Debussy, and Brahms. The critics reacted far more favorably toward the St. Louis Symphony's conductor than they had to the Cleveland Orchestra's own maestro. According to Elwell, "the whole orchestra, in fact, sounded better than it has for some time."

But nothing Cleveland had heard in recent memory could approach the thunderbolt that struck immediately thereafter when Szell returned for a three-week guest stint. His all-Beethoven program on December 20 and 22 essentially clinched the post for him. Conducting the *Egmont* overture, "Emperor" Concerto (with Serkin as soloist), and the Seventh Symphony, Szell confirmed the potent impression he had made the previous season, shaping performances that left listeners captivated. The headlines the day after the opening Beethoven concert told most of the story: "Szell, Serkin Thrill With Severance Beethoven Bill" (*News*); "Szell Enraptures Severance Crowd, Serkin is Applauded" (*Plain Dealer*); "Szell, Serkin in Year's Best Symphony Concert" (*Press*). "This was surely not the same orchestra we have been listening to all season," wrote Elwell, obliterating Golschmann's achievement. "It was rather something that has to do with dreams, and dreams, perhaps, of the future."

Szell hadn't even conducted his second week of concerts, and the town was already buzzing with anticipation. The day of Szell's second program, the *Press*'s Widder wrote about the dilemma facing Cleveland: Would the victor be Szell, Golschmann, or Leinsdorf? "The massive tranquility of Severance Hall belies the seething conductorial situation," he wrote. "The advent of George Szell on Dec. 20 sharply intensified a situation in which the present conductor, Erich Leinsdorf, is far from secure. One group of orchestra supporters was already vigorously beating the drums for Vladimir Golschmann, director of the St. Louis Orchestra." Szell's Beethoven concert, wrote Widder, had galvanized the public as never before. "Cleveland can probably have Mr. Szell—but on his terms, and his terms only. I think Mr. Szell is the kind of a conductor who must have absolute power—both in direction of music and selection of personnel—to achieve his artistic goals. Of course that is what makes him the man who can produce music as he does." Szell had the ability to "produce 'box office' at home, abroad and on records because musically he has IT."

With various board factions preparing to make their separate cases early in January, Szell continued to astonish Cleveland during his second and third programs. For his second week, he conducted Tchaikovsky's "Pathétique" Symphony, the suite from Stravinsky's *Firebird*, and Ravel's *La valse*. To open his third program, he introduced Bartók's Concerto for Orchestra to Cleveland, and included another work he and the orchestra would perform often over the next 24 years, Brahms's First Symphony. Once again, the press went mad with superlatives.

Now the public was talking, and the Musical Arts Association was listening. Letters poured in suggesting or demanding that Szell be hired. The orchestra's executive committee met to consider the groundswell of support for Szell. By the first week in January, the decision had been made: Szell would be pursued; Leinsdorf would go. Telling Leinsdorf was up to board president Thomas L. Sidlo, who invited the conductor to his Cleveland Heights home to discuss the inevitable. Leinsdorf, calm and philosophical, agreed to write a letter of resignation that would be read to the trustees when the Szell announcement was made. This was slightly presumptuous on Sidlo's part: Szell hadn't yet been offered the job.

The resignation letter that Leinsdorf devised at Sidlo's request is a poignant document. He wrote that he held nothing against the trustees for the circumstances that had prevented him from doing his job: "All those difficulties arose from the unpredictable events which are part of war and crisis. Since we cannot be held responsible for 'force majeure', we have no reproaches in our hearts and can rejoice in the feeling of personal friendship and esteem. The main purpose for all of us remains: to help the growth of music; whatever we can do toward that goal must be done in our different roles." Leinsdorf was burning no bridges—at least not for the moment; his view of these circumstances is far less circumspect in his feisty memoirs, *Cadenza*.

✿   ✿   ✿

On January 15, Szell engaged in a shrewd negotiating game with Vosburgh, Sidlo, and trustees Percy Brown and Lewis B. Williams at the Cleveland Hotel. The conductor had the upper hand. He would speak with each man only individually before agreeing on a contract. Szell's conditions regarding personnel, programming, scheduling, touring, recording, broadcasting, soloists, guest conductors, and leaves of absence had to be met before he would consider talking salary. As Sidlo was to tell the board, with what might be termed gargantuan understatement, "Dr. Szell is no easy-going person."

The contract Szell signed on January 15 gave him powers that no other Cleveland Orchestra conductor had come close to holding. His three-year agreement called for the orchestra to be increased by eight players and for every effort to be made to reengage flutist Maurice Sharp, clarinetist Emerson Both, bassoonist George Goslee, and hornist Philip Farkas as principal players. The orchestra's current budget would be considered a minimum level, and Szell would have a full week of rehearsals before the opening week of the 1946–47 season. Another aesthetic issue Szell insisted upon in his contract must have made the local Sherwin Williams Company happy: "You have requested that the Association arrange to repaint the stage-setting with three to five coats of hard paint in plain ivory color before September 1, 1946, and the Association agrees to do so upon the understanding that the color chosen will be in harmony with the color scheme of the rest of the hall."

The salary Szell demanded for each of his first three years in Cleveland—$40,000—is mentioned only in the contract's final paragraph. The fee represented a sizable jump from the $30,000 salaries of Sokoloff and Rodzinski and something of a slap in the face for Leinsdorf, who earned only $18,000. Several days after the pact was signed, Sidlo had Szell's title changed in the contract from "Conductor" to "Musical Director and Conductor" to reflect added responsibility and control. None of his predecessors had been given such an option.

Sidlo announced the results of the negotiations to the board on January 24, when he described the background that had led to this course of action. "For the first time in the entire history of the Orchestra, a conductor has occupied our podium concerning whom there developed such general approval and acceptance as has never before been known," he told trustees.

"So much so that the task of choosing a regular conductor was virtually taken out of our hands and the choice made for us by audience and public. Concertgoers, musicians, critics and the general public generally have been so overwhelmingly in favor of Mr. Szell that to have refused to engage him would have been difficult to explain. We faced a public demand which if unheeded might easily have exposed us to charges of willful disregard or defiance."

Sidlo reported that nothing Szell had discussed during negotiations had seemed arbitrary or unreasonable. He said the conductor had come up with the $40,000 salary figure in part because "the work involved in bringing back an Orchestra which in his opinion had slipped markedly during the past two years was something not to be lightly dismissed; that he was so constituted he could not give less than his utmost at all times, whether in rehearsal or performance, and that he did not think he needed to tell us that this was an extremely wearing process." The demands Szell made would add 15 percent to the orchestra's budget, according to Sidlo, who would increase the figure to 20 percent a few months later. The budget would be $480,000 for the 1946–47 season compared with $400,000 for the previous season, attributable partly to a rise in musician salaries. Minimum weekly scale was rising from $76 to $85.

Achieving growth with Szell promised to be extremely challenging, Sidlo noted before the board voted on the proposed contract. Szell is "a worker, a terrific worker, an artist so dedicated to his art as to be unwilling to give anything but his best, and equally unwilling to accept anything but the best from others," Sidlo said. "Of this though I feel certain—that if we will do our part, he will do his, and that with good will, determined purpose, and everyone co-operating, it will not be long before we shall see results that will open our eyes and gladden our hearts." The board voted unanimously to hire Szell, despite premeeting lobbying for Golschmann by A. A. Brewster, Eleanor Painter Strong, and Elizabeth Blossom.

News of Szell's appointment spread through the audience at Severance Hall that night during the orchestra's concert, for which the chronically unfortunate Leinsdorf was on the podium. Not only had Szell taken away his job that day, but Vladimir Horowitz, the scheduled soloist, had become ill and cancelled his performances that week of the Liszt First Piano Concerto (to be replaced by Beryl Rubinstein).

Clevelanders found out about the Szell announcement by word of mouth or radio. A newspaper strike that had begun on January 5 kept the city's three newspapers silent until February 6, though an article written by Elmore Bacon for the *News* was printed in a dummy paper that was ready in case the strike ended. The story—dated January 25, 1946, the day after the board meeting at which the new conductor was chosen—said Leinsdorf had requested that his candidacy be dropped (a variation on the truth) and that Szell was delighted to have been named to the post. "I shall do my best to justify the confidence and warm affection the Cleveland public has so generously showered upon me," read a Szell statement. "The Musical Arts Association has expressed its desire to make the Cleveland Orchestra second to none in quality of performance. To this end I shall dedicate all my efforts." It is likely that radio listeners were the only ones who heard these words, especially the key phrase "second to none," which Szell and orchestra officials would continue to employ throughout his tenure.

The Cleveland papers got in on the act only after the New York print media had their say about the change from Leinsdorf to Szell. Some observers were already skeptical. Irving Kolodin speculated in the *New York Sun* that Cleveland for Szell might be "the anteroom for the Philharmonic as it was for Rodzinski . . . There are more than a few who feel that Szell's routing to Cleveland is merely an incident in his career, that he is being groomed for better things." Kolodin wrote those provocative, though ultimately inaccurate, words on the basis of the New York Philharmonic's first performance of the Bartók Concerto for Orchestra under Szell the previous day, just a month after he led the work's Cleveland premiere.

Time magazine announced the Szell appointment by referring to the conductor as "a tall, near-bald, thick-spectacled Czech-Hungarian, who conducted the Berlin State Opera B.H. (Before Hitler)." Referring to Cleveland, Szell was quoted with explosive words from which he was never to waver: "A new leaf will be turned over with a bang! People talk about the New York, the Boston, and the Philadelphia. Now they will talk about the New York, the Boston, the Philadelphia and the Cleveland." Widder finally chimed in on the subject in the *Press* by announcing that the orchestra would have at least 20 new players for Szell's first season—the eight additional players stipulated in the new boss's contract and numerous personnel changes Szell was planning to make.

Szell got down to the business of molding his orchestra without wasting any time. The pink slips he had Vosburgh hand out soon after his appointment included one for the orchestra's only female violinist, Evelyn Botnick, who had been hired by Leinsdorf. According to Botnick, Szell subscribed to the European attitude that orchestras were mainly for men. The presence of Alice Chalifoux as harpist didn't much concern him, since the harp isn't used in the repertoire for which he felt the most affinity—music of the Classical era. But a woman violinist was another matter. "I had to reaudition for all the first chairs," recalled Botnick. "They all voted for me 100 percent. They put up a real big fight about keeping me. It was very rewarding." Although she would come to respect Szell above all other conductors, Botnick's presence in the orchestra "was like a bone in his throat," she said.

✿   ✿   ✿

"Erich Leinsdorf deserves better," declared an editorial in the *Press*, though it praised the Szell appointment nonetheless. "And Cleveland deserves better from its Musical Arts Association, which, after all, is custodian and not owner of the community's principal musical interest. It isn't good for the future business of acquiring talent that this city should be known for an ungracious brush-off to a good man who leaves." Sidlo apologized the next day. "There is justification for criticism," he said, "and it is due to my failure to release a letter I wrote Mr. Leinsdorf. I deeply regret anyone should have been pained at this seeming lack of consideration."

Leinsdorf wasn't about to depart before leaving some lasting sign that he had, after all, been conductor of the Cleveland Orchestra. He had been contemplating making recordings with the ensemble for Columbia since the ban imposed by American Federation of Musicians president James C. Petrillo was lifted in November 1944. The repertoire for these records changed often, and the possibility that Leinsdorf might have to share sessions with Szell and another conductor had turned the process into an ordeal. To make matters worse, by the time he actually stood before the microphones at Severance Hall, Leinsdorf was recording in the shadow of the Szell appointment, with an orchestra whose members were fully aware that a quarter of the players would be gone in two months.

All of the discs featuring Leinsdorf and the Cleveland Orchestra were made on February 22, 24, and 25, 1946, at Severance Hall. In three three-hour sessions, the conductor recorded 13 works, including three complete symphonies (Dvořák's Sixth, Rimsky-Korsakov's Second—known as "Antar"—and Schumann's First) and excerpts from Debussy's *Pelléas et Mélisande*. The remaining pieces were Viennese miniatures by Mozart, Schubert, Brahms, and members of the Strauss family, each of which could fit onto a 4½-minute side of a 78 rpm phonograph record.

The recordings suggest that board member Percy Brown may have been right: perhaps Leinsdorf *was* a mistake for Cleveland, particularly at this early point in his symphonic career. Granted, the conductor had had little time to shape the orchestra as he might have liked, and conditions weren't conducive to optimum performance. But the Leinsdorf-Cleveland recordings in general are not competitive with performances by other major conductors and orchestras of the period or later. Technology is not the culprit: although limited by the 78 rpm format, the sound is clear and natural, giving a fair idea of the Cleveland Orchestra during this time.

The best performance is the Rimsky-Korsakov "Antar" Symphony, the first piece Leinsdorf and the orchestra recorded. Szell's observation that the ensemble had "slipped markedly" in two years is not apparent in this recording, which finds the orchestra in crisp, responsive form. Also worth hearing are the *Pelléas* excerpts, which are included in the orchestra's 75th-anniversary compact disc collection. They reveal Leinsdorf's strengths as an opera conductor. Of the remaining recordings, the Viennese tidbits are variable in stylishness, and the Schumann and Dvořák symphonies are generally unimpressive. The Leinsdorf recordings reveal good discipline and solid solo playing, though Szell would have much work to do to bring unanimity of purpose to this orchestra.

✿   ✿   ✿

The same week Leinsdorf was making his recordings in Cleveland, Szell was at the Met preparing Verdi's *Otello* with Torsten Ralf in the title role, Stella Roman as Desdemona, and Leonard Warren as Iago. *The Plain Dealer's* J. C. Daschbach attended one of the rehearsals and sent back a story quoting a magnanimous Szell on the subject of making music. "We musicians are very fortunate, for we make our living doing the thing we like best to do," said Szell. "Music is not a task. It is something that is a delight to the performer as well as to the audience. That is, if it is well done. And the person who does not take delight in his music cannot produce a pleasing performance." Szell clearly was playing to the crowd. "Rehearsals should not be a grind. They should be enjoyable periods when we play for the sole reason that we like to play. We should enjoy these periods of creating a production that is to be a pleasure to the audience. We should not approach it as a job, but as the thing we want most to do for our own pleasure."

A member of the Met orchestra called Szell "an exacting director" whose "aim is always perfection. When things go right he is in a good mood. When they don't, we hear from him in no uncertain terms. But we know that he knows music and that all of his striving is only that we give the best performance that is humanly possible."

Cleveland, and the rest of the country, could hear the results of Szell's striving. The *Otello* premiere was broadcast on February 23, a performance preserved on tape, as is his vibrant conducting of *Der Rosenkavalier* on the

Met broadcast of a week earlier. Cleveland would get to experience Szell's operatic gifts in person just two months later (April 26), when he led *Rosenkavalier* during the Met's annual tour week at Public Hall.

Sidlo was counting on Szell not only to take the Cleveland Orchestra into the rarefied artistic realm inhabited by the New York Philharmonic, Boston Symphony, and Philadelphia Orchestra, but also to help the ensemble's bottom line through radio, recordings, and ticket sales. The budgets of the eastern orchestras were more than double Cleveland's at this time and their earnings almost triple. "But let the Orchestra strike fire with its audience the way it did a year ago and the way it did last December under Mr. Szell's magnetic baton, and our objective will soon be on the way of achievement," Sidlo said.

By mid-May, one objective was reached: subscription sales for Szell's first season had already topped the entire amount for the 1945–46 season. Still, Sidlo—aware that the institution had to continually raise more money to ward off deficits—hoped to increase the orchestra's earnings to between $75,000 and $100,000 a year. To spur others to donate more, he announced he was doubling his contribution.

While Sidlo and his colleagues were discussing dollars, Szell was beginning to reveal his compulsion to control every aspect of the orchestra's artistic operations (and other matters, as well). He wrote to program editor and assistant manager George H. L. Smith that he thought it best not to announce the entire repertoire early in order for news of the programming to have more of an impact during the season itself. He urged Smith to explore the possibility of purchasing four tuben, the brass instruments Richard Wagner had created with Hans Richter for the *Ring* cycle and which other composers, like Bruckner, used in their works. On the subject of auditions, Szell was planning to hear potential orchestra members in early April at the Met by invitation.

Szell was about to get nearly his every contractual wish concerning players. Three of the four wind principals he had requested to return—Farkas, Goslee, and Sharp—would do so. (Emerson Both opted to remain with NBC in Chicago.) Among other musicians returning were clarinetist Robert McGinnis (who had been in the navy and was then living in New York), oboist Ernest Serpentini (who had gone to the Pittsburgh Symphony), hornist Ernani Angelucci (who would come back after a brief tenure with the Philadelphia Orchestra), and six players who had been serving in the military. Szell's new concertmaster was to be Samuel Thaviu (concertmaster in Pittsburgh for three years), replacing Joseph Knitzer, who said he was leaving to pursue solo and teaching careers but actually was dismissed by Szell for being a "sourpuss" as concertmaster.

Many of these personnel changes were announced in April, just as Leinsdorf was ending his bumpy ride in Cleveland. He led his final concerts as conductor on April 18 and 20 with his transcription of Brahms's Quintet, Op. 34, Wagner's "Good Friday Spell" from *Parsifal*, and Strauss's *Till Eulenspiegel*. He was saluted by the orchestra with a standing ovation at the start of the first concert and received a gift from Sidlo at intermission. These performances were not to be his last encounters with the Cleveland Orchestra, though he wouldn't be back during Szell's tenure.

Leinsdorf would go on to serve in top positions with the Rochester Philharmonic, New York City Opera, and Boston Symphony. In February 1971, he appeared with the Cleveland Orchestra at Carnegie Hall for the first time since 1946, an occasion that was "as happy and gratifying an evening as I can recall." Leinsdorf also toured New Zealand and Australia with the orchestra in 1973 and was a regular presence as a guest conductor for more than a decade thereafter. And during the eventual transition between Lorin Maazel and Christoph von Dohnányi, he served in an unofficial supervisory capacity, conducting often in the hall where he had had such a frustrating time in the 1940s.

❊   ❊   ❊

Szell spent the months preceding his ascent to the Cleveland podium establishing himself as artistic chief and overseer of institutional policy. He didn't intend to be an ivory-tower figure. One of his first major announcements was the creation of a program giving two apprentice conductors the opportunity to be in residence for a full season to observe rehearsals and work under his guidance. They would be paid the minimum union scale of $85 a week for preparing scores and parts, conducting at rehearsals, and playing piano or another instrument when needed. The Kulas Foundation, founded by orchestra trustee E. J. Kulas, was donating $5,000 for two conductors who would have to pass a series of rigorous musical tests for Szell.

Szell planned to undertake the lion's share of subscription concerts his first season, giving several programs to Rudolph Ringwall and one each to guest conductors Bruno Walter, Igor Stravinsky, and Georges Enesco. The repertoire for Szell's inaugural year was beginning to emerge; he intended to work on a fair number of the pieces during the preseason rehearsal week with the orchestra. Among the new compositions Szell was thinking of conducting was Shostakovich's Ninth Symphony, which had received its world

premiere the previous November by the Leningrad Philharmonic under
Evgeny Mravinsky. Szell had obtained performance rights without seeing
the score, but once he did he was "so insulted by the irresponsible empti-
ness and boring vulgarity" of the piece that he decided not to perform it.
(And he would never conduct a Shostakovich symphony in Cleveland.)

The stage now was set for the new adventure. Szell was tinkering meticulously (some would say ruthlessly) with personnel, and massaging repertoire and many other details. Tickets sales were skyrocketing. Sidlo was delighted, especially after years of tumult and uncertainty. Every great orchestra, he told the board, had to grow slowly and to struggle. "You return
to the task somewhat discouraged but still determined, and you make a little more progress; until the day comes at last, if you are lucky, when you have
attained something fine and beautiful, something worth all the toil and sacrifice. That has been our good fortune, and in consequence we are on the
threshold of a golden era. We face the greatest prospect that Cleveland and
the Cleveland Orchestra have ever been presented with."

The lawyer known as "Mr. Music" never spoke truer words.

PART THREE

REACHING THE TOP

1946–1970

— 16 —

Genius George

What did Cleveland really know about the conductor who had enthralled its audience and captured its orchestra's podium? The public was aware of the most crucial matter: George Szell could make music with a probing intensity that was rare in any era. Still, it would take time for Cleveland musicians and patrons to realize the depth of the new conductor's knowledge and experience. His acclaimed performances with the NBC Symphony and the Metropolitan Opera had given him an artistic cachet that in turn added instant stature to the Cleveland Orchestra. But the 49-year-old Szell was no overnight success. He had chalked up one triumph after another—and a few setbacks, as well—since growing up a wunderkind in Vienna.

Szell considered himself Viennese, though this was only partly true. He was born Georg Szell on June 7, 1897, in Budapest, Hungary, to a Hungarian father and a Slovakian mother. An only child, Szell moved to Vienna with his parents in 1900 or 1903, according to various sources. Probably for business reasons, the family converted from Judaism to Catholicism upon arrival in Vienna, a notoriously anti-Semitic city. Szell's father ran a firm that *Time* magazine later would describe as "a private door-shaking police force for Vienna's gentry." In his adopted city, the young Georg absorbed music in the environment that had welcomed Mozart, Beethoven, Brahms, and Bruckner. He walked the same streets as some of the day's formidable musical geniuses, including Gustav Mahler and Arnold Schoenberg. He heard Mahler conduct Mozart's *Don Giovanni* in the innovative production designed by Alfred Roller. And he quickly showed signs that he was a prodigious musician. Trained by a number of fine teachers (one was Max Reger in Leipzig), Szell began to attract attention for his wizardly abilities as composer and pianist.

A major turning point in Szell's life was his introduction to his piano teacher, Richard Robert. Having fallen ill with pneumonia, the boy was treated by a doctor who invited the Szell family for an evening at his home.

The doctor's daughter played a waltz on the piano, after which Georg went home and wrote out the piece perfectly. Through the doctor, the young musician was introduced to Robert, who agreed to hear the boy and accepted him as a pupil.

Szell's progress was swift. In 1908, the 11-year-old made his debut, as pianist and composer, at Vienna's gilded Musikvereinsaal with the Wiener Tonkünstler, led by Oskar Nedbal, in Mozart's Piano Concerto in A major, K. 488. The program included an overture by Szell and his Rondo for Piano and Orchestra. He began traveling the same year, when he made a 10-concert European tour. Among the cities he visited was London, where Mozart had amazed the public in 1764 and 1765, and where Szell now did likewise. Indeed, while he was there, the *Daily Mail* dubbed him "the new Mozart." Interviewing Szell, the reporter gave him a theme and asked that he improvise variations. "Is this for piano only, or for orchestra?" the interviewer inquired, about the result. "For orchestra," said Szell. "I am 'hearing' all the instruments." It was an ability with which he later would startle Cleveland. "Do you remember everything you hear?" queried the reporter. "Always—when it is good music. I cannot always play it when I return from the concert, but I can write it all straight away—every note I have heard—and I never forget what I have once heard."

And Szell heard the best in Vienna, with which he developed a love-hate relationship. "I got a lot out of Vienna without being infected by its phony *Gemütlichkeit*," he said years later, referring to the so-called Viennese charm. At the Court Opera, Szell attended performances conducted by Bruno Walter (Mahler's assistant). He heard the Vienna Philharmonic under Arthur Nikisch, director of both the Berlin Philharmonic and the Leipzig Gewandhaus Orchestra. Nikisch had a powerful impact on Szell, who idolized the Hungarian conductor's mesmerizing music-making, if not his flamboyant podium personality.

Soon, Szell's compositions—expertly crafted works in Brahmsian style—were published by the Viennese firm Universal Edition. Still, Szell didn't take this aspect of his musical life too seriously. Eager to salute his friend on his 16th birthday, pianist Rudolf Serkin—also a Robert student—obtained several Szell pieces and played them for him. Szell didn't like what he heard. "Serkin! How can you play such trash?" he remarked. Later in life, he would do whatever he could to suppress performances of his music.

But Szell wasn't destined to be a composer, anyway. He had determined at age 12 or 13 that he would become a conductor. Though the beginnings of his podium career are hazy, history has accepted that his conducting debut occurred during the summer of 1913 in Bad Kissingen, the Bavarian spa town where his parents had taken him for a vacation. The Vienna Symphony was in residence there for concerts under Martin Spörr, who evidently hurt his arm—or, by one account, was hit in the groin by a tennis ball—and had to withdraw from a performance. No one seemed available to replace him until 16-year-old Szell, who had been watching rehearsals, was summoned to take over. The performance, which included Rossini's *William Tell* overture, was a victory for the aspiring maestro, whose future thus was set.

Szell's formidable gifts soon netted him more engagements—with Berlin's Blüthner Orchestra and at the Berlin Royal Opera, where he met a towering figure who would influence his career: German composer Richard Strauss. For a while, Strauss and Szell were close colleagues, and the former found one of the latter's feats remarkable: Szell could play Strauss's *Till Eulenspiegel* by memory at the piano and simulate the sound of a percussion instrument by cascading about the keyboard with his cufflinks.

The composer soon entrusted important musical matters to his brilliant disciple. The most famous episode in their relationship happened either in November 1916 (Szell's claim) or sometime in 1917 on the occasion of the very first recording of Strauss's *Don Juan*. According to Szell, Strauss instructed him to rehearse the Berlin Royal Opera orchestra before the early-morning recording session so that he could get some extra sleep. When the session was scheduled to begin, Strauss was nowhere to be seen. A budget-conscious Deutsche Grammophon executive told Szell to begin recording. Strauss hadn't arrived after the first four minutes and was still missing when Szell was told to start the second four minutes. Then Szell noticed the composer standing nearby. "Well, in this case one can cheerfully bite the dust if one sees such a young generation coming along," Strauss said. He instructed the producers to use the first eight minutes. By another account, the composer said: "Now I can die happy, with a young fellow like this to take over." Whatever his statement, Strauss conducted the last eight minutes, making for an excitingly schizophrenic recorded debut for *Don Juan*: Szell's portion is headlong and impassioned; Strauss's is expansive and majestic. (Only Strauss's name appears on the record label.)

Strauss made use of Szell not only at recording sessions but also during performances. On January 28, 1917, when Strauss conducted the revised version of his opera, *Ariadne auf Naxos*, at the Zurich Opera, Szell played the prominent piano part in the orchestra. Among those in the audience was the conductor Otto Klemperer, who had heard Szell perform Chopin's Second Piano Concerto in Prague eight years earlier. Klemperer was looking for a conductor to succeed him at the Municipal Opera in Strasbourg.

When Strauss recommended Szell for the job, Klemperer made it possible for Szell to appear as guest conductor, which led to his appointment. Szell lied about his age to get the job.

Szell worked in Strasbourg for a year and then served as an assistant conductor and coach at the German Opera in Prague for two years. He gained more operatic experience in Darmstadt and Düsseldorf before returning to the Berlin State Opera (formerly the Berlin Royal Opera) in 1925 as first conductor under Erich Kleiber, who that year was preparing the world premiere of Alban Berg's *Wozzeck*.

In 1929, Szell became general musical director of the German Opera and conductor of the Philharmonic in Prague—posts that had been held by Mahler, Klemperer, Kleiber, and Alexander von Zemlinsky. Then, a year into his tenure, he had a life-changing experience: he attended a concert by Arturo Toscanini and the New York Philharmonic. The qualities that Szell heard in Toscanini and the Philharmonic could be considered his own mantra, as Szell later told the *New York Times*: "The clarity of texture; the precision of ensemble; the rightness of balances; the virtuosity of every section, every solo-player of the orchestra—then at its peak—in the service of an interpretive concept of evident, self-effacing integrity, enforced with irresistible will power and unflagging ardor, set new, undreamed-of standards literally overnight."

Szell had a decisive effect on performance standards in Prague. "From the musicians he conducted, quite a few of whom were friends of mine, I had gathered that he was a fearsome character who bullied them with a ferocious temper and an encyclopedic knowledge of music that enabled him to win all arguments," wrote Joseph Wechsberg in a 1965 profile of Szell in *The New Yorker*. "He certainly made the orchestra sound better than it ever had before, and after listening to his performances of Mozart, Wagner, and Strauss, I had become one of his enthusiastic admirers."

Szell had plenty of detractors who believed he was a supreme artist but a cold and unforgiving human being. When Norwegian soprano Kirsten Flagstad auditioned for the Metropolitan Opera's Artur Bodanzky in St. Moritz in 1934, he suggested that she go to Prague to study with Szell. Flagstad spent 10 days in Prague, where Szell coached her in Wagner roles. He was confident that the Met would find the soprano well prepared. "But how stern and harsh he was with me during those ten days!" Flagstad said in her memoirs. "He would get so irritated over the most trivial mistake. I got quite scared at times. We spent one hour a day together on my Metropolitan roles. In-between I stayed in my hotel room and put in as many hours of study as I could possibly stand without collapsing."

At least one person in Prague evidently found Szell entrancing—Helene Schulz Teltsch, a divorcee with two young sons. After they were married in 1938, the couple became virtually inseparable. Helene would learn to deal with her husband's temper, obsession with perfection, and bulldozer approach to gourmet cooking (he made a total mess of the kitchen while concocting a fancy dish)—and to welcome his reliance on her ear for music as well. She would also see a side of Szell that few knew existed—the warm, loving, even sentimental husband whose letters to his wife begin with such endearments as "My Mugele" or "Dear Mugi" and are signed "Pussi" or "Pussi Teddybear."

Szell's early period in Prague coincided with his debut in the United States. During the 1930–31 and 1931–32 seasons, he appeared as a guest with the St. Louis Symphony, which was looking for a conductor. Szell's chief competitor was Vladimir Golschmann, a debonair Frenchman whose way with the ladies helped win him the post. For the next few years, Szell toiled productively in Prague, until the threat of Nazism became uncomfortable. Not one, but two separate posts solved the problem, at least temporarily: In 1937, Szell was named conductor of the Scottish Orchestra in Glasgow and principal guest conductor of the Residentie Orchestra in The Hague.

One guest conductor at the Residentie Orchestra was Toscanini, who discovered a vastly improved ensemble. Szell had to turn down Toscanini's invitation to conduct the NBC Symphony in 1939: he was committed to engagements with orchestras of the Australian Broadcasting Company in 1938 and 1939. When the outbreak of World War II convinced Szell that he couldn't return to Europe, he took Helene to New York City, where he accepted a position teaching composition at the Mannes School of Music on Manhattan's East Side and devising orchestral transcriptions for a publisher. He also studied the top American orchestras and played chamber music with friends. During the summers of 1939 and 1940, Szell led the Los Angeles Philharmonic at the Hollywood Bowl.

Finally, in 1941, he conducted Toscanini's NBC Symphony. His success led to five more concerts, though the master didn't always appreciate Szell's rehearsal methods. Pianist Oscar Levant told of an NBC Symphony rehearsal that Szell was conducting: "It was Beethoven's Second Symphony and each bar was diagnosed, torn apart and put together until finally Toscanini couldn't stand it any longer and harangued at Szell, 'It's my orchestra! My orchestra and my intellectual capacity for the interpretation of Beethoven! It's an insult to me!' "

However insulting Szell could be, his gifts must have been apparent. He began receiving invitations from other American orchestras to appear as guest conductor. In 1942, Edward Johnson, the Metropolitan Opera's manager, hired him, mainly to conduct German repertoire. Szell made his Met debut on December 9, 1942, leading Strauss's *Salome*. "A virtuoso job on a difficult and complex work," wrote the *New York Herald Tribune*'s Virgil Thomson; "the score glowed and pulsated," noted the *New York Evening Post*'s Oscar Thompson. Szell remained very busy that December (and well into 1943) at the Met, also conducting Wagner's *Tannhäuser* and Mussorgsky's *Boris Godunov*.

The month Szell made his Met debut, Artur Rodzinski was negotiating to become the New York Philharmonic's musical director starting with the 1943–44 season. Within weeks, Szell was a candidate for the Cleveland post, though the job that time would go to Erich Leinsdorf. But Szell's concerts at Severance Hall in November 1944 and December 1945 would completely derail Leinsdorf's Cleveland career, laying the foundation for a historic orchestral partnership.

Raves and Raids

"Second to none." They sounded like fighting words. George Szell hadn't even led a note as musical director and conductor of the Cleveland Orchestra, and already he was setting the gears in motion for a wholesale transformation. Musicians deemed unworthy of the orchestra were out. Valued principal players who had left were back in. The personnel list, at 92 musicians, was the largest in the orchestra's history. Szell was exerting his will in areas where his predecessors had barely set foot, such as program books and season brochures. Ticket sales and fund-raising were soaring.

Szell began the musical metamorphosis by holding a full week of rehearsals prior to the first week of his inaugural season, an expensive feat that Nikolai Sokoloff, Artur Rodzinski, or Erich Leinsdorf could not have pulled off. The orchestra was obligated to provide up to nine services (rehearsals or performances) per week in 1946, usually playing five rehearsals (starting on Mondays) and two subscription concerts (Thursday and Saturday). Holding nine preseason rehearsals in October, Szell read through many of the works he and the orchestra were scheduled to perform that season. With five opening-week rehearsals added, the orchestra had an unprecedented 14 rehearsals before playing its first concert of the season. The artistic benefits could only have been enormous.

Szell rehearsals became renowned for being efficient, productive, and grueling. "Rehearsals were a matter of life and death. So were performances," recalled Kurt Loebel, who joined the violin section in 1947 and stayed for 50 years. Szell often would begin a rehearsal by conducting a piece from start to finish and then methodically dissect details, adjust balances, correct rhythms, and exhort his players to listen to one another as if they were members of a large string quartet. Szell viewed the ideal orchestra as an enormous chamber group in which every strand of sound could be heard, unless it wasn't supposed to be.

He shared his philosophy of orchestral playing with critic-musicologist

Paul Henry Lang: "I personally like complete homogeneity of sound, phrasing and articulation within each section, and then—when the ensemble is
perfect—the proper balance between sections plus complete flexibility—so
that in each movement one or more principal voices can be accompanied by
the others. To put it simply: the most sensitive ensemble playing." Szell bris-
tled when anyone mentioned the so-called "sound" of the Cleveland
Orchestra, believing that the style of music should determine the sound, not
any particular defining qualities of the orchestra. He preferred to concentrate on matters of phrasing and, especially, articulation, "which is so much
more important than anything else, because it means, absolutely, the delivery of the music for the proper understanding on the part of the listener."

This delivery wasn't easy. "He wouldn't allow you to think for yourself,"
said Daniel Majeske, whom Szell appointed concertmaster in 1969. "He
spelled out everything in millimeters and micrograms. He certainly could
have been a pharmacist, because he used to talk about weighing all of these
things on a pharmacist's scale as far as how you were going to make this
nuance."

Accusations of rehearsal mania would rage throughout Szell's tenure. On
one occasion, he was working on Mozart's "Haffner" Symphony when he
told his musicians, "Well, that went so well we really don't have to bother
with it anymore except one little spot in the first movement we need to touch
up." Some touch-up it was, according to Klaus George Roy, the orchestra's
program annotator from 1958 to 1988. "It was just like at the dentist's—the
little spot became larger and larger," he said. "The whole first movement was
rehearsed, all the other three movements were rehearsed. By evening it was
dead. He killed it with overrehearsal." Roy attributed Szell's obsession with
rehearsing in part to his drive for perfection: "That was a real weakness in
him. He was never done rehearsing, not even in the performance. They used
to say he even rehearsed the inspiration."

"He was prepared to sacrifice the spontaneity of the performance to make
his point for the orchestra," recalled Louis Lane, a member of the orchestra's conducting staff for 27 years. "And he did it and he knew he was doing
it and he was willing to do that for the sake of future development."

John Mack, who would become principal oboe in 1965, said Szell could
have been writing his own epitaph in rehearsal one morning, when he told
the orchestra, "I want this phrase to sound completely spontaneous—however, as a result of meticulous planning." The musicians couldn't contain
themselves. "We all roared with laughter," said Mack. But laughter wasn't a
frequent sound during Szell rehearsals. Cloyd Duff, the orchestra's princi-

pal timpanist for almost 40 years, remembered the uncompromising sense of purpose the conductor brought to the preparation of every type of music. "He never took a chance on things," said Duff. "He would even rehearse the 'Star-Spangled Banner.' We were probably the greatest overrehearsed orchestra in the world."

❀   ❀   ❀

While Szell was fine-tuning the ensemble for his first season, Cleveland played host to numerous stage events of varied appeal. Billy Rose's touring production of *Carmen Jones* (music by Georges Bizet, text by Oscar Hammerstein II) was on the boards at the Hanna Theatre. Music Hall was presenting the San Carlo Opera Company in *Lucia di Lammermoor*, *Carmen* (again Bizet, minus Hammerstein), *Rigoletto*, *Madama Butterfly*, and *Aida*. On a less exalted level, burlesque was thriving at the Roxy Theatre at East Ninth and Chester.

Stirred into this eclectic mix on October 17 and 19 at Severance Hall were Szell's inaugural concerts, a calling-card program comprising Weber's *Oberon* overture, Debussy's *Afternoon of a Faun*, Strauss's *Don Juan*, and Beethoven's "Eroica" Symphony. These works, which would be heard often under Szell's baton for the next 24 years, helped the conductor astound the Cleveland audience, as a breathless Herbert Elwell noted the next morning on the front page (above the fold) of *The Plain Dealer*: "This is it, the kind of Cleveland Orchestra we have been waiting for . . . the kind which will unquestionably be able to hold its head high and go out and make a name for itself among the finest orchestras of the world." Along with smoothness in the strings and better tuning and blending of instruments, Elwell was impressed that the orchestra had become so unified in such a short period. The playing had a "full, warm singing tone" and was marked by "vital propulsion." Elwell immediately discounted any hint that the new conductor might be a cold fish. "Above all Szell is not afraid to inject romantic feeling into music which calls for it, yet when the rigidity of classic architecture is demanded, it is there in the full glory of finely delineated proportions, as was so convincingly evident in the noble enfoldment [*sic*] of Beethoven's 'Eroica,' which occupied the last half of the program." Oscar Smith reported in the *Akron Beacon Journal* that "The ensemble hasn't had such tone quality, fine precision and delicate shades of expression in three years—since the days of Artur Rodzinski, in fact. Szell apparently has brought the orchestra out of its guest-conductor slump."

Szell's upbeat, and surprisingly giddy, assessment of the first concert suggests that even the perfectionist conductor could bask in his accomplishment. "The opening night went splendidly and the orchestra played simply magnificently; in fact, as beautifully and as well integrated as I had expected them to play after a year's work," Szell wrote to Bruno Zirato, assistant manager of the New York Philharmonic, two days after the first concert. "I shall send you clippings as soon as I can obtain them. At the present moment the papers are sold out."

Szell's second week of concerts held several significant firsts for Cleveland, the most important being the debut of pianist Leon Fleisher in the Schumann concerto. The 18-year-old Fleisher, from San Francisco, was to become one of the conductor's favorite soloists in concert and in the recording studio. Along with the pianist's debut, the concerts of October 24 and 26 brought performances of what would become two Szell standards, Berlioz's *Roman Carnival Overture* and Brahms's Second Symphony, and the Cleveland premiere of three of the *Four Sea Interludes* from Britten's opera, *Peter Grimes*. Szell would later be excoriated for failing to pay sufficient attention to contemporary music, yet here he was, in the second week of his tenure, conducting the Britten pieces, which were only a year old at the time.

Szell largely steered clear of the 20th century for his third week, focusing instead on beloved Czech works that would also become Cleveland standards (Smetana's *My Country*, Janáček's Sinfonietta, Dvořák's "New World", all of which he recorded with the orchestra). But his fourth program found a balance between the old—Mendelssohn's Violin Concerto, with Erica Morini, and Schubert's C major Symphony—and the recent, with the Cleveland premiere of William Grant Still's *In Memoriam: The Colored Soldiers Who Died for Democracy*. Despite his efforts on behalf of 20th-century music, Szell quickly earned a reputation as a conductor who seemed only to pay lip service to the moderns, especially American composers. At one point during Szell's first season, trustee Percy Brown read the riot act to Gardner Read, a composer and faculty member at the Cleveland Institute of Music, who had told colleagues that Szell was refusing to consider performing any works by Clevelanders. "Gave him long lecture on 'Self,' and pursuing Geo Szell, and advised him to keep his mouth shut," Brown wrote in his notebook. Read agreed to sign an apology to Szell.

❉   ❉   ❉

Szell needed only four weeks—and probably far fewer—to determine that certain changes in the orchestra's personnel would be necessary by the end of the season. One of the casualties would be concertmaster Samuel Thaviu.

Szell had been so intent on getting rid of Joseph Knitzer as concertmaster that he had offered Thaviu a one-year contract, even though he was already thinking of offering the job to another violinist for the following season.

Thaviu didn't know that something fishy was going on. He had signed the Cleveland contract partly as a means of escaping the wrath of another great, autocratic conductor, Fritz Reiner, under whom he had played concertmaster in the Pittsburgh Symphony for three years. In the fall of 1946, Thaviu had every reason to believe he was fulfilling his Cleveland duties satisfactorily. Upon returning in early December from a guest-conducting stint with the Chicago Symphony, Szell led a program containing a work in which the concertmaster must shine, Strauss's *Till Eulenspiegel*. The featured artist several weeks later on the final program of 1946 was none other than Thaviu, in his solo debut with the ensemble in the Dvořák Violin Concerto. At what point Thaviu realized that things weren't going so well in Cleveland isn't clear. But he may have picked up a crucial signal when he advised Szell that he and his wife were on the verge of buying a house in Shaker Heights. "I wouldn't," Szell cautioned.

Given the chronology of events, Szell's actions could be viewed as "underhanded," as Louis Lane later called them. The previous year, Szell had been a guest conductor of the Detroit Symphony, whose concertmaster was a superb Russian-born violinist he had known as a member of the NBC Symphony. Szell was impressed not only by Josef Gingold's elegant artistry, but also by the violinist's qualities of leadership and humanity, which he believed would serve Cleveland well. On the way to a Cleveland Orchestra tour concert at the University of Michigan in Ann Arbor in November 1946, Szell made a stop in Detroit and quietly offered him the concertmaster post. Gingold initially declined, pledging loyalty to the Detroit orchestra. On a second try, Szell outlined his plan to take the Cleveland Orchestra to the top and told Gingold that he had 20 minutes to make a decision. A contract was signed. Szell and Gingold agreed to button their lips until the appropriate moment.

Back in Cleveland, board president Thomas L. Sidlo and the trustees could hardly contain their elation over the results of Szell's opening months. Along with soaring ticket sales, the new partnership was earning rave reviews at home and on tour. Their Saturday night radio broadcasts were getting higher ratings than programs by the Boston, NBC, New York, and Philadelphia orchestras. Things were looking so good financially that Sidlo predicted the Cleveland Orchestra would finish the year in the black.

Now, from a position of growing strength, Szell pushed his plans forward. He asked the board to increase the orchestra's season to 30 weeks in order to retain excellent players and draw new talent, thereby improving the quality of the ensemble. Although the minimum annual salary was only $2,400 (half the orchestra was earning more), the musicians had told the board they would forgo a weekly wage increase for the time being if the seasons were longer. With 12 weeks of summer concerts added under this plan (at lower weekly rates), the season would be extended to 42 weeks, a major jump from previous years. One of the prime goals in terms of season length, said Sidlo, was to gain "absolute equality with the Big Four," meaning the orchestras of Boston, Chicago, New York, and Philadelphia. The 30-week plan for the 1947–48 season was unanimously approved.

As Szell continued his inaugural season, he was preparing for a veritable bloodbath on the personnel front. The end of January 1947 brought the news that Thaviu would leave at the close of the season (no reason given) and that principal hornist Philip Farkas planned to abandon music for a year to go into his father's advertising business in Chicago. Two weeks later, principal oboist Philip Kirchner—who had been with the orchestra since its first season—and principal cellist Harry Fuchs announced they were departing. In the *Press*, Milton Widder referred to the "wave of resignations of principal players." An editorial in the *Press* reflected the confusion and anger that some Clevelanders were feeling as a result of the so-called resignations. "Is it absolutely necessary to rip up the personnel of the orchestra to achieve another extra measure of perfection? Is it necessary to put the orchestra personnel on pins and needles of fears for their jobs in the pursuit of that same mirage of perfection?" The editorial is respectful of Szell, "an artist of great virtuosity" and "high intelligence," but oddly disdainful of Rodzinski, "who would not have understood or cared" about the issue.

The Rodzinski reference actually was timely, on two counts. In mid-December, Szell invited the orchestra's former conductor to return as a guest, though Rodzinski declined to give him a definite answer, citing the board's previous view that such an invitation would be "a delicate matter." His hesitancy was explained by what soon followed: On February 3, 1947, Rodzinski abruptly resigned from the New York Philharmonic, accusing manager Arthur Judson of conspiracy and lack of ethics, and three days later signed a contract to become conductor of the Chicago Symphony.

Then came the raids, unsuccessful and otherwise. Upon signing in Chicago, Rodzinski tried to hire three principal players from Cleveland— clarinetist Robert McGinnis, hornist Farkas, and trumpeter Louis Davidson. None accepted the offer. Szell had more luck, although a small storm ensued. The day after Rodzinski's failed raid was announced, Szell's surreptitious hiring of Gingold hit the news. Karl Krueger, musical director of the Detroit Symphony, accused Szell of pirating his orchestra. Szell, rightly, sneered at claims made by the people in Detroit. "Any organization is entitled to approach any artist in perfectly good faith for a time for which he is not legally committed to another organization," he told a reporter. Krueger wasn't about to let the matter rest. He wrote Szell a letter that he released to the press. "I cannot for a moment believe that the estimable members of the governing body of the Cleveland Orchestra could be guilty of collusion with you in your snide negotiations in this case," wrote Krueger. "For Mr. Gingold I have only the warmest good wishes. But whether Mr. Gingold is active in Cleveland or Detroit is quite beside the point. The issue in this instance is your method. To me it appears reprehensible." Sticks and stones. Szell had his concertmaster. The abundance of orchestral brouhaha caused mirth in the media. *Downbeat*, the jazz magazine, headlined an article, "Sympho Slugfests Not for Fun!—Longhair Scraps Put Even The Dorseys to Shame." Other headline writers had a field day: "Sour Notes! Musicians Off Beat in Contract" (*Portland [Ore.] Journal*); "Cleveland Orchestra Director Pooh Poohs 'Piracy' Charges" (*Dayton News*); "Krueger Blasts Raid on Detroit Symphony" (*Detroit News*).

Szell was not to be distracted from the business of making music in Cleveland. Before the dust had settled on the Gingold affair, the conductor led the world premiere of Hindemith's Concerto for Piano and Orchestra, with Jesus Maria Sanroma as soloist. More evidence of Szell's commitment to contemporary music came in March 1947, when he led the first Cleveland performances of Schoenberg's Theme and Variations for Orchestra (the composer's 1943 arrangement of a band piece). The city's music critics were divided over the piece: Arthur Loesser, in the *Press*, found it trite; Herbert Elwell called it ingenious.

Behind the scenes, the orchestra was simmering with resentment over the "forced 'resignations' and general bad feelings created by the conductor," wrote a concertgoer in a letter to the editor in the *Press*. Szell agreed to speak with the orchestra committee about the issue, but he gave only a brief speech and "stalked out of the room," reported the *Press*. Orchestra manager Carl Vosburgh defended Szell's methods and insisted that some of the players weren't returning because they had asked for more money than the orchestra could afford.

The public was taking an interest in the altercations. Another letter to the editor in the *Press* put the matter in pointed context. "Szell has shown apparent coldness, arbitrariness and precise brutality, which are very hard to understand in a man of such intelligence," wrote the letter writer. "Is it true, as many charge, that these mid-European maestros can't come over here and operate with human decent contacts [*sic*] with the musicians they direct?" Szell had created an atmosphere in which "the musicians at the orchestra are scared for their lives." The fright would last another 23 years.

In an attempt to cool everyone down, Vosburgh announced that 87 of the orchestra's 92 players had been offered contracts for the coming season. Thirteen had declined. Two of the five players who had not been offered contracts were being given the chance to reaudition for Szell. At most, Vosburgh said, the orchestra would have 18 new players (it would turn out to be 20), not significantly higher than previous years—17 changes in 1945–46, 14 in 1944–45, 16 in 1943–44, and 17 in 1942–43. What is striking is the fact that within five years the orchestra experienced a massive 84 personnel changes—more players than Rodzinski ever had during his tenure.

However stormy the weather had become in Cleveland, no one could deny that Szell was fulfilling his mandate. The orchestra wasn't yet second to none, but it clearly was moving upward in a swift artistic arc. As his first season drew to a close, Szell balanced the new with the old on one program—the Vaughan Williams Symphony No. 5 paired with Brahms's Piano Concerto No. 1, the latter featuring his Viennese friend, Rudolf Serkin. "The two oldest cronies in Cleveland today," as Szell expressed it. He concluded the season April 17 and 19, 1947, with music by one of the composers who would help him put the orchestra on the classical map, Beethoven. The lineup was prime Szell territory: the *Leonore* Overture No. 3 and the fourth and fifth symphonies. "George Szell's conducting of the Cleveland Orchestra in a Beethoven program last night at Severance Hall brought to a brilliant close the Thursday night series of the most successful season in the orchestra's history," wrote Elwell.

✻   ✻   ✻

Between these final concerts, Szell and the orchestra made a series of tests for Columbia Records, which had come to town for its first recordings with the new pairing. Szell previously had said he wouldn't record until the orchestra had reached a certain level. Even with players who were on their way out, however, he now apparently was eager to begin. For the three days of recording sessions (immediately after the closing concerts), he chose music he had conducted at Severance Hall in recent weeks—six Dvořák Slavonic Dances, Beethoven's Symphony No. 4, and Mozart's Symphony No. 39. Szell would never alter his recording routine in Cleveland. He would fully rehearse and perform the works before preserving them for posterity. Most of them would be recorded the day after the Thursday night concert or over the weekend.

The marked changes in personality and technical ability that the orchestra had undergone in one season under Szell can be heard on the three recordings they made on April 21, 22, and 23, 1947. The ensemble that sounds so loose and unbalanced on Leinsdorf's recordings of 14 months before now emerges as tightly wound and cohesive. Szell's fastidious attention to articulation and rhythm is already in place, though he doesn't yet have the string section to pull off his ideals of precision or finesse. Nor is the wind section completely settled. Flutist Maurice Sharp, clarinetist McGinniss (leaving the orchestra after these sessions), and bassoonist George Goslee are marvelous section leaders and soloists. But oboist Kirchner, who sounds wonderful on recordings with Sokoloff and Rodzinski, had become so nasal that his playing fully justifies Szell's decision to show him the door.

These recordings provide an early glimpse of the Cleveland Orchestra the world would come to know. Szell's penchant for clarity and ensemble unity is stamped is all over the performances. The recordings also explode a number of Szell myths regarding rigid pacing, lack of warmth, and harshness of sound. There would be times when the Cleveland Orchestra under Szell indeed could be accused of sounding strident and cool. But the earliest recordings are finely wrought, elegant performances.

Szell's affinity for Czech repertoire is apparent in the Slavonic Dances, which burst with robust energy and affectionate nuances. If the orchestra was shaking in its boots over the conductor's handling of personnel issues, the anxiety isn't evident in the playing. Dvořák's heartwarming celebrations of national dance idioms unfold with utter naturalness. The Beethoven Fourth Symphony, performed twice by the orchestra in the preceding days, sounds lived-in and refined to a high gloss. Szell doesn't follow Beethoven's metronome markings slavishly; many slow tempos are slower than marked, and even the quick tempos are less manic than Szell could be. The result is aristocratic classicism, full of rhythmic zest and order, but also motivated phrasing and meticulous detail. This would be the first Szell-Cleveland recording released, in December 1947.

The third recording session was devoted to the Mozart Symphony No. 39, another work that established the orchestra's distinctive classical style. It is a superb performance, nuanced and relaxed.

❀   ❀   ❀

Planning for his second season in the spring of 1947, Szell gave Vosburgh permission to assign associate conductor Rudolph Ringwall or Josef Gingold (who hadn't yet arrived as concertmaster) the responsibility for hiring two good violinists, "male or female," but to go without extra players rather "than

have the section spoiled by deadwood just in order to show off numbers."
Even so, the numbers were up. For the 1947–48 season, the orchestra would
have 95 musicians, including two apprentice conductors, Seymour Lipkin
and Louis Lane, whom Szell had hired to succeed his first season's appren-
tices, Theodore Bloomfield and John Boda. The new season was to include
appearances by two guest conductors, Alsatia's Charles Münch and
Czechoslovakia's Václav Talich.

As would be his custom throughout his Cleveland tenure, Szell spent the
summer of 1947 in Europe, golfing and preparing for performances. His
scheduled operatic engagements at the Glyndebourne and Edinburgh
music festivals never took place, Szell wrote to Vosburgh, because the casts
were incompetent and the festivals mismanaged. Rudolf Bing, head of
Glyndebourne at the time, tells a somewhat different tale in his juicy memoirs, *5000 Nights at the Opera*. Szell had been hired to conduct Verdi's
Macbeth and Mozart's *The Marriage of Figaro* at both festivals. Arriving for
rehearsals at Glyndebourne, he flew into a rage about a young, inexperienced American soprano who had been hired to sing Susanna in *Figaro*.
According to Bing, Szell actually was miffed because he assumed that the
freelance orchestra was not likely to be a top-notch ensemble. Whatever the
reasons, Szell—"a nasty man, God rest his soul," noted the former
Glyndebourne chief—left in a huff. As Bing, soon to be general manager of
the Metropolitan Opera, tartly summed up the situation, "it would not be
the last time George Szell walked out on me."

– 18 –

Honing the Instrument

A conductor can be immensely gifted as an interpreter and programmer, but what will result if the orchestra at his fingertips cannot live up to what he hears in his head? George Szell was unwilling to find out. With his first successful season completed, he had beguiled the ears of the public and justified the unwavering support of the board. Now he had to find more musicians who would enable him to create his ideal symphonic instrument. The building process wouldn't be pretty.

From the time Szell accepted the Cleveland post until the moment six years later when he declared his mission essentially accomplished, the ensemble went through almost 90 personnel changes—enough to staff an entire orchestra. Players who were unable, or unwilling, to put up with Szell's rigorous standards and anxiety-provoking temperament remained only a short time. Among the musicians who joined during the late 1940s and early 1950s were a large number who would play longtime roles in the orchestra's rise to prominence, and not only in principal positions.

Szell was putting his dream ensemble in place meticulously and sometimes deviously, as in the case of Josef Gingold. By the start of his second season (1947–48), he had brought in four principals—concertmaster Gingold, cellist Ernst Silberstein, oboist Bert Gassman (who had been an orchestra member from 1930 to 1944), and clarinetist Bernard Portnoy—to replace players he had let go. A number of musicians who would stay in Cleveland for most of their careers also arrived at this time: Kurt Loebel (violin), William Kiraly (viola), Laszlo Krausz (viola), Martin Simon (cello), Irving Nathanson (bass), and William Hebert (piccolo). Their identity as Cleveland Orchestra players would be inextricably linked with Szell.

In Gingold, the conductor found a concertmaster who may have exceeded even his lofty expectations. Born in 1909 in Brest Litovsk, Russia, Gingold began playing violin at a young age and moved to the United States in 1920. He received his first "decent bow" from Josef Fuchs, future concertmaster of the Cleveland Orchestra, and studied with Vladimir Graffman before making his New York recital debut in 1926. After studies in Brussels with Eugene Ysaye, Gingold returned to America, where he earned his first paychecks playing assistant concertmaster on Broadway in Jerome Kern's *The Cat and the Fiddle*. The experience taught him two crucial lessons. "First, never take your eyes off the baton for a split second; no two performances are alike," Gingold told an interviewer. "Second, what may be the hundredth performance for you is the first performance for the audience. Never become a *routinier*."

He played several other shows and then moved out of the pit in 1937 to become a founding member of Toscanini's NBC Symphony, which Szell first conducted in 1941. Two years later, Gingold became concertmaster of the Detroit Symphony, which led to a reunion with Szell in 1945 and his furtive Cleveland appointment a year later. Gingold's impact on the Cleveland Orchestra in 1947 was almost instantaneous. Where his two immediate predecessors had failed, especially in bonding with colleagues, the new concertmaster was a triumph. A violinist of uncommon warmth and flair, he was also a diplomat, nurturer, and father figure who knew how to handle delicate situations.

Part of Gingold's sweet, impish nature was his ability to doubletalk to the point where "nine words out of ten [had] no meaning at all," according to violinist Arnold Steinhardt, who sat next to Gingold in Cleveland for five seasons as assistant concertmaster. With Szell on the warpath, Gingold would defuse the tension by stopping a rehearsal to ask about bowings. Then he would "launch into this doubletalk, interspersed with a few strategically placed string-playing terms," recalled Steinhardt. "The orchestra would hold its breath. Szell would study his score for some time and say, 'Well, in *this* case, I'll leave the bowing up to you.' He never caught on—or never wanted to admit that he didn't understand. It was *heroic* of Joe."

Gingold, like virtually everyone who came into Szell's orbit, had an intricate relationship with the conductor. Szell trusted his concertmaster but often abused him and occasionally accused him, unjustly, of ruining a performance by changing a microscopic detail. The most patient of gentlemen, Gingold kept his cool unless Szell was entirely unreasonable. Then the concertmaster would let the conductor know, in private, that he couldn't treat him this way. Szell eventually would patch things up, at least in the short term, and even socialize with Gingold and his wife, though he would always be critical. "More salt," Szell once commanded upon tasting a dish that was simmering on the Gingold stove.

As concertmaster, Gingold often took over, judiciously, where the boss left off. "Musically, Joe made up for Szell's limitations," Steinhardt recalled.

"Szell thought he knew everything and would impose his own bowings. But Joe truly knows everything there is to know about bowings. When the orchestra's string sound became tight and lacking in sheen, he'd suggest using more bow to get more suppleness. When Szell had lapses in his conducting technique—especially in twentieth-century music—Joe would discreetly lead the ensemble. Joe practiced the orchestral parts as thoroughly as solo pieces."

✧   ✧   ✧

A formal audition hadn't been necessary in Gingold's case. Szell liked what he heard and closed the deal himself, as did other conductors of the time. Before musicians' unions gained power in the mid-1960s, the orchestra hiring process was not democratic. There were no screens, established audition procedures, or player committees to influence the final decision. A conductor hired whom he wished at whatever price he wanted (within reason). Szell sometimes turned to an assistant or principal player to find a replacement. But the majority of musicians who hoped to join the Cleveland Orchestra had to face the conductor one on one, either onstage at Severance Hall or in a hotel room or concert hall in another city.

An audition with Szell could be a daunting experience. Kurt Loebel, a Viennese-born violinist who fled from the Nazis in 1939 with his instrument, a suitcase, and the equivalent of $30, played for Szell during the summer of 1947 at Steinway Hall in Manhattan. The audition included a Mozart violin concerto, which went well, and Beethoven's Eighth Symphony, which didn't. Szell told Loebel to come back several days later, when a contract for the third stand in the first violin section was offered. Loebel naively said he was playing second stand in the Dallas Symphony at the time, suggesting that third stand was beneath him, and he told the conductor he needed to consult his wife. "Mr. Loebel, take it or leave it," Szell boomed. The contract was signed, beginning Loebel's 50-year tenure in the orchestra. "To come to Cleveland was not to come to Cleveland, it was to come to George Szell," said Loebel. "We paid a dear price for it. It was hell, but it was great, for the most part."

No musician who auditioned for the Cleveland Orchestra could be guaranteed that Szell would listen for long. Once, he was sitting in Severance Hall with Gingold and staff conductor Louis Lane when a violinist from another major orchestra walked onstage. The fiddler tuned for several minutes, becoming more and more out of tune. A smile came across the man's face as he finally prepared to play. "Thank you very much," Szell announced, before the candidate had sounded a real note. "That will be all."

Szell generally could tell within seconds whether a musician would fit into the Cleveland Orchestra. At other times, he kept a candidate for an hour or more if the player piqued his interest. Szell began auditions by requesting a solo piece, partly to relax the musician, partly to gauge technique and musical intelligence. This would be followed either by another solo work or with orchestral excerpts, including heavy doses of Mozart for string players. Those who passed the initial scrutiny might be asked to alter phrasing or style in order for Szell to see how flexible the musician could be. In some instances, depending upon the conductor's mood and the player's ability, auditions turned into mini-lessons, with Szell suggesting bowings, fingerings (for string, wind, and brass players alike), and phrasing that would help the candidate reach specific musical goals.

Landing a job in Szell's Cleveland Orchestra promised artistic exhilaration, if not necessarily contentment or security. Even players who respected Szell highly considered him a tyrannical master with a sharp tongue who could make life miserable for everyone. "It came, I think, from the fact that he was a child prodigy," said program annotator Klaus George Roy. "He always had his own way. He was an only child. He was the be-all and end-all for his parents and everyone else, and he became a man who learned that his word was law, and that is not good for a personality." A perfectionist who tolerated no errors, Szell could wither a player with a remark or by hurling a stinging glance from behind his thick spectacles, which won him the name "Dr. Cyclops." Intimidation came naturally to Szell, though he may not always have realized he was causing undue stress. "Look out—the last time you played it, it was perfect!" he told a wind player, as if this would help.

Szell's perfectionism and need to control extended to virtually every aspect of the orchestra and its operations—including nonmusical ones. Szell gave advice to cleaning women at Severance Hall, even telling them what brand of toilet paper to install in the rest rooms. He insisted that his male players wear coats and ties at all times when on tour—except, perhaps, while sleeping. One player lost his job after Szell noticed that he had purchased a new car instead of a fine instrument. Another musician who fell down with his expensive violin in hand wasn't asked if he had hurt himself: Szell wanted to know if the instrument was damaged.

Szell gave guest artists tips on the best places to stay in Cleveland and where to buy groceries (Russo's on Cedar Hill, he informed mezzo-soprano Janet Baker). He personally negotiated all orchestra salaries above minimum scale, a situation that led to inequities—third-chair players, for example, making more than the principal—that weren't addressed until after his death. He told players what to eat on tour and kept close tabs on the health of his players—perhaps out of human concern but mostly to make sure that the orchestra's ensemble skills were never compromised. One time, Szell expressed scorn over an ailment that put several players out of commission temporarily. "The hernias in the Orchestra are precarious," he complained in a written note. "Why does Hernia recovery take all that long??"

Program annotator Roy experienced Szell's domineering personality on numerous occasions, though one experience stuck out. Asked to drive the conductor to the orchestra's concert in Ashland, Ohio, Roy picked up Szell at the conductor's Shaker Heights home and told him that he didn't know how to get to the highway. No problem, Szell answered. As Roy drove through Shaker Square and began to make a turn, the car suddenly gave a violent lurch. Roy thought he would have to tell Szell that his car had had a flat. But it hadn't. Szell, though deep in thought about the Mozart symphony he was going to conduct that night, had reached out with his left hand and turned the steering wheel in the opposite direction. When they arrived back at Szell's home after the concert, the conductor told Roy, "Thank you, very well driven."

To everyone but a handful of trustees and friends, Szell was always addressed as "Mr. Szell." He put on different faces for different people. He was pleasant but standoffish with the public: he didn't like small talk. He viewed trustees as colleagues. They set institutional policies and gave him full artistic responsibility. They also raised the money that enabled him to run his musical machine. Szell kept close tabs on his staff, occasionally meddling in day-to-day details.

The musicians saw another Szell—the despotic conductor who expected the highest standards and would allow nothing to stand in his way. The results were exceptional. So was the tension. "Every Monday-morning rehearsal had to be a Carnegie Hall performance," recalled harpist Alice Chalifoux. "A lot of people got ulcers and had to go to psychoanalysts." Chalifoux's view was confirmed by Michael Maxwell, who became assistant manager in 1966 and general manager in 1970. "About forty percent of the musicians included some form of psychiatric care on their insurance claims," Maxwell said. "That is probably shared by others of the major orchestra group. The pressures can be staggering."

As forbidding and compulsive as he often could be, however, Szell showed signs of humanity and even impish humor. He occasionally helped musicians in emotional or financial distress. He did so quietly to avoid appearing vulnerable or to let anyone take advantage of him. And he could reveal a dry wit. Violinist Arnold Steinhardt wrote of the time Szell drove him to his physical for the Ohio National Guard, membership in which would keep the young assistant concertmaster out of the draft. One requirement of the physical was a urine specimen. As Steinhardt "emerged from the bathroom clutching my container of steaming liquid, Szell continued to scrutinize me," the violinist wrote. "The warm amber liquid sloshed in its jar as I walked past him with as much dignity as I could muster. I reached the door, and I heard Szell's voice, with its clipped German accent: 'Imported or domestic?' "

The conductor could also show a lighter side when confronted with someone strong, clever, or foolish enough to stand up to him. Louis Lane was a 22-year-old student at the Eastman School of Music in Rochester, New York, when he auditioned to be an apprentice conductor in 1947. Candidates had to conduct a Mozart, Beethoven, or Brahms symphony while Szell played the score at the piano. Lane chose Mozart's Symphony No. 28, one of the composer's less-performed symphonies. Szell asked him why he picked this work. Lane answered, "I thought you might not know it so well." Szell was amused: "Well, that's a very good point, because as a matter of fact, this is a work I have never conducted." Lane got the job.

✿   ✿   ✿

Prior to the first week of the 1947–48 season, the orchestra once again underwent a full extra week of rehearsals, for a total of 14 by opening night, October 9, 1947. At Severance Hall, Szell conducted works by Weber, Debussy, Smetana, and Brahms. The first five weeks of Szell programs included a bounty of the Classical and Romantic works that would become the conductor's specialties in Cleveland (Beethoven's Seventh Symphony, Schumann's Fourth, Mendelssohn's "Italian," Mahler's *Das Lied von der Erde*, Bruckner's Eighth Symphony). Recording activity for Columbia continued in late November, just before American Federation of Musicians president James C. Petrillo imposed another recording ban to protect his members from losing employment because of the proliferation of records. The repertoire comprised Hindemith's Symphonic Metamorphosis, the Schumann Fourth Symphony, and the Mendelssohn "Italian" Symphony (which was released in April 1952, after the first and second movements were rerecorded in December 1951). The Hindemith and Schumann performances find a strengthened orchestra responding to Szell with increased intensity and finesse. He would record all of these works again during his Cleveland tenure, partly to take advantage of advances in recording technology.

That fall Szell and the orchestra gave their debut performance of Aaron

Copland's Third Symphony, which was only a year old. When a Cleveland interviewer asked Copland about his modern style, the composer noted, "If you think I chew nails for breakfast, you should hear what the younger generation in New York is producing these days. They already regard my music as soft and not daring enough." At least one conservative local critic, the *Press*'s Arthur Loesser, found the composer's music "manly, direct and terse. There will be some who find some of his harmonic procedures unattractive, and there will be elderly people who will wince at some of the percussion effects. Nevertheless, the sincere strength and the mature craft evinced by this symphony will not fail to impress most earnest music lovers." Szell must have admired the piece; he also performed it with the New York Philharmonic.

Szell didn't fare particularly well when the Cleveland Orchestra ventured to Carnegie Hall in February for its first New York appearance with its new conductor—and its first concert there in seven years. Szell led Hindemith's Symphonic Metamorphosis, Schumann's Fourth Symphony, Smetana's *Vltava*, and Beethoven's Piano Concerto No. 4, with Artur Schnabel as soloist. Virgil Thomson's impressions in the *Herald Tribune* were mixed:

> The Cleveland Orchestra is a highly satisfactory musical instrument. Its string section, in particular, is a homogeneous body both rich in tone and powerful. The wind sections, too, so far as could be judged in one evening, are suave and skillful, particularly the woods. Indeed, the ensemble is in every sense a serious and proper one . . . Hearing George Szell with his own orchestra, which is also a first-class one, is hearing him, I presume, at his best. Well, that best remains workmanlike and more than merely respectable, but also something less than genuinely enlightening. Like his predecessor in Cleveland, Artur Rodzinski, he is a good foreman but not an interpreter of any especial grace or grand inspiration. And almost anything in the nature of poetry escapes him.

With these last sentences, Thomson voiced complaints that would dog Szell throughout his Cleveland years, and which the conductor would counter on occasion. "The borderline is very thin between clarity and coolness, self-discipline and severity," Szell told Joseph Wechsberg in his 1965 *New Yorker* profile. "There exist different nuances of warmth—from the chaste warmth of Mozart to the sensuous warmth of Tchaikovsky, from the noble passion of 'Fidelio' to the lascivious passion of 'Salome.' I cannot pour chocolate sauce over asparagus."

More positive, and equally perceptive, about the first Szell-Cleveland concert at Carnegie Hall was Olin Downes in the *Times*. "This is an admirable orchestra, one of which any city in the world could be proud. It is remarkably disciplined, strong in all of its divisions, completely competent. It can play pianissimo, as well as fortissimo, and Mr. Szell sees to it that it does so." Then Downes pinpointed another quality that would become associated with Cleveland under Szell: "If there is one conspicuous difference between this orchestra and those nearer home, it is the important one of the quality of the strings. They incline toward dryness. Mr. Szell is a musician, one could say, who thinks in terms of expressive phrases and classic architecture before he comes to the matter of the purely sensuous or color characteristic of tone. There were moments last night when he showed that the latter consideration was not foreign to him, but the orchestral tone could have more richness, smoothness and shimmer."

These reviews are fair and accurate, especially when placed in historical perspective. The orchestra's strings, if not necessarily dry, would certainly remain lean throughout the Szell years, lacking the lushness found in the Philadelphia Orchestra or the forceful personality of the New York Philharmonic. James Levine, later an apprentice conductor to Szell in Cleveland, once heard Szell exult in the "beautiful, big warm fiddle tone" of the Berlin Philharmonic. "I bit my tongue," Levine recalled. "It was all I could do not to say, 'But, Uncle George, it's because whenever a violinist auditions with you who has that kind of sound, you reject him in favor of one who comes in with a little wiry sound, who has all the sixteenth notes in the right place.' Of course, I didn't say that, but it was interesting how he appreciated the Berlin Philharmonic sound and didn't realize that everything he did in Cleveland was counterproducing that sort of sound."

Szell and his ensemble returned from Carnegie Hall in February 1948 to face a busy schedule of first performances together, including Sibelius's Seventh Symphony and Elgar's *Enigma Variations*. Szell emphasized Mozart's importance to the orchestra with performances of five piano concertos, two apiece played by Schnabel and Robert Casadesus and one by Rudolf Serkin. Another piano-playing Rudolf—Firkusny, a Szell colleague from Prague—made his debut with the orchestra in March in Beethoven's "Emperor" Concerto. A month later, apprentice conductor and pianist Seymour Lipkin, who was "deathly afraid" of Szell, according to Lane, performed the Schumann concerto under the conductor, just two weeks before winning the Rachmaninoff Fund's first national piano competition at Carnegie Hall—and saying farewell to Cleveland.

✻   ✻   ✻

The orchestra was improving with every purposeful motion of Szell's baton, and the conductor was becoming more confident about showing off his ensemble. For the first four weeks of the 1948–49 season, he led only one work featuring a soloist (the Grieg Piano Concerto, with Menahem Pressler) and focused largely on such beloved fare as Wagner's *Meistersinger* prelude and *Flying Dutchman* overture, Tchaikovsky's Fourth Symphony, Ravel's *La valse*, Schumann's First Symphony, Brahms's Third Symphony, and his own orchestration of Smetana's "From My Life" string quartet (which he and the orchestra would record the following spring).

Szell's utterly serious rehearsal methods and Eurocentric sensibility encountered a local obstacle in the midst of these concerts. The Cleveland Indians were playing the Boston Braves in baseball's World Series. Many of the orchestra's musicians were big Indians fans, and were listening to the radio broadcast "when rehearsal was called for stage," reported the *Press*. "Disgustedly they left the radio and assembled for the playing of Berlioz's 'Minuet.' When Conductor George Szell poised his baton for the start the band broke out with: 'Take Me Out to the Ball Game,' leaving Szell with a puzzled and bewildered look. Not until the tune was explained to him did he understand the significance of the gag."

Days later, he had a stunning impact on Severance patrons with the first Cleveland performance of Mahler's Ninth Symphony, which, as was customary for that period, took up the program's first half (and a long one, at almost 90 minutes). It was followed by a far less challenging work (at least for orchestra and listeners), Chopin's Piano Concerto No. 1, with Sigi (later Alexis) Weissenberg, as soloist. Two weeks later, Arthur Loesser, music critic of the *Press*, again cast away concerns about conflict of interest and appeared as soloist, under Szell, in Beethoven's First Piano Concerto.

The regular chorus of praise the orchestra was receiving from Cleveland critics was beginning to be matched by evaluations from out of town, including New York. When Szell and the orchestra gave their second concert together at Carnegie Hall in February 1949, the *Times*'s Olin Downes noticed a big difference: "The Cleveland Orchestra, which Mr. Szell is training with such effect, would appear by comparison between this performance and the one it gave here only a season ago to have developed conspicuously in point of sonority and of technical finish."

The growth can be heard on the Columbia recordings Szell and the orchestra made two months later. The three works taped at Severance Hall on

April 25, 26, and 27 had been performed earlier in the season—Smetana's "From My Life" quartet (Szell's orchestration), *Till Eulenspiegel*, and Haydn's "Oxford" Symphony. In Smetana's ultra-romantic work, the orchestra finally sounds like Szell's own ensemble—the playing is crisp and ultra-sophisticated. *Till Eulenspiegel* and Haydn's "Oxford" Symphony also receive the fastidious Szell treatment. The Strauss tone poem is a brisk romp—even faster in spots than Rodzinski's Cleveland recording of nine years before. Szell's refreshing classicism pervades the Haydn, a performance in which the distinctive Cleveland exactness is already in place. The conductor always urged his players to play short articulations very short, an entreaty that can be discerned here in the way notes line up like military regiments, yet within beautifully proportioned phrases. With these three recordings, it is possible to hear just what the growing Cleveland-Szell fuss was all about.

Despite the fact that the fuss was getting more expensive, as Szell had anticipated, the board was stirred to move onward. Trustees gave the go-ahead to expand the season from 22 pairs of subscription concerts to 24—as long as the Boston Symphony's season but four weeks short of Chicago, New York, and Philadelphia. Szell would conduct 18 of the 24 pairs, with Dimitri Mitropoulos, William Steinberg, and Bruno Walter appearing as guest conductors. Single tickets were priced from $1.50 to $3.60.

Buoyed by the support of the board, President Thomas L. Sidlo continued to push for additional fund-raising aimed at keeping the orchestra on its upward path. He put on his best orator's cap to bolster the trustees' morale, loosen their financial portfolios, and urge them to sign up more contributors. "Let us remind ourselves again that we are not called upon to create the Orchestra, or to provide its endowment, or build its home," said Sidlo. "Those things have all been done for us. All we are called upon to do is to hold on to what we have, an assignment which should be child's play compared to the Herculean task of the founders of the Orchestra."

One of Szell's formidable tasks before the 1949–50 season was replacing no fewer than 15 players. Among the hires were a number of musicians who would become longtime orchestra members. A crucial new player, in more ways than one, was principal violist Abraham Skernick, succeeding Marcel Dick. Skernick, who had studied violin and viola at Juilliard and then majored in math and physics at Brooklyn College, played assistant principal viola in the St. Louis Symphony and principal in the Baltimore Symphony before winning the Cleveland post.

Skernick became one of Szell's closest associates—and the musician the conductor trusted most for the rest of his life. Szell admired his principal vi-

olist as person and artist. He gave him many opportunities to appear as
soloist in performance and recording. (Skernick's playing on Cleveland
recordings of Strauss's *Don Quixote* and Mozart's Sinfonia Concertante for
Violin and Viola is especially superb.) The conductor turned to Skernick for
advice on all sorts of matters. And Szell, like most conductors—even great
ones—a bundle of insecurities, looked at Skernick often during rehearsals
and performances for nods of approval. The orchestra also benefited from
the relationship. Skernick intervened on behalf of colleagues on issues ranging from the conductor's rash behavior to travel money while on tour. He
would calm Szell down hundreds of times during the 21 years they made
music together in Cleveland.

✿   ✿   ✿

That Szell had arrived in the right place at the right time was now abundantly
clear. The end of World War II saw the country edging toward prosperity,
and with it the Cleveland Orchestra board was ready to give their authoritative conductor the support he needed to realize his artistic goals. There
may have been more than a few people in the community, and within the orchestra, who didn't appreciate the way Szell treated his players. But no one
could argue with the musical results, at least on a technical level. With the
Cleveland audience's hunger to experience symphonic music on a higher
and higher level, and the board willing to make this possible, Szell could not
have landed in a more welcoming environment.

Another sign that he intended to challenge his musicians and to push the
boundaries of the symphonic art in Cleveland came when Szell began the
1949–50 season with two weeks of purely orchestral programs. He even programmed Virgil Thomson's *Louisiana Story*, despite the fact that the composer-critic had been less than complimentary to him in the *New York
Herald Tribune* several seasons before. (Thomson would return Szell's favor
two months after the *Louisiana Story* performances with a rave review for
what had become the orchestra's annual Carnegie Hall concert.)

By now, Szell was established not only in Cleveland, but also as a guest
conductor of other major American ensembles. He had led concerts with
the orchestras of St. Louis, New York, Boston, Detroit, Chicago, and
Philadelphia, as well as the NBC Symphony. He gave his opinion about the
world's major orchestras toward the end of 1949 to the Associated Press:
"The orchestras in Vienna and Amsterdam are the two leading ones in
Europe, and although they have fine qualities they cannot compare with the
best American orchestras."

Cleveland was closing in on comparison with the best ensembles. Still, it would take a good deal more rigorous Szell training and the hiring of key players to push the orchestra to the top. Those players included principal oboist Marc Lifschey, whose move to Cleveland in 1950 marked the start of one of the most illustrious and turbulent careers in the orchestra's history. Lifschey had auditioned the previous year in Cleveland, but his tendency to make disruptive breathing sounds prompted Szell instead to hire another player. When it became clear that that musician wasn't working out, Szell called Lifschey. "We would have engaged you except for this habit you have of snorting and sniffing while you play," Szell said. "And if you can rid yourself of this habit, I can practically promise you the job next year."

Although the orchestra's reputation had grown, there were some in Cleveland and elsewhere who believed the ensemble had come farther still than generally realized. Board member Percy Brown, who might be excused for lack of objectivity, was agog after Szell conducted a Beethoven program in March 1950 that included the local debut of a 21-year-old pianist, Gary Graffman. "Geo. Szell certainly can conduct Beethoven superbly. Best in U.S.A!" Brown wrote in his notebook. A week later, a more objective observer, Bruno Walter, stepped onto the Severance podium to conduct Vaughan Williams's *Fantasia on 'Greensleeves'* and the first symphonies of Beethoven and Mahler. "Let me congratulate you upon the excellent work by which this orchestra has been raised to its present high rank among the finest in the musical world," he wrote to Sidlo days after his concerts. "I am sure your audiences and citizens in general will be proud of such achievement and recognize its importance for Cleveland as a musical center and thereby for the culture of our country." Szell was less reserved about the situation. "Cleve. Orch. now second to none in U.S.A.," Brown quoted the conductor in his notebook. "Says Philadelphia has the material if there were brains in leadership. Boston bound to decline. Likes Chicago string section."

Szell was reengaged for three more seasons in Cleveland.

Another conductor who was impressed by the orchestra during this period was Dimitri Mitropoulos, who came to town soon after being named conductor of the New York Philharmonic. At Severance Hall, he led a program of works by William Schuman, Webern, Saint-Saëns, and Rachmaninoff. "I really honestly believe that the Cleveland Orchestra today is one of the greatest in our country, without any doubt, and this is certainly due to the invaluable efforts and greatness of an artist like Mr. George Szell," Mitropoulos wrote to general manager Carl Vosburgh. "With such orchestras existing, America can really compete with the whole world in matters of cultural achievement."

Maybe so, but orchestras, as well as other arts and entertainment institutions, were battling competition from another source—television. Although the offerings on the little square box were still few, the novelty of the device and the fact that programs entered living rooms at virtually no cost prompted audiences to stay home rather than travel to theaters, movie houses, and concert halls. Radio listening plunged. This wasn't good news for orchestras, which relied heavily on ticket sales and revenue from radio broadcasts. Concerts at Severance Hall were largely sold out for the first few years of Szell's tenure, but as television continued to insinuate itself into the public consciousness, "it was like a bomb had dropped on the audience," said Louis Lane. "In fact, the Sunday afternoon concerts were devastated by it and they never recovered."

Orchestra budgets were also affected by the 20 percent federal admissions tax, which Congress had imposed on nonprofit organizations during World War II to help the war effort. Sidlo wrote to Margaret Truman in January 1949 asking that she speak to her father, President Truman, about the tax. "I don't know if there is anything I can do about this," she wrote back, "but I shall be delighted to talk it over with Dad and show him your letter. We shall see how things work out." They wouldn't work out quickly. A year later, the tax was still in place. Now, in mid-1950, Sidlo was turning to Szell to address the issue in public. Whenever the tax was finally cancelled, Sidlo wanted the orchestra to keep the 20 percent amount that the federal government had added to ticket prices. Sidlo asked Szell to write a statement, to be ready for release to newspapers and radio, that would "persuade even the hard-boiled ticket subscriber that it is essential for the Association to retain this freed tax money for its own uses in order to provide additional insurance for keeping the Orchestra at its present high level."

Given the effects of television and the admissions tax, as well as the constant difficulty in raising money, members of the Musical Arts Association were becoming nervous about the orchestra's future. Percy Brown discussed the matter with fellow trustees Leroy Davenport and Henry Curtiss, who proposed a gloomy solution. "Henry thinks we should cut down and admit Cleveland's inability to maintain present high standards," wrote Brown. A day later, an entry in Brown's notebook revealed another set of problems: "The orchestra board is in a mess—E. J. Kulas wants to be President and is heartily disliked. Also he dislikes Bob Heller and Frank Taplin . . . Heller hates Kulas. Kulas + Heller dislike Carl Osborne. Heller asks to be retained as V.P. Geo. Szell insists I go back as V.P. (over Heller). Don't want to." Onstage, the artistic results were looming toward transcendence. Backstage, struggle and melodrama were the norm.

✣   ✣   ✣

On August 23, 1950, an era ended in Cleveland when Adella Prentiss Hughes died at the age of 80. She had not been directly involved in orchestra affairs since her forced retirement in 1943. But she had written her memoirs, and maintained a presence at Severance Hall until illness kept her away. Sidlo paid tribute to Hughes in a statement to the board: "She did so many things herself that she often made the rest of us feel like slackers. She had just one dominant and driving purpose, and that was to keep everyone stirred to greater interest and greater effort on behalf of the Cleveland Orchestra, to make 'her' Orchestra the peer of any in the land."

The orchestra opened its 1950–51 season with a work in Hughes's memory, Mozart's *Masonic Funeral Music*, which Szell followed with a scheduled program the late manager no doubt would have savored: Brahms's Haydn Variations, Debussy's *Afternoon of a Faun* and *Fêtes*, Casella's *Paganiniana* (in its first Cleveland performance), and Beethoven's Fifth.

In addition to oboist Lifschey, the orchestra at this time welcomed several other players who would take part in its rise under Szell. The departure of principal hornist Frank Brouk for Chicago radio station WGN after four seasons in Cleveland brought the arrival of Ross Taylor, a graduate of Juilliard whom Szell hired from the fourth-horn chair of the New York Philharmonic. "I have never heard such an exhausting audition," recalled Louis Lane. "Szell listened to him audition for about an hour and quarter on all of the most difficult literature from the repertoire." Taylor finally protested that his lip was giving out, so Szell dismissed him but soon engaged the horn player, not entirely convinced he'd done the right thing, according to Lane. Three weeks into his Cleveland tenure, Taylor won acclaim for his playing of the famous solo in Tchaikovsky's Fifth Symphony. (Yet he was to prove erratic due to nerves. In 1955, when Szell decided to promote Myron Bloom from third horn to first, he helped Taylor obtain the principal post in the San Francisco Symphony. Several years later, Taylor committed suicide.)

Along with the arrival of new players, Cleveland welcomed a handful of guest conductors each season. The practice of engaging podium guests dated back to the time of Nikolai Sokoloff, who had realized that he probably would have dropped dead if he'd continued to lead the entire subscription season. Moreover, musicians and audiences appreciated the chance to hear other conductors' interpretations of the symphonic literature. Then Szell arrived. He was so popular that patrons began to expect him to be around most, if not all, of the time. Szell devoted more weeks each season to his own orchestra than most conductors of major American ensembles. But he also enjoyed working with other orchestras, especially the New York Philharmonic. The situation was proving to be a problem. Vosburgh urged Szell not to be gone so much. "Tom and I have had many questions from not only members of the board but from many of our audiences as to why our conductor is away for such an extended period," he wrote to Szell in New York. "If we have had these complaints, rest assured that many other members of the board have had similar ones." Guest conductors were a challenge for another reason: they were expensive, particularly the greatest, such as Bruno Walter, Leopold Stokowski, and Pierre Monteux. Worse, some guest conductors didn't sell tickets. For this reason, Vosburgh suggested not asking Mitropoulos back.

Szell knew what he had in Cleveland. Soon after his annual Philharmonic engagement, which included Beethoven's Sixth Symphony, he returned to Severance Hall to conduct the same work on a Beethoven program featuring Jascha Heifetz in the Violin Concerto. "Taking all things into consideration," Szell told the *Press*, "the Cleveland Orchestra is a much, much finer organization than the New York." How that statement may have been received in New York is unclear, but the Philharmonic must not have been too miffed, for Szell continued to be associated with the orchestra for the rest of his life.

He wasn't the only one who believed that Cleveland was an orchestra on a rapid ascent. In December 1950, Leopold Stokowski made his debut with the ensemble conducting a typically eclectic program: Bach's Toccata and Fugue in D minor, Three Chorale Preludes, and Passacaglia and Fugue in C minor (in the conductor's own transcriptions), Shostakovich's Symphony No. 6, and Tchaikovsky's *Romeo and Juliet*. His effect on the Cleveland Orchestra was magical. "Stokowski did nothing except say, 'With the beat, gentlemen.' Or occasionally he would say, 'You sir. You are playing the same bowing as your stand partner. Have you no individuality?' " recalled Louis Lane. "That was all he ever said and in fifteen minutes it sounded like the old Philadelphia Orchestra of 1936." A tape of the concert confirms the distinctive brand of symphonic alchemy that Stokowski exerted on the Cleveland Orchestra, and vice versa. "Your orchestra is superb," Stokowski wrote to Szell. "My first rehearsal was a joy. You have created a truly marvelous instrument. Sincere congratulations on your great achievement."

Stokowski's appearance with the orchestra created a stir. "The manner in which both the orchestra and the Severance Hall audiences took the famous maestro to heart and his evident enjoyment in conducting here has led some to wonder whether he has his eyes on the Szell baton," Elmore Bacon speculated in the *News*, not content to stop there. "The marked success that Director Szell has won in conducting the New York Philharmonic Symphony the past four weeks has started Severance Hall fans to discussing whether or not the New Yorkers would like to have him there permanently to take over the post now held by Dimitri Mitropoulos."

Szell was harboring no thoughts of abandoning Cleveland for New York. He was more certain than ever that he had achieved most of the goals he had set in 1946. "The Orchestra is really TOPS," he wrote to Artur Rubinstein in early 1952. "I mean it and, as you know, I am not in the habit of kidding myself." Elwell must have had a sixth sense on the subject. "As the weeks go by, George Szell continues his interpretive triumphs with the Cleveland Orchestra at Severance Hall," he wrote in *The Plain Dealer*. "When he arrives at a point where you think the orchestra has just about reached its top of perfection, he surprises you by going on to even higher levels of virtuosic refinement and brilliance."

Orchestra Ascending

*T*he musicians of the Cleveland Orchestra may have been aware of the upward artistic sweep into which they were drawn, but at least half still weren't earning enough money to make ends meet. A new contract in the spring of 1948 had raised the minimum weekly pay from $85 to $90. Being a member of George Szell's orchestra was exhilarating. For years to come, it would also be a part-time job. "I was in my 20s when I came," said Louis Lane, who arrived as apprentice conductor in 1947. "I would make friends. I remember particularly a family on the West Side that was very hospitable to me. The first time I was taken over there and introduced to the mother and father by my friend, the father said . . . 'So you're a member of the Cleveland Orchestra. How nice. And how do you make your living?' "

The ensemble's winter season in 1948–49 remained 30 weeks long, while the summer season (6 weeks in 1948; 12 in 1949) paid far lower wages. Public Hall was not air-conditioned, which made everyone miserable. Because of a strange union rule, only musicians who had been in the orchestra for at least two years were eligible to play summer seasons. "I could do nothing" in the summer of 1948, said violinist Kurt Loebel. "I would play weddings, receptions. But it was chicken feed." When the musicians tried to get management to match summer scale to the higher winter scale, they were told that the summer seasons were less pressured without Szell around. The musicians countered that groceries cost the same during the summer. The argument didn't work.

The 1949–50 season nearly didn't happen. Negotiations between the board and the musicians' union had come to a stalemate in March 1949. The union wanted to increase the minimum weekly scale to $98, but many trustees weren't convinced. Board president Thomas L. Sidlo finally said that the situation would have to be dealt with sooner rather than later. "We have a first-rate Orchestra, but . . . with a second-grade payroll," he told trustees. "We are aspiring to be one of the finest orchestras, with a budget that is less than two-thirds that of Boston, New York or Philadelphia."

The Cleveland musicians had become increasingly proud of their abilities under Szell, but their pay didn't reflect the quality of the product. "They feel that they are as fine players as those who make up the other great orchestras, and that they should be compensated accordingly, or at least somewhere near accordingly," said Sidlo. Parity was an issue that would never again fail to emerge at contract time, and it wouldn't be fully addressed for a long while. Sidlo, noting that the cancellation of the coming season would "arouse feelings of astonishment and resentment on the part of concertgoers, Friends, etc.," urged trustees to consent to the wage increase. He was ready to hand in a letter of resignation if the board decided to retrench. They didn't. The raise was approved.

By 1952, most of the players were still trapped in financial purgatory. Only principal players were making salaries that could be termed adequate. In addition to their prestigious orchestra duties, they were in demand as teachers, soloists, and chamber musicians. Rank-and-file players weren't so fortunate. Of the ensemble's 95 members, 57 were supplementing their incomes through jobs unrelated to music. The Cleveland market didn't, and never would, offer sufficient freelance opportunities in radio, television, or recording, to the detriment of the orchestra members' bank accounts, if not their artistry.

The winter season in 1952–53 was still only 30 weeks, for which more than half the orchestra earned the new weekly minimum scale of $108, or annual compensation of $3,240. The summer season had been cut back to six weeks (at the reduced scale), in part because of flagging attendance at sweltering performances in Public Auditorium.

The musicians continued to grapple with low salaries, mirage-like pension plans, and sporadic recording activity. In 1953, most players still earned an annual wage that placed them on "the borderline of poverty," an orchestra committee document later stated. "Cleveland Orchestra members were sinking into poverty at the very time when the standard of living for carpenters, plumbers, factory workers, etc., was rising well into the middle economic class." Musicians' union officials appeared determined to maintain absolute power over their members, who continued to receive little help at contract time. The orchestra committee—the panel of five musicians chosen by their colleagues to deal with labor issues—held its first meeting with Local 4 officials during the fall of 1953, when it was informed that the players would receive no raise the following season.

In contrast to his players, Szell was being paid $48,000 a year in Cleveland, and had many lucrative engagements elsewhere.

Cleveland musicians survived in two basic ways: they left for better-pay-

ing symphonic positions elsewhere or squeezed in other jobs between rehearsals and concerts. Most worked as salesmen, hawking everything from
cars and insurance to real estate, liquor, clothing, Fuller brushes, chickens,
and hosiery. In a survey for the *Press*, James Frankel discovered that the musicians were involved in numerous other vocations: "drill press operator,
electric meter reader, lab technician, operator of bolt making machines,
baker's assistant, farmer, hardware clerk, turret lathe operator, grocery
clerk, chiropractor, sample stapler in a suit factory . . . light bulb sorter, government translator, jeweler, landscape gardener, timekeeper, hotel night
clerk, short order cook, librarian, mink breeder, painter, entomologist, elevator operator, race track usher and operator of a Dairy Queen milk bar."

There was no denying that these sometime clerks, cooks, and salespeo-
ple came together to form an orchestra of remarkable accomplishment. As
Szell told *Time* magazine in early 1953 (upon signing a new three-year contract), his ensemble was "as good as any conductor could wish for." What's
more, the institutional picture seemed rosy—the endowment was up to $5
million, and the Musical Arts Association had raised $110,000 to retire the
annual deficit.

When Public Hall was closed for the summer of 1953 to undergo redec-
oration and the installation of an air-conditioning system, Sidlo initially announced that the summer season would resume only in 1954. Szell, who
never conducted the Cleveland Summer Orchestra, wasn't happy about the
predicament. "Not only for the sake of continuity but for the sake of the orchestra men, it is terribly important we have pops going in the summer," he
told the *Press*. Szell was worried that the orchestra would lose players if they
didn't have summer work. He was also concerned that his tightly molded ensemble would lose some of its special abilities during the six-month hiatus
between concert seasons.

Then a clever, if brief, solution was found. *Cleveland News* reporter
Ernest Wittenberg suggested that the Cleveland Summer Orchestra play in
Cleveland Stadium before Indians games. The Musical Arts Association, the
Cleveland Baseball Company, the city of Cleveland, and the Cleveland
Federation of Musicians embraced the proposal. Twelve concerts, planned
for June, July, and August 1953, would begin an hour and a half before baseball games. "The orchestra of 70 men, under the direction of Louis Lane,
will play its 15th series of concerts under the lights on a special stage to be
constructed behind the outfield fence in center field," noted a front-page
story in the *News*. "It is expected that the musicians will play before the
largest audiences ever assembled for a pop concert anywhere in the world."
Wittenberg contributed tidbits about the programs: "Louis Lane, conduc-

tor of the Cleveland Summer Orchestra, said today he will limit his pre-night baseball 'pop' concerts to light, lilting music that everyone knows." And soon the concerts had a catchy name: Indipops.

The *News* promoted the undertaking on June 2, the day of the first concert, with a banner headline: "Beethoven Up—Play Ball! First Stadium 'Pop' Tonight." At concert time, only 2,000 fans were in the stadium. Attendance increased to 17,000 by game time. The first program, heard through three enormous speakers, included music by Wagner, Porter, Sousa, and Johann Strauss II. Arthur Loesser's review the next day in the *Press* was headlined, "Acoustics, Orchestra Excellent at Stadium." Years later, Lane—who had taken over direction of the Cleveland Summer Orchestra from Rudolph Ringwall in May 1952—recalled the experience with mixed sentiments: "It was quite an effort on my part to find music that was loud most of the time and sufficiently popular. We played a lot of marches and a few waltzes."

✿   ✿   ✿

At Severance Hall, dry acoustics continued to be a thorn in the orchestra's side. Szell had been urging the Musical Arts Association to act on the matter since he arrived in town. In 1949, the orchestra hired Clifford M. Swan, an acoustical consultant who had been involved in the design and construction of many American concert halls, to test Severance. "Your auditorium is beautiful and luxurious," noted Swan in a letter to the Musical Arts Association, "but it is also 'dead.' One is responsible for the other. Usually, the problem is to add absorption; here it is to remove some." The main culprits were carpeting throughout the hall and heavy curtains in the two stage boxes, which were devouring sound and keeping the reverberation time low. (He suggested an optimum reverberation time of 2.4 seconds, which would even be unreasonably high 50 years later.) Swan concluded that the stage shell didn't have enough hard surfaces to project the orchestra. The price tag for the project: $25,000.

With the orchestra and the board busy with other matters, not another word was heard on the acoustical issue until the spring of 1953, when Szell received support from a musician who held innovative views on the subject of sound: Leopold Stokowski, former conductor of the Philadelphia Orchestra. The imposing maestro led two weeks of concerts at Severance Hall, and was taken aback by the Severance acoustics. "I only wish you had a hall with acoustics worthy of your great Art," he informed Szell. "In some of the rehearsals I listened to certain passages on the stage, and then went down in the hall to listen to them in the places where the public would hear them. I was deeply impressed by the difference. On the stage it sounded wonderful. In the hall it sounded quite differently. In the hall the music was dry and half dead-sounding. On the stage it sounded glorious." He told Szell he would be happy to assist in making improvements.

Stokowski said the same things to Sidlo, who passed on to trustees the suggestion that changes in the shape of the stage shell, and greater use of plywood, would help the acoustics. The board hired Robert S. Shankland, a physicist at Case Institute of Technology, to test the hall. Working with colleague Arthur H. Benade, Shankland determined that the reverberation time in Severance was an unusually low 1.45 seconds with the hall empty. In a report to Szell, he proposed removing the heavy carpeting and drapes (which was done that year), using denser wooden materials for the stage shell, and installing a new hardwood stage floor. Shankland's study would eventually be adopted when the full stage renovation was carried out in 1958. During the summer of 1953, Szell hit the roof when he heard that the plywood on the new shell would be covered with a thin layer of linen in order for new paint to adhere. "This would completely offset the effect of the plywood!" Szell wrote to orchestra manager Carl Vosburgh from Switzerland. "The HARD SURFACE is the crucial thing! Therefore: the paint directly on the plywood—no further covering material!" Vosburgh wrote back that linen glued to the plywood would make the surface harder, and placated the maestro—for the moment.

✻   ✻   ✻

Vosburgh also was trying to improve the recording situation. Cleveland trailed far behind the orchestras of New York and Philadelphia in public recognition because Columbia Records wasn't paying much attention to Szell and company. From April 1949 through January 1952, Szell recorded only 6¾ works, including the rerecording of the first two movements of Mendelssohn's "Italian" Symphony. During the rest of 1952, the orchestra recorded Szell performances of Schumann's Second Symphony and Brahms's Piano Concerto No. 1, with Rudolf Serkin as soloist, and Igor Stravinsky conducted his own complete *Pulcinella* and Symphony in C. In 1953, Szell recorded only one work in Cleveland—Bach's Violin Concerto No. 2, with Zino Francescatti. Under an unusual agreement, the ensemble was known as the Columbia Symphony Orchestra, a name the recording company also used for freelance orchestras in New York and Los Angeles.

One pianist who might have recorded with the Cleveland Orchestra under different circumstances was Szell himself. In October 1951, he made his debut as piano soloist with his ensemble performing (and himself conducting, from the keyboard) Mozart's Piano Concerto No. 23, K. 488. In *The Plain Dealer*, Herbert Elwell called the performance "an ideal esthetic marriage. For the soloist it was like having a wife so devoted that she says exactly the right thing at the right time. An official conductor in this menage would have been like a crowd of three." Loesser, an excellent pianist himself, also was impressed: "Szell proved emphatically what we had good reason to believe right along: That he is a pianist of high expressive attainments, in addition to being a profound master of the classics."

Szell's pianistic debut gave Vosburgh the idea of asking Columbia to record Szell as soloist with his orchestra. "This certainly was one of the high spots of the orchestra in the 34-year history," Vosburgh wrote to Richard Gilbert at Columbia Records about the Mozart performances. Gilbert wrote back that recording Szell playing Mozart with members of the Cleveland Orchestra would be prohibitively expensive because the entire ensemble would have to be paid for the sessions.

Clearly, changes in the orchestra's recording arrangement were needed. Columbia responded to Vosburgh's harangues by turning to its subsidiary label, Epic (which initially had recorded European orchestras), to issue Cleveland Orchestra recordings at lower prices than those released on the Columbia Masterworks label. The *Sturm und Drang* with Columbia was destined to last for years—in fact, past Szell's death in 1970. RCA, Mercury, and Capitol (Angel Records) had approached Cleveland about the possibility of recording, but no new deals had been struck.

Columbia kept dangling options that Vosburgh and Szell were unwilling to accept. At one point, the manager had just about enough. "George, I feel we have one of the great orchestras and one of the great conductors of the world and I think this is recognized nationally if not worldwide," he wrote to Szell in July 1954. "I feel very definitely that we are not just another one of the so-called major orchestras of this country. I think our treatment by Columbia has been lousy, stinking and I could go on and on. With an organization such as we have I think we are comparable to a little puppy meekly sitting and begging its master and then condescendingly from time to time Columbia tosses us some little bone or scrap left over from the overloaded 'platter' of the Philharmonic or Philadelphia Orchestras."

James Frankel touched upon the recording situation in a *Press* article about orchestra deficits. "The present contract with Columbia that produces about two records a year is ridiculous in an era when discs are being pressed in greater quantities than ever before," he wrote. "During Artur

Rodzinski's decade here, the symphony made 19 works for Columbia on old-fashioned 78 rpm discs. In Szell's nine years the orchestra has recorded only 14 pieces—this in the LP era!"

Szell was generating some of the recording controversy himself by making a number of albums with the New York Philharmonic for Columbia. "Now Szell is in competition with himself (and his own organization)," wrote Milton Widder in the *Press*. When Szell next did record with Cleveland, they played Mozart, Bach, and Tartini concertos with pianist Robert Casadesus and violinist Joseph Szigeti, but again under the name Columbia Symphony Orchestra. The Epic contract took effect with recording sessions in April 1954, when Szell and the Cleveland Orchesta—this time credited under its own name—taped Haydn symphonies no. 88 and 104.

      ❖   ❖   ❖

Szell served up a series of rich symphonic meals for the start of the 1952–53 season, beginning with two weeks of purely orchestral fare by Berlioz, Debussy, Sibelius, Verdi, Bartók, and Tchaikovsky. The third program brought Szell back as pianist-conductor in another Mozart concerto (K. 595), which shared the bill with two of his specialties, Delius's *Irmelin* prelude and Smetana's *The Moldau*, and the first Cleveland performances of Howard Hanson's Symphony No. 2 ("Romantic"), conducted by the composer.

Several days into 1953, Szell paid tribute to pianist Beryl Rubinstein, who had died on December 29, with performances of Mozart's *Masonic Funeral Music* to open concerts devoted largely to light New Year's fare. Just before these concerts, Szell was reengaged by the Metropolitan Opera to conduct German repertoire (at the same time Pierre Monteux was hired to conduct French repertoire).

New York recognition of Szell and his orchestra was continuing apace. Irving Kolodin attended their Carnegie Hall concert in February 1953 (*Benvenuto Cellini* overture, Schubert's C major Symphony, Beethoven's "Emperor" Concerto, with pianist Clifford Curzon as soloist) and wrote glowingly in the *Saturday Review*: "It is an orchestra with much more of a 'family' feeling than most of those we hear in New York. That is, one is conscious not so much of individual choirs or individual desk soloists as of a unity of feeling, a similarity of response associated with the best chamber music playing."

In the spring of 1953, Szell led the orchestra in performances of Verdi's Requiem that marked the debut of the Cleveland Orchestra Chorus in its new incarnation. The orchestra had maintained a chorus before, but it had been disbanded during World War II for financial reasons, and also because many tenors and basses had gone into the armed forces. Szell had begun laying the groundwork for the creation of a volunteer orchestra chorus in 1951, when he conducted Beethoven's Ninth Symphony with a chorus of singers from Western Reserve University, Fairmount Presbyterian Church, and Church of the Covenant prepared by Russell L. Gee and Robert M. Stofer. Before a repeat of the Beethoven with the same forces the following year, Szell announced "the establishment of a permanent Cleveland Orchestra chorus" that would appear with the orchestra in one or two major choral works each season. Gee, a member of the music department at Western Reserve University and choirmaster at Fairmount Presbyterian Church, and Stofer, choirmaster at Church of the Covenant, were engaged as co-directors. "The joy and emotional satisfaction of creative participation in the great choral works of musical literature with a great symphony orchestra will be obvious to all who have once had the experience," Szell said. "It is my hope to make this experience available in the years to come."

Members of the Cleveland Orchestra Chorus would experience the awkward relationship common to choruses connected with major American orchestras. As unpaid volunteers (even though many of them are trained singers), they inevitably feel at times like second-class citizens, however excellent their collective artistry. But in exchange, they get to work with the finest conductors—and to taste musical glory.

At the official debut of the Cleveland Orchestra Chorus in the Verdi Requiem in 1953, Szell led performances with a starry array of soloists: soprano Herva Nelli, alto Nell Rankin, tenor Jan Peerce, and bass Nicola Moscona. Loesser and Elwell barely mentioned the new chorus in their reviews, the latter noting only that it "responded wonderfully." Elmore Bacon, in the *News*, went a bit farther, saying that the chorus "responded to every Szell demand with a purity of tone and a smoothness of shading most satisfying. It gave a full-throated response in the opening Kyrie and the Sanctus and provided also dramatically effective moments of spiritual calm."

❊   ❊   ❊

Dealing with musicians, board members, budgets, and sundry other details was beginning to take a toll on Vosburgh, who also kept watch over Szell's house and made sure that his beloved Cadillac was in top condition. In June 1953, he complained to Szell that he wasn't feeling well. The conductor advised him to seek medical help immediately. Vosburgh, always close to Szell, did as he was told. "Your paragraph regarding the migraines came in at the appropriate moment as I am seeing my doctor late this afternoon,"

Vosburgh wrote to Szell. "I really think what I need is a vacation and a rest as there has actually been no let-up so far as I am concerned."

One of Vosburgh's major burdens lifted the same month when Percy Brown, Szell's closest ally in Cleveland, was named president of the Musical Arts Association. He succeeded Sidlo, whose health had been failing for some time—and whose effectiveness as a leader had long been waning. The 6-foot, 4-inch Brown, a native of Concord, Massachusettes, had come to Cleveland in 1924 to open the local office of the stock brokerage firm Hornblower & Weeks. He had given bountiful time and money to local organizations, serving as chairman of the Community Fund, president and treasurer of the Institute of Music, president of the Chamber of Commerce, and chairman of Case Institute's finance committee. With his wife, Helen, a pianist and teacher, he had helped bring Szell to Cleveland.

Brown considered development of the summer pops season his first mission. He appointed Edgar A. Hahn, a trustee who managed the orchestra's summer seasons, to collaborate with Vosburgh and others. "I'm going to have a team, just like Ike does with his cabinet," said Brown, a staunch Republican. "These men will run the show. If they don't do it well, they'll get their knuckles rapped." Brown knew that the summer seasons were crucial to the orchestra: "If you want a top-flight musician you still have to go to New York, and we have to attract them there. That's why we have to build up the summer program." He singled out recordings as another top priority: "We also should record more. Recordings build up a pension fund and everybody has a pension fund but us." Even so, the Cleveland Orchestra had a great deal more than most institutions of its kind, noted Brown: "A $6,000,000 endowment fund, a $3,000,000 hall—worth $5,500,000 now, even with depreciation—and one of the top three symphonies are an awful responsibility."

As Brown was putting his policies in place, another trustee was emerging who would help chart the orchestra's course for more than three decades. Frank E. Joseph, a prominent lawyer and civic leader who would be affectionately designated as "Cleveland's most accomplished and effective worrier," had begun to contribute important ideas. He believed the board could function well only if responsibilities were divided among numerous committees. Joseph urged his colleagues to communicate with other local and national institutions to figure out solutions to organizational problems.

❈   ❈   ❈

Szell's annual vacation and conducting engagements in Europe during the summer of 1953 had the usual effect: they made him eager to get back to work with his own orchestra. His arrival in Cleveland in late September, however, wasn't exactly a public-relations person's dream. Szell let slip to reporters that he admired European manners. "I'm still polite from Europe," he said. "In 10 minutes, I'll be as vulgar as the rest of you." The result was a wave of protest from Clevelanders who took offense at being told they were hicks. One Cleveland Heights reader of the *Press* didn't hold back:

> Each year I await, with bated breath, George Szell's comments upon his return to the United States from his European vacation. Each year I receive fresh proof that as a social observer Szell makes a fine musician. I'm sure that none of us would be so vulgar as to point out to Szell that we support and admire our conductors in this country even though we spell our culture with a small c. But any well-trained, 10-year-old, American child might point out to him that it is rude to sneer at those who have applauded you. We might even call it vulgar.

Szell responded by saying he meant to direct the remark not at the general public, but at journalists (hardly a judicious statement, either). At the orchestra's first rehearsal of the season, he offered another apology: as the *Press* reported, Szell told his musicians that he was "sorry they were subjected to the Pop Concert setup this summer at the Stadium; it seems he felt that mixing music with baseball was undignified."

Despite the labor issues that were bringing conflict to Severance Hall, the orchestra was more consistent and refined than ever. The opening program of the 1953–54 season—works by Beethoven, Blacher, Stravinsky, and Brahms—drew strong approval from Elwell: "George Szell now has such a dependable organization that little rehearsing is needed in order to open the new season at the same artistic level on which he closed last spring."

Soon after finishing his fall concerts in Cleveland, Szell was off to New York for his annual guest stint with the Philharmonic and performances of Wagner's *Tannhäuser* at the Metropolitan Opera. While he was gone, Swiss conductor Ernest Ansermet returned after a five-year absence to lead works by Beethoven, Debussy, and Bartók. "Your orchestra is as fine as an orchestra can be," he wrote to Szell.

Szell probably needed to hear such words: his engagement at the Met had turned out to be a disaster. He led only four performances of *Tannhäuser* before resigning abruptly, informing Met general manager Rudolf Bing (on whom he'd first walked out at the Glyndebourne Festival in England in 1947) that conditions at the opera house were deplorable. Thus was rekindled one of the most famous artistic feuds of the era. Bing wrote to Szell:

"We both, alas, are beyond the school boy age; does it give you any particular satisfaction to hurt the Metropolitan as your walking out this season inevitably would?" Szell's answer went straight to the heart of many issues. Pointing to his "forty years of active experience in opera," Szell charged that "the Metropolitan is really 'hurt'—and very seriously—by your own improvidence and casualness, your many errors of judgment and by the dilettantism and incompetence I have encountered and observed in various departments during the past few weeks." The incompetence included the "scandalous mechanical breakdown of the change of scenery in Act I of the performance on Saturday afternoon, January 9th"—during a live radio broadcast, no less.

Szell's resignation took everyone by surprise, even Vosburgh, who had been in New York for several of the performances. The incident brought about Bing's celebrated statement about the conductor: When someone suggested that Szell was his own worst enemy, Bing retorted, "Not while I'm alive."

Szell returned to Cleveland for the rest of the season. At the end of January 1954, he held a 12-day conductors' workshop, during which 28 aspiring maestros were in residence at Severance Hall to discuss their art and observe the orchestra in rehearsal and performance. These performances would have revealed Szell's abundant strengths, as well as his limitations. "In a physical sense—in the sense of stick technique—he wasn't a born conductor," said violinist Kurt Loebel. "Sometimes he was a bit awkward and he probably knew that himself. He had to overcome those things. It was an intellectual effort, an effort controlled by his mind to technically achieve what he wanted to say musically." Timpanist Cloyd Duff recalled that Szell's stick technique was not always definite, which sometimes forced the musicians to guess exactly where notes should be placed: "Sometimes when he used a casual beat—what we call a bounce beat, with no bottom to it—Szell gave you a choice. But you never dared to take the wrong choice."

The musicians believed that Szell often chose the wrong repertoire, focusing too heavily on standard fare. "Cut down on Tchaikovsky and Beethoven, give us more Bach and Bartók, say the men of the Cleveland Orchestra. Give Franck's Symphony in D minor a rest, play more Mahler. More of Shostakovich's Fifth Symphony and less of Beethoven's Fifth. And let's see more of Jascha Heifetz," noted James Frankel in a poll in the *Press*. "The findings brought out a thorough weariness of standard concert pieces and a craving for masterpieces which the men feel are being neglected." The men—and women—of the orchestra must have realized that their wishes were unlikely to be granted. Although Szell would pay attention to recent and neglected music throughout his tenure, more and more by calling upon colleagues to conduct these works, mainstream Austro-Germanic music would always be central to the character of his orchestra.

Still, Szell and the ensemble weren't convincing enough patrons to pull themselves away from their television sets or other activities long enough to attend concerts. Budgetary pressures prompted consternation among trustees. Of major concern was retaining Szell himself. He had made it clear when he signed on in 1946 that the board must constantly raise more money to make improvements possible. "If we were to reduce the size of our orchestra (we now have just under 100 men) he would have grounds for resigning—yet we are drawing upon our sacred surplus to meet our deficit," Percy Brown told the trustees, referring to the use of endowment money to pay off debts. "Of course, we can always go back to a second position with a comfortable number of, say, 70 men, and a comfortable second-rate conductor, for we can always have symphonic music with our Endowment Fund, but do we want to pass up this position of leadership in the musical world which has been attained under the fourteen years' chairmanship of Mr. Sidlo?"

There would be no retreat now—or ever—at Severance Hall. Yet, things couldn't have been called settled. While Szell was enjoying triumphs with the Vienna Philharmonic and playing golf in Switzerland during the summer of 1954, Vosburgh was contending with paltry attendance at the Pops, despite the new air-conditioning system at Public Hall. "Frankly, I am beginning to believe that Cleveland is just not interested in summer concerts," he wrote to concertmaster Josef Gingold. In addition, Vosburgh was still fuming about the orchestra's treatment by Columbia Records.

❖   ❖   ❖

The 1954–55 season brought to the orchestra five players who stayed one or two seasons and a musician who became a crucial participant in Cleveland's symphonic metamorphosis, hornist Myron Bloom. A native Clevelander, Bloom studied with Martin Morris, the orchestra's second horn player, before attending the Eastman School of Music and the Juilliard School of Music, where his teacher was the New York Philharmonic's James Chambers. As guest conductor of the Philharmonic, Szell had admired Chambers's playing, and he decided Cleveland should adopt his horn style. Halfway into his first season in Cleveland as third horn, Bloom was contacted by the Chicago Symphony and offered the post of principal horn, without an audition. "I went to Szell immediately," said Bloom, who had come to Cleveland from the principal chair of the New Orleans

Philharmonic. "I told him I wanted to go. He said, 'Haven't you heard? You're now the first horn of the Cleveland Orchestra.'"

Like Abraham Skernick and Robert Marcellus, the orchestra's principal clarinetist since 1953, Bloom helped to define the orchestra's character under Szell, whom he came to revere as a conductor with "a mind and a heart, although you didn't see the heart very often. He had a total understanding of music." Bloom was a hornist of unusual daring, producing a large sound and employing a pulsating vibrato to bring expressive intensity to lyrical lines. Szell's penchant for achieving orchestral clarity through rhythmic precision and short, almost machine-gun-like articulation was taken up enthusiastically by Bloom, who cultivated a bold, poetic, and occasionally edgy style of horn playing. Bloom considered Szell his musical father, especially following one incident when the conductor consoled him after the pressure of playing principal horn became unbearable. In March 1957, Szell was especially hard on him while preparing *Till Eulenspiegel*, whose famously mischievous horn solo is among the most challenging in the orchestral repertoire. Bloom had to calm his anxiety by confronting Szell: "Before I could say a word, I burst into tears. And he was so . . . sensitive. He embraced me. He was incredible."

Till Eulenspiegel is one of the first works in which Bloom can be heard with the orchestra (not yet as principal but as third horn). The piece was recorded in December 1954 by Szell and the orchestra as one of three works for the Book-of-the-Month Club. (The other two were Bach's Suite for Orchestra No. 3, and Smetana's *Ma Vlast*.) Each record contained music on one side and an analysis on the other. The discs were sold only to club members. Because Szell and his musicians were serving as free agents, the ensemble was called the Music Appreciation Orchestra. The recordings were made in Masonic Auditorium, the orchestra's former home. Originally, the Book-of-the-Month Club wanted Szell to make these records with the New York Philharmonic, but Szell persuaded club officials to use his own ensemble. "I did this not only because I prefer to work with members of our Orchestra," he wrote to Percy Brown, "but also because I was eager for them to get some extra income, particularly in the present unfortunate situation, where no recording income whatsoever is assured for them as yet." The following October, Szell and the orchestra recorded five more works for the Book-of-the-Month Club: Brahms's *Academic Festival Overture* and Variations on a Theme by Haydn, Mozart's Symphony No. 39, Schumann's Symphony No. 4, and Stravinsky's *Firebird* suite.

In these recordings, the "Music Appreciation Orchestra" is the Cleveland Orchestra at its Szell-motivated best. The Bach suite demonstrates the conductor's affinity for baroque style. *Ma Vlast* receives a majestic performance. For some reason, the *Till Eulenspiegel* reading is a bit offhand and dry, though the final moments finally give the whimsical narrative its due charm.

The orchestra is even more splendid on the October 1955 recordings. The two Brahms scores are less authoritative and detailed than Szell's later Columbia recordings, but only marginally so. Mozart's Symphony No. 39 shows Szell and the orchestra in prime Classical form. Ensemble is meticulous in Schumann's Fourth Symphony, as is the conductor's attention to nuances and rhythmic buoyancy. Stravinsky's *Firebird* suite is especially intriguing: It was recorded less than two months before the composer arrived at Severance Hall to conduct the orchestra in recordings of his own music. Szell had coached his musicians in Stravinsky's style down to the smallest subtlety. The *Firebird* performance is lucid, poetic, and fierce.

✳   ✳   ✳

The first week of March 1955 brought distinguished musical visitors to Cleveland. Between two concerts conducted by Szell at Severance Hall, Herbert von Karajan and the Berlin Philharmonic made a stop at Music Hall to perform Mozart's "Haffner" Symphony, the Prelude and "Liebestod" from Wagner's *Tristan und Isolde*, and Brahms's First Symphony. Wagner lovers in Cleveland had an opportunity to compare: Szell's program that week ended with the composer's *Rienzi* overture. Another direct comparison was possible three weeks later, when Max Rudolf led the Cleveland Orchestra in the same Brahms symphony Karajan had conducted.

By this time, Vosburgh was out of the office, having felt ill since returning from the Cleveland Orchestra's annual eastern tour the previous month. One letter he received in mid-March came from principal hornist Ross Taylor, who, in shaky handwriting, submitted his (forced) resignation. "May I say that it is with considerable regret that I write it; if San Francisco weren't both my and my wife's home town I should certainly have preferred to stay with this superb orchestra and with the great conductor who created and sustains it at such a lofty level," wrote Taylor. "I don't know if this will come to you in person at this time, but when it does, I want to wish you a rapid recovery."

There would be none. On March 28, Vosburgh died of coronary thrombosis at St. Luke's Hospital in Cleveland at age 59. To pay tribute to his valued colleague, Szell conducted Mozart's *Masonic Funeral Music* the following week to begin two programs featuring pianist Artur Rubinstein. Vosburgh had served the orchestra for 32 years.

The manager chosen to succeed Vosburgh had ample orchestral experience, though his stay in Cleveland would be brief. William McKelvy Martin, 47, came from the Pittsburgh Symphony, which he had served as manager for three years and as associate manager for one year. Previously, he had been assistant manager of the Los Angeles Philharmonic. Szell decided Martin was for Cleveland after learning that he had revolutionized the fund-raising program in Pittsburgh. "This is what I want. Let's get him," he told Percy Brown. Martin was hired quickly, perhaps too swiftly for Szell to get to know him or his work well. Theirs was not to be a successful pairing, as that of Vosburgh and Szell had been.

Vosburgh's death didn't prevent the realization of several goals he had been close to achieving. Six weeks after he died, the orchestra signed a five-year agreement with Epic Records, the subsidiary of Columbia. The musicians were guaranteed $300 each for the first year, and the Musical Arts Association would earn royalties on every release. At the same time, the players won their first three-year contract, a victory that would precipitate a new era in labor activity by militant orchestra members. The weekly minimum was raised from $115 to $125, still behind the major eastern orchestras.

The board also was in for major changes. In late May, former president Thomas L. Sidlo died at the age of 67. Around the same time, Percy Brown decided to step down as president after two years, both for health reasons and, according to his son, Edward, because "he did not have the urge for power." The power was transferred in June to Frank E. Taplin, Jr., a director of the White Motor Company and the North American Coal Corporation, whose two-year presidency would be marked by major advances and upheavals.

— 20 —

Peak Performance

George Szell embarked on his 10th season with the orchestra functioning at the lofty artistic level he had aimed to achieve since his arrival in Cleveland, though he would never back away from the impossible goal of perfection. Now there was other unfinished business. The notorious acoustics of Severance Hall would have to be improved dramatically if Szell was to reveal the true greatness of the orchestra he had fashioned in his formidable image. An extended outdoor summer festival, to assure musical continuity and job security, was also high on his list of priorities. And then there was the matter of the chorus, which Szell had concluded was going nowhere under co-directors Russell Gee and Robert Stofer.

But uppermost in Szell's mind was the need to show off his orchestra in Europe. Although the ensemble was now renowned in the United States, the countries that gave birth to most of the music Szell cared about still were barely aware of it. A plan to take the orchestra to the Edinburgh Festival in 1949 had failed, which may have been a good thing. At that time, just two years after he had taken over, the new maestro didn't have the requisite personnel in place, and only a handful of his Cleveland recordings had been released.

By the 1955–56 season, however, the orchestra *was* in superb shape, and it had made numerous recordings under Szell, who was getting impatient. Major American orchestras had started to tour across the Atlantic, leaving Cleveland behind. "Pretty soon the Cleveland Orchestra will be one of the few outfits without an announced tour abroad—which I would deem extremely detrimental to prestige and morale," Szell wrote to board president Frank Taplin early in 1956. Actually, the Cleveland Orchestra had already announced a European tour—vaguely. Taplin had been in contact with the New York–based American National Theater and Academy (ANTA), which the U.S. government had charged with managing an international exchange program in response to the Soviet Union's program for sending artists abroad. In August 1955, with ANTA approval, the Cleveland Orchestra announced that it intended to make its first European tour, without giving many specifics. The trip would probably occur in 1957, last five or six weeks, and cost about $250,000. Half the money was expected to come from concert fees. ANTA and the orchestra would supply the other half.

Szell wanted the orchestra to charge top fees for its European concerts, but he received a reality check on the matter from the Paris-based agency, Bureau Artistique International, which would manage the tour. "As to the Orchestra's fees in Europe, it is very difficult to judge for the time being how much we could obtain, as the Cleveland Orchestra is unfortunately completely unknown in Europe," a representative informed Szell. "I think that sometimes it might be necessary to give concerts at the Orchestra's own risk." This didn't sit well with Szell. "I think that I should emphasize at this point," he wrote back, "that the Cleveland Orchestra, although a comparatively young one, is in every respect fully the equal of the American orchestras heard up to now in Europe and, in some respects, even superior to them, in particular as far as warmth of tone, subtlety of ensemble playing, general artistic attitude, and mastery of the various styles of music is concerned." However confident Szell may have been at this point, plans for his orchestra's first European journey would proceed extremely slowly.

❁ ❁ ❁

The tempo of personnel changes was much more swift. At the start of the 1955–56 season, 13 musicians joined the orchestra, including several who would stay well beyond the Szell era. "Retirements and jobs with other symphonies account for the bulk of the changes," reported the *Press*. One new violinist this season was Detroit-born Daniel Majeske, a former navy musician who would move up in the first violin section and eventually serve as concertmaster under three music directors.

Szell was thinking about the long term. He was pleased with the lengthened season, enlarged roster, and higher performance standards he had established in Cleveland. He made this clear when he told the *Press* that "the orchestra today is an instrument of artistic expression ranking with the best in the world, and with certain qualities I do not find in any other orchestra at the present moment." But Szell wasn't ready to settle for the status quo. "While all this is gratifying, I am not yet satisfied and will not be satisfied until we are able to have a summer season for the full orchestra comparable to the orchestras on the eastern seaboard," he said. "Only then will we be able to offer to all our musicians employment fully as attractive as any in the country. This requires the establishment of a large attractive open-air area with a fine music shed and adequate parking space."

Szell also said he hoped the orchestra could be more active in radio and television. He would consider performing operatic productions at Severance Hall if the orchestra could find a sponsor to foot the massive bill. And he noted that a pension fund for the musicians was needed to keep and attract the best players. In a 10th-season interview in the *News* (headlined, almost entirely inaccurately, "Szell Starts 11th Year Here, Still Likes 'New' Music"), Szell mustered all his powers of diplomacy to defend the new. "There is really no dearth of composers," he said. "They are legion. But really inspired musical works are not so plentiful."

Szell acted on his view by conducting no works that were even remotely modern during the first three weeks of the 1955–56 season. Mozart, a composer with whom Szell and the orchestra would become indelibly associated, was a regular musical presence this season. During his fifth program, Szell conducted the Symphony No. 40, which, the *Cleveland Press*'s Arthur Loesser wrote, "was given an exemplary performance, wonderfully drawn, shaded and colored." Herbert Elwell countered in *The Plain Dealer* that Szell's Mozart "must be better than this. This was one of those virtuosic performances, with tempi so swift as to make the music sound slick, trivial and ambiguous in style." Two weeks later, Elwell sang a different tune following Szell's performance of the Symphony No. 41, and he used whimsical language to convey his approval. "Let no one cast any asparagus, this time, at Szell's Mozart," he wrote. "His 'Jupiter' was as fine a performance as I have heard him or any other conductor achieve. It had not only precision and fitness, but variety of mood, flexibility of tempi, and a dozen other virtues that made it a vitally glowing experience."

Before the end of 1955, Szell recorded Beethoven's Fifth Symphony and Schubert's "Unfinished" Symphony (both for Epic), and Stravinsky conducted his own *Le baiser de la fée* ballet (for Columbia). The Stravinsky score, in a crisp, lucid account showing the orchestra at its responsive best, can be heard on a remastered Sony Classical disc, along with the composer's Symphony in C and complete *Pulcinella*, which he had recorded at Severance Hall in 1952. More Mozart under Szell soon followed for Columbia—the Piano Concerto No. 12, with Robert Casadesus as soloist, and Concerto for Two Pianos, featuring Casadesus and his wife, Gaby, who were among Szell's closest friends and colleagues for several decades.

✧ ✧ ✧

In December 1955, a storm broke out at Severance Hall. The board, acting on Szell's wishes, voted not to renew Rudolph Ringwall's contract, ending his 30 years of service to the orchestra. The trustees also voted to hire Robert

Shaw as associate conductor. Shaw, who was already enormously respected as a choral conductor, had studied with Szell in 1942 at the Mannes School of Music in New York. Szell long had wanted to get rid of Ringwall, whom he and many orchestra members felt was no longer effective. And the orchestra's boss was determined that the Cleveland Orchestra Chorus be brought to a level worthy of his ensemble.

No one could have anticipated the furor that the dismissal of the 65-year-old Ringwall would spark. Lillian Baldwin, who had raised the orchestra's educational concerts to national prominence since 1929 through programs devised under "the Cleveland Plan," took Ringwall's firing—and the hiring of Shaw, who had no experience with children's programs—as a sign that the orchestra was retreating from its educational mission. The previous year, Szell had referred to one of Baldwin's programs in derogatory terms. "Why do you play trash for our children?" he asked her. "I blush with shame at the concerts you give our children." Szell had never had much input into children's concerts. And, curiously, the program he objected to—colorful works by Wolf-Ferrari, Vaughan Williams, Coates, Grainger, Sibelius, Lecuona, and Herbert—could hardly have been termed trashy. "When Szell came," recalled harpist Alice Chalifoux, "he wanted the kids to hear Mozart, and they didn't give a damn about Mozart. Ringwall did things that children understand at age 6, 7 and 8."

At first, Baldwin gave Shaw the benefit of the doubt. She met with him several times to discuss his ideas about educational concerts (he had none). Her conclusion was unhappy. "The conferences convinced me that I would only spend a heartbreaking year in a losing fight against the long determination to end the Orchestra's children's concerts as we have known them," wrote Baldwin in her resignation letter to Taplin. "Since no one has been appointed by the Cleveland Board of Education to take my place as liaison person between the schools and the Orchestra, I assume that Mr. Shaw will have to plan next season's programs. In fairness to him I must not delay this, to me, incredible letter. I simply cannot believe that with April concerts I shall be saying goodbye to 'my' young audiences!"

Taplin tried to heal the rift in a letter a few days later. "We all love the Orchestra and the Children's Concerts, and we have much to keep us busy," he wrote to Baldwin. "We want you to stay on as Consultant on Music Education during the important period which lies ahead. You may be sure of our loyalty to and interest in this work which lies so close to your heart." Baldwin didn't buy it. She was finished with Szell, who she felt had never been helpful with children's concerts, and the orchestra, which she had served tirelessly for 26 years. One member of the Cleveland Board of

Education came to Baldwin's defense by throwing brickbats at Szell for calling Ringwall "only a violinist." Alfred A. Benesch fumed, ridiculously, that Szell was "like Truman and Liberace, only a piano player."

Shaw was caught in the middle of the controversy. Admired as founder of the Collegiate Chorale and as assistant to Arturo Toscanini for NBC Symphony performances requiring chorus, he had ventured slowly into symphonic music as conductor of the San Diego Symphony, an orchestra far below Cleveland's level. Shaw knew that he would gain immeasurable orchestral experience working with Szell in Cleveland. For Szell, hiring Shaw meant killing two birds with one stone: he would get rid of Ringwall and obtain the superb chorus that had eluded him. Shaw deemed his new job a situation he couldn't pass up. "Some people seem to regard this as the big switch," he said of his turn toward orchestral conducting, "but I'm not one of them. There's a great opportunity out there to work with a fine orchestra and a master conductor like Szell. I expect to learn a lot." He would do just that. "The first year I was there I conducted more than 80 concerts," he later said. "And for twelve years I had the hottest orchestral property in the U.S. to learn on."

Many observers in Cleveland were delighted with the choice of Shaw. His appointment "is the best thing to happen to the Cleveland Orchestra since the resignation of Rodzinski," a concertgoer wrote to Taplin. "We had almost decided to give up our seats next season, but now will look forward to at least a few more interesting programs. My heartiest congratulations for a very pleasant Christmas surprise." He revised one statement in a postscript. "In rereading, I realized my first sentence is ambiguous. I thought Rodzinski was great—not so Szell."

Shaw had plans to build the Cleveland Orchestra Chorus into a volunteer organization without peer. "I'd like to audition 600 singers right after Labor Day, choose 200 of them and start right away on chorus work," Shaw said in January 1956. "I want to build the best chorus in the United States. I may even form a new Midwest professional chorus from this group." By the time the first open auditions were held the following September, more than 1,800 singers had signed up for tryouts. Shaw whittled the number down to 240 and called the first rehearsal. At the stroke of 8 p.m., the doors to the rehearsal room were locked. Shaw had 200 singers in place. The other 40 were dismissed. "I'm sorry," Shaw told the rejected singers. "You will not ever be a member of this chorus. When I say 8:00, it is 8:00. It's not 8:01."

Szell and Shaw would have major disagreements throughout Shaw's 11 years in Cleveland as associate conductor and director of choruses. Critics would be quick to point out, too obviously, that Shaw was not in Szell's league as a symphonic conductor. Shaw, an admitted slow learner, would suffer knowing that he could never approach Szell's achievements. Even so, no one would deny the transformation Shaw wrought on the Cleveland Orchestra Chorus, which finally met Szell's exacting standards. "It is astonishing—like some sort of magic," he told Shaw. "Simply by the quality of the beat one can make an instant change in tone, tempo, balance or color. This chorus is simply more responsive than an orchestra."

Soon after the Baldwin-Ringwall-Shaw affair, another controversy began to brew. Szell had decided that William McKelvy Martin, the orchestra's new manager, was inadequate, and he demanded that Taplin take action. The board president's Band-Aid solution diminished Martin's powers by splitting his duties with George H. L. Smith, the program annotator who had been associate manager for several years. Smith was promoted to co-manager, a post in which, it would turn out, he was thoroughly miscast.

❊   ❊   ❊

All of these events were being played out as Severance Hall was approaching its 25th anniversary. The orchestra prepared to mark the milestone with gala concerts. One former Clevelander who had hoped to attend was Nikolai Sokoloff, the orchestra's founding conductor, who was living in California at the time. But the weather didn't cooperate the day he was supposed to travel, and his flight to Cleveland was cancelled. "Will be with you in spirit," he wrote in a telegram to Taplin. "Severance Hall and orchestra will always remain dear to me. Much of my life went into the creating of both. Certain Cleveland will cherish its orchestra and Severance Hall evermore."

In a retrospective, *The Plain Dealer*'s Herbert Elwell stated that Szell was the greatest thing ever to happen to the Cleveland Orchestra, though he was not inclined to denigrate the orchestra's previous leaders. He noted that Sokoloff "had one gift that has not been equaled in any of his successors. This was an uncanny, almost clairvoyant sense about putting together interesting and satisfying programs." He was equally admiring of Rodzinski, who "has never been surpassed in certain fields, such as the interpretation of Tchaikovsky and Strauss." These former Cleveland conductors were part of a field, Elwell said, that had become crowded: "Sokoloff once observed that if you threw a brick out of a window of almost any hotel in New York, in all probability it would land on the head of an unemployed conductor."

❊   ❊   ❊

Szell showed an increased penchant for things European. Of eight composers he commissioned for scores to celebrate the orchestra's 40th season, six were from Europe: Boris Blacher, Henri Dutilleux, Bohuslav Martinů, Robert Moevs, Gottfried von Einem, and Sir William Walton. (The others, Paul Creston and Howard Hanson, were American.) Szell's Eurocentricity on many subjects had not gone unnoticed in Cleveland, where the board was called upon to counter objections to Szell's attitude. As Percy Brown, now chairman of the board, told trustees:

> At various times criticisms have reached me as to Mr. Szell running off to Europe each summer and deserting Cleveland. To such I would reply that I do not think he is fully appreciated by Clevelanders. Many of us rate him as an outstanding musician and conductor, but others seem to feel that he is kind of a hired man who is expected to be here twelve months in the year. The fact is, he is under contract for only thirty weeks out of the 52. He is in demand throughout Europe and one major orchestra in this country tried to hire him away from us this past year.

No documentation can be found to suggest which orchestra this may have been.

The fact that Szell derived enormous satisfaction from working in Europe cannot be denied. He was bubbling with news during the summer of 1956, when he conducted Mozart's *The Abduction from the Seraglio* at the Salzburg Festival. He sent co-manager Smith a list of things he wanted people in Cleveland to know about his European endeavors, including the news that this "peach of a [Mozart] performance" would be broadcast in the U.S. in early September. Szell told Smith that he had been invited to conduct a new opera and a Mozart program with the Vienna Philharmonic at Salzburg the following year, when he would also be engaged for the Berlin, Vienna, and Prague festivals. In addition, Herbert von Karajan had requested that he conduct *Salome* at the Vienna State Opera during the 1957–58 season. Clearly, Szell realized the importance of well-timed publicity. "Perhaps you save items 2–5 until after Labor Day, when readers are back in town," he advised Smith.

❖   ❖   ❖

Europe was on Szell's mind for other reasons. Part of his original mission in Cleveland had involved the heightening of the orchestra's identity. The ultimate destination was Europe. He was determined to introduce his orchestra to cities where classical music had been taken seriously for centuries. In September 1956, Szell exulted that the first foreign tour with his ensemble was about to become reality. Writing to Anatole Heller at the

Bureau Artistique International in Paris, he outlined preliminary ideas for
the tour, which was to run from May 5 to June 18, 1957. The orchestra was
not to play more than six concerts per week, Szell told Heller, and only five
if travel was necessary between cities. The American National Theatre and
Academy (ANTA), which was organizing the tour, wanted Szell and his ensemble to perform not only in major cities, such as London, but also in what
they termed "secondary" cities (Bordeaux, Lyon) and some behind the Iron
Curtain, such as Prague (which would be cancelled at the last moment) and
Belgrade (which would never make the itinerary). Szell was willing to use
his considerable influence to demand the proper fees and dates for his orchestra. Asked to conduct at the Prague Festival, he intended to tell the festival director "he cannot have me conduct in Prague at all unless he takes
the C.O."

The orchestra that Szell would take to Europe now was consistently rising to the peak of performance he had been working toward since arriving
in Cleveland. The splendor can be heard in two sets of excerpts from
Wagner music dramas performed and recorded in November 1956 at
Severance Hall. Szell's keen way with Wagner's textures and dramatic
propulsion are vividly apparent in the sequences from *Tannhäuser, Tristan
und Isolde*, and *Götterdämmerung* that were taped live by Herbert Heller,
an electronics engineer at Cleveland's Clevite Corporation, during the concert on November 1. Heller had been hired by the Institute of Radio
Engineers to make some of the earliest multichannel three-track recordings
in the United States. He taped Szell, the ensemble, and soprano Margaret
Harshaw in Wagner performances that are preserved on the orchestra's
Szell Compact-Disc Centennial Edition.

A day later, minus Harshaw, Szell and his musicians recorded excerpts
from the *Ring* cycle, including portions from *Die Walküre, Siegfried*, and
Götterdämmerung, for Epic. Szell's authority in this repertoire—he had
conducted a complete *Ring*, as well as *Salome,* at the Berlin State Opera in
1924 without any rehearsal—comes blazing forth in these accounts. As always, Szell creates a sense of urgency but makes sure that every important
strand is heard. The orchestra is superbly cohesive and precise. In most respects, these glowing performances would only be superseded in 1968,
when Szell and the orchestra rerecorded the excerpts with better sound for
Columbia.

Severance Hall was also the scene this season of the debut of one of the
most iconoclastic and brilliant musicians of the era, pianist Glenn Gould,
who performed Beethoven's Piano Concerto No. 2. "His playing was almost
shy in its intimate understatement," wrote Elwell. "The piano part crept in

on tiptoe to dance with astonishing swiftness, lightness and grace, while it also exuded sweet pathos. Effeminate? No, but charmingly and amusingly boyish, as were some of the pianist's mannerisms." These mannerisms tested Szell's patience. During rehearsals, Gould made constant adjustments to the low chair he used instead of a piano bench. Szell finally had enough. "Perhaps if we were to slice one sixteenth of an inch off your derrière, Mr. Gould, we could begin," he is reported to have said (though some claim an English word was spoken in place of the French). Szell later told Louis Lane he wouldn't work with Gould again. "His habits annoy me, but he's a great artist. We must have him back and so why don't you take him next season?" When Lane did so in 1962, collaborating with Gould in performances of the postponed Bach concerto and Strauss's *Burleske*, Szell was in the audience for the final concert. At intermission, he spoke to Lane by phone, uttering a line that became famous: "That nut is a genius."

✧   ✧   ✧

A few days before Szell and the orchestra left for Europe, the Musical Arts Association announced the hiring of A. Beverly Barksdale, a tall, soft-spoken Southerner who was serving as supervisor of music at the Toledo Museum of Art, to be associate manager, succeeding William McKelvy Martin. A former basso from Greenville, South Carolina, who had received music degrees from Louisiana State University, studied at the Juilliard School of Music in New York, and taken voice lessons with the Metropolitan Opera's Pasquale Amato, Barksdale was set to begin work in August.

The tour was bound to be one of the grandest, and bumpiest, adventures in the orchestra's history. During their 1957 European debut, the ensemble was set to perform 33 works by 20 composers in 22 cities and feature five eminent soloists: pianists Robert Casadesus, Leon Fleisher, and Rudolf Serkin; violinist Wolfgang Schneiderhan; and soprano Elisabeth Schwarzkopf.

Szell and his players weren't prepared for the joys and rigors of international touring, especially in the Iron Curtain cities of Katowice, Poznan, Lodz, and Warsaw, Poland, where services could be appalling. "Only a few hotels could be obtained, and these were distinctly second rate," wrote Elwell after the tour. "Most of the members had to live in the train in which they were traveling." The conditions didn't hinder the Clevelanders' generosity. They brought along strings, reeds, and mouthpieces for musicians who didn't have access to fine musical supplies. Principal trumpet Louis Davidson gave a $300 instrument to a Polish player, who told him, "You have changed my life." The orchestra evidently changed the lives of countless

Poles. In Katowice, Szell began the concert with a performance of Mozart's "Jupiter" Symphony that elicited 11 curtain calls.

Such concerts helped Szell change the world's view of an orchestra from the Yankee heartlands. "In a scant six weeks, the Cleveland Orchestra did much to dispel those [European] theories which regard America's midwest as the epitome of provincialism," reported *Hi-Fi Music at Home* after the tour. "Its double goal was well met: superb musicianship won many followers for the orchestra, while its actual presence and performances gathered praise and esteem for America in the international cultural competition."

Cleveland's entry in that competition began in Antwerp with a program of Berlioz, Schumann, Creston, Smetana, and Wagner and continued the next night at the Brussels Palais des Beaux Arts, where Szell conducted music by Rossini, Beethoven, Barber, and Ravel. The reaction of a Brussels journalist established a critical trend for the tour—fabulous ensemble, questionable interpretations. "A prodigious orchestra. One of the best I have ever heard. They achieve perfection," wrote the critic, before dropping a few salvos. "All effects are exaggerated. When they have fortissimo, it's double fortissimo. When they play andante, it's too much andante. Effects are overdone. Maybe this is the way the public likes it over there. More nuance, however, would be welcome." Many European critics were to find the Cleveland conductor's tempos too fast.

Szell had hoped to take his orchestra to Prague, where he had held the top conducting post at the German Opera, to perform two concerts in Smetana Hall during the renowned Prague Spring Festival. A week into the tour, Czech officials suddenly refused to issue visas for the Cleveland entourage, without giving a reason. The Communist government relented the next day but cancelled the engagement two weeks later. The second Prague concert was quickly replaced by a performance at Berlin's Hochschule für Musik. It was Szell's first visit to the city in more than a quarter of a century. "I hardly recognized Berlin," he told the Associated Press. "I did not know that Berlin was that much destroyed by the war. I drove around to look at the streets where I had lived 28 years ago, but I could not find them."

During the tour, unsettling news came from the renowned orchestra of another European city. On May 28, the Concertgebouw Orchestra of Amsterdam announced that Szell had agreed to serve as its second regular conductor for a three-year period, sharing the podium with Eduard Van Beinum. The announcement led to speculation that Szell might leave Cleveland. "Is this the initial break that will ultimately see the departure of Szell?" wrote Paul Mooney in the *Cleveland Press*. "With a glance at conductorial permanency records, it is odds on. Szell has enjoyed 11 successful

seasons in Cleveland, whipping the orchestra to its top position in the musical world and parading it in the present triumphant tour. Has he reached
the goal he set up for himself here and now . . . launched out for a new one?"

He hadn't. Szell had no intention of departing from Cleveland, especially
since he and his orchestra were now flying so high musically in Europe.
However, things weren't always soaring backstage. While Szell and the ensemble were in Paris, acting manager George H. L. Smith resigned from his
post "because of intolerable treatment by George Szell." Taplin put it another way: "Have today released George Smith of all duties and responsibilities as acting manager and assistant secretary," he wrote to orchestra
trustee Frank E. Joseph, who was on the verge of succeeding Taplin as board
president. Taplin appointed bass player Olin Trogdon, also the orchestra's
personnel manager, as successor to Smith for the rest of the tour.

Taplin told the Associated Press he had fired Smith for "non-performance," a veiled reference to the manager's incompetence in losing the orchestra's payroll in a hotel lobby during the tour. Smith told the *Press* that
Szell, while in Stuttgart, "suddenly turned on me for no reason at all and behaved like a perfectly ridiculous beast. He caused a perfectly horrible
scene." This account was confirmed by none other than Szell's secretary, Peg
Glove, who abruptly quit her post in protest when informed that Smith had
resigned. Glove told the *Press* the incident "was magnified due to the strenuousness of the trip. Mr. Szell lost his temper, but I'd rather not go into details. He insulted Mr. Smith in front of a lot of people." Several weeks later,
the Smith case assumed another dimension. His wife was granted a divorce,
and Glove was named as "the other woman in an alleged triangle." Glove
quickly denied the charge. "Mrs. Smith is a fool," she said. "She has no right
to do this to other people. This is all absolute nonsense . . . I'm a happily-
married woman." (Not long thereafter, Glove was back at Severance Hall as
Szell's secretary. She remained in the post until 1970, after the conductor's
death.)

These episodes were mere distractions on a tour that finally placed the
Cleveland Orchestra among the great international ensembles. As timpanist
Cloyd Duff recalled, "we returned home and found out that we were better
than most people thought we were here." In virtually every city, audiences
were euphoric and critics raved, even if Szell's music-making didn't always
suit their tastes. "No finer orchestra playing has yet been heard in the
Festival Hall, and I doubt whether anything superior is to be heard anywhere else," wrote the critic of *The New Statesman and Nation* in London.
"They play with the loving spontaneity of a fine European orchestra, as well
as with the discipline, blend, and unanimity characteristic of America."

Combat, a newspaper in Paris, hailed Cleveland's "magnificent sonority, movement and cohesion." Yet the same critic viewed Szell as "an India rubber jumping jack" whose performances had "little or no deep life, free flow or heart."

Weeks after the tour, Herbert Elwell provided a different perspective from home (the orchestra's early international tours were not covered by Cleveland critics). He theorized that the European journey brought out qualities in the orchestra and its boss that weren't always apparent in Cleveland. "In these excellent [European] halls, Conductor George Szell found no need to drive his men, as he sometimes does, and as he relaxed, they did also, with the result that they played better and sounded better than they ever have before." He also said that the tour had made Europeans aware of the city and raised the orchestra's morale.

> The Cleveland Orchestra may well be entering a new era in its history, an era of increased artistic merit and greater usefulness to the community and to the world. In these last years, it has gone through much strife and bickering. Generously interpreted, these internal convulsions might be regarded as growing pains. No great artistic achievement was ever attained without pain and struggle. Let us hope that the most severe and violent of these unfortunate incidents are now things of the past, and that from now on, affairs of the orchestral family will run a smoother course.

On these last matters, Elwell was dreaming. The realities of running so complex an organism as an orchestra would always involve internal strife. What mattered was the product, which Szell had raised to world-class status. "Exploit to the utmost the <u>simply incredible</u> success of the Orchestra in Europe," Szell wrote to Frank Joseph after the tour. "Impress upon the AMERICAN—not only the Cleveland—public the fact that the C.O. has definitely been recognized internationally as one of the very very topranking Orchestras of the world. This has to be pounded in, kept alive, reiterated, in the most effective way, or else, the European success will have been squandered."

The success would not be squandered. On the contrary, the orchestra was headed for a prolonged golden age under its uncompromising boss.

Resounding Success

The Cleveland Orchestra's defining qualities reached full bloom in 1957 and 1958. The city finally realized what it had. The success of the European tour convinced the hometown that its orchestra was as good as, or better than, ensembles in metropolises far larger or more glamorous. Halfway into George Szell's tenure, the institution engendered pride and envy for its distinctive approach to orchestral playing.

Most important was the debut in Europe. Szell had not demonstrated the greatest skill in dealing with people, especially his players. But he had rarely been wrong when it came to artistic matters. Despite criticism of his conducting, Szell's orchestra had performed throughout Europe with almost devastating ensemble brilliance and refinement. Many of the benefits were to be domestic. "That European trip and the incredible success of the orchestra was the greatest thing that could have happened at this particular stage of the orchestra's development," Szell told *The Plain Dealer* before opening night in 1957. The tour persuaded the musicians that they were "as excellent as musical audiences and critics of the European capitals found them to be."

More positive developments awaited the orchestra at the beginning of its 12th season under Szell. After a hiatus of 15 years, weekly radio broadcasts from Severance Hall were set to resume in November 1957. Twenty one-hour programs would be heard on Saturday nights by listeners to more than 200 stations of the Columbia Broadcasting System, which was paying the Musical Arts Association $10,000 to underwrite the series. Among the listeners delighted to learn about the broadcasts was Joe Pugh Lindsay, a music lover in Tutwiler, Mississippi, who had been exchanging annual letters with Szell. "As I am to have the privilege of enjoying your concerts this year, I want to be a real Friend of the Cleveland Orchestra. I am enclosing a dollar for the maintenance fund," wrote Lindsay. "Music has always been such a joy to me because I never have been able to get around very well, having been afflicted with cerebral palsy. Also, hearing great music, especially in the wonderful way that you perform it, always uplifts me, and makes me feel very near to God."

Szell continued to ensure great music-making by hiring players who could live up to his rigorous standards. Among the new members at the start of the 1957–58 season were three whose contributions would prove lasting and even groundbreaking. Two violinists arrived who were to be connected with the orchestra not only musically but also politically: Gino Raffaelli and Leonard Samuels became active on the orchestra committee. The arrival of Donald White, a cellist from Richmond, Indiana, was noted in a *Plain Dealer* headline: "Orchestra Here Signs First Negro." After studying with former Cleveland Orchestra principal cellist Leonard Rose, White played in the National Orchestral Association in New York and as first assistant cello in the Hartford Symphony Orchestra before being engaged by Szell for Cleveland. "We heard a group of cellists who came to audition and of them Mr. White was unquestionably the best," recalled assistant conductor Louis Lane.

Dealing with personnel was only one of the challenges facing the orchestra's new manager, A. Beverly Barksdale, who had arrived in Ohio in 1940 to start an educational program for children and adults at the Toledo Museum of Art. As supervisor of music, he managed the museum's admired Peristyle Concerts series, which presented international artists and ensembles. In Cleveland, Barksdale was to discover quickly that working with Szell, though always stimulating, was often grueling. Szell never missed an opportunity to tell his courtly manager that he could do better, or that he had made big mistakes. About Barksdale's suggestion that the orchestra perform Bach's B minor Mass at Oberlin College, Szell offered a withering reply in December 1957: "My initial reaction would be that the mere idea of doing a repeat performance after a full month has elapsed, with a completely changed team of soloists and just one squeezed-in rehearsal is so puerile as to not even be worthy of serious discussion." Barksdale would endure this type of ranting throughout his association with the conductor.

Szell wasn't the only Cleveland Orchestra conductor to try Barksdale's bountiful patience at this time. Artur Rodzinski had accepted an invitation from Szell to return as a guest for the first time in 15 years, to lead two programs in December 1958. "The dates for 2 weeks are acceptable and I would like to repeat my first and last program which I conducted in Cleveland," Rodzinski wrote to Szell in November 1957, when the ensemble's former boss said he would like "the highest fee the Cleveland Orchestra ever paid a guest conductor." Barksdale wrote back that such a fee would be $2,000 per week. In *Our Two Lives,* Halina Rodzinski says her husband's Cleveland

engagement was dropped because he asked an "exorbitant fee." Whatever
the price, the orchestra's former conductor responded to Barksdale's entreaty for a quick answer with the same indecision Carl Vosburgh had encountered during his rocky 10-year relationship with the mercurial maestro.
"Right now I have a small complication of a professional nature which makes
it impossible for me to give you a definite answer before the end of
February," Rodzinski wrote to Barksdale. If Cleveland had waited until
then, answered Barksdale, "and had then found that you were unable to
come, it would have been impossible for us to secure a guest conductor or
conductors of sufficient importance. We had wanted to make your return to
Cleveland a great occasion and still hope that we may be able to do so in another season."

It wouldn't happen. Even the original dates would not have worked out:
the 66-year-old Rodzinski died on November 27, 1958, three weeks before
the proposed Cleveland engagement. He died in Boston a few days after he
had led a performance of *Tristan und Isolde*—the first opera he had presented in Cleveland in 1933—at Chicago's Lyric Opera, with Birgit Nilsson
as the heroine. Halina Rodzinski told a reporter that her husband had given
Wagner's music drama "everything he had in Chicago. He was tremendous.
The critics raved. There were standing ovations every time. But it finished
him." Summing up Rodzinski's career at the helm of the orchestras of
Cleveland, New York, and Chicago, the *New York Times*'s Howard Taubman
paid tribute to an artist who was complicated but forceful: "If Rodzinski left
turbulence in his wake, he filled his music-making with excitement. He was
a passionate fighter for his convictions."

❊   ❊   ❊

Rodzinski, who had arrived in Cleveland during a depression and left during a world war, had failed in several areas in which Szell was having sensational success, such as increases in personnel and subscription weeks. Now
another Szell coup was pending. The Musical Arts Association had finally
approved plans to liven up the dry acoustics of Severance Hall and asked
Heinrich Keilholz, the German recording engineer whom Szell had hand-
picked for the project, to submit drawings for a new shell, which he did in
January 1958. His proposal was not original: It was based closely on recommendations made to the Musical Arts Association by Robert C. Shankland,
the Case Institute of Technology physicist who had tested the acoustics in
1953. The renovation, estimated at $300,000, was set for the summer of
1958, while the orchestra was on break.

Observers already were predicting that the new shell would make the brasses even louder than before. Szell predicted otherwise. "The brassiness is due precisely to the fact that the sound now is so stifled that only the brasses get through because the strings & woods are killed," he wrote to Barksdale. "After the change the sound will be more balanced, i.e. mellower and yet more brilliant, with the brasses not sticking out any more." Szell's prediction wouldn't prove entirely accurate, but the strings indeed would be infinitely more prominent than before.

Specific acoustical plans weren't released to the public until early July 1958, when the Musical Arts Association announced its intention "to permit the Cleveland Orchestra to be heard with greater resonance and richness." To do so, a substantial shell would replace the flimsy 1953 stage set of plywood with muslin glued to the surface. Vinyl tile would replace carpeting in the aisles. One aim was to increase the reverberation time. "We not only want to hear a pin drop," said trustee Walter K. Bailey, "but we want to hear it drop longer." Another crucial goal of the renovation was improved clarity of sound. It was to be accomplished without touching the regal Art Deco beauty of the auditorium, if not the stage. "With our new setup the orchestra will be enabled to play more easily and with no forcing," Barksdale said. "Our old setup was more for theater and not so much for a concert hall."

The new shell, a Danish modern design that made the stage look like a recording studio, was constructed of layers of light wood (basswood, maple plywood) covered by a thin veneer of maple plywood. Between the basswood core and a layer of maple plywood, an air space was filled with sand to a height of nine feet. The convex curves on the shell walls were designed to blend the instruments onstage and project the sound into the hall. The stage's new red-oak floor (the original floor was pine) initially was topped by risers, or platforms, that were considered vital for volume and projection. Szell and the orchestra found the risers problematic. They emphasized, rather than diminished, the dreaded "brassiness." David Zauder, who joined the orchestra's trumpet section in 1958, just as the new acoustics were about to be unveiled, said the sound was superb for works for small ensemble. But when it came to large symphonic pieces, the results could be "unbearably loud and raucous," Zauder recalled. Eventually, Szell got rid of the risers, though timpanist Cloyd Duff continued to play on a small platform throughout his tenure.

Long before anyone sat on the new stage, Szell closely reviewed every aspect of the renovation, including color schemes. "I am as pleased as punch with the progress report on Severance Hall. Please make sure that it is not overlooked to change the ghastly blue paint [on the stage shell] which William McKelvy Shithead Martin put in on his own back to the color matching the rest of the auditorium," he wrote to Barksdale in mid-July from Europe. Szell was playing golf in Switzerland in late August when the orchestra played its first notes on the new stage under Louis Lane in preparation for recording sessions of popular repertoire. He wasn't surprised to learn that the musicians weren't ecstatic. "It must have been a real shock to them, indeed, after being used to a dead hall, to have to adjust themselves to a rehearsal-acoustic to which other Orchestras are used as a matter of course," Szell wrote. "The fact is that a good hall MUST have excessive reverberation when empty." A few days later, Szell wrote to Barksdale again with suggestions for cutting down the avalanche of sound, as well as a few warnings: "Two main considerations must be very firmly in our minds: 1. I am not going to settle for some outlandish, anticonventional seating of the Orchestra. 2. The opening concert must not be played under conditions calling for an apology for an unfinished or poorly accomplished job." From Hamburg, acoustician Keilholz sent his own advice, including covering parts of the shell with absorption materials temporarily to find the areas where reflections were unreasonable.

Some of the earliest notes sounded in the new acoustical environment were captured on the recordings Lane and the orchestra made on August 21 and 22, 1958. Adjutor "Pappy" Theroux, a French-born recording engineer whose association with the orchestra dated back to the Rodzinski era, was in charge of the Epic sessions. Theroux wrote to Szell that the recording sessions had gone well but that he was concerned about one aspect of the shell. "Pappy objects that the wooden surfaces of the set have been 'filled and highly lacquered'," Szell wrote to Barksdale. "WHO THE HELL HAS GIVEN INSTRUCTIONS FOR LACQUERING???? Is it not possible in this world to get a piece of work executed without self-defeating idiotic blunders ???" Szell believed the so-called lacquering would hinder projection. Barksdale soothed him by telling him that a thin finish had to be applied to keep the wood stable and sealed from Cleveland's unpredictable climate. He had received assurances from physicist Shankland that the coat was needed. Barksdale also told Szell he believed a few speeches were needed to kick off the opening concert in the new shell, but Szell quickly shot him down. "Heavens, NO, NO, let the new sound speak for itself !!!" he wrote from Paris.

Szell was back in Cleveland soon to check out the acoustics with Keilholz, who walked "along the balcony with his little Geiger counter to test the reverberation," recalled Lane. "He had a little starter's pistol." Keilholz, who had worked on the shell design with Cleveland architect Edward A. Flynn, prepared people in the hall for his pistol shots—which helped him measure reverberation time—by shouting, "Achtung, Schuss!" (roughly, "Watch out for the shot!") Students who had been invited to attend the rehearsal had to be asked to refrain from laughter to avoid upsetting the measurement equipment. Klaus George Roy, the Viennese-born composer, musicologist, and critic who had just arrived at Severance Hall to serve as program annotator and editor, translated Keilholz's reaction to the acoustics upon hearing the orchestra for the first time in the new environment: "In very simple terms, it feels as if after a foggy night the daylight has finally come."

Szell also proclaimed the renovation a success. "Tomorrow night for the first time, Cleveland will hear its orchestra," he told guests at a preview rehearsal on October 7. He had planned a juicy opening program virtually guaranteed to delight the audience: Wagner's Act I prelude to *Die Meistersinger*, Brahms's Fourth Symphony, Walton's Partita (one of the 40th-anniversary commissions, which had received its premiere the previous January in a very different Severance Hall), and Stravinsky's *Firebird* suite. The *Meistersinger* prelude was the first piece Szell rehearsed in the new shell, an experience recounted years later by violinist Bernhard Goldschmidt. "Is this really an orchestra? Is this a recording?" he recalled of that first rehearsal. "That feeling never left me—that fantastic sound and balance built in this group. There are miracles happening here."

Several aspects of the acoustical renovation weren't quite so miraculous. The modernist shell had a wondrous effect in revealing the true personality of the Cleveland Orchestra, but it was out of character visually with the auditorium's Art Deco architecture. The transformation of a multipurpose hall into a bona fide concert hall now made operatic productions cumbersome. And it completely cut off sonic access to the E. M. Skinner pipe organ. Efforts to project the organ through speakers at the back of the new shell proved inadequate.

Even so, there was no doubt that Szell and the orchestra had pulled off another triumph. "From the opening heraldry chords of Wagner's thickly textured 'Meistersinger' Prelude," wrote Bain Murray, serving as guest critic in *The Plain Dealer*, "the capacity opening-night audience knew that at last the Cleveland Orchestra had a hall worthy of its finest efforts."

❖   ❖   ❖

Carnegie Hall, where the orchestra had played on occasion over the decades, was becoming the ensemble's home away from home—and one of its most important links with the international music world. In February and March 1958, Szell and his ensemble had begun the first of an annual three-concert series at the New York landmark, where audiences were large and enthusiastic, and where critics hailed the team as virtually untouchable. "Cleveland can be proud of its orchestra, one of the really great ensembles of the world," wrote Paul Henry Lang in the *Herald Tribune* of one of the 1958 concerts. The orchestra's board once again displayed visionary thinking by agreeing to commit itself to the Carnegie series. "Such a step, while expensive in the beginning, is deemed necessary for the further solidifying of the Orchestra's national standing," Barksdale told trustees. "We expect the series of three announced for next season to be even more successful financially and prestige-wise."

The Carnegie concerts the following season indeed bolstered the orchestra's stature, though opinion would always be divided about Szell's interpretive gifts. "The Cleveland Orchestra behaves as if it intends to make a firm place for itself on the New York scene," wrote the *New York Times* of an all-Beethoven concert on February 4, 1959, that included the Symphony No. 6 ("Pastoral"). The *World-Telegram* noted, "the true revelation was the 'Pastoral.' If there has been a better, or even equal, performance of this symphonic landscape since the reign of Toscanini, I have forgotten it or never heard it." Another review, in the *Herald Tribune*, said that the orchestra reflected Szell's personality: "Its playing is everywhere solid, sane, secure and sober. It is a marvelous mechanism operating on gears that know neither imperfection nor inefficiency." The critic wasn't done: "However, a number like the 'Pastoral' Symphony needs a bit more in the way of sunshine and springtime if it is to be wholly successful in performance. As Mr. Szell gave us the piece, there was not a note out of place, though the kind of smiling grace and lightness that account for the work's poetic impetus was quite lacking."

The day of this concert, the musicians reluctantly agreed to participate in a photo shoot at an unusual New York location. "Orchestra Slowly Thwarts Subway Stunt," read the headline in the *Times*. Photos of the musicians playing or posing accompanied the story. One image featured Lawrence Angell trying to stick a bass through closed subway doors. "The Cleveland Orchestra, one of the best-disciplined groups in the country, staged an insurrection this morning when herded into subway cars for publicity," wrote Murray Schumach. The caption under the photos told more. "Furioso: A thoughtful press agent had provided a rented bull fiddle for just such a picture as this. The musicians rebelled. Said a subway man: 'So much temperament!' "

❀   ❀   ❀

In his early months as the orchestra's manager, Barksdale had to learn how to deal with big New York artist managers, especially Sol Hurok, the powerful impresario who represented many of the classical world's stellar artists. Hurok had wanted Barksdale to engage some of the younger performers on his roster. By this time, Barksdale had almost completely booked the orchestra's 1958–59 season, leaving virtually no dates for soloists until the following season. Hurok said he would keep the dates for two major artists Cleveland wanted most, pianist Artur Rubinstein and violinist Nathan Milstein, in pencil until Szell contacted him personally. "This is the kind of blackmail I have heard about but have never experienced before. Practically every important manager had been accused of it some time or other," Barksdale wrote to Szell in Vienna. "I have not had enough contact with [Hurok] to know when he is bluffing and when he isn't. Actually, we have based our whole season around the special week with Rubinstein. At this point I don't know whom we could get to fill such a spot."

Barksdale didn't have to lose any sleep in the end. Both Rubinstein and Milstein appeared during the 1958–59 season—the pianist in two special concerts under Szell in which he played the Tchaikovsky First Piano Concerto and the Chopin concerto, Beethoven's "Emperor" Concerto, and Rachmaninoff's Second Piano Concerto; and Milstein in the Tchaikovsky Violin Concerto. Rubinstein wasn't the only pianist for whom Szell displayed unusual affection. Leon Fleisher had become a favorite artist at Severance Hall, where he collaborated with Szell often in some of the most penetrating recordings of major piano repertoire. As he did for many young artists, Szell served as mentor to Fleisher. After Van Cliburn won first prize in the Tchaikovsky competition in Moscow, Szell guided Fleisher away from the first Tchaikovsky concerto—with which Cliburn had dazzled Muscovites—for upcoming Cleveland concerts and recording sessions. "Consequently, we have changed both your recording repertoire and your repertoire for your appearances with us here to consist of the G major Beethoven and the Mozart K. 503," Szell wrote to Fleisher. "I hope you are as happy as I am with this new turn of events and I also want to emphasize that my scheduling you for two concertos on the same program is an important testimony to your increased prestige so far as our audiences are concerned."

The issue of soloists was a major concern for the orchestra, both at Severance Hall and elsewhere. Renowned artists were big lures, especially when they performed works that audiences adored. On November 15, 1958, the Cleveland audience found itself in an enviable pickle when two great sopranos appeared in the city. At Severance Hall with the Cleveland Orchestra and Szell, Elisabeth Schwarzkopf sang Mozart's concert aria, "Ch'io mi scordi di te," K. 505, and Strauss's *Four Last Songs*. At Music Hall, Maria Callas—who had been fired early that very week by the Metropolitan Opera's Rudolf Bing—gave a concert with a pickup orchestra of Cleveland musicians led by Nicola Rescigno. The situation prompted heated remarks from both Barksdale and G. Bernardi, manager of the Cleveland Opera Association, sponsor of the Callas concert. "We brought Schwarzkopf here twice before and took it on the chin, losing money on each concert," Bernardi told the *News*. "To have booked that woman the same night we are presenting Callas is thoughtless. They give us a lot of competition when they do a thing like that. I wouldn't do it for spite." Barksdale countered that the orchestra had announced Schwarzkopf's engagement the previous spring and Bernardi should have known about it. Meanwhile, the divas were a bit more civil. Schwarzkopf told the *News* she admired Callas and hoped to see her while they were in Cleveland. Callas became slightly tempestuous when asked by *The Plain Dealer* whether she considered herself a tempestuous person. "That's what they always ask!" she answered. "It is so boring!"

Orchestra trustees didn't have diva problems on their hands at this time; they were embroiled in a debate over securing Jack Benny, the beloved entertainer and sometime fiddler, to appear with the orchestra to raise money for the Pension Fund. "If Frank + Seelbach are opposed to engaging a comedian to help on Pension Fund I cannot but rejoice that our trustees have such a lively concern about the dignity of our organization and I am willing to let the matter rest right there," Szell informed Barksdale. "I myself am against Jack Benny. Danny Kaye seems to me a different proposition. Again, it's up to you. Of course, in any such concert, it would have to be Danny Kaye as sole conductor."

But the option of engaging Benny would prove too good an opportunity to pass up. The laconic comedian, whose main shtick revolved around his seemingly parsimonious personality, had raised a lot of money for other symphony orchestras. He played a Stradivarius violin passably well, and he was one of the funniest men on earth. Szell showed Benny nothing but respect when he arrived in November 1960 for the benefit, even joking around with the comedian for photographers. The concert turned out to be a gala event. Lane and Robert Shaw led the orchestra before Szell conducted Smetana's *Bartered Bride* overture and teamed with Benny for Sarasate's *Zigeunerweisen* and Saint-Saëns's Introduction and Rondo Capriccioso. "For the many Benny fans of three decades of entertainment it must have been something of a surprise to learn and hear that their man does have something of a violin soloist's technique," wrote Frank Hruby, the new music critic at the *Cleveland Press*, whose father and other relatives had played in the orchestra. "Sometimes, though, when the going got rough he would get help from the concertmaster or other violinists of the orchestra, after which the helper would be summarily 'fired.' Even the cymbal player was sent off for making too much noise for the sensitive soloist's nerves." The evening grossed $45,370, the largest amount yet raised at a single Cleveland Orchestra performance. Of that figure, $42,000 went to the pension fund.

A relationship with the entertainment industry had been contemplated even earlier. Late in 1958, John Cox, a member of the viola section, contacted Barksdale about the possibility of the Cleveland Orchestra serving as a recording orchestra for the motion-picture industry before and after the regular season. Cox had learned that Hollywood studios were eager to get rid of their staff orchestras (and thus avoid high union wages) by employing other ensembles on a per service basis, as was done in Europe. Szell gave the idea his blessing (though he wouldn't, of course, conduct these sessions, which would be held while he was vacationing and performing in Europe). "I probably do not need to point out the high international standing of The Cleveland Orchestra," Barksdale wrote to Charles S. Boren at the Association of Motion Picture Producers in Los Angeles. "Most of its members are in residence here the year round and would welcome the opportunity of earning additional income. During the past summer we completely renovated the interior of Severance Hall and have found it to be an ideal location for recording. Our Epic records which have been released since the first of January will testify to this." But there was to be no glamorous future in Hollywood for the orchestra. Boren wasn't interested.

❖   ❖   ❖

Szell may have been particularly eager to find extra work for his players because the added income might have eased the pressure they had begun to exert on their recalcitrant musicians' union. Contracts still were negotiated with virtually no input from players. The union discussed salaries and conditions with orchestra management, and the two parties came to terms. Musicians not in a position to negotiate individual contracts above union scale—almost everyone but principal players—had to accept what they were offered by Szell or Barksdale. Szell, ever the control freak, wouldn't stand for any decrease in his powers as musical director. Any move on the part of the players to improve job security (i.e. have a say in hiring and firing) would prompt him to threaten resignation or fret that labor matters could become messy. "As I have not heard from you about it, I fear that

Union negotiations have not yet started," Szell wrote to Barksdale from Vienna in late 1957. "This would conform to their customary delaying tactics of which I have warned you because they get us into a tough, unmaneuverable spot! Try to push them, PLEASE!"

The musicians, led by their most militant members, appealed to the orchestra's board to find enlightened ways to deal with labor issues. Their goal was to increase summer employment and, ideally, establish a 52-week season:

> It is our belief, having shown such confidence and progressiveness as it has shown in establishing the Pension Fund, higher wage scales and now the remodeling of Severance Hall, that now the Musical Arts Association would probably want to pioneer a new type of contract with the orchestra. Such action would focus the attention of the entire musical world on those men of the Musical Arts Association who are so forward looking as to be the first to revise their approach to the musician. That which is in view here is the old approach of seasonal pay which American educators have been glad to abandon and which fails to recognize the needs of the one so paid.

However rambunctious he may have believed the musicians were being, Szell still clearly basked in his accomplishments in Cleveland. He confirmed this once again in May 1958 by signing his sixth contract, covering the four seasons beginning with 1958–59. "I don't think I would accept a permanent conductorship anywhere else," Szell told a reporter. "Of course, in this profession, you cannot say anything is definitely permanent."

His annual salary in Cleveland certainly wasn't. It had risen from $40,000 per season starting in 1946 to $48,000 from 1949 to 1956 and $52,000 to 1958. In 1958, Szell's new contract provided $36,000 in annual base salary for four seasons and a Contingent Deferred Compensation Plan (essentially a pension fund) of $80,250, or a total of $188,250 for the period. By contrast, Barksdale signed a two-year contract in 1958 at $17,500 per season.

※   ※   ※

The orchestra's exhilarating liberation from acoustical dryness at Severance Hall in 1958 happened in time for a series of important performances and recording sessions. Szell showcased contemporary fare by leading the intermezzo from Barber's opera *Vanessa* (new early that year) and Copland's *Appalachian Spring* suite (not new, but at least recent). Pianist Guiomar Novaes had the honor of being the first soloist to play in the new shell, performing Chopin's Second Piano Concerto. "It's tremendous," she told the *Press*. "I wish we had one like it in Brazil." Dietrich Fischer-Dieskau, the celebrated German baritone who had been forced to cancel his Cleveland debut the previous season due to illness, finally made it in late October to perform an aria from Handel's *Berenice* and Mahler's *Songs of a Wayfarer*.

During the same period, Epic, buoyed by the orchestra's newfound prestige in Europe and Severance's enhanced acoustics, began recording Szell's cycle of the complete Schumann symphonies, starting with the First Symphony. Many listeners still consider these performances to be definitive, despite (or due to) Szell's occasional "orchestral retouches," as he called them, of Schumann's supposedly unwieldy instrumentation. Szell's first Cleveland recording of Dvořák's Symphony No. 8 followed soon after the Schumann.

Not all news was good in the fall of 1958. Little more than a week after Rodzinski's death on November 27, another devoted advocate for music in Cleveland was gone. On December 8, longtime orchestra trustee, former board president, and Szell ally Percy Brown was on his way to lunch at the Union Club when he collapsed at the corner of Euclid Avenue and East 12th Street, the victim of a heart attack at age 71. "I shall not even try to describe the crushing impact of the news of Percy's death," Szell wrote to Barksdale from Amsterdam. "Even if we knew that his health has not been the best lately, the message of the actual catastrophe was a tremendous blow." After much discussion with Helen Brown about the nature of a memorial concert for her husband, Szell settled on a program of works that he believed reflected his friend's dignity and spirit: Bach's Brandenburg Concerto No. 3, Mozart's Symphony No. 40, and Beethoven's "Pastoral" Symphony.

❀   ❀   ❀

Critics at home and on tour now consistently mentioned the Cleveland Orchestra in the same breath with only a few other international ensembles. For many observers, Cleveland had become synonymous with the best in the orchestral realm. Szell received due credit for the disciplined elegance and clarity he instilled in the ensemble, even as his sometimes propulsive, hard, and unyielding performances could leave listeners chilled. "Perhaps it is only in the imagination, but the orchestra seems to have assumed that brilliant edge it gets prior to its New York City performances," wrote the *Press*'s Hruby of a Beethoven-Berlioz-Walton program under Szell in January 1959. "And with it comes a certain tension which lends an intense, breathless quality to everything . . . it tends to overcharge a work such as the Beethoven Eighth Symphony. This tenseness could account for the surprising number of ragged attacks in the Beethoven. These had become almost non-existent in our orchestra in recent years."

Szell had other ways of filling an audience with anxiety. Perhaps the most stunning public example of the conductor's temper during his Cleveland years occurred on April 9, 1959, when he was scheduled to begin an all-Tchaikovsky program with the *Romeo and Juliet* fantasy-overture. The audience seemed unusually restless, and a great deal of coughing could be heard. A few bars into the Tchaikovsky, Szell decided it was time to put his foot down—and his baton as well. "I'll give you five minutes to clear your throats," he growled at the crowd, whereupon he stalked offstage. According to Elwell, Szell returned exactly five minutes later and gave another speech: "We are trying to do our best. Won't you try to do likewise and exercise a little self control and refrain from disturbing the performance?" What followed evidently was a perilous account of *Romeo and Juliet*. "The orchestra was driven unmercifully at speeds which would certainly be frowned upon by traffic officers, if not music critics," wrote Elwell. Szell defended his behavior after the concert. "This is the first time in my 13 years here that I've had to do this, but last night I had no choice," he said. "It was unbearable. I just couldn't go on. The audience was making more noise than the orchestra."

The noise continued the next day on the editorial page of the *Press*: "George Szell should understand that there are limits to rudeness on the part of anybody, no matter how gifted, or fortunately placed among men. His outburst at the audience last evening, in the precise manner that he did it, was inexcusable. He ought to have more compassion upon the people who sustain both himself and his orchestra in their enviable position in the world of music." Nevertheless, Klaus G. Roy recalled, "the audience, duly chastened, behaved itself for the rest of the season. Coughing resumed in the fall." (According to Roy, Sir Thomas Beecham once took much less time to put an end to audience distractions at Severance Hall: "Without losing a beat, he said, 'Shut up!' ")

Szell found himself on the defensive once again two weeks after the coughing incident when he was asked about the conservative programming he and his orchestra were taking to Carnegie Hall each year. "I think that New Yorkers are entitled to a high-level classical program once in a while," he told the Associated Press. "I bring New York what it doesn't get any more. I bring what it used to be able to count on, but can no more, from the conducting and the programs of Toscanini and Bruno Walter."

Just the previous month, ironically, Szell had discussed his Cleveland record of performing more modern music than most American orchestras.

"I think that that is part of an orchestra's job," he was quoted as saying in New York's *World-Telegram*. The truth of the matter was that Szell's tolerance for contemporary music was steadily waning. Even Stravinsky, the legendary 20th-century composer whose early masterpieces Szell revered (though he conducted few of them because he had trouble with changing meters), was no longer in the maestro's favor by 1959. "While in Zurich, I have secured the American first performance of the latest (quite possibly the last) work of Stravinsky," Szell informed Barksdale, referring to the Movements for Piano and Orchestra. "I saw already 2 of the movements. It is written in the post-Webernian small-fart-burp-belch-hiccup-technique with the fitting rhythmical quirks." Not surprisingly, Szell never conducted the score in Cleveland.

Decades later, Lane confirmed that his mentor began losing his appetite for "temporary music," as Szell called it, around 1960, though he continued to conduct select new and recent works during the following years. "One day in his office he was looking at a new score and finally he slammed it shut and handed it to me and said, 'I think I'm old enough to concentrate on the music I really like. Why don't you do this?' "

Artistic Morality

Week after week, George Szell and his musicians treated audiences to supercharged, illuminating performances. Seats for Thursday night Severance Hall concerts—opening night for each subscription program—were virtually impossible to obtain. Patrons began to cling to their tickets, keeping subscriptions in the family by handing them down in their wills.

For all his ability, Szell continued to draw mixed responses from critics, especially outside Cleveland. Some viewed him as a musical god, others as commanding but pedantic. No one disagreed about his impact on his ensemble, which now could do almost no wrong. "Good orchestras are common and great orchestras not unknown in Carnegie Hall," wrote Irving Kolodin in *Saturday Review* in 1962. "But Szell's is, currently, in a category of its own for the blazing enthusiasm these players bring to their thoroughly disciplined effort. They are good and they know they are good, but they are not so surfeited with it to lean back and relax. This is front-of-the-chair playing, a treat to hear."

As if they could ever lean back and relax. Szell drove his players to the brink. Behind the Cleveland discipline and pride lay perennial discontent. The musicians respected the conductor for his consummate musicianship and superior intellect, but they abhorred his caustic tongue and unsympathetic manner. "Szell is one of the world's great musicians and a cold, cold sonofabitch," remarked a young conductor who had been a disciple. More than a few psychiatrists in Cleveland were beneficiaries of the Szell era.

Among the musicians who experienced Szell's overbearing personality was Arnold Steinhardt, who won the 1958 Leventritt International Violin Competition—Szell was on the panel of judges—and came to Cleveland as assistant concertmaster a year later. He spent five seasons in awe and fear of Szell before deciding that the symphonic life wasn't for him. "For all its glorious sound, the orchestra was much like a feudal kingdom," Steinhardt later wrote. "Szell was the ruler of an empire composed of the nobility (the section heads), and vassals and serfs (section string players, second woodwind and brass players). At least, that is the way Szell seemed to view himself and the rest of us." Among the nobility was principal hornist Myron Bloom, who claimed Szell's dictatorial stance was largely a facade. "What was underneath was pure gold," Bloom said. "You never felt that Szell was commanding you to do what he wanted. He wanted to make music with you. He was helping you."

Yet Szell often played the role of autocrat to the hilt, prompting even members of the Berlin Philharmonic—an orchestra that shared international prominence with Cleveland and the Vienna Philharmonic—to remark on the tolerance level of Cleveland's musicians. "It's ironic," said a member of Szell's ensemble. "Over there, they have democracy. Here, we have the Third Reich."

Szell achieved such success in Cleveland partly because he was a unique musician and partly because he was allowed to reign supreme. He belonged to a waning generation of European conductors who grew up when authority—in some cases, tragically—wasn't questioned. Toscanini, Rodzinski, Reiner, Szell, and others were products of cultures that responded unswervingly to strong leaders. These conductors allowed no encroachment in matters affecting artistic policy. To say the least, they gazed contemptuously on those institutions known as musicians' unions.

Szell's players continued to clamor for treatment commensurate with their growing prestige. This made the conductor resentful and angry—even ready to literally walk out the door. In his later Cleveland years, he kept a signed resignation letter ready in case the musicians stepped beyond what he believed were reasonable bounds regarding job security.

The dictatorship that they found despicable was spelled out plainly in their contracts:

> Rights of Conductor: The Conductor shall have full power to control all performances and rehearsals including the power to regulate the pitch of the Orchestra, to determine the seating of Musicians, to establish reasonable rules as to conduct and performance, and to regulate all phases of the musical effort, as well as deportment and order.
>
> The Musician will comply to the best of his ability with all such requirements and instructions.

Ruler, vassals, and serfs.

✲ ✲ ✲

In the late 1950s, two longtime principal players decided to seek other (possibly more lucrative or less draining) employment. The first was Marc Lifschey, the eloquent and increasingly temperamental principal oboist—and a Szell favorite since his arrival in 1950. Lifschey won the principal spot in the Metropolitan Opera Orchestra in early 1959, to begin the following fall. He was also heading back to New York to care for his ailing father. He wasn't leaving Cleveland without regret. "Mr. Szell's inspired leadership and vast knowledge have contributed so very much to my growth as a musician, and I will always treasure the many wonderful friendships I've formed with members of the orchestra," Lifschey wrote in his resignation letter. "In my relationship with the management I have only experienced courtesy, understanding and helpfulness. All of these things have indeed made my stay here memorable."

To succeed Lifschey, Szell hired Alfred Genovese, principal oboe of the St. Louis Symphony, who appeared to be an excellent addition. He can be heard on all of the Szell-Cleveland recordings from the 1959–60 season, which reveal a highly lyrical player, especially in the fifth symphonies of Tchaikovsky and Prokofiev, Schubert's "Unfinished" Symphony, Dvořák's Seventh Symphony, and Schumann's Fourth Symphony. The public, understandably, would become confused by Szell's subsequent decision to get rid of Genovese by the end of the season. "He has a beautiful tone, and in many minds, including my own, he is the best first oboe the orchestra has had," wrote Herbert Elwell in *The Plain Dealer* upon hearing the news. "For no visibly good reason Genovese suddenly has been fired. Conductor Szell owes Clevelanders an explanation for this action." The explanation wasn't exactly forthcoming. Answering a castigating letter to the editor in *The Plain Dealer* from Frieda Schumacher, a beloved Cleveland piano teacher and harpsichordist, Szell said that he had made arrangements for Lifschey and Genovese to switch places—Lifschey back to Cleveland, Genovese to the Met. "This exchange was arranged in the best interest of all individuals and organizations concerned," he wrote.

Szell had given Genovese no warning that he might be sacked. Peg Glove, the conductor's secretary, handed the oboist a message informing him of the change. "I had no desire to leave Cleveland and, until that time, no plans to do so," Genovese wrote in a letter to the editor in the *Press*. "I had established my family in Cleveland in what I considered a permanent residence and bought furniture for it. In fact, the Cleveland Orchestra had a two-year option on my services in addition to my one-year contract. Even if I had wanted to take a better job elsewhere, I would not have been free for three years." For Genovese, Cleveland was to be a brief detour on a distinguished career. After playing for many years at the Met, he served as longtime principal oboe of the Boston Symphony.

The other musician Szell was losing was Josef Gingold, a 13-year veteran as concertmaster. During the crucial years when the orchestra first achieved global acclaim, Gingold had helped Szell to mold the ensemble's distinctive personality. Gingold regarded Szell as a genius, and Szell held Gingold in the highest regard. But the conductor would still browbeat his sweet-tempered concertmaster. Now, Gingold was prepared to forgo the excitement of orchestral performance—and the mistreatment from the podium—for the more peaceful satisfactions of academia. He accepted an invitation to join the faculty at Indiana University's School of Music in Bloomington. Upon arriving there in the fall of 1960, his relief was clear. "For the first time in fourteen years, I sleep well every night," he told a colleague.

Sweet dreams most likely were only sporadic for Beverly Barksdale as he continued to keep the orchestra's complex daily affairs in order. Upon the announcement of Gingold's departure, Szell charged Barksdale with the delicate mission of finding candidates for the concertmaster post. Among the names Szell and Gingold suggested were Broadus Earle, Zvi Zeitlin, Robert Gerle, Jacob Krachmalnick, Oscar Shumsky, Michael Tree, Daniel Gilet, and Norman Carol. Tree, later violist of the Guarneri String Quartet, and Carol, who would become concertmaster of the Philadelphia Orchestra, came to Severance Hall to audition for Szell. In the end, he settled on Rafael Druian, the Russian-born, Cuban-bred concertmaster of the Minneapolis Symphony.

Gingold, generous as always, provided his successor with sage advice on tuning the orchestra during rehearsals, performances, and recording sessions. He suggested that Druian follow Szell's bowings, which "are positively ingenious," and readily seek the conductor's counsel. About his colleagues, Gingold had nothing but praise:

> You will find that the musicians in the Orchestra are not only superb instrumentalists but are the finest gentlemen that one could hope to meet anywhere. For the past thirteen years I can truthfully say that I have never known a group of human beings whose enthusiasm and traits of character have been so fine. You will also find them most cooperative in any musical matters that you should wish to carry through.

Szell's severe character and Utopian standards, and the orchestra's unsettled labor situation, led to further significant reshaping of the ensemble.

From 1959 through 1962, the orchestra underwent 31 personnel changes, almost a third of the membership. The new players during these seasons included many who would stay for the rest of their careers—thanks to the eventual achievement of a 52-week season and contracts on a par with the nation's other top ensembles.

❧   ❧   ❧

For an orchestra that was reaching such artistic heights on a regular basis, Cleveland had problems that wouldn't go away. One of the most vexing was its recording situation. Columbia Records had remained steadfast in promoting Bernstein's New York Philharmonic and Ormandy's Philadelphia Orchestra ahead of its Ohio clients. Szell and Barksdale continued to look quietly for another recording company in case Columbia showed an inclination to dump Cleveland. The most promising prospect was RCA, which was facing the end of Fritz Reiner's tenure at the helm of the Chicago Symphony in 1962.

Szell had been approached by Eric Oldberg, president of the Chicago Symphony board, about the possibility of succeeding Reiner. Szell thought seriously about the invitation but decided instead to use it in negotiations with RCA and Columbia. He didn't want Barksdale to be the negotiator in this instance. Szell suggested that Edgar Vincent, the Cleveland Orchestra's New York press representative, discuss the matter with RCA's Alan Kayes. "He should intimate to Kayes that he has an idea that Chicago has been offered me but that he also seems to sense that I am rather unlikely to make the change after having brought Cleveland to where it stands now," Szell wrote to Barksdale. "He then should continue to say that he has an idea that if RCA would like to switch its Chicago contract on to Cleveland they would find us very receptive and prepared to make every effort to get out of our present contract."

As Szell and Barksdale groused endlessly to Columbia, the company began giving a few inches. Columbia's Jane Friedmann was delighted when Szell agreed to serve as pianist in recordings of the Mozart and Beethoven piano-wind quintets with Cleveland principal players—though the project never happened. Another unrealized ambition was Friedmann's suggestion that orchestra principals record trumpet, oboe, and violin concertos by Haydn, Handel, and Mozart under Szell. Barksdale did prove his mettle as a negotiator, however, achieving improvements in the orchestra's Columbia contract in terms of royalty rate, publicity, promotion, and sales.

One work Columbia hoped Szell would record was Richard Strauss's giddy *Burleske* with André Previn—best known as a film composer, conductor, and jazz pianist—as piano soloist. Szell had never met Previn, so Columbia set up a meeting when Szell was in Los Angeles for concerts with the Philharmonic. Previn arrived at Szell's room at the Beverly Wilshire Hotel and engaged in small talk. Then Szell said, "Well, let's go through the piece." One problem: the room had no piano. Szell proceeded to tell Previn to play the piece on a table. "Well, I was still young and inexperienced, I suppose, and in awe of the great conductor, so I didn't walk out," recalled Previn. "I sat down and started whacking away at this table." Soon Szell stopped him: "No, no, no. It needs to be faster." He wasn't kidding. Nor, perhaps, was Previn: "Well, maestro, the reason it sounds so slow is that I'm simply not used to this table. My dining room table at home has much better action." With that, Szell dismissed him—"I don't consider that funny, young man. You may go"—and the recording was off.

Cleveland's relationship with Columbia, while productive, would always be fraught with tension. Szell had often fought with producer Howard Scott, whom he blamed for ruining the sound on the orchestra's Columbia recordings, but who at least had a fine musical background. When Scott retired in 1961, after a decade of working with Szell, the conductor became upset that Schuyler Chapin, a Columbia producer who was not a trained musician, might be his successor. Columbia instead assigned Thomas Frost and then Paul Myers to produce Cleveland's recordings for the rest of the 1960s, a period of remarkable activity before the microphones for Szell and his orchestra.

❊   ❊   ❊

It was a remarkable period outside the recording studio as well. In the spring of 1960, Szell took the orchestra on a monthlong U.S. tour comprising 29 concerts in 25 cities, including their first journey together to the West Coast. The critical response went beyond anything their press office could have concocted. *San Diego Union* music critic Alan M. Kriegsman, later winner of a Pulitzer Prize for dance criticism at the *Washington Post*, opened his review of a program of works by Berlioz, Smetana, Strauss, and Brahms with a paragraph of hyperbole. "I have never had any special yearning for an early death, but after the Cleveland Orchestra concert Sunday night at the Russ, I was overcome by an irresistible urge to end it all then and there, that I might shuffle off this mortal coil with these sounds as my valedictory," he wrote. "Only one thing stayed the stiletto—the thought that someday the orchestra might come back."

While in San Francisco, Szell enumerated for an interviewer the three things required to maintain a first-rate symphony orchestra. "You need money, because orchestras always cost money," he told the *San Francisco Examiner*. "You need a conductor at the helm who knows his business. And you need a board of directors who won't interfere with the conductor, but who will go out and raise money. It's the God-given function of symphony committees to do just that—raise money for music."

And the Cleveland Orchestra needed money in 1960. The Musical Arts Association was projecting deficits of nearly $900,000 over the next three years, prompting officials to announce the first major fund-raising campaign in decades. Cleveland no longer claimed the prominent families that could retire orchestra deficits by signing a check, so the orchestra had to appeal to other sources of support. The board found that corporations in Cleveland were donating 21 percent of the total contributions received by the orchestra, while business communities in other American cities were far more generous. In Detroit, corporations were providing a whopping 72 percent of the orchestra's total budget, and the numbers were also higher in Minneapolis (65 percent), Houston (60 percent), and Pittsburgh (35 percent). Frank E. Joseph, Cleveland's board president, believed his city could do better to support its triumphant ensemble. "When our major athletic teams win a championship it is good for Cleveland. The orchestra is a never-failing champion year in and year out. Certainly the corporations have a stake in it."

New help came from the orchestra's Women's Committee, which had spent most of its 40-year life nurturing educational concerts. The need to raise money galvanized these volunteers. They were led by a determined and tireless president, Dorothy Humel, a concert pianist who had appeared as soloist with the orchestra in six Twilight and summer pops concerts. Humel was a prime force in increasing Women's Committee membership from 960 to 1,512 over two years. A student of Jose Iturbi, Arthur Loesser, and Charles Rychlik, and treasurer of her family's business, Humel Construction, she brought the orchestra to the attention of the community through successful telethon campaigns to sell subscriptions, preconcert talks by program annotator Klaus G. Roy, and the committee's first major fund-raiser, a fashion show on March 1, 1960, that added almost $12,000 to the orchestra's coffers.

✻   ✻   ✻

The orchestra needed to appeal to the public for money because the musicians' salaries were starting to rise. They weren't ascending nearly as quickly as the players would have liked, however, and their union wasn't much help.

As in the past, officials of Cleveland's Local 4 wanted to control every aspect of negotiations, allowing the musicians little say. Musicians couldn't vote on contracts. They couldn't even convince the union to let their appointed lawyer participate in negotiating sessions. In April 1961, a federal judge dismissed a suit that orchestra players had filed to obtain the right to vote on contracts. The judge had agreed with Local 4 that the Landrum-Griffin Act precluded union members from such a vote. The result was a new three-year contract ratified by the union and the Musical Arts Association, despite an 85 to 10 vote by the orchestra against the contract. The agreement provided a weekly raise of $5, to a minimum of $155 for the first year, with annual raises of $10 each for the remaining two years. "None of the major objectives of the orchestra members have been achieved," said an orchestra member. "Rather than a three-year contract we want $175 minimums for the first year, job security, traveling condition improvements and equal pay for overtime and extra services."

They wouldn't get them, though they would try. The musicians once again filed a suit against the union, stating that the contract had been signed contrary to the wishes of the majority. When the union tried to take orchestra members to court for "promoting disunity," 16 players filed yet another suit to prevent a trial and to obtain $320,000 in damages from union officers and executive board members. The trial never happened, and the contract eventually was upheld.

But Szell continued to get the willies when labor issues became prickly. The resulting ranting was directed at Barksdale. In December 1960, the conductor sent his manager a heated letter on the subject:

> I fear that you may lend an all-too-willing ear to certain wishes. You will have to realize that the present negotiations require more cold-blooded toughness than previous ones and you may have to condition yourself to an attitude not quite natural for your make-up. I stick to what I have already said: The Orchestra is welcome to all the money the Association can give them without wrecking our organization but regarding working conditions and 'Job Security' guarantees we have reached the limit. I am firmly determined not to sign a new contract if we cannot get a workable long term Union Contract and I may be compelled to ask the Trustees to release me from my present one, effective the close of the present season, if the Union presses demands that are unworkable or detrimental to the artistic standards.

As always, Szell was uncompromising, but not totally without justification, in light of the results he and his orchestra were achieving.

At least Barksdale often was sympathetic to the musicians' plight. He told Szell he agreed with the orchestra's lawyer that the players should have a hand in ratifying their own contract, as well as representation at the bargaining table. Still, Barksdale knew he was treading on dangerous ground. "I hope and pray that no word of all this may leak to the newspapers because it could have a very disastrous effect on our Fund Campaign, which is just now going into high gear," he wrote to Szell. "We have a great deal more money from many fewer contributors than we have ever had at this point in the year." The musicians welcomed Barksdale's support even as they remained confused. "We can not understand why our own union officials, if they bargain in good faith, should have any objection to our presence as observers," violinist Gino Raffaelli wrote to Barksdale. "We fail to understand why they wish to conceal their efforts from us as they bargain in our behalf."

A central bone of contention continued to be salary, which even the American Federation of Musicians found was far below what was deemed acceptable in other fields. An AFM study of annual wages in 1960 showed that the average weekly salary in the orchestras of Boston, Chicago, Cleveland, New York, and Philadelphia—the so-called "Big Five"—was $167. The figure would have been impressive if the musicians had been employed 52 weeks, but most orchestra seasons ran only 30 weeks. Nationwide the scenario was much worse. "In fact, the average annual wage for the 2,500 or so full time symphony players in the United States was $75 a week!!" noted the *Daily Sentinal Tribune* in Bowling Green. "So it is small wonder that even the greatest orchestras have trouble filling and maintaining positions." Cleveland's labor troubles were similar to those found at the other big orchestras, though its salaries remained below those of the major ensembles on the East Coast.

The issue of job security kept Szell on the offensive and Barksdale on the defensive. "Yesterday I had my first session with the Union and was presented the enclosed demands. I am sure that some of these will make you angry, but remember that no food is eaten as hot as it is cooked," Barksdale wrote to Szell. "As nearly as I can determine from the few people who will talk to me about this, the demands for job security grow out of fear of what will happen when Szell is no longer here. [Fritz] Reiner's wholesale changes in Chicago a few years ago and the more recent ones in St. Louis, seemed to have had a profound effect on the thinking of orchestras elsewhere. Rafael [Druian] says this is true in Minneapolis and understands that it is so in Detroit and Pittsburgh." Szell would have none of such talk, or of his manager's continuing inability to act decisively. "If you work to drive me out of Cleveland through these relapses into lethargy and inefficiency, you could not have chosen a more propitious moment. Make up your mind!" he ordered.

Five months later, in May 1961, Szell was in a better mood. He wrote to his manager offering thanks "for a fine and difficult season" and congratulating him for "unruffleability, which, with many other distinguished qualities, stood you in such good stead during this season of Union negotiations of uncommon thorniness."

The answers to the orchestra's problems were becoming clearer to Cleveland's trustees: the players needed higher salaries and longer seasons. And publicity about squabbles between the musicians and their union wasn't helping the orchestra's fund-raising efforts. "Many of our supporters view the thing, to put it mildly, with distaste," Barksdale said. "But George Szell, musical director and conductor, has kept the men together as a smoothly functioning team. So far, their differences have not affected the quality of the music—because the orchestra this year is playing better than ever."

It was playing better amid annual budgets that were riding a seesaw— normal procedure for an American orchestra at the time. Cleveland was facing a $220,000 deficit for the 1962–63 season. A season earlier, the bottom line had listed a $7,000 surplus, the first year in the black since 1955–56.

❊   ❊   ❊

Barksdale's comment about the quality of the music-making in Cleveland reflected the zeal and commitment with which Szell and his players went about their work. Escalating budgets, onerous deficits, union arrogance, and unsatisfactory contracts—none of these elements seemed to have an effect when a rehearsal was in session or a performance began at Severance Hall.

By the early 1960s, the orchestra was functioning like a supremely refined chamber ensemble in which every player knew his or her place in the musical scheme. The famous statement Szell made about his orchestra—"We start rehearsing where the vast majority of orchestras finish performing"— may have offended other worthy ensembles and conductors. But program annotator Klaus G. Roy often witnessed the truth of Szell's comment:

> I recall very clearly sometimes coming in on a Monday morning, going up in the balcony and hearing the first rehearsal of the week and being absolutely overwhelmed by a Brahms 1st, for example, that [Szell] would play through without stopping. I would say, 'My gosh, this is ready for a

34. Members of the Cleveland Orchestra, shown with a train conductor, on tour in September 1941: violinist Felix Eyle, left, concertmaster Josef Fuchs, principal oboist Philip Kirchner, violinist David Klinger, and manager Carl Vosburgh.

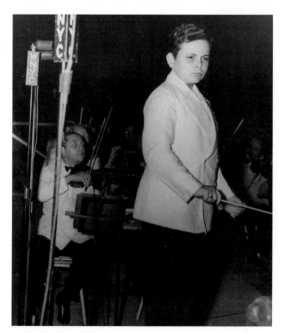

35. Stern young maestro: Lorin Maazel conducts an orchestra in New York City circa 1943.

36. Erich Leinsdorf in concert with the orchestra at Severance Hall during his brief tenure as conductor (1943–1946).

37. Leinsdorf meets with soprano Dorothy Maynor before her Severance Hall debut in December 1943.

38. A publicity still of Georg Szell during his period on the conducting staff at the Berlin State Opera in the 1920s.

39. Szell urges his orchestra to play more softly during a rehearsal in the late 1940s.

40. Szell and Thomas L. Sidlo, the orchestra's board president from 1939 to 1953, greet one another toward the end of the conductor's first season in the spring of 1947.

41. The horn section of the Cleveland Orchestra in the late 1940s (left to right): Charles Blabolil, Erwin Miersch, Ernani Angelucci, Martin Morris, Frank Brouk, and Roy Waas.

42. Josef Gingold, the orchestra's concert-master from 1947 to 1960, was adored for his expressive artistry and sweet temperament.

43. Leonard Rose served as principal cellist from 1939 to 1943, when Rodzinski took him to the New York Philharmonic. Rose later had a distinguished career as soloist and chamber musician.

44. Principal harpist Alice Chalifoux uses her harp case as a dressing room.

45. Myron Bloom served as the orchestra's principal horn from 1955 to 1977.

46. Louis Lane and the orchestra perform an "Indipops" concert at Cleveland Municipal Stadium before a Cleveland Indians game in 1953.

47. Rudolph Ringwall and Lillian Baldwin meet with students after an educational concert at Severance Hall in the 1950s.

48. Cleveland Mayor Anthony J. Celebrezze and his wife enter a Severance Hall box with Percy and Helen Brown (who were instrumental in bringing Szell to Cleveland) in the mid-1950s.

49. Three Cleveland musicians who were associated with the orchestra for many decades: pianist Beryl Rubinstein, left, composer-conductor Arthur Shepherd, and composer-critic Herbert Elwell in the 1950s.

50. Frank E. Taplin, Jr., served as president of the Musical Arts Association from 1955 to 1957, when he helped plan the orchestra's first European tour. He is shown at the Metropolitan Opera House at Lincoln Center, where he later served on the board.

51. Marc Lifschey's tenure as principal oboe from 1950 to 1965, with one year off to play in the Metropolitan Opera Orchestra, was marked by sublime artistry and tussles with Szell.

52. Robert Shaw leads an orchestra rehearsal at Severance Hall in the early 1960s.

53. Cleveland Orchestra players take a break in Warsaw during the orchestra's first European tour in 1957.

54. The Collinwood High School Band welcomes the Cleveland Orchestra home after its triumphant 1957 European tour.

55. Workers erect the modernistic "Szell shell" at Severance Hall during the summer of 1958.

56. Program annotator Klaus George Roy and acoustical consultant Heinrich Keilholz test out the sound in the new shell at Severance Hall in 1958.

57. Cleveland youngsters sit in boxes at Severance Hall during a children's concert, circa 1960.

58. General manager A. Beverly Barksdale preparing to narrate *The Nutcracker* in December 1958.

59. French cellist Pierre Fournier rehearses with Szell and the orchestra in 1963.

60. Szell in conversation with principal bassoonist George Goslee in the mid-1960s.

61. Szell coaches James Levine during a rehearsal at Severance Hall in the mid-1960s. Levine would go on to become artistic director of the Metropolitan Opera.

62. Szell in concert at Severance Hall. Also shown are violists Edward Ormond, left, and Abraham Skernick.

63. Szell and Pierre Boulez outside Severance Hall in the late 1960s.

64. Two prominent Cleveland lawyers who served as presidents and chairmen of the Cleveland Orchestra: Alfred M. Rankin and Frank E. Joseph.

65. Members of the orchestra's wind, brass, and percussion sections during a Severance Hall rehearsal in the mid-1960s.

66. Rafael Druian, shown gazing at a drawing of Szell, was concertmaster from 1960 to 1969, when he resigned suddenly over a rehearsal mixup.

67. Christopher Jaffe, Louis Lane, Szell, and Peter van Dijk look over a model for Blossom Music Center.

68. Szell rehearses the orchestra at Carnegie Hall circa 1966.

69. Szell conducts the Cleveland Orchestra and the audience in the national anthem on opening night of Blossom Music Center (July 19, 1968). Emily Blossom and Frank E. Joseph join in at right.

70. Szell poses in front of a similar portrait of Igor Stravinsky at the Academy of Music in Philadelphia in 1956.

recording!' I was just overwhelmed. Mr. Szell said, 'Now we start to work.' I knew what he was doing, but it was amazing how the orchestra would be further along than you can possibly imagine in the first run-through. And for sheer emotional impact these first rehearsals were sometimes the most fantastic.

Guest conductors reacted in similarly emotional fashion to the phenomenon. In December 1960, Romanian conductor Georges Georgescu, who had studied in Berlin with Arthur Nikisch and assisted Richard Strauss at the same time as Szell, came to Severance Hall to make his Cleveland debut. He opened his first rehearsal with Strauss's *Ein Heldenleben*, playing it through without stopping. "And at the end he started to cry," recalled Louis Lane. As Georgescu told the orchestra, "This is the most beautiful performance I have ever heard. Why do we rehearse?"

More than a few conductors over the years would be stumped, or undone, by the orchestra's ability to approach technical perfection so quickly. One guest called standing before the orchestra "a frightening experience—you feel that you're facing a hundred little Szells." Conductors who couldn't surmount the fear found themselves unable to get results. The orchestra could lead some maestros to believe that they were better than they actually were. "Sometimes, but rarely, a Friday morning guest conductor, in rehearsal, was not quite up to the task," recalled Roy. "Yet the performance itself would be fabulous. 'He wasn't half bad!' I said to Danny Majeske. The cool reply: 'We are the Cleveland Orchestra.' "

The orchestra learned from a master intimidator. In spite of Szell's encyclopedic knowledge of music (and many other subjects) and lofty abilities as conductor and pianist, his attitude often rubbed colleagues the wrong way, even if he was undeniably right. Two great violinists in particular had difficulty coping with the Szell hauteur—Henryk Szeryng and Nathan Milstein. When Szeryng came to Severance Hall in February 1961 to play Prokofiev's Violin Concerto No. 1, Szell stormed offstage during a rehearsal following a dispute with the soloist. As Szell told a reporter, "It was useless to rehearse again. We had rehearsed yesterday and there was no improvement of understanding." The artistic outcome of the rift was noted by Elwell in his *Plain Dealer* review: "It was an extremely brilliant and at the same time a curious performance, reminding one in some ways of a tennis match. Szell set tempos, some of them at terrific speed, and allowing the soloist not the slightest margin for any expressive liberties." According to Lane, Szeryng was the main cause of the deep freeze: "Charming man in his own way as he was, [he] had an ego which was impenetrable! It was colossal. I would call it intergalactic in scope. He was impervious to suggestions. Impervious! It was always a very uneasy event." When Milstein and Szell disagreed, they fought it out on a more visceral basis: they screamed at each other in German.

Even with its contentious leader, the orchestra could demonstrate solidarity on moral issues. In March 1961, the musicians raised their collective voice in support of cellist Donald White. During a tour through southeastern states with Szell, the orchestra was scheduled to give a Sunday matinee concert in Birmingham, Alabama. "At the time of this tour, it was widely known that The Cleveland Orchestra had a Negro cellist," Barksdale later wrote to Szell. White at first was refused entry to the concert hall by a guard, who relented only after orchestra members intervened and identified him as a colleague. Informed of the incident, the hall manager told Barksdale that a city ordinance forbade blacks and whites from appearing onstage together. Whereupon Barksdale told the manager that the entire Cleveland Orchestra would play or no Cleveland Orchestra would play, a stand supported by Szell. After Barksdale spoke to the mayor of Birmingham by phone, the concert was allowed to proceed without further ado. "At the end of the concert, several people came backstage to thank us for taking this courageous stand," recalled Barksdale.

Not surprisingly, Szell wasn't afraid to make his views known even when it meant taking on an entire orchestra and its conductor. After guest conducting the San Francisco Symphony for one week in March 1962, he abruptly skipped town, leaving his second scheduled week to the ensemble's music director, Enrique Jorda. Szell initially let the orchestra's management announce that he was "tired and was forced to withdraw." The suspected reason that Szell had fled—because he believed the San Francisco orchestra to be in terrible shape—caused a furor. Alfred V. Frankenstein, music critic of the *San Francisco Chronicle* and program annotator of the San Francisco Symphony, wrote to Szell complaining that rumors circulating around the country about his cancellation were hurting the orchestra and Jorda: "It would therefore be a just, proper, and pleasant gesture if Mr. Jorda could be invited to serve as guest conductor in Clevel. next season. I hastily add that I propose this entirely on my own, and that Jorda would be furious at me if he knew I was doing it."

Writing back in elegant, scathing prose that was quickly reprinted in many American newspapers, Szell denounced the conflict of interest inherent in Frankenstein's dual jobs and then went to the heart of the matter: "It is entirely out of order for you to suggest my taking a step designed to be interpreted as implicit approval of what I found to be the saddest state of musical affairs I have encountered in any American or European city during

the almost fifty years of my active conducting career." Jorda couldn't survive
the bald attack on his ability, or evade the reality that he wasn't up to the job.
Two months later, he announced his resignation as San Francisco's music director. The fracas brought an editorial condemnation of Szell from
Frankenstein's *Chronicle*—"the airy vagueness of this incredible indict-
ment, plus Szell's refusal to specify and enlarge, seriously diminishes its va-
lidity"—and articles throughout the country discussing the conductor's displeasure with orchestral standards in San Francisco.

Szell could blow off the controversy easily. His own orchestra was riding
a wave of acclaim virtually unequalled in the United States. "The secret of
this phenomenal symphonic development in the Mid-West is George Szell
himself, a singular breed of aristocratic and not infrequently autocratic musical genius that is completely uncompromising where musical values are
concerned," wrote Ronald Eyer in the *New York Herald Tribune* preceding
the orchestra's annual Carnegie Hall concerts in February 1962. Szell told
Eyer that accomplishing greatness meant loving music more than oneself:

> It is a matter of artistic morality. It is necessary to find and bring in play-
> ers who have artistic morality and, of course, have the funds to afford them.
> It is necessary to keep the musicians interested in the music for its own
> sake, and it is my job to inspire them every day at the rehearsal period from
> 10 to 12:30 with a sense of selfless devotion to the musical purpose.

A great orchestra must have star quality "without star mentality," Szell said.

By now, there were few concerns about a shortage of excellence. "Mr.
Szell has lifted the Cleveland Orchestra almost overnight," wrote a somewhat slow-on-the-draw critic after the 1962 Carnegie Hall concerts, "into a
position where it rivals the world's finest symphonic organizations." One of
those rivals had recently visited Cleveland for its Severance Hall debut as a
benefit for the Cleveland Orchestra Maintenance Fund. The Berlin
Philharmonic and its imposing conductor, Herbert von Karajan, performed
Bach's Suite No. 2, Stravinsky's Symphony in C, and Strauss's *Also sprach
Zarathustra* on November 1, 1961. "In contrast to the crystalline clarity of
our Cleveland Orchestra," wrote Frank Hruby in the *Press*, "the Berlin
Philharmonic concentrates on a rich, rounded sound." And at a much higher
pitch, as Karajan and others quickly discovered. When Berlin's keyboardist
fell ill before the Cleveland concert, Szell volunteered Lane to play the
organ part in Strauss's sonic blockbuster. The Berlin orchestra tuned to
A=446, while the Severance organ was pitched at the lower 440, where the
Cleveland ensemble had played for decades (and still does today).

Zarathustra must have had a startling start. "It was fine except that where the big C major chord cuts off, it sounded like I was playing B major," recalled Lane. "It was such a shocking difference between their pitch standard and the organ that Karajan looked over . . . and then of course he realized what had happened and grinned."

Karajan was one of two legendary conductors who stood on the Severance stage that season. The other was Leopold Stokowski, Cleveland's only regular-season guest conductor in 1961–62. For his concerts on March 8 and 10, 1962, the maestro with the stormy white hair and batonless technique devised a typically inventive program—works by Gabrieli, Bach, Shostakovich, and Beethoven. He arranged the orchestra according to his unusual seating plan—all strings to his left, with cellos and basses on platforms, and all winds to his right ("Topsy-turvy," as Szell once described it). Stokowski couldn't be bothered with criticism of this arrangement. "I have asked the intellectuals what is so good about the traditional seating," he told the *Press*. "They have given me no good answers."

An even more legendary musical figure stood before Cleveland musicians this season, but not in front of the orchestra and not at Severance Hall. In June 1962, at the invitation of revered cellist Pablo Casals, Robert Shaw took 120 members of the Cleveland Orchestra Chorus to the Casals Festival in San Juan, Puerto Rico, for the first of three annual visits. Shaw conducted four chorales from Bach's *St. John Passion* and Schubert's "Ständchen" and Mass in G major, while the 85-year-old Casals led Beethoven's Ninth Symphony and his own oratorio, *El pessebre*. The chorus repeated the Schubert mass (under Shaw) and Casals's oratorio (under the composer) at Carnegie Hall the following week.

The relationship between Casals and the Cleveland Orchestra Chorus didn't begin well. At the first rehearsal in San Juan, Casals could not make himself clear to the singers and became increasingly frustrated. According to Kathleen Shamp, a chorus member at the time, Shaw finally took his ensemble aside. "It isn't everyone who has the chance to pick up the pieces for the really great ones," he said. "You have that opportunity. You *know* what he wants—don't give him what he's conducting, give him what he *wants*." The chorus was told to watch the orchestra's concertmaster, Alexander "Sascha" Schneider, during the performance. "It was truly heavenly," recalled Shamp, "and then the little maestro beamed at us with tears streaming from his eyes, and clasping his breast in joy—and Shaw stood at the back of the auditorium beaming like a [Cheshire] cat."

❧   ❧   ❧

In September 1962, Szell and his musicians joined a distinguished roster of conductors and orchestras that had been invited to appear during the inaugural performances at New York's Philharmonic Hall, the first venue to open at Lincoln Center, the performing arts complex in midtown Manhattan. In addition to Szell and Cleveland, Lincoln Center had lined up Leonard Bernstein and the New York Philharmonic, Erich Leinsdorf and the Boston Symphony, Eugene Ormandy and the Philadelphia Orchestra, and Ernest Ansermet and the Metropolitan Opera.

Months in advance, Szell was skeptical that acoustician Leo Beranek could succeed at Lincoln Center. "Trust Beranek, something will be botched at Philharmonic Hall," he wrote to Barksdale. The impending disaster predicted by Szell—partly the result of numerous architectural changes made during the design phase—was confirmed in a letter from Barksdale weeks before the opening. "Stokowski was invited to attend one of the acoustical rehearsals of the Philharmonic in Lincoln Center in late May," the manager wrote. "He made a grand entrance onto the stage and paused dramatically at the edge. He clapped his hands, waited a minute, and said very slowly, 'Gentlemen, you have called me too late.'"

Whatever the prognostications, Szell and his orchestra made such a big impression in New York on September 27 that some observers hardly noticed the acoustics. "In the Lincoln Center parade of orchestras through Philharmonic Hall this week, the Cleveland Orchestra fared best," wrote Miles Kastendieck in the *New York Journal-American*. "That Mr. Szell towered over the other conductors of the week helps explain why the concert was so satisfying. He helped clarify how fine the new hall really is." The concert's soloist was Isaac Stern (in the Brahms Violin Concerto).

Stern had headed the 1960 campaign to save Carnegie Hall from the wrecker's ball, a demise that could have sent every visiting American and foreign orchestra to Philharmonic Hall. By 1960, Szell and Cleveland were fixtures at Carnegie, and the conductor intended to take a wait-and-hear attitude on the new hall. "I agree a hundred percent with you that we should stick to Carnegie as long as we don't know how good Lincoln Center is acoustically, but would it not be wise to be governed by what Boston and Philadelphia are going to do?" he wrote to Barksdale. "If ALL Orchestras should move to the new Hall, wouldn't we alone . . . playing at Carnegie,— when audiences have been conditioned to the new neighborhood and premises,—make a rather provincial off-brand impression? Could you possibly get holds at Carnegie with escape clauses? If they refuse this, then by all means let's stick to Carnegie." Cleveland would do so for at least the next four decades.

On the subject of Philharmonic Hall, Szell was typically forthright. It is "an acoustic failure. But it is not beyond repair if proper recommendations are followed." Even when the hall was remodeled in 1963, Szell wasn't convinced that the right solutions had been found: "Let me give you a little simile. Imagine a woman, lame, a hunchback, cross-eyed and with two warts. They've removed the warts." A year later, his patience was gone: "Tear the place down and start over again; the hall is an insult to music." After the opening week, Szell never again led the Cleveland Orchestra at Lincoln Center, though he would continue to be a frequent guest there with the New York Philharmonic.

✻   ✻   ✻

As Szell and his orchestra were making the most of the present, the 1962–63 season offered opportunities to embrace the future and commemorate the past. In December 1962, Szell had dinner in Baden-Baden, Germany, with Pierre Boulez, the radical and brilliant French composer-conductor whom Cleveland's musical director had invited to be a guest at Severance Hall. At this point, Szell didn't see Boulez in any official conducting role with his orchestra. But he knew Boulez could provide the perfect Gallic and contemporary balance to his own repertoire, which was increasingly focused on mainstream Austro-Germanic masterpieces from the 18th and 19th centuries. Boulez was in such demand as a conductor that his Cleveland debut had to be put off until March 1965. "The program is already fixed and including a new piece he is just writing," Szell wrote to Barksdale. The new piece was to be *Figures, Doubles, Prisms*.

The "cold squire of Severance"—as Milton Widder had dubbed Szell in the *Press*—was about to celebrate what was believed to be his 50th anniversary as a conductor. He agreed to cooperate in anniversary events, "particularly those of which the C.O. can benefit—if I am spared functions of the Lion—Elk—Kiwanis—etc. type." One of the commemorative articles for which he allowed himself to be interviewed was a February 1963 *Time* magazine piece. It repeated the story about the 16-year-old Szell, vacationing with his parents in Bad Kissingen, an upscale German spa, in July 1913, triumphing as replacement of the indisposed conductor of the Vienna Philharmonic.

But certain details don't click. The orchestra was the Vienna Symphony, not the Philharmonic. Nor is it certain that Szell conducted the Vienna Symphony at all that summer. Researching the subject for the anniversary,

Barksdale wrote to Josef Deutz, the German consul to Cleveland, requesting confirmation of Szell's conducting debut in July 1913. The manager must have been mortified by Deutz's response. The consul responded that he had checked with the State Spa Administration in Bad Kissingen, which had informed him that no Szells had registered at the spa in July 1913. The names of Szell's parents showed up in the registry for September 4, 1913, and the local newspaper on that date included a review of a chamber music soiree held the previous night featuring "a still very young piano virtuoso from Vienna, Georg Szell, [who] introduced himself in a very promising way not only as a master of his instrument, but also as the creator of an appealing piano quintet." A week later, the paper reported that Szell performed "in a concert together with the Frankfurt Opera Singer Miss Charlotte Uhr under the conductor Richard Mandl." Bad Kissingen could provide no evidence of a Szell appearance as conductor. Barksdale was not inclined to put the brakes on the Szell celebration. "Roy Hide this away," he scribbled at the top of the Deutz letter, which he forwarded to program annotator Klaus G. Roy.

The anniversary, accurate or not, was marked with concerts in Cleveland and extensive testimonials in major newspapers and magazines. Szell even made the cover of the February 22, 1963, issue of *Time*, which extolled his virtues and reveled in his vices in a long article full of colorful, if not entirely accurate, observations. Relishing the *Time* spread above all was Szell: "It's official! It's official! It's in print—I'm a bastard!"

Few were arguing this point.

— 23 —

Dreaming Big

By 1963, six years had passed since the Cleveland Orchestra's triumphant debut in Europe. Now the Soviet Union was beckoning, and George Szell wasn't happy. Beverly Barksdale had mentioned the subject of Russia to the conductor in 1959, when the State Department had been informed of the manager's interest in pursuing such an engagement for the orchestra. Testy Cold War relations between the United States and Soviet Union, however, slowed discussions to a crawl.

Matters heated up considerably in July 1963, when Szell received a report from the State Department's Office of Cultural Presentations proposing that "two of the top U.S. symphonies" go to Europe as goodwill ambassadors. At this point, Szell assumed that both orchestras—Cleveland and Pittsburgh—would make the tours in 1965. The report, from the Advisory Committee on the Arts, contained a tentative plan that didn't please the Eurocentric Szell (who was himself a member of the committee): the Cleveland Orchestra would go to Russia for six weeks and then to Scandinavia and other countries in Western Europe; the Pittsburgh Symphony drew the plum assignment of performing at the prestigious Edinburgh, Lucerne, and Salzburg music festivals, as well as in other cities.

Szell, who had last gone to the Soviet Union in 1935 to conduct the Leningrad Philharmonic, suggested that the Cleveland and Pittsburgh itineraries be switched, partly on flimsy linguistic grounds. "There are only two members of the Cleveland Orchestra who speak Russian, none to my knowledge any of the Scandinavian Languages," Szell wrote to Glenn G. Wolfe at the State Department (occasionally resorting to the third person). "The other great Orchestras have a much larger Russian-speaking contingent in their personnel. Szell speaks neither Russian nor any of the Scandinavian Languages. On the other hand, he is completely fluent in 4 Western European Languages (English, French, German, Italian) with a modest working knowledge of Dutch, Hungarian & Czech. The personnel [of] the

Cleveland Orchestra contains quite a number of members speaking French & German."

Aside from the language issue, Szell told Wolfe that the great European music festivals had "expressed keen interest in appearances of the Cleveland Orchestra,—not to mention a large number of other cities in France, Germany, Austria, Holland etc." Only the support of the State Department was needed to make the tour a reality, the conductor noted, adding a veiled putdown of Steinberg and Pittsburgh: "The question seems to arise whether it would be wise in the general sense of the Cultural Presentations Program to deny to all of these countries and cities the American Orchestra they specifically want to have and to force another on them—if the one they would like to have is being sent across the Atlantic anyway."

Szell was not to have his way. Pittsburgh was set for 1964. The Cleveland Orchestra would tour the Soviet Union and Europe in the spring of 1965.

✻   ✻   ✻

Szell opened the 1963–64 season with works by Berlioz, Ravel, Walton, and Hindemith, proceeded with the pairing of the Beethoven fifth and Bruckner third symphonies, and went entirely Russian the third week with music by Kabalevsky, Liadov, Shostakovich (the Cleveland premiere of the Cello Concerto, Op. 107, with Mstislav Rostropovich as soloist), and Mussorgsky. The orchestra and Szell recorded the Beethoven, Liadov's *The Enchanted Lake*, and Mussorgsky's *Pictures at an Exhibition* (in the Ravel orchestration) for Epic in the midst of these performances.

Relations with Columbia Records and Epic, its classical subsidiary, were still shaky. Szell and Barksdale continued to believe that the company was barely promoting the Cleveland Orchestra. When RCA again pursued a contract with Cleveland, Barksdale answered that no discussions about repertoire could ensue until the matter of royalties was resolved. He was playing two hands at once. Even as he maintained contact with RCA, Barksdale negotiated with Columbia to drop the Epic arrangement and market the orchestra, aggressively, on the more prestigious Columbia label. "Is this not the time for there to be at least partial atonement for the sins of omission of past years and to bring an end to the second-class treatment we have known for so long?" Barksdale wrote to a Columbia official. The last work from Szell and the orchestra bearing the Epic label was Beethoven's Symphony No. 2, recorded in October 1964.

Szell took exception to another aspect of Columbia's promotion: he deplored many of the cover designs the company used for Cleveland Orchestra releases. Many Szell letters to Columbia detail his contempt for the artwork and for the people who designed it. "To castigate the moronic qualities of these perpetrators was inevitable for if I were to assume that these designs were made by competent, conscientious and cultured craftsmen, I would be compelled to consider them a silly hoax or a calculated insult," Szell complained to Columbia. The issue wouldn't go away for the rest of the conductor's tenure.

Another issue that would persist was the musicians' demand for higher salaries and longer seasons. Around the time the tour to the Soviet Union was announced, the Cleveland Federation of Musicians said it would begin negotiating for an expanded season in Cleveland. The New York Philharmonic was scheduled to become the first American orchestra to enjoy a 52-week contract starting with the 1964–65 season; the Philadelphia Orchestra would be the second a year later. Cleveland was stalled at 32 weeks. First, the union had to come to terms with its own members, who still had no say in contract negotiations. In December 1963, the union adopted a resolution stating that a strike could be implemented if at least 60 percent of the orchestra voted to reject a contract. This step, nevertheless, would not end tensions between the musicians and their local, or with the Musical Arts Association. Szell's absolute power to hire and fire players had become an increasingly sticky issue among the musicians, who believed they had the right to binding arbitration if they disagreed with a conductor's decision not to renew a member's contract. The orchestra committee knew they would have little effect in this regard while Szell was musical director. So they requested that their next contract include a provision stating that such arbitration would begin only after Szell had stepped down. They were in for quite a fight.

※　　※　　※

The celebrations of Szell's (purported) 50th anniversary as a conductor continued during the 1963–64 season. In an anniversary interview, Szell said that he couldn't easily define the qualities a conductor needed to excel in his field: "He should be equipped with the gift of leadership and should be a pedagogue, a diplomat, a poet and a lion-tamer all rolled into one. First and foremost, he should have the magnetism which compels others to do his exact bidding whether they like it or not, but preferably he should be able to make them like it." In his case, not everyone did or would like it, even though they realized Szell was a master. One musician who recognized Szell's superior musical qualities was a new orchestra member at the start of the 1963–64 season—a teenaged virtuoso destined to become an inspired soloist. Lynn Harrell was 18 when he auditioned for Szell and 19 when he took a seat in the cello section. His association with Szell began unsteadily, and his time in Cleveland wouldn't be easy. Yet it would linger as one of the cellist's most sublime musical experiences.

Robert Shaw, Harrell's godfather, had arranged for the cellist (son of the distinguished baritone Mack Harrell) to play for Szell. Both of Harrell's parents were dead, and "the world seemed a cold, unfriendly place to me," the young musician recalled. Szell didn't help. He took one look at the robust cellist before his Severance Hall audition and said, "I've heard so much about you. I'm bound to be disappointed." He evidently was. When Harrell played the Dvořák concerto, Szell gave little positive reinforcement. "Thus was laid out in a stroke my whole difficult relationship with this extraordinary musical giant over the next eight years," remembered Harrell. He bore the brunt of Szell's "caustic sarcasm, his withering looks, his harsh criticism" and emerged a better musician: "Sometimes, I dream of him. I see him on the podium above me holding the orchestra tight, like a puppeteer with a hundred strings on his fingers. He sang to us endlessly; he would try 50 different ways to explain a musical phrase to us; he spent hours with key players, haunted by the sound he knew they could deliver."

Harrell's rise in the cello section would be hastened at the end of the 1963–64 season by the departure of principal cellist Jules Eskin for the same post in the Boston Symphony.

Eskin's successor for one season was Gerald Appleman, like Eskin and Harrell a student of former principal cellist Leonard Rose. At first Appleman shared duties with co-principal Ernst Silberstein. Szell then made Appleman and Harrell alternating principals before promoting Harrell to the principal spot, precipitating Appleman's departure for the New York Philharmonic. However, Harrell's promotion came with a drawback: once he became principal, concertmaster Rafael Druian "took a great dislike to Lynn and constantly complained to Mr. Szell about everything he did," recalled Louis Lane.

Eskin's resignation prompted a sobering commentary on the orchestra's financial situation from Barksdale. "While Cleveland can attract top musicians because of its high standards," he told *The Plain Dealer*, "it finds it increasingly difficult to hold them in competition with orchestras who pay more and have longer seasons. To keep the orchestra topnotch means that there will have to be even greater support from individuals, business and industry."

The responsibility for raising the money to hold on to players largely was entrusted to board president Frank E. Joseph, who already had devoted countless hours to the cultivation of new local sources of income. In the early 1960s, the kindly lawyer faced monumental challenges with the orchestra, including the familiar demand for higher salaries and a 52-week season. Finances weren't terrible in 1963: the orchestra's deficit for the previous season had been a mere $2,000 on a budget of $1.4 million. Subscription sales for the 1963–64 season were at a record 3,295, up from the previous year's record of 3,181.

Yet Joseph knew that the orchestra could no longer expect money to pour in from a limited number of well-heeled donors. "When Severance Hall was originally built it was thought that only the so-called four hundred families would support classical music," he wrote in an article for the magazine *Fine Arts*. "The annual deficit of The Cleveland Orchestra was paid by one or two wealthy men. The income tax and inheritance tax radically changed that picture and made a broader base of support imperative. As a result, we began to employ every reasonable device to have more and more of our citizens listening to The Cleveland Orchestra, working for The Cleveland Orchestra and contributing to The Cleveland Orchestra."

❉   ❉   ❉

Audiences listening to the orchestra at Severance Hall in the fall of 1963 heard several Cleveland premieres led by Szell before he left town for his annual engagement with the New York Philharmonic. Robert Casadesus appeared as soloist in his own Concerto for Two Pianos with his wife, Gaby. A week later, Copland's Nonet for Strings had its Cleveland debut on a program with Haydn's Nelson Mass and Mozart's Violin Concerto No. 4 (played by Arnold Steinhardt, who would leave at the end of the season to pursue a solo career and then become a founding member of the Guarneri String Quartet). Szell and Casadesus were reunited a month later for a Beethoven program with the New York Philharmonic during one of the most tragic weeks in American history: On November 22, President John F. Kennedy was assassinated in Dallas. A day later, Szell led the funeral march from the "Eroica" in Kennedy's memory. Shaw was presiding in Cleveland that week, conducting works by Bach, Mozart, Hindemith, and Stravinsky, with pianist Claude Frank making his Cleveland Orchestra debut.

Another sad event affected the orchestra at this time. Fritz Reiner, former music director of the Chicago Symphony who had been scheduled to appear as a guest conductor at Severance Hall in March 1964, died in late October 1963 at age 74. Reiner's replacement was Igor Stravinsky, who shared the podium with his assistant, Robert Craft. The 81-year-old composer, who had first conducted the orchestra in 1925, recorded his Ode and

Jeu de cartes for Columbia between the March performances, when Craft also recorded Schoenberg's Five Pieces for Orchestra. The engagement—the great Russian composer's last with the Cleveland Orchestra—was remembered affectionately by program annotator Klaus G. Roy: "Stravinsky had the habit of fortifying himself before rehearsals and performances by a drink or two of fine Scotch from a silver flask," Roy wrote in a program essay in April 1982. "One rehearsal morning, he filled the cap of the flask—but suddenly stopped before putting it to his lips, and with a small bow handed the cap to me for a first sip. It was, without question, the most memorable drink of my life."

Stravinsky wasn't the only composer that season to have an impact at Severance Hall. Samuel Barber returned just after New Year's 1964 to hear Szell conduct the Cleveland premiere of his Piano Concerto—which had won the 1963 Pulitzer Prize in music—with John Browning as soloist. The American composer was anticipating not only the first Cleveland performances of his concerto but also a recording for Columbia and more performances (with the same forces) in the Soviet Union and Europe in 1965. Between rehearsals, Barber told a reporter he was impressed with "the wonderful atmosphere at Severance Hall of music-making in a simple and profound way. It is perhaps the highest level of working that I know in this country."

Between Barber and Stravinsky, another composer, this one deceased, brought enormous attention to Szell and the orchestra in Cleveland and New York. Szell had conducted the first Cleveland performances of Mahler's Ninth Symphony in November 1948 and then waited almost 16 years to conduct it again with his orchestra. In his review, Herbert Elwell provided bittersweet evidence that his impending retirement in May 1964, after 33 years as music critic of *The Plain Dealer*, was warranted. "Mahler's music sounds insufferably old-fashioned, quaint and frustrated, especially in what it picked up from Richard Strauss," he wrote. "The orchestra was magnificent in its struggle against a lost cause."

Mahler received a more dignified reception in New York. "A magician conducted a hundred magicians—each of them shaped and trained in the image of the master—in Carnegie Hall last night," wrote Louis Biancolli in the *World-Telegram & Sun*. "Which is another way of saying that George Szell and the Cleveland Orchestra were back in New York to prove that no matter what anybody has done so far this season, they could—and did—go them all one better." In the *Times*, Harold C. Schonberg seconded this opinion: "Mr. Szell and his men played the Ninth with extraordinary tensile strength, with clarity and force, with sensitivity and color. It may not have been everybody's Mahler, for some may have found this severe approach unidiomatic. But to many others the performance surely must have thrown new light on this problematic masterpiece." David R. Denby, later admired as film critic for *New York* magazine and *The New Yorker*, was a student at Columbia University when he reviewed Szell's Mahler for the *Columbia Daily Spectator*. He hailed the orchestra but found Szell's interpretation lacking in intensity: "One must remember the vast difference in temperament between the composer and his interpreter: Mahler took great (almost dangerous) emotional risks, while except for a rather explosive temper, Szell is a tight, disciplined man."

Perhaps the most favorable assessment came from Michael Steinberg, reviewing the New York concert for the *Boston Globe*. He called the orchestra "at this time unequaled" and said "it is because of its unanimity as an orchestra even more than for its surpassing virtuosity in other ways that I would call the Cleveland Orchestra uniquely great, or perhaps even uniquely an orchestra." Steinberg reserved his loftiest praise for principal hornist Myron Bloom: "In moment after moment, whether in the declamatory style, the lyric, or the grotesque, Myron Bloom demonstrated that he is easily the most varied, resourceful, and artistic horn player before the public now." The review caused Bloom a momentary blush. "The next day in Boston, when I got in the elevator, there was Szell," Bloom recalled. "We were alone, and he said, 'Can I touch you?' A perfect straight line." (Szell wasn't always so solicitous to his valued principal hornist: on another occasion after a concert, again in an elevator, he told Bloom, "That kind of playing has to be eradicated!")

After the second of the orchestra's three Carnegie Hall concerts in February 1964, Alan Rich wrote in the *New York Herald Tribune*: "It was interesting, in fact, how much the Cleveland Mozart sounds like the Mozart we heard the previous evening by the Vienna Symphony. The same clarity, balance and lightness of tone, the same beautiful blend among strings, and between strings and winds: the Cleveland Orchestra seems to be, in the best sense, our most un-American orchestra."

❋   ❋   ❋

As the critics reached dizzying heights in their praise for the Cleveland Orchestra, its musicians continued their quest for professional recognition by the public—and by their employers. An interview with guest conductor Sixten Ehrling in *The Plain Dealer* in March 1964 prompted violinist Gino

Raffaelli, chairman of the orchestra committee, to demand a retraction for quotes suggesting (incorrectly, it turned out) that Ehrling opposed federal arts subsidies—the National Endowment for the Arts was in the process of being proposed to Congress—and that American musicians were to be pitied:

> We—symphony musicians as a group throughout the country—are trying hard to dispel the idea prevailing in this country that music is 'really only a part-time job' and that 'struggle' or deprivation of some kind is necessary for art. Finally, there is a strong intimation that symphony musicians maintain their excellence principally for fear of losing their positions. This is also quite uncomplimentary to us. Professional integrity and responsibility are far more often the motivation for maintaining artistic standards.

They needed another motivation: an adequate contract—and they weren't yet getting one. Negotiations for a new three-year agreement led to an impasse in May, when the musicians voted 69 to 30 to reject an offer that would have raised the weekly minimum from $175 to $180, with further $5 increases in following years, and increased the season from 32 to 38 weeks, not including summer activity. The key point of contention concerned working conditions for the 10-week foreign tour scheduled for 1965. Szell reacted to the musicians' vote with a letter rebuking them for creating "a dangerous atmosphere" and threatening the foreign tour, not to mention his musical directorship. "Don't over-estimate the significance of the European Tour to me personally," he wrote (significantly mentioning Europe but not the Soviet Union). "I have worked for it for years—not for my sake, for your sake because of the tremendous and moral uplift it gives you and also because of the increased income, and, last but not [least], the pleasures and delights of Europe. Now, you are probably aware of the fact that the pleasures and delights of Europe are mine every year for four months without working myself to death. If I work myself to death, I do it only because of the supreme joy it gives me to make music with a body of musicians as unique and distinguished as you are."

How distinguished? Szell continued: "Rudi Serkin, the other day, said to me after our concerts, 'there never was an orchestra like this.' I would like to go one step further and without any exaggeration and megalomania say, I don't think it likely that there ever or very soon will be an orchestra like this because we understand one another musically, deeply and closely, and I don't recall a relationship of a conductor and an orchestra in the 50 or 60 years I can remember that could have competed with this. It is up to you,

Ladies and Gentlemen, to make the wise decision continuing this and it is equally up to you to destroy it."

A few days later, the musicians, by a vote of 85 to 12, decided to continue, with a little help from negotiators. The outcome was somewhat encouraging to them. The three-year contract raised the weekly minimum to $185 for two years and $190 in the third year. The musicians received one week of paid vacation the first year, two the second, and three the third. The regular season was extended to 38 weeks and the summer season to 10, bringing the musicians closer to year-round employment. The players received increases for extra rehearsals and concerts, a jump in their expense payment on tour, additional fees for tours of six days or longer, and improvements in their medical and pension plans. "These are great gains," said board president Joseph. "However, in view of the training and skills required, the men deserve them. If Cleveland wants the greatest symphony orchestra in the world it is going to have to pay for it. I am asking every lover of good music to increase his giving in the fund raising." Cleveland would have to pay $350,000 for the coming year.

The issue of summer employment, which had been plaguing the orchestra for decades, was now more urgent than ever. With other major orchestras extending their seasons to 52 weeks, Cleveland had to find a way to match its conterparts or continue to risk losing players. Joseph had begun to explore the subject in 1958, while visiting the Boston Symphony's Tanglewood festival in western Massachusetts. He would become the motivating force behind a Cleveland summer facility. The signing of the orchestra's contract in May 1964 increased the tempo on establishment of a summer home. Szell had the issue on his mind while in Europe that summer, when he read a story about Meadowbrook, the Detroit Symphony's alfresco home, in the *New York Times*. "Let's try to find out more about architect & acoustician and let's inspect the place," Szell wrote to Barksdale. "We may have to build one soon for ourselves."

Barksdale was already on the lookout. He informed Szell that he had met with representatives of Cleveland's City Planning Commission to inspect "very tentative drawings for a kind of cultural complex which would be built down in Erieview," the urban renewal district bordered by Lakeside and Chester avenues and East 9th and East 12th streets. "The fact that it has become known that we are interested in finding a location for a more or less permanent summer home for the orchestra has fired the imagination of many people." Officials in University Circle were interested in proposing a summer facility near Severance Hall. Other inquiries came from Bratenahl, a wealthy community just east of the city on the shores of Lake Erie, where there was a possibility of converting a 40-acre golf course into a concert site. James D. Ireland, an orchestra trustee, suggested that board members check out another piece of land, his own 38-acre Bratenahl property.

In November 1964, the Musical Arts Association announced its intention to build a summer home, but nothing about the location. By this time, the Bratenahl sites were out. The engineering firm of William Gould & Associates was hired to search for a minimum of 100 acres, "but preferably 200," for a pavilion seating at least 5,000 people, a lawn area for another 5,000, and parking for 3,500 cars. Opening of the festival was set for 1967. Along with the pavilion for outdoor and indoor concerts (with walls that could be closed electronically in inclement weather) and parking areas, the original plan included a second performance space for ballet and opera, and a summer music school modeled after the admired programs at the Tanglewood and Aspen festivals. These elements would be implemented in phases, beginning with the massive pavilion. "We're sensitive to the fact that Severance Hall is the smallest music hall used by any of the 18 major symphony orchestras," Joseph told the *Press*. "We're handicapped. We could use another 500 seats and we don't want to make the same mistake again." He told another journalist that the orchestra had to take an ambitious course: "We want to dream big, so future generations won't blame us for thinking too small!"

❋   ❋   ❋

In September 1964, George Szell was once again eager to show Europe that an American orchestra could tower over any of its Continental counterparts. "In fact, this is what they criticize us for," he told Robert Finn, Elwell's successor at *The Plain Dealer*. "They say our orchestras are inhuman, they are so perfect. But most of the criticism is directed not at the orchestras themselves, but at the conductors."

More than a bit of Szell's own criticism over the next six years would be directed toward James Levine, a prodigiously gifted 20-year-old pianist and conductor from Cincinnati. Levine had participated at a young age in the Marlboro Music Festival, run by Szell's boyhood friend, Rudolf Serkin, where a number of Cleveland Orchestra members spent summers playing chamber music with distinguished colleagues and talented students. After serving on the jury of an American conductors project funded by the Ford Foundation, Szell asked Levine to come to Cleveland. Szell and Levine were to have a meaningful but turbulent relationship complicated by the former's stern personality and the latter's independent streak. At first, Szell couldn't wait to give his young apprentice a chance to prove himself. On the third program of the 1964–65 season, he allowed Levine to make his debut conducting Chopin's Piano Concerto No. 2, with pianist Ann Schein, also in her debut with the orchestra. Szell devoted many private coaching sessions to Levine, during which they discussed and dissected important orchestral and operatic scores at the piano. (As part of his orchestral duties, Levine was given keyboard parts, including several during the 1965 foreign tour.)

Levine's first assignment at Severance Hall in September 1964 was to play harpsichord in performances of Stravinsky's *The Rake's Progress* with the Lake Erie Opera Theater, which was in its inaugural season of full-scale productions with members of the Cleveland Orchestra in the pit conducted by the company's musical director, Louis Lane. The inaugural season also included the double bill of Puccini's *Il Tabarro* and *Gianni Schicchi*. The company made a distinguished, if brief, contribution to Cleveland's musical life, giving the local premieres of the Stravinsky opera, Prokofiev's *The Love for Three Oranges*, Poulenc's *Dialogues of the Carmelites* and Richard Strauss's *Capriccio*.

As Levine developed his exceptional conducting gifts, local musicians and audiences took notice. He began an association with the Cleveland Institute of Music. He brought members of the Cleveland Orchestra, the University Circle Orchestra, and a freelance group known as the Philharmonia Chorale together to form the Cleveland Concert Associates, which presented a remarkable array of internationally known singers in acclaimed concert performances of Mozart's *Don Giovanni*, Verdi's *Simon Boccanegra* and *Don Carlo*, and Beethoven's *Fidelio* at Severance Hall. Cheerful, inexhaustible, and unquestionably destined for great things, Levine became so revered that a group of music lovers formed a small society, known as the Levinites, to hail their hero.

Szell was not a member. He became increasingly distressed that Levine seemed to show little interest in attending rehearsals. At one point, Szell decided to telephone him and say that he was forbidden to enter Severance Hall again. Lane talked Szell out of making the call. Levine would acknowledge that he learned an enormous amount from Szell about classical style— and also about methods of making music and handling orchestras that weren't to his taste. "I find that forcing an orchestra shuts it down," Levine later told an interviewer. "The sound shuts down and becomes crushed, dry, grainy, hard, not vocal, and that was one of my biggest objections to Szell's music-making—the lack of vocal legato, vocal line, breath. It was interesting because, of course, the man was phenomenally perceptive and illuminating about structure—classical structure, particularly—and the chamber-style balances that he could get were fabulous, but I always wished for a greater line, greater vocality, greater breath, and greater physical sensuality, less abstraction."

Aside from Levine, the 1964–65 season brought to the orchestra a number of musicians whose tenures would range from one to 15 seasons, the longest being bass trombonist Edwin Anderson. The quickest casualty was a French violinist, Liliane Caillon, whom Szell fired before the season was out. The reason, according to longtime violinist Evelyn Botnick, was that Caillon became pregnant, a condition Szell may have believed was intolerable in an ensemble that needed to be at full strength at all times. Botnick said she never would have thought of having a family while playing in the Cleveland Orchestra under Szell. At the time, most female members who had children had given birth before they joined Szell's ensemble. An exception was Catherine Dalschaert, a New Zealand–born, Australian-reared violinist whose Belgian husband, Stephane, also played violin in the orchestra. Dalschaert gave birth to her second child in 1964, hours after playing a concert under Szell. Informed of the birth the next day, the conductor was astonished. "What do you mean?" he said to the happy father. "She was here last night. Those Australians—they're a tough lot." The Dalschaerts, who had arrived in Cleveland in 1960, left in 1967 to play in the better-paid Philadelphia Orchestra.

Szell could be narrow-minded on more than just the issue of gender. In the mid-1960s, he continued to become more conservative musically, leaning farther toward the mainstream repertoire he loved most. For the opening weeks of the 1964–65 season, he concentrated on Haydn, Mozart, Beethoven, Brahms, Mendelssohn, Schumann, Smetana, Strauss, Debussy, and other established masters, while taking but a few detours for recent music by Mennin, Barber, and Walton. October was an especially productive recording month for Szell and the orchestra, who taped Beethoven's first and second symphonies—their last recordings on the Epic label—and Brahms's Symphony No. 3, several Dvořák Slavonic dances, and three works inspired by the music of other composers (Walton's Variations on a Theme by Hindemith, Hindemith's Symphonic Metamorphosis on Themes by Weber, and Brahms's Variations on a Theme by Haydn) for Columbia.

These recordings convey an artistic attitude upon which Szell expanded when he spoke at the dedication of the Oberlin Conservatory's new facilities in late October 1964. "The lot of the musician is not and should not be an easy one," he said. "It should be based on the joy to shoulder responsibility to the composer, and to discharge that responsibility." Another responsibility Szell held dear—that his musicians comport themselves with dignity at all times—became an issue the same month, when Barksdale was compelled to send a memo to the orchestra's male players. "Both Mr. Szell and I have had unfavorable comments from subscribers regarding the short socks worn by some of the men," the manager wrote. "May I remind you once more that you should wear socks of sufficient length to completely cover the exposed part of the leg. The 'over the calf' type is preferable."

The musicians were going to dress smartly for their forthcoming tour to the Soviet Union and Europe, for which the orchestra was planning a big civic send-off in April 1965. Frank Joseph was thinking ahead. In November 1964, he wrote to Earl Warren, Chief Justice of the U.S. Supreme Court, inviting him and his wife to attend the April event. Joseph had met Warren when the orchestra played in Washington, D.C., the previous February. Now he was taking the opportunity to tell Warren how much the tour meant to the orchestra and the nation. "We are told that this is the finest kind of American propaganda, because it really isn't propaganda at all," wrote Joseph. "It is hoped that the impact will be much greater than all the books and debates and that the people who hear this beautiful music will be automatically convinced that the country that produced it can't be as bad as their leaders would have them believe."

Meanwhile, longstanding tensions between Szell and Marc Lifschey, his superb but mercurial principal oboist, led to a final break. During the first rehearsal of 1965 (for performances of Prokofiev's Fifth Symphony), Szell stopped to question Lifschey's pitch. "Now Marc, what's wrong? You've got to correct this. What's the problem?" Lifschey didn't miss a beat: "That's the way I play it. If it doesn't suit you, you can get someone else to play it." To which Szell responded, softly, "Mr. Lifschey, you may leave the orchestra." The incident constituted the oboist's firing, concluding one of the most distinguished careers in the orchestra's history. Lifschey tried to apologize to Szell, who wouldn't listen. Within a week, Szell had appointed Robert Zupnick, the orchestra's assistant principal oboe, and Adrian Gnam, a 25-year-old musician studying at Columbia University, as co-principals.

The Lifschey incident, plans for the foreign tour, and a series of important performances (including the world premiere, finally, of Henri Dutilleux's *Cinq Métaboles*, only seven seasons late as a 40th-anniversary commission) took a toll on Szell. To add to his burdens, the 67-year-old conductor entered University Hospitals in late February 1965 for prostate surgery. The obstruction in his urinary tract proved to be benign. At least Szell didn't have to step onto any podiums in March. The big musical event in Cleveland that month was the U.S. conducting debut of French composer-conductor Pierre Boulez, whom Szell long had been eager to introduce with his orchestra. Boulez arrived with a program ideally suited to his lucid and adventurous gifts: pieces by Rameau, his own *Figures, Doubles, Prisms* (U.S. premiere), Debussy's *Gigues, Rondes de printemps*, and *Jeux* (the last for the first time in Cleveland), and Stravinsky's *Song of the Nightingale*.

The reaction, predictably, was mixed. In a *Plain Dealer* review folksily headlined "Boulez Bowls 'Em Over, Debussy Sends 'Em," Finn admired the "ravishingly beautiful performances of three fine works of Debussy" and noted a curious phenomenon after the Debussy pieces: "A large portion of the audience, perhaps a fifth or a quarter of the whole, simply got up and walked out. I was dumbfounded. Was this some sort of spontaneous protest against Boulez or—heaven help us!—against the Debussy classics? Then I realized that these people, evidently unable to tell Debussy from the Stravinsky that came after it, thought the concert was over! It was a display of musical ignorance and reflects no credit to those involved."

❁   ❁   ❁

A second European tour was what Szell wanted for his orchestra above any other artistic endeavor. To ensure the tour and to avert a strike for the 1964–65 season, he made the first major concession of his Cleveland career: he allowed a clause in the union contract about terminating individual contracts to be changed to the musicians' advantage. Then, however, Szell had the Musical Arts Association add a clause to his *own* new contract, signed in February 1965, stating that he could cancel his contract at the end of any season during which his recommendation to dismiss a player was overruled.

All of these matters were settled, for the moment, as Szell and his musicians ended their season with programs in preparation for the tour. A note of sadness intervened in early April, when Leon Fleisher, who had been scheduled to play piano concertos by Mozart, Beethoven, and Grieg during the tour, was forced to cancel after he began having difficulties with his right hand that were believed to be the result of a pulled tendon. The condition would be diagnosed as repetitive stress syndrome, derailing Fleisher's playing career, and compelling him to concentrate on left-hand repertoire. Initially, Fleisher thought he might be able to meet up with Szell and the orchestra after their appearances in the Soviet Union, but it wasn't to be.

Finally, the time came to embark on the 10-week, 44-concert tour to the Soviet Union, Scandinavia, and Western Europe, including appearances at music festivals in Helsinki, Bergen, Prague, Vienna, and Amsterdam. On April 13, 1965, 117 musicians, staff, and family members boarded a Pan American–chartered Boeing 707 at Cleveland Hopkins International Airport for the flight to London and then on to Moscow. The concerts wouldn't begin until April 16, giving the musicians time to recover from jet lag, take in the novel atmosphere of a Communist society, keep their playing in shape, and, in the case of cellist Albert Michelsen, make up for lost time. In Moscow, Michelsen was reunited with his sister, Yelena, a retired dentist, after a 40-year separation. "We lost contact during the war, and then we hunted and hunted through the Red Cross," the cellist told United Press International. "Finally we established contact and when it looked certain the orchestra would come to Russia two years ago, my sister literally counted the days and the hours until we met."

Szell and the orchestra hadn't exactly arrived in the Soviet Union at the most propitious moment. Fighting in Vietnam was escalating, causing tension between the United States and the U.S.S.R. Yet Szell and the others were never subjected to any political friction while traveling behind the Iron Curtain. The orchestra became the first American ensemble to perform in the Soviet Union in six years with its April 16 concert in Bolshoi Hall of the Moscow Conservatory, where Szell conducted a Berlioz-Barber-Schubert program. The Muscovites shouted enough bravos to bring Szell back for 20 curtain calls and four encores. He could not keep the orchestra further: Following the concert, 35 of the ensemble's Jewish players were scheduled to go to the Israeli Embassy to observe Passover as guests of Israeli Ambassador Yosef Tekoah.

In Moscow, Lane conducted a program split between American fare (Gershwin, Bernstein, Elwell) and European repertoire (Sibelius and Stravinsky). A number of the Clevelanders weren't finished playing once their orchestra concerts were done in Moscow (or later in Kiev): flutist John Rautenberg and percussionists Richard Weiner, Joseph Adato, and Robert Matson headed to youth cafes for jam sessions with local jazz musicians. The orchestra's fifth, and final, concert in Moscow included a performance of Prokofiev's Fifth Symphony that received a special stamp of approval from the composer's widow, Lina. Thanking Szell profusely backstage, she kept repeating, "What a marvelous interpretation! What a marvelous interpretation!" A few days later, motivated by raves from the Soviet press, the orchestra voted unanimously to give up a free day and accept an invitation from the Georgian Ministry of Culture to perform an extra concert on May 1, the international Communist holiday, in Tblisi, capital of the Georgian Republic. "We consider to be asked to play on this holiday is a great gesture of goodwill and an unusual honor," said Barksdale. The goodwill gesture also came from Szell, who agreed to forgo a rehearsal in Helsinki later in the tour to make the Tblisi concert possible.

After one concert in Kiev, Szell again was called back to the stage 20 times. The orchestra gave three acclaimed performances in Georgia before the May Day concert. "The reception we are getting here is like the kind you get when you hit a grand slam homer in the bottom of the ninth inning," said violinist Kurt Loebel.

"Armenians Won't Let Szell Stop," read a dramatic headline in *The Plain Dealer.* "When violinist Gino Raffaelli was spotted on the street, the volatile Armenians demanded an impromptu sidewalk recital," noted *Time* magazine. "He complied." In Yerevan, the Armenian capital, "hundreds of fans attempted to batter their way into the concert hall, and heavy police reinforcements had to be rushed in to quell the riot." Browning's performance of the Barber Piano Concerto "attracted an avid following of young girls, who stormed the stage crying 'John, John . . . oh, John!' " The orchestra was treated as musical royalty in Leningrad, where its third concert was attended by three great violinists—Isaac Stern, David Oistrakh, and Leonid Kogan. For Szell, the five weeks of cultural exchange with the Soviet Union had provided crucial lessons: "It is the only contact that functions even when political relations are bad. It is the best means of teaching people to know and appreciate each other, despite all the dividing factors, and show them that in a higher sense they all belong together."

From Leningrad, Szell and his musicians headed to Helsinki, where they performed Sibelius's Seventh Symphony with three of the composer's daughters in attendance. While in Helsinki, Szell received the Sibelius Medal, and the orchestra took the short trip north to Ainola to visit the home and grave of the country's musical hero. "Since Mrs. Sibelius is 93 and in rather frail condition, just a few of us were invited into the house," Barksdale later told trustees. "Afterward we returned to the apple orchard where [the composer] is buried under a simple bronze slab bearing his name. There Mr. Szell laid a wreath from The Cleveland Orchestra. As this was going on a few of the men looked back toward the house and saw Mrs. Sibelius standing on a small balcony watching the proceedings. She withdrew as soon as she saw that she had been observed."

Among the listeners in Warsaw was a large contingent from the Warsaw Philharmonic Orchestra, whose conductor, Witold Rowicki, said the experience "was the greatest lesson for the Warsaw Philharmonic in how we should play. We heard Maestro Szell and the Cleveland Orchestra here eight years ago and have always considered it the greatest orchestra that played on our stage. It was confirmed again tonight." Responded Szell: "I have been a little frightened by that legend and am very happy we made good." So good that even Warsaw cab drivers had opinions about the orchestra. "In the afternoon we took a taxi to visit the old city and by chance had an English speaking driver," recalled Barksdale. "When he learned who we were he said: 'Why you play only one concert? You could play every night for a week and still be sold out.' " The Polish press may have helped: One newspaper headlined its review, "Wizards from Cleveland." Days later, a French newspaper offered a variation: "Cleveland Conquered Paris."

But the commander of the conquering forces was behaving poorly. Szell, who never wanted to go to the Soviet Union in the first place, was in a bad mood throughout the early portion of the tour, and he drove the orchestra to the edge. There were many possible reasons: the loss of oboist Lifschey in January and pianist Fleisher just before the tour; his prostate operation in February; news that his Shaker Heights home had been ransacked in his absence. "He was scared and neurotic about the tour," remembered violinist Loebel. "He said, 'In Vienna the critics are going to roast me.' He was behaving miserably. He screamed. He gave dirty looks. Helene was ready to leave for her sister's. He screamed at the TV crew. He was unbearable, out of control, a bastard about everything." Finally, the musicians asked the orchestra committee to confront Szell in Bergen, Norway. They told him that if he didn't stop acting unreasonably, no one would attend rehearsal the next day. "From that point on, he was a totally different person—nice and controlled," Loebel said. "It proved he was like a child who sees how far he can go."

With Szell calmed down and eager to continue through Europe, the orchestra played a concert in Bergen's Festival Hall that was seen on European television by millions of viewers—the biggest audience in the ensemble's history to that point. From Bergen, they proceeded to Berlin and its new concert hall, the Philharmonie, home of the Berlin Philharmonic and its conductor-for-life, Herbert von Karajan. In Prague, where they became the first American orchestra to visit Czechoslovakia since Toscanini and the New York Philharmonic in 1930, Szell was reunited with the city he had served as conductor at the German Opera. Prague hailed him as "Our Szell." He was called back to the stage 16 times in Bratislava, where Cleveland became the first American orchestra ever to pay a visit. Then came Vienna, where Szell and the orchestra were celebrated, rather than roasted, for their concerts, which included a Gershwin program led by Lane. "This orchestra does not need to improve," said Rudolf Weisshappel, critic of the *Kurier*. "Its standard is perfect. It could not be better."

In London, critics couldn't find enough words of praise. "The Cleveland players show the most unobtrusive and artistic kind of virtuosity," wrote Andrew Porter in the *Financial Times*. "There is no striving for fat, sleek, overfed tone, nor any attempt to wow us with brazen clangour. On the other hand, their controlled soft playing (especially in the finale of the Bartók [Concerto for Orchestra]), can be breathtaking in effect"

After concerts in Amsterdam and Scheveningen, Holland, the orchestra returned to Cleveland, where more than 5,000 people greeted the musicians at the airport.

Just as the State Department had expected, the tour's artistic achievements were complemented by invaluable personal contact. In each city, the orchestra's players visited conservatories, where they listened to young musicians, gave them lessons and advice, and presented them with American recordings. They brought orchestral scores for Soviet composers who otherwise would have had little access to these materials. Barksdale realized that Szell and the orchestra had accomplished their mission when they were feted in Tblisi by the local composers' union. One composer approached Barksdale, handed him a glass of schnapps, and proposed a toast that the manager deemed the most beautiful of the tour: "To your loved ones at home who may be worried about you because they don't know that you are among friends."

– 24 –

Summer Music

George Szell had annual postseason rituals. Each year, he followed his final Severance Hall concerts with a summer stay in the part of the world he loved most—Europe. When he wasn't conducting, Szell holed up at swanky Swiss hotels to play golf (badly) and study scores (supremely well) for the coming season's concerts. The respite from his orchestral duties gave him time to ponder subjects that needed special scrutiny. In the summer of 1965, the subject was a summer home for the Cleveland Orchestra.

It was an issue important to the orchestra's musicians, who for almost four decades had inched along toward full employment. After the 1927 and 1928 series of concerts at Edgewater and Gordon parks under Rudolph Ringwall, the musicians went without summer employment until their independently-organized Promenade concerts in 1932 and 1933 at Severance Hall. They waited until 1936 to play again during the summer, this time as the Great Lakes Symphony Orchestra at the Great Lakes Exposition, and skipped the next summer before playing light operas at the Aquastage at the East Ninth Street pier in 1938. A year later, the Cleveland Summer Orchestra established itself at Public Auditorium, where it remained a fixture except for the one summer, 1953, when it performed during Indians games while the auditorium was fitted with air-conditioning.

In 1965, the Musical Arts Association began seriously following through on Szell's desire to build a permanent summer home. Frank E. Joseph, his friend and board president, and Beverly Barksdale, the orchestra's manager, had been exploring possible sites for an outdoor facility with help from a local consulting firm, William A. Gould Associates. Eleven parcels of land reportedly were offered as outright gifts, but none met the standards established by Gould. Aside from inquiries by the city of Cleveland, Bratenahl, and University Circle, the orchestra was being courted from the east by Painesville in Lake County and from the south by the Brandywine ski resort and the town of Peninsula in Summit County. "Our site developers studied over 80 different sites," Peter Reed, the corporate lawyer who was serving as chairman of the site committee, later told the board. *Plain Dealer* music critic Robert Finn was eager to write about the sites, but Joseph gently told him that he couldn't yet discuss specifics. "If we ever get 'Joseph's Folly' off the sidewalk, I hope you will be my guest!" he wrote to Finn in May 1965.

Two months later, the association considered a 200-acre site in Peninsula among five final proposals for a summer facility. The project was becoming more crucial by the minute. "The Cleveland Orchestra has become the best [ambassador] of good will this city has," Joseph told the *Press*. "This summer festival is the only way we can keep these skilled musicians here. We have guaranteed them 48 weeks of employment and despite everything—winter concerts, the pops, country club dates—we cannot extend the season without this summer project."

Szell was all for the project, but only if it met his stringent requirements and didn't conflict with another project being discussed—a third European tour, in the summer of 1967, to the music festivals of Edinburgh, Lucerne, and Salzburg. "While it is of course IMPERATIVE to have such an installation for the summer, it seems to me even more important to have it turn out to be exceptional, absolutely first rate, terribly attractive, and not merely a provincial imitation of Tanglewood et al," Szell cautioned Barksdale from picture-postcard Switzerland. "In view of the fact that we are at a disadvantage, geographically as well as demographically and not overblessed with striking scenic beauty in our immediate vicinity, I consider it of vital importance to have the chosen area and its 'furnishings' as beautiful, attractive and functionally perfect as possible. If this goal should be jeopardized by having to rush to meet a deadline we might find ourselves with something on our hands that costs enough money but is not the really right thing."

Barksdale, an eternal optimist, still wanted to stick to the original schedule, which called for the festival to open in 1967. "I hope that we can actually acquire a site by the end of 1965 and begin architectural and landscape planning. Site preparation, including landscaping, would begin in the late spring of 1966," he wrote to Szell. "If this can be adhered to, we should have the basic work done and the pavilion or shed, administrative headquarters, eating facilities, etc., ready by the summer of 1967. Somewhere within the next year we must decide if we want to inaugurate the school simultaneously with the festival or bring it in the second year, etc. For this we need your thinking."

The school was the brainchild of Szell and Louis Lane, the orchestra's associate conductor, who would take charge of the program. Szell envisioned the Blossom Festival School as a forum to train gifted students in chamber music, which he deemed essential in achieving the kind of intimacy, balance, and cohesion he had drilled into the Cleveland Orchestra. One aspect of the program would extend Szell's influence on the musical world even further: orchestra members would teach private lessons and coach chamber music sessions, thus passing down their conductor's approach to many aspects of performance. The faculty would include Kent instructors, renowned guests (such as former concertmaster Josef Gingold), and conductors appearing at Blossom, such as Pierre Boulez, who could work with students on chamber orchestra repertoire. The Blossom school, later renamed Kent/Blossom, would become one of the nation's foremost summer music programs, training students who would go on to top orchestra, chamber music, and university jobs. Many members of the Cleveland Orchestra received important performance experience at the school.

By late 1965, Barksdale and Joseph realized that Szell was right about the timeline. Pushing for a 1967 opening would be impractical, especially with a European tour scheduled for the same period. All of the sites being considered had proved problematic in terms of location, infrastructure, airplane traffic noise, and other concerns. Another dilemma affecting the project was the musicians' contract, which provided lower minimum salaries for summer concerts ($150 per week) than for the winter season ($185). In late March 1966, the orchestra rejected a new summer contract proposed by the Musical Arts Association, threatening a strike. The Detroit Symphony had recently settled on a year-round minimum weekly scale of $185. "This comparison with Detroit is of great importance to most of our Orchestra," Barksdale told trustees. He chose the phrase "most of our orchestra" carefully: only 85 of the ensemble's 111 members—the Cleveland Orchestra minus its principal players and a few others—constituted the Cleveland Summer Orchestra. In early April, the trustees decided to make the summer minimum equal to the winter minimum. Ninety-eight musicians voted to approve the contract, bringing the orchestra "a step closer to year-round employment," said hornist Roy Waas, a member of the orchestra committee. "It gives us a total of 45 weeks employment this year and 49 next year."

The contract equalizing the winter and summer rates was another incentive for orchestra trustees and officials to press forward on the summer home. After much debate, they chose more than 500 acres of wooded land north of Akron, and south of Peninsula, in Summit County. "We considered that site and a site about three and half miles farther north, which was in a way even more beautiful," recalled Lane. "But while we were out there a big jet started its landing pattern for Cleveland Hopkins [airport] and that was the end of that. It was amazing how much [difference] three miles makes to the sound of a jet which is flying low." Barksdale could hardly contain his glee upon notifying Szell about the property. "We have had meetings in Cleveland and near Akron with all kinds of officials including township trustees, zoning boards and the like," he wrote. "Everyone is excited over the prospect of our locating in the valley region and we have been promised all assistance from the township and any zoning restrictions we require."

News of the purchase broke in late June 1966. The festival would be located in Northampton Township (later incorporated into the city of Cuyahoga Falls) on a site "described as having a natural amphitheater sloping toward a wooded ravine," reported the *Press*. "A large, flat nearby area will be used for parking three to four thousand cars." The location seemed well-nigh ideal, at least for music lovers in Akron, who could drive to the festival in less than 20 minutes. It would take Clevelanders about 40 minutes from the East Side and 55 minutes from the West Side. The pavilion would hold nearly 5,000 people, with space on a sweeping lawn for another 5,000— a number that would eventually rise to 15,000. The *Press* boasted, a bit overzealously, that the festival would be "the largest ever to be developed and the first ever created completely by any orchestra." The first festival season was scheduled for mid-July to late August 1968.

Orchestra members were so intrigued with the prospect of their own summer home that they made noises about traveling to the site to check it out. Barksdale asked them to be patient. "Please do not attempt to visit our proposed summer site on your own until after we actually have title to it," he wrote in a memo. "The transfer of ownership (closing) will take place mid-August and only then will we have free access. Unauthorized entrance would be trespassing. We urge your cooperation."

Barksdale certainly had cooperation on the project from a large contingent of trustees, including site committee chairman Reed, who negotiated the purchase of the summer-home property. Reed reported the particulars to the board in July 1966: the Musical Arts Association was buying 571 acres in Northampton Township from Seibert Development Enterprises, Inc., for $521,000. As acoustical consultant, he recommended that the association hire Christopher Jaffe, an acoustician from Connecticut admired for his successful indoor and outdoor stage shells, to collaborate with the Cleveland architectural firm of Shafer, Flynn and Van Dijk, which had worked on the 1958 Severance Hall stage renovation. "Why don't we build the world's biggest amphitheater?" Jaffe asked Barksdale and architect Peter van Dijk during a study tour of outdoor concert facilities, including the Philadelphia Orchestra's Saratoga and the Boston Symphony's Tanglewood. To show them what he meant, Jaffe drew a possible shape for a pavilion on a paper napkin.

The meeting in July 1966 at which Reed announced the summer home plans included another important piece of business: Joseph asked the board to approve naming the facility Blossom Music Center in honor of the family that had supported the orchestra so generously throughout its history. There was some concern that the name "Blossom" might confuse the public into thinking the venue had something to do with a flower. Some board members "weren't sure people would understand that it's actually a family name and not some name pulled out like 'Tanglewood,'" according to Michael Maxwell, the orchestra's assistant manager at the time. Nevertheless, the name was adopted unanimously. The Blossom family responded by donating $1.3 million, a large portion of which would be used for Blossom Music Center. The remainder would go to the orchestra's endowment fund to help meet a $2 million challenge grant from the Ford Foundation. Elizabeth Blossom, the family matriarch and widow of Dudley S. Blossom, had one desire for the center: "I do hope that the tickets won't be too high priced so that everyone who loves good music will be able to attend." In thanking the Blossoms for their longtime support, Joseph wrote that the board considered them to be more deserving of the honor than any other Cleveland family. He also suggested that being responsible for a great orchestra sometimes could be an unenviable challenge. "The crises have been frequent, the problems many and the thank you's few," he wrote to Emily Blossom, widow of Dudley S. Blossom, Jr. "But what you and your fine family did was so perfect and heartwarming that it is reward enough."

A hint of what Joseph meant by "problems" soon cropped up. A number of board members were unhappy that "big name" architects hadn't been hired to design Blossom Music Center. Once Shafer, Flynn and Van Dijk submitted sketches, the board decided that it might consider hiring a nationally known architect or two as consultants. The opposition leaders finally met with Flynn and van Dijk ("the most brilliant young architect to arrive on the Cleveland scene in a number of years," according to Barksdale) and proposed two possible consultants: Walter Gropius, the founder of the modernist Bauhaus movement, and Pietro Belluschi, who was designing the new Juilliard School for Lincoln Center. The latter was chosen.

Even before any designs were in, Blossom Music Center was beginning to generate national interest. Robert C. Marsh, the *Chicago Sun-Times* critic who had been hired by Cleveland's World Publishing Company to write a 50th-anniversary book about the Cleveland Orchestra, let his readers know about the orchestra's summer home. "Wags are already referring to it as the Szellsburg Festival, and this quip contains more wisdom than most," wrote Marsh. "In 20 years as music director George Szell has made the Cleveland Orchestra one of the supreme symphonic ensembles in the world. The presence of himself and his players in a new summer music site gives it dignity, prestige and an international image of the highest artistic quality, comparable with Salzburg in the days when Toscanini and Bruno Walter were dominant figures on the musical scene." The comparison with Salzburg would never hold water.

Nor, it seems, would the property where the festival would be located. Literally. Even after four wells were dug at the site, officials of the Akron Department of Public Services couldn't find sufficient water for the facility. They promised to install an adequate (and expensive) water main—and before any work could start, hidden gas pipes had to be located. Whatever the challenges, the site promised to be a stunning place to hear music, symphonic or otherwise. "The only reason why 500 acres were available to us," said Reed, "was that the rugged contours of the land made it unsuitable for industry, but the natural bowl made it perfect for the orchestra."

Not surprisingly, Szell maintained firm control of the design process. He encouraged Barksdale to "build now a fire" under the architects and acoustician Jaffe, who was instructed to supply detailed scale drawings of diffusive surfaces for the orchestra shell, ceiling, and other areas in the pavilion. Taking a lesson from the Severance Hall stage renovation, Szell wanted to make sure that the Blossom stage could direct sound in specific directions. "It is quite possible, that a place with partly open side-walls (equivalent to sound absorbers) should not have excessive volume," he advised Barksdale, even as he pushed him to get the project moving. "I leave it to you to drive these people _energetically_ to work and to work out more than just approximate sketches. Frankly, I am getting concerned about the slow pace of progress and would regret it, if my disappointment should force me to disassociate myself from the whole project, but I am determined not to waste much more time on it if the others proceed at snails pace and talk instead of work."

With the successful reconstruction of the Severance stage in mind, Szell convinced the board to engage Heinrich Keilholz (whom he had wanted as acoustician in the first place) as acoustical consultant for Blossom. The situation would prove difficult. The architects, who had developed a productive working relationship with Jaffe, ignored many of Keilholz's early design suggestions. When Jaffe read a story in _The Plain Dealer_ announcing that Keilholz had been named consultant, he withdrew and the German recording engineer—technically, he was not an acoustician—was handed the Blossom job. Szell prevailed, as usual.

One property owner near Blossom would not prevail. A. W. Heck, who had land 1½ miles south of the future Blossom Music Center, had begun to build an airstrip, posing potential sound problems for the orchestra and its audiences. An injunction from the local zoning commission to halt construction was denied by the courts, which said Heck had the right to do as he pleased. While the case was being appealed, the orchestra requested that zoning resolutions be changed to prevent similar nuisances. Ten months later, the Court of Appeals issued a permanent injunction against construction of private airports in the vicinity.

The Blossom facility originally was intended to include adjacent land for the new school, for which the University of Akron was interested in providing administrative services. So was another admired institution, this one next door to Severance Hall. John S. Millis, president of Western Reserve University, received the association's memorandum, "A Proposed Peninsula Cultural Center," but couldn't attend a meeting about the festival and school. He tried to stall any decision on educational plans, and got the ensemble's name wrong in the process. "The Cleveland Symphony should not settle for any educational enterprise less distinguished than the Orchestra itself," Millis wrote Barksdale. "This will therefore require the creation of [an] entity able to call upon the scholarly and musical resources of many institutions."

But the Musical Arts Association had already found a potential collaborator. It was exploring the project with Kent State University, whose main campus lay 10 miles east of the site in Portage County. The initial concept for the school was ambitious. "Such a facility, separate from but adjoining the Center, might include a graduate school of music as well as educational programs in the dramatic and graphic arts," read an orchestra press release announcing talks between the orchestra and Kent State. As negotiations continued, the school appeared headed for a spot on 37 acres next to the Blossom site that Kent State would purchase from the Himmelright family. The university would share costs with the association for an access road and water facilities, as well as "future costs of area maintenance, policing the area, and similar problems."

✻　　✻　　✻

Before school or festival could be developed, the orchestra had to raise the money to build Blossom—$6.6 million. The association announced that it would embark on a major capital fund drive, the Half-Century Fund, to help match a $2 million Ford Foundation challenge grant. "This is the first capital fund effort on behalf of the Cleveland Orchestra since the endowment campaign in 1929 at the time Severance Hall was being planned," said

Joseph. Of the total, $4.36 million was to be used for construction of Blossom and the remainder for an endowment to maintain the facility.

Money was becoming a pressing issue for the trustees, who had also been studying the possibility of building an annex onto Severance Hall. The orchestra's home needed expansion, especially for storage space and women's facilities (more and more female musicians were joining the orchestra in the 1960s). The project would require a major infusion of cash, and the trustees decided this was no time to get involved in two construction projects. Although the orchestra had balanced its budgets for the four years preceding 1967, Joseph feared that inflation—caused in part by U.S. involvement in the Vietnam War—would not allow it to do so in coming years, so it was also no time to allow recording engineer Keilholz to spend orchestra dollars in a manner the trustees viewed as extravagant. One concern was the sound-reinforcement equipment Keilholz wanted to purchase for the pavilion. He was opting for European equipment at $120,000. Reed told him he must use American equipment that was equal in quality and priced at $70,000.

Another money-saving compromise particularly irked Szell. He had insisted that the Blossom stage be air-conditioned for the comfort of the musicians and the quality of the music-making (since the weather could affect both human and instrumental response). When Barksdale and trustees realized that they needed to cut corners, they asked Szell if he would agree to a one-season delay in the air-conditioning. Project engineers believed a cooling system wouldn't be effective anyway, because the ceiling over the pavilion would reach a height of 90 feet. The ductwork, nevertheless, was scheduled for installation, enabling air-conditioning units to be connected later if the first season showed that they were necessary. This saved $70,000, at least in the short term.

✿   ✿   ✿

Once ground was broken for Blossom on July 2, 1967, Szell and his staff could get down to the most important business—programming the center's first season and making plans for the school. These would prove to be complex and often puzzling endeavors. One conductor Szell hoped to secure for the opening festival was Leopold Stokowski, who was 85 and still active. "I am writing to you, the dean of the world's conductors, to extend a cordial invitation to participate in the inaugural season of this Festival," wrote Szell. "I would feel personally honored if you would consent to conduct one or two concerts next August." But Stokowski wouldn't. Aaron Copland would agree to conduct, but not to teach at the Blossom school. "As you can possibly imagine, my conducting plus composing activities in recent years have made it impossible for me to do any further teaching, even for short periods," Copland informed Szell. "When I resigned from Tanglewood in 1965, I really was resigning from all such academic connections. There just isn't time to do everything!"

The orchestra succeeded in signing more than a few celebrated artists for the inaugural season. The roster of conductors was set to include Copland, Karel Ančerl, Charles Münch (who would cancel and be replaced by Stanislaw Skrowaczewski), and William Steinberg, along with Lane and Robert Shaw. Few festivals could do better than Blossom's first list of soloists: pianists Van Cliburn, Rudolf Firkusny, Philippe Entremont, and Vladimir Ashkenazy; soprano Elisabeth Schwarzkopf; violinist Edith Peinemann (who considered Szell her mentor); and clarinetist Benny Goodman. The Blossom facility's flexibility would be tested by the New York City Ballet in works by founder George Balanchine and Jerome Robbins, accompanied by the Cleveland Orchestra in the pit.

As the inaugural season approached, Szell talked about the center with *The Plain Dealer*'s Robert Finn, who likened the opening of Blossom to the opening of Lincoln Center, which had not been completely finished when the first notes were sounded. "Ah, but we hope our acoustics will not be that bad," Szell retorted. He also hoped that audiences would understand the essentially conservative nature of his Blossom programming. "There are always people growing up who have never heard the standard pieces in live performance, in the flesh," said Szell. "No matter how often you have heard a Beethoven symphony by yourself in your living room, there is something unique about hearing it for the first time in communion with a lot of other people. The experience has a 'oneness,' and 'unrepeatability.' "

The Blossom Festival School was beginning to shape up both chorally and instrumentally. The choral institute the first season would be run by Clayton Krehbiel, the orchestra's director of choruses since 1967 as successor to Shaw, who had left to become music director of the Atlanta Symphony Orchestra. Sixty-nine graduate students were admitted to the choral program, including 16 on scholarship who would comprise a chamber chorus. The instrumental program would have about a dozen wind players, two dozen string players, and three pianists, who would attend on scholarship. So far, the collaboration between the orchestra and Kent State University was going beautifully. "[Every] time we have mentioned additional scholarships, the Kent people have just swallowed hard, dug down and come up with the money," said director Lane. "They have been marvelous about it."

Relations between the orchestra and Kent State would not always be so cordial, and the Blossom school would never have a campus next to the facility, but the program would thrive.

❁   ❁   ❁

Steels Corners Road in Northampton Township was a narrow thoroughfare when Blossom Music Center was about to open in 1968. The two-lane dirt road, which would have posed more than a little discomfort for concertgoers on their way to a gorgeous, if unfinished, summer facility, was resurfaced just in time for the first concert on July 19, though it wouldn't be widened until after the inaugural festival. Even so, Blossom had become a reality, a decades-long dream of the orchestra, and especially of its musicians, who finally—50 years after the ensemble's founding—could revel in full-year employment. The completion of Blossom sent signals that the orchestra didn't flinch from challenges and that the public was taking increased ownership of its renowned institution. By the time the summer home was ready to open, the board had received donations of more than $4 million for its Half-Century Fund, an amount qualifying the orchestra for the $2 million Ford Foundation grant. "The Cleveland Orchestra has a record of achieving what it sets out to do and, under George Szell, it has combined this with a dedication to the highest artistic standards," wrote Marsh in the *Chicago Sun-Times*.

Many listeners who had never before attended an orchestra concert would experience those standards, an important motivation for Szell in pushing the project. "The whole idea of the Blossom Festival is to give the greatest possible number of people the opportunity to hear the orchestra," he told the *Akron Beacon Journal*. Szell was in an expansive mood just before the opening: "I believe that Blossom Music Center will become, almost overnight, one of the important summer music festivals of the world," he said in a *Press* interview.

Overnight international success wouldn't happen, though reaction to Blossom generally was positive. Music critics from major American papers and magazines traveled to Northampton Township to assess the new summer home, including Harold C. Schonberg of the *New York Times*. His first report began on an ominous note reflecting a troubled era: "For a while it appeared that the inaugural concert of the Blossom Music Center, with the Cleveland Orchestra conducted by George Szell, would have to be cancelled. Two nights ago, there were race disturbances in nearby Akron, and Mayor John Ballard placed a curfew on the city. But tonight he modified the curfew so that Akron music lovers could drive to the festival. There they could pick up a pass to show to Akron police on the way back to town. The whole thing is rather frightening, but that is America this summer of 1968."

But the *Times* critic had nothing but praise for the Blossom pavilion itself, which some observers compared to a clamshell and others to a spaceship. Noting Peter van Dijk's studies with the eminent architect Eero Saarinen, Schonberg wrote "there is something of Saarinen in the soaring, daring steel arch that springs from the earth and, at an angle, encircles the entire building. It is an exciting building, and it went up in less than a year. Heinrich Keilholz, the acoustic consultant, came from Germany a few weeks ago, looked at what had happened since he had last been on the site, and threw up his hands in amazement. 'Only in America.' " Most importantly, the acoustician had created a superb outdoor facility for music. "Mr. Keilholz has done an impressive job in keeping the sound clear and detailed, and there is a strong bass response," wrote Schonberg, who may not have known at the time that Christopher Jaffe had done virtually all of the acoustical work. "Naturally the areas outside the pavilion have to be amplified. There are also interior loudspeakers [not used during the opening concert], governed by an operator at the rear of the hall." The outdoor sound system had taken some clever and tricky planning, since the blend of sound from the stage and sound from the speakers could have produced an echo effect on the lawn. The solution: an electronic delay system that synchronizes the distant sonic projections, even though eyes watching from the lawn perceive what appears to be an orchestra out of sync with its own sound.

Emily Blossom, who sat in the Blossom family box on opening night with her 86-year-old mother-in-law, Mrs. Dudley S. Blossom, may have best expressed the pervasive feeling of accomplishment when she stood before the orchestra during the opening ceremony to speak on behalf of her family. "Don't waste time while you're dreaming," she told the audience. "It is obvious no one did," responded Thomas Willis, music critic of the *Chicago Tribune*. "But more important still, no one took short cuts." Irving Kolodin put a Biblical spin on the phenomenon in the *Saturday Review*. "Perhaps only in the name of a family called Blossom could a wilderness, even when fertilized by $6,500,000, produce a major music center seating nearly 5,000 in a mere eleven months from ground-breaking to gala opening," he wrote. "Unlike Moses, whose objective was to lead his children out of the wilderness, it is the clear intent of Szell to lead his people, chosen and unchosen, into this now refined wilderness off Ohio's Route 8, 28 miles south of [Cleveland], and 10 miles northwest of Akron."

Cleveland papers were equally impressed. "The verdict on Blossom Music Center—or at least on its opening concert last night—is simplicity itself," Robert Finn remarked in a front-page story in *The Plain Dealer*. "The place is a visual, musical, acoustical and artistic triumph." The *Press*'s Frank Hruby described the occasion in mythical terms: "In one jump, the Cleveland Orchestra landed squarely among the world's major summer music festivals with none of the struggling tent-to-barn-to-platform warm-up business. Rather, it would compare to the birth of the full-grown Athena from the head of Zeus." The critics spent so much time rhapsodizing about Blossom's visual, acoustical, and civic triumphs that, perhaps naturally, they tended to place the inaugural concert's music-making in second place. Of 11 long paragraphs in the *New York Times*, only one (the last) mentions the performance, and then only the Beethoven Ninth Symphony featuring Phyllis Curtin, Jane Hobson, Ernst Haefliger, Thomas Paul, and the Cleveland Orchestra Chorus. "The music received a typical Szell interpretation—taut, tensile, logically shaped and powerful in its impact," Schonberg wrote. "One had expected no less."

An audiotape recorded from the concert's live color telecast on WKYC (Channel 3), "Blossom Center: Opening Night," confirms Schonberg's assessment of the Ninth. The same basic qualities he noted in the Ninth Symphony can be discerned in the program's opening work, Beethoven's *The Consecration of the House* overture, though the trumpets are miked so closely that they sound edgy. Even so, Szell's command of the idiom and of the orchestral resources results in a bold, probing performance. The Ninth's "Ode to Joy" causes the inevitable eruption from the audience, which invests the occasion with a special brand of adulatory intensity. The audience wasn't large on opening night (5,963), possibly a partial manifestation of the racial unrest in nearby Akron.

Szell conducted six concerts during the first Blossom season. He devoted the three concerts of his first weekend entirely to Beethoven, who, along with *The Consecration of the House* and the Ninth Symphony, was represented by the *Egmont* overture, third and fourth piano concertos (played by Rudolf Firkusny on consecutive evenings), and the Seventh Symphony. Szell concentrated solely on Brahms during the second concert of his second week, during which Edith Peinemann played the Violin Concerto. The two other concerts that weekend featured soprano Elisabeth Schwarzkopf: the first in Strauss songs and the Mahler Fourth Symphony (performed after Haydn's Symphony No. 93), and the second in three Mozart arias and Strauss's Four Last Songs (flanked by Mozart's "Jupiter" Symphony and Strauss's *Death and Transfiguration*).

Several non-orchestra events kept Blossom audiences happy the first season. Among the special attractions were trumpeter Herb Alpert and the

Tijuana Brass, who lured 13,600 people to Northampton Township, snarling traffic for three miles and creating a two-hour drive for some Cleveland listeners. Sitar player Ravi Shankar gave a concert, as did legendary jazz trumpeter Louis Armstrong. But orchestra lovers could also feast on beloved repertoire: Rachmaninoff's Second Piano Concerto, played by Van Cliburn; Rachmaninoff's Third Piano Concerto, with Vladimir Ashkenazy; Tchaikovsky's Symphony No. 5, under Skrowaczewski; Tchaikovsky's Piano Concerto No. 1, featuring Byron Janis; excerpts from Wagner music dramas, conducted by William Steinberg and sung by soprano Doris Jung and tenor Jon Vickers; Dvořák's Cello Concerto, with Pierre Fournier and led by Karel Ančerl; the Berlioz Requiem, under former associate conductor and director of choruses Robert Shaw; and Carl Orff's colorful cantata *Carmina Burana*, conducted by Lane.

One sound frequently heard at Blossom was not so welcome. Finn put it deftly in *The Plain Dealer*. "At least once during each concert at Blossom Music Center it happens: VA-ROOM! From somewhere backstage comes a loud, hollow crash, the sort of noise some giant door might make slamming in an echo chamber," he reported. "Listeners look at each other, puzzled. Conductors fume, inwardly because the bang always comes during a soft, slow passage. Those in charge at Blossom again vow to run the elusive noise to earth." The noise, it turned out, came from steel beams high in the pavilion that contracted when the night air turned cool. The "Blossom boom," as it came to be called, occurred twice a day when the pavilion ceiling heated and cooled. Pressure between small beams and large beams caused a buildup of pressure to 30,000 pounds, resulting in the noise. With changes in the composition of the sliding brackets between the beams, the sound was silenced by the 1971 Blossom season. Another problem with the pavilion during the first season was solved in an ingenious, if messy, way. The main beam of the roof tempted young people to climb on and frolic. Officials solved this dilemma by coating the beam with axle grease.

The end of the first Blossom season brought both good and bittersweet news, as well as fresh threats from Szell. Still obsessing about the air-conditioning, the conductor barraged Barksdale with harsh letters on the subject, claiming that the cooling system somehow could be made to work. It would have to. "Even if the term 'Airconditioning' cannot be taken in its orthodox meaning in such a space, a combination of exhaust and cooling or what-have-you is certainly thinkable and should be possible in the day and age of space-flight," Szell wrote from Salzburg. "I plan to explain to press and public my withdrawal from Blossom in a mutually agreed-upon release, and, if needs be, my own way."

On a cheerier note, the inaugural seven-week Blossom season attracted 191,175 concertgoers and netted earned income of $536,119. Although operating expenses of $878,417 resulted in an operating deficit of $342,298, the total included orchestra salaries ($247,875) and one-time opening expenses ($94,423). The center thus basically broke even its first season. Blossom-goers had attended 19 orchestra concerts, four ballet performances, and eight popular attractions. Most of the audience came from outside Cuyahoga County. Less than 4 percent came from outside Ohio. The success of the first season would lead to a 12-week season in 1969, along with a restaurant and a newly paved and widened Steels Corners Road.

Szell had told Harold Schonberg of the *New York Times* that he would "exercise complete artistic control" over Blossom. "He will select the guest conductors ('those I can trust') and soloists, scan the programs, 'keep an eye on the school.' " As he looked ahead, Szell suggested to Barksdale that Blossom embrace a more popular course, both in repertoire and guest artists, than the orchestra was inclined to offer at Severance Hall: "If I were you, I'd go—during the summer—brutally, but not indecently, for sure-fire-income and leave the riskier things for the winter-season—although there are financial hazards as well."

As one era began, another ended. Frank E. Joseph, who had succeeded in turning "Joseph's Folly" into a triumph, had decided to step down as the orchestra board's president—or up, actually, since he would take over the far less burdensome post of chairman. He would be succeeded by Alfred M. Rankin, another prominent Cleveland lawyer, who had been a trustee since 1948. In his final speech to the trustees as president, Joseph reflected on the orchestra's achievements and looked to the future without sidestepping reality. "Along with every other orchestra and, in fact, every other non-profit organization, inflation has caught up with us and we are in a financial bind that literally scares the daylights out of me," he said. "However, if I waited to make this move until the Cleveland Orchestra had no problems, I would have this job for the rest of my life. During these 12 years The Cleveland Orchestra has had hundreds of problems and hundreds of crises, and I have poured an inordinate amount of blood, sweat and tears into trying to overcome them. It hasn't been easy. However, I can honestly and truthfully say that I have gotten a lot more out of the job than I have put into it."

The creation of Blossom Music Center put an end to a dilemma that had plagued the orchestra for decades—the issue of year-round employment. In the process, it opened up a new world for thousands of concertgoers—many of them longtime orchestra lovers, others who had never (or would never) set foot in Severance Hall.

Musicians and
Miracles

B efore the opening of Blossom Music Center and the expansion of the summer season, the musicians of the Cleveland Orchestra struggled to achieve the salaries, pensions, and say in labor negotiations they believed they deserved. This discord was a major factor in the 37 personnel changes from 1965 to 1967—an enormous number for an ensemble hailed as one of the world's best. Still, pride in the institution and the ironclad work ethic established by George Szell kept standards lofty, even with a persistent undercurrent of grumbling about labor issues.

Some of the grumbling came from Szell. To avoid a strike that would have obliterated the orchestra's 1965 tour to the Soviet Union and Europe, he had relented slightly in his demand that he retain complete powers in matters of job security. Now, with that tour in the past, Szell reopened old wounds. "I am herewith giving notice of termination of our present agreement effective the end of the '66–'67 season. This I am doing merely to avoid becoming prisoner of a situation in which I could not work," Szell wrote to Frank E. Joseph. "To clarify my motives completely, let me say that I view with extreme alarm the continuing and growing tendency of the American orchestras to usurp the functions of musical director and management, in particular in the question of hiring and firing."

Szell wrote this biting letter on October 4, 1965, two days after he completed one of his most transcendent Cleveland recordings for Columbia— Mahler's Symphony No. 4, with soprano Judith Raskin as soloist. As usual, the recording was begun the morning after the first concert at which Szell led the work. The recording gives no hint of the tensions mounting at Severance Hall. Szell is the consummate classicist in this, the first of only two complete Mahler symphonies he recorded in Cleveland, the other being the Sixth in 1967. (Szell and the orchestra also recorded the first two movements of the unfinished Tenth Symphony in 1958.) To every phrase of the Fourth Symphony, Szell brings order and logic, as well as affection. The playing couldn't be warmer, and Raskin is ineffably poignant in the last movement. The performance still holds a firm place among the great Mahler Fourths in recording history.

It is also the first commercial recording featuring principal oboist John Mack, former principal of the National Symphony Orchestra in Washington, D.C. Mack arrived the week before the Mahler recording as successor to Adrian Gnam, whom Szell had deemed unsuited to be principal oboe after testing him for several months as acting co-principal in place of the fired Marc Lifschey. (Mack had been a candidate for principal oboe in 1959 when Lifschey was about to leave for the Metropolitan Opera.) Mack can be heard to wonderful effect in his very first concert with the orchestra on September 23, 1965, in Ravel's *Le tombeau de Couperin*, a performance preserved on the orchestra's 75th-Anniversary Compact Disc Edition. Over the years, the oboist discovered what he believed to be the key to Szell's remarkable sense of balance. "If you were a player who had a solo passage, Szell would direct his attention during that solo to you so single-mindedly that it was a rejection of the rest of the orchestra, and they psychologically accepted that, fell back, and let their concentration go toward you," Mack recalled. "It was as though the light had been turned on you and all other lights had been turned out."

Between the two subscription concerts the first week of the 1965–66 season, an important chapter closed in Cleveland Orchestra history. On September 24, Nikolai Sokoloff, the ensemble's founding conductor, died in La Jolla, California, at the age of 79. After leaving Cleveland, he had conducted the New York Orchestra (1933–35), organized and directed the Work Projects Administration's Federal Music Project (1935–38), served as music director of the Seattle Symphony (1938–40), and conducted summer concerts of the San Diego Symphony.

The concert of September 23, 1965, was not only Mack's debut with the orchestra but the first performance at Severance Hall taped and broadcast by WCLV, the Cleveland classical radio station (95.5 FM) that had been on the air since 1962. In March 1965, a month before the orchestra left for its 10-week tour to the Soviet Union and Europe, general manager A. Beverly Barksdale had asked WCLV if the station would like to broadcast its hometown orchestra. (It already was broadcasting the Philadelphia Orchestra and Boston Symphony.) With Cleveland's ensemble set to perform abroad, Barksdale told WCLV that it could begin a broadcast series using tapes collected from the tour. Once the orchestra returned, WCLV received help from Richard Kaye, an engineer at WCRB, a Boston classical music station that had been a pioneer in the industry. WCRB and the Boston Symphony had come up with an ingenious idea: they created a plan to divert all money from broadcast rentals to the orchestra's pension fund, thus avoiding the prohibitive expense of paying the musicians directly for their services. WCLV and the Cleveland Orchestra began their relationship by adopting the plan.

Kaye came to Cleveland in September 1965 to assist WCLV in placing microphones throughout Severance Hall. At Boston's Symphony Hall, WCRB used only two microphones, but Kaye found that Severance Hall needed up to eight. Robert Conrad, co-founder of WCLV, quickly realized that Szell was starting to lose the top end of his hearing. "He wanted more string sound" on the broadcast tapes, recalled Conrad, the "voice" of the Cleveland Orchestra broadcasts since 1965. "We decided he wasn't hearing the strings. It's a normal [problem] at that age." Then another dilemma cropped up: after the season's first program was taped, WCLV gave Szell a copy of the performances. At the orchestra's next rehearsal, the conductor made the mistake of telling the musicians that he had listened to the tape "and this is what I want to fix." As in 1956, when they complained about Szell listening to concert tapes every week, the musicians demanded that the conductor be given no more tapes to scrutinize.

The WCLV broadcasts, however, also brought the orchestra under the delighted scrutiny of listeners throughout the U.S. National distribution of the concerts began on October 31, 1965, when 80 stations paid $15 to $100 weekly to air the tapes. The syndication continued on the pension fund system until 1984, when Standard Oil of Ohio (later BP) picked up the sponsorship (about $1 million a year), the musicians were paid directly for broadcasts, and distribution jumped from 100 to almost 300 stations. When the price of oil dropped to $15 a barrel in 1992, BP dropped its exclusive sponsorship, which was taken up by a consortium of eight Cleveland corporations and later by *The Plain Dealer*, the Cleveland Clinic Foundation, and, to a lesser extent, BP.

✻   ✻   ✻

In the fall of 1965, Szell remained the consummate professional, despite his threat to step down if the labor situation affected his authority. He led seven subscription programs at Severance Hall before the end of the year, continuing to lean increasingly toward the symphonic works he adored and away from "temporary music" with performances of symphonies by Mozart, Beethoven, Schumann, and Sibelius. A pianistic dynasty arrived at Severance Hall in January 1966, when the teenaged Peter Serkin made his

Cleveland debut in Mozart's Piano Concerto No. 17 (the first of many appearances with the orchestra over the next four decades), and his father, Rudolf, was soloist the following week in Brahms's Second Piano Concerto, which he recorded with Szell and the ensemble amid the performances.

A week after the Brahms concerto was preserved by Columbia, Szell and his musicians recorded Bruckner's Third Symphony, a session described zestfully in the *Press*: "Violin players set up a betting pool ($12) on how many notes there were in the 1st Violin part. During recording lulls Kurt Loebel counted them and found 15,986 notes. Stephane Dalschaert won the pool of $11. He gave Loebel $1 for counting."

The orchestra's musicians now tended to view the Musical Arts Association as unusually unsympathetic. They had been lobbying for better wages and benefits, but they also wanted some respect, which they believed they were getting neither from the association nor from Local 4 (the Cleveland Federation of Musicians). Negotiations for the three-year contract in 1964 had stalled on the issue of salaries for the 1965 European tour, which, since partly scheduled after the winter season, management intended to budget under the less expensive summer contract. Management tried another questionable ploy in February 1966 as plans for the 1967 European festival tour were being rushed to completion. "Resolved, that the Orchestra membership express to management its strong resentment of the recent negotiating tactics," wrote hornist Martin Morris, secretary of the orchestra committee, to Barksdale. "The membership objects to the pressures exerted in order to secure the Orchestra's consent to a European tour with [only] four days notice and after presumably withholding information, which, had it been presented in reasonable time, would have afforded a fair chance for relaxed, thorough and unhurried discussion." Orchestra members were fuming the day Morris wrote his letter (February 5, 1966), when they voted to reject a new summer contract but accept terms for the proposed European festival tour in August 1967. The tour vote was hardly an endorsement—67 to 39—but at least the trip was saved. "This will be a grand tour," Barksdale told *The Plain Dealer*. "No other orchestra has ever gone to all three of the festivals in one swoop."

The Cleveland Orchestra had never received (nor ever would receive) much support for touring or any other endeavor from the city of Cleveland. Weeks after the orchestra agreed to the terms for the 1967 European tour, board president Joseph attempted to obtain $25,000 from City Hall. "In cities having major symphony orchestras, some form of municipal financial support is perhaps more the rule than the exception," he wrote to city council president James V. Stanton. "We are fully aware of the financial stringencies of the City of Cleveland and of the conflicting pressures and demands which are made upon available funds. We do, however, strongly feel, and we hope that the Council will agree, that the maintenance of our Orchestra at its present level of excellence is a major responsibility of all who are interested in the growth and welfare of this City." Every Cleveland administration for the rest of the century would be asked to fulfill its part of the responsibility. Few would respond positively.

✻ ✻ ✻

Most aspects of the orchestra's operations were proceeding splendidly in 1966. Following one of the ensemble's Carnegie Hall concerts in February, the *New York Herald Tribune*'s Alan Rich had only accolades for Szell's performances of works by Rossini, Mozart, and Bruckner. "Year by year, this annual visit comes to represent one of the truly important events in New York's orchestral season, a demonstration of orchestral playing, and of unity between conductor and instrument, that is unique among American ensembles," Rich wrote. "This is a wonderful city to live in (barring a few small matters here and there) but it is awfully nice to be a vicarious Clevelander for a few weeks every year. Godspeed, and a quick return, Mr. Szell!"

The orchestra returned to Cleveland to welcome a phenomenal 20-year-old Israeli violinist to Severance Hall—Itzhak Perlman, who made his debut in the Tchaikovsky concerto under Louis Lane. The following week, Szell and his musicians gave the Cleveland premiere of the massive, and quirky, Busoni Piano Concerto (with Pietro Scarpini as soloist), which they had performed the previous month at Carnegie Hall.

In March 1966, the orchestra announced the appointment of Michael Maxwell, promotion director and an assistant to the manager of the New York Philharmonic, as assistant manager. He would begin booking artists and making tour arrangements in July, when George P. Carmer, the orchestra's comptroller and assistant manager, would receive a new title, assistant general manager. A 30-year-old native of New Zealand, Maxwell had worked for the Philharmonia Orchestra of London (where he met Szell in 1961 when Cleveland's musical director was a guest conductor), managed the 1963 North American tour of the Royal Philharmonic, and served as manager of the Princeton Chamber Orchestra before going to the New York Philharmonic. Szell, an annual guest of the Philharmonic, invited Maxwell to join his orchestra's staff.

Controversy erupted weeks after Maxwell's appointment when the orchestra announced that 10 members would leave at the end of the season. The number, which would rise to 12, wasn't the big issue. The headline on a front-page *Plain Dealer* story stated that the musicians were departing because they were bored, a claim that prompted a flurry of letter writing by orchestra players. "Anyone reading the entire article could see that not one person of the 10 who are leaving is doing so because of monotony but because of other reasons—among which working conditions and salary are important factors," wrote assistant concertmaster Daniel Majeske. "The Cleveland Orchestra under George Szell has continuously proved itself to be the 'Rolls Royce of the world's orchestras.' It has done this at home and as far away as the Soviet Union as well as on records. But this excellence is not reflected in such practical things as pay and pension." The orchestras of Boston, Chicago, New York, and Philadelphia, asserted Majeske, were paying their musicians up to $3,000 more per year, and pensions were much higher. "A man presently retiring from the Cleveland Orchestra with 47 years' service receives a pension of $130.50 a month. If he has 25 years of service he receives $100 a month. My main purpose in making these things public is to point out that these are things that a man thinks about when he decides to leave an organization. The fact that the work is difficult is not minded when adequate compensation is given. The marvelous playing of our colleagues is not boring but facing a $100 a month pension is frightening these days."

The heightened intensity apparent in the orchestra's performance of Brahms's Fourth Symphony under Szell on Columbia Records may have something to do with the fact that the *Plain Dealer* story ran on April 9, 1966, the morning "an angry Cleveland Orchestra" assembled to complete the Brahms recording. "We state categorically that both the headline and the article itself were false and misleading. The esprit de corps, the high morale, the satisfaction with the growth and development of our orchestra—all these are shared by the membership to an uncommonly high degree," the orchestra committee wrote in a letter to the editor in *The Plain Dealer*. "As for the matter of boredom, which figures so sensationally in the headline, there are many attributes of symphonic playing. It is extremely exacting, often physically and emotionally tiring, sometimes nerve-wracking, but above all, stimulating, and, in the very nature of the work, basically pleasurable."

Soon the orchestra took a grueling spring tour to 12 Midwestern and Western states—27 concerts in 29 days, led by Szell, Lane, and conducting assistant Michael Charry. The orchestra committee let management know afterwards that the musicians had been displeased with the schedule, travel arrangements, and backstage facilities. Their complaints didn't affect their performances. "In the 20 years it has been under Szell's guidance it has always been one of the most superbly disciplined of all orchestras. It still is," wrote Albert Goldberg in the *Los Angeles Times*. "The ensemble is virtually flawless and the most minute detail invariably emerges with the ultimate degree of polish. Nothing is left to chance and the element of accident is reduced to an absolute minimum." At previous performances, Goldberg had detected a certain "coldness and rigidity about this mechanical perfection. The orchestra was a drillmaster's dream but it was not the musically responsive instrument it has now become."

In San Francisco, the *Examiner's* Alexander Fried recounted a conversation he'd once had with the conductor. "You can't be a 'good guy' and whip an orchestra into shape. It's a tough process," said Szell. "It isn't only a matter of adding an overlay of fine players. Everyone has to make a good sound. If you have only three weak violinists, their bad tone can spoil a whole section. Then every player has to grow. The fact of maturing—of getting better and better—plays a great role. Every player has to integrate himself in the orchestra's style, so that all respond to the conductor and to each other with absolute spontaneity."

Szell was not averse to allowing his orchestra to adapt to the style of a vastly different but worthy conductor. If he had been, he wouldn't have invited Herbert von Karajan, permanent conductor of the Berlin Philharmonic and director of the Salzburg Festival, to conduct the Cleveland Orchestra during its 1967 European festival tour. Nor would he have pursued Karajan to be a guest at Severance Hall in 1968. Szell and Karajan couldn't have been more diametrically opposed as musicians. Where Szell favored lucidity, crispness, and precision, Karajan focused on beauty of orchestral sound and smooth phrasing. Yet Szell admired Karajan, who was scheduled to conduct Metropolitan Opera performances of Wagner's *Die Walküre* in March 1968, when Szell hoped he would also come to Cleveland. This plan wouldn't work out, but Karajan did agree to conduct the Cleveland Orchestra in Europe in August 1967 in repertoire that was still in limbo as of June 1966. "RE his programs with the C.O. in Salzburg + Lucerne he sent word I should go ahead and schedule myself whatever I damn well please and he will work around it," Szell wrote to Barksdale.

Had it been up to certain factions in Cleveland, Karajan wouldn't have conducted the orchestra in Europe or anywhere else. The announcement of his engagement prompted an inflammatory article in the *Sun Press* headlined, "Hitler's Conductor to Lead Cleveland Orchestra." The unsigned story resorted to provocative prose. "Known currently by his friends and enemies alike as 'Herr Musik Diktator,' von Karajan joined the Nazi Party in 1935 when Adolf Hitler was bringing a heavy political hand to bear on German music. Von Karajan was 26. In order to take the post of opera director in Aachen, he became a Nazi." But Karajan's past opportunism did not change the fact that he was a superlative conductor. Szell, never prone to discussing politics in public, kept quiet on the subject. Discretion was urged by others as well. "One Cleveland musician, herself a Jew, said flatly that von Karajan was a great conductor and should not be the object of race neurosis," the *Sun Press* reported.

Weeks later, the issue had died down, and the orchestra was busy preparing for its 1966–67 season, another prelude to a European tour. "I must say that the almost embarrassingly fine reputation of this orchestra is something that exceeded what I expected 20 years ago. Not 10 years ago," Szell told the *Cleveland Press*. "Ten years ago I expected it. Why do I say embarrassing? Well, perhaps that is not a good word. It is embarrassing only in that it obligates you to keep up ever rising standards."

The ascent in artistic standards was perceived by management to have been accompanied recently by "a marked decline in standards of deportment and a corresponding rise in tardiness and absence among members of the orchestra," according to Barksdale in a letter to the musicians. The orchestra's trade agreement still allowed fines—"liquidated damages," as the language read—to be imposed on players deemed guilty of such infractions. The money went into the pension fund. The issue infuriated the players, who would fight to have the offending paragraphs stricken from their contract.

The day before the opening of the 1966–67 season, Szell and his musicians taped a documentary for the *Bell Telephone Hour*. A dress rehearsal, with family and friends serving as the audience, stood in for a performance. "This could be of great help locally in the big fund raising campaign we have ahead of us," Barksdale informed the orchestra. But the NBC program, whose grandiose title, "The Cleveland Orchestra: One Man's Triumph," suggested that Szell alone had brought about the ensemble's success, turned out to be an embarrassment. It showed an atypically benevolent Szell in genial rehearsals with his orchestra and coaching sessions with his staff conductors. Szell's conversation with an uncomfortable Lane couldn't be less spontaneous. The atmosphere is sycophantic; Szell comes off as a grandfatherly icon. The orchestra itself gets short shrift. Months after the program aired, the musicians still hadn't been paid for the overtime the filming had necessitated.

❧ ❧ ❧

Despite consistently remarkable artistic achievements, the orchestra was entering a period of unprecedented uncertainty. With plans for Blossom Music Center moving forward, the Musical Arts Association had to raise enormous sums of money. The orchestra had not conducted a major capital campaign since its endowment was established and Severance Hall was built in the early 1930s. And the board faced a familiar challenge: the Cleveland Federation of Musicians still would not permit the players to be represented by their own lawyer in labor negotiations. Union officials insisted that they negotiate directly with orchestra management, without input from the musicians or outside legal counsel. In January 1967, board member Joseph E. Adams reported to trustees that "the atmosphere is bleak and that the Orchestra Committee continues to shun meetings between Union and Management representatives."

Szell and the orchestra largely kept their heads amid the furor brewing during the 1966–67 season. They performed the year's biggest work in early February—Beethoven's *Missa Solemnis*, which soared and thundered in Szell's commanding account featuring soprano Saramae Endich, contralto Florence Kopleff, tenor Ernst Haefliger, bass Ezio Flagello, and the Cleveland Orchestra Chorus, in one of its final assignments with director of choruses and associate conductor Shaw before his departure to become music director of the Atlanta Symphony. This interpretation is one of the gems included in the orchestra's Szell Centennial Compact Disc Edition. When these forces took the *Missa Solemnis* to Carnegie Hall three months after the Cleveland concerts, the *New York Times* employed no restraint: "One must go back to Toscanini for this kind of 'Missa Solemnis.' "

The reference to Toscanini was timely: the world had just begun marking the centennial of the conductor's birth. Szell wrote an appreciation of his mentor for *Time* magazine that appeared in the issue of March 27, 1967, the day of the 100th anniversary. In striking ways, Szell's performance of the *Missa Solemnis* mirrors the qualities he noted when he heard Toscanini conduct the New York Philharmonic in Prague in 1930.

Szell's ardor could get the best of him. While rehearsing the *Missa Solemnis* in Cleveland, he railed so vehemently at the musicians that they walked off the stage and sat in main floor seats in protest while Szell stood backstage with arms defiantly crossed. "There was a cough. A seat creaked. The clock ticked," reported a wire story. "After a half hour Szell walked out and said, 'It was nothing personal.' " The rehearsal continued without further incident. Two days later, Szell received a mild reprimand from musicians' union president Anthony A. Granata: "As a great conductor, you are entitled to the utmost respect from your musicians. As artists and human beings, they in turn are worthy of your highest consideration."

Granata wouldn't always live up to his own words. As negotiating sessions with management for a new orchestra contract continued in the spring of 1967, he remained steadfast in his refusal to allow the musicians' lawyer, Bernard A. Berkman, to present a contract proposal. Cellist Warren Downs, chairman of the orchestra committee, tried to put the ludicrous situation in perspective in a letter to management. "A businessman who did not have legal counsel in a complex contract would be considered a fool," Downs wrote. "Why should musicians with little or no business experience be looked upon with suspicion because they wish similar expert advice?" Curiously, the union had agreed to let the orchestra hire Berkman the previous summer but in November barred him from negotiating sessions. Even when 98 of the 110 musicians signed a petition asking that the union change its mind, officials turned a deaf ear, evidently determined to retain power. Now the orchestra realized it might have to go out on strike for the first time in its history. The fallout was already starting: by spring, 11 musicians told management that they intended to leave at the end of the season. The number would rise to 14.

A solution to the contract fracas appeared to arrive on May 10, the day before the first of the orchestra's final performances of the season. The *Press* reported that the board's Joseph E. Adams had presented the musicians with a five-year contract that would increase their agreement to 52 weeks and make Cleveland "the highest paid of any orchestra in the United States." The new contract would raise the annual minimum from $11,700 (for the 1967–68 season) to $14,300 (for the 1971–72 season). The minimum weekly salary would go from the current $190 to $275 in the fifth year. Union president Granata hailed the contract. Berkman, the orchestra's lawyer, said the proposal showed "callous disregard for minimal standards of decent employer-employee relations." The contract "bears little resemblance to the extravagant [claims] made for it by management and the union, in their joint effort to sell the package to orchestra members," Berkman told *The Plain Dealer*. Furthermore, management's statement that the orchestra would become the country's highest paid was untrue, the lawyer continued, noting that the Metropolitan Opera Orchestra was guaranteeing its musicians at least $335 a week. The members of the Cleveland Orchestra "are not seeking as high wage rates as the plumbers have recently received," said

Berkman. "But they feel they are entitled to live decently, provide for their families and their old age, and have dignity and respect on the job. As the finest symphony orchestra in the world and as substantial contributors to the cultural enrichment of Greater Cleveland and the nation, they are entitled to no less."

Once Berkman spoke, the orchestra acted. The musicians rejected the contract offer by a vote of 78 to 18, portending cancellation of the Lake Erie Opera Theater's two-week season in September, as well as threatening an important milestone. "We hope last night's massive strike vote will induce a re-examination of management's attitude," Berkman told the *Press*. "Otherwise next season's 50th anniversary of the orchestra will be celebrated by the sound of silence." The European tour in August was not in jeopardy, because it fell under a separate contract. Bain Murray spelled out more aspects of the labor situation in the *Sun Press*, revealing that members of the Boston Symphony received $5,000 a year in pension, whereas Cleveland musicians received about $1,400. Berkman told Murray that the orchestra had no grievance procedure, which was standard elsewhere. "Under the present contract, management can fire a man if he misses two services (rehearsals, etc.) or concerts for whatever reason, if, in the conductor's opinion, his excuses are invalid," Murray wrote. "Hence, the orchestra feels that job security and seniority benefits are nil."

The board, meanwhile, was struggling to come up with any solution to the contract debacle. Adams told the trustees that the matter revolved around the association's right to run the orchestra. He suggested that the issue wouldn't be resolved with the current orchestra committee and lawyer in power. Association treasurer Alfred M. Rankin wondered if the musicians would be able to find other orchestral positions if they decided to depart now. Barksdale told him there was no such likelihood.

With no negotiations scheduled, the orchestra played its pops season, and Barksdale continued putting the finishing touches on plans for the European tour. He also began making inquiries for another foreign trip proposed for 1970, the orchestra's first visit to Japan. Szell, who had turned 70 on June 7, advised Barksdale in early July that the new tour might work out fine: "May 70 for Japan is okay with me—if we are still alive + working . . ." In mid-July, the union and orchestra management tried to resuscitate contract talks. Granata said he had received new contract demands from the players, and he would invite the five-member orchestra committee, but not their lawyer, to a bargaining session. Announcing resumption of the talks, the *Press* stated, "the orchestra will strike Sept. 4 unless a settlement can be reached."

✼   ✼   ✼

August brought a brief hiatus from labor negotiations, allowing the orchestra and its conductor to concentrate on music-making. In early August, Szell entered a New York studio to make his first recording as a pianist in almost two decades. Before the advent of the long-playing record in 1948, he had recorded Mozart chamber works with the Budapest String Quartet and violin sonatas with Joseph Szigeti for Columbia. Now the company convinced him to record Mozart sonatas with his concertmaster, Rafael Druian. As usual, Szell remained intensely self-critical. When Columbia engineer Paul Myers told him, "it's so good," Szell couldn't muster similar enthusiasm. "It's all right," he answered.

Then it was back to Cleveland to rehearse the orchestra for the Salzburg, Edinburgh, and Lucerne festivals, where Szell and his musicians were scheduled to give 11 concerts and perform 20 works. *Chicago Sun-Times* critic Robert C. Marsh, whose book about the orchestra was about to be published, attended a rehearsal at Severance Hall and captured Szell calling his players to musical arms. In each city "we shall find the international audience assembled and waiting for us," Szell said. "I don't mind telling you that the reputation we have in Europe is such that they expect miracles, but I am fully confident that we can provide the kind of performances these audiences should receive."

Szell's confidence, as usual, was well founded. After the orchestra's first Salzburg program on August 13, "audiences cheered and critics lyricized," reported *The Plain Dealer*. The music critic of *Die Kurier*, from Vienna, said Beethoven's "Eroica" received "a fascinating performance." Two nights later, Szell conducted a Brahms-Mozart-Ravel program that elicited a rave review in Vienna's *Die Presse* bearing the headline, "Precision and Virtuosity."

But the most anticipated Salzburg concert was the third. In Szell's place stood Herbert von Karajan, director of the festival and "music director of Europe," who had three rehearsals with the orchestra and appeared in two different capacities at the performance. On the program's first half, he conducted while playing third piano in Mozart's Concerto in C major for Three Pianos, with Jörg Demus and Christoph Eschenbach as colleagues. It was his first public keyboard performance in years. "I just decided to try my comeback as a pianist with the Cleveland Orchestra because of my admiration for the American musicians," said Karajan.

After intermission, he put his individual stamp on Prokofiev's Fifth Symphony. Karajan's approach surprised no one more than Szell. "In the interval of the rehearsal he came and said he was suffering from nervous shock because the moment I started he realized that I was doing exactly the contrary of all the things he had taught the orchestra," Karajan said years later. "It seemed like a complete breakdown; but after a few minutes they were playing as if they had always played this way." Szell endeared himself to Karajan. "Half an hour before the first orchestra rehearsal was due to start in Salzburg, he invited me to talk to him," Karajan recalled. "We chatted about trivialities. Only later did I realize that, having trained his orchestra to be extremely punctual, he wanted to be sure that I would make a good, punctual impression on them. And immediately before the concert he called the cello section of the orchestra to a special rehearsal which I really wouldn't have considered necessary, but he wanted his players to make the very best impression on me."

Karajan and the Cleveland musicians also made a favorable impression on listeners. "The Salzburg audience has been looking forward to attending the rare combination of master Karajan and the computer-like perfectionists from Cleveland," reported *Die Kurier*. "At the end, the enthralled crowd made no secret of its enthusiasm. It was a perfect interpretation and a great experience." Nevertheless, the orchestra found working with Karajan somewhat weird. According to Louis Lane, the musicians contemplated playing a merry prank on the lofty Austrian conductor: "Karajan liked to conduct with his eyes closed. And [the players] wanted to make a bet . . . after the first movement of the Prokofiev Fifth they would all quietly disappear and [see] whether he would notice—on the downbeat there would be nobody there!" They didn't follow through with their conspiracy, and the evening was a triumph.

The next stop on the 1967 itinerary was Edinburgh. The ensemble made its debut at Usher Hall with four concerts—two featuring pianist Clifford Curzon (in Mozart's Piano Concerto No. 24 and Beethoven's "Emperor") and one with violinist Leonid Kogan (Beethoven's Romance and Mozart's A major Violin Concerto). Keith Nichols, a British trombonist in town to play at the festival with another orchestra, initially told a reporter that he was skeptical of Cleveland's reputation. "Really, now, no orchestra can be that good," he said. By concert's end, he had changed his tune: "Incredible, just incredible. I've never heard such tonal balance . . . just fantastic."

For the first time on the tour, however, the critical reception was mixed. David Cairns, writing in the *Financial Times*, was swept away, mostly by the ensemble: "What an orchestra it is! Is there any other that combines to such a degree force and delicacy, extreme homogeneity and individuality, freedom of artistic expression? They play wonderfully together yet with hardly a trace of regimentation. Every player seems aware of every other player yet remains an individual. There is smoothness without facelessness, brilliance without asperity; nothing overemphasised, and everything alive." In the *Guardian*, Neville Cardus wrote the first of several laudatory reviews of the Edinburgh engagement. "During the third suite of Bach the string playing of the celestial air was not of this world," he noted. "If, after passing out, any of us should awaken to hear such strains, we shall at once know that, after all, we have arrived at the right place."

Noel Goodwin, writing in the *Scottish Daily Express*, dissented, calling the performance "a very run of the mill concert to begin an international festival." He didn't like the programming, Szell's Bach, or even his Mozart, whose "emotional temperature stayed well below blood-heat for most of its course." Another critic, Eric Mason in the *Scottish Daily Mail*, described the orchestra's Edinburgh programming as "disappointingly unadventurous," though he said, "it would be churlish not to salute the high quality of the performances George Szell and his players gave last night." Among the champions of the orchestra's third program was Conrad Wilson, in *The Scotsman*, who wrote that the orchestra "began with a performance of 'Don Juan' so magnificent, so pulsating in its vitality and ravishing in its beauty that for several minutes during the rest of the programme one found oneself neither knowing nor caring what was being played."

Cardus topped all of his colleagues with one review "that I cannot read without blushing," Szell later said. Even the distinguished critic-musicologist knew he might be treading on hyperbolic turf when assessing the "Eroica" as performed by Szell and company. "Here I must call on the muse of caution, less I become adjectivally indiscreet. Not since Toscanini have I heard this greatest of all symphonies explored and unfolded with so much power of dramatic illumination, with so firm and comprehensive a vision," wrote Cardus. "The full strength and scope of the Cleveland Orchestra actually expanded a canvas, the horizon, and the great sky of the symphony, storm, wreck, clouds, the heavenly vistas and all. I can make no bigger compliment to Szell and his orchestra than this—that this interpretation more than ever brought home the incredible genius of the Eroica, the terrific voltage of it, the inexhaustible musical thinking in it, the immeasurable human compass of it."

With their Edinburgh concerts done, Szell and the orchestra headed to the Lucerne festival, but not before making a stop in London to record works by Mozart and Beethoven for Columbia at the EMI Abbey Road studios, the company's principal recording site since the 1930s (and also the place where the Beatles made some of their most famous albums). The repertoire during the single recording session included Beethoven's *Fidelio* and *Leonore* No. 1 overtures, and Mozart's Symphony No. 40. Paul Myers, the British-born engineer who produced the orchestra's recordings in Cleveland, was on hand for the session. According to *Gramophone* magazine, Cleveland became the first major American orchestra to record in Britain.

The Mozart symphony figured in the first of the orchestra's three Lucerne programs under Szell. Then Karajan was back on the podium for the tour's swan song, a repeat of the Salzburg program. He told the Associated Press that Cleveland was "indisputably the best of all American orchestras."

❊   ❊   ❊

It was more than likely, however, that Cleveland's was not the happiest of all American orchestras. The tour's artistic accomplishments did not quell the musicians' dissatisfaction over their contract. The orchestra committee spent part of the tour drafting a letter to subscribers detailing the ensemble's fractious history of labor relations and praising the Musical Arts Association for its "tremendous fund-raising efforts." The letter warned subscribers that they might not hear any music at Severance Hall at the start of the 1967–68 season: "It is therefore with the deepest regret and sadness that we note that unless significant progress is made in the next few weeks to break the deadlock in negotiations which currently exists, we will have no reasonable alternative but to lay down our instruments and refuse to respond to Mr. Szell's opening downbeat next season."

Orchestra trustee Joseph Adams once again placed the onus on the musicians, saying that the Musical Arts Association had been trying to negotiate for months, to no avail. "We earnestly hope that, when the orchestra returns Friday from its triumphs in Europe, common sense will prevail and representatives of the orchestra will participate in discussions of the contract," he said. But the harsh reality of the situation was expressed by an orchestra member at the end of the tour. "We played at our best and nearly surpassed ourselves. This was our last concert. We are now on strike."

The strike began on September 11, the day the old contract expired. "The orchestra members are seeking a $300 weekly minimum wage, a better pension plan, improved overtime provisions, a sick-leave program and other fringe benefits," reported the *New York Times* that day. The story added an ominous forecast: "Many people here believe that if the orchestra does not begin its season as scheduled, Mr. Szell will either guest conduct in the United States or Europe, or even accept another conducting post."

Rebuffed again by union and management, the orchestra committee drafted a second letter to subscribers describing what they believed to be cavalier treatment. "Why were we not kept informed of events during the progress of these 36 hard-fought (but secret) bargaining table battles?" stated the letter. "Why this desperate attempt from the other side of the table to rehabilitate the union as our champion?" The orchestra decided it was time to go straight to the public with a handout detailing their grievances: no legal representation, lower pay than many other major orchestras, no guaranteed sick leave, no seniority rights, paltry pension, more weekly concerts and rehearsals than the other major orchestras.

It was too late. On September 17, their union squeezed through a new three-year contract by accepting an orchestra vote of 50 in favor and 42 against on the basis of majority rule, despite the fact that a 1963 union bylaw stated that an affirmative vote must account for at least 60 percent of the players. The strike had lasted seven days. The new contract raised minimum weekly salaries from $190 to $225 for the 1967–68 season, $240 for 1968–69, and $255 for 1969–70. A 52-week season was guaranteed for the first time, thanks largely to the creation of Blossom Music Center. The contract included other improvements, some of them meager, in pensions, medical coverage, life insurance, travel pay, vacations, and holidays. Orchestra committee member Warren Downs told *The Plain Dealer* that the union had changed the bylaw illegally to push the contract through. Berkman announced that the orchestra had "instructed me to institute legal action on their behalf to set aside the vote."

While Berkman did so, the orchestra's 1967–68 season went on as planned, with 14 new players in the ensemble, including one, tuba player Ronald Bishop, whom Szell had plucked from the San Francisco Symphony. Bishop's hiring led to tuba problems in San Francisco when the union told management it had to hire a local player. The orchestra countered that there were no first-class tubists in the San Francisco area. Finally, the union relented and the orchestra hired Chester Roberts, who had just ended his 17-year tenure with . . . the Cleveland Orchestra. Also during this period, two Cleveland musicians were promoted—Daniel Majeske to associate concertmaster and James Levine to assistant conductor.

Szell was scheduled to conduct 35 of the season's 64 subscription performances, with help from Lane, Shaw, Pierre Boulez, and Claudio Abbado, and then follow his European vacation with six concerts during the inaugural season of Blossom Music Center. On October 6, 1967, music lovers could choose between two great international orchestras: Cleveland, under Szell, playing works by Piston, Glazunov, Delius, and Dvořák at Severance Hall;

and the Vienna Philharmonic, led by Karl Böhm, performing the Beethoven sixth and Brahms first symphonies at Public Hall.

The day after these concerts, 62 members of the Cleveland Orchestra asked the common pleas court to void their new contract. Even more interesting news hit Cleveland the next day: Szell was being named senior guest conductor and musical advisor of the New York Philharmonic starting with the 1969–70 season. The appointment would not affect Szell's Cleveland activities, since he would guest conduct in New York during periods he had previously devoted to Europe. But the Philharmonic had initially offered Szell the post of musical director as successor to Leonard Bernstein, who would have welcomed the move:

> I can't tell you how pleased I am at the news that you have accepted to guide the fortunes of my orchestra after I depart. My heart is filled with relief to know that these musicians will be safe in your masterly hands, and with gratitude to you for agreeing. I only wish (and have wished from the beginning, and had so advised the Philharmonic management) that you could have accepted the full directorship; but of course I understand very well your deep commitments in Cleveland. In any case, I am joyful, and send you my warmest affection and thanks. You are the only man I have ever believed right for this moment in Philharmonic history.

Even at this anxious moment, the future looked bright for the Cleveland Orchestra. The musicians had finally secured year-round employment. The Musical Arts Association could proceed with plans to open Blossom Music Center in July 1968. Szell was staying. And Pierre Boulez was developing a closer bond with the Cleveland Orchestra. The French conductor-composer, who had turned down a permanent guest spot with the New York Philharmonic, would accept a similar offer as guest conductor in Cleveland through the 1971–72 season, leading to speculation that he was being groomed to be Szell's successor. "No other kind of long-range commitment has been made to him, or even discussed," Barksdale said in March 1968. "I want to stress that." (Boulez later confirmed that he never had talks with Cleveland officials about becoming the orchestra's music director.) Yet Boulez was becoming a frequent presence by 1967. While Szell was conducting in Europe in November, Boulez led three weeks of programs comprising works by Schubert, Debussy, Stravinsky, Haydn, Berlioz, Handel, Berg, and Beethoven. "Everything is going extremely well with Boulez," Barksdale informed Szell. "I have spoken with a number of men who tell me that they enjoy working with him very much. Certainly the audiences have been enthusiastic. He said he is enjoying his stay and continually marvels at the quality of the Orchestra."

The orchestra was destined to be in pristine condition when Boulez arrived for his concerts in the fall of 1967. Szell had just spent a month maintaining his ensemble's exceptional standards, which can be heard in a work captured in a Columbia recording in October—Mahler's Symphony No. 6. Remarkably, this was the first time the orchestra ever played the symphony, though that is not apparent in Szell's intensely dramatic, expressive, and detailed performance. The Sixth marked the orchestra's final commercial Mahler recording.

While in town in November 1967, Boulez made his first recordings with the orchestra for Columbia: Debussy's *Danses sacrée et profane*, with harpist Alice Chalifoux as soloist, and *Images pour orchestre*. The same week, management announced that the ensemble would give its debut performances in Japan in May 1970, including five concerts at the International Exposition in Osaka as the United States's principal cultural representative, one in Nagoya, and five in Tokyo. Szell would lead nine of the concerts. The remaining two, according to the *Press*, would be led by a guest conductor to be named.

Despite the important recordings for Columbia from this period, the orchestra's relations with the company were on the decline. Cleveland's three-year contract with Columbia had expired at the end of September 1967 and only been extended for two years. Columbia had slashed its guarantee of 16 sides per year to 5. Barksdale urged Szell to take up these and other issues with Columbia's Goddard Lieberson. "How is it possible that this could be done to an organization which has been hailed in America and abroad as one of the greatest orchestras in the world?" Barksdale demanded in a letter to Szell. "Does he have any idea what effect this has on the morale of the Orchestra? How can you explain this to the Orchestra and to the supporting organization in Cleveland? Despite the guarantees of equal promotion and everything else in the most recent contract, Cleveland has continued to run a very poor third to Philadelphia and New York."

This was one reason why Barksdale asked Columbia to allow Cleveland to make recordings for EMI, which was pursuing Szell to record the five Beethoven piano concertos later in the 1967–68 season with Emil Gilels. "It is in behalf of the musicians that we request your permission for EMI to hold these sessions," Barksdale wrote to Clive Davis at CBS Records. "Surely, in the light of the pitifully small recording we have from CBS, this is not an unreasonable request. It would be logical for EMI to do this since they issue most of our recordings abroad." Permission was granted. The recording sessions with Gilels on April 29 and 30, and May 1 and 4, 1968—not preceded by public performances—would be the orchestra's first for Angel Records, the American subsidiary of EMI.

Gilels wasn't the only eminent Soviet artist who came to Cleveland that season. In December 1967, David Oistrakh performed double duty at Severance Hall. He appeared as soloist in the Brahms Violin Concerto under Szell, and then made his American conducting debut leading Shostakovich's Tenth Symphony. Szell initially had been reluctant to let Oistrakh conduct this work. "SHOSTAKOVICH TENTH LONG CRAP MAY REQUIRE REHEARSAL OVERTIME BUT AGREE IF FEASIBLE REGARDS SZELL," he wired. Oistrakh was to figure prominently in EMI recording plans in Cleveland. Angel Records proposed that Szell consider collaborating with Oistrakh in recordings of the Brahms Violin Concerto and Double Concerto (with cellist Mstislav Rostropovich), both of which were made, as well as two that were not: Beethoven's Violin Concerto and Triple Concerto, with Rostropovich and pianist Sviatoslav Richter.

Although Szell never got around to recording the Verdi Requiem, which EMI had hoped he would, he did conduct it several times during his Cleveland tenure, including performances in February 1968 at Severance and Carnegie halls with his orchestra and chorus (now prepared by Clayton Krehbiel) and a vibrant vocal quartet composed of soprano Gabriella Tucci, alto Janet Baker, tenor Pierre Duval, and bass Martti Talvela. "George Szell conducted the Cleveland Orchestra in the Verdi Requiem last night in Carnegie Hall, and better performances do not come around," said the *New York Times*. "Not since Toscanini has there been equivalent power and passion, line and control, in this great piece of music. Drama was there, but also shape. Every marking in the score was observed, but there was not the slightest feeling of pedantry. Mr. Szell was at his peak last night."

✿   ✿   ✿

Szell was also forceful coming to James Levine's defense in April when the Selective Service Board in Cincinnati reclassified the young assistant conductor as 1-A. Cleveland needed Levine, Szell advised the board, to conduct educational concerts, play piano in the orchestra, and "be prepared at all times to substitute for a scheduled conductor in the event of an emergency, and he had to do this on March 7, 8 and 9, when a guest conductor was ill. In addition, he is an excellent pianist and is frequently needed to play in the Orchestra. In past letters addressed to you, I have indicated that he would be difficult to replace. This is even more so today with the expanded number of concerts, a longer playing season and his growing responsibilities. I continually look for new talent and have found no one who could adequately replace him." Levine was not drafted.

Szell's continual search had turned up at least one new talent, though not as a prospective assistant. For a guest-conducting stint in Cleveland he was considering a European-based American who had last led the ensemble in summer pops concerts in 1952: Lorin Maazel, music director of the Deutsche Oper Berlin. Maazel attended the Cleveland Orchestra's concert in Philadelphia in February 1968, when he visited Szell after the performance and was reunited with Michael Maxwell, whom he had known from guest conducting stints with the Philharmonia Orchestra of London. Two months after the Philadelphia meeting, Maazel was having no success finding a period that was mutually agreeable to himself and the Cleveland Orchestra for a guest engagement. "This seems to be the case of the 2 herons in the classic Russian fable who would not mate, because they were never in the mood for marriage at the same time," Maazel wrote to Szell from Berlin, adding, in a handwritten postscript, "Perhaps we can give the fable a happy ending—!" Szell answered in kind: "I share your wish to give the fable a happy ending and shall examine what can be done in the foreseeable future."

But the foreseeable future for Szell was shorter than he knew. He would not have the opportunity to bring Maazel to Cleveland, at least not directly. The fable would indeed have its ending—perhaps happy, perhaps otherwise. It was just not an ending that either party could have predicted.

Departure

*F*or the first two decades of his tenure as musical director and conductor of the Cleveland Orchestra, George Szell signed three- or four-year contracts with the Musical Arts Association. These agreements suggested that he felt confident about renewing the relationship for an extended period. Then, in 1965, Szell sent a subtle signal that he had begun to become aware of his own mortality: he signed only a two-year contract (for the 1965–66 and 1966–67 seasons) and decided to negotiate subsequent contracts on a season-to-season basis. This awareness is also clear from language added to the 1965 contract: "Should death intervene at any time during the period of your active service or during service thereafter in an advisory and consultative capacity, the Association will immediately pay Helene Szell, if then living, the sum of Five Thousand Dollars."

Szell's skills as a negotiator in the mid-1960s were as keen as they had been in 1946, when he achieved all of his initial contractual demands. Now, in 1968, he had amassed a healthy retirement fund ($157,050) provided by the Musical Arts Association and settled upon annual salaries that would make his future even more comfortable ($82,500 for the 1968–69 season; $100,000 for the 1969–70 season).

He had reason to be at least somewhat content. By 1968, after the opening season of Blossom Music Center, the orchestra appeared to have settled into a period of relative calm. The musicians finally were employed 52 weeks a year, and the added stability prompted fewer departures than in recent times. Artistically, Szell and his ensemble enjoyed a reputation on a par with the two finest European orchestras, the Berlin and Vienna philharmonics, partly as a result of their 1967 tour to the Salzburg, Edinburgh, and Lucerne festivals.

Even so, worrisome issues continued to beset the Cleveland Orchestra in 1968. The players remained skeptical of management—and of their own union for pushing through the 1967 contract against the wishes of almost half of the musicians. The ensemble's recording activity with Columbia was waning, which would mean less income, and audiences at Severance Hall were diminishing as inflation was rising.

One aspect of Cleveland Orchestra life would remain constant, however: amid the changes and challenges, Szell and his musicians never allowed discipline or standards to waver. "If there has to be chaos," Szell said, "it must be organized chaos."

Stepping into the fray to help the orchestra face these challenges was Alfred M. Rankin, who succeeded Frank E. Joseph as president of the Musical Arts Association in October 1968. Like Joseph and one of his predecessors, Thomas L. Sidlo, Rankin was a skilled lawyer and music lover who knew how to handle thorny business issues but relied heavily on others—the general manager, mainly—for artistic advice. Rankin took the reins just as the 52-week contract, Blossom, and America's economy were starting to send orchestra finances out of control. Even more troublesome, relations among management and the musicians continued to unravel. A study commissioned from McKinsey & Company, a management consulting firm, suggested organizational changes to bring these parties closer. As a result, new responsibilities were assigned to Michael Maxwell, who was given the title of assistant manager-orchestra affairs. He was to handle all aspects of the musicians' contracts. Maxwell's added responsibilities were leading him somewhere, though no one knew quite where at this point.

✶   ✶   ✶

Columbia Records was winding down more than three decades of activity with the orchestra, whose recordings had not proved as lucrative as Columbia releases by the New York Philharmonic and Philadelphia Orchestra. In the fall of 1968, Columbia agreed to record a mere 10 sides per year (for a two-year period) in Cleveland—six with Szell and four with Louis Lane or a guest conductor. Despite its flagging interest, the company came to town in October 1968 and recorded several superb performances. Szell's special handling of Classical repertoire is evident in crystal-clear accounts of Haydn's Symphony No. 96 ("Miracle") and Mozart's *Eine kleine Nachtmusik* and piano concertos nos. 15 and 17 with Robert Casadesus as soloist. On a grander note, there is Wagner, a composer Szell treated without the layers of sonic cholesterol many conductors apply to this music. Szell's 1956 Epic recording of excerpts from Wagner's *Ring* cycle was refined and powerful, but it was recorded in mono. The 1968 Columbia version, in stereo, reveals far more nuances and shadings. The orchestra wasn't necessarily better in 1968 than in 1956, but the recording technology helped bring out qualities that previously couldn't have emerged.

With Szell away for performances in Europe in late October and November 1968, Cleveland heard the debut of a maestro who immediately enjoyed the orchestra's approval—and who seemed to stand out as a conductor with a future in town: Hungarian conductor István Kertész introduced himself in performances of Mahler's Symphony No. 2 ("Resurrection"). Although he was out of town, Szell wasn't ignoring matters in Cleveland. Reacting to a story in the November 15, 1968, issue of *Time* magazine about dress codes for bank tellers, he fired off a note to general manager A. Beverly Barksdale. Scribbling on an advertisement next to the story, he decried the possibility of miniskirts on Severance Hall personnel. "If I see a single one on my return, there will be a scandal; I shall be insulting to the utmost of my ability," Szell wrote. "If you have no sense of propriety or no guts to enforce it, others must press you. I, for one, am nauseated by what I have sometimes to see.—G.S." And, in a postscript: "They can go half naked during their own time if they so desire, but at work, in the hall, they must made to conform with certain standards of appearance!!!"

Soon after New Year's 1969, Szell conducted Brahms's *Tragic Overture* in memory of Arthur Loesser, the local pianist, teacher, author, and critic who had just died at age 74, and also recorded more works for Columbia, among them Haydn's Symphony No. 95, and Prokofiev's *Lieutenant Kijé* suite. These works were part of another program the same month that included the U.S. orchestral debut of Christoph Eschenbach, the 28-year-old German pianist who had performed with the ensemble at the Salzburg and Lucerne festivals in 1967. Eschenbach, who played Mozart's Piano Concerto No. 19 at his Severance Hall debut, was encouraged to take up the baton by Szell. He did so, and later would show Cleveland the results.

✻   ✻   ✻

Pierre Boulez, as guest conductor, was drawing closer to the Cleveland Orchestra than to any other American ensemble in early 1969. In February, he accepted the post of principal guest conductor, beginning with the 1969 Blossom festival and extending through the 1971–72 season. The commitment required him to conduct five weeks at Severance Hall during the 1969–70 season and six to eight weeks the following seasons, as well as three weeks at Blossom each summer. Barksdale already was negotiating with Columbia for Cleveland recordings conducted by Boulez.

The French conductor-composer had received guidance in all of his American conducting decisions from Szell, who was still serving as musical advisor to the Philharmonic, following Leonard Bernstein's departure as music director. Boulez initially pledged allegiance to Cleveland, but then a tempting offer came from New York. "I remember the date," he recalled. "I thought it was a joke: April 1, 1969." He continued to seek counsel from Szell, who told him to accept the post of music director of the Philharmonic. "You will agree with me that New York is certainly the city,—especially from a contemporary point of view—where one could try most daringly—and yet within the possible," Boulez wrote to Szell in French. "The dimensions of the city, the manifold opportunities in other fields—theatres, galleries, museums—facilitate the adaptation of the public to a re-modeled repertoire. I think that a new pattern can be tried only in a big city, where different audiences can coincide (over-lap, meet). I have, therefore, decided to try this adventure to the extent to which [it] is possible."

On June 10, 1969, after two months of pondering and negotiating, Boulez was officially announced as Bernstein's successor at the Philharmonic, starting with the 1971–72 season. The three-year appointment would not affect his contracted Cleveland engagements, and evidently didn't convince some Clevelanders that Boulez was out of the running as a possible Szell successor. "The Frenchman's escalating guest conducting arrangements in Cleveland have led to widespread speculation that he is heir apparent to George Szell here," wrote Robert Finn in *The Plain Dealer*. "His acceptance of the New York post would seem to postpone that possibility for five years or so, but not to eliminate it."

❊   ❊   ❊

The second half of the 1968–69 season at Severance Hall was a dizzying ride. In February, Szell and Barksdale began talks with EMI to record songs by Hugo Wolf with baritone Dietrich Fischer-Dieskau. In March, the orchestra announced that it would make its debut in Japan in May 1970 with Szell conducting 12 concerts and Boulez leading three. An outstanding performance in April turned out to be a swan song. As a very premature warm-up for Japan, concertmaster Rafael Druian and Boulez performed the Berg Violin Concerto on an eclectic program including works by Webern, Debussy, Mozart, and Ravel. A month later, Druian resigned in a huff over a rehearsal mix-up. Szell and the orchestra were recording Brahms concertos for EMI with violinist David Oistrakh and cellist Mstislav Rostropovich when Druian arrived at Severance Hall one morning thinking a rehearsal was scheduled. Discovering that he hadn't been informed of the rehearsal's cancellation, the concertmaster demanded an apology from Szell. "I'm not apologizing. It's not my mistake," the conductor said. Druian walked out, his contract was terminated, and associate concertmaster Daniel Majeske moved over to the concertmaster chair for the recordings and for the rest of the season's subscription concerts. A week later, Majeske was officially appointed concertmaster.

In mid-May, the board concluded that major financial trouble lay just ahead. "The orchestra may face death next year unless the 1969–70 season is better financially than past seasons have been," the Associated Press reported on May 19. Deficits for the previous two seasons had forced the board to draw $2 million from the endowment fund. Rankin and Joseph speculated that mounting deficits could cause the endowment to be "wiped out" and the orchestra to "disband or face bankruptcy." The budget had been $2.9 million for 1967–68; for 1968–69 it was forecast as $3.5 million—$1.2 million more than projected operating income. Cleveland wasn't in the hot water alone. It was considering joining the other "Big Five" orchestras—Boston, Chicago, New York, Philadelphia—in seeking funds from the federal government, national foundations, and corporate donors. By November, the number of American orchestras that had come together to ask the federal government for help to avoid bankruptcy had grown to 77. "Meeting in New York City," Finn reported in *The Plain Dealer*, "the orchestra officials were told that the nation's 88 principal orchestras posted a new cash loss of over $5 million for last season and that this figure will hit $13 million by the end of the 1971–72 season."

The orchestra's budget in 1969 wasn't helped by falling ticket sales at Severance Hall and Blossom Music Center, despite the second summer season's impressive array of guests, including violinist Itzhak Perlman, former principal cellist Leonard Rose, soprano Judith Raskin, and the New York City Ballet. By mid-July 1969, single-ticket sales for the orchestra at Blossom were far lower than the inaugural year, with attendance dropping by a third or even half for some performances. A number of trustees believed the orchestra was suffering from a "negative press," due in part to the "loss of Boulez to New York" and the "loss of George Szell to New York," though Boulez hadn't yet left for the Philharmonic and Szell was only a part-time caretaker for the same orchestra. Other trustees charged that the Musical Arts Association had to sell its orchestra more forcefully to the public.

Szell had cut back his 1969 Blossom schedule to three concerts. None of the orchestra's concerts came close to the attendance record set by the rock group Blood, Sweat and Tears, which drew 24,364 fans on August 26 and kept traffic bumper to bumper for miles (and hours). Buoyed largely by such popular attractions, Blossom ended its second season showing significant gains: overall attendance was 323,161, up from 191,175 for the shorter 1968 Blossom season.

✼   ✼   ✼

After 23 years of service, Barksdale had decided, not necessarily of his own volition, to step down as general manager when his contract expired in June 1970. The orchestra's "success has brought with it such leaping costs of operation, including the 52-week season and the magnificent new venture of Blossom, that on re-examination of today's priorities in orchestra management, I see too many critical needs—unrelated to the arts—which are now becoming the prime duties of anyone in my position," Barksdale wrote in his resignation letter. "Such changes in emphasis would mean a change in direction for me which I feel I should not make at this point." Barksdale may indeed have realized that his interest did not lie in financial planning and labor issues. But he was also tired of Szell's abuse.

For his part, Szell was weary of a manager who, while meticulous and smart, tended to think too long before acting. When Maxwell received an invitation to become general manager of the Detroit Symphony in mid-1969, Szell seized the opportunity to keep him in Cleveland by having him promoted to the top administrative post. Barksdale, forced out of his job prematurely, at least was given the chance to depart with dignity. His "resignation" was announced in newspapers on September 24 and Maxwell's appointment (effective June 1, 1970) on September 29. By November, Barksdale had already landed on his feet: He was appointed general manager of the Cleveland Museum of Art, to start on July 1, 1970, returning him to the museum world he had inhabited before coming to Cleveland in 1957.

✼   ✼   ✼

The stability that full-year employment now brought to the orchestra was reflected in the tiny number of personnel changes at the start of the 1969–70 season. Only four musicians joined in September 1969, the smallest contingent in the orchestra's history. Szell opened the 1969–70 season with works he had conducted often in Cleveland: Smetana's *Bartered Bride* overture, Haydn's Symphony No. 97 (recorded for Columbia the following week, along with a Haydn work the orchestra had never played before, the Symphony No. 98), Debussy's *Afternoon of a Faun,* Wagner's *Siegfried Idyll,* and Strauss's *Till Eulenspiegel.* Cellist Michael Haber, a new orchestra member, recalled being amazed by what he heard when Szell began the season's first rehearsal with the Smetana overture. Only a calming pat on the arm from his stand partner, Theodore Baar, kept Haber from freezing with fear. A week later, when he heard the concert's radio broadcast, Haber said he couldn't believe he had played in such a fantastic performance.

To a few people in Cleveland, Szell seemed different at the start of the season. "I already saw a change in him," Maxwell said. "He was very contemplative, very introspective, worried about something. And in hindsight he already knew he had this bone cancer." But the subject was not raised. Szell would never discuss his health at Severance Hall. The musicians had no inkling that their conductor was ill. Whatever Szell may have been feeling this fall, he made one of his greatest Cleveland recordings in October for Angel Records, an elevating performance of Bruckner's Symphony No. 8. The recording stands as a summation of Szell's art. It vibrantly reflects the score's grandeur, lyricism, and earthiness, and the orchestral playing claims a luminous quality rarely achieved in Bruckner.

Transcendence of the same kind pervaded another work Szell conducted this season, Mahler's *Das Lied von der Erde*. Szell had agreed to record the song cycle in two sessions for Columbia amid performances in February 1970 with mezzo-soprano Janet Baker and tenor Richard Lewis. The sticking point was the tenor: Lewis could not be considered for the Cleveland recording because he had recently recorded the work with Eugene Ormandy and the Philadelphia Orchestra for Columbia. A solution seemed to arrive when Columbia and Cleveland found that Canadian tenor Jon Vickers could be available for two days in February for the recording. Then a sticky technicality emerged—a national rule from the American Federation of Musicians allowing an orchestra to rehearse material for recording only if scheduled for a performance before the recording. Vickers wasn't scheduled for a performance, and Szell, not unreasonably, insisted that the orchestra have a rehearsal with Vickers before recording. But since the tenor's recording sessions would take place *after* the first performance at Severance Hall, the musicians were bound by the AFM rule. The *Das Lied* recording for Columbia was cancelled. "I am really heartsick over 'Das Lied' as I wanted to see this great performance recorded before I left the Orchestra," Barksdale complained to CBS Records.

Fortunately, the Severance *Das Lied* in February 1970 was preserved by WCLV. It is among the Szell performances included in the orchestra's 75th Anniversary Compact Disc Edition—a richly expressive interpretation, full of subtlety and controlled power, as well as ineffable beauty in the final song, "Der Abschied," in which the orchestra's radiance complements Baker's searching artistry. A week after the Severance concerts, "George Szell, looking trim and fit, and his Cleveland Orchestra, sounding trim and fit," according to the *New York Times*, repeated the work at Carnegie Hall, again with Baker and Lewis. "As for Mr. Szell, he was of course the dominating force, in complete command, thoroughly in control. There might have been some in the audience who would have said overcontrolled; who would have said that everything—the ritards, the balances, the dynamics—was so carefully calculated as to kill any feeling of spontaneity. Mr. Szell has been accused of pedanticism in the past. But it is also possible to confuse perfect preparation with pedanticism."

※   ※   ※

Whatever health problems Szell may have had at this point did not prevent him from participating actively in the orchestra's current activities or looking to the future. In September, he solidified plans for New York Philharmonic concerts through the 1971–72 season. Soon thereafter, he received a letter from Robert Shaw, his former associate conductor, now in his third season as music director of the Atlanta Symphony, inviting Szell to be a guest conductor. "We would be honored beyond measure and dearly 'love' to have you visit us at any moment of your 'availability'," Shaw wrote. Yet another request followed: Eugene Ormandy asked Szell to return as a guest conductor with the Philadelphia Orchestra during the 1972–73 season.

In October 1969, Szell proceeded as usual in Cleveland, making recordings for Columbia and Angel, and performing with favorite soloists at Severance Hall. In the following weeks, when Szell was out of town, Louis Lane led the ensemble's first performances of Mahler's Symphony No. 3, and Japanese conductor Seiji Ozawa introduced himself to local audiences in Prokofiev's *Romeo and Juliet* suite, Nielsen's Symphony No. 5, and the Cleveland premiere of Toru Takemitsu's *November Steps No. 1*. Finn, in *The Plain Dealer*, was dazzled by the Takemitsu but not overly impressed with Ozawa. "There is nothing at all subtle about this lad, let me tell you. Everything is fast and loud and the tendency is to stride from one musical event to the next with hardly a breath or transition," wrote Finn. "Ozawa's performances dwelt constantly on the slopes of a volcano."

Columbia's plans to release Cleveland from its recording contract at the end of 1969, and to terminate their agreement entirely in October 1971, had prompted EMI/Angel to step up its recording schedule with Szell and the orchestra. One project that had been in the works for Szell and Cleveland—an album of Wolf songs featuring baritone Dietrich Fischer-Dieskau scheduled for sessions in January 1971—was cancelled at this time because EMI decided it could be recorded less expensively in London. Yet EMI was anticipating exciting things for Cleveland, especially with Szell in such a cooperative frame of mind. "Dr. Szell is quite willing to have the orchestra record with guest conductors provided they have international stature and the balance of recorded output between his own performances and those of others is properly maintained," Angel's John Coveney wrote to Brown Meggs at Capitol Industries, the American subsidiary of EMI.

Amid the season's music-making, the Musical Arts Association was facing hard facts. The orchestra had to raise $1 million for its Sustaining Fund by the end of May, according to Rankin, "if the orchestra as we know it is to continue." The financial situation led to talk about the possibility of a short-ened season or other cutbacks, but by late February half the goal had been reached. By this time, musicians and management were already immersed in negotiations for a new three-year contract. The players were asking for minimums of $290 for the 1970–71 season, $310 for 1972–73, and $340 for 1973–74. One of their proposals stipulated that the size of the orchestra not be reduced. They also asked for something they had never been granted: "a voice in the selection of the Musical Director."

There was no reason to expect that a search for a new musical director would begin anytime soon. Szell was planning a heavy schedule through 1970, including 16 concerts in March and April with the New York Philharmonic and the Cleveland Orchestra's first tour to Asia, which now comprised concerts in Japan and Korea (preceded by three western U.S. cities) in May. He had commitments in August and September with the Vienna, Berlin, and London philharmonics at the Salzburg, Lucerne, and Edinburgh festivals, respectively, and a concert with the West German Radio Symphony Orchestra in Cologne before returning to Cleveland to begin the 1970–71 season. In signing on for the Cleveland Orchestra's Asian tour, Szell had withdrawn from the 1970 season at Blossom Music Center, which announced a conducting roster consisting of Leonard Bernstein (in his debut with the orchestra), Bernard Haitink, André Previn, Aaron Copland, Sixten Ehrling, Rafael Frühbeck de Burgos, and Stanislaw Skrowaczewski.

✿   ✿   ✿

Despite appearances, Szell was not well. A week after the February per-formance at Carnegie Hall, he was out of commission with what was re-ported as German measles. A note from a New York doctor confirmed the nature of the sickness: "This is to certify that Dr. George Szell is under my care for febrile illness (101.4 [degrees]) probably of viral origin. It is manda-tory that he remain confined to bed." While Szell was confined, Lane took over the orchestra's remaining tour concerts, including performances of Mozart's Piano Concerto No. 14 (with Rudolf Firkusny) and Bruckner's

Eighth Symphony that marked his Carnegie Hall debut. The concert received raves, though critics couldn't help but make comparisons. "Lane, although he had had only one rehearsal with the orchestra in the work, plainly knew the score cold, and whether what was heard were his ideas or Szell's, Lane clearly knew how to get at them," wrote the *New York Times*. "The orchestra was at its best." Leighton Kerner, in *Women's Wear Daily*, was less happy: "George Szell, having been hit in his mid-70s with the German measles, was, if not replaced, at least substituted for by his four-decades-younger associate, Louis Lane."

Szell recovered sufficiently to lead the 16 Philharmonic concerts in March and April. Before heading to New York, he attended Boulez's first Cleveland program in March—Bartók's Piano Concerto No. 1, with Daniel Barenboim as soloist, and Mahler's Fifth Symphony. After playing the Bartók, Barenboim sat in a box with Szell "with the score, listening to Boulez conducting. I never saw him again."

The same month, the unique relationship between WCLV, a for-profit corporation, and the Cleveland Orchestra, a not-for-profit organization, expanded beyond collaborating on concert broadcasts. WCLV devoted an entire broadcast weekend to listener requests for archival tapes of orchestra performances, for which hundreds of listeners made donations. The original goal for the first WCLV-Cleveland Orchestra Marathon was $10,000, which was reached within 24 hours. The weekend's total was $33,000. From 1970 to 1996, WCLV raised $4 million for the orchestra through the annual marathons, which were broadcast from area malls and Severance Hall, with orchestra members, conductors, and local and visiting celebrities appearing on the air.

Around the time of the first WCLV marathon, the orchestra made two announcements: Szell would conduct 12 pairs of concerts during the 1970–71 season, his 25th with the orchestra; and Kenneth Haas, the 27-year-old assistant to the general manager of the New York Philharmonic, would become the Cleveland Orchestra's assistant manager on July 1.

An announcement of a different kind appeared in early April in a full-page ad in local newspapers:

> The Cleveland Orchestra is in trouble. Loud, unavoidable, cymbal-crashing trouble. This year our operating deficit has risen to $1,000,000. And despite our endowment fund, excellent ticket sales, a vigorous drive for business support and other fund-raising activities, we have not been able to make up the deficit. This is why, for the first time in our history, we're asking you and everyone in Northeast Ohio to help. We're asking

you to show your pride in the Orchestra. We're asking you to join with others in securing the future of the Orchestra. Every dollar will help. Every $5. Every $10 . . . You say it with money, we'll say it with music.

The orchestra was doing exactly that with Boulez and Szell, who returned in late April to prepare for the Asian tour, end the season, and make several recordings. On April 27, 28, and 29, 1970, Angel Records captured Szell and the orchestra in exceptional performances of Schubert's C major Symphony and Dvořák's Eighth Symphony and Slavonic Dances, Op. 46, No. 3, and Op. 72, No. 2. The day after the last recording session, Szell was supposed to attend a ceremony at Baldwin-Wallace College's Riemenschneider Bach Institute to receive an honorary membership, along with his old friend, conductor Max Rudolf. But Szell wasn't well enough to be there. His wife, Helene, went in his place.

Days later, hundreds of college campuses around the country became the scene of student protests over the U.S. invasion of Cambodia on April 30. On May 4, world attention shifted to Kent State University, where the Ohio National Guard's attempt to curb unrest led to violence. Guardsmen killed four Kent State students and wounded nine others, marking a dark day in America's, and certainly Ohio's, history. The news of Kent State weighed heavily on Szell, who had become increasingly introspective as his health continued to decline. "He was just worried about the state of the world and the state of society and the state of everything," Maxwell recalled. "It was preying on his mind."

Szell revealed his feelings about Kent State at the start of the final Severance Hall program of the season on May 7. Before conducting Weber's *Oberon* overture, he addressed the audience, which had greeted him with an ovation: "Ladies and gentlemen, my gratitude for your warm reception is very deep and very genuine. But now I would like to ask of you a favor. Would you please join me in standing silently for a few minutes in simple human recognition of the tragic events of this week?" The program contained two works that had helped him establish the orchestra's reputation in repertoire of the Classical era: Mozart's Symphony No. 40 and Beethoven's "Eroica." Bain Murray captured the aura of the occasion in the *Sun Press*: "The orchestra's final concert, which was to have been a send-off for the Orient tour, turned out to be a tense, probing and meaningful experience. It was marked by music that deals in freedom and grief."

✿   ✿   ✿

A day after the final Severance performance of the season, Szell and the orchestra left for their three-week tour to Japan and Korea. First, they stopped
in Portland, Oregon, and Seattle, Washington, for concerts that were unanimously hailed. "In the past 24 years," wrote the *Oregon Journal*, "Szell has
molded the Cleveland Orchestra in his image, a polished ensemble so responsive to his direction that the impression is given of reaction to his baton
as immediate and accurate as the keys of a piano to a virtuoso at the keyboard." The *Seattle Post-Intelligencer* was even more direct: "This is the
finest symphony orchestra in the world."

The orchestra arrived in the Far East on May 13 and played its first con-
cert in Osaka, Japan, on May 15 during Expo 70. The only other major orchestras invited to the world exposition were those of Berlin and New York.
Cleveland's two concerts in Osaka featured prime Szell fare: Weber's
Oberon overture, Mozart's Symphony No. 40, Sibelius's Symphony No. 2,
Smetana's *Bartered Bride* overture, Prokofiev's Piano Concerto No. 3 (with
Gary Graffman), and Beethoven's "Eroica." After the second Osaka concert,
which ended with the Beethoven, Szell was brought back to the stage 12
times before he led two encores. He was kept onstage by 3,000 listeners in
their 20s and 30s who refused to leave. "He shook as many hands as he could
and then charmingly gave up, waving his right hand in mock pain as he
backed into the wings and beckoned for the orchestra to follow," reported
the *Sun Press*. A young Japanese woman, serving as interpreter, continued
to send Szell onstage. At one point, he asked if he had to go back again. "Oh,
yes, Dr. Szell," the woman said, in her thick accent. "Japanese people love
to crap!" According to Lane, Szell "suddenly exploded with laughter and
went back out another couple times just absolutely roaring with laughter. I
don't know what the audience thought. The orchestra was mystified by the
whole thing."

After concerts in Kyoto and Nagoya under Szell, the orchestra traveled
to Tokyo for two concerts with Szell and one with Boulez at Ueno Bunka
Kaikan Hall. The first concert, on May 22, ended with the Sibelius Second
Symphony, a performance of incandescent beauty and expressive depth that
is preserved on the orchestra's 75th Anniversary Compact Disc Edition. The
concert was taped by a Japanese television station and broadcast several
weeks later in Cleveland, after which a technician erased the tape.
Following the first Tokyo concert, Szell attended a supper given by Japanese
hosts. Orchestra trustee Dorothy Humel sat between Szell and a Japanese
man who told her that the Cleveland Orchestra was the best orchestra in the
world—better than the Berlin Philharmonic, which had just played in

Japan. He said discussions had already begun about bringing Cleveland back in 1973 or 1974. Humel related these remarks to Szell, who looked at her and said, "I won't be here."

A fourth concert in Tokyo was preceded by a performance at the Nakajima Sports Center in the northern city of Sapporo, where Szell gave a party at a geisha house that was renowned for having the best lobster in town. The guests were served by geisha girls, recalled Lane, "who fed us at the table. The head geisha who was an older woman, not perhaps as attractive as some of the younger ones, was very attentive. She was the only one that spoke English. So that was all right, but Szell kept looking over at mine and said to me, 'I think you got the better deal, Lane.' "

The adventures continued in Seoul, South Korea, and then in Anchorage, Alaska, for the last concert of the tour, in a high school auditorium. The occasion was preceded by a drunken episode that left one of the orchestra's most contentious members, principal trombonist Robert Boyd, unable to play the concert. Changes in the program, necessitated by the removal of works with trombones, replaced Berlioz's *Roman Carnival* overture and Walton's Variations on a Theme by Hindemith with the *Oberon* overture and Mozart's Symphony No. 40. Eugene Kilinski, the orchestra's associate chief librarian at the time, later suggested that the changes might not have had to do entirely with trombones. "Did he have some premonition that this might be his last concert ever?" Kilinski wrote a year after Szell's death. "If so, would he not want to perform the music he loved best, music which in the eyes of the world he conducted greater than anyone else within living memory?"

During the last piece, Beethoven's "Eroica," Szell stopped conducting for an instant. "I felt a chill through my body," recalled cellist Michael Haber. "I remember thinking something was terribly wrong."

❖   ❖   ❖

Something *was* terribly wrong with Szell, and everyone around him had begun to notice. "He looked like the wrath of God, and he wanted me to take him home, but I wouldn't," Frank Joseph recalled of meeting Szell at Hopkins Airport upon the orchestra's return. "I told him he had to go to the hospital." Days later, Kurt Loebel sent Szell a letter on behalf of the orchestra committee:

> With the memories of the recent tour still fresh in our minds, there are some impressions and thoughts we would like to share with you. Many members of the orchestra were unaware of your illness during most of the

Szell responded on June 5, two days before his 73rd birthday:

> Your kind letter, which was read to me over the phone, has moved me and I want to thank you and your colleagues most warmly for the sentiments you voice. I was much too tired on our last flight, otherwise I would have said a few words over the P.A. system of the plane to the effect that I have been keenly aware of the help every member of the Orchestra gave me during the whole tour. Without this help I could not have got through the tour at all.

By mid-June, Szell was recovering from exhaustion and a fever at University Hospitals, where his wife allowed only close friends and associates to see him. One frequent visitor was Lane, who was preparing to conduct Mozart's *Don Giovanni* at the Lake George Opera. "Bring your score over and we'll go through it," Szell told him. They had had several sessions and scheduled another when Szell was stricken by a heart attack on Thursday, June 18. Two weeks later, he was out of intensive care and receiving messages from colleagues. "Please set the tempo for your recuperation 'Presto Assai' so that before long we will be able to give the world a truly definitive Tchaikovsky 4th and more Wagner excepts," wrote Andrew Kazdin, producer of the orchestra's most recent Columbia recordings.

Szell's hospitalization coincided with a period of tense negotiations between management and the musicians for the new labor contract. Adding to the tension, several male players had decided that the conductor's ban on facial hair could no longer be justified; they began growing beards and mustaches. Maxwell threatened to take the matter to the union, but other issues were pressing.

The 1970 Blossom season had begun with a touring production of *Fiddler on the Roof* and a Viennese program with the orchestra conducted by Lane. The opening festival concerts in early July promised to be especially exciting. Along with the debut of Dutch conductor Bernard Haitink, the orchestra was about to meet Leonard Bernstein for the first time. He was engaged to conduct a benefit performance of Mahler's Symphony No. 2 ("Resurrection"), with mezzo-soprano Christa Ludwig, soprano Lorna Haywood, and the combined Blossom Festival and Cleveland Orchestra choruses. The charismatic maestro was as extravagant as ever, throwing himself into rehearsals with Mahlerian fervor and telling Szell's players that they were remarkable. One of Bernstein's assessments was particularly unrestrained and memorable. "You guys are so fucking good" is the phrase musicians who were there best recall. Bernstein was more genteel when he met with trustees socially after a rehearsal. "I gave them so much in so little time and they picked it up like this," he said, snapping his fingers. "No orchestra in the world could do what this orchestra did."

Bernstein had a mission in Cleveland, aside from the Mahler: he wanted to visit Szell in the hospital. Maxwell drove him to University Hospitals, where they proceeded toward Szell's room. But Helene Szell was standing guard when Bernstein, wearing a string of worry beads given to him by Maria Callas, hugged the conductor's wife and asked to see Szell. She refused. Bernstein "was crestfallen," remembered Maxwell. Mrs. Szell remembered something else about the conductor, who was dressed from neck to toes in one chic color: "He looked like a white cupcake." Bernstein's performance of the Mahler Second, as heard on a tape, is expansive, loving, and piercingly moving, rising to ecstatic heights in the final choral pages. *The Plain Dealer*'s Finn termed it "quite simply, one of the greatest occasions in Blossom's history and perhaps in that of the orchestra itself."

The euphoria wouldn't last. On July 16, local newspapers carried stories announcing the cancellation of Szell's appearances in August and September at the Salzburg, Lucerne, and Edinburgh festivals. Separately and privately, board president Rankin presented a statement to orchestra and union representatives laying out his perception of financial reality. The orchestra's operating deficit was $1.05 million, a staggering jump from the figure of $311,000 three years before. According to Rankin, "any economic agreement which we make must fall within the limits of our resources and our anticipated public support. Any other course of action inevitably would lead to curtailments which would have a detrimental effect upon the quality of the Orchestra or result in bankruptcy . . . We have no hidden resources and we have no additional borrowing capacity."

To ward off bankruptcy, the board had proposed reducing the number of work weeks, possibly reducing the size of the orchestra, and canceling all contracts if financial concerns made this necessary. Now Rankin was proposing that the musicians think "in terms not of compensation increases but rather of some adjustment to protect your present compensation from inflationary erosion." Essentially, the new proposal amounted to a renewal of the old three-year contract with "adjustments" of $10 per week during the first year of the contract and $7.50 for each succeeding season. The musicians did not appreciate this line of thinking. But the board didn't like at least one particular aspect of the musicians' thinking: the players wanted an equal voice in the selection of a new musical director, and they wanted "an audition committee for new members to become effective if and when a new Musical Director is chosen."

Events already set in motion were bringing the prospect of such a choice nearer every day. Szell's condition, despite optimism at the beginning of July, was worsening quickly. Although his wife allowed him few visitors, Szell was reunited with violinist Edith Peinemann, who was in town to play the Berg concerto with the orchestra and Boulez on July 19 at Blossom. "They were like father and daughter," said Maxwell. "And she'd go into his room and feed him soup and just be with him along with Helene."

On July 24, at the urging of Frank Joseph, a doctor wrote a note stating that Szell would not be able to conduct the fall concerts of the Cleveland Orchestra. Although Severance Hall was saying nothing about Szell's health, Frank Hruby wrote the same day in the *Press* that the orchestra was searching for conductors to replace Szell for the opening months of the 1970–71 season. Surveying the possibilities, Hruby suggested Bernstein and Karajan, and then two younger conductors—Lorin Maazel and Zubin Mehta. "Some of the artists listed above would also be candidates for permanent conductor in the event of Szell's retirement," he wrote. "One assumes that orchestra officials are giving thought to this eventuality and are doing something about it. The Musical Arts Assn. has been conspicuously successful in bringing superior artists to the orchestra's music stand. Nikolai Sokoloff, Artur Rodzinski and, 25 years ago, George Szell. One therefore can feel optimistic about the future of the orchestra."

Unbeknownst to Hruby and others, Szell was now critically ill, and Maxwell had already replaced him with other conductors, not just for the fall, but for the entire 1970–71 season. The new roster included Boulez, Lane, Eugene Ormandy, Rafael Kubelik, Erich Leinsdorf, and Georg (Jerzy) Semkow, as well as assistant conductors. Kubelik, Leinsdorf, and Semkow were signed to share conducting duties for an East Coast tour in February 1971. In light of the situation, Rankin took the initiative in advising Mrs. Szell of the changes and offering hope. "A number of guest conductors with whom we have conferred have said that they are only providing their services out of respect for George and the Orchestra and will gladly step aside if George is able to resume conducting. I am confident that the others would, if asked, do likewise," Rankin wrote. "As far as the Trustees and Officers of the Association are concerned, we shall sorely miss George's genius and his music this fall and we will begrudge every moment of his absence."

These words, written on July 28, came the day the association agreed to a compromise on the musicians' demand for a say in the choice of the next musical director. The compromise would represent a small triumph for the players: the association would include one orchestra member—selected by the orchestra—on a committee established to make conductor recommendations. News that Szell would not conduct at all during the 1970–71 season became public the next day in local and national newspapers. In a story about Szell in the *Chicago Sun-Times* the same day, Robert C. Marsh noted that the Cleveland ensemble, "like the Chicago Symphony, is negotiating a new union contract, and Cleveland has a history of labor strife considerably more bitter than any this city has known."

On June 30, Cleveland found out how bitter. The orchestra committee issued a newsletter to orchestra members detailing its negotiating troubles. Among the subjects was the need for management to recognize the players as professionals "by relaxing present humiliating and punitive measures dealing with fines, tardiness, absences, and sick leave procedure at home and on tour, compassionate leave, grievance procedures and dismissal for cause." The committee was willing to take a hardball stance to achieve a fair contract:

It is not our intention to negotiate away the quality of our achievements. We feel that what we are asking for is consistent with our ability to maintain our own high standards and the performing excellence of the Orchestra. We are a great orchestra with a musical uniqueness and particular quality of dedication and pride in what we can do that is not to be found in any other orchestra in the world. It is something that belongs to all of us, for each of us by his concerted efforts and conscientiousness, in response to great musical leadership and training, has labored to bring it about.

That night at Blossom, the musicians were applying their efforts to Brahms's Piano Concerto No. 1, with Mischa Dichter as soloist and Boulez on the podium, when the phone rang backstage. Szell had just died, at 9:50 p.m., of complications from the heart attack he had suffered the previous month. News of Szell's deteriorating condition had spread throughout the day, but the orchestra wouldn't learn of his death until after the concert. Boulez, informed by Lane at intermission of the titan's departure, agreed to say nothing to the musicians. Most accounts state that Lane later broke the news to the players in a meeting in the basement of the Blossom pavilion; Lane claims Barksdale made the announcement—though the latter had by then already retired as general manager. Whoever delivered the message to the musicians, "the shock of the news left them numb," wrote Finn. "They filed out silently to cars and buses, each with his own private thoughts, no one much inclined toward conversation." Boulez was able to offer Finn a few words about Szell: "For me it was like a pupil and teacher. This orchestra brought me his lessons."

It had been a horrible week for the conducting world. On Tuesday, Sir John Barbirolli had died in London at the age of 70. On Wednesday, Romanian conductor Jonel Perlea—who had conducted the Cleveland Orchestra once, in 1956—had died in New York at 69. Then, on Thursday, Szell.

The Plain Dealer saluted him in an editorial the next day: "Few men did more to enhance Cleveland's reputation than did the late George Szell. To many people around the world he and the Cleveland Orchestra symbolized the city . . . . Szell will be best remembered for what he leaves behind—the Cleveland Orchestra. Seldom has a richer legacy been left to a city."

– PART FOUR –

UNWAVERING
COMMITMENT

1970–2000

– *27* –

Discord

The death of George Szell thrust Michael Maxwell, the orchestra's brand-new general manager, into a role he hadn't counted on. "The board left me to pick up and I, in essence, became the *de facto* music director for two years," recalled Maxwell. "It was a wonderful time and I relished it." He particularly savored scheduling and programming the 1971–72 and 1972–73 seasons. "My principal concern: preserve the reputation of the Cleveland Orchestra by carrying on as usual with the best available conductors and soloists." Maxwell carried on with a zeal that would alienate him from staff and musicians. He would exert absolute authority over every aspect of the orchestra's operations.

Ironically, Szell had begun to become disenchanted with his young manager's abilities during the Asian tour. Although he had been sufficiently impressed with Maxwell at the New York Philharmonic to hire him for Cleveland and later get him promoted from assistant general manager to general manager, Szell didn't appreciate the way Maxwell handled tour details in Japan. As the conductor lay dying in his hospital bed, he told Louis Lane that he had made a big mistake. It was a rare admission for Szell, who prided himself on being in control at every moment. Now it was Maxwell who would assume control.

Sadness, grief, confusion, anger, fear, and ambition hung in the air after the death of the fastidious, demanding conductor who had raised the Cleveland Orchestra to international renown. In some ways Szell's death held out a promise of relief. After 24 years of autocratic rule, many of his musicians were ready for a more enlightened form of leadership. While the players admired their late conductor's commanding artistic gifts, his rigid discipline had worn them down to the point where they hungered to be treated with more civility. Szell had achieved greatness through heightened musical powers and an utter lack of democracy.

A new building process had to begin in Cleveland. The musicians were determined to obtain a contract that would keep them on par with the country's other major orchestras. The Musical Arts Association, facing mounting deficits, was determined to avoid further financial erosion by offering only small increases in salaries and benefits. Now the board suddenly had to contend with a crucial artistic matter in which most trustees had no experience (and which the institution hadn't faced in 24 years): the search for a new conductor. As all of these issues came crashing down on the Cleveland Orchestra, Maxwell began running the show as self-appointed artistic boss. Cleveland was in for the rockiest of transitions.

                              ✻   ✻   ✻

On August 1, two days after Szell's death, the orchestra began its concert at Blossom Music Center with an unconducted performance of the Air from Bach's Suite No. 3 in the conductor's memory. Aaron Copland, an old Szell friend, led the remainder of the program (works by Schubert, Copland, Roussel, and Ravel). A formal memorial concert was held at Severance Hall on August 3, when the strings again played the Bach and the orchestra followed with Beethoven's *Leonore* Overture No. 3 and Mozart's Symphony No. 40 under Lane, Szell's assistant for 23 years. Lane now was preparing to play a bigger role, or so he thought. Several weeks after the memorial concert, he was named resident conductor. At the same time, Pierre Boulez was appointed musical advisor. For Boulez, the title was largely honorary. His input during the two years after Szell's death has since been greatly exaggerated, as Boulez himself has noted. He didn't do much more than conduct about four weeks of concerts each season—and fill many programs with contemporary fare that outraged a large portion of the public. His limited responsibilities in Cleveland had much to do with his job change: he was getting ready to become music director of the New York Philharmonic.

Upon his appointment as resident conductor, an optimistic Lane told *The Plain Dealer* that the orchestra's programming now would differ from that favored by Szell. "Obviously the repertoire will be affected to a great extent," he said. "Because of my own interests and that of guest conductors, there will be more emphasis on 20th-century music. We will not abandon Beethoven and Brahms, but we will move out of the 19th-century Germanic main line. It will probably be a healthy change." Lane expressed optimism about the orchestra's prospects: "The orchestra is in a period of transition and uncertainty as to the direction it will take. The executive committee, the trustees and the administrative staff are all determined that it will not be downward."

A day after the Szell memorial concert, the musicians rejected management's proposed three-year contract by a vote of 84 to 14. The weekly minimum offered was $255, with $20 extra for Blossom concerts. The players were seeking $290. Management offered a $10 raise for the first year and $7.50 for each of the two remaining years of the new contract. The board intended to "absolutely refuse any change in the economic figures or in the musical directorship or management prerogatives." Despite the labor problems, the musicians vowed "to cooperate in any way they could to keep the high standards of excellence that Mr. Szell had set."

Several conductors associated with the Cleveland Orchestra were eager to help out. Days after Szell's death, as sympathetic letters and telegrams from musicians who had idolized the conductor continued to pour in, messages from István Kertész and Robert Shaw arrived offering their services whenever needed. In mid-August, the board began discussing the formation of a search committee to initiate the succession process. Board chairman Frank E. Joseph, who had been with Szell when he died, wrote to an orchestra member that he didn't look forward to the hazy future facing the orchestra, or to the prospect of replacing his late friend:

> We have some horrendous financial and other problems at the Cleveland Orchestra and all of us will be under various degrees of strains and tensions for some time to come. If we hope to realize our common goal of maintaining the high standards George Szell set, we are going to have to realize that each of us is doing the best he knows how under difficult conditions and try to understand each other's problems and be willing to help solve them. That is the only way we can keep the Cleveland Orchestra in its present position of pre-eminence and that, after all, would be the finest memorial to George Szell.

One of the orchestra's problems revolved around recording, or more precisely the lack of it. Columbia Records was about to end its 31-year association with the orchestra, and the news from Angel (EMI) Records was equally grim. With Szell's death, Angel general manager Robert Myers told *The Plain Dealer*, the company had no further plans to record the Cleveland Orchestra. Recording might resume, Myers said, depending upon Szell's successor.

A new contract for the musicians looked increasingly remote. The players had proposed that language be added to the contract stating that the size of the orchestra would be maintained at its present level. In an early round of negotiations, management suggested that a reduction of orchestra personnel might be necessary because of financial conditions. The musicians weren't going to stand for that. "It is not our intention to consent to the decline of the Cleveland Orchestra as we know it. It is a jewel in the hat of Cleveland," the orchestra committee stated in a newsletter to the general public in mid-August. Citing their part in establishing a great orchestra, the musicians now wanted "a say in our destiny," including a voice in selecting a new musical director, an audition committee, recognition of the orchestra committee, and input into seating changes within sections. The Musical Arts Association initially would reject all of these proposals.

Amid the acrimony, the orchestra continued playing at Blossom, mustering all of its professionalism and pride to perform at its customary high level. The remaining summer concerts were entrusted to Lane, Morton Gould, Rafael Frühbeck de Burgos (in his debut), Sixten Ehrling, and Stanislaw Skrowaczewski. A few days after the end of the Blossom season, the orchestra—no longer locked out of negotiations by the musicians' union—rejected management's latest offer by a vote of 79 to 17.

At 12:01 a.m. on September 7, the second strike in the orchestra's history began, threatening the opening of the 1970–71 season at Severance Hall. The big sticking points remained salary and job security. "They're afraid that a new conductor may come in, clean house, eventually get rid of some of them and bring in some of his friends," said Anthony A. Granata, president of the Cleveland Federation of Musicians. Robert Finn put the musicians' situation in a more whimsical perspective in *The Plain Dealer*: "The passing of George Szell has given them an opportunity they have lacked for 24 years. They are like men suddenly liberated from a no-sweets diet. They are heading for the pastry shop with a firm gait." Maxwell tried to get the orchestra's attention on September 18, the day of the scheduled opening, by addressing the subject of a new musical director. In a letter to each musician, he said that a new conductor would be chosen "with your help," but that the conductor could not function if his actions were subject to veto by the players. "Instead, he must command your respect and cooperation to maintain the greatness of the Orchestra he inherits," wrote Maxwell. "We have, from the beginning, offered you a voice in the selection of the new Musical Director, but we will not agree to your participation in his duties, whether it be audition procedures and decisions, or the seating of Orchestra personnel."

On September 18, the musicians and their audience experienced the first cancellation of the season's opening in the orchestra's 53-year history. Finn treated the situation with much-needed good humor in a non-review the morning after the elusive first night:

> The Cleveland Orchestra's 1970–71 season did not open last night with the first of two programs offering all five of the Beethoven piano concer-

tos. Pianist Anton Kuerti (a former Clevelander) did not give fine performances—or any performances at all—of the first, second and fourth concertos. Resident conductor Louis Lane was not on the podium. The orchestra did not play well, badly—or at all.

On September 20, the orchestra voted 77 to 18 to reject another offer, and in the days following the musicians walked picket lines outside Severance Hall. Many players found carrying placards "very foreign to our nature," as violist Ben Selcer told the *Press*. "It's quite repugnant to me and to everyone else doing it." His sign read, "For Mutual Respect." The musicians placed an advertisement in local newspapers comparing the association's offer with the contracts of the country's other four top major orchestras (Boston, Chicago, New York, Philadelphia). The new Cleveland proposal, said the ad, would give the players the lowest salary, longest working hours, least vacation time, worst medical coverage, and lowest pension.

The board was not budging. "We have repeatedly informed the members of the Orchestra and the communities at large that our financial capacity can no longer be compared with that of the other four orchestras," board president Alfred M. Rankin told the trustees. In a refrain that would be repeated often in the near and distant future, Rankin said the other four orchestras could draw from larger population bases. They had larger halls and therefore more earned income. Cleveland's recording royalties were negligible compared to theirs. And the Cleveland Orchestra received no funding from the city, county, or state, as did its counterparts. Maxwell provided the most pointed and condescending evaluation of the situation. "It is a testing time for us all, not only to stand firm but also to approach our challenges with flexibility and an open mind," he told the board. "To this degree, we ask our musicians to most carefully search their consciences for their true understanding of what it is to be an artist and a professional musician. In a world of changing values, it seems to me that attitude plays an important role and a musician's attitude towards his work must reflect his artistic integrity."

The musicians didn't hear these exact words, but they were getting the message. When the board made another offer, the musicians rejected the proposal by 70 to 27. The orchestra committee addressed their grievances two days later, on October 9, in a letter to the trustees. The letter decried the lack of first-class working conditions and suggested that management and the board weren't really interested in maintaining the orchestra's quality. With the drop in recording activity, the musicians noted that the new contract would put their salaries below the level of the 1969–70 season. The players were intent upon achieving financial parity with the other "Big Five" orchestras, partly to guarantee that the best musicians could be drawn to Cleveland. It didn't help, then, when the players were told that their new scale would be the highest among the orchestras *just below* the "Big Five" category.

The board briefly took up the possibility of canceling the rest of the season, risking the loss of musicians, but Rankin urged his colleagues to convince the players that the dire financial situation was real and to salvage the season.

The season was saved when the board increased the minimum weekly salary figures, giving the musicians $10 raises (instead of $7.50) for the last two years of the contract. The players expressed enormous reluctance over the contract, voting 59 to 34 to accept the offer. This ended a wearying 41-day strike that had cancelled nine concerts at Severance Hall and performances in Akron and Oberlin. "I really feel, by the orchestra accepting the contract, that the musicians have sacrificed an awful lot," said Michael V. Scigliano, secretary-treasurer of the Cleveland Federation of Musicians. The players' gains were minimal in areas aside from wages. The contract stated that the orchestra could select one musician to serve on the board's search committee for a new musical director. The board's intention to maintain the orchestra at a minimum of 100 players—there were 105 at the time—was included in a new clause. The pension plan, still an embarrassment, gave retired musicians a maximum of $2,500 per year and future retirees $3,000 annually after 25 years of service. The contract did nothing to change the musicians' view that the association considered them little more than hired labor.

The trustees' reaction to the new contract appeared to confirm this view: among board members, there was quiet jubilation. Joseph termed the settlement a "major victory" for the association. Rankin assessed the mood of the orchestra, correctly, as "somewhat bitter, especially among the more radical musicians," a telling comment at a time when the Vietnam War was polarizing the nation. "A by-product of the settlement," said Rankin, "may be the disillusion of the majority of the Orchestra with their more militant leaders. In addition, the Association has set an example that it hopes will be followed by other orchestras in future negotiations." The board was crowing a bit because its settlement would prompt a three-year increase in weekly scale totaling only $330,000, a significantly lower figure than hikes in recent orchestra settlements in Chicago ($800,000 over the same period) and New York ($1.2 million).

❁   ❁   ❁

With the strike settled, everyone at Severance Hall could get back to business—some to make music, some to seek out a new musical director. The
board had appointed a search committee consisting of Maxwell, Rankin,
Joseph, Lane, and trustees Joseph Adams and Paul J. Vignos, Jr. The orchestra would name principal violist Abraham Skernick as its representative. Maxwell had been thinking about potential candidates for Szell's successor even before the new contract was signed. In mid-October 1970, he
suggested to colleagues on the search committee that they attend upcoming concerts led by two possible candidates: Lorin Maazel, who was about
to conduct two weeks with the Philadelphia Orchestra, and Zubin Mehta,
music director of the Los Angeles Philharmonic, who had three concerts
with the New York Philharmonic.

Eugene Ormandy, the longtime music director of the Philadelphia
Orchestra, was in town the week after the end of the strike to open the delayed season and to make his debut with the Cleveland Orchestra, conducting Beethoven programs. In an interview, Ormandy described Szell, his
Hungarian countryman, as an "inflexible perfectionist" and himself as a
"flexible perfectionist." He said his approach to working with orchestral musicians was different from Szell's. "You have to remember that each one of
them started out to be a Heifetz; and you have to treat them that way. I
started out [as] a violinist myself," said Ormandy. "I try to think of how they
feel. Musicians do not like to be *told* what to do. It is better just to *suggest*."

Most of the 46 conductors on the board's list of possible candidates in the
fall of 1970 had never stood before the Cleveland Orchestra. Neither Szell
nor the board apparently had given much thought to the matter of his eventual successor. Few of the names on the 1970 list would be taken seriously,
anyway. In October 1970, Joseph and his wife, Martha, set out to hear
Maazel in Philadelphia and Mehta in New York. The board chairman was
eager to get the process off on the right footing. He suggested to Maxwell
that the search committee meet "to decide the qualifications of the person
for whom we are looking and the best procedures for going about it.
Personally, I am in favor of soliciting both criteria and specific suggestions
from our Trustees, orchestra members, performers, music institutes, etc."

Already there was talk that one candidate was ahead of the pack. "When
the musical rumor mills start grinding, the name they most frequently churn
out as leading candidate for conductorship of the Cleveland Orchestra is
that of Lorin Maazel," reported Finn in *The Plain Dealer* on October 26,
1970, after an interview with the conductor in Philadelphia. Maazel told
Finn that he had been engaged to be a guest conductor in Cleveland for the

following two seasons. Finn also discovered that Maazel's contracts with the Deutsche Oper Berlin and the Berlin Radio Symphony were about to expire. One Maazel comment in the interview may have raised some eyebrows: He said he had never met Michael Maxwell. But Maazel actually had known the Cleveland Orchestra's general manager for nine years, since May 1961, when Maazel was a guest conductor with the Philharmonia Orchestra of London, of which Maxwell was orchestra manager.

Beside Finn, Maazel met with at least one other person from Cleveland while in Philadelphia in October 1970—Maxwell. The manager had lunch with the conductor and his second wife, pianist Israela Margalit, and then spoke privately with Maazel. "This question is not official, and I'm not here with any authority to discuss it," Maxwell said, "but if you were to be approached about the Cleveland position, would you be interested?" Maazel answered, "Yes."

Within weeks, the Cleveland Conductor Contest was generating plenty of buzz. Mehta, without giving a reason, announced that he had turned down invitations to guest conduct the orchestra for the next two seasons, effectively removing himself from the race. Then another prospective candidate showed up at Severance Hall in November—Claudio Abbado, who had cancelled his debut two seasons before due to illness. Now the dashing director of Milan's La Scala Opera was raring to go in Cleveland. He told *The Plain Dealer* that he would be able to accept the Cleveland post but didn't like the American penchant for revealing the list of candidates. "It becomes a contest where someone always has to be eliminated. I hate contests," said Abbado, although he had won one—the New York Philharmonic's Mitropoulos Prize. "They don't have anything to do with music."

Abbado's two weeks of concerts evidently had everything to do with music. Audiences responded enthusiastically, the orchestra was impressed, and critics rhapsodized. "His Cleveland debut on the Severance podium these past two weeks has been more than successful; it has been sensational," wrote Bain Murray in the *Sun Press*. "In this short span of time Abbado has made our tense, gloomy orchestra musicians smile again and he ignited them into playing that was brilliant, warm, controlled and electrifying." Murray suggested that the search committee "might well bring the search to a halt and settle on a man who in two weeks won the respect and admiration of the Cleveland Orchestra."

Alfred Rankin, as board president, ultimately would choose Szell's successor. He was doing his homework. Soon after Abbado's concerts, he asked concertmaster Daniel Majeske if a conductor who had never appeared with the Cleveland Orchestra could be engaged as musical director (as had been the unfortunate case with the appointment of Erich Leinsdorf in 1943). "I think this could be quite disastrous and would produce many undesirable kinds of possibilities," answered Majeske. "I feel we have already seen some outstanding possibilities in the way men like Abbado or Kertész are responded to by the orchestra. It seems to me to be necessary to remember that orchestras have different personalities as [much] as people [do] and therefore react differently to the same conductor. Therefore a success with another orchestra does not guarantee the same here."

By early December, the search committee presented to the board the names of five candidates—Abbado, Frühbeck de Burgos, Kertész, Maazel, and Seiji Ozawa. Among those "discarded" at this time were Mehta, who actually had discarded the orchestra first, and Daniel Barenboim (who would state erroneously in his memoirs that he had been pursued for the job).

Soon after the candidates were presented, Maxwell told the board that the committee had drawn up prerequisites for the musical director. "The committee," he said, "believes that the new Musical Director should be a younger man but one far enough along in his career to have acquired an international reputation. Generally speaking, this means a conductor who is between 35 and 45 years old." Among the other criteria: broad repertoire; ability to produce balanced programs; innovation in generating new audiences; willingness to become a full member of the community; ability to attract new recording and TV work; and willingness to continue to appear in other major musical capitals to enhance both the conductor's and the orchestra's international reputations. Maxwell informed the trustees that no conductor could probably arrive as musical director until the 1973–74 season. The 1972–73 season was already completely booked with guest conductors. For the 1971–72 season, the orchestra would play under a preposterous number of conductors—15—partly as a result of late changes brought about by Szell's death.

One of the conductors scheduled for the current season was Leinsdorf, who had last appeared with the orchestra in April 1946. He was engaged to lead five weeks of concerts at Severance Hall, as well as performances on tour. But his history of misfortune in Cleveland wasn't quite over. Leinsdorf's first three programs during the season's opening weeks were cancelled by the musicians' strike. Now, in January 1971, a back ailment forced him to withdraw from his program of works by Mozart and Bruckner, which Lane took over. Finally, in early February, Leinsdorf walked into Severance Hall for the first time in 25 years and was reunited with an almost completely different orchestra for rehearsals of the Mozart-Bruckner program he would lead two weeks later at Carnegie Hall.

Leinsdorf's rehearsals came a week after another respected conductor, Rafael Kubelik, entered Severance Hall to make his debut with the orchestra in two subscription programs (in place of Szell). Like Leinsdorf, the Czech-born music director of the Bavarian Radio Orchestra had experienced early misfortune in the United States. In 1950, Kubelik became music director of the Chicago Symphony as successor to Artur Rodzinski. Kubelik endured three years of castigation from the *Chicago Tribune*'s caustic music critic, Claudia Cassidy, before heading back to Europe. In January 1971 in Cleveland, the reception for Kubelik in prime Szell repertoire— works by Schumann, Bartók, Mozart, and Brahms, with baritone Dietrich Fischer-Dieskau as soloist—was far more approving. The following month, Kubelik shared the orchestra's podium with Leinsdorf and Georg (Jerzy) Semkow during an East Coast tour that garnered praise for the ensemble but reservations about the conductors' interpretations. The concerts provided confirmation that Szell's death had not affected the orchestra's quality. Writing about one of the Carnegie Hall programs, the *New York Times*'s Harold C. Schonberg noted, "the great Cleveland Orchestra played well for Mr. Kubelik. It remains one of the miracle groups of the world."

Meanwhile, Abbado, who was serving as guest conductor of the Philadelphia Orchestra, had Cleveland on his mind. "After Philadelphia, I think that is the best orchestra," he told the *Philadelphia Inquirer* in mid-February 1971. "Such discipline. When you put down your baton, there is silence. You say what you want, and they do it." The interview noted that Abbado's commitments to the Vienna Philharmonic were not so great as "to make him drop his Cleveland aspirations."

Toward the end of the 1970–71 season, audience members at Severance Hall were expressing displeasure at the shift away from Szell's mainstream repertoire and toward more 20th-century fare. Maxwell told the board "that Mr. Boulez' recent programs, which some subscribers found to overly emphasize the modern repertoire, would not have seemed so objectionable in the context of Mr. Szell's weeks of the standard repertoire." Many of the season's programs after Szell's death had been refashioned by Maxwell, to the dismay of Lane, who had little input in the process despite his status as resident conductor. Maxwell had taken over, controlling every artistic decision and guiding Joseph and Rankin—brilliant, accomplished leaders, but not musicians—through his personal agenda for the orchestra's artistic future. He spent several weeks in Europe in early spring 1971 discussing a potential tour for the ensemble in May 1973 and exploring the possibilities for recording, which looked bleak. Among Maxwell's stops during his European trip was Berlin, where he had scheduled a visit with Maazel.

One maestro who shared his wisdom about conductor searches at this time had been a visitor to Cleveland since 1910. Leopold Stokowski was in town in May 1971 to lead the final concerts of the Severance Hall season—and, it would turn out, his final concerts with the orchestra. "No, I am not a candidate for the Cleveland Orchestra conducting post," the 89-year-old conductor of the American Symphony Orchestra cheerfully told the *Press*. "There are many talented conductors around. I'm sure, if you are patient, you will find the right one."

The musicians of the Cleveland Orchestra weren't particularly patient, and they weren't confident that management was going to find the right conductor—and they were decidedly miffed that the process was unfolding without their input, despite what Maxwell had promised them. Maxwell's familiarity with Maazel had already sent signals. Then an incident occurred that added weight to the musicians' suspicions that Maazel was the top candidate. Maxwell appeared on a local television show, hosted by jewelry magnate Larry Robinson, with Frank and Martha Joseph and principal clarinetist Robert Marcellus to discuss orchestra matters. After the taping, the Josephs were driving Marcellus and Maxwell home when the clarinetist asked the manager to name an ideal candidate for musical director. Maxwell proceeded to give him a list of Maazel's virtues. "There is no doubt in my mind," recalled Maxwell, "that this conversation led to the speculative gossip that went through the orchestra that Maazel was my preordained choice, and that the selection process was a sham."

Maazel *was*, in fact, Maxwell's personal choice "for quite specific reasons," Maxwell noted almost three decades later. "Although he had not conducted the orchestra at that point I knew him and his work with the Philharmonia in London, in concert and in EMI recordings we made. But first, he was American, and would be the first to lead a 'big five' orchestra since Bernstein." (The nationality can be disputed: Maazel was born in France, and he had spent most of his career in Europe.)

No one else at the time was talking much about anyone *but* Maazel. By early June, Finn believed the field had been narrowed down to Abbado, Maazel, Frühbeck de Burgos, and Kertész, and he added Kubelik as a "distant long-shot possibility." But he focused mostly on the man who was set to make his Blossom debut on July 9 and 10. "Maazel's situation at Blossom this summer will be extraordinary and more than a little unfair to him. The rumors that he is the nominee persist despite his public denial of any such knowledge and despite the fact that he has not conducted our orchestra since he was a prodigy of 13 or so," wrote Finn in *The Plain Dealer*, forgetting that the 22-year-old Maazel had led the Cleveland Summer Orchestra in two popular programs at Public Hall in 1952. "He is still an unknown, though highly recommended, quantity here. His two Blossom programs are full of Szell specialties and, coming as he does at the very start of the Blossom season, he will be directly on trial every minute, whether he likes it or not. Hardly a situation calculated to promote peace of mind."

※   ※   ※

In mid-June, Maazel wrote to Maxwell, accepting an invitation. "This is simply to confirm that I shall be delighted to be the house guest of Mr. and Mrs. Alfred Rankin (my eldest daughter will <u>not</u> be coming with me)," Maazel wrote. The note is telling: No other guest artist during the 1971 Blossom season stayed at the home of the orchestra's board president, or any trustee. Most were housed at the Holiday Inn in Fairlawn, not far from Blossom.

More evidence that Maxwell was setting Maazel up to be the next musical director can be found in a memo the manager sent Rankin at the end of June. Maazel's conducting dates for July 1971 and the 1971–72 and 1972–73 seasons are attached to the memo, confirming what the conductor told Finn the previous October in Philadelphia. But there is more. "Further to our conversation the other evening," Maxwell wrote to Rankin, "I have very carefully looked at the schedule for the 1973–74 [season] as well as the outline for both 1974–75 and 1975–76 to see what a basic concert commitment would be to us from the Musical Director." Maazel's name is typed next to specific weeks for these three seasons.

Aside from the formality of Maazel's Blossom concerts and negotiations for a contract, the search essentially was over.

Though only Maxwell, Rankin, and Joseph knew it for sure, the musicians, public, and critics continued to speculate that Maazel was the man. Frank Hruby extracted interesting comments from the conductor prior to his Blossom concerts. "At the invitation of your manager Michael Maxwell I will be doing considerable guest work there in Cleveland for the next two years," Maazel said in an interview in the *Press*. "What ultimately transpires after that I have no way of knowing. I would be delighted to consider a role in Cleveland's musical affairs." Maazel called the ensemble "a wonderful orchestra—what we call a marvelous sound body—a fine instrument indeed," and said any thought of the Cleveland post would depend not only on the number of concerts and where, but on "coming to agreement [on] what would appear to be extra-musical considerations." Maazel assured Hruby that "all of this is extremely premature, and as far as I know the Cleveland Orchestra may be considering other conductors."

Finn upped the ante. "It is doubtful if any pair of concerts in the whole

53-year history of the Cleveland Orchestra has carried with it quite the air of expectancy, speculation, and rumor that surrounds the concerts at Blossom Music Center this Friday and Saturday nights," he wrote. "In all I have read about the three previous conductorial changes in our orchestra's history, there seems to be nothing comparable." Finn noted that many observers believed the conductor was "signed, sealed and delivered for the job." He dismissed the idea that Maazel's programs, filled with Szell "specialties," amounted to auditions for the job:

> Pity Lorin Maazel, nevertheless! He will be on exhibit like a prize Hereford at a cattle show. Blossom Music Center will be crawling with conductor watchers, all toting their mental scales, microscopes, slide rules and calipers. And if anything in this world is certain, it is this: after Friday night's concert a minimum of 37 people will ask the various critics: 'Well, whaddaya think? Is he the man or isn't he?' Me, I'm going to sneak out a back way before anyone can ask.

After making his escape from Maazel's first concert on July 9, Finn wrote a laudatory review. "For those able to shut out of their minds all the advance publicity, propaganda and speculation and simply listen to the music-making, what emerged was a very fine concert, beautifully executed by the orchestra and conducted by a musician of enormous accomplishment and self-assurance," he said of performances of Berlioz's *Roman Carnival* overture, Beethoven's Piano Concerto No. 3 (with John Browning) and Bartók's Concerto for Orchestra.

Finn's observations were similar to those made by John von Rhein in the *Akron Beacon Journal*—"Whether he has his eye on the throne or not, Maazel's was an auspicious debut; round two follows tonight"— and Boris Nelson in the *Toledo Blade*—"The Cleveland Orchestra could do a lot worse than hanging its future on this conductor . . ." But the *Sun Press*'s Bain Murray deemed the conductor's music-making "glib, superficial." Maazel's second program on July 11—Mozart's *The Impresario* overture, Prokofiev's Third Piano Concerto (with Byron Janis), and Brahms's Third Symphony—elicited only marginal approbation, as well as a whiff of sarcasm, from *The Plain Dealer*'s Wilma Salisbury. About the Brahms, she wrote:

> Maazel's attitude seemed to be that of an arrogant curator who unveils a masterpiece saying 'Voila! Here is a great work of art which I, Lorin Maazel, have personally selected and now present for your pleasure.' This self-conscious approach emphasizes the interpretation rather than the

creation and keeps the listener on the surface of the composition rather than drawing him into the heart and soul. It is nonetheless a perfectly valid way of making music.

The players sensed that something was brewing during rehearsals for these Blossom concerts. At one point, Maazel turned to principal cellist Lynn Harrell, who was about to leave the orchestra to pursue a solo career, and said, "I hear we're losing you." The issue of the search process wasn't the only bone of contention: Maazel's idiosyncratic way of making music—with all sorts of odd modifications of tempo and mannered inflections—didn't sit well with many players, including principal hornist Myron Bloom. "That's not according to the text," Bloom called out at a Blossom rehearsal. (Maazel and Bloom were destined to become enemies. When the conductor later began calling principal players by their first names, the hornist protested, again in front of his colleagues. "Mr. Bloom to you," he said.)

In July 1971, tension within the orchestra was palpable. When the search committee met the day after Maazel's last Blossom concert, principal violist and search committee member Abraham Skernick believed an announcement concerning the musical directorship was imminent. But the committee reached no consensus and set its next meeting for September. Skernick quickly discussed the developments with his orchestra colleagues, who took a vote expressing no confidence in Maazel as possible musical director. The vote, more a protest against the search process than against Maazel, was conveyed to Maxwell, as was the players' specified desire to evaluate upcoming Blossom concerts by Kertész, Frühbeck de Burgos, and Barenboim.

A few board members also believed the die had already been cast. Helen Brown, whose husband, Percy, had been the sole dissenter on the board committee when Leinsdorf was appointed conductor in 1943, wrote separate letters to Joseph and Rankin asking that a decision not be made until the full board could vote. "I feel closer to you than any of the other members of the 'Selection Committee,' so I want to ask you if I am being just too naive, too unsophisticated or too downright trusting to discount all the rumors flying around that our future conductor has already been chosen?!?" she wrote to Joseph. She was equally passionate to Rankin: "How much better it is to go slowly, let the Orchestra Family, at least, have a voice, than try to cram something down their throats as Adella Prentiss Hughes did in that lamentable era. Please, I implore you, do not allow history to repeat itself under different names. The future is much too perilous." Joseph wrote back saying that Szell's successor would not be chosen without a vote of the full board. But he warned that a decision had to be made soon. "If we go too long without anyone at the helm, I think we raise many risks both in the area of orchestra morale and in the area of fund raising," wrote Joseph. "It would be impossible to hear every leading candidate at Severance Hall because we are booked up and they are booked up. My personal hope is that the Search Committee can come to some decision this fall."

Maazel had been the favorite of Maxwell, Rankin, and Joseph up to this point. Now he was about to become the legal successor to George Szell. Less than two weeks after Maazel's Blossom concerts, Rankin drew up an agreement that he planned to present to the conductor on August 7 in London during a trip with his wife, Clara, and Maxwell.

Meanwhile, rumors continued to fly, including an item in the *Press* calling Maazel and Abbado the top candidates—and Abbado the favorite. Amid the suspense, a candidate whom the orchestra liked enormously, Kertész, arrived at Blossom for a concert Salisbury called "the most satisfying performance of the summer season." She praised the Hungarian conductor even as she offered a veiled criticism of Maazel: "A musician of mystique, an artist free of arrogance, a performer of extraordinary gifts, Kertész, 41, ranks as one of the foremost conductors of his generation—and one of few worthy of the Cleveland Orchestra." Kertész's success prompted the musicians to action. On August 5, local papers announced that the players would conduct a preference poll on their choice for musical director on August 8. "There have been persistent rumors that Maazel will get the post, but management has emphasized that no decision has been made yet," wrote Finn.

It had, however. On Saturday, August 7, as the orchestra was preparing to play works by Schubert, Brahms, and Bruch under Barenboim at Blossom, Maazel and Rankin secretly made the decision official in London:

This letter constitutes an Agreement whereby The Musical Arts Association offers you the position, which you accept, as Musical Director and Conductor of The Cleveland Orchestra. The term of this Agreement shall be for a period of five years commencing with the 1972–73 winter season.

It is agreed that you will function with the full authority and all the responsibilities of Musical Director, to include the selection and placement of the Orchestra's personnel within the framework of the Trade Agreement with the Cleveland Federation of Musicians, the choice of guest conductors, and program policies as evaluated with the General Manager, all these to be effective from the 1973–74 winter season.

You agree to provide The Musical Arts Association with seven (7) weeks in the 1973–74 winter season, the number of concerts and the compensation therefore to be negotiated with your agent, Hurok Concerts, Inc. Similarly, it is agreed that the contract for your services in the 1972–73 season, including concerts at Blossom Music Center in 1973, will remain in full force.

You agree to provide The Musical Arts Association with fourteen (14) weeks in the 1974–75 season, two of these weeks to be at Blossom Music Center in 1975, with a maximum of fifty-two (52) concerts. Your compensation will be one hundred and ten thousand dollars ($110,000) therefore.

In the 1975–76 and 1976–77 seasons, you agree to provide The Musical Arts Association with eighteen (18) weeks each season, two weeks in each to be at Blossom Music Center, with a maximum of sixty (60) and a maximum of sixty-five (65) concerts in each season, as determined by the General Manager. Your compensation will be one hundred and twenty-five thousand dollars ($125,000) in the 1975–76 season, and one hundred and forty thousand dollars ($140,000) in the 1976–77 season.

While this letter sets forth our basic Agreement, it is understood that a formal contract of employment will be evolved and executed before the fall of 1973. Such contract will embody all the articles of this Agreement effective for the 1973–74 season, and any further articles that may be mutually agreed, including your election of method of your compensation.

It is understood that this Agreement shall be effective and binding only after your appointment as Musical Director and Conductor is formally approved at a meeting of the Board of Trustees of The Musical Arts Association.

Your signature below indicates your understanding and acceptance of this Agreement.

While Maxwell and Rankin were away, two other "candidates"— Frühbeck de Burgos and Barenboim—received mixed reviews for their Blossom concerts. Finn wrote of the former: "If he should be chosen, it is obvious things at Severance Hall might be debatable, but they would never, never be dull." Salisbury, on the latter, said: "[He] jabbed at the ensemble as if it were a fencing partner. He pummeled it like a punching bag, caressed it like polished marble, molded it like clay."

Both conductors—and, even moreso, Maazel—were pummeled in the musicians' preference poll on August 8, less than 24 hours after Maazel signed the agreement with Rankin. When the votes of the 98 players attending the meeting were tallied, Kertész was the runaway victor, with 76 first-choice votes, followed by Abbado (13), Frühbeck de Burgos (4), Barenboim (3), and Maazel (2). Leinsdorf and Bernard Haitink, also on the list, received no first-choice votes. The session had been strategically planned. "We have it from good sources that the Musical Arts Assn. (parent body of the Cleveland Orchestra) may be ready to announce the new musical director soon—in a week or so," violinist Bert Siegel, representing the orchestra committee, told the *Press*.

Rankin could have responded with "no comment." But two days after the poll, he stated, accurately, that no announcement would be made before fall and, disingenuously, that the matter was still up in the air. "This expression of preference will, of course, be one of the factors which will be taken into consideration in the next meeting of our search committee," he told *The Plain Dealer*. "The search committee has not as yet completed its deliberations and therefore has not finalized a recommendation for presentation to the trustees." The recommendation, according to violinist Siegel, was supposed to include input from the musicians. The day the orchestra poll was announced, Siegel claimed that Joseph had once stated that no conductor would be appointed whom the majority of players opposed. Joseph told the trustees that he couldn't recall making such a claim; Skernick later pinpointed the statement to a social occasion Joseph and the musicians attended in Russia during the 1965 tour.

Maxwell, speaking at a board meeting, called the poll "embarrassing to the guest conductors who must now come to Cleveland knowing of the Orchestra's ratings, as well as to the new Musical Director if he is indeed one of those who received few votes." He told the trustees that he and Rankin had met recently with Maazel in London and later informed him of the poll so that he could possibly "reconsider his candidacy." These issues were presented to the board six days after Maazel signed the agreement (which was not mentioned at the meeting).

However embarrassed the orchestra's guest conductors may have been by the poll, only one responded in any tangible way to the developments— the man who received the most votes. During his Blossom engagement in late July, Kertész told Maxwell that he didn't think he had a chance to become Cleveland's musical director. He was canceling his two weeks of concerts at Severance Hall in October. Somehow, Kertész's management had led him to believe that Leinsdorf had been chosen (once again) to be the Cleveland Orchestra's next boss. With this bogus information, Kertész vowed to extend his contract with the Cologne Opera. News of Kertész's cancellation made the newspapers three days after the orchestra poll. Then, on August 20, Kertész was quoted to the effect that he still wanted the job. "I've never made a secret of it, especially since the death of George Szell, that I would love to become the music director of the Cleveland Orchestra," he said. "In case the post were offered, I could accept it." Commenting on the search, Joseph said "the recommendations of the orchestra will weigh heavily in the consideration of the trustees, who have final authority in naming the next music director."

The pressure to bring the matter to closure was weighing heavily on everyone with an interest in the orchestra. Joseph was concerned about reactions that were bound to occur. "I know you agree with me that Mike Bloom is one of the most talented members of the Orchestra," he wrote to Rankin. "He seems to be very torn and emotional, and I do think it would be helpful if you would have a talk with him. We don't want to lose him when the new conductor is announced." Toward the end of August, Joseph's conscience shifted into overdrive. Again writing to Rankin, he said that something would have to give soon: "I just don't think we can keep on with a stony silence in view of all of the very many letters and telephone calls I have been receiving. There is a wide feeling that we selected a successor conductor long ago and that the Search Committee is just so much window dressing."

Members of the board were beginning to get itchy, too. Some trustees with friends in the orchestra were eager to discuss the general anguish among the musicians. Frank K. Griesinger advised board colleague Paul Vignos, a member of the search committee, that he was leaning toward Kertész and hoped that the trustees would receive complete information on the candidates before a full vote. "I feel very strongly that if we are to keep our men believing that we have an enterprise in which all of us are working together for a common objective," Griesinger wrote, "we must give proper weight to their musical judgment, as that judgment may be superior to the musical judgment of those of us who are not professional musicians."

Rankin and Joseph had not been ignoring the judgment of orchestra professionals. Rankin, wanting to make sure that Maazel was a better option than Kertész, discussed the two conductors with the cultivated and demanding Ernest Fleischmann, who had known both men while serving as manager of the London Symphony. Fleischmann initially balked at the inquiry, believing it amounted to an "inquisition." But he told Rankin that Kertész and Maazel were complete opposites: Maazel had a larger repertoire and greater intellect; Kertész was interested mainly in 18th- and 19th-century European music, and he needed a "father" figure to function well. Fleischmann suggested making Kertész and Maazel a team in Cleveland.

Another figure whom Rankin turned to for support in the "nomination" of Maazel was Boulez, who was just starting his tenure as music director of the New York Philharmonic. Boulez told Rankin that he believed Maazel to be the right choice, though he was aware that the Cleveland Orchestra wasn't happy. "Do you think it would be even <u>tasteful</u> to send a word of congratulation to the orchestra after the appointment has been made public?" Boulez asked Rankin in a note attached to his recommendation letter. "You will feel the pulse of the 'patient', and tell me what is your opinion."

At this point, almost six weeks after Maazel had signed the agreement in London, only Rankin, Joseph, Maxwell, Boulez, and a few others knew that the outcome of the search had been decided. The board's executive committee was not informed of the decision at its meeting on September 13. Rankin told colleagues that a comprehensive list of candidates would be reviewed on September 29, when the search committee would make its final report. One trustee, Peter Reed, suggested postponing a decision to alleviate the polarization caused by the Maazel-Kertész situation, but no one supported him. Other trustees expressed the view that Kertész should be rejected as a candidate because his remarks to Salisbury about wanting the job were insulting to the board. But soon Kertész was no longer available for the job. On September 18, Finn reported that the conductor had extended his contract with the Cologne Opera until 1979 and accepted the directorship of the city's Gürzenich Orchestra. He had had no communication with the powers-that-be in Cleveland in recent weeks. "Cleveland was and still is my dream," Kertész told Finn. "The orchestra and the audience are very fine. We are all very young, and 1979 is not very far away."

❀   ❀   ❀

The opening program of the orchestra's 1971–72 season looked like a lineup Szell would have relished conducting: Dvořák's *Carnival* overture, Mozart's Violin Concerto No. 5 (with Majeske as soloist), "Tabor" from Smetana's *Ma Vlast*, and Janáček's Sinfonietta. The conductor was Karel Ančerl, the noted Czech musician. "I greatly admire Szell for the way he built up his orchestra," he told the *Press*. "It is my ideal."

Despite Kertész's withdrawal, members of the orchestra committee made a last-ditch effort to ward off what was viewed, with alarm, as the inevitable. They appeared on the Channel 5 WEWS-TV news, on September 28 to ask that the trustees act with "selflessness, dignity, integrity and dedication" and not choose a conductor who had been rejected by most of the players. The gesture was futile. Three days later, the search committee went through the motions and made its report to the executive committee, which was sanctioned to recommend that trustees appoint Maazel as musical director for a five-year term starting in September 1972. The full board meeting followed at the Union Club, with Rankin calling the decision "the unanimous recommendation of the Executive Committee and the members of the Search Committee other than Louis Lane and Mr. Skernick, the Orchestra representative." He then engaged in a series of curious explanations possibly intended to blur the exclusivity of the process. "It would be fanciful to assume that we have arrived at this point according to a preconceived plan," said Rankin. "Statements by Trustees with respect to candidates soon became common knowledge among the Orchestra membership. Very shortly remarks favoring the candidacy of Maazel were translated into alleged commitments; and the absence of remarks favoring the candidacy of Kertész were [sic] translated into disinterest or indifference."

To bolster the choice, Rankin ran down a list of Maazel's qualifications, (including the odd observation that "he is very much of a human being"). "To quote from my proposed letter to the Orchestra—'in the course of our extensive conversations, we have found him to be dedicated to musical excellence, thoughtful and considerate, witty, perhaps a bit reserved, sensitive to the feelings and requirements of both musicians and management, eager to serve and clearly capable of dynamic commitment to this great Orchestra.'" Rankin acknowledged that some orchestra members considered Maazel unqualified on musical grounds, but that many prominent figures in the music business held him in highest regard. One objection to Maazel, he noted, concerned his reputation as "a disciplinarian." "Following the Orchestra's long period of tight discipline," he stated, "which included some conflicts, many members of the Orchestra are anxious to avoid a return to what they see as strict control."

At least one trustee believed the search process itself was being too strictly controlled. Frank Griesinger told the board that requests by principal players to appear before the search committee—and by the orchestra committee to appear before the trustees—had been rejected. He said that Rankin had denied Griesinger's own request to allow Skernick and Lane to address the trustees during this meeting. Griesinger recommended defeat of a motion to appoint Maazel, and he moved that the trustees be given the chance to discuss the qualifications of other candidates. Joseph countered that he had conferred with many respected figures in the orchestra world who told him that Maazel was right for Cleveland, and he insisted, once again, that the musicians' opinions were not being ignored. He said that the situation regarding the players "is indeed a source of great concern."

It was not enough of a concern to keep the motion to appoint Maazel from being brought to a vote "and passed by an overwhelming majority," according to the minutes of the October 1 meeting. The majority was not exactly overwhelming, however, as Bain Murray recounted in the *Sun Press*. Of the board's 58 trustees, only 38 attended the meeting, enough for a quorum. But "twelve of the 36 [*sic*] voted against Maazel's appointment," wrote Murray. "Many of the Trustees did not feel qualified to make this decision; others, who have more of a musical background, were out of town during the Blossom season when most of the candidates appeared." The implication is that board members were not notified (in advance, or at all) that Maazel was even a candidate for the job. Otherwise, they might have changed their summer plans and been present for his Blossom concerts. Whatever the vote, the orchestra was informed of the appointment in a letter from Rankin and Joseph that was hand delivered to the home of each musician immediately after the board meeting. "We have, of course, been mindful of the differing views which have been expressed from time to time during the past year, including your own, and all of these views were given serious attention," the letter said. A reporter for the *Press* who was waiting at the Union Club was able to get a brief story in the afternoon paper headlined "Maazel Named by Orchestra," though the story was vague on details.

The next morning, the musicians "were angry and upset about the naming of Lorin Maazel to the post of orchestra conductor," the *Press* reported. "All but two, anyway. Two voted for Maazel in a recent informal popularity poll of potential future conductors." Violinist Siegel, never shy with the media, said he planned to attend a weep-in party: "The search committee was a sham. The committee never once took a vote on where the committee actually stood. We heard rumors a year ago that Maazel would be named. We heard Pierre Boulez recommended him to the board way back when." Despite the fact that the search process had outraged the musicians, Siegel said the orchestra objected to Maazel on a purely artistic basis: "We do not like his music-making. It doesn't fit in with the legacy of the Szell tradition."

From Berlin, Maazel sent a telegram to the orchestra and told the *Press* that the job was "the most important musical position in the United States. There is no better orchestra than the Cleveland Orchestra. I am very happy." In a statement to the media, the orchestra committee proclaimed a "day of great sadness in the Cleveland musical community." But the sadness did not affect their concert that week under Karel Ančerl at Severance Hall. "Whatever their personal reactions to the news of the hour about their futures," wrote Finn, "they still sounded like the Cleveland Orchestra."

They wouldn't, however, honor Maxwell's request for another public comment about the appointment: "We emphasize that the orchestra will give their best for Mr. Maazel as they have in the past given of their talents for Mr. Szell; in view, however, of the manner in which the search for our

new music director was conducted, we do not wish at this time to participate in any public statement, nor find that a reply to the cablegram is appropriate." Only 16 months into his tenure as general manager, Maxwell
had, in effect, lost the confidence of the orchestra.

At least one orchestra member *did* make a public statement—principal
trombonist Robert Boyd, who admitted that he was one of the two players
who voted for Maazel in the preference poll. (The other was second bassoonist Vaclav Laksar.) In a letter to the editor of *The Plain Dealer*, Boyd
wrote that Szell probably wouldn't have garnered even two votes in a popularity contest when he won the Cleveland post in 1946. Boyd also con-
tended, based on Maazel's performance of the Bartók Concerto for Orchestra at Blossom, that he was "the young Szell's equal in every respect."
Another letter to the editor in *The Plain Dealer* the same day from an
orchestra patron countered that the board had made a mockery of the
process and "dare to compare [Maazel] to the late George Szell. All this is
in bad taste."

The patron wasn't the only one who found the situation uncomfortable.
"You can well imagine that I have not taken very kindly to having been
caught in the cross-fire," Maazel wrote to Rankin in late October. "For the
moment, my only desire is to work in as professional a way as possible while
guest conducting in December, after which there will be plenty of time to
set things straight."

– 28 –

Following a Giant

*I*n appointing Lorin Maazel to the Cleveland Orchestra, did the Musical
Arts Association make a mammoth blunder? At least 96 of the orchestra's musicians appeared to think so. Twelve of the 38 trustees who had been
present to vote on the subject had disagreed with the board's decision. At
that point, the atmosphere was so fraught with emotion that no one—not
even Maazel—could anticipate how the new partnership would fare. The
musicians were disgusted that their management and board had so totally
disregarded their views. Many people who heard Maazel's two Blossom concerts proclaimed him unfit to stand on the podium that George Szell had occupied for 24 years. They were quick to pass judgment. Maazel may not have
possessed Szell's impeccable taste, but the orchestra's new music director
would soon prove himself to have extravagant qualifications for the job.

Like Szell, he had been working toward such a position since he was a
child. Lorin Varencove Maazel was born on March 6, 1930, in Neuilly-sur-
Seine, a suburb of Paris, where his father, a New York–born actor-singer
named Lincoln, was studying voice. The Maazels moved to Los Angeles
when Lorin was two. Lincoln and his wife, Marie, were to discover that their
precocious son had perfect pitch. Hearing the high-pitched swoosh of a toilet one day, the four-year-old declared to his mother, "That's A-flat." In 1935,
he began studying violin. A year later, he took up piano and started conducting lessons with Vladimir Bakaleinikoff, former music director of the
Moscow Artists Theater. Lorin was a chubby boy of eight in short pants
when, on July 13, 1938, he stood before an orchestra for the first time. He
led the University of Idaho Orchestra in Schubert's "Unfinished"
Symphony, in Moscow, Idaho. It wasn't his only impressive feat: five days
later, he was soloist in the first movement of Viotti's Violin Concerto No. 23.

The mini-maestro's conducting gifts began to draw national attention
during the summer of 1939, the year the Maazel family moved to Pittsburgh
to be near Bakaleinikoff, who had become Fritz Reiner's assistant conductor at the Pittsburgh Symphony. That summer, at the National Music Camp

in Interlochen, Michigan, Maazel conducted an orchestra of 150 American college students. Olin Downes, music critic of the *New York Times*, heard the concert and wrote a column about the wunderkind, making note of "the most disconcerting of all music's phenomenons: the child prodigy. In this class there is now a special case: Lorin Maazel, who soon will make his appearance at the New York World's Fair. Neither a Paganini *redivivus*, nor a pianist, nor a boy soprano . . . Lorin is, by God, a conductor! And naturally he directs from memory."

The boy went on to conduct most of American's top orchestras. "He was a high-class carnival act, traveling the country and leading big orchestras before curious audiences—the way the child Mozart was summoned two centuries ago to give clavier recitals for the crowned heads of Europe," one journalist later noted of Maazel's youthful career. Maazel triumphed over one situation that would have sent most youngsters crying for their mothers: At the first rehearsal for his New York Philharmonic debut, the 10-year-old encountered musicians sucking contemptuously on lollipops. But they were soon won over by Maazel's obvious talent. Among his high-profile concerts during the summer of 1941 was his debut with the NBC Symphony, at the invitation of Arturo Toscanini.

Maazel had been a teenager for only eight days when he stepped in front of the Cleveland Orchestra for the first time, still in short pants, on March 14, 1943. Two years later, conducting in long pants, Maazel was finding it difficult to impress anybody. "I was dropped as soon as I lost my market value," he later said. But Reiner, the exceptional and stern conductor of the Pittsburgh Symphony, recognized Maazel's gift. He invited the young conductor to his home on Sundays to discuss scores. Maazel was a good enough violinist to join the Pittsburgh Symphony, on the last stand of the second violin section, in 1948, after Reiner had departed. For three seasons, Maazel served as the orchestra's apprentice conductor and as first violinist in the Fine Arts Quartet, while studying liberal arts at the University of Pittsburgh. In 1951, he participated in the conducting seminar at Tanglewood, where one of his fellow students was a young German named Christoph von Dohnányi. A year later, with a recommendation from a family friend, poet Joseph Grucci (whose journal *Pivot* later would include the conductor's first published poems), Maazel received a Fulbright Fellowship to study baroque music at the Conservatory of Santa Cecilia in Rome. The same year, he married Miriam Sandbank, a Brazilian-born concert pianist.

Before heading for Italy, Maazel had his second engagement with the Cleveland Orchestra (this one actually with the Cleveland Summer Orchestra), for which he conducted two concerts in July 1952. He would later say that his real professional conducting debut occurred in 1953, when he made his European debut leading Italy's Orchestra of Catania in place of an indisposed Pierre Dervaux. Soon, Maazel was in demand throughout Europe. He conducted the Vienna and Berlin philharmonic orchestras and made recordings for Deutsche Grammophon. In 1960, at the invitation of Wieland Wagner, he became the first American, and the youngest person up to that time, to conduct at the Bayreuth Festival. He led six performances of *Lohengrin*. In 1965, he landed not one but two posts in West Berlin—chief conductor of the Berlin Radio Symphony and general music director of the Deutsche Oper.

America also beckoned in the 1960s, when Maazel appeared with the New York Philharmonic, Philadelphia Orchestra, and Boston Symphony. He made his only appearances at the Metropolitan Opera during the 1962–63 season, leading eight performances each of Mozart's *Don Giovanni* and Strauss's *Der Rosenkavalier*. Maazel's conducting at the Met generally was not admired. Of a preserved Saturday afternoon radio broadcast of *Rosenkavalier*, Paul Jackson notes: "Nostalgia recedes into nothingness in the face of his driving tempos and harsh orchestral sound, especially from the overly aggressive battery [percussion]." He was more successful operatically in Europe, where he conducted at most of the major houses and led Wieland Wagner's 1968 production of the *Ring* cycle at Bayreuth.

By the early 1970s, Maazel clearly had the credentials to lead a major American orchestra. When he accepted the Cleveland post, he could boast of achievements that few, if any, colleagues could match. "I'm starting this position with the repertoire and experience most conductors have when they retire," Maazel told *The Plain Dealer.* "I could conduct 20 years of concerts in Cleveland and never open another score because I have a repertoire of over 1,000 works. I've conducted 3,000 concerts around the world."

Only five had been with the Cleveland Orchestra.

✿　　✿　　✿

"Personally I have not the slightest reservation that we have the right man and that he will maintain the high musical standards to which we have become accustomed," board chairman Frank E. Joseph wrote to a disgruntled concertgoer after Maazel's appointment in October 1971. "I think you should give him a chance to show what he can do." Maazel intended to make an immediate good impression. Upon his appointment, he told the *New York Times* that he planned to avoid symphonic cycles and to give audiences programs that would sound good, not just look impressive on paper. "And I don't believe we're going to do anything for music by spitting in the faces of

longtime music-lovers," he said. "I want the museum of the concert hall to
be just that, but one with masterpieces from all periods."

He was brimming with ideas, such as splitting the ensemble into smaller
groups to make the orchestra more accessible to more people. "My first aim,
of course, is to keep the orchestra in the very front line of American music,
and I want to usher the orchestra and the community into our decade,"
Maazel said in the *Philadelphia Inquirer*. "I think the changes that have
been going on in music are cumulative, and I sense in Cleveland a real desire for change. There are whirlpools of dissension everywhere about what
the orchestra should be and do. There is no real pattern, no consensus, and
because that is true, I don't think we can respond in just one way." Maazel
hoped to respond by making the orchestra "a model for other orchestras. I
have found a young and eager organization in Cleveland, and I think it will
be interesting to work with it."

Interesting even though his appointment had engendered such controversy. "I'm a strong personality and considered by my generation a leading
conductor," said Maazel in an Associated Press interview. "Naturally, when
one of the five highest paid conductors in the world, and I happen to be one,
is engaged to conduct an orchestra which has no peer, the members wonder, 'What is going to happen? Are we going to lose our identity?' It's perfectly natural. I'm the first to understand it."

Understanding Maazel would be another matter, especially musically. He
was eager to discuss his approach to music-making in the AP interview. With
these words, he pinpointed artistic characteristics that would divide Cleveland audiences:

> I don't believe in the mechanical reproduction of what is on the print-
> ed page. You can't do it anyway; the language of music notation is subject
> to an infinite number of interpretations. But I don't think you can afford
> to be free in your interpretation until you have submitted yourself to dis-
> cipline. As the Greeks have taught us, freedom is attained through disci-
> pline. After you know what the composer has written down and observe
> everything, then you're free to take liberties—because they are not liber-
> ties. They are interpretations of what in your considered and instinctual
> opinion the composer is really trying to say. I haven't set out to interpret
> more as I've gotten older and gained more experience and discipline, but
> it has been an inevitable result.

Cleveland soon had another chance to gauge Maazel's interpretive
personality. He returned in December, less than three months after his

appointment, for his Severance Hall debut. His concerts were preceded by activities around the city, including events that gave him the chance to charm the public, change a few minds, and speak—in generalities—about his plans for the orchestra. He talked about possibly taking the musicians into schools and using television to gain wider exposure. There were to be "special programs" and "new formats." About the controversy his appointment generated, he said, "I hope it keeps up. It would be bad if everybody just forgot us."

No one was likely to forget about Maazel, as Robert Finn suggested in his review of the new music director's first concert in Cleveland since his appointment. "Twenty-five years ago, when George Szell took over the Cleveland Orchestra, he announced flatly, 'A new leaf will be turned over with a bang!' Another such bang is to be heard in Severance Hall this weekend with the debut there of Lorin Maazel, who will become Szell's successor nine months hence," Finn wrote of the program—Beethoven's *Leonore* Overture No. 2, Chopin's E minor Piano Concerto and Sibelius's Fifth Symphony. As his soloist, Maazel brought Israela Margalit, who had become his second wife in 1969 (and had given birth to their first child, Illan Sean, in August 1971).

Finn spent most of his review describing the Sibelius performance, which he called a shrewd choice. "It is Maazel's kind of piece: big in sound, epic in concept, full of inherent drama and of 'effects' that lend themselves to the kind of exaggeration he favors. It is no work for a literalist conductor, and Lorin Maazel is no literalist. Pianissimos are superhushed, climaxes become towering technicolor sound structures, rhythm and accent are subject to all kinds of modification. Every dramatic implication in the score, whether stormy or subdued, is musically underlined threefold." Finn acknowledged the exciting nature of the interpretation, while noting that Maazel's music-making was "at the opposite end of the musical universe from what has been the Cleveland norm for so long. At Severance Hall, the big, bold stroke of primary color has replaced the musical blueprint." The end of the review offered an overall assessment of the conductor, and of his future impact on the orchestra: "Lorin Maazel is a strong personality. Where his ideas suit the music, they create real sparks. Where they do not, they become annoying mannerisms. One thing is sure: very little is understated at a Maazel concert. Cleveland has reached a sharp turning in the musical road."

The musicians had told management that they would not stand when the conductor arrived onstage for his debut. The dispute wasn't resolved until moments before the concert, when the players agreed to rise only after Maazel gave them a welcoming gesture. Even so, the orchestra clearly was still smarting. Frank Hruby, reviewing the concert in the *Press*, wrote, "The audience rated a higher score than the majority of the players. So help me, there were pouts and sneers onstage and a general reluctance to respond graciously to the situation. Of the customary courtesies the occasion called for, there were precious little." This review, and a follow-up column chastising the musicians for snubbing their future boss, won the critic a slap on the wrist from the orchestra committee in a letter to the editor of the *Press*.

At least Hruby was generally positive about the performances. The same couldn't be said for two other observers. Bain Murray, in the *Sun Press*, brought up the matter of taste with a hint of sarcasm and a reference to Leonard Bernstein: "We are in for a heart-on-the-sleeve type of music-making. This is legitimate. One finds it easily in Philadelphia, Hollywood, and in pre-Boulez New York. And for those who want their symphonies in technicolor, we now can supply this commodity in Cleveland." Don Robertson, a feisty Cleveland novelist and columnist who watched the concert's live television broadcast on WKYC, wrote about the experience a month later in the *Press*. He didn't mince words, calling the event "absolutely dreadful."

> The orchestra members were coldly professional, and they played all the notes, but their antipathy towards Maazel was so obvious you could have scooped it with a shovel. As for the new maestro, his readings were fussy, nervous and superficial, and he never once let himself get caught up in the music. He gyrated a great deal, and his face was marvelously expressive (perhaps for the benefit of the TV camera), but everything came out plastic. In short, the entire affair was a calamity.

With his Severance debut complete, the future music director departed from the podium for the rest of the 1971–72 season. Performances were led by Louis Lane, Pierre Boulez, Michael Charry, and a host of guest conductors (Erich Leinsdorf, Bernard Haitink, Rafael Frühbeck de Burgos, Daniel Barenboim, André Previn, Rafael Kubelik). The programming, devised mostly by general manager Michael Maxwell, was veering away from the 18th and 19th centuries and zealously toward the 20th. No Beethoven symphonies were played and only five works by Mozart. Boulez filled his four programs with music by Stravinsky, Bartók, Schoenberg, and Mahler. Lane brought works by Donald Erb and Easley Blackwood. Other conductors focused on such composers as Josef Suk, Alban Berg, Anton Webern, Manuel de Falla, Russell Smith, and Sir William Walton.

Leinsdorf, whose tenure as the orchestra's boss had been fraught with frustration in the 1940s, was finally a success in the 1970s. He was on the podium, and at the piano, for a special program on January 17, 1972, featuring the great Russian cellist Mstislav Rostropovich, who had been allowed to leave the Soviet Union only recently after a year under official watch for having spoken out in defense of dissident writer Alexander Solzhenitsyn. The cellist played the Dvořák concerto and Tchaikovsky's Rococo Variations under Leinsdorf's baton, teamed with the conductor-pianist in Beethoven's Variations on Themes from *The Magic Flute*, and gave a solo encore of an unaccompanied Bach sarabande.

One former possibility for the orchestra's podium, Daniel Barenboim, arrived in early February to make his Severance Hall debut. He also shared an East Coast tour with Leinsdorf, taking the orchestra to Carnegie Hall for a Mozart-Liszt-Bruckner program that "stirred a mild tremor or two," according to the *New York Times*. Barenboim's performance of Bruckner's Seventh Symphony, the *Times* said, possessed wide fluctuations in tempo and expressive detailing that was uncommon in this music. "The orchestra, forced to follow Mr. Barenboim's musical impulses from moment to moment, did so with hair-trigger precision (if a few brass bloopers are ignored). It was as if the orchestra were the conductor, alertly following an opera singer's every breath. This takes great finesse and Cleveland has it."

Barenboim fared less well in Washington, D.C., where his program of music by Schubert, Liszt, and Beethoven with the ensemble earned an unsavory headline in the *Washington Star*: "Barenboim Lays Egg With Great Orchestra." As the critic put it, "Among orchestra players, there is a cynical saying that there are no bad orchestras, but that there are conductors who can make good orchestras sound bad. Daniel Barenboim should have proven once and for all that this is true by his performance with the Cleveland Orchestra at the Kennedy Center on Black Sunday, the 12th of February, when he succeeded in making what is presumably the world's greatest symphony orchestra sound second class." Days later, Irving Lowens, the *Star*'s chief music critic, wrote of a Mozart-Weill-Prokofiev program in the same hall, "With Erich Leinsdorf on the podium, at any rate, the Cleveland Orchestra still sounds like one of the greatest in the world."

Overseas, meanwhile, things weren't so cheerful for Maazel. In early March 1972, he asked to be relieved of his duties as associate principal conductor of the New Philharmonia Orchestra of London. Some accounts claimed that Maazel had lost his temper with the trombone section and stormed out of a rehearsal. Others said Maazel blamed management for not consulting him on programming and artists. Management countered that the conductor's ideas were too expensive.

Maazel returned to Cleveland in May 1972 with his wife and son for a party given in their honor by the Greater Cleveland Growth Association at the Sheraton-Cleveland Hotel. He was eager to begin his tenure with the Cleveland Orchestra. "Our job is to make it fun," he told *The Plain Dealer*, "and to make people realize that they want us as much as we want them."

When Walter Susskind, music director of the St. Louis Symphony, took the Cleveland musicians on a western tour in late May and early June, the response to the orchestra was once again ecstatic. "Years ago, Alfred Frankenstein coined the phrase 'One hundred men and a genius' for George Szell's Cleveland Orchestra," wrote a reviewer for the *San Francisco Chronicle*, where Frankenstein had been longtime music critic. "Saturday evening in the Opera House it was 'one hundred men and a nice guy,' but either way, the Cleveland Orchestra remains one of the sensations of the universe." (The fact that women had been members of the orchestra throughout its history seemed utterly lost on some observers.)

❖   ❖   ❖

Maazel soon was back again for two programs at Blossom that drew passionate responses from critics. Wilma Salisbury, reviewing the first concert of music by Brahms, Bartók, and Sibelius in *The Plain Dealer*, noted that Maazel had reseated the orchestra—the cellos moved directly to the right of the podium, where Szell had placed the violas. She said the "orchestra made a fat, rumbly sound—suitable for fat, rumbly music, but utterly uncharacteristic of the Cleveland Orchestra with its wonderful Haydn-Mozart-Beethoven affinity." Of Maazel's performance of Sibelius's Second Symphony, Salisbury wrote that the conductor "was constantly on the lookout for spots to 'do' something: stretch a phrase, pause before a downbeat, wallow in sound, bloat a nuance, crash into an accent, dramatize a transition, race through a scherzo, slobber over a sentimental tune, prolong a grandiose climax." Of the second program of works by Barber, Lalo, and Rimsky-Korsakov, Finn observed that Maazel "plays on the Cleveland Orchestra as if it were a great rumbling organ, where his predecessor treated it like a string quartet. It is a complete shift in musical values which listeners are going to have to get used to."

Maazel's concerts were not the only highlights of the fifth Blossom season. Lane took the honors for extravagance by conducting the first Northeast Ohio performance of Mahler's Symphony No. 8 ("Symphony of a Thousand") with 480 performers onstage.

The Blossom season ended with a bang, of the satirical type. In a biting parody headlined "A Fable for Orchestral Critics," Salisbury devised a tale of a beautiful bird named Cleve Ork whose owners "built for him an elegant gilded cage in the heart of the city's cultural area" and imported one of the greatest Ork trainers in the world, Dr. George. Under its trainer, Cleve's voice "developed into one of the most glorious ever heard among the world-wide species known as Ork." But Dr. George died, and the owners ignored Cleve and hired "a man who was not a trainer at all, but rather a glittering showman who had been putting great Orks through their paces ever since he was a little boy. His name was Childe Lorin. And he must have been a magician, for the first time he stepped into Cleve's gilded cage, he performed a miracle: He raised his magic baton, brought it down like a whiplash and presto—poof! Cleve was transformed instantly from a beautiful delicate bird into a high-strung thoroughbred stallion." Only when "one of Dr. George's spiritual descendants" came to town and "spoke softly to the high-strung horse [would Cleve] revert to form, fly back to his gilded cage and sing gloriously as in days of yore."

Maazel, in Salisbury's estimation, had become Public Enemy No. 1 in Cleveland, even before he had conducted a note as music director. Maxwell, evidently infuriated by Salisbury's article and her review of the Sibelius Second at Blossom, wrote an essay, "A View of Musical Criticism," that was printed in the second program book of the 1972–73 season. Maxwell made no direct mention of Salisbury in the essay, but he quoted her Sibelius review and offered a prescription for critical competence:

> In short, I need trust in my critic, and a credibility must be established that could govern my attitudes toward interpretation or performance. If my critic can achieve this he will be thrice blessed because, as an arbiter and judge, he himself will be a cultural force of importance, as well as a man (or woman) of importance to his editor, and will command the attention and respect, not only of his readers, but the artists he evaluates as well.

Salisbury wasn't the only listener already disenchanted with Maazel. One concertgoer informed board president Alfred Rankin in early September that she was concerned about the Musical Arts Association's "floundering" and the orchestra's "petulance": "We who love music and have for years listened lovingly and supported faithfully our glorious Cleveland Orchestra are disheartened. For our own sakes we shall attend and support so long as we are able. But the highest joy is gone. It will take years for the Association and the players to undo the mischief already done—if that can ever be."

In this heated atmosphere came words of reason from Robert Finn. He pointed out that the "exciting new era" promised by the orchestra actually wouldn't begin until the following season, when Maazel would be on the podium for at least 14 programs. The conductor could only commit himself for six weeks during the current season, hardly enough time to make a decisive imprint on the orchestra's personality. "The real significance of 1972–73 is that the post-Szell interregnum is finally ending and a future course, for good or ill, has been charted," wrote Finn. "Musically, this season looks resolutely backward, but in terms of the Cleveland Orchestra's future it is like the pregnant pause before a new conductor's downbeat."

Maazel was already showing signs that he would have a long-term impact on the orchestra. Decca Records (London Records in the United States), with whom he had made dozens of recordings in Europe, was interested in beginning a relationship with Maazel and the Cleveland Orchestra, if the Musical Arts Association would pay orchestra costs up front. A tour to Australia and New Zealand in October 1973 had become available after the Chicago Symphony withdrew from participating in the (much delayed) opening week of the $100 million Sydney Opera House. Maxwell was negotiating a tour that would comprise 18 concerts in Honolulu, New Zealand, and Australia.

Maazel received a symbolic endorsement when Ormandy came to town to conduct performances of Mahler's Symphony No. 2, known as the "Resurrection." The veteran music director of the Philadelphia Orchestra gave the Cleveland Orchestra Women's Committee a cheerleading speech at a luncheon. "There is a great similarity between Lorin Maazel and myself," said Ormandy. "He is following a giant, George Szell, as I followed a giant, Leopold Stokowski. I survived and he will survive. He is a terribly talented young man, a young man who should be here many years."

Coincidentally, it was Ormandy who had told Maxwell about another talented young man in 1971, when Cleveland was looking for a choral director to succeed Margaret Hillis (who had replaced Clayton Krehbiel in 1969). He was Robert Page, longtime director of choral activities at Temple University and music director and conductor of the Mendelssohn Choir of Philadelphia. Both of Page's ensembles performed on occasion with the Philadelphia Orchestra. "Oh, he's wonderful," Ormandy told Maxwell. "I just think he's the greatest choral director and I really lean on him for everything I need in terms of the chorus unless we're using the Westminster Choir or some other group." The high-spirited Page arrived in Cleveland in the fall of 1972, just as Maazel was about to make his first appearance as music director, and became a close colleague.

❀   ❀   ❀

Finally, two months into the 1972–73 season, Maazel arrived to make his debut as music director of the Cleveland Orchestra. He chose an enormously dramatic work, the Verdi Requiem, for performances on November 24 and 26 featuring soprano Martina Arroyo, mezzo-soprano Shirley Verrett, tenor Placido Domingo, bass Bonaldo Giaotti, and the Cleveland Orchestra Chorus. Before these concerts, he had a few things to get off his chest. Maazel began his first rehearsal as music director not with music, but with a 40-minute talk—"the longest speech ever given by a conductor to this orchestra in my time," noted violinist Kurt Loebel, who jotted down notes about the speech. Maazel spoke about the need to find new audiences, especially young people. He told the players he would ask guest conductors to include worthy modern works on their programs. He touched upon the controversy over his appointment and his problematic relationship with the musicians. He called the media unreliable. Then, his marathon oration complete, Maazel rehearsed the Verdi. "There seemed little doubt that he has perfect pitch, probably a photographic memory and a fine baton technique," Loebel recalled. However, he noted, "At this point he seemed somewhat cold, superficial and theatrical."

Maazel repeated some of his remarks in the *New York Times* the same week, saying he was "instituting a regime for total repertoire." The approach would embrace important contemporary works that had not been performed in Cleveland. "I hope to get around the idea of doing a novelty for novelty's sake and then playing Beethoven's Fifth so that the audience will forget the new work," he said. The new team of Maazel and Cleveland then swiftly introduced itself to New York, taking the Verdi Requiem to Carnegie Hall immediately after the Severance performances, with Nicolai Gedda singing the tenor part and Cesare Siepi replacing Giaotti. Harold C. Schonberg, the *New York Times* critic who had been such a Szell champion, suggested that the successor would work out fine. "His ideas were completely different from Mr. Szell's. His pacings, especially in the opening movement, were considerably slower, and his attention to dynamic contrast much more marked. At the very opening Mr. Maazel made it clear that this was to be 'his' performance," Schonberg wrote. "This was very impressive conducting, no matter what one may have thought of the conductor's approach. Working, as always, without a score, Mr. Maazel had every note and phrase in mind, he got exactly what he wanted, and for a space of an hour and a half he did create a world of his own, and he swept the audience along with him." The *New York Post* called Maazel's performance "unsettled" and "too theatrical."

On their return to Severance days later, Maazel and the orchestra performed Mozart's Symphony No. 38 (prime Szell territory) and Tchaikovsky's
"Manfred" Symphony (which Szell never conducted in Cleveland).
Salisbury once again noted how different the orchestra sounded under the
new boss, though not always, this time, to the music's disadvantage. "Gone
was the crisp, transparent elegance for which the Cleveland Orchestra's
Mozart has been justly celebrated in the past. In its place was a concept
heavy, romantic and antithetical to the Mozartean manner," she wrote. "The
orchestra also did not sound like its former refined self in the Tchaikovsky
opus. On the contrary, it took on the character of a fantastic Russian tonal
giant: overwhelming, sensual and deep-throated. At times the sonority was
mellow, at times, gruff, at times brilliant . . . In response to its master's authoritative leadership, the orchestra produced mountains of gorgeous tone
. . . achieving some of its most unified playing of the season."

✻   ✻   ✻

Maazel had no intention of monopolizing the orchestra's podium. Like
Maxwell, he was eager to engage the best conductors to serve as guests, including Herbert von Karajan, who had brought his Berlin Philharmonic to
Severance Hall in November 1961. But the Austrian conductor again was
proving elusive, as he had several years before when Szell tried to bring him
to Cleveland. In 1973, Karajan turned down another offer to guest conduct.
Maazel tried to change Karajan's mind by offering to give up one of his own
weeks with the orchestra if arrangements could be made.

The subject of guests was very much on the minds of Cleveland's musicians and audiences this season, when Maazel was only available to lead four
weeks at Severance Hall. Barenboim, who had taken such a beating during
the orchestra's East Coast tour a year before, didn't fare terribly well on his
return in January 1973, either, conducting a performance of Schubert's
"Great" C major Symphony that "was simply too exaggerated for comfort,"
according to Finn. The critic also ran hot and cold on cellist Jacqueline du
Pré (Barenboim's wife), who played the Lalo concerto "with defiant brilliance, paying far more attention to strong, gutsy articulation than to beauty
of tone or stylistic niceties."

The early months of 1973 featured a stream of former candidates for
music director, including Abbado and István Kertész, who, with Barenboim,
took the orchestra on a two-week East Coast tour. The major repertoire
ranged from Stravinsky's *The Rite of Spring* and Mahler's Sixth Symphony
(both led by Abbado) to Dvořák's Eighth Symphony (Kertész) to Schubert's
"Great" C major Symphony (Barenboim). Michael Steinberg, who had

raved about Szell's performance of Mahler's Ninth Symphony at Carnegie Hall in 1964, heard Abbado and the Cleveland Orchestra play Mahler's Sixth in Boston. "Wednesday's performance was vintage Cleveland: a sound with a cutting edge like a diamond, incredibly concentrated and compact, highly characterized, yet with a perfection of blend—the voicings of those brass chords played as though by a single instrument!—that speaks for uncommon care in assembling and training," wrote Steinberg in the *Boston Globe*. "Beyond those conventional, though remarkable, virtuosities, there was the orchestra's flexibility and capacity for instant response, the prerequisite for Abbado's Rubato style. If finer Mahler is available today, it is from an orchestra and a conductor I have never heard of."

A week later, on February 13, 1973, Kertész led the orchestra in a Mozart-Mahler-Dvořák program (a lineup Szell might well have conducted) at Carnegie Hall. It was his last concert with the ensemble he would have inherited had the musicians had their way. Two months later, the 43-year-old Kertész drowned while swimming in the Mediterranean Sea off the coast of Israel.

✻   ✻   ✻

Maazel had several crucial missions to accomplish upon taking over the Cleveland Orchestra. In the two-year period after Szell's death, subscriptions had plummeted, and the orchestra had stopped recording and touring internationally. Maazel's arrival now brought a sharp increase in ticket sales—and also an invitation from Decca Records to record Prokofiev's complete ballet, *Romeo and Juliet*. The prospect of continuing the orchestra's recording activity renewed the board's excitement over Maazel even as it created a bit of concern. "I think the jackets on some of Lorin Maazel's recent recordings are offensive," Frank Joseph wrote to Maxwell in March 1973 without specifying which jackets he found inelegant. "I would hope that we would not try to market Cleveland Orchestra recordings with pictures of naked women."

Another area in which Maazel hoped to make headway was community outreach. Unlike his predecessor, who had shown little interest in this realm, the new music director believed the orchestra had to become a more inclusive resource, and he knew where to start—children in the city's schools. An annual concert at Public Hall would feature a chorus of up to, or sometimes even more than, 1,000 students. Maazel's first such project, on May 19, 1973, was a program comprising music from *Porgy and Bess*, Copland's *A Lincoln Portrait* (narrated by actor Mel Ferrer), and the "Ode to Joy" from Beethoven's Ninth Symphony, sung in English by nearly 900 singers from

27 Greater Cleveland high schools. Tickets cost $1, and an audience of almost 5,000 attended the concert.

By the time of this successful event, Maazel had completed his first Severance Hall season. He had returned in March for programs of works by Stravinsky, Bartók, Ravel, Bach, Beethoven (with Vladimir Ashkenazy in the C minor Piano Concerto), and Brahms. With Brahms's First Symphony, Maazel introduced his highly idiosyncratic—some would say objectionable—approach to the German composer. "Maazel's performance was grossly overinterpreted, with all kinds of exaggerated ritards, accents and tempo fluctuations," wrote Finn. "Maazel's intention apparently was to 'split the ears of the groundlings,' but the result was heavy-handed and, to my ears, utterly unconvincing." Maazel next led two Strauss blockbusters, *Also sprach Zarathustra* and *Don Quixote* (with former principal cellist Leonard Rose doing the solo honors and principal violist Abraham Skernick again portraying Sancho Panza), and wrapped up his Severance season with one of the most sublime and challenging creations in all of music, Beethoven's *Missa Solemnis*. His performance garnered an unpromising headline on Finn's review: "Loud, Louder."

The jury was still out on Maazel, as Finn suggested in an analysis of the conductor's inaugural season in *The Plain Dealer*. Certain composers had received stellar handling by the new man in town, he noted, while others (especially Mozart and Brahms) had been the victims of conductorial perverseness. "The players, I think, have come to respect Maazel's undeniable technical proficiency and musical knowledge," wrote Finn. "No one that I know of has charged that he is a poor conductor in the purely technical sense. But I do not think the men yet trust his interpretive instincts, nor have they really warmed up to him yet as a person."

Actually, more than a few musicians and listeners were moving into Maazel's camp. Others would never be convinced that the Musical Arts Association had made the right choice. Maazel had unwittingly generated enough controversy to keep both admirers and detractors fascinated with the town's new conductor.

– 29 –

Maazel in Charge

Lorin Maazel couldn't devote himself entirely to his new job as music director of the Cleveland Orchestra during the 1972–73 season. He still had commitments in Europe that made it impossible for him to be at Severance Hall for more than about half the time he would need to make a discernible impact. Now, in the spring of 1973, Maazel was ready to begin making that impact, including a mission that was vitally important to the orchestra: conducting its first recording in almost three years.

On June 4, 5, and 6, 1973, the new boss and his musicians took up temporary residence at Masonic Auditorium—where the orchestra hadn't recorded in 16 years—to tape Prokofiev's complete *Romeo and Juliet* for Decca Records. Breaking with a Cleveland tradition established by George Szell, the Prokofiev was not recorded immediately after a public performance. Maazel rehearsed the work on May 11 and 12 and performed it only once with the orchestra during a special nonsubscription concert on May 12.

The Prokofiev recording represented a new way of working in Cleveland, partly as a result of Maazel's remarkable memory and incisive baton technique. He had arrived at Severance Hall having solved the technical problems in virtually the entire major orchestral repertoire, including the most complex scores, to the point where conducting them was no longer a challenge. The gift was compromised by a weakness: too much facility, not enough depth. Finding conducting so easy, Maazel often appeared to be gliding across the surface of a score or experimenting, as if to ward off boredom, by imposing what came across as interpretive eccentricities and distortions.

As an American who had spent the past two decades living in Europe, Maazel had a highly personal view of interpretive matters. "There's a certain reticence about expressing oneself for fear of exhibiting bad taste," Maazel told the *Washington Post* a week before recording the Prokofiev in Cleveland. "So that, unless a player is encouraged along these lines, he'll often end up with a kind of fine, respectable 'no taste.' I'm not talking about just turning a phrase tastefully, and tipping one's hat to the stylistic niceties. I'm talking about the daring—at the risk of overstatement or understatement—the Europeans seem to have; the impetus to say, 'I'm going to infuse this phrase with my direct feeling about this music.' "

Maazel's sterling Cleveland recording of the Prokofiev ballet is certainly a reflection of his music-making at its most forthright and impassioned. The fact that the orchestra had only performed *Romeo and Juliet* with its new conductor at a single concert three weeks before had little effect on the final product. Maazel could rehearse quickly and show the musicians every detail with his baton. Even if there were slight flaws during the recording session due to insufficient rehearsal, Decca could create a seamless performance by making a composite of takes. However it was achieved, the Prokofiev recording shows that the Cleveland Orchestra had lost none of its ensemble cohesion, energy, or focus in the three years since Szell's death. The playing is balanced, ravishing, fierce, and vividly dramatic. The three-record album was released quickly, in late August 1973, to hit the stores before André Previn's new account of the complete score with the London Symphony on EMI.

Maazel and the orchestra spent part of the week before the Prokofiev recording sessions performing in Washington, D.C. Paul Hume, the long-time *Washington Post* music critic who had so adored Cleveland under Szell, had a mixed reaction. After hearing the new combination in a Wagner program, Hume was alarmed: "Not in many years under Szell did I hear that orchestra in some of the trouble that plagued it Wednesday night: ragged entrances from the trumpets in Brünnhilde's immolation scene, rough going for the horns in the Rhine journey and far too often an uneven allotment of sound (an area in which Szell was a miracle worker)." The next day, he registered more optimism while reviewing the conductor's performance of the Verdi Requiem. "Had the soloists been up to the level of the chorus and orchestra, Maazel would have given us a great, memorable evening," wrote Hume. "For the record, the same problem used to plague Toscanini." During the same engagement, Maazel conducted a program consisting of Mozart's Symphony No. 38 and Beethoven's Ninth Symphony, which prompted varying responses from the *Post*'s Alan M. Kriegsman. He wrote that Maazel couldn't match Szell in the Mozart, while the Ninth "struck me as excellent but still palpably short of profound or memorable."

✿   ✿   ✿

Attendance at Blossom Music Center increased 23 percent for the 1973 season—to a total of 370,390 patrons. But the orchestra had nothing to do with

the increase, which was attributed to popular music concerts and performances by the National Ballet of Washington. The orchestra actually experienced a slight drop in attendance that summer, despite the presence of
Maazel for two concerts and programs featuring such soloists as pianists
Alfred Brendel, Malcolm Frager, Eugene Istomin, and Alexis Weissenberg,
and violinists Sergiu Luca, Gyorgy Pauk, and Edith Peinemann. The conducting roster, aside from Maazel, might have been less of a draw for the
general public: Matthias Bamert, Stanislaw Skrowaczewski, Kazuyoshi
Akiyama, Aldo Ceccato, and Louis Lane. In contrast to Blossom, subscription sales for the orchestra's upcoming Severance Hall season—the first
with Maazel in town long enough to be considered a full-fledged music director—were showing a 33 percent rise from the previous year.

✻   ✻   ✻

The orchestra opened the 1973–74 season on the road—and a long road it
was—with its first tour to New Zealand and Australia (also its first interna-
tional tour with Maazel). It was an action-packed journey, both logistically
and musically. The orchestra racked up almost 30,000 miles during the trip.
The voluminous repertoire included two Beethoven symphonies and two
Brahms symphonies, as well as symphonies by Bruckner, Dvořák, Mozart,
William Schuman, Shostakovich, and Tchaikovsky—plus music by Barber,
Copland, Debussy, Ravel, Rossini, Richard Strauss, Stravinsky, Wagner,
Weber, and the world premiere of a work by Australian composer Nigel
Butterley. The conducting responsibilities were not undertaken solely by
Maazel, who could make only the final four concerts at the new Sydney
Opera House because of previous engagements in Berlin. Leinsdorf and
Skrowaczewski shared the early portions of the tour, starting in Honolulu
and proceeding to New Zealand and Australia (where the two conductors
cuddled koala bears for press photographers).

En route to New Zealand, the orchestra revealed a virtuosic talent that
went beyond music-making. "The top internationally famous Cleveland
Orchestra arrived by air in Wellington today, but the veteran guest conductor, Erich Leinsdorf, was not boasting of basses and bassoons—but of the
106-man orchestra's beer consumption," reported *The Evening Post* in
Wellington. The orchestra evidently had set a beer-drinking record on the
flight over from Hawaii. "Airline staff told us we had drunk more beer than
anyone else had done on the 8½-hour flight," said Leinsdorf. "It's not a bad
record. And it shows that the members were not drinking hard liquor."

The beer didn't hinder the orchestra when it mattered (nor did a crip-
pling series of labor strikes in Australia). Newspapers described the ensem-

ble as the "whirlwind from Cleveland," and used virtually every superlative to describe its playing. After concerts in Auckland, Wellington, and Christchurch, New Zealand, the orchestra headed to the Australian cities of Brisbane, Canberra, Adelaide, and Melbourne—where Leinsdorf received an engraved boomerang from the orchestra as a gift—before linking up with Maazel in Sydney. There, the orchestra became the first foreign ensemble to perform during the opening week of the controversial, shell-roofed Sydney Opera House. The $140 million facility, with four performance halls, was already considered by many to be a white elephant. Leinsdorf decried the "opera auditorium seating 1,400, an absurdly small number, no close parking facilities, no elevators for ailing people, long walks to and from the halls, and a concert hall of indifferent acoustical properties." The orchestra's soloist in Sydney certainly didn't have any trouble being heard: Birgit Nilsson, the reigning dramatic soprano of the era, collaborated with Maazel and his players in "Abscheulicher" from Beethoven's *Fidelio* and the closing scene from Strauss's *Salome*.

The *Sydney Morning Herald*'s Roger Covell, who had visited Cleveland the previous April to hear the orchestra under Bernard Haitink, wrote of its opening concert in the opera house's concert hall that the ensemble might have been created to perform in the new auditorium, in which the audience surrounded the stage. Maazel "conducted 'Zarathustra' and every other piece of music on the programme with fierce relish, uninhibited emphasis and total command of the traffic of the scores," he said.

Along with raves about the playing came reservations about the orchestra's programming and about Maazel. *The Sydney Sun* compared Maazel unfavorably with Szell: "Under its present incumbent, Lorin Maazel, the orchestra displayed all the characteristics of a typical American 'hard sell.' And I infinitely preferred the hard Szell to the hard sell." *The Melbourne Age* took the orchestra to task for bringing to Australia "the European memories of yesterday. The music from Wagner's *Tannhäuser*, Beethoven's Fifth, Brahms's Second and the Shostakovich Fifth hardly warrants the airfare from the USA." The writer went on to lobby for works by American composers: "Perhaps there is no national pride left, no rejoicing in one's own abilities, no more adventure but only a nostalgic day dream in the mausoleums of European history. Oh Benjamin Franklin, America is in need of thee." Actually, the orchestra's American tally on this tour wasn't so terrible: it played Barber's *Medea's Dance of Vengeance*, Copland's *Appalachian Spring*, and William Schuman's Symphony No. 7.

Foreign critics who covered the opening of the opera house weren't much taken by what they heard either. Martin Bernheimer, the smart and tart music critic of the *Los Angeles Times*, wrote about the first night with typical flamboyance. "Lorin Maazel, the controversial heir to George Szell's baton, chose an unremittingly extroverted program and conducted it with tremendous skill and razzle-dazzle to match," he observed. "No one could gainsay the surface brilliance of the Maazel-Cleveland Shostakovich ('Festive Overture'), Stravinsky ('Petrouchka') and Strauss ('Also Sprach Zarathustra'). But those who savor subtlety and warmth as well as snappy bombast left the concert with a nagging feeling of frustration." In London's *Financial Times*, Andrew Porter noted "with regret that the Cleveland Orchestra on tour, under Maazel, was not the superlative instrument admired in Severance and Carnegie halls; and that Maazel—in *Petrouchka*, in *Also sprach Zarathustra*—seemed bent on beating up a supercharged Chicago or LSO [London Symphony Orchestra] type brilliance, the eschewal of which was once a Cleveland virtue."

The tour's final concert in Sydney included the premiere of Nigel Butterley's *Fire in the Heavens*, whose title was appropriated by Cleveland station WKYC for a television documentary about the tour (the program's full title was *Fire in the Heavens: The Cleveland Orchestra Down Under*). One performance from this concert was taped by the Australian Broadcasting Commission and released the following year on a Columbia Special Projects recording—Maazel's interpretation of Brahms's Symphony No. 1. The recording finds the orchestra unfazed by the long journey but sometimes challenged by its music director's surprising handling of the score. The first three movements are full of dramatic effects that impede their flow, but the performance at least reveals the famed Cleveland discipline and "the superlative instrument" that critic Porter didn't experience at a different Sydney concert.

✣ ✣ ✣

Upon their return to Cleveland on October 7, 1973, following a circuitous route home because of a strike by radar technicians at the Sydney airport, the musicians had only two days off before starting rehearsals for the opening of the new season at Severance Hall. Maazel, unhappy that the orchestra had had to rehearse and perform for four days straight in Sydney, gave his players a (mercifully short) cheerleading speech before digging into Berlioz's *Symphonie fantastique*. "You came through magnificently, particularly in Sydney, where we had our backs to the wall," Maazel said of the unreasonable schedule. "I promise you that shan't happen again." The musicians shuffled their feet in approval.

The rehearsal that followed went remarkably smoothly, belying the fact that Maazel and the orchestra had ever been at odds. On one violinist's fingering, the conductor—himself an accomplished violinist—offered congratulations. "I've been wanting to tell you to play it that way, but I haven't had the chance," he said. "You must have anticipated my madness. Or maybe we're both geniuses." Maazel even made a reference to—and a slight criticism of—Szell's achievement as he tried to obtain the right effect. "I don't want to get caught between the devil and the deep blue sea, but I'd like to get a more grotesque, uncultivated sound here," Maazel explained. "I know it's hard to play that way after all these years of practicing to make homogeneous music, but let's try it."

Maazel spent only a week at Severance Hall in October before returning to Berlin for more responsibilities at the Deutsche Oper. But Cleveland didn't suffer from any lack of diversion or drama during the music director's absence. For the second week of subscription concerts, the orchestra welcomed back Louis Lane—whose contract as resident conductor was set to expire at the end of December—for the Cleveland premiere of Olivier Messiaen's *Turangalîla-symphonie*, with the composer's wife, Yvonne Loriod, as pianist and her sister, Jeanne Loriod, playing the electronic instrument known as the Ondes Martenot. No one much liked the work, which the *Sun Press*'s Bain Murray termed "a disaster," and asserted, "It has to be the worst piece of 20th century music that Louis Lane has ever played in Severance Hall." Leinsdorf followed toward the end of October 1973, opening a two-week engagement with *Song of the Birds* by Pablo Casals in memory of the great Spanish cellist and composer, who had died only days before at age 96. Sadder news for Cleveland during this period was the announcement in early November that Robert Marcellus, the orchestra's principal clarinetist since 1953, had been forced to abandon his performing career due to diabetic retinopathy. Eye specialists had told Marcellus that his sight would worsen if he continued playing. Observers may have known that something was wrong when Marcellus didn't join the orchestra in New Zealand and Australia, or during the opening weeks of the Severance Hall season.

❂   ❂   ❂

The orchestra had extended its contract to make the tour possible, but now the extension was running out, and the musicians were once again making noises about a strike. Board president Alfred M. Rankin reiterated what many board presidents had told the players, comparing the Cleveland Orchestra to other major orchestras in terms of concert and recording income, local demographics, subscription attendance, and hall capacity.

Rankin noted that Severance Hall, with 2,000 seats, was by far the smallest of the auditoriums in which the major American orchestras played. The players, many paid the minimum weekly scale of $285, were requesting a weekly increase of $80 over two years. Management was offering $30 over three years. The musicians weren't buying the association's arguments, especially since the trustees had recently boasted to the public that the Cleveland Orchestra had raised more money than any orchestra but the Chicago Symphony. In their own message to the public, the players pointed out that their take-home pay ranked 13th among the country's major orchestras:

> Let's examine the logic of the position of the Musical Arts Association. If the Cleveland Orchestra is a first rank Orchestra; the Association is second in fund raising, and the Orchestra is seventh in producing income; but the salary of the members is thirteenth, then there are some serious questions to be asked. If the gap in contracts between the Cleveland and other Orchestras continues to widen, our Orchestra will no longer attract first rate musicians and present members will be encouraged to leave our ranks.

A few trustees were sympathetic to the musicians' views, especially Robert C. Weiskopf, a conductor who had founded the Suburban Symphony Orchestra, a community ensemble in Beachwood, but made his living in the family business, Cleveland Cotton Products. Weiskopf encouraged his Musical Arts Association colleagues "to empower the negotiating team to act for the best possible contract"—for the players—"and to state the Board's commitment to excellence." Inspired by Weiskopf, Rankin told the trustees that the board would have to borrow from future revenue and "live dangerously." Rankin also laid to rest a suggestion that the orchestra's personnel be reduced to cut costs. Even so, talks between the musicians and management dragged on until late January 1974, when the players voted 83 to 2 to strike unless a reasonable agreement was offered soon. It came a few days later. The musicians voted 84 to 13 to accept a 42-month contract giving them a hike of $65 to a weekly minimum of $350 plus a new hospitalization plan providing half of family costs. The price tag for the Musical Arts Association was $800,000.

Settling the contract saved performances that have become legends of the Maazel era. Days after the labor dispute ended, the conductor led concert performances of Richard Strauss's opera, *Elektra*, with a cast headed by Ursula Schröder-Feinen (Elektra), Astrid Varnay (Klytemnestra), Roberta Knie (Chrysothemis), Kenneth Riegel (Aegisthus), and José van Dam

(Orestes). As heard on a broadcast tape drawn from the two Severance performances, the combination of Maazel's highly charged conducting and the orchestra's extravagant, yet controlled playing makes for Strauss of almost frightening intensity, as well as tonal radiance. The Cleveland critics captured the excitement. "It was on all counts a masterful realization of the Strauss epic," wrote Frank Hruby in the *Press*. "It was a virtuoso performance in the better sense of the word." Bain Murray, never a Maazel champion, registered astonishment in the *Sun Press*: "The orchestra played with tremendous sweep, precision and power under Maazel's direction. Maazel seems to be at his best in truly theatrical music and he brought off a stunning production which one expects will be well-received in New York."

It was. The performance at Carnegie Hall on February 4, 1974, two days after the final Severance concert, garnered superlative reviews. "It was an exciting evening," wrote Harold C. Schonberg in the *New York Times*. "There was, of course, the great Cleveland Orchestra, a group of virtuoso players that no opera house orchestra, certainly in this country, could come near equaling. There was the equally virtuosic Mr. Maazel, on his very best musical behavior, conducting with brilliance, superb rhythm and a determination to extract every last bit of color from the score." Alan Rich, music critic of *New York* magazine, reviewed the second Maazel-Cleveland Carnegie program: Mozart's D minor Piano Concerto, with Rudolf Firkusny as soloist, and Stravinsky's complete *Firebird*. "Maazel Tov," read the headline on Rich's article:

> Lorin Maazel's appointment as conductor of the Cleveland Orchestra was greeted, when announced, with widespread grumbling within the orchestra. Yet, the orchestra I heard two weeks ago in Carnegie Hall did not sound at all discontented; the Cleveland is once again the superb organization it was under Georg [*sic*] Szell. It plays with marvelous clarity, a tone just a shade drier than that of some ensembles, but with a vivid attack and a tension that were a joy to hear . . . If the Cleveland is no longer first among American ensembles, that is the fault of Georg Solti [with the Chicago Symphony], not Maazel; it is, in any case, a group that restores one's faith in the state of the symphony."

One of the orchestra's concerts during the 1973–74 season achieved notoriety for reasons beyond the artistic. Even before playing a note at an educational program at Lakewood Civic Auditorium in early April under conducting assistant James Judd, the musicians were pelted with paper clips hurled by students from Lakewood public schools. After two pieces, and despite warnings from Judd and narrator Reuben Silver, the attacks continued. The musicians finally had enough and left the stage. The incident made the national news, though it wasn't a first-time occurrence. "Members of the orchestra reported yesterday that they are showered with paper clips, spitballs and metal objects during at least four or five of the 40 educational concerts they perform each season," reported *The Plain Dealer*. "The heaviest bombardment has been in Severance Hall." In an editorial titled "Make the punks face the music," the newspaper lashed out at the youthful offenders: "The performance of the punks in the audience does more than give the city of Lakewood and its school system a black eye. It also is tantamount to stealing money from the serious students in Lakewood's middle schools and high school who paid their way into the hall with the expectation of learning something. It also could discourage music appreciation groups from underwriting similar programs in the future."

Attention quickly reverted from the ridiculous to the sublime: the orchestra's subscription concerts the same week included the local debut of Romanian pianist Radu Lupu in the Schumann concerto (under Lawrence Foster, also making his debut). The Cleveland premiere of Ralph Vaughan Williams's *A Sea Symphony* followed soon thereafter on April 18 under director of choruses Robert Page. Fittingly, perhaps, the work by a 20th-century British composer of conservative leanings was dedicated to the memory of a similar American composer—Herbert Elwell, *The Plain Dealer's* former music critic, who had died the day before this concert.

✿   ✿   ✿

Having traveled 30,000 miles at the start of the 1973–74 Severance Hall season, the orchestra now embarked on another long journey at season's end. In mid-May 1974, the orchestra headed to Japan, exactly four years after its first visit there. Maazel led concerts in Spokane, Seattle, and Portland before conducting 12 performances in Japan (Kobe, Osaka, Nagoya, Nagano, Tokyo, Sendai, and Akita). The repertoire included standard fare by Bartók, Beethoven, Berlioz, Gershwin (*An American in Paris*), Prokofiev, Ravel, and Richard Strauss, plus familiar encores.

The Japanese welcomed Maazel and the orchestra with typical politeness, as well as a bit of nostalgia for the ensemble's previous engagement. Dick Feagler, the colorful *Cleveland Press* reporter and columnist, traveled with the entourage and sent back a story that recounted a testy encounter between Maazel and a reporter in Osaka:

"We had the honor of hearing the Cleveland Orchestra under Maestro

George Szell," Mr. [Junichino] Kawatsuka remarked. "Would you be content to merely take over the heritage of maestro Szell?"

Everybody swigged a little orange pop at that question and maestro Maazel donned his sunglasses and Mrs. Maazel lit up a small cigar.

"I think I get the gist of that," maestro Maazel said. "Any conductor that follows Szell has his work cut out for him. I want to continue in the tradition of great music-making but great music-making cannot become a ritual, as it will if it is an imitation. The need is not to imitate, not to repeat but to renew."

Even so, Maazel fared extremely well with the critics in Japan. *The Daily Yomiura*'s critic didn't allow the past to get in the way of the present: "Let it be said that the Cleveland Orchestra is still in good hands."

Decca (London) Records also seemed to think so. Soon after Maazel and the orchestra began their 1974 season at Blossom Music Center, they spent three days of sessions at Masonic Auditorium recording ballet music from Verdi operas (*Otello, Don Carlos*, and *I vespri siciliani*), Ravel's *Daphnis et Chloé* (complete), and three Gershwin scores (*Rhapsody in Blue*, with pianist Ivan Davis; *An American in Paris*; and *Cuban Overture*). A week later, the British firm signed a three-year deal with the Musical Arts Association to make 13 albums in Cleveland. It was the orchestra's first recording contract since Columbia had severed its relationship with Cleveland in 1970.

Almost severed. Under the terms of its contract, Columbia still owed the Cleveland Orchestra one last LP. The company requested that Michael Tilson Thomas, who was scheduled to make his debut with the orchestra at Blossom in August 1974, record Carl Orff's orgiastic cantata, *Carmina Burana*. Maazel resented the recording but could do nothing to stop it. The work was taped days after the Blossom performance, with the Cleveland Orchestra Chorus, tenor Kenneth Riegel, and baritone Peter Binder repeating their assignments. Judith Blegen had been hired to sing the soprano part, but since she couldn't participate at Blossom (where Susan Davenny Wyner did the honors) or during the recording session, she dubbed in her lines at Columbia studios in New York the following month. The recording became a best-seller and won the chorus a Grammy Award in 1976.

However divided the orchestra and audiences may have been over Maazel, they couldn't complain about the general health of the institution in the two years since he had become music director. The ensemble's international touring business was booming, at last a new recording contract was signed, and now the financial picture was looking better, partly from the efforts of Anthony J. Poderis, who had become the orchestra's first director of development in 1972. For the 1973–74 season, the Musical Arts Association reported a significant drop in the annual deficit, from $232,900 the previous year to $32,400 for the most recent season. The gains were attributed to ticket-sale revenue, fund-raising, a grant from the Ohio Arts Council, and increased Blossom attendance.

Despite Cleveland's rising fortunes, one Northeast Ohio critic, John von Rhein of the *Akron Beacon Journal*, was less than pleased with the way the orchestra was handling matters at Blossom. "Ah, the irony of it all! Blossom Music Center, the youngest Summer pleasure dome among those operated by our major American orchestras, seems to have contracted a bad case of 'programmingosclerosis,' commonly known as stodgy scheduling," wrote von Rhein, who later became music critic of the *Chicago Tribune*. "The disease is not usually fatal, and is often curable if it is detected in its early stages. Its symptoms are a preponderance of Tchaikovsky in particular and standard repertory in general on symphony concerts, and a refusal to stray from time-honored formulas." The programming evidently didn't turn off audiences: Blossom set an attendance record for the 1974 season with a total of 403,166 people.

✿   ✿   ✿

Among Maazel's crucial responsibilities as music director was hiring the right people for the right jobs, which he did in most cases. Many players hired by Artur Rodzinski, Leinsdorf, and Szell were preparing to retire in the mid-1970s, though the orchestra's pitiful pension plan ($3,000 a year for musicians with at least 25 years' service) prompted more than a few members to stay put. Irrepressible harpist Alice Chalifoux, however, was ready to depart after 43 seasons as a principal player. She decided to call it quits on a wintry night in early 1974 "at the corner of Courtland and Shaker" in Shaker Heights. "I was sliding all over the place. It was 11 o'clock at night. I said, 'I'm not going to do this anymore.' The next morning, I resigned. It took them about three months to believe me." The harpist actually had another reason for leaving: Maazel, whom she had come to dislike intensely. "The boys said if they got up a petition, would I stay? I said, no. Maazel called me. 'You just need a rest. Take a week off.' " Her decision was also based on artistic matters. "He would look at you and give you this heavy beat and I resented it. He talked so much and his musical taste was so bad."

Lisa Wellbaum, the Chalifoux student who succeeded her teacher as principal harpist, had something of a trial by fire during her first concerts with the orchestra: the opening program of the 1974–75 Severance Hall season included Mahler's Fifth Symphony, whose famous Adagietto is an ineffably poignant piece for strings and harp. *The Plain Dealer*'s Robert Finn echoed some of Chalifoux's misgivings about Maazel in his review of this concert: "Maazel's performance of the Mahler Fifth Thursday night was a mixture of brilliant ideas and inconsistencies. In the first two of its five movements the emphasis was on huge orchestral climaxes, inflated dynamics and heavy accents. Then, starting with the scherzo, the focus changed. Maazel began showing the most finely calculated care for delicate orchestral balances, precise dynamic shadings and subtle blends of instrumental timbres."

The orchestra, in fact, was playing superlatively well for Maazel, as audiences and critics (mostly) were acknowledging. After so many years under the strict, unyielding rule of Szell, the ensemble was assuming a more expansive and flexible character. (It was also much louder, as some detractors were quick to point out.) These qualities were partly the result of Maazel's choice of works, including contemporary scores that stretched the musicians, and partly due to his increased presence—up to 23 weeks a season, including tours. Yet another factor entered into the change. "He gave the orchestra a chance to play," said trumpeter David Zauder, also the orchestra's personnel manager at the time. "He said, 'Just play. I'm not going to tell you where to breathe. You're free to express yourself.' With his stick, you couldn't get lost. The choice [of Maazel as music director] wound up being extremely beneficial."

These positive developments gave at least one person, general manager Michael Maxwell, the opportunity to crow, telling the trustees that the ensemble "has not sounded so well in many, many years. The Orchestra's famed technical expertise has now been given the advantage of a fluidity and a natural beauty that is quite remarkable. This certainly allows the Orchestra to adapt to many performing styles and to present happily a great variety of repertoire each year."

Maxwell's observations were accurate. But his crowing days were numbered.

Image Making

*L*ike it or not, Cleveland had to face an inevitable fact: Lorin Maazel was not George Szell. In the Central European repertoire in which his predecessor had excelled, Maazel was hard pressed to convince anyone that he possessed comparable insight or focus. Audiences, and especially the orchestra's musicians, often found Maazel's oddly shaped performances of Beethoven and Brahms symphonies to be trying experiences. In one way, however, Maazel turned a seeming disadvantage (succeeding Szell) into an advantage by exploring artistic territory that Szell had ignored or embraced only reluctantly. During his 24-year tenure in Cleveland, Szell had paid scant attention to educational concerts. Maazel enthusiastically participated in many of these important programs, including the Public Hall concerts he devised featuring singers from area high schools. And where Szell had appeared merely to be doing his duty in the area of 20th-century repertoire, Maazel showed missionary zeal. In the 1970s, the new music director broadened the Cleveland Orchestra's already superior abilities by programming works that challenged its virtuosity in new ways. The orchestra would always be principally admired for the special qualities it brought to music of the 18th and 19th centuries. But Maazel, with his remarkable memory and command of every detail in even the most complex scores, pushed the orchestra well beyond its previous artistic boundaries.

By his third season in Cleveland, he was having a noticeable impact on the orchestra—and he knew it. "The Cleveland Orchestra used to be a jewel within a jewel box," Maazel told the *New York Times* before taking his ensemble to Carnegie Hall for five concerts in February 1975. "The orchestra is still a jewel, but occasionally we take it out of the box now—otherwise it might gather dust." Stephen E. Rubin, author of the *Times* article (schmaltzily headlined "Lorin Maazel: His Heart Belongs to Cleveland"), acknowledged the conductor's contribution by noting that "while the Cleveland Orchestra is still regarded as very special, it has shed its elitist image."

Maazel clearly was reshaping the ensemble in his image. Comparing himself with Szell, he told Rubin: "My temperament is obviously different, and in the course of working with the orchestra, its sound must inevitably change to reflect me. I think now there is a kind of bloom, a breadth, a warmth." He ascribed these qualities in part to the fact that he was a violin player, whereas Szell had been a pianist. "My training is structural," Maazel said, "but my intuition is a melodic singing one. While not losing transparency, clarity, balance and precision, there is this string player's sound to the orchestra now that perhaps it didn't have before. I'm not saying it's better; it's different— a fusion of precision and warmth."

That fusion was leading the orchestra beyond Szell's Classical regimentation toward more elastic music-making. Some conductors who had appeared with Szell's orchestra had been frustrated by the tightness. After once leading Tchaikovsky's "Manfred" Symphony at Blossom Music Center, William Steinberg had come offstage elated but perplexed. "They play wonderfully, but they are so inflexible," he said. Steinberg "couldn't make them play with the kind of movement and coloration that he was looking for," recalled Michael Maxwell. "They were really hidebound by the application of a playing technique and tradition imposed on them by their music director."

Under Maazel the orchestra began what would prove to be an enduring tradition of involvement with music of the present and recent past. In November 1974, he invited Aaron Copland back to Severance Hall as part of a plan to bring attention to one eminent, living composer during an entire week of performances and community events centered on that composer's art. The composer would attend rehearsals and concerts and, if so inclined, conduct the orchestra. The annual series, a mini-festival of sorts, was dubbed "Great Composers of Our Time" (which later would become "Composers of Our Time," suggesting, perhaps, that history would have to decide if a composer was great or not).

By inviting Copland, America's most esteemed living composer, as the inaugural honoree, Maazel could emphasize that worthy serious music was not the exclusive domain of European composers, alive or otherwise. In the process, he restored a practice that had languished during the Szell era: appearances by noted composers who could conduct or appear as soloist, a tradition that dated back to the days of founding conductor Nikolai Sokoloff and his successor, Artur Rodzinski. Szell, on the other hand, had gradually shifted most of the responsibility for new music to Louis Lane.

As part of his weeklong stay in Cleveland, Copland rehearsed a student orchestra at the Cleveland Institute of Music and heard a concert of his chamber music at the Cleveland Museum of Art, which screened several movies for which Copland had written the scores. He participated in a colloquium at Cleveland State University and appeared on local radio and television programs. One Cleveland television station followed Copland around during his visit and made a documentary. The main event of the week was Copland's guest-conducting engagement with the Cleveland Orchestra, a program comprising his Piano Concerto (with Leo Smit as soloist), *Inscapes*, *El salón México*, *Fanfare for the Common Man*, and Symphony No. 3.

The composer relished the tribute. "I'm recently back from my unforgettable week in Cleveland—for which I have <u>you</u> to thank most profusely!" Copland wrote to Maazel. "Everyone was wonderfully cooperative—the orchestra, the staff, the TV people, the schools, etc. etc. And last, but not least, the audience. I shall never forget that audience's response as I stepped on the stage, before conducting a note. It was really something. It seems to me you have hit on a formula which other orchestras might do well to emulate."

✿   ✿   ✿

Another American composer was on Maazel's mind at this time—George Gershwin. Decca Records had decided to give *Porgy and Bess*—the Gershwin opera that Rodzinski had wanted to premiere at Severance Hall in 1935—its first-ever complete recording in stereo with Maazel and the Cleveland Orchestra. The recording was set for August 1975 at Masonic Auditorium following a concert performance at Blossom Music Center. As of November 1974, Maazel was talking about a cast headed by Robert Merrill (Porgy), Martina Arroyo (Bess), Marilyn Horne (Serena), Leona Mitchell (Clara and backup for Bess), Betty Allen (Maria), Willard White (Jim), and André Montal (Sportin' Life). It didn't seem to matter to Maazel or Decca that casting two white singers, Merrill and Horne, would ignore the wishes of the opera's creators, who had specified black singers for all of the principal roles. The casting issues wouldn't be resolved for months.

Meanwhile, other projects were claiming Maazel's attention. One of his favorites was the orchestra's second Public Hall concert featuring local students as choristers, in January 1975. The program's climax featured 1,400 singers from 30 Greater Cleveland high schools in the finale from Mahler's Symphony No. 2 ("Resurrection"), with soprano Leona Mitchell and mezzo-soprano Katherine Ciesinski as soloists. "It is a thrill to work with young people who sing beautifully," Maazel told the *Press*, once again sponsor of the event. "Great music is for a great number of people." Rudolph

Ringwall, who had led hundreds of Cleveland Orchestra programs for children, attended the concert. The 83-year-old conductor wrote to Maazel that
the Mahler performance was "inspirational under your direction."

The audience of 4,500 at the Public Hall performance included a healthy
number of people who had never heard an orchestra concert. Among the
initiates was Frank Robinson, new manager of the Cleveland Indians and
the first black manager of a major league team. Robinson was invited to appear as narrator in Benjamin Britten's *A Young Person's Guide to the
Orchestra*, which precipitated a whimsical exchange between him and *Press*
reporter Bob Sudyk days before the performance:

> "Ever heard of Benjamin Britten?"
> "Nope."
> "You will introduce the different instruments."
> "You kiddin'?"
> "What's the difference between a clarinet and oboe for openers?"
> "You blow 'em I guess. Don't you?"
> "Are you a little apprehensive about all this?"
> "Yep," laughed Robinson, the only baseball player voted most-valuable
> in both leagues and perhaps the first and last manager to narrate for a sym-
> phony orchestra.
> "I guess this is my year for new adventures."
> Indeed.

Maazel continued to invite major conductors (such as Gennady
Rozhdestvensky and Kurt Masur) to make their Cleveland debuts, hold
symposia for young conductors (as Szell had in the early 1950s), and spend
longer periods with the orchestra than even his predecessor had. "Only now
am I really doing what a music director should do—conducting his orchestra a good five months of the year, taking it on tour, getting around to a wider
spectrum of the repertory," Maazel told Robert Finn in *The Plain Dealer*.
Beefing up the roster of guest conductors was an important part of the
process. "We want to hear them all, and then the ones we like we will invite
back," said Maazel. "I do think that by the end of this five years we will have
heard from just about every major conductor except [Herbert von] Karajan,
who just does not guest conduct much at all. Karajan and I are very good
friends. We had dinner not long ago and he assured me that if there is one
orchestra he will guest conduct sometime in the future, it will be the
Cleveland Orchestra."

By programming more 20th-century repertoire and contemporary works, Maazel flexed the orchestra's stylistic and technical muscles. Among the pieces he scheduled to receive their first performances in coming years were eight works by American composers, commissioned for the orchestra's tribute to the U.S. bicentennial. The first four scores—by Maazel (for orchestra, reciting chorus, and solo violinist, a work that never materialized), George Walker, Donald Harris, and Raymond Premru—were scheduled for the 1975–76 season. Three others would be performed the following season, as well as a piece by Jacob Druckman funded by the National Endowment for the Arts as part of a group commission of six major symphonic works by Americans. The orchestras of Boston, Chicago, Cleveland, Los Angeles, New York, and Philadelphia were each to give the world premiere of one of the pieces, which then would be taken up by the other orchestras.

The Cleveland Orchestra was hardly veering madly over the cliff of contemporary music, however. Maazel balanced new works with older ones, and he gave guest conductors ample leeway to choose mainstream repertoire to go along with 20th-century fare. The only recording the orchestra made between *Carmina Burana* for Columbia in August 1974 and *Porgy and Bess* for Decca in August 1975 was a performance of Beethoven's Eighth Symphony under Rafael Kubelik for Deutsche Grammophon in April 1975. The German recording company had come up with a novel idea for the Czech conductor: record the complete Beethoven symphonies, but each with a different major international orchestra. The Cleveland entry in this series almost didn't get made. Because the recording was a studio job, Deutsche Grammophon initially intended to pay only the 75 orchestra members who were needed for the Eighth Symphony. Some musicians who were not taking part tried to persuade their colleagues to refuse to play if the entire orchestra wasn't compensated. "Many recordings of this kind have been made in the past without protest and so this last minute dispute comes as a surprise," assistant manager Kenneth Haas told the trustees days before the scheduled sessions. "The staff is in communication with several officials of the American Federation of Musicians in Cleveland and in New York and it is hoped that this dispute can be resolved so that this recording is not lost." The dispute was ultimately resolved, and the result was a felicitous performance of the Eighth Symphony. When the entire Beethoven set was released, the British magazine *Gramophone* called the Kubelik-Cleveland recording "a finely scaled, musically satisfying account."

❈   ❈   ❈

The 1974–75 Severance Hall season ended early, in mid-April, with concerts featuring Rudolf Serkin in the Brahms Second Piano Concerto, so that

Maazel and the orchestra could make a three-week, 15-concert tour to Mexico, Nicaragua, Venezuela, Brazil, Argentina, and Miami Beach and Orlando, Florida. South America was a new destination for the orchestra, which received ecstatic reviews in Caracas, Rio de Janeiro, and Buenos Aires. In Rio, Maazel spoke to reporters in Spanish and Portuguese, saying that the orchestra's quality was due to the generous support of Cleveland citizens and the work Szell had done to maintain the highest level of artistry. Back in Cleveland, though, Maazel was "still fighting the memory of George Szell," wrote *The Plain Dealer's* Finn. "He has begun playing many of Szell's speciality pieces (as indeed he should), and next year is leading a Schumann cycle, an act of special courage in George Szell's Cleveland."

But Maazel was also about to break ground with *Porgy and Bess*. It not only would be the first time the complete opera was recorded in stereo, it would also be the orchestra's first opera recording (and the British firm's first opera recording in the United States). Maazel agreed to the cast of singers that Decca/London producer Terry McEwen finally proposed for principal roles: Willard White (replacing Robert Merrill, who had backed out of the project) as Porgy, Leona Mitchell as Bess, Barbara Hendricks as Clara, Florence Quivar as Serena, McHenry Boatwright as Crown, François Clemmons as Sportin' Life, Arthur Thompson as Jake, and Barbara Conrad as Maria.

Maazel, like Rodzinski in 1935, considered *Porgy and Bess* an opera. "It is not an operetta, a musical comedy, nor is it a jazz drama, Black Blues, or pre-Soul," Maazel wrote in a liner note for the recording. "We performed and recorded it as an opera, as one worthy of the same care and devotion we would have accorded any operatic masterpiece. Gershwin's compassion for individuals is Verdian, his comprehension of them, Mozartean. His grasp of the folk-spirit is as firm and subtle as Moussorgsky's, his melodic inventiveness rivals Bellini's, ingenious and innovative are his compositional techniques." Maazel and Decca had decided that every note Gershwin had composed for *Porgy* would be included: "The reinstated sections are of the richest inspiration, and serve to realign the internal balance of the work."

Maxwell had hoped that the opera's only surviving creator, 78-year-old Ira Gershwin, would attend the concert performance at Blossom on August 16, but it wasn't to happen. "Alas, I shall not be able to be with you but of course you have my highest hopes for a grand and successful evening," Gershwin wrote to Maxwell in late July from Beverly Hills. The Blossom evening turned out to be the grand success that Gershwin had wished for, as did the recording. During four days of sessions (August 18 through 21) at Masonic

Auditorium, Maazel, the orchestra, the Cleveland Orchestra Chorus and Children's Chorus, and the Blossom cast preserved a striking performance of a piece that had been sliced and diced over the decades. The recording restores 37 passages that are usually cut—a total of 28 minutes of music. Maazel, originally unopposed to the idea of casting Robert Merrill as Porgy, told the *New York Times* that it was a good idea to use unknown black singers, in part to give them exposure. He predicted, correctly, that three of the principals (White, Mitchell, and Quivar) would become stars.

Maazel later confirmed his (revised) view of the casting in an interview in *Gramophone* magazine:

> There's a stipulation in the score that all the performers must be black, the reason being that in the 1930s, black Americans simply didn't get any opportunities to appear, or at least opportunities commensurate with their talents, and this was one way the Gershwin estate saw to it that there would always be some jobs for black singers on the assumption that the work would continue to be popular.

McEwen and Maazel sensed that they had a hit on their hands months before the recording's release. "FIRST OPPORTUNITY SATURDAY NIGHT TO LISTEN TO PORGY COMPLETE WITH KNOWLEDGEABLE FRIENDS," McEwen telegrammed Maazel in November 1975. "IN 26 YEARS WITH THIS COMPANY I'VE NEVER HEARD A MORE GRIPPING OR BEAUTIFUL OPERATIC RECORDING. A THOUSAND BLESSINGS UPON YOU." Maazel was equally taken with their achievement. "I had to listen to the tapes critically, but I must say that to my mind the result is simply stunning," he wrote to McEwen. "The cast is superb, and the atmosphere is incredibly intense, yet touching and infinitely poignant. A dream has truly come true."

Months later, critics and other listeners would also find much to admire. "Fortunately, for this excellent recording, the normally Bach- and Beethoven-bound Cleveland orchestra forgets the concert room and remembers they are American, since the jazz figurations have no embarrassing terrors," wrote David Simmons in London's *Tribune* (exaggerating the ensemble's relationship with Bach). "The difficult solos are all assumed by excellent black artists, and this recording should emancipate them for wider audiences. The conductor, Lorin Maazel, has a triumph too, escaping from the stranglehold of 'dead' classics with ease, authority and style." Peter G. Davis, reviewing the recording in the *New York Times*, discerned a shortage of theatrical presence in Maazel's performance, but mostly was impressed:

"For all its passing flaws, this new recording is an indispensable document and an often moving account of an operatic masterpiece."

For Maazel, the finest accolade may have come from an unquestionably authoritative source—pianist-songwriter Kay Swift, who thanked the conductor in a handwritten letter:

> As I was a close friend of George Gershwin and knew all of the others connected with the original production of "Porgy and Bess" ([librettist DuBose] Heywood, Ira Gershwin—the latter still a good friend—and the entire cast) I want to thank you for giving us the extraordinary recording of the opera's complete score. It seems to me that in this set of platters you have brought to light the work that George Gershwin had in mind when creating it. You evidently saw [it] exactly as he saw it. No other recording ever has—but then, of course you know that.
>
> As an ASCAP composer, I was lucky enough to hear each segment of "Porgy" while it was being composed and orchestrated. I even lent my "no-voice," along with the Gershwin brothers' no-voices, to sing all the parts, which sounded dreadful but was thrilling to me.
>
> You have given a number of people (among them, musicians) an understanding of the opera that has astonished those whom I know. My family has accused me of giving away these albums like popcorn. I'll continue to do so as long as I can, for I am very sure that this is America's only great opera, performed just <u>right</u>.

Back home, Dennis Dooley penned a gleeful review for *Cleveland Magazine* that pinpointed part of the conductor's achievement with the orchestra. "The recording, finally, says a lot about Maazel—his musical tastes, his savvy, his popular bent," Dooley noted. "Can anyone, for instance, even for a moment imagine George Szell, God bless him, ever recording *Porgy and Bess*?"

On the other hand, many could not imagine Maazel venturing onto Szell's musical terrain, which he did with an unabashed confidence that belied any hint that he was intimidated by his predecessor. Days after recording *Porgy* in Cleveland, Maazel and the orchestra taped Brahms's Symphony No. 1, inaugurating what would be a much-debated Brahms symphony cycle for London/Decca. Szell, an acknowledged master in this repertoire, had recorded an acclaimed set of the Brahms symphonies in Cleveland for Columbia. Maazel perhaps was fated to encounter resistance to his emphatic, indulgent performances of these pieces. A similar polarization of response would surround the Maazel-Cleveland Beethoven symphony cycle for Columbia. But neither Szell nor anyone else can hold a monopoly on the masterpieces that audiences need to hear and orchestras must play. Maazel *had* to conduct works that had been closely associated with Szell.

He did so three weeks after the triumph of *Porgy and Bess*, when he and the orchestra made their first European tour together—and the ensemble's first trip to the region since the 1967 festival tour conducted by Szell and Karajan. The 1975 trip was supposed to pay tribute to the American bicentennial, though only two pieces (Ives's *Three Places in New England* and Barber's *The School for Scandal* overture, the latter an encore) fit the bill. The fact that the orchestra and the conductor were American may have been enough to satisfy bicentennial qualifications. Even so, Maazel also programmed repertoire, such as Beethoven's "Eroica," that was bound to elicit comparison with Szell.

The tour was tightly packed with appearances, perhaps too tightly: 21 concerts in 28 days. In one five-day period in September 1975, Maazel and company performed in London; Brussels and Ghent, Belgium; Leverkusen, Germany (near Cologne); and Sint Niklaas, Belgium. In a seven-day period, they played seven concerts—in Vienna (two) and Linz, Austria; and Nuremberg, Ludwigshafen, Landau, and Bonn, Germany. In yet another five-day period, the entourage traveled from Düsseldorf to Frankfurt to Hoechst, Germany (all for one concert, which was taped for television), to Paris to Geneva to Barcelona. Neither Maazel nor the musicians were pleased. The schedule was "absolutely unacceptable," he later wrote to Maxwell.

> We all recognized at the time that it was necessary because of several factors to appear in as many cities as possible, the principal factor, of course, was the fear of the local promoter that he would not be able to 'sell' The Cleveland Orchestra for more than one concert in each city. This is no longer the case, and we must not subject our Orchestra members to the strains and rigors of one-night stands in these areas.

As a reward for suffering those rigors, the orchestra and Maazel were greeted by enthusiastic audiences, though European critics didn't always seem to know what to make of the Cleveland musicians. In London, the orchestra played for a capacity crowd of 7,000 at the Albert Hall. "My one worry is to run out of superlatives," wrote a reviewer in *The Daily Telegraph*. The estimable William Mann, of the *London Times*, had misgivings about Maazel's performance of Beethoven's "Eroica," calling it "extremely pompous, retouched and bumped-up." Generally, however, Mann remained enthusiastic about the orchestra. "If they are not, on this showing, the awesome virtuoso instrument that we remember from the era of Georg Szell, they are still a splendid one, as was made plain in the suite from Bartók's *Miraculous Mandarin* ballet of which Maazel and his Clevelanders gave a thrilling account, barbarous, voluptuous and as clean as a whistle."

If British critics were enchanted with the Cleveland Orchestra, so was the ensemble's leader. "I feel very much like the President of the United States, or anybody who has got right to the top," Maazel told *The Daily Mail*. "Quite frankly, I can't imagine accepting a position after this. I'm a completely contented human being, totally fulfilled." On the phone from Berlin, he told Robert Finn that it was important to reintroduce the orchestra to listeners who may have forgotten what they had been missing: "The Cleveland Orchestra has not been talked about much in Europe in recent years, and there was a lot of speculation about us in the cities here—was it really a good orchestra? I'm happy to be able to serve that good reputation."

However, Jean Cotte, music critic of *France-Soir*, wasn't sure that Maazel was helping the orchestra's reputation. The ensemble's Paris concert, on October 1, promised to be one of the tour's highlights, a program that included the Schumann Piano Concerto featuring Arthur Rubinstein. But Cotte used Rubinstein's magisterial artistry to put down American orchestras in general and the Cleveland Orchestra in particular. "I saw these robots come alive for a moment, while Arthur Rubinstein was playing the Schumann concerto," wrote Cotte. "Rubinstein is 88 years of vitality, love, passion for music. It is he who succeeded in giving this orchestra what it lacks: freshness, spontaneity, youth."

While Cotte was sizing up the orchestra in Paris, Finn was doing the same in Cleveland. In spite of the tremors that had hit Cleveland when the new music director arrived, he noted, the orchestra's future looked healthy. Listeners would just have to live with the conductor's quirks. "Maazel is seen by his critics as an erratic conductor, who can be wonderfully exciting in one piece and perversely mannered in the next," Finn wrote. "He is certainly not a conductor who leaves people lukewarm." The board showed its confidence in Maazel in the midst of the European tour by extending his contract through the 1980–81 season.

Upon returning to Cleveland, Maazel had no reason not to boast about the trip. "Its success has been truly gratifying," he wrote to Terry McEwen at London Records. "The general consensus seems to be that The Cleveland is in fact perhaps the finest playing ensemble on stage today. Of course, we had expected no comparisons to be made—we simply gave the best concerts we could." It was the right moment for McEwen to bring up an important topic. Would Maazel agree to conduct another concert performance of *Porgy and Bess*, this time at Carnegie Hall in February 1976, to kick off the release of the recording? McEwen wrote:

> The success of <u>Porgy</u> is, in my opinion, going to contribute enormously to a whole new image which is bigger and more universal than ever before. The success of your two most recent records, Ravel and Gershwin, followed by Verdi and <u>Porgy</u>, are, I believe, going to confirm what many of us have thought has been coming since you arrived in Cleveland. The Cleveland Orchestra will no longer be considered exclusively a German Classical/Romantic group, but a great orchestra for <u>everybody's</u> enjoyment, and that category is enjoyed by almost no other orchestra in the world today.

Maazel agreed that a Carnegie performance would be a splendid idea, and he even joined Maxwell in trying to convince orchestra members to play the concert, which would be scheduled on one of their official days off. The musicians' contract prohibited them from playing a performance on a day off without their consent. To receive permission, Maazel and Maxwell manned the phones and called each musician individually. "What do you do when the boss calls and asks for a favor? Say no?" one player said in the *Press*. But Maxwell would receive the players' consent too late to schedule the *Porgy* performance in New York. The episode would lead to his departure.

Maazel had become increasingly displeased with the way his general manager had scheduled tours and neglected to follow through on grants and projects (including the musicians' contracts for the *Porgy* concert). There was growing discontent on both sides. Maxwell had noticed changes in Maazel, especially after the conductor signed his new, four-year contract. Generally cooperative during his first three years as music director, Maazel had become more autocratic on numerous matters. He had also begun acting with a mixture of irresponsibility and eccentricity, according to Maxwell, upsetting working relationships with management and the orchestra. Some of Maazel's programs were becoming unwieldy and exhausting, such as a big Mahler symphony preceded by too many other works. Occasionally, Maazel would arrive late for rehearsal or show up in a grumpy mood and wearing sunglasses. "These aberrations became irritations," recalled Maxwell.

There were others. On the podium, Maazel wore tails made especially for him by a tailor in Italy. At one point, he came up with the idea of dressing the entire Cleveland Orchestra in suave new suits, which he thought would give the ensemble a distinctive look. Maxwell and board president Alfred

Rankin actually visited a Cleveland tailoring company to see if such an endeavor would be possible. The cost would have been exorbitant—and what would the orchestra do when extra players were needed or when a musician retired? Another abortive Maazel brainstorm involved Blossom Music Center, where he envisioned installing a canvas tent over the vast lawn area to shelter the crowd from storms. Blossom architect Peter van Dijk came up with a design. Then financial reality set in and the idea died.

Maxwell's failure to secure the musicians' consent quickly enough to schedule the *Porgy* concert performance proved the last straw for Maazel. He told Rankin he could no longer work with the manager, who was informed in late January 1976 that he would have to go. Rankin put the best face on the situation for the public, telling the *Press* that Maxwell had "acquired a host of friends in Cleveland and has earned the admiration and respect of the musical community." The *Press* told readers "Severance Hall will no longer be Maxwell House, as of Sept. 1." It was to be transformed into Haas House. Thirty-three-year-old Kenneth Haas, the 6-foot, 7-inch former assistant manager who had left Cleveland the previous July to become general manager of the Cincinnati Symphony, was announced as Maxwell's successor. The relationship between Maazel and Haas would flow much more smoothly. With only a modest musical background, Haas could pose no artistic challenges to the conductor.

✼   ✼   ✼

Maxwell wasn't the only person on the way out at Severance Hall. Three weeks after the general manager's "resignation" was announced, a front-page story in *The Plain Dealer*, headlined "Sour notes in Orchestra," reported that principal players Abraham Skernick and David Shifrin would leave at the end of the season for university jobs. Violist Skernick told Wilma Salisbury he was departing after 27 years because the board was letting things slip, and the orchestra wasn't keeping up with its peers in terms of salary and pension. Trustees denied both charges (although the orchestra's annual pension of $3,000 clearly could not compete with the pension Skernick would receive at Indiana University—$14,000). Clarinetist Schifrin said he enjoyed "being a free spirit" and looked forward to a more flexible life at the University of Michigan. Both musicians told Salisbury only part of the story. Skernick, the player closest to Szell for more than two decades, had come to dislike Maazel and his music-making. The *Detroit News* reported that Maazel and Skernick had met after the Salisbury article and reached a reconciliation. "I'm leaving in concern, not in anger," Skernick said. "I'm not thinking of today, but tomorrow." Shifrin simply wasn't fitting in, Maazel had decided. "He didn't resign, he was fired," the conductor told the *Lorain Journal*.

Another treasured Szell principal player, hornist Myron Bloom, had fled Maazel by taking a sabbatical during the 1975–76 season to be guest principal with the Orchestre de Paris—"the worst orchestra that ever existed," Bloom later said—at the invitation of Daniel Barenboim. Bloom became so unhappy playing in the Paris orchestra that he called Kenneth Haas to ask if he could return to Cleveland. Haas said that if Bloom was in his chair for the first rehearsal the following week, the job was still his. Bloom hopped on a Concorde, which developed engine trouble and was forced to land in Goose Bay, Labrador, where another plane was summoned. By the time Bloom arrived in Washington, D.C., Haas's deadline had passed. Bloom returned to Paris without calling Cleveland to explain, and he remained in the Orchestre de Paris until he accepted a teaching post at Indiana University in 1985. After an audition that drew 90 applicants and 17 actual candidates, Maazel chose Richard Solis, an orchestra member since 1971, to be principal horn. He would occupy the endowed George Szell Memorial Chair.

The fact that Maazel was getting under the skin of more than a few of his musicians was made clear in a *Plain Dealer* profile of the conductor in May 1976, just as the 1975–76 season was ending. Scott Eyman was present for a Maazel rehearsal of Schumann's Symphony No. 2 when things unraveled. "Suddenly the relative serenity of the last quarter-hour vanishes; in response to a muttered comment and giggled reply from two cellists, Maazel explodes—quietly, with the erudite, venomous coldness of an ironic college prof," Eyman reported, quoting the conductor's steely reprimand: "I expect discipline over there and I'm not getting it. It's part of your contract and I expect you to fulfill it. It's also part of your responsibility, the responsibility of your freedom to make your comments in a decent fashion. If you have anything to say, say it out loud."

As always, the tension bouncing off the walls at Severance Hall didn't affect the level of the music-making. The orchestra was playing with the same strict discipline that had been its hallmark for decades. The musicians wouldn't have had it any other way.

Roller Coaster

*B*y the end of his fourth season as music director of the Cleveland Orchestra, Lorin Maazel had achieved more than anyone had expected. The London/Decca recordings were providing crucial exposure and income. Superb new players had replaced retiring or departing musicians. Contemporary music was alive in Maazel's "Music of Today" series and the "Great Composers of Our Time" concerts, which were bringing major creative voices to town. Four international tours had confirmed the orchestra's status among the finest in the world—and more trips were in the works.

Maazel's enormous repertoire and seemingly endless energy allowed him to program major scores within short periods, though there would always be arguments about whether he dipped below the surface of these pieces. During three weeks of concerts he led during the 1976 summer season at Blossom Music Center, he conducted such diverse and challenging fare as the Verdi Requiem, Tchaikovsky's Sixth Symphony, excerpts from *Porgy and Bess* (mostly with the cast of the recording, but with Simon Estes as Porgy), Mahler's Second Symphony, and Prokofiev's Fifth Symphony. With Beethoven's *Fidelio*, he moved closer to realizing one of his goals—establishing a concert version of a beloved opera as an annual Blossom event.

If Maazel had had his way, Blossom would have become something far more ambitious. Over the next few years he planned to build it into "one of the world's finest festivals of music. We want to create a real festival—the kind that are presented at Bayreuth or Salzburg. We're not talking about having another Hollywood Bowl or Ravinia," Maazel told the *Press* soon after the 1976 season. An artist who thought Maazel had the ability to make a big impact was soprano Beverly Sills, who had just recorded Massenet's opera *Thais* with him in London for EMI (with Maazel also playing the violin solo in the famous "Meditation"). A former Clevelander, Sills appeared at Blossom under the baton of Julius Rudel in August 1976 and told *The Plain Dealer* that the city needed an opera company—and she knew who should start it. "You have a great symphony orchestra, a great hall (Severance) and a great summer music festival," Sills said. "I would not start an eensy-teensy company here. I would take Lorin Maazel and the Cleveland Symphony [*sic*] and do Mozart operas. With Maazel, you have an enormous talent, know-how and experience. With the conductor and orchestra, you already have 50% of the opera. It would be a dream way to start an opera company."

Taking up the same subject in the *Press*, Frank Hruby informed Sills that Anthony Addison had started a small student summer troupe at the Cleveland Institute of Music and that David Bamberger was forming his own professional company. "Oh, I've worked with him at the New York City Opera," Sills said of Bamberger. "Very gifted man. I hope that things get going for him there. Cleveland can certainly afford its own opera company." (Bamberger would eventually establish a local troupe, New Cleveland Opera Company, later renamed Cleveland Opera.)

Maazel did have an operatic triumph—one of his greatest—during the first week of the 1976–77 season, but not in Cleveland. Upon finishing the opening concerts at Severance Hall—Strauss's *Ein Heldenleben* and Bartók's Concerto for Orchestra—he decided to fly to Washington, D.C., to catch a Kennedy Center performance of Verdi's *Otello* by the Paris Opera with Sir Georg Solti conducting. The morning of the performance, Maazel answered a phone call at his Shaker Heights home from Martin Feinstein, executive director of the Kennedy Center. "Martin, I'm glad you called," said Maazel. "I was thinking of catching 'Otello'." Feinstein's answer: "How'd you like to conduct it?" Solti had fallen ill with the flu, and the Paris Opera had no one to conduct. Maazel, who had led *Otello* many times (but not the Paris production), agreed to save the performance on less than 12 hours' notice, conducting the work from memory. Maazel didn't think this was such a big deal: "I have never done anything like this in my entire operatic career before. But Martin called me, and he was in a terrible bind. And I had the night off." Others felt Maazel's feat *was* a big deal. "By the second act it was obvious to everyone that there was no cause for any kind of nervousness, but rather that a formidable performance was being built," wrote Paul Hume in the *Washington Post*.

Maazel appeared to be inexhaustible. The night after *Otello*, he was back at Severance Hall with his orchestra, conducting a concert in his "Explorations" series, which presented major symphonic works accompanied by spoken poetry, narratives, even excerpts from plays. On this occasion, Maazel led two Brahms scores—Variations on a Theme by Haydn and the Third Symphony—with Stephen Klein providing spoken program notes.

And he still wasn't done for the week. Two nights later, Maazel returned to the podium for the second subscription program of the season, conducting works by Bartók, Shostakovich, and Falla. His penchant for juggling assignments manifested itself in yet another form that fall: he began a three-year tenure as principal guest conductor of the New Philharmonia Orchestra of London (which he had left in acrimony in 1972). Later in the 1976–77 season, he would accept a similar post with the French National Orchestra.

Faced with such heavy workloads, however, even Maazel wouldn't always prove tireless. At times, he struggled to keep his art on the loftiest level. His Cleveland tenure had become a wild ride of magnificent, illuminating, weird, maddening, and indifferent performances, depending upon the repertoire and the conductor's frame of mind. Maazel was also starting to show signs that he fit squarely into the orchestra's tradition of exacting, temperamental music directors. He could turn surly and hostile not only in rehearsal but also in the midst of a performance, if something didn't go as he thought it should. In October 1976, he lost his cool during a rehearsal of the Saint-Saëns's Piano Concerto No. 5, with Aldo Ciccolini as soloist, and fumed to the orchestra about getting on "with the bloody notes." As in the case of similar stormy incidents involving Nikolai Sokoloff, Artur Rodzinski, and George Szell, the orchestra committee complained to management about Maazel's behavior. But this time the players failed to extract an apology. Maazel wrote a long, defensive letter to general manager Kenneth Haas. "I stand on my record of moderate, firm leadership," he wrote. "I believe I conduct the affairs of our musical state in a gentlemanly, courteous and equilibrated fashion. Even in provoking circumstances, I believe I have generally shown much forbearance. I shall continue to fulfill my duties of Music Director with regard to rehearsal discipline and individual behavior."

❖   ❖   ❖

One of the principal reasons Michael Maxwell had pushed so vigorously to engage Maazel was the conductor's contract with Decca Records. Since being dumped by both Columbia Records and EMI after Szell's death, the orchestra essentially had ceased recording. Now Maazel was helping Cleveland return to the field with a vengeance. In late 1976, the ensemble renewed its contract with Decca (for five years and a total of 20 records) and reached an agreement with Columbia Records for two discs per year for two years.

A third recording company entered the picture in January 1977—a fledgling Cleveland-based firm called Advent Records (later Telarc Records), which specialized in high-fidelity products of extraordinary sonic realism. Run by Robert Woods, a former singer, the company actually was stepping back into a previous technological era, using a recording method that inscribed sound directly onto master discs. "The result is in effect a live performance without the opportunity for retakes to correct mistakes," reported *The Plain Dealer*. Maazel and the orchestra made their first direct-to-disc recording of short works by Berlioz, Falla, Bizet, and Tchaikovsky in mid-January. Upon the disc's release, Irving Lowens waxed rapturous in the *Washington Star*: "I was knocked into the middle of next week. If the Cleveland Orchestra sounds this good in the flesh when it shows up in the Kennedy Center later in the week for a Brahms cycle, you'll leave the hall walking on clouds."

Not everyone would be as enthusiastic about Maazel's conducting. Many critics in the late 1970s listened to his London/Decca recording of the four Brahms symphonies—and later of his Cleveland set of the Beethoven symphonies on Columbia—in continuing awe of the orchestra but with more than a little concern about Maazel's interpretive choices. In the *New York Times*, John Rockwell called the Brahms set a "contradictory, sometimes infuriating affair, as is so much of that vastly talented but persistently mannered conductor's work . . . though the performances 'work' in some basic sense, Mr. Maazel sounds sweet and spineless, mucking up the line with unpersuasive personalizations and loosening his grip on the basic pulse that has to underlie even the most extreme indulgences in rubato." Indeed, Maazel takes an unusually dark view of these pieces, even the affable Second Symphony, often adding a dramatic, ponderous emphasis that weighs the music down. The orchestral playing throughout is warm, cohesive, and vibrant, and Maazel's ability to enhance clarity, like Szell's, pays bountiful dividends. But his approach too often has a dispiriting effect on the music.

Other pieces that Maazel recorded in Cleveland, especially large, colorful scores, would benefit from his attention to precision, balance, and texture. His recording of Respighi tone poems (*Roman Festivals, Pines of Rome*) is a radiant experience. "There is really no point in making comparisons here," wrote *Gramophone* magazine. "Maazel's account of *Roman Festivals* is something of a revelation—by far the finest recording this work has ever received . . . the superb orchestral virtuosity is marvellously controlled here by Maazel."

That virtuosity and control were headed for an extensive showcasing before the microphones. With Telarc, London/Decca, and Columbia, Maazel and the orchestra would record almost 60 more works over the next six years.

The Maazel roller coaster was racing at top speed, and its twists and turns were unpredictable. Paying tribute to the (recently deceased) German composer Boris Blacher in the "Great Composers of Our Time" series during the 1975–76 season and honoring Sir Michael Tippett in 1977, Maazel continued to expand Cleveland's connection with recent music. At the same time, his performances with the orchestra could go any which way, depending upon his mood or his view of the music. Some concertgoers avoided Severance Hall whenever Maazel touched anything by Mozart, Beethoven, Brahms, or other composers who had been interpreted superbly by Szell.

Those who were drifting away from the orchestra under Maazel could take refuge in performances at Severance Hall or Blossom Music Center by other prominent artists. In September 1977, tenor Luciano Pavarotti, in his prime, gave a recital of songs and arias at Blossom with pianist John Wustman, thoroughly enchanting the crowd. The singer's triumph led Maazel and Haas to hatch a plan to bring him back in a concert version of a beloved opera at Blossom. "Regarding our Boheme in 1980, Pavarotti has not yet signed his contract but he is expected back in the U.S. before the end of April and his manager tells us that he will have a final decision at that time," wrote the manager to the conductor. The final decision would be a resounding "No." A Blossom audience had already experienced operatic electricity in July 1977, when Sarah Caldwell (whose Opera Company of Boston was now being run by Michael Maxwell, the orchestra's former general manager) made her debut at the orchestra's summer home conducting the local premiere of excerpts from Prokofiev's opera, *War and Peace*. Hruby called the concert "one of Blossom Center's milestone performances."

Soon after Caldwell, a maestro of even more wondrous artistry, Klaus Tennstedt, elicited an ecstatic response from audiences and critics in two concerts at Blossom. The intense, chain-smoking German conductor, whose spectacular U.S. debut at Tanglewood with the Boston Symphony three years earlier had catapulted him to international fame, led the Cleveland musicians in a Mozart-Bruckner program the first night and a Mozart-Haydn-Tchaikovsky-Stravinsky lineup the next. In praising Tennstedt, Wilma Salisbury offered an implied criticism of Maazel: "When a musician of exceptional integrity leads the Cleveland Orchestra, the music pours out with the naturalness of a flowing stream."

❧   ❧   ❧

Money had been pouring out of the orchestra's coffers in a steady stream since the early 1970s thanks to escalating operating costs and musicians' salaries and benefits, as well as expenses for Blossom. The deficit for fiscal year 1975–76 was $339,500, the largest since 1971–72. This figure brought the accumulated deficit (for debts of several recent seasons) to $971,500. A year later, the figure hit $1.04 million, good reason for the Musical Arts Association to embark on a fund-raising campaign to raise $20 million for the endowment (which stood at $12 million—not nearly high enough to produce significant annual income). Although the accumulated deficit would rise once again, to $1.06 million, for 1976–77, the annual shortfall was only $70,010, making it the smallest operating deficit in three seasons. The endowment campaign became particularly necessary after the musicians accepted a new three-year contract in May 1977 that boosted the weekly minimum from $350 to $450. The last figure still kept the ensemble's minimum behind those in Chicago and New York. But, finally, Cleveland pensions were budging, from $3,000 per year—for a musician who retired at 60 or later with 30 years' service—to $7,500. The mandatory retirement age was raised from 65 to 67. After decades of struggle, orchestral musicians were finding Cleveland more and more attractive as a place to make a living.

✳   ✳   ✳

The first release in Maazel's Beethoven cycle for Columbia, the Fifth Symphony, received little international applause. Typical of the critical reaction was a review in *Gramophone* magazine: "As a start of Maazel's complete Cleveland Beethoven cycle this new recording is both strange and unpropitious. It is a performance which eschews real revolutionary ardour, and circumscribes splendor and imaginative quiet."

Yet Maazel received high praise from Alan Rich in *New York* magazine after the critic heard him conduct the orchestra in February 1978:

> I never stop wondering whether the players in any orchestra ever realize how good their total ensemble is, but if there are players in Cleveland with good ears, it would be interesting to know how willing they are to eat their words. I don't know Maazel well enough to know whether he is lovable or not, but I do know that the orchestra he brought to Carnegie Hall last weekend is not only one of the most spectacular musical organizations anywhere in the world today but is also the work of one of the most supremely gifted music directors.

Conductors also were impressed with Maazel's impact on the orchestra. William Steinberg, who had been frustrated by what he believed to be an inflexibility instilled by Szell, was complimentary after leading a Brahms

program in March 1978. "I wish to say that your orchestra is really extraordinary and I have no doubt that you will keep it at that point," he wrote to
Maazel.

Two months later, a conductor of very different talents kept the musicians
on the edge of their seats—and helped raise much-needed funds in the
process. Danny Kaye, the comedian best known for his neurotic film characters, was no symphonic novice; he had conducted orchestras around the
country, including one at a major university (Yale). His antics on the podium
had generated vast sums of money. Kaye's "shtick technique" was virtually
unparalleled. He could reduce an orchestra and its patrons to convulsions
by conducting Rimsky-Korsakov's "Flight of the Bumble Bee" with a fly
swatter or by imitating a geriatric conductor who no longer knew which way
to face. And he was highly musical, despite the fact that he couldn't read a
note. "I do it all by ear," Kaye told Salisbury. "And I will sing you every bar."

A gourmet cook and classical music maven, the merry maestro had won
the approval of many professional conductors for the depth of his knowledge and the clarity with which he communicated with musicians. "I don't
know about musical theory," Kaye said, "but I know that if you have 10 different cooks following the same recipe, each one will do something different; and if you have 10 different conductors for the same piece you can have
10 different interpretations." During the Cleveland concert, he sang a
Japanese duet with orchestra violinist Keiko Furiyoshi and "shot" concertmaster Daniel Majeske backstage for not following orders. Kaye called the
Cleveland Orchestra the finest ensemble that he had ever conducted, as-
suring trustees that he had never said this to any other orchestra. Whether
Kaye was being whimsical didn't matter—the trustees were celebrating because the concert raised $170,000.

Soon the Musical Arts Association was able to announce that it had ended
the previous fiscal year in the black. The $1 million debt was gone and re-
placed by a $21,446 surplus. Along with the Kaye concert donations, grants
and fund-raising had done the job. It was the first time since the 1961–62
season that the institution could boast of being debt free.

A few days after the orchestra revealed this financial news, the musicians
and Maazel left for their second Asian tour together. The three-week trip
included 15 concerts in Hong Kong, Seoul, Tokyo, Nagoya, Osaka,
Fukuoka, and Hiroshima. In Hong Kong, where the orchestra gave five concerts, Majeske played the Beethoven Violin Concerto, and John Mack was
soloist in the Mozart Oboe Concerto. The reviews confirmed Cleveland's
standing in the music world. Upon its return, the ensemble welcomed two

staff conductors: British-born Andrew Massey, who became assistant conductor, and Israel's Yoel Levi, a conducting assistant who would rise quickly to the position of resident conductor.

The board was in a celebratory mood throughout the fall of 1978, due to healthier finances, the triumphant foreign tour, and continued recording activity (royalties were up to $78,000 from $50,000 the previous year). The trustees now paused to salute Alfred Rankin on his decade as president of the Musical Arts Association. "At all times, even during trying union negotiations, Al never permitted any of us to forget that our reason for being was the orchestra—that the musicians (both orchestra and chorus) were the number one members of the team, and that we were one family," association vice president Richard Tullis told the board. "When things were blackest financially, he never let us talk about reducing quality or quantity of music. He stuck to a very tough course for ten difficult years, and he has won! And all of us have won with him."

For its 60th anniversary, marked on December 10, 1978, the orchestra invited back two former concertmasters, Josef Gingold and Rafael Druian, to play a Vivaldi four-violin concerto with Majeske and associate concertmaster Raymond Kobler. Another former orchestra principal, cellist Leonard Rose, also took the stage, as did violinist Isaac Stern and soprano Beverly Sills. To bring historic resonance to the anniversary, Maazel led Victor Herbert's *American Fantasy*, the very first work the orchestra had performed in December 1918. Not only that, he showed his skill as a host by playing piano for whimsical turns with Stern and Sills. Seated in the audience were three people with close ties to the orchestra: Halina Rodzinski, widow of the ensemble's second conductor; pianist Gaby Casadesus, widow of pianist Robert Casadesus; and former staff conductor Louis Lane, who was in town to lead the orchestra that week in subscription concerts for the first time in five years.

The 60th-anniversary concert was taped by WVIZ and broadcast nationally on PBS stations the following March, when an Associated Press story referred to the event in the context of Cleveland's recent fiscal troubles. With Dennis Kucinich, "the boy mayor," running the government, the city had defaulted in December 1978—five days after the orchestra's celebratory concert—on $14 million in payments to the Cleveland Electrical Illuminating Company and five local banks. "Mention Cleveland these days and most people think of political infighting and financial disaster," said the AP story. "Well, why not think of Beethoven, Beverly Sills and birthdays instead?"

Beethoven was on the minds of the Musical Arts Association for another reason. The trustees had been discussing ways to develop Blossom Music Center, which had not yet captured the fancy of the international musical world or grown to the satisfaction of the orchestra's music director. Maazel had stated his desire for Blossom to reach the level of such prestigious European festivals as Bayreuth and Salzburg, which may have been wishful thinking but was also a valiant effort to push the facility beyond regional appeal. The board reacted to Maazel's wishes by proposing to study the possibility of "an annual Beethoven festival, at Blossom, of international scope and significance" and to make an aggressive attempt to "capture for The Cleveland Orchestra a leading TV and recording role."

Beethoven could also have been in the air at this time because the orchestra's recording of the nine symphonies under Maazel was being released in a boxed set by Columbia. John Rockwell, who had been unmoved by Maazel's Brahms cycle, shaped his *New York Times* review of the Beethoven cycle into an analysis of the conductor's seemingly capricious artistry:

> Lorin Maazel remains one of the most fascinating enigmas among contemporary conductors, and his orchestral recordings with the Cleveland Orchestra, on two record labels, contribute to the enigma as much as they help resolve it . . . This critic has encountered Mr. Maazel in concert many times over the years, in widely varying repertory and with widely varying orchestras. The performances are nearly always first-class in terms of execution. But too often they sound bored or willful from an interpretive standpoint, and Mr. Maazel's sometimes seemingly fitful concentration on the interpretive soul of the music has been confirmed by musicians who have played under him.

Dismissing Maazel's Cleveland recording of Rimsky-Korsakov's *Scheherazade* as "fatally detached," Rockwell registered admiration for performances of Berlioz's *Harold in Italy*, Strauss's *Ein Heldenleben*, and Prokofiev's Fifth Symphony before generally hailing the Beethoven cycle. "The music-making is full-bodied, intense, hearty, and impassioned, much as the popular image of Beethoven himself suggests . . . . At their frequent best, these are performances that really demand to be heard—even in the absurdly overcrowded field of complete Beethoven symphony sets. The First, Second, Fourth and Eighth symphonies are breath-taking, and the Fifth and Seventh are truly exciting, as well."

The accolades continued in May 1979, when Maazel and the orchestra won the Deutsche Schallplattenpreis (German Record Prize) for their recording of the "Eroica."

✻   ✻   ✻

The orchestra and its boss were thriving. Along with six other American orchestras, Cleveland was chosen to participate in an AT&T program that would distribute $10 million over four years to cover deficits for tours to areas around the country not exposed to live concerts by major orchestras. Another healthy show of support ($320,000) arrived from the National Endowment for the Arts, which granted a total of $10.8 million to 109 orchestras. On the heels of these windfalls, the orchestra announced that it had eluded a deficit for the second year in a row. The 1978–79 season ended with a surplus of $23,760, up from $21,446 the previous year. Just a few years earlier, the orchestra had been on the brink of financial disaster.

Maazel gave every indication that he was buoyed by his success in Cleveland. In a *Press* interview in August 1979, he boasted of the orchestra's accomplishments. "When I took over in 1972 the orchestra had 25% subscription, no recording or tours in sight, was poorly paid and heavily in debt. Eight years later, we have 60 LPs, every possible international prize, 83% subscription and tours right and left," he said. He also noted that "for the first time in 16 years we are financially in the black," calling Cleveland the only symphony orchestra in the country that could make this claim.

But the city's roller-coaster ride with its controversial maestro was about to take yet another unexpected turn.

Longtime Lame Duck

The Cleveland Orchestra's European tour in September 1979 was an ordeal. Twenty concerts in 26 days. Travel from Cleveland to Zurich, Lucerne, Stockholm, Oslo, Göteborg, Malmö, Berlin, Munich, Mannheim, Bonn, Düsseldorf, Brussels, Linz, Vienna, Budapest, Paris, and London. Repertoire weighty enough to test the endurance of even the most stalwart lips and limbs: the four Brahms symphonies, Bruckner's Eighth Symphony, Strauss's *Ein Heldenleben*, orchestral excerpts from Wagner music dramas, and hefty encores as well.

But for sheer drama, nothing could compare with the rumors that kept the Cleveland musicians on the edges of their seats. Soon after the orchestra arrived in Europe, word began circulating that Maazel was a candidate for the directorship of the Vienna State Opera, a post formerly held by Gustav Mahler, Richard Strauss, and Herbert von Karajan. The other name being bandied about was that of Christoph von Dohnányi, the German conductor who headed another fine European opera house, the Hamburg State Opera. As his tour with the orchestra proceeded, Maazel appeared to emerge as the top contender, a situation that made its way back to Cleveland on September 19. Robert Finn reported developments that day in *The Plain Dealer*, saying an announcement was expected on September 21. "Most speculation assumes that Maazel will assume the Vienna post after his Cleveland contract expires in 1981," wrote Finn. "Thus he would have two more full seasons at Severance Hall." The story said Musical Arts Association president Alfred M. Rankin, who was flying to Vienna for the news conference, denied that Maazel would leave Cleveland upon taking up the Vienna post. "I do not expect that any commitment [Maazel] may make to the Vienna State Opera will interfere with his Cleveland commitments," said Rankin, adding that he would discuss an extension of Maazel's Cleveland contract with his music director while in Vienna.

Two days later, orchestra members were the first to learn that the news about Vienna was true. Each player received a memo from Maazel on orchestra stationery:

> A press conference is being held today to announce my appointment as General Manager and Artistic Director of the Vienna State Opera starting September 1, 1982. In accepting this position, I agree to conduct a maximum of thirty opera performances per year so that I would be free to meet the challenge that the administration of this magnificent opera house represents. The flexibility that this arrangement provides will also allow me to negotiate meaningfully with the Musical Arts Association, which had proposed and continues to propose that I stay on as Music Director of The Cleveland Orchestra through the 1984/85 season. I hope that we can work out means by which the future interests of the Orchestra can best be served for I enjoy our relationship immensely and am very proud of our achievements.

Back home, *The Plain Dealer* had already made its opinion known regarding Maazel's future as music director. The day before the Vienna news conference, an editorial stated that if Maazel were to take the opera post, "we believe it would be a mistake for him to be kept on as head of the Cleveland Orchestra." Maazel's new position would take him away from the orchestra for prolonged periods, leaving Cleveland's ensemble "with a split personality." There was no reason why Maazel shouldn't receive a contract extension if he didn't take the Vienna post, but if he did, the editorial naively stated, "the Musical Arts Association should begin immediately to accept applications from the numerous highly qualified persons who undoubtedly would covet the honor of leading the Cleveland Orchestra."

With the unexpected news from Vienna came yet another surprise: Rankin had no intention of letting go of Maazel, whom he had hired. The board president said the orchestra could now complete negotiations "to extend [Maazel's] music directorship through the 1984–85 season." Maazel called the Cleveland and Vienna posts "complementary." Many observers begged to differ, saying the orchestra would be best served if Maazel stepped down upon becoming chief at the Vienna State Opera. By October 10, the board was told that Maazel would extend his Cleveland contract through the 1981–82 season but then depart to devote himself to his duties in Vienna. One confusing point regarding the appointment was clarified. Maazel had intended to finish the tour and then return to Vienna afterward, when the news about the opera post would be released in Cleveland and

Vienna at the same time. But the speculation in the European press had compelled Viennese officials to make the announcement earlier.

Now that Rankin and Maazel had changed their tune—"I did not mean to give that impression," Maazel said of his initial intention to hold two posts at once—the board could come up with solutions for the orchestra's future. It announced that Maazel would lead 12 subscription weeks during the 1981–82 season and become music director emeritus for a three-year term (1982–85), for four to six weeks per season. The orchestra would begin to search for a new music director to take up the post, if possible, at the start of the 1982–83 season. As conductor emeritus, Maazel would conduct concerts, recordings, and television productions. However hopeful the board president and the music director may have been, the board was informed that an extended relationship wasn't necessarily a sure thing: "[Maazel's] contract for services as Conductor Emeritus does contain certain mutual options for renegotiation when a new Music Director is engaged."

❧   ❧   ❧

Thus began the longest search for a music director in the orchestra's history. Robert Finn began the speculation in *The Plain Dealer* by saying that the "[Klaus] Tennstedt groupies, for example, are in full cry. You can, without much trouble, compile a list of eight or 10 conductors who ought at least to be investigated. The identity of Maazel's successor will supplant at last the presidential desires of Edward M. Kennedy as fodder for speculation." He scolded Rankin and Maazel for their initial statements—"equivocation, pure and simple"—that the conductor could serve Vienna and Cleveland at once. And Finn noted the absence of a strong lobby for any conductor: "You will recall that it was only about a month after George Szell died when the rumors became rampant that Maazel had the Cleveland job wrapped up— rumors that eventually proved true. I do not get this feeling now. I think the board is starting with a clean slate."

The slate was cleaner, perhaps, than the Cleveland board might have liked. Many of the candidates who could have succeeded Maazel had been rejected in 1971. The Cleveland area still couldn't compete with larger American and European cities in terms of international clout, artistic or otherwise. The city's economy was in dire straits, and the downtown area was feeling the effects of suburban sprawl. The shortage of first-class hotels and restaurants hardly made the city appealing to conductors—and guest artists—accustomed to the finest amenities.

When they began considering strategies for finding a successor, trustees and management were determined to avoid the fiasco surrounding Maazel's appointment. General manager Kenneth Haas and board member Thomas J. Quigley met with the orchestra's Artistic Advisory Committee and determined that the musicians needed to have more input in the search. Rather than one player on the search committee—as dictated by the orchestra contract—the board intended to involve a larger number as consultants.

Finn continued to do his bit to stir up interest. He devised a list of former candidates (Claudio Abbado, Bernard Haitink, Daniel Barenboim) and possible new candidates (James Levine, Klaus Tennstedt, Michael Tilson Thomas, Andrew Davis, Colin Davis, Carlo Maria Giulini, Stanislaw Skrowaczewski, André Previn), and ruled out Erich Leinsdorf and Antal Dorati as too old. He noted that the music directors of the other "Big Five" orchestras—Seiji Ozawa (Boston), Sir Georg Solti (Chicago), Zubin Mehta (New York), and Riccardo Muti (Philadelphia)—were unlikely to leave their posts for Cleveland.

A favorite seemed to be Tennstedt, whose candidacy was being pushed by the so-called "Klausketeers," a group of enthusiasts who published an occasional newsletter about their conducting hero. Tennstedt provided plenty of fuel for speculation when he came to Severance Hall in December 1979 for two weeks of subscription concerts (works by Weber, Wagner, Bruckner, Beethoven, Bartók, and Dvořák). "This being the Important Season when the Musical Arts Association is having visions of new musical directors dancing in its collective head, at least one of those sugarplum apparitions must look a lot like Klaus Tennstedt," wrote Frank Hruby in the *Press*. "Which wouldn't be too far out of line with the first faint rumors stirring about."

Rankin was being extra careful to keep the search process as open as possible. He proposed that a 12-member Ad Hoc Committee on the Artistic Direction of the Orchestra comprise "a musician selected by the Orchestra, the five members of the Orchestra's Artistic Advisory Committee, the MAA president, four vice-presidents, and the General Manager." The committee would recommend qualified conductors to the board, which would also seek advice from other informed sources, though, he noted, "the selection of a new Music Director rests exclusively with the Trustees."

❧   ❧   ❧

The buzz about the future was a distraction, but the orchestra's performance schedule went forward as planned. In January 1980, the Musical Arts Association inaugurated one of the institution's most significant annual events, the Martin Luther King Jr. Celebration Concert, to be held on or near the late civil rights leader's birthday. The first concert was held on

January 15 with Andrew Davis conducting Beethoven's Ninth Symphony with the Cleveland Orchestra Chorus, the Prestonian Choral Ensemble, and soloists Janet Alcorn, Barbara Conrad, Curtis Rayam, and John Cheek. (The concerts were collaborations between the Musical Arts Association and the Greater Cleveland Interchurch Council until 1986, when, at the request of Cleveland city council president George Forbes and Mayor George V. Voinovich, subsequent concerts were presented with input from the city. Concerts alternated between Cory United Methodist Church, where Dr. King gave his last speech in Cleveland, and Severance Hall.)

In a now-familiar refrain, Maazel continued to receive polarized international appraisals for his work with the orchestra. After their performance of Mahler's Fifth Symphony in New York in mid-February, Harold C. Schonberg wrote admiringly of Maazel's interpretation and his effect on the musicians. "The Cleveland Orchestra remains one of the top groups in the world," he noted in the *New York Times*. "George Szell left a virtuoso orchestra that plays like a chamber-music ensemble, and Mr. Maazel has retained that quality. It is a wonderful group that performs with a quality of elasticity, with a feeling that there is always something in reserve, with clear textures and absolute precision." But a week later in the *London Times*, Paul Griffiths offered damning words about the new Maazel-Cleveland recording of Debussy's *Nocturnes, Iberia,* and *Jeux,* saying it was marred by "an inappropriate style . . . performance and recording combine to offer glossy colours and clear statement instead of hint and subterfuge. The resulting glamour, most unwelcome in a swooning account of *Jeux,* is enhanced by forced rhythms and heavily marked accelerations."

Meanwhile, the rumor mill ground on. In early March, the *Chicago Tribune* reported that Claudio Abbado had turned down an offer to be Maazel's successor in Cleveland. Haas quickly tried to set the record straight. "The position has not been discussed with nor offered to any conductor, including Mr. Abbado," he told *The Plain Dealer*. "Any suggestion as to the basis of his quoted remarks would only be speculation on our part." Abbado, who had been on the list of Cleveland candidates in 1971, hadn't conducted at Severance Hall since 1973. The orchestra announced that it hoped the Ad Hoc Committee on Artistic Direction would submit its recommendations for music-director candidates by September. Six months after Maazel's Vienna announcement, Haas had a list of 36 possible conductors. Along with accepting real input from orchestra members, the board agreed to diverge from its previous search process by doing away with any age criteria for candidates to avoid limiting the field, as they may unwittingly have done in 1971 (when the age preference was 35 to 45).

❀   ❀   ❀

No matter who was scheduled to be on the podium in mid-1980, there was a distinct possibility that there would be no orchestra to conduct. The orchestra had rejected the Musical Arts Association's first offer for a new labor contract. The old agreement was set to expire in March, and negotiations between the musicians and management were going badly. Of the 105 issues originally on the table, 35 were still unresolved by mid-May, including 20 involving money. The possibility of a strike threated the 1980 Blossom Music Center season—including the special attractions, as all performers would be members of the American Federation of Musicians. The board knew what the players were demanding. "It is clear that the necessity to maintain a competitive position with other orchestras will require a large financial settlement," Rankin told the trustees.

On July 1, the musicians announced that they were ready to follow through on their intention to strike. They walked out the next day, putting up a picket line (in full concert dress) at the entrance of Blossom Music Center and essentially shutting down the facility. Principal percussionist Richard Weiner, chairman of the orchestra's negotiating committee, told *The Plain Dealer* that musicians and management were far apart on such issues as "wage scales, workload, pension plan, vacations, life insurance and dental insurance, audition procedures, touring conditions, seniority pay, a rotation plan for string sections, unpaid leaves of absence and unpaid optional weeks off." The orchestra needed to stay in competition with the country's other top ensembles on these issues. "The Cleveland Orchestra works harder, is paid less, tours more and receives fewer benefits than other major orchestras," Weiner said. "The situation has deteriorated for so long that it is a monumental task to catch up." Even the federal mediator who had been meeting with both parties for two months had been unable to make much headway.

Blossom offered little more than the quiet pacing of picketing feet for the next two weeks, when seven orchestra concerts, including three that were to have been led by Maazel, and seven popular events were cancelled. Among the casualties were performances that were supposed to feature the Scottish National Orchestra Chorus. For pop fans, the cancellation of a concert by the Doobie Brothers was infinitely more irksome.

As the strike dragged on, orchestra players explained to the media exactly why they felt it necessary to keep up with other major ensembles on economic issues. "We joined the orchestra because it was the Cleveland Orchestra," one musician said. "But if we cannot draw the top players because they know of the discrepancy in salary here, in 10 years, the Cleveland Orchestra very well might be a second-rate group." Haas remarked that every orchestra was having difficulty finding qualified applicants, but Weiner disagreed. "This kind of erosion of talent pool in Cleveland is insidious," he said. "It creeps up on you. If Chicago gets 200 people and we get 20, maybe we're not hearing the best people."

Finally, in mid-July, the orchestra and management were able to come to terms. The agreement moved the musicians from eleventh in pay to fifth place, putting Cleveland back where it belonged among the so-called "Big Five" orchestras. The new 3½-year contract was touted, grandiosely, by the Musical Arts Association as the "largest salary increase in the history of American orchestras." It raised the minimum weekly salary from $450 to $500, with an increase to $610 by March 1982 (when the annual minimum pay would be $34,060). The pension was increased from $7,500 to $10,000 a year for musicians aged 60 or older, and a seniority clause was added providing extra pay after 10 and 20 years' service. The musicians were also going to enjoy eight weeks of paid vacation.

The strike ended in time for a significant event: a program on August 1 marking the 10th anniversary of Szell's death. As they had done at Blossom a decade earlier, the strings began with an unconducted reading of the Air from Bach's Third Suite, followed by Louis Lane—Szell's longtime assistant—conducting typical Szell fare: Mozart's Symphony No. 40, Hindemith's Symphonic Metamorphosis on Themes by Weber (replacing Prokofiev's Third Piano Concerto, due to John Browning's illness), and Schumann's "Rhenish" Symphony.

✤   ✤   ✤

With Vienna looming, Maazel's Cleveland activity in the recording studio was waning quickly. In 1980, he made only two recordings—a virtuosic but bizarrely distorted performance of Stravinsky's *The Rite of Spring* for Telarc, and a forceful reading of Tchaikovsky's Fifth Symphony for Columbia. Maazel would complete his series of Cleveland recordings with five works in 1981 (Shostakovich's Fifth Symphony and Tchaikovsky's *Nutcracker* suite, *Romeo and Juliet* fantasy-overture, and fourth and sixth symphonies) and one in 1982 (his second Cleveland recording of Berlioz's *Symphonie fantastique*, made less than two weeks before his final concerts as music director).

Maazel's mind may have been on Vienna, but he was still in full command in Cleveland. He was engaged to lead 13 weeks of subscription concerts during the 1980–81 season, when he conducted such novel fare as Luciano

Berio's *Coro* (featuring the Cologne Radio Chorus), Luigi Dallapiccola's *Canti di Prigionia*, Peter Mennin's Symphony No. 8, and the world premiere of Morton Gould's *Burchfield Gallery*. Maazel also led a concert celebrating the 50th anniversary of Severance Hall (with the same program of works by Bach, Loeffler, and Brahms that Nikolai Sokoloff had conducted on February 5, 1931, at the hall's opening) and performances of Beethoven's *Missa Solemnis*, which had been cancelled the previous summer due to the orchestra strike. The financial news was good at the start of the 1980–81 season. For the third year in a row, the orchestra's fiscal year (1979–80) had ended with a small surplus—$9,600, compared with $23,760 and $21,446 for the two previous years.

News about the orchestra's search for a music director wasn't nearly as upbeat. In fact, there was no news. More than a year after Maazel had announced his intention to leave, the Musical Arts Association still was unable to find the conductor who would lead the institution into the future. By November 1980, Rankin was telling the trustees that they would have to remain patient. "You may be confident that the matter has been given the highest priority and will continue to receive our most careful attention," he informed the board. "A public announcement will be made at the earliest possible moment." In the next breath, Rankin announced that the orchestra would play under guest conductors during the 1982–83 season and possibly have a new music director in place for the 1983–84 season.

Few of the guest conductors scheduled for the 1980–81 season would prove to be music director material, at least at this point in their careers. Antal Dorati, 74, and Erich Leinsdorf, 68, were unlikely to be considered for another major post anywhere, especially Leinsdorf, who had vowed never again to take up such a job after his sour experience as music director of the Boston Symphony. Jesús López-Cobos, Giuseppe Patanè, and James Conlon, while impressive, didn't seem right for the orchestra. The only other guest conductor this season was the extroverted Rafael Frühbeck de Burgos, a candidate in 1971, whose style didn't quite mesh with Cleveland's ultra-refined personality, either.

The prospects looked somewhat brighter when the roster of conductors was announced for the 1981 season at Blossom Music Center. Among the guests were Germany's Michael Gielen and Christoph Eschenbach and two British conductors—Sir Colin Davis, music director of London's Royal Opera House at Covent Garden, and Andrew Davis (no relation), music director of the Toronto Symphony. The season hummed along nicely. Then, on August 21, Sir Colin stepped onto the podium and sent surges of hope through the Blossom pavilion with a gloriously evocative and majestic per-

71. An audience enjoys a concert by the Cleveland Orchestra at its summer home, Blossom Music Center.

72.. A view of the interior of the pavilion at Blossom Music Center. It has been hailed for its superb acoustics.

73. Szell shares the stage at Tokyo's Uemo Bunka Kaikan Hall with his musicians and two Japanese girls during the last tour of his life in May 1970.

74. Principal tuba player Ronald Bishop, Helene Szell, principal oboist John Mack, and Szell confer onstage in a high-school auditorium in Anchorage, Alaska, in May 1970 before the last concert of Szell's life.

75. Members of the Cleveland Orchestra and staff conductor Louis Lane bow their heads during the memorial service for George Szell at Severance Hall on August 3, 1970.

76. General manager Michael Maxwell and music director Lorin Maazel share a happy moment during the orchestra's 1973 Australian tour.

77. Pianist Arthur Rubinstein makes a point to Maazel in 1975.

78. Maazel gives a young violinist a few tips after a Key Concert at Severance Hall in 1975.

79. David Zauder played cornet and trumpet in the orchestra for four decades and succeeded Olin Trogdon as personnel manager.

80. Baton hijinks: Comedian Danny Kaye and Maazel compare stick techniques before a benefit concert in 1978.

81. Maazel serves as host to violinist Isaac Stern and soprano Beverly Sills during the orchestra's 60th-anniversary concert in December 1978.

82. Erich Leinsdorf at Severance Hall in the fall of 1982,
when he began expanded conducting duties during the transition between Lorin Maazel and Christoph von Dohnányi.

83. Dohnányi and general manager Kenneth Haas at the conductor's first press conference
as music director-designate in August 1982.

84. Christoph von Dohnányi and soprano Anja Silja, then his wife, perform with the orchestra during a gala benefit concert at Severance Hall in February 1983.

85. Members of the orchestra on strike for a better labor contract at Blossom Music Center in July 1980.

86. Christoph von Dohnányi conducts the orchestra at Blossom Music Center in the late 1980s.

87. Ward Smith was the orchestra's board president from 1983 to 1995.

88. Violinist Kurt Loebel was a member of the orchestra for 50 seasons, starting in 1947.

89. Dohnányi, center, and executive director Thomas Morris, right, celebrate completion of the orchestra's Beethoven symphony cycle for Telarc Records in October 1988 with company officials Elaine Martone, Robert Woods, and Jack Renner.

90. Jahja Ling welcomes Polish composer Witold Lutoslawski to a rehearsal of the Cleveland Orchestra Youth Orchestra in the early 1990s.

91. An audience in the grand foyer at Severance Hall for one of the orchestra's annual concerts marking the birthday of Dr. Martin Luther King, Jr.

92. Robert Shaw and Pierre Boulez flank Dohnányi backstage in Paris in 1990 during an orchestra tour.

93. Daniel Majeske served as concertmaster from 1969 until his death in 1993.

94. Dohnányi conducts the orchestra at Severance Hall in the early 1990s.

95. The orchestra and Dohnányi at a recording session of Wagner's *Das Rheingold* in December 1993 on a platform built over the main-floor seats at Severance Hall.

96. The orchestra and Dohnányi rehearse at the Felsenreitschule (Rock Riding School) in Salzburg, Austria, in 1994. Scenes in the movie *The Sound of Music* were filmed here.

97. Dohnányi and the orchestra perform in a gymnasium in Shanghai, China, in 1998.

98. After Szell's death, violinist Leonard Samuels grew a beard and ponytail, making him the most recognizable member of the orchestra until his death in 1995, two weeks before his scheduled retirement.

99. Richard J. Bogomolny became president of the Musical Arts Association in 1995.

100. The main auditorium at Severance Hall undergoes renovation in the late 1990s.

101. Franz Welser-Möst, shown conducting the orchestra at Severance Hall, was appointed the ensemble's seventh music director on June 7, 1999.

102. The reopening of Severance Hall is marked by a gala concert on January 8, 2000.

103. A crowd gathers for the Cleveland Orchestra's annual 4th-of-July concert on Public Square (on July 3, 2000).

formance of Sibelius's Symphony No. 2. "The Cleveland Orchestra responded superbly to Davis," wrote Finn the next day. "They were clearly on his wavelength, and he on theirs. This was an exciting concert, a truly significant Cleveland debut, and one of the memorable nights of recent Blossom seasons."

Suddenly, everyone—including the board—was talking about the possibility of a courtship leading to marriage. Less than three weeks after Sir Colin's two Blossom concerts, Rankin and Haas sent the knighted conductor a letter: "We are pleased to propose that you become Music Director of The Cleveland Orchestra as of September, 1984, under terms to be mutually agreed." Sir Colin would not agree; his family, he said, came first and, after all, he had a very satisfying job at Covent Garden. The Cleveland Orchestra was back at the drawing board, two full years after Maazel had accepted the Vienna post—and only eight months away from his last concerts as music director.

In early November, Rankin gave the board another update on the music director search, putting an optimistic spin on the situation, though only he, Haas, and perhaps a few others knew that Davis had turned down the post (the rejection would never be publicly addressed): "You may be sure that our negotiations with conductor candidates are proceeding in a positive and encouraging manner, and we continue to plan for a new director who will assume conducting responsibilities in the 1983/84 season or at the latest in the 1984/85 season."

By this time, the orchestra world at large had noticed that Cleveland was having inordinate trouble choosing Maazel's successor. The *New York Times* added to the embarrassment, taking up the subject in November in an article headlined "Help Wanted: A 'Big 5' Music Director." Its author, Judith Karp, noted: "Mr. Haas is acutely aware that the main handicap in filling the post is the city's reputation as a dull, insular factory town. But he says, 'People are always pleasantly surprised, if not shocked, when they get here . . . There are some 85 cultural and educational institutions here, and the population is very aware of the national treasure it has in this orchestra.'" A member of the orchestra suggested to Karp that the ensemble had an image problem in comparison to its "Big Five" colleagues. "We don't have the electricity of New York, the gentry atmosphere of Boston, the brute strength of Chicago or the sheen of Philadelphia," the musician said. Another unidentified player uttered chilling words about the situation: "Whoever comes in next will make or break this orchestra."

The 1981–82 season didn't appear to hold much promise. An unusually large number of guest conductors—nine, not including staff conductors

Yoel Levi and Robert Page—had been engaged for Maazel's last season, when the music director was scheduled to conduct only seven subscription programs, about half the number he had led during previous seasons. The guest roster included conductors who had appeared with the orchestra before: Marriner, Mata, Leinsdorf, Eschenbach, Andrew Davis, and Sir Colin Davis.

Only three guests would be new to Cleveland: Simon Rattle, the 27-year-old Liverpool-born firebrand with the Beatle-like mop of hair; Charles Dutoit, the Swiss-born music director of the Montreal Symphony; and Christoph von Dohnányi, general music director of the Hamburg State Opera and Maazel's sole competitor in 1979 for the Vienna State Opera post.

Rattle and Dutoit were scheduled for late in the season, close to Maazel's final concerts. But their appearances would prove irrelevant to the search, anyway. The man destined to become the orchestra's sixth music director was about to make his debut at Severance Hall.

Christoph von Who?

O n Tuesday, December 1, 1981, the musicians of the Cleveland Orchestra arrived at Severance Hall as usual for their first rehearsal of the
week. By the lunch break, the players sensed that a viable candidate had arrived: A conductor they had never met before had begun to make a big impression. The wavy-haired gentleman with the tongue-twisting name was
Christoph von Dohnányi, a German conductor with a reputation for keen
orchestral skills and an affinity for the composers of the second Viennese
school (Schoenberg, Berg, and Webern). But he was leading none of this
music at his Cleveland debut. Instead, the program included works by
Dvořák and Bartók, the Hungarian composer who had been a colleague of
his grandfather, admired composer, conductor, and pianist Ernö (or Ernst
von) Dohnányi, who had appeared as a guest conductor with the Cleveland
Orchestra in 1924.

The excitement at rehearsals continued to mount, as Robert Finn noted
in his *Plain Dealer* review of the first concert: "The intelligence reports out
of Severance Hall rehearsals earlier this week had been all enthusiastic.
Guest conductor Christoph Von [*sic*] Dohnányi was going to be something
quite special in his debut with the Cleveland Orchestra. I went to Thursday
night's concert with high anticipation." Still, to Finn's ears, the expectations
weren't met. The guest's performance of Dvořák's Symphony No. 8 was
"frankly outrageous, a heavy-handed and exaggerated parody of one of the
most beautiful symphonies in the repertory." He was in the minority, and
not only among critics: the audience and even the musicians would disagree.
The end of the Dvořák was followed by a rare phenomenon for a Cleveland
Orchestra concert: the players applauded the conductor with corporate ex-
uberance, as if they had experienced a decisive moment in their professional
lives. In the *Cleveland Press*, Frank Hruby wrote, "The Dvořák Eighth was
given an exhilarating performance. Dohnányi was but the one zillionth conductor to do the work with the Cleveland Orchestra, but this by no means
[meant] that he simply turned it on and let it run. He explored every nook

and cranny of the luscious work, fashioned them to not only his own liking, but to the audience's as well."

At last, a conductor who seemed to identify with Cleveland's traditions, including its highly disciplined work ethic, had stepped onto the podium. It wasn't a moment too soon. After considering a list of 60 or so conductors, the Musical Arts Association was still coming up empty handed. Sir Colin Davis had turned down the job, and interviews with Kurt Masur, Claudio Abbado, and others—"the usual suspects," according to trustee Ward Smith—had gone nowhere. After Dohnányi's concerts, the musicians on the Ad Hoc Committee on Artistic Direction quickly arranged to talk with general manager Kenneth Haas about their authoritative guest.

The following week, when back trouble forced Erich Leinsdorf to cancel his two weeks of concerts in early January, Haas phoned Dohnányi in Hamburg to see if he might take over these programs. Dohnányi told him he was booked. But he also said that his concerts with the orchestra had been unusually satisfying. Haas, a savvy manager, could read the subtext. He initiated talks with Dohnányi and his New York agent, the Colbert Agency, and began a series of long-distance phone conversations with the conductor on many artistic topics. The decision to offer Dohnányi the post was made on January 25 by the trustees on the search committee (Rankin, Smith, Claude Blair, Thomas Quigley, and Herbert Strawbridge). While the orchestra was in the Far East (Japan, Hong Kong, and Manila, with a final stop in Honolulu) in February for a three-week tour with Lorin Maazel, Dohnányi stopped in Cleveland on his way to an engagement with the Chicago Symphony. On February 28 at Rankin's Gates Mills home, board members presented Dohnányi with the contract that Smith and Haas had written on a typewriter at Smith's home. The four-year agreement named him music director of the Cleveland Orchestra, starting in September 1984. Later the same day, Dohnányi—wearing sunglasses—visited the Cleveland Museum of Art.

The Cleveland public and media never got wind of the deal. The trustees and musicians who knew of it did a superb job of buttoning their lips. On the morning of March 12, the board met to approve Dohnányi's appointment. Within the hour, the orchestra—ready to go onstage for a matinee conducted by Simon Rattle, who had made his debut the night before—was told the news. "Those audience members and ushers outside the hall [heard] three bursts of applause," recounted James Badal in *Northern Ohio Live* magazine. The *Cleveland Press* and *Akron Beacon Journal*, both afternoon papers, reported the appointment hours after the announcement. *The*

Plain Dealer ran the story on its front page the next morning. Reaction by concertgoers and people in the music business ranged from bewilderment to surprise to curiosity to delight.

The first order of business was trying to decipher the new maestro's redundant surname. The German "von" implies aristocracy. So does the Hungarian "i" at the end of "Dohnányi." Should he be referred to as "von Dohnányi" or just "Dohnányi"? (The latter proved to be accurate.) And the pronunciation—was it doe-NON-yee or doe-NON-ee, or either one with the emphasis on the first syllable? The definitive answer, the public soon discovered, was DOCH-non-ee, with the "ch" sounded as in "Bach." Musicians and staff at Severance Hall would come up with their own solution: they would refer to the conductor as CvD.

Now Cleveland could begin to learn more about the dark-horse candidate who would succeed Maazel. Dohnányi actually was not unfamiliar to the United States or the classical music world in general. He had been a guest conductor with the St. Louis Symphony, Chicago Symphony, and New York Philharmonic and led productions at the Metropolitan Opera, Lyric Opera of Chicago, and San Francisco Opera. He had made recordings for Decca of music by Berg, Grieg, Mendelssohn, Mozart, Schoenberg, Strauss, and Stravinsky. And his extensive European career had ranged from top posts at the Frankfurt and Hamburg operas to engagements at other major opera houses and at the Salzburg Festival. Dohnányi would bring a bonus to town: his wife, Anja Silja, the former reigning, and provocative, dramatic soprano at Germany's Bayreuth Festival. The Dohnányis would move to Cleveland with their three young, blond-haired children—Julia, Benedikt, and Olga.

These tidbits didn't even begin to reveal Dohnányi's fascinating and turbulent past. He was born on September 8, 1929, in Berlin, to Hans and Christine von Dohnányi. Hans, son of Ernst von Dohnányi, was a noted lawyer. Christine was a member of the Bonhoeffer family that included her brother, the noted Protestant theologian Dietrich Bonhoeffer. Music had played a prominent role in the lives of the Dohnányis and Bonhoeffers for generations. Ernst von Dohnányi was firmly ensconced in the pantheon of Hungarian composers that included Béla Bartók and Zoltán Kodály, colleagues in Budapest during the early decades of the 20th century. Clara Bonhoeffer, Christoph's great-grandmother, had studied piano with Franz Liszt and Clara Schumann. Gatherings of the Dohnányi and Bonhoeffer broods invariably included sessions of chamber music, during which family members played instruments or sang. In this stimulating environment, young Christoph developed an early love of learning and music. He began with piano studies at age five; soon his grandfather was helping him create little pieces at the piano.

The family's happiness would be interrupted with cruel severity. As Hans von Dohnányi rose in the German government to posts on the supreme court and in the military intelligence service (the Abwehr), he became increasingly dismayed by Hitler's persecution of the Jews. With Dietrich Bonhoeffer and other conspirators, he devised several plans to kill Hitler. Hans delivered a bomb to an officer in the Abwehr, who placed it on Hitler's private plane on March 13, 1943. The bomb didn't go off. Days later, while the Dohnányi and Bonhoeffer families were preparing for a birthday celebration, another plot failed, this one to bomb a Berlin arsenal where Hitler was holding a meeting. The Gestapo arrested Dohnányi, his wife (who soon was released), and Dietrich Bonhoeffer. A year later, family members Rüdiger Schleicher and Klaus Bonhoeffer, who also had taken part in resistance efforts, joined them in prison.

In the year preceding the arrests, the families had been forced to move often to avoid bombing raids. The journey led them to Leipzig, Berlin, and the Benedictine cloister at Ettal before they finally reached grandfather Bonhoeffer's farm in the Berlin suburb of Sakrow. Dohnányi vividly recalled the day (April 5, 1943) when his parents were arrested. "I was very young at 13, and you really had to fight for your daily food," he said. "We knew our parents were very much against this Hitler system." While in Sakrow, Christoph stayed in touch with his father and and his uncle Dietrich, sharing general news and details about his flute studies (he had begun playing the instrument in 1939) in a series of poignant letters. "My flute teacher has now come back again," he wrote to Bonhoeffer. "He's been in Spain. I can go to him tomorrow. He lives in Steiglitz. That's not exactly the best place for air raids. He takes his fourteen flutes—I believe that's the number he has with him into the cellar each time there's an alert." One note from Bonhoeffer to Dohnányi's parents concerns the young musician: "A letter from Christoph has just come. It's surprising how he keeps thinking of writing. What a view of life a fourteen-year-old must get when he has to write to his father and godfather in prison for months on end. He cannot have many illusions about the world now; I suppose all these happenings must mean the end of his childhood."

Even from prison, Hans von Dohnányi tried to continue his resistance work, using special codes to deliver messages to colleagues. In early 1945, he delayed his trial by eating food laden with diphtheria cultures that his wife had smuggled to him. His illness prompted the Nazis to send him to a concentration camp. The end was swift: Hans was hanged at Sachsenhausen on April 9, 1945, the same day Dietrich Bonhoeffer was hanged at Flossenburg. Klaus Bonhoeffer and Rüdiger Schleicher were shot on April 23 at a Berlin prison. Hitler committed suicide a week later. In mid-May, the Germans surrendered at Reims.

✤   ✤   ✤

In the years following the war, Christoph and his older brother, Klaus, vowed to help rebuild their country and restore order and justice. Both entered law school, though one of them would stray: Christoph would discover that the urge to make music was stronger than his desire to be a lawyer. In 1948, he entered the Musikhochschule in Munich, where he won the city's Richard Strauss Prize for conducting and composition. While a student, he made his debut at the Munich Opera, but not as a conductor: he served as an extra (initially as a smuggler in *Carmen*), coached singers, played piano for such conductors as Hans Knappertsbusch and Joseph Keilberth, and ran the wind machine in Wagner's *Der fliegende Holländer*. His experiences firmed his resolve to be a professional musician, and he decided to travel to the United States to study with his grandfather. Ernst von Dohnányi had left Europe—after being accused of not taking a forceful enough stand against Hitler—and accepted a teaching job at Florida State University in Tallahassee. Grandfather and grandson had a difficult relationship when they were reunited in 1951. Ernst came from the musical world of the Romantics; Christoph followed contemporary trends. The grandson found the experience rewarding but stressful. "It's very funny: I composed a violin concerto, which I put on his piano one day. That night, he came down and corrected it. He wrote on it, 'Why is it so ugly here when it could be done so nicely?' He changed it to Brahms style."

While in the United States, Christoph learned English. In the summer of 1952, he studied conducting with Seymour Lipkin at Leonard Bernstein's summer institute at Tanglewood. During one conducting session, Lipkin chastised Dohnányi for his treatment of a passage in Haydn's Symphony No. 88. Then "a voice from the back of the hall echoed forth: 'You may do whatever you like!' " Dohnányi would never forget Bernstein's words.

Upon his return to Europe that fall, Dohnányi was hired by Georg Solti to be an opera and ballet coach at the Frankfurt Opera. In Frankfurt, he learned his craft thoroughly backstage and led his first theatrical performances (operettas by Franz von Suppé and Johann Strauss II). In time, Solti promoted him to principal conductor, giving him the experience he needed to land his first major job, general music director at the opera house in the small northern German city of Lübeck, in 1957. Dohnányi was not only the youngest conductor to serve in that post, he was also following in massive footsteps: Wilhelm Furtwängler had begun his career there. In six years in Lübeck, Dohnányi conducted his first performances of some of the great works of the operatic repertoire, such as *The Marriage of Figaro*, *Die Meistersinger*, and *Der Rosenkavalier*, and he began making orchestral appearances (his debut was with the Tonkünstler Orchestra of Vienna).

His next posts were in Cologne, where he was director of the West German Radio Symphony, and in Kassel, where he served as music director of the opera house. During his time with the orchestra in Cologne, Dohnányi performed an enormous amount of contemporary music, including works by the politically impassioned German composer Hans Werner Henze, who chose Dohnányi to conduct his operas *Der junge Lord* in Berlin in 1965 and *The Bassarids* in Salzburg in 1966. Two years later, Dohnányi succeeded Solti as Intendant (artistic and executive director) and chief conductor at the Frankfurt Opera, where, with productions of *Figaro* and *Das Rheingold*, he became one of the few conductors also to serve as a stage director. Dohnányi's imaginative work in Frankfurt—including cost-cutting measures that resulted in pared-down, innovative productions—led to his appointment as Intendant and principal conductor at the Hamburg State Opera in 1977.

As in Lübeck, Dohnányi was successor to a formidable list of directors, among them Gustav Mahler and Otto Klemperer. The new boss balanced traditional works with contemporary pieces, and once again served as stage director (for productions of *Rheingold* and *Fidelio*). But Hamburg was a handful. The opera house, built in 1874, had been bombed in 1943 air raids, leaving only the stage house intact. A new auditorium fitted onto the old house in 1955 didn't solve the problem of outmoded stage machinery, which hampered the quality of productions. Perhaps as vexing was the situation with the orchestra musicians, who also played in the Hamburg Philharmonic. Since the opera presented 220 performances a season, many musicians would play rehearsals of a particular work but not the performances. A conductor could step into the pit and encounter dozens of players he had never seen, or heard, before. "Now we know why Toscanini, Szell, de Sabata, Kleiber and Solti left opera," said Dohnányi. "They weren't satisfied with the musical standards. I don't believe it necessarily has to be this way. But if you want to get the best, you have to fight for it." The mayor of Hamburg, his brother Klaus, could do nothing to help him solve the problems at the opera house.

And so, when Cleveland came calling in 1982, Dohnányi was more than happy to answer. "I would have left any opera house at least [by] 1987," he said. "[By] then, I would have done 25 years as the chief in opera houses. That's a long time. It takes a lot of energy. And I want to do concerts."

✸   ✸   ✸

Dohnányi would have to wait a bit longer. In Cleveland, the orchestra's 1982–83 season already was completely booked with an absurdly high number of guest conductors—13, necessary during the long transition period.

Maazel, for his final two programs, chose beloved fare: Mendelssohn's Piano Concerto in G minor (with Rudolf Firkusny) and Beethoven's "Eroica" for the first week, and the Verdi Requiem (the piece with which he had begun his tenure in 1972) for his Severance swan song. He made his last Cleveland recording on May 10 (his second recording with the orchestra of Berlioz's *Symphonie fantastique*), and he told management that he was withdrawing from all engagements in the United States in the coming years to concentrate on Vienna, essentially throwing the "conductor emeritus" post in the board's face.

At its end, Maazel's tenure drew varied assessments. The *Cleveland Press* was positive; other papers were reserved. In *The Plain Dealer*, Robert Finn noted that the best summation of the relationship between Maazel and the players came from a local musician who was not a member of the orchestra: "It was not a happy marriage, but it *worked!*" According to Finn, Maazel's "greatest pride as he leaves can be that he is handing over to his successor a first-rate orchestra. He inherited one, and he kept it that way. Our greatest regret as a public is that we never *really* got used to his interpretive vagaries."

Maazel's relationship with the orchestra wasn't over when he conducted his last Cleveland concert on May 15. He took the ensemble on a short tour the following week to Avery Fisher Hall at Lincoln Center, Woolsey Hall at Yale University, and Carnegie Hall. As at Severance Hall the previous week, Maazel's final concert brought a nice touch of symmetry to his tenure in Cleveland: the Verdi Requiem was also the work with which he had introduced himself to New York with the orchestra in 1972. Even so, few critics were much impressed with Maazel's farewell performances, in Cleveland or New York. In the *New York Times*, Donal Henahan found little to recommend about the conductor's way with Beethoven's third and fifth symphonies: "The showmanship and baton techniques were on display constantly so that instead of power and expressiveness that a conductor of his experience could be expected to find in these scores, we had a mere acting-out of the music's surface meaning for the benefit of the audience." Peter G.

Davis, in *New York* magazine, said the orchestra's New York engagement comprised "four impeccably groomed but strangely dispiriting concerts."

Of the national critics, only Thor Eckert, Jr., in the *Christian Science Monitor*, offered Maazel praise, though tempered by disappointment. "He leaves his successor, Christoph von Dohnányi, the best orchestra, overall, in the United States, rivaled only by the Berlin Philharmonic and the Concertgebouw for virtuosity. Above all, there is a distinctiveness of timbre in this faultless ensemble wedded to startling purity of tone," wrote Eckert, also assessing Maazel's Cleveland recording legacy. "His Brahms set proved a total bungle interpretively. The Beethoven cycle on Columbia Records is only average, a superb orchestra notwithstanding. On the Telarc label is a Stravinsky 'Rite of Spring' that is eccentric as can be, yet so superbly recorded, so utterly representative of the best of this fabulous ensemble, that it should be required listening to all who love great orchestral playing."

Upon leaving Cleveland, Maazel settled in for what was to be a productive but tense tenure at the Vienna State Opera. Politics quickly convinced Maazel that Vienna was not the place for him, at least on a permanent basis. He left after only 18 months and spent the following years as musical supervisor to the Pittsburgh Symphony until he agreed to become its music director in 1988. In the early 1990s, he won the top post with the Bavarian Radio Symphony Orchestra in Munich, at an annual salary reported to be between $3 million and $4 million. Since his departure in 1982, he has not conducted the Cleveland Orchestra.

❋   ❋   ❋

Dohnányi didn't stay away from Cleveland for long after his appointment. In August 1982, in the middle of the Blossom season, he spent a week in Northeast Ohio meeting with musicians, trustees, and staff. He sat in a Blossom box with his wife for a concert on August 6 led by Riccardo Chailly. The program, assisted by the Blossom Festival Chorus, comprised Verdi's *Nabucco* overture, "Stabat Mater," and "Te Deum," and Tchaikovsky's Fifth Symphony, repertoire that could give the music director–designate (a title he had assumed in June) a good notion of the orchestra's stylistic flexibility. The Dohnányis surprised everyone the following night by venturing onto the lawn to sit on a blanket, munch on sandwiches, chat with well-wishers, and listen to a second Chailly concert (works by Verdi, Rachmaninoff, and Mussorgsky). Dohnányi told reporters that he wanted to sit there to get another perspective on Blossom. He may already have begun hatching ideas for the orchestra's outdoor concert hall.

Aside from Chailly's appearances, the 1982 Blossom season was notable for concerts featuring cellist Yo-Yo Ma and flutist James Galway and a concert performance of Puccini's *Madama Butterfly* under James Conlon with Leona Mitchell as Cio-Cio San. Only two area newspapers—the *Akron Beacon Journal* and *The Plain Dealer*—covered the Blossom events, the venerable *Cleveland Press* having folded in June. At the end of the Blossom season, a beloved member of the orchestra said farewell after 50 seasons as principal flute—Maurice "Mo" Sharp. "I'll miss out on music director No. 6—Christoph von Dohnányi—but I played under him in December," Sharp told the *Press*. "Liked him very much. In fact, we all did." Sharp's successor was Jeffrey Khaner, a young graduate of the Curtis Institute of Music in Philadelphia, and the only musician to join the orchestra for the 1982–83 season.

❈   ❈   ❈

Now began the first of two seasons of transition. The orchestra was not going to be rudderless. Resident conductor Yoel Levi was assuming additional concert responsibilities, though the most prevalent podium figure would be Erich Leinsdorf, who was scheduled for six weeks of subscription programs at Severance Hall. "I am the bridge between the regimes," said Leinsdorf. "I am responsible for keeping what has been accomplished. It is my responsibility to keep it on a very high level." Much higher, in fact, than during his ill-fated tenure as the orchestra's conductor. "In looking back 40 years, I was not ready for the task," he told the *Akron Beacon Journal*. "It was not of my doing, being inducted into the Army. But it had a shocking effect on me and the organization." The conducting roster for the 1982–83 season also included Antal Dorati, Andrew Davis, Aldo Ceccato, Dennis Russell Davies, Klaus Tennstedt, Kurt Masur, James Conlon, Vladimir Ashkenazy (the Russian-born pianist, in his Cleveland conducting debut), Rafael Frühbeck de Burgos, and Chailly.

The season began with good news. A new orchestra contract would raise the minimum weekly salary from $610 to $680 over the course of the three-year agreement. The Musical Arts Association announced that it had posted a surplus of $15,000—on a budget of just under $14 million—for the fiscal year ending May 31, 1982. And the board of the Musical Arts Association was elated that it had hired a music director of such distinguished pedigree—and with so much potential for Cleveland. Haas addressed the issue at the annual meeting:

It is a tremendous pleasure to be able to tell you that your patience has been more than rewarded, and that we have found in Christoph von

Dohnányi everything that we hoped for in a new artistic director. He combines relative youth (with its vitality, energy, and new ideas) with remarkable talent, and the necessary experience, maturity and knowledge of the European tradition to be an effective and strong leader for our players. He is recognized around the world, but not over-exposed; his prize-winning recordings represent him well, but he has refrained thus far from recording the basic classical repertoire and is therefore free to do so with our Orchestra.

Dohnányi found himself free to make a quick trip to Cleveland in February 1983, before embarking on a series of guest engagements with American orchestras, to conduct a benefit concert for the pension fund. On February 6, he stood onstage at Severance Hall for a gala program consisting of Beethoven's *Leonore* Overture No. 3 and Symphony No. 8, Schoenberg's Six Songs (with Silja, in her debut with the orchestra, as soloist), and Strauss's *Till Eulenspiegel*. Several critics sensed good times for Cleveland. "This looks like an extraordinary love affair that is blossoming between Cleveland and the orchestra's new leader," wrote Betty Dietz Krebs in the *Dayton Daily News*. Conversely, reactions in the *Columbus Dispatch* and *Cincinnati Enquirer* raised questions about Dohnányi's fitness for the job. Even so, according to board minutes, the benefit concert "did wonders for the Orchestra's esprit, for the audience's enthusiasm, and for the balance sheet as well."

In the five weeks following the gala Severance concert, Dohnányi solidified his stature by appearing with the Detroit Symphony, Pittsburgh Symphony, and New York Philharmonic. Finn went to Pittsburgh to hear the conductor again in the Dvořák Eighth Symphony. "As leader of the censure faction—admittedly a minority—I can report that the Pittsburgh performance was in no significant respect different from the Cleveland one," he wrote. "Both Pittsburgh critics liked it—but I still found it episodic, heavy-handed and mannered sometimes to the point of eccentricity."

Even as Dohnányi began establishing his relationship with Cleveland, Maazel was still being closely linked with his former ensemble. In a *Time* magazine article in April 1983, Michael Walsh, again rating America's major orchestras like sports teams, theorized that there no longer existed a "Big Five" of orchestras, but instead a "Big Nine," adding St. Louis, Los Angeles, San Francisco, and Pittsburgh to the longtime list of Boston, Chicago, Cleveland, New York, and Philadelphia. Cleveland fared extremely well, in Walsh's estimation, if not as high as possible. "Under the late George Szell, the Clevelanders were honed into an ensemble of breathtaking precision eminently suited to the music of Mozart," he wrote. "During the regime of Conductor Lorin Maazel, Szell's high technical standards were maintained, but the sound of the Orchestra became fuller, richer, and more flexible and thus up to the challenge of the romantic repertory. By the end of Maazel's tenure, The Cleveland Orchestra was the best-sounding band in the land. Today's standards have unavoidably slipped a bit as the Orchestra awaits the arrival in 1984–85 of Maazel's German-born successor, Christoph von Dohnányi." The last comment may have been true, but it was not something the Musical Arts Association was willing to swallow. "There is no record," Haas told the board, "that Mr. Walsh has actually heard the Orchestra play during the ten months since Mr. Maazel departed."

✿　　✿　　✿

With the orchestra's future maestro away for the opening of the Severance Hall season, Leinsdorf and Kurt Masur did the honors. One of Leinsdorf's programs celebrated the 40th anniversary of his first concert with the orchestra. When Dohnányi finally arrived, he conducted an inventive program: Schubert's "Unfinished" Symphony, Mozart's Adagio in C major for English Horn, Reicha's Scene for English Horn (both with the orchestra's Felix Kraus as eloquent soloist), and Beethoven's "Eroica." During the two days after these concerts, he made his first recordings in Cleveland—the Schubert "Unfinished" and Beethoven third and eighth symphonies for Telarc. "The recording sessions went extraordinarily well," Haas told the board, "and were climaxed by spontaneous cheers from the musicians for Mr. Dohnányi at the conclusion of the recordings."

When Dohnányi's first Telarc discs were released the following March, national critics suggested that the pairing of Cleveland and its music director–designate was bearing fine fruit even before the conductor's tenure had actually begun. "Dohnányi is a conductor solidly in the same Central European tradition that produced Szell," stated the *Washington Post*. "By any objective standard, Telarc has presented first-class interpretations, performed by an orchestra that is unquestionably one of the world's greatest and presented in glowing color and impressive vitality." Even more impressed was the *Milwaukee Sentinel*: "The curtain has gone up on what promises to be an historic era for The Cleveland Orchestra. Under its new Music Director, Christoph von Dohnányi, the Orchestra that George Szell raised to greatness has created two magnificent inaugural recordings that echo its golden age . . . an orchestra in spectacular form at the hands of an original and masterly conductor." These reviews appeared just as Dohnányi was back at Severance Hall in April 1984 to bring yet more originality to the orchestra's programming by pairing Mendelssohn's "Scottish" Symphony with Stravinsky's opera-oratorio, *Oedipus Rex*.

The orchestra's board sensed that a special time was about to begin. Dohnányi "is clearly well on his way to achieving, in the United States, the same superstar status he enjoys in Europe," Haas told trustees. "He is, as many of you have discovered, a warm, outgoing, and genuine man who is filled with ideas and most eager to begin his collaboration with all of us on future growth of the Orchestra, Severance Hall, Blossom Music Center, and the City of Cleveland."

There were other reasons for the board, the musicians, and the community to feel good on the eve of their new orchestral era. The orchestra's radio broadcasts soon would be heard on almost 160 stations, twice the previous number. The broadcasts promised to net the Musical Arts Association $80,000 a year and increase weekly fees for the musicians. And subscriptions for Dohnányi's first season were already showing a jump of 4,000 from the previous season.

Still, nothing en route to the conductor's inaugural season proved quite so impressive as the night of August 18, 1984, at Blossom Music Center. In the middle of the overture to Mozart's *The Magic Flute*, an electrical storm knocked out power to the Cuyahoga Valley, plunging orchestra, conductor, and audience into utter darkness. The musicians didn't flinch—Dohnányi probably didn't either—and played the overture perfectly to the end. The chamber music skills that Szell had ingrained in the ensemble were still magically in place.

Upwards Again

As Christoph von Dohnányi took over the reins of the Cleveland Orchestra in September 1984, the musicians and the public—including audiences outside the United States—were eager to find out if the new conductor could live up to the artistic excitement he had already generated. By now, the players already knew that his baton technique was efficient, rather than obsessively exact or even beautiful, as had been the case with Lorin Maazel. It also had become clear—despite Robert Finn's initial charge of wild distortion—that Dohnányi was a musician for whom the composer came first. Like George Szell, he had a reputation as an intellectual addicted to the pursuit of knowledge. He pored over scores as if they were books. He devoured historical materials to explore the composers and the periods in which they lived. He trusted the tempo and expressive markings in the music and tried to remain faithful to them in performance. His penchant for detailed, extensive, and often tedious rehearsing resembled Szell's fastidious way of working—but without the brusque personality. Compared to Maazel's glib and aloof rehearsal manner, Dohnányi came across as serious, thorough, and gentlemanly.

The fact that he could make penetrating music and devise arresting programs was vividly apparent as his first season unfolded. For his first four weeks as music director, Dohnányi focused largely on Austro-Germanic works, though not necessarily the most obvious choices. His inaugural program began with Mozart's "Prague" Symphony and closed with Schumann's Symphony No. 2; between them, he welcomed Itzhak Perlman as soloist in a 20th-century masterpiece, the Berg Violin Concerto. Audience and critical response was fervently enthusiastic. The last of the opening-weekend performances was telecast live to Europe and later shown on PBS in the United States. The second week brought another stellar soloist, 81-year-old Rudolf Serkin, to play Mozart's Piano Concerto No. 22, K. 482, on a program that included J. C. Bach's Sinfonia, Op. 18, No. 3, and Dvořák's "New World" Symphony.

Dohnányi's third program deserved a medal for inventiveness. The concluding piece was Strauss's extravagantly colorful *Also sprach Zarathustra* (popular, in part, because of Stanley Kubrick's use of the majestic opening bars in his film *2001: A Space Odyssey*). The program's opening work was a novelty, and a challenging one: Schoenberg's unfinished oratorio, *Die Jakobsleiter (Jacob's Ladder)*, in its United States premiere. Dohnányi's long identification with Schoenberg's music had given him a stature in this repertoire equaled only by that of Pierre Boulez. The oratorio performances at Severance Hall stunned the audience, which didn't expect to find the piece at all alluring but sat in hushed wonder as Dohnányi, the orchestra, the Cleveland Orchestra Chorus, and an exceptional roster of singers made it a moving experience. A month later, when Dohnányi and the orchestra took the work to Carnegie Hall for their New York debut together, critics raved. Andrew Porter, in *The New Yorker*, called it "a remarkable performance. The new music director has begun bravely."

Programming the Schoenberg wasn't Dohnányi's only act of courage during his inaugural year. He led the first Cleveland performances of repertoire as diverse as Carl Ruggles's *Men and Mountains,* Hans Pfitzner's Violin Concerto (with Edith Peinemann), and Haydn's Symphony No. 64, as well as Charles Wuorinen's *Movers and Shakers* (a commissioned work "celebrating the players of the Cleveland Orchestra") and Stravinsky's ballet-oratorio *Renard* with dancers from the Cleveland Ballet and choreography by their artistic director, Dennis Nahat. One highly animated Dohnányi program paired Stravinsky's *Petrouchka* with Orff's bawdy cantata, *Carmina Burana.* For the year's "Great Composers of Our Time" series, he invited longtime friend Hans Werner Henze to conduct two programs that included three of the German composer's own works, two pieces by Mozart, and a score that easily won the season's prize for most original (and unappetizing) title, David Lang's *Eating Living Monkeys*. Along with Dohnányi and Henze, the conducting roster included Robert Page, Simon Rattle, Erich Leinsdorf, Helmuth Rilling (leading the *St. John Passion* to mark the 300th anniversary of Bach's birth), Yoel Levi, and Christoph Eschenbach.

Among the benefits that Dohnányi brought to Cleveland was his affiliation with Decca/London Records, which acknowledged the electricity between conductor and musicians by signing a contract to make 10 compact discs over three years. The relationship began during Dohnányi's second month as music director with recordings of Dvořák's eighth and ninth symphonies and the Scherzo Capriccioso, Op. 66, that are prime examples of collaborative vitality. Decca/London wasn't the only recording company interested in Dohnányi and the orchestra at this time: Telarc, which had made the conductor's first recordings in Cleveland the previous year, was committed to two discs per year for four years. Their major project would be a set of the complete Beethoven symphonies. "The orchestra is in a fortunate position, as most orchestras do not have ongoing recording commitments," general manager Kenneth Haas told the board.

The Dvořák recordings were made following Dohnányi's first tour with the orchestra, a two-week trip in October that included 11 concerts in Louisville, Cincinnati, Ann Arbor, Ames, Chicago, Boston, and New York. Dohnányi discussed his orchestral credo in a pretour interview in the *New York Times*:

> I think good orchestras have a strong desire for a strong personality. They *want* to know what to do. But the relationship between human beings—the whole social structure—has changed. Conductors today have to *convince* an orchestra by their technique, their musicianship. Music is not a democracy; music is the meaning of one person. I love the idea of democracy; of all the bad possibilities, it is probably the best. But I think that Americans have learned democracy better than Germans. . . You see it in the Cleveland Orchestra: they have a *desire* for a strong person, but that person has to give his life to them and to music, and only then will they follow.

The orchestra clearly was following him. Reviews throughout the tour were almost entirely positive. "Dohnányi is a real musical firecracker," wrote Ellen Pfeifer in the *Boston Herald*. The *Chicago Tribune*'s John von Rhein (formerly of the *Akron Beacon Journal*) noted that "the Cleveland sounded in every important respect like the patrician ensemble one remembers from the Szell years, but also a warmer and rather more mellow instrument . . . under [Dohnányi's] firm leadership the orchestra seems to be functioning near the top of its wonted form. The portents are encouraging." Harris Goldsmith, assessing the Beethoven-Schubert Telarc recordings in *Opus* magazine, wrote: "The Clevelanders appear to have made a wise choice, and we can look forward to a fruitful association between Maestro Dohnányi and his new orchestra. These recordings represent an auspicious beginning."

At the end of the 1984–85 Severance Hall season, conductor and musicians made another short tour, this one to six cities, again including Boston and New York. The *Christian Science Monitor*'s Thor Eckert, Jr., wrote, "the Cleveland is one of America's unique orchestras. I can think of no higher compliment to its new Music Director than to say that so far he is a conductor truly worthy of his orchestra." David Patrick Stearns, in *USA Today*, enthused that Dohnányi "has become an overnight sensation in the USA" and that "the group is crowning its most artistically acclaimed season in years" with the tour. *The New Yorker's* Porter attended the orchestra's two May concerts in New York and came away with mixed impressions. At this point, he was ready to name the Philadelphia Orchestra under Riccardo Muti as the country's top ensemble. "The Cleveland under Dohnányi has still to regain the distinction and character that the Cleveland under Szell once had. I don't have a clear idea of Dohnányi; I've not heard enough of him in basic classical repertory, and what I have heard hasn't tempted me."

In May 1985, the orchestra's board was pinching itself to make sure its good fortune was real. Trustees had begun the season celebrating the fact that the orchestra's deficit had been cut in half ($53,312 for the 1983–84 season, down from the previous year's $107,907), and now they were ending the season celebrating the start of what was looking like a grand era. "The first season with Mr. Dohnányi as Music Director has exceeded our greatest expectations," said Haas. "It has been a wonderful year, not only in terms of sales and attendance, but also in the spirit of the Orchestra musicians who are very much unified behind their new leader." Haas, board chairman Alfred M. Rankin, and new board president Ward Smith quickly took advantage of the situation, negotiating a new contract with Dohnányi that extended his tenure through the 1992–93 season.

Even as Dohnányi was making an elegant splash, another conductor who had arrived in Cleveland at the same moment was beginning to have an impact on the orchestra—Jahja Ling. The Indonesian-born musician, trained as a pianist and conductor at the Juilliard School and the Yale School of Music, had come to Dohnányi's attention in the fall of 1983, when the music director–designate was looking for a conductor to succeed Yoel Levi in Cleveland the following year. While in San Francisco to conduct operas by Strauss and Janáček, Dohnányi stopped in on a rehearsal of the San Francisco Symphony Youth Orchestra, which had gained international attention under Ling, its vivacious music director (and also associate conductor of the San Francisco Symphony). Dohnányi watched Ling rehearse for five minutes and decided he wanted him for Cleveland. He invited Ling to a conductors' symposium at Severance Hall in February, when an associate conductor would be chosen. Ling won the post handily. His first season in Cleveland was so successful that he was promoted to resident conductor. By the end of the 1984–85 season, the Musical Arts Association was starting to make plans for Ling to conduct an ensemble that he would create, the Cleveland Orchestra Youth Orchestra.

❀   ❀   ❀

Dohnányi could have finished his first season by conducting a handful of concerts at Blossom Music Center—the pattern set by Szell and Maazel—and been done with it. But he had something else in mind. After spending most of his professional life in opera, he wasn't prepared to wean himself totally from the genre. He believed he could make imaginative use of the vast spaces at Blossom by presenting a production of Mozart's *Die Zauberflöte* (*The Magic Flute*) that he would not only conduct, but also stage. The production, the first full-length staged opera in Blossom's history, was scheduled for the last week of the 1985 season.

In order to rehearse *The Magic Flute* and prepare the stage for the inventive concept devised by Dohnányi and his theatrical assistants (local director Joseph Garry, Jr., and European associate Wolfgang Buecker), the orchestra gave no concerts during the two weeks preceding the two performances. His design team included Franco Colavecchia (sets), Judith Dolan (costumes), and F. Mitchell Dana (lighting). The conductor had one unorthodox idea that didn't add much to the masterpiece: the presence of Mozart (portrayed by stage and film actor Peter Firth, who had performed the role of the composer in Peter Schaffer's play, *Amadeus*) as narrator and opera guide. But the device didn't prove a major distraction. Dohnányi's staging balanced fantasy with sacred solemnity, romance with uproarious antics. Most importantly, he proved to be a Mozart conductor of consummate taste and refinement who could capitalize on the Cleveland Orchestra's gifts in this repertoire. Guiding a cast headed by Judith Blegen (Pamina), Mikael Melbye (Papageno), Celina Lindsley (Queen of the Night), and John Macurdy (Sarastro), the conductor/stage director found the heart and spirit of a work that is at once intricate and simple. *The Plain Dealer*'s Wilma Salisbury was delighted: "Christoph von Dohnányi's imaginative production of 'The Magic Flute' by Mozart is an investment in an experiment that paid off with a brilliant success for the Cleveland Orchestra." The *Columbus Dispatch*'s Barbara Zuck, who had been skeptical of Dohnányi after his benefit concert with the orchestra in February 1983, called the production "the Ohio musical event of the summer."

It was an expensive event. Budgeted at $350,000, the production wound up costing $561,000. The principal funding had come from the Cleveland Foundation, a venerable institution with a special interest in social issues and the arts, which provided a $100,000 grant with the stipulation that it be matched—which it was—by other sponsors. More than 15,000 opera-goers showed up for the performances, generating almost $200,000 in ticket sales. The Musical Arts Association was left with a huge pile of bills, leading the board to consider other options for presenting opera at Blossom. The Cleveland Foundation, buoyed by the artistic success of the Mozart production, immediately showed interest in discussing "the future of opera in the Cleveland area and the role that the Association and the Foundation might assume." The association board already had something up its sleeve for the 1986 Blossom season: a possible collaboration with a foreign opera company.

✾   ✾   ✾

Recording promised to add funds to the association's coffers. The Cleveland Orchestra was scheduled to record 11 works during the 1985–86 season for Decca/London and Telarc. On the former label, there were to be performances of Dvořák's Seventh Symphony (under Dohnányi), Beethoven's third and fifth piano concertos (played and conducted by Vladimir Ashkenazy), works by Debussy (Ashkenazy), music by Gershwin (Riccardo Chailly), and Stravinsky's *The Rite of Spring* (Chailly).

Telarc was continuing its Beethoven symphony cycle with Dohnányi with the Ninth Symphony, a recording that would prove oddly problematic. The first challenge was vocal. James King, the distinguished American Heldentenor, sang the Severance Hall performances, which convinced Dohnányi that he was past his prime and not suitable for the recording. Luckily, German tenor Siegfried Jerusalem was available for the sessions. The recording went smoothly and everyone went home. Then Telarc realized that the discs could never be released: a ruinous electronic hum was present throughout the performance. Somehow, the orchestra was able to reassemble the same vocal quartet (Jerusalem, with soprano Carol Vaness, mezzo-soprano Janice Taylor, and bass Robert Lloyd) and rerecord the symphony two weeks later. The Beethoven Ninth recording had come at a crucial moment: Dohnányi, the orchestra, and the Cleveland Orchestra Chorus were scheduled to perform the work during the conductor's first European tour with his ensemble in February 1986, when the recording would be on the market.

Before heading across the Atlantic, the orchestra announced that there would, once again, be opera at Blossom during the 1986 season. Gérard Mortier, general director of the National Opera of Belgium and a former Dohnányi assistant at the Hamburg State Opera, had attended *The Magic Flute* at Blossom and decided that a collaboration with the orchestra might be possible. He came up with the idea of having Dohnányi conduct a new production of Lehár's operetta, *The Merry Widow*, with Silja in the title role, first in Brussels in April 1986 and then at Blossom for three performances the following August. The joint production would save the orchestra almost $200,000 in set and costume construction costs. A contract was signed. The yearlong relationship was set to begin during the European tour with the orchestra's performances in Brussels and Antwerp under the auspices of Mortier's company. It would include performances at Blossom by Maurice Béjart's Ballet of the Twentieth Century, resident company of the National Opera of Belgium.

Then a slight hitch turned up: David Bamberger, general director of Cleveland Opera, notified the orchestra that his troupe had already scheduled a 10th-anniversary production of the Lehár operetta for the fall of 1986, with Roberta Peters in the title role and Franz Allers conducting. The situation prompted polite discussions between the two institutions. The Musical Arts Association offered the costumes from its *Merry Widow* to Cleveland Opera, at no cost, and Cleveland Opera agreed to let the orchestra know its plans for the coming years to avoid conflicts. But Bamberger declined use of the costumes, anticipating that Mortier's company—one of the most provocative and innovative in Europe—intended to produce "an anti-*Merry Widow Merry Widow*."

❊   ❊   ❊

The orchestra was faring extremely well at home and on the national scene. When Dohnányi and the ensemble played two concerts at Carnegie Hall in December 1985, critics from the *New York Times* responded largely with high praise. "With each succeeding visit to New York, the Cleveland Orchestra underlines the absolute rightness of its affiliation with Christoph von Dohnányi," wrote Bernard Holland. "Mr. Dohnányi became the orchestra's music director last season, and it is pleasing indeed to hear this collective instrument—so finely tuned by George Szell and so well-maintained by Lorin Maazel—now directed toward the seriousness of musical purpose its new conductor offers." Holland's colleague, Will Crutchfield, devoted most of his review of the second concert to Silja's performance of Schoenberg's monodrama, *Erwartung*, even as he noted a few reservations about Dohnányi's account of Beethoven's Fifth Symphony: "It was a real performance, not memorable, but alive. The last time I heard the Cleveland play this symphony (under Lorin Maazel in 1982), it was hard to care whether the next phrase came or didn't. Mr. Dohnányi has certainly changed that."

❊   ❊   ❊

Europe was waiting to hear what kind of impact Dohnányi was having on the orchestra. First, however, an impact of a very different kind was felt at Severance Hall days before the orchestra left for its four-week foreign tour. On Friday morning, January 31, 1986, Dohnányi and the ensemble were in the midst of the first movement of Dvořák's Seventh Symphony during a matinee when the building began to shake. It was a historic moment for the orchestra: performing during a local earthquake, which was felt throughout Northeast Ohio but did no damage. The hall, filled for the concert, emptied quickly, starting with the musicians (who were holding valuable instruments). Management offered patrons half-priced tickets for concerts later in the season.

Dohnányi and his players now were ready to play 21 concerts in 17 European cities, the orchestra's first trip abroad in the middle of winter. They brought along the Cleveland Orchestra Chorus for performances of Beethoven's Ninth Symphony in London and Brussels (after which the chorus and director Robert Page collaborated with the Belgian National Opera Orchestra in Brahms's *A German Requiem*). In contrast with Szell, who had scheduled 33 works for his first European tour in 1957, Dohnányi opted to tour with only 12, including symphonies by Beethoven, Bruckner, Dvořák, Mendelssohn, Schumann, and Tchaikovsky, and other works by Ives, Mozart, Ravel, Schoenberg, Strauss, and Zemlinsky.

European critics, especially in London, were divided about the performances, praising the ensemble with little reservation but taking exception to some of Dohnányi's interpretive choices, especially in Beethoven's Ninth Symphony. "In full charge for little over a year, he is, I fancy, in the process of giving it a more human 'face' with some slackenings of its former parade-ground discipline, with cool, vibrato-less woodwind, skirling [*sic*] brass and, when suitable, very precise, bastinadolike percussion," wrote Christopher Grier in the *London Standard*. The reviews prompted a brief dip in orchestra morale after so much euphoria in the United States. But one British critic may have made the most astute observation of all: "Unfortunately, London is not the best place to judge American orchestras, with players either jet-lagged from new arrival or exhausted at the end of a long tour," wrote Edward Greenfield in *The Guardian*, "but with just a few allowances for that first ailment Cleveland standards are still a marvel." Belgian critics were more favorable, writing of the orchestra's "triumph" and "perfection of unity." *De Standaard*, the major Brussels paper, called Cleveland "an American orchestra that plays in a European way and that finds a beautiful balance between technical ability and interpretive depth. Christoph von Dohnányi continues in the footsteps of his predecessors with dignity, leading the ensemble both technically and artistically to ever higher peaks."

The orchestra gave its first Warsaw concerts since 1965 at the National Philharmonic Hall. In Vienna, it sounded appropriately golden in the gilded Musikverein. A stop in Paris was notable partly for a near disaster at Orly Airport as the orchestra's plane came close to colliding with another Air France jet while landing. West Berlin opened its arms to native son Dohnányi and his musicians, who played at the Philharmonie, home of the Berlin Philharmonic. "If the Cleveland Orchestra didn't exist, we would have to invent it right away," wrote the critic of the *Berliner Morgenpost*. "The orchestra plays with a peerless instrumental refinement. It is one of the best orchestras in the world." In Hamburg, where Dohnányi maintained a residence, the concert caused some critical rethinking. Carl-Heinz Mann, music critic of the *Hamburger Abendblatt* wrote of Dohnányi, "when he was in Hamburg, he was known as a somewhat cool person, and now we see him as a full-blooded musician, full of temperament. Yesterday he showed us that he is a truly great conductor."

By the end of the tour, the musicians were grumbling about the length of the trip and the questionable decision to travel during winter. At the same time, the new music director was registering delight with the orchestra and disdain for certain critical quibbles. "I think the Cleveland Orchestra proved that it's just a stupid prejudice of the European audiences that American orchestras only play fast and loud," Dohnányi said. "I think our success with this unusual programming was outstanding."

The tour's success was compounded when Teldec, the European recording company formerly known as Telefunken, invited Dohnányi and the orchestra to record the four Brahms symphonies starting in the fall of 1986. This meant the orchestra would be recording with three companies at once: Teldec, Decca/London, and Telarc. Sales of Telarc recordings already were providing more royalties than anticipated, almost $120,000 above projections. And the orchestra needed the money: trustees were estimating a deficit of almost $750,000 for the 1985–86 season, partly due to the expensive *Magic Flute* production at Blossom. They were projecting an $800,000 deficit for the 1986–87 season.

✿   ✿   ✿

At least there was cause for hope that *The Merry Widow* might generate a healthy influx of cash at Blossom. The Brussels production opened in April to general acclaim, including a review in the *International Herald Tribune* that said, "the Brussels Opera is doing Lehár's *The Merry Widow* in a production that is a model of its kind. It is flamboyantly and wittily staged by Jürgen Tamchina. The spirited cast is headed brilliantly by Anja Silja, and

Christoph von Dohnányi conducts with a subtle elegance and style that would not be wasted on Mozart." The following month, Silja made her debut with the Opera Company of Boston in Janáček's *The Makropoulos Affair* and was dubbed "the Garbo of opera" by the *Boston Globe*.

A major event occurred at Blossom before Silja arrived in *The Merry Widow*. Returning to the facility for the first time since his 1970 performance of Mahler's Second Symphony with the Cleveland Orchestra, Leonard Bernstein conducted the New York Philharmonic in his *Candide* overture and *Serenade* (with Philharmonic concertmaster Glenn Dicterow as soloist) and an account of Tchaikovsky's "Pathétique" Symphony that generated major debates. Many Cleveland Orchestra musicians and listeners were infuriated by Bernstein's concept, an expansive and neurotic approach—the antithesis of a Szell performance. Others found it unique and imaginative. At the end of the concert, Bernstein rushed about the stage and hugged every member of the Philharmonic.

For the Blossom performances of *The Merry Widow*, audiences wrapped themselves up in blankets both in the pavilion and on the lawn to ward off unseasonably frigid weather. They found the Brussels version of Lehár's beloved operetta a bit bizarre. The production verged on camp and included odd touches, such as the presence of an enormous stuffed bear in one scene. Some operetta lovers had trouble fathoming a Wagnerian soprano such as Silja in the title role. But this was a sophisticated and exceedingly merry *Merry Widow*, sparked by the high-charged personalities of its gifted (and, during rehearsals, argumentative) husband-and-wife team. Silja proved mesmerizing, if vocally steely, in the title role. Dohnányi emphasized the score's humor and sensuality. The three performances drew 17,000 patrons and generated more income than expected.

✳   ✳   ✳

Dohnányi's third season as music director continued along the adventurous path he had laid out during his first two seasons. He achieved programmatic variety partly by encouraging guest conductors to explore neglected works or those the orchestra had never performed. His own repertoire for the season included Carl Ruggles's *Sun Treader*, Britten's *An American Overture*, and Zemlinsky's suite from *The Mermaid*. But there were other unusual offerings: Debussy's *The Martyrdom of St. Sebastian* (conducted by Michael Tilson Thomas), Bernstein's Divertimento (Ling), Oskar Morawetz's *Memorial to Martin Luther King* (Masur, with principal cellist Stephen Geber as soloist), and Franck's *Psyche* (Ashkenazy).

Among the most notable concerts were the two weeks of performances that brought Pierre Boulez back to Cleveland after a 14-year absence. The orchestra's former principal guest conductor and musical advisor was the honoree in the "Great Composers of Our Time" series in November 1986, when he led works by Stravinsky, Ravel, and Bartók, and the Cleveland premieres of his own *Notations* and *Improvisations sur Mallarmé I and III.* "In addition to his significance as a composer, Boulez is a great conductor," wrote Mark Kanny in the *Pittsburgh Post-Gazette* after the first program. "His ear is phenomenal, and his beat is uniquely explicit. Boulez does not use a baton, but indicates time with his right hand, using his thumb and fingers to indicate rhythmic details. No one conducts 20th-century music more expertly." The engagement was the start of another long-term relationship between the orchestra and Boulez.

The week Boulez arrived, an important figure at Severance Hall announced that he soon would depart. Kenneth Haas, who had been associated with the orchestra since 1970, had decided to accept the post of managing director of the Boston Symphony, citing the need to face new and different challenges. He had served the Cleveland Orchestra with distinction, guiding the institution with a firm hand and enormous charm. Finding a successor as skilled as Haas—who was set to begin in Boston in February 1987—would prove almost as difficult as finding a new conductor.

In the months before his departure, Haas began to explore Severance Hall maintenance issues. Since his first season, Dohnányi had been interested in restoring the disused E. M. Skinner pipe organ. At that time, Haas had hired architect Peter van Dijk, designer of Blossom Music Center, and acoustician Christopher Jaffe, originally van Dijk's Blossom collaborator, to devise a proposed renovation of Szell's 1958 shell that would incorporate the organ pipes and make the organ usable. Now, in late 1986, Dohnányi was pressing again for the organ project to move forward. But Severance needed modernization of its offices, including its computer systems, and other improvements, at a possible cost of $10 million. The organ project was postponed.

A project that moved ahead was the Cleveland Orchestra Youth Orchestra, with Jahja Ling as music director. The creation of the orchestra was made possible with a $250,000 commitment from the Martha Holden Jennings Foundation. Ling auditioned hundreds of local teenagers to form an ensemble that would play the major symphonic repertoire. The musicians would receive coaching from members of the Cleveland Orchestra. At the inaugural concert in February 1987, Ling conducted excerpts from Bernstein's *West Side Story*, Haydn's Symphony No. 104, and Dvořák's Symphony No. 8. "The performance was astonishingly good, and bodes well

506 THE CLEVELAND ORCHESTRA STORY

for the future of this foundation-funded long-range project," wrote Robert Finn in *The Plain Dealer*. "The younger players produced a good, solid symphonic sonority, and they were on top of most of the technical challenges. Ling did not spare them, either; his tempos and interpretive demands in the three pieces were exactly what they might have been had he been conducting the Cleveland Orchestra itself."

Dohnányi was in town at the same time to conduct two weeks of concerts and lead a trip to Boston's Symphony Hall and New York's Carnegie Hall in March. After the Carnegie Hall concert—Sibelius's Symphony No. 7, Prokofiev's Violin Concerto No. 2 (with Kyung Wha Chung), and Janáček's Sinfonietta—Donal Henahan once again hailed the marriage of conductor and orchestra. Maazel and the Cleveland Orchestra "always struck one as a classic mismatch, despite his long and generally successful tenure as music director of the ensemble he inherited from the late George Szell," Henahan wrote in the *New York Times*. "Christoph von Dohnányi, on the other hand, gives the impression of always having been music director of the Cleveland, although he is now only in his third season in that post. Temperamentally and technically, the Berlin-born conductor suits Cleveland perfectly. What he wants from an orchestra—chamber-music clarity, instrumental precision and well-tempered passion—are what his orchestra with its Szell heritage is best able to give."

Those qualities can be heard on the Decca/London, Telarc, and Teldec discs that would make the orchestra the most-recorded American ensemble for more than five years. In 1987, Cleveland was basking in the glow of its recording activity, which was generating excellent sales and effusive reviews. Writing about the Dohnányi recording of Dvořák's "New World" Symphony in *Time* magazine, Michael Walsh described the combination of conductor and musicians in admiring terms: "Rich, detailed and burnished, this handsome 'New World' Symphony shows why the Cleveland under its German-born leader is now the best-sounding orchestra in the country. Pass the word."

A Veritable Explosion

The Cleveland Orchestra and music director Christoph von Dohnányi were thriving in the mid-1980s, especially when it came to recordings. They were making discs for three companies (Decca, Telarc, and Teldec), which were preserving performances of many works that George Szell and Lorin Maazel had recorded with the orchestra. As these recordings were made, the orchestra continued to evolve under Dohnányi, attaining a level of refinement missing during the Maazel era, and the roster of musicians underwent changes with the retirement of longtime members and the hiring of excellent young players.

As the decade unfolded, recording promised to become even more central to the orchestra's agenda. To succeed Kenneth Haas as executive director, the Musical Arts Association chose Thomas W. Morris, a recording enthusiast whose appointment before the 1987–88 season caused more than a little discussion among musicians, patrons, and the media. Haas had left Cleveland in February 1987 to become managing director of the Boston Symphony—a post held previously by Morris, a longtime friend and colleague in the orchestra business. But this was not just a simple case of switching jobs. Morris had initially stepped down from his post with the Boston Symphony in January 1986, after 17 years, to do consulting for the Concertgebouw Orchestra of Amsterdam and other major European and American arts institutions.

An audiophile who rummaged through record bins and delighted in finding obscure gems, Morris recognized how important recording was for the orchestra. The month he arrived, the ensemble named Vladimir Ashkenazy principal guest conductor, partly because he was under contract to Decca. Dohnányi's stock was rising so rapidly at this time that Decca signed him to make four records a year in Cleveland and one annually with the Vienna Philharmonic. With its Decca, Telarc, and Teldec deals, Cleveland was to make "six or seven records annually with our Music Director, which is an unprecedented volume of recording activity for any major symphony orchestra," Morris told the board weeks after his arrival. "This must be considered an essential part of the international visibility of the Orchestra."

A native of Rochester, New York, Morris had studied piano and percussion, attended Princeton University, and received a master's degree in business administration at the Wharton School of Finance. He worked briefly with the Cincinnati Symphony before joining the staff of the Boston Symphony in 1969, becoming assistant manager in 1971 and general manager in 1973. With his experience as a musician (he occasionally played percussion in the Boston Pops under Arthur Fiedler), Morris brought to Cleveland the type of musical expertise that Haas had left entirely to conductors. "My interest is in the creative side. That's why I'm in the business," Morris told *The Plain Dealer.* "Don't forget, my degree at Princeton was in music. My hands-on experience in the business side was in Boston. Artistic initiatives and planning are what have driven [me]. The business decisions will then flow logically from that."

In the three months between his appointment and his arrival, Morris had begun to develop a fruitful working relationship with Dohnányi. "We have to understand each other musically as well as organizationally," Morris said. "I love talking music with Christoph."

Morris pursued recording deals with considerable skill and enthusiasm. "One of the prime thrusts in this administration is in recording," he told the board in November 1987. "The expanded recording activity demonstrates the reputation of Mr. Dohnányi and The Cleveland Orchestra in the international world of music; it will enhance the visibility of the Orchestra; and it will provide a long-term source of funds through royalties." In 1987, the orchestra recorded seven works with Dohnányi and four with Ashkenazy. "This whole picture could change quickly," observed James Badal in the *Cleveland Edition,* the weekly alternative-press newspaper, "for the world of the recording business continues to be a volatile arena, especially in the classics where costs routinely soar and sales cannot be counted on to dutifully follow. For now, at any rate, Cleveland is the king."

By April 1988, Morris could tell Musical Arts Association trustees that the orchestra was flourishing as never before in the area he loved best: "There is a veritable explosion in recording activity." The orchestra was scheduled to record 16 discs in the coming year with Dohnányi for Decca and Telarc and with Ashkenazy for Decca.

Dohnányi's Cleveland recordings continued to impress critics at home and abroad. Just as the orchestra was landing in Europe for a four-week tour in May 1989, the June issue of the British audiophile magazine *Gramophone* hit newsstands with Dohnányi on its cover. Inside were reviews of no fewer than 14 works the conductor and his orchestra had recorded for Decca, Telarc, and Teldec. In an interview, Dohnányi discussed his method for recording in Cleveland: "My approach is, and it's partly because of timing, that we play these pieces in concert before—three times or so—then we record. The session begins, tuning, balancing for the record people, then we start to play the whole piece. Then we listen to it, have a real break and then I fix the ten or so spots with the orchestra where something has gone wrong; and then we play the piece once again so there is music-making—there's no cutting and sticking bits together."

✿   ✿   ✿

The orchestra's visibility was enhanced not only by recordings but by foreign tours. In late September 1987, after the opening three weeks of the 1987–88 season, Dohnányi and the ensemble headed to the Far East, where classi-cal recording sales per capita were the highest in the world. The 13-concert tour included performances of music by Beethoven, Bartók, Schumann, Tchaikovsky, and others and took the group throughout Japan, and also to the new National Concert Hall in Taipei, Taiwan. Neither the conductor nor the players were strangers to the region. The orchestra had performed in Japan on four previous tours (1970, 1974, 1978, and 1982), and Dohnányi had appeared there with the Vienna Philharmonic and the Hamburg State Opera. In 1987, Japanese reporters showed great interest in upcoming Dohnányi-Cleveland recording projects.

The orchestra's early tour performances generated small audiences, probably due to high ticket prices (up to U.S. $91). Perhaps the unfamiliar combination of Dohnányi and Cleveland was another factor. "If the orches-tra comes back a few more times, it'll be the rage," Morris said. "This is ex-actly the kind of music they go bonkers over." By contrast, the closing con-certs in Tokyo were sold out, and the houses for the three Taipei perform-ances—where Cleveland became the first foreign ensemble to play during the inaugural weeks of the National Concert Hall—were almost full. The Taipei auditorium proved stunning, with African rosewood walls, 106 chan-deliers, a pipe organ with more than 4,000 pipes, and silent air-conditioning units beneath every seat.

In May 1989 the orchestra made its first European trip organized with Morris's input. Even before Dohnányi and his musicians departed for the 16-city, 20-concert tour, the executive director took a bold step to bolster the orchestra's international reputation. He hired Roger W. Wright as artistic administrator, a new position. Wright, a 32-year-old native of Manchester, England, had served as senior producer for the BBC Symphony Orchestra in London. He arrived in Cleveland in the spring of 1989 to work with Dohnányi and Morris on repertoire and soloists. His musical intelligence and charm would serve the orchestra well.

The 1989 European tour was scheduled to end in the British capital with a performance of Janáček's *Glagolitic Mass* featuring the Cleveland Orchestra Chorus in its final tour concert prepared by Robert Page. But Dohnányi cancelled the London performance in mid-May, when he fell ill with the flu in Cleveland and handed over the Severance Hall rehearsals and performances to resident conductor Jahja Ling. The music director wrote to the chorus that he wouldn't have had sufficient time to rehearse the piece before the performance at London's Royal Festival Hall: "As London is the most competitive musical environment in the world, we cannot afford to do less than the very best of which we are capable." The chorus wasn't left completely unoccupied. It had been engaged to precede the London concert with performances of Prokofiev's *Alexander Nevsky* in Belgium and the Netherlands and Mendelssohn's *Elijah* in West Germany and Luxembourg. The Janáček cancellation left the disappointed choristers with three days to sightsee—and to attend the concert they were supposed to sing—before returning to Cleveland. Otherwise, the orchestra's hectic 1989 tour to Brussels, Antwerp, Amsterdam, Frankfurt, Prague, Vienna, Munich, Stuttgart, Geneva, Zurich, Strasbourg, Cologne, Hamburg, West and East Berlin (five months before the fall of the Berlin Wall), and London promised to eclipse the frigid 1986 winter tour in every way.

Dohnányi had been music director for almost five years. He had shaped the orchestra into a more elegant and balanced instrument than it had been under Maazel—something closer to Szell's concept, if without the pervasive rhythmic intensity. "The Ferrari of orchestras will make two rounds of the track in Belgium next week," wrote *Le Soir*, before the 1989 European tour. "In command will be one of the conductors who is the most complete, the most scrupulous of his generation, Christoph von Dohnányi, on the threshold of his 60th year, who has clear-eyed vision, a calm energy, a charming manner and incredible talent."

Among the stops was Prague, where the orchestra made its first appearance since performing there under Szell in 1965. "Disciplined, technically perfect, and very equal in all sections. The result is a full sonic spectrum," noted a Prague critic. In the Austrian capital, where the Vienna Philharmonic has always been rated above all others on the planet, the city's dominant music critic put aside chauvinism and dealt directly with artistry. "Were we not so happily married to the Vienna Philharmonic, we would seriously have to consider such a relationship with the Cleveland Orchestra,"

wrote Franz Endler. "Dohnányi is a master of interpretation and at the same
time he is one of the conductors who demands the same mastery from his
musicians." The response was universally positive in London, where reviews
of Dohnányi and Cleveland had been lukewarm in 1986. "George Szell gave
the Cleveland Orchestra its fabled precision and unflagging seriousness of
purpose during his reign of considerable terror in the 1950s and 1960s,"
wrote Richard Morrison in *The Times*. "Personnel must have changed since
then, but under Christoph von Dohnányi, its present music director, the orchestra sounds just as lean, tense and rigorously drilled. Do they shoot
sloppy instrumentalists in Cleveland, or is it just something they tell the
players to encourage them?"

At the end of the 1988 Blossom Music Center season, four longtime members of the orchestra had retired: violist Vitold Kushleika, who had joined in
1944 during Erich Leinsdorf's abbreviated tenure, and three principal players—Leinsdorf appointee George Goslee (bassoon) and Szell appointees
William Hebert (piccolo) and Bernard Adelstein (trumpet). The Cleveland
ensemble had been getting increasingly younger during the 1980s with the
retirement of Rodzinski, Leinsdorf, and Szell appointees. (By the end of the
decade, players hired by Dohnányi accounted for more than a fifth of the
orchestra.)

Dohnányi again showed his knack for maintaining the orchestra's traditions by choosing superb ensemble players to replace them: David McGill,
former principal bassoonist of the Toronto Symphony, and a musician of
remarkable elegance and technical perfection (he would leave in 1997 to become principal in the Chicago Symphony); Michael Sachs, who emerged
from the fourth chair of the Houston Symphony to win Cleveland's top
trumpet post; and Thomas Robertello, an excellent piccolo player who,
upon deciding that the instrument wasn't enough for him, left after a season
for the Pittsburgh Symphony's flute section (and was succeeded in
Cleveland by a supremely gifted piccoloist, Mary Kay Fink). Virtuosic hornist Eric Ruske, who had arrived at the start of Dohnányi's tenure to become
associate principal horn, departed in 1988 to pursue a solo career. His successor was Richard King, a 20-year-old player from Philadelphia's Curtis
Institute of Music, who, like Ruske, was initially refused an audition.

Despite its growing prestige over the decades, the Cleveland Orchestra
often seemed to function as a training ground for musicians—especially
concertmasters—destined for careers in other major ensembles. Until
Cleveland achieved a 52-week contract in 1967, the prime reason for the

player exodus, aside from Szell's rigorous methods, had been money: the orchestra, with relatively short seasons, couldn't pay nearly as much as the big orchestras on the East Coast. Lifestyle also figured into the decision of some musicians to leave. Especially during the 1960s, '70s, and early '80s, when bedeviled by Rust Belt economic woes and tales of burning rivers, Cleveland couldn't compete in amenities with such metropolises as New York, Boston, Chicago, Philadelphia, Los Angeles, and San Francisco. Many Cleveland musicians realized that if they wanted to move up, they had to move elsewhere. Associate concertmaster Cecilia Arzewski seized the chance to become concertmaster in Atlanta (where she succeeded William Preucil, who had left to join the Cleveland Quartet). Martin Chalifour, Arzewski's Cleveland successor and Preucil's former stand partner in Atlanta, would leave Cleveland in 1995 to become concertmaster of the Los Angeles Philharmonic. Sheryl Staples, Chalifour's Cleveland successor, would depart in 1998 to become principal associate concertmaster of the New York Philharmonic. Perhaps the most stunning example of rapid advancement in Cleveland Orchestra history—and another example of the orchestra having difficulty keeping certain extraordinary musicians—was the case of Emmanuelle Boisvert, whom Dohnányi appointed to the last desk of the second violin section in 1986. In September 1988, she won the post of concertmaster with the Detroit Symphony at the age of 25.

Two other personnel changes marked the end of eras for the orchestra in 1988. In August, Klaus George Roy, who had served with enormous distinction as program annotator and editor since 1958, cleaned off his stacked desk in the basement of Severance Hall and headed into a future filled with lectures, composing, travel, and frequent letters to the editor of *The Plain Dealer*. (His successor was James. R. Oestreich, former editor of *Fanfare* magazine, whose tenure at Severance would last only until the following spring, when he became an editor and critic at the *New York Times*. After Oestreich, Peter Laki, a brilliant Hungarian-born singer and musicologist, became program annotator.)

In October 1988, Robert Page announced that he would depart as director of choruses and assistant conductor after the 1988–89 season. He had prepared the Cleveland Orchestra Chorus for hundreds of performances and a number of admired recordings and conducted both subscription and Christmas concerts. "In four years of working with Bob, there have been many memorable collaborations," Dohnányi said upon the announcement of Page's decision. But Dohnányi and Page had not always agreed on artistic issues. As Page's successor, Dohnányi hired Gareth Morrell. The 33-year-old British musician had prepared the BBC Symphony Chorus for a

Dohnányi performance of Schoenberg's *Die Jakobsleiter* in London and served as orchestra keyboardist when Cleveland's music director led Strauss's *Salome* at Covent Garden.

In 1990, the orchestra lost yet another high-profile player to one of its competitors: after eight seasons in Cleveland, principal flutist Jeffrey Khaner announced that he would leave at the end of the season to become principal with the Philadelphia Orchestra. The change would lead to a controversial move—Dohnányi's decision to hire Joshua Smith, a 20-year-old Khaner student at the Curtis Institute of Music in Philadelphia, for the Cleveland post. Smith won the job after two auditions, despite the fact that he had never held a principal position anywhere (and had done little orchestral playing at Curtis). But Smith wasn't a total stranger to Northeast Ohio: he had studied at the Blossom Festival School, the joint summer program run by the orchestra and Kent State University, in 1988 and 1989. There he had worked with John Mack, the orchestra's principal oboist, who would coach him again during the summer of 1990. The new flutist was destined to be one of Dohnányi's most inspired hires.

❊   ❊   ❊

Principal guest conductor Vladimir Ashkenazy, who, like Dohnányi, had a contract with Decca, enhanced the orchestra's recording situation. Even so, conducting stints by the acclaimed concert-pianist-turned-maestro tended to polarize listeners. When he led the orchestra in a program of music by Mozart (the Clarinet Concerto, with Franklin Cohen), and Sibelius (*The Swan of Tuonela* and Fourth Symphony) at Carnegie Hall in February 1988, two pianist-critics had divergent views of his conducting abilities. "For all his virtuosity and seriousness as an instrumentalist, I am convinced Mr. Ashkenazy will end up a better conductor than he ever was a pianist," wrote Bernard Holland in the *New York Times*. "Vladimir Ashkenazy's musicality cannot be denied, but his metamorphosis from pianist to conductor of the Cleveland Orchestra is still incomplete," stated Harris Goldsmith in the *New York Post*.

But Ashkenazy easily won over many Cleveland Orchestra musicians, who admired his interpretive sensitivity and his serious, soft-spoken personality. He forged particularly strong relationships with several orchestra players, including Cohen, with whom he recorded works by Brahms and Schumann for Decca. Although his orchestral performances could sound loosely structured and rhythmically lax, Ashkenazy showed unusual affinity for certain scores, such as works by Shostakovich and Sibelius.

If some audience members had had their wish, Ashkenazy might one day have been a candidate to succeed Dohnányi. Early in 1988, it appeared that someone might try to whisk the orchestra's boss away, at least for part of the year. "The conductor most sought-after to fill one of the London vacancies is rumored to be Christoph von Dohnányi, currently happily placed with the Cleveland Orchestra," reported the *Financial Times*. "His most recent London appearance was with the BBC Symphony in an uncharacteristic program of Ives, Glass (a new piece to Europe, *The Light*), and Bartók, which demonstrated in its sovereign control of texture and positive knack of characterization just why Dohnányi has become such a hot property." Artistically, Dohnányi was also becoming a hot property in the United States. After taking his orchestra to Carnegie Hall in late January and early February 1988, Dohnányi received laudatory reviews that further solidified his reputation. One Dohnányi program—Schoenberg's *Pelléas und Mélisande*, Mussorgsky's *Night on the Bare Mountain*, and the New York premiere of Philip Glass's *The Light* (which had received its world premiere in Cleveland that season)—elicited a rapturous notice from Tim Page in *Newsday*: "What an orchestra this is: It has all the brilliance of the Chicago Symphony with none of its vulgarity, the plush elegance of the Philadelphia Orchestra and the affinity for new music that we associate with the St. Louis Symphony. Dohnányi's conducting was meticulous and unsentimental. He clearly understands this music [Glass], which has defeated many traditional conductors." *The New Yorker*'s Andrew Porter, who had been only mildly taken with Dohnányi and Cleveland several years before, was now a convert, partly as a result of their performance of Bruckner's Seventh Symphony at Carnegie Hall. "Mr. Dohnányi and his orchestra cast a spell of attention such as is rarely encountered in New York's concert halls. Beauty of sound, eloquence of individual phrasing, balance of long periods, and a sense of high purpose were united," wrote Porter. "New York's orchestral season began, as I wrote in October, with two noble Carnegie concerts from the Vienna Philharmonic and Leonard Bernstein. Nothing that I heard after them, until the Cleveland-Dohnányi Bruckner Seventh, reached that level."

But Dohnányi wasn't faring so well in U. S. engagements outside Cleveland and New York. In December 1988, he made his debut with the Philadelphia Orchestra at the Academy of Music with performances of Bruckner's Ninth Symphony. The results were refined but short of electric. Nothing in Dohnányi's recent past, though, could have prepared him for the failure of his engagement with the Boston Symphony in February 1989. He was scheduled for two weeks of debut concerts. Dohnányi pushed the ensemble hard to achieve his goals, especially in Brahms's First Symphony. The rehearsals went badly, and the concerts never reached the heights that

Boston critics expected. "Dohnányi and the Cleveland Orchestra almost immediately forged one of those rare, alchemical bonds between music director and orchestra," wrote Richard Dyer in the *Boston Globe*. "It is probably betraying no secrets to reveal that such a bond was not immediately established during the first week of rehearsals with the Boston Symphony; that it does not yet exist was audibly evident last night."

There would be no second week of concerts. At the end of the first week in Boston, Dohnányi withdrew from the rest of his engagement, claiming illness, and was replaced by Jesús López-Cobos. Quick to defend Dohnányi, Kenneth Haas, his former Cleveland colleague, said "He had very hard working rehearsals; some enjoyed them and some didn't. That's the way it is with a strong conductor and strong musicians. He had a different approach, a very keen idea about how he likes the music to sound." From Cleveland, Morris told the *Globe* that Dohnányi was in bed with bronchitis.

✿   ✿   ✿

One of Dohnányi's greatest strengths as music director—programming—was becoming increasingly evident. During three concerts at Carnegie Hall in January 1989, he led the orchestra in a vast array of works, including Ferruccio Busoni's quirky Piano Concerto (with Garrick Ohlsson as soloist), Sir Michael Tippett's Concerto for Violin, Viola, Cello, and Orchestra, Varèse's *Amériques*, and pieces by Mozart, Beethoven, Delius, Villa-Lobos, Bach, and Bartók. "A genuine festive spirit pervaded the Cleveland Orchestra's recent three-day visit to Carnegie Hall, and it took me a while to figure out why," wrote Peter G. Davis in *New York* magazine. "Surely the audience had not come as stargazers—Christoph von Dohnányi is an excellent conductor but not the type who asks to be worshiped. Nor is the Cleveland one of the world's great cult orchestras, a splendid band though it may be. No, what made these concerts special was, amazingly enough, the music itself."

Cleveland's music director was succeeding where Pierre Boulez had failed as music director of the New York Philharmonic. Dohnányi's "imaginatively planned, venturesome programs almost always flatter an individual's intelligence without threatening or overly provoking the majority," Davis wrote.

A great deal of valuable, attractive music has been written in this century by composers who never belonged to radical camps, right or left. They tend to be neglected, and Dohnányi is reminding us of their work, along with tougher contemporary masterpieces that are still underplayed and

need a boost. Heard within this context, even the classics can sound fresh
and startling once again, especially when played so honestly and with a
minimum of fancy embroidery. Most so-called music festivals offer much
less.

At home, Dohnányi's adventurous programming had been drawing complaints from the public (though it would win him and the orchestra prestigious awards from the American Society of Composers, Authors and
Publishers). But, Dohnányi told the board, "giving the public 'safe' programming is dangerous to maintaining art and in no way provides for the
music of tomorrow. A balance of programming is essential and recognizes
that audiences over the next twenty years will be changing. We must perform only the music we love and think is important."

In August 1989, the Musical Arts Association announced that the orchestra had a deficit of $2.3 million for 1988–89, the largest shortfall in its
history for a single season. More ominously, the accumulated deficit had
risen to more than $4 million. Board president Ward Smith said the trustees
were "treating this as a crisis." The solutions were clear—raising more
money and keeping costs down—but a plan wasn't in place.

Dohnányi, who had lectured the trustees earlier in the season about the
orchestra's importance to Cleveland, came before the board for a second
time to plead his case for rectifying the money problems:

> The primary reason for the Cleveland Orchestra's outstanding quality
> is the same one that causes it financial difficulty—it resides in a small city.
> There are too many distractions for musicians, and a music director, in
> large cities such as New York, Boston, London, Paris, etc. For example, a
> musician with the New York Philharmonic may take advantage of the pos-
> sibility of playing as an extra in the Metropolitan Opera, thereby diluting
> energies and creating an overwhelming workload. In more major cities,
> the music director must fight for things we take for granted in Cleveland.
> Time off here, including vacation and optional leave, is thought out in the
> interest of the quality of the orchestra, and not as a means of pursuing
> other jobs. By having so many loyal members of the Cleveland Orchestra,
> the spirit of music-making is stabilized.

He cautioned trustees not to try to save money by reducing the size of the
orchestra, whose crucial balance between strings, winds, brasses would be
compromised. Among other warnings: avoid presenting the orchestra in
pops concerts, which generally are conducted by "fourth- or fifth-rate con-

ductors and are very damaging to the overall quality of the orchestra"; view fund-raising not as support for the musicians, but as support aimed at enabling the community to attend concerts; beware of other orchestras tempting Cleveland Orchestra players away with offers of higher salaries.

As they absorbed these comments, the trustees came to the crux of the dilemma: the future of Blossom Music Center. They could get rid of the special attractions (which were not generating the expected revenues), discontinue orchestra concerts at Blossom, or find an outside promoter to lease the special-attraction business. Since the center had been created as the orchestra's summer home, but also needed extra revenue to survive, the final option was the only realistic alternative.

In January 1990, the Musical Arts Association announced that it would turn over the booking of special attractions—sometimes referred to as "rock-and-roll concerts" by board members—to MCA Concerts of Los Angeles. The firm, a division of MCA Entertainment Group, had vast experience, and success, with outdoor concert facilities. Board president Smith expected the new arrangement to help operating costs at Blossom "go down fairly markedly." It would also help reduce and eventually retire the orchestra's $4 million accumulated deficit. Observers were taking a wait-and-see attitude toward the arrangement. "Besides helping in a long-term solution to the orchestra's financial problems, the move might enable the orchestra administration to concentrate on upgrading symphonic programming at Blossom so it can realize its full potential," wrote Robert Finn in *The Plain Dealer*. But one person was not happy with the move. Dohnányi preferred "an Orchestra-only approach" to Blossom.

✿   ✿   ✿

At least recording and touring were going well. Decca had decided to move recording sessions from Masonic Auditorium to Severance Hall starting in the summer of 1990. The company planned to build a temporary stage over the seats on the main floor to bring the orchestra out into the larger acoustical space. At the same time, Morris was transforming the orchestra's touring agenda. The musicians had been unhappy about making extended foreign tours crammed with one-night stands. Tours now would no longer exceed three weeks. They would have more performances in fewer cities. Two such trips were scheduled for 1990: the first to the Far East in May and June for concerts in Hong Kong and Japan; the second, in August and September, to major European music festivals, including Salzburg, which was interested in a multiyear agreement with Cleveland.

Herbert von Karajan, longtime director of the festival and conductor of the Berlin Philharmonic, had invited Dohnányi to bring his orchestra to Salzburg. Recalling his experience leading the Cleveland Orchestra at the Salzburg and Lucerne festivals in 1967, Karajan told Dohnányi that Cleveland was the only ensemble he had ever conducted that left him with nothing to say after three rehearsals. (Karajan never heard the orchestra again at Salzburg: he died in 1989.)

Salzburg, indeed, proved the most electrifying destination on the orchestra's 1990 European tour, a 12-concert trip that also took Dohnányi and the musicians—and, for three performances, Mitsuko Uchida as soloist in the Schoenberg Piano Concerto—to Munich, Lucerne, London, Ghent, Brussels, Bonn, Düsseldorf, Amsterdam, and Paris. Gérard Mortier, head of the Théâtre de la Monnaie in Brussels and a former Dohnányi assistant at the Frankfurt and Hamburg operas, had been hired to succeed Karajan as director of the Salzburg Festival. The orchestra, which had last played in Salzburg in 1967 under Szell, was now close to signing a deal for a long-term residency at the festival starting in 1992. "Salzburg is really THE festival," said Dohnányi during the 1990 tour. "The orchestra has to be there more frequently." Austrian critics weren't about to disagree. After the ensemble's first concert at the festival's Felsenreitschule (Rock Riding School, where scenes in the movie *The Sound of Music* had been filmed), Viennese critic Franz Endler added to the praise he had heaped on orchestra and conductor the previous year: "Together they are virtually unbeatable."

Yet European critics had varying reactions to Dohnányi's interpretations. Some believed him to be stern and inflexible; others praised his elegant orchestral command and, in the words of Max Loppert in London's *Financial Times*, his "intelligence, honesty and rigorous musicianship. This seems to be Christoph von Dohnányi's special seal on a great orchestra: a virtuosity which has nothing to do with splashy effects-making and everything to do with a quality of concentrated responsiveness between departments and in the whole ensemble."

The official announcement of the Salzburg Festival residency wasn't made until January 1991, when Mortier came to Cleveland to hold a press conference with Morris. "I am committed to presenting the best the world has to offer on our stages," Mortier said. "It is in this spirit that I am proud to announce an ongoing collaboration with Christoph von Dohnányi and the Cleveland Orchestra." The orchestra was to become the first American ensemble to establish such a relationship with the Salzburg Festival. The agreement called for residencies in 1992, 1994, and 1995, with the possibility of further collaborations.

By the time these developments were announced, Dohnányi had made room on his summer schedule for more European engagements. In November 1990, the orchestra announced that Leonard Slatkin, music director of the St. Louis Symphony, would become the first Blossom Festival Director with the summer of 1991. The orchestra tried to present the appointment in the best possible light, noting that Slatkin was eager to transform Blossom's programming and present an abundance of American music. Dohnányi would continue to appear occasionally at the orchestra's summer home, largely to prepare programs for the Salzburg residencies. But Slatkin's hiring effectively signaled Dohnányi's withdrawal from Blossom, where he had been unable to carry out his adventurous vision.

Music Dramas

The Cleveland Orchestra entered the 1990s reaching out in an almost dizzying number of directions. Touring was flourishing, especially with the prospect of the residencies at the Salzburg Festival starting in 1992. Recordings continued to herald the orchestra's artistry and the city's name around the world. Under Christoph von Dohnányi, whose contract had been extended to 1995, the ensemble sounded as polished and articulate as it ever had, prompting one journalist to observe, "the results reach a pinnacle not even attained under the legendary George Szell." Despite persistent problems with the budget, the board had managed to cut the annual deficit from $2.2 million to $1.1 million.

At home, the orchestra was wending its way into the lives of more and more people. On July 3, 1990, the musicians and resident conductor Jahja Ling gave their first concert on Public Square in downtown Cleveland for a crowd of more than 75,000. Later in the year, BP America—successor to John D. Rockefeller's Standard Oil of Ohio—pledged a five-year grant of $1.8 million to the orchestra for a new series of free summer concerts at North Coast Harbor, also in downtown Cleveland, in addition to its $1 million sponsorship of the ensemble's syndicated radio concerts (originating at WCLV-FM). A week after the BP windfall, the Cleveland Foundation announced that it was giving the orchestra a $2.1 million grant for community programs, operating support, youth activities, and performances of new music.

Ticket sales jumped 25 percent for the 1990 season at Blossom Music Center, and average attendance at orchestra concerts there was 5,167, the second-highest total in the center's history. During the Blossom season, the musicians signed a new three-year contract, a month before the deadline. The biggest artistic news of the period was the announcement of a project of extraordinary daring—some would say foolishness—that would serve as the centerpiece in the orchestra's upcoming 75th-anniversary celebration: concert performances of Wagner's *Ring* cycle under Dohnányi at Severance

Hall during the 1992–93 and 1993–94 seasons to coincide with Decca/London recordings of the four music dramas.

The orchestra was still doing extremely well in the recording business. Along with its Decca, Telarc, and Teldec agreements, Cleveland was about to enter into a long-term recording contract with Deutsche Grammophon, the German recording company, to produce discs with Pierre Boulez. They began recording for Deutsche Grammophon in March 1991 with works by Debussy (including *Afternoon of a Faun,* with flutist Joshua Smith in his first season as a principal player in any orchestra) and Stravinsky (*Petrouchka* and *The Rite of Spring*). Boulez had recorded *The Rite* with the orchestra in 1969 for Columbia—a performance of exceptional rhythmic vitality. The 1991 recording shows the ensemble in equally charismatic form. Boulez's conducting is still crisp and lucid, and more expansive in the final "Danse sacrale."

During the 1989–90 and 1990–91 seasons, Dohnányi recorded two dozen pieces, finishing his Beethoven symphony cycle for Telarc and recording Bruckner and Mahler symphonies for Decca. Ashkenazy was active with the ensemble for Decca, inaugurating a Brahms symphony cycle (Dohnányi had just completed one in Cleveland for Teldec) and recording works by Dvořák and Ravel.

✣   ✣   ✣

Martin Bernheimer, the *Los Angeles Times*'s Pulitzer Prize–winning music critic, put the ensemble's abilities into a national context when Dohnányi and the orchestra played at the Orange County Performing Arts Center as part of a West Coast tour in October 1991:

> Americans love their Best Games. We live by qualitative lists—rating and ranking movies, cars, detergents, wardrobes, scientists, journalists, refrigerators, politicians, ballclubs and recordings with equal, stubbornly constant zeal. It is a silly game, but someone has to play it. Even in the arts. When it comes to orchestras we traditionally think of the Big Five: New York, Boston, Chicago, Philadelphia and Cleveland (not necessarily in that order). Los Angeles, Pittsburgh, St. Louis and San Francisco usually follow as upstart afterthoughts. One of these decades, the perceptions may change. At the moment, New York, Philadelphia and Chicago are in a state of directorial flux, and Boston seems to be in the doldrums. That may leave Cleveland alone at the top.

To keep the orchestra there, the board knew it had to take even firmer control of the financial situation, which was improving, despite a recession. The new relationship with MCA Concerts at Blossom had begun to make a difference. In the fall of 1991, the orchestra reported that its operating deficit for the 1990–91 season was $756,000, the lowest since a shortfall of $605,000 for the 1987–88 season. Speaking to the trustees in December 1991, board president Ward Smith underscored the orchestra's stature: "We are once more at the peak of our reputation. There is no more respected Orchestra in the United States." Executive director Thomas W. Morris assserted that the orchestra stood "at the center of the community's self-esteem. Where else can you drive into a gasoline station, as my wife did several years ago when we moved to Cleveland, and have the attendant, recognizing she was new to the community, volunteer, 'You will really love it here. We have a really great Orchestra'?"

        ✻   ✻   ✻

For Dohnányi, the residency at the Salzburg Festival in 1992—part of a tour that included concerts at the Promenade Concerts (or Proms) at London's Royal Albert Hall—was crucial to his orchestra's global identity. "If there is a problem with Cleveland, it's that it's a connoisseur's orchestra," he said. "Musical insiders know that it's one of the best, but the normal European market connects more easily with Boston or New York. From a public relations point of view, Salzburg will make this orchestra the absolute equal of the other five or six leading orchestras of the world." He was once again in an expansive mood on the eve of the tour. Dohnányi said his musicians were likely to come under extraordinary scrutiny in Salzburg, where the Cleveland Orchestra would be the first American ensemble ever to open the series of orchestral concerts at the festival—"something like the Olympics of classical music," as *The Plain Dealer*'s Steven Litt described it. "Everything will be watched in a very, very meticulous way and, maybe, not in an entirely objective way," said Dohnányi, referring to well-known European critical prejudices. "So we will go in and do what we do without looking to the right or the left."

They began at the Proms in London, where the BBC taped one of their two concerts for television broadcast. During the engagement, Dohnányi's supposed lack of spontaneity was again raised by the media. "In recent years London critics have accused Dohnányi of being note-perfect but sometimes dull," wrote Elaine Guregian in the *Akron Beacon Journal*. "They have said that his leadership of the Cleveland Orchestra is overly fastidious . . . . Whatever people said, though, the general audience's reaction to the orchestra at this weekend's concerts was overwhelmingly positive." The

London critics, while admiring the orchestra almost without reservation, re-mained divided over Dohnányi. "Distinctly short on passion, let alone mor-bidity of any kind," wrote Barry Millington in *The Times* of Dohnányi's per-formance of Berlioz's *Symphonie fantastique*. But Millington praised per-formances of Beethoven's Fifth Symphony and Schumann's Fourth Symphony. A bit of chauvinism entered Geoffrey Norris's review of the same concert in *The Daily Telegraph*. He wrote of Dohnányi's Beethoven that "the underlying rhythmic impulse was sluggish, and the individual points, pauses and surprises, which can make the symphony so riveting, were dis-guised in what the Americans would call an overview of the piece." Richard Fairman in *The Financial Times*, was perhaps most succinct: "Dohnányi needs to let himself go more."

Gérard Mortier, the Salzburg Festival's new director, came to Dohnányi's defense. "What they're saying is a cliché," he said "A lot of critics think a con-ductor is good if he has beautiful hair. Dohnányi is not one of the glamour conductors. I like him because he has great analytical knowledge, and yet at the same time, he doesn't lose his poetic flair." The musicians were fed up, too. "There were 10 years of [Lorin] Maazel and eight years of [Christoph von] Dohnányi," observed violinist Kurt Loebel, "but it's still viewed as Szell's orchestra."

❖   ❖   ❖

Finally, in the fall of 1992, Dohnányi inaugurated his dream project: Wag-ner's *Der Ring des Nibelungen* with his orchestra. The conductor had been urging Decca to let him record the *Ring*, one of the towering works of Western art (and one of the longest: 15 hours of music). Decca had made the first (resplendent) stereo recording of the cycle from 1959 to 1966 with Georg Solti, the Vienna Philharmonic, and stellar casts. Company officials suggested that Dohnányi also record the work in Vienna, but he insisted upon the Cleveland Orchestra. Decca listened. Under Dohnányi, the en-semble would become the first symphony orchestra in the United States to record Wagner's entire magnum opus (the Metropolitan Opera Orchestra had already recorded the cycle for Deutsche Grammophon, conducted by James Levine).

Dohnányi initiated his immersion into the *Ring* in October 1992—a month before the start of his Severance Hall Wagnerfest—at the Vienna State Opera, where he began at the beginning with *Das Rheingold*. At the helm of the great Vienna Philharmonic, Dohnányi signaled that his *Ring* would avoid the usual Wagnerian monumentalism and instead focus on mu-sical and verbal clarity.

Decca and Dohnányi had opted to start their Cleveland *Ring* recording with *Die Walküre*, the second opera in the cycle. The casts for the concert performances at Severance Hall and the recording were not going to be identical, because of scheduling difficulties. German soprano Gabriele Schnaut, as Brünnhilde, and Danish tenor Poul Elming, as Siegmund, couldn't be in Cleveland in the weeks before the recording. British soprano Anne Evans and German tenor Robert Schunk sang these roles, respectively, at the concert performances, which included Alessandra Marc as Sieglinde, Robert Hale as Wotan, Alfred Muff as Hunding, and former Bayreuth Festival diva Anja Silja as Fricka (for the first time in her career). Dohnányi's two performances of *Walküre* at Severance were even more remarkable than the Vienna performances in orchestral majesty and transparency. The singing was not always of the kind to send a Wagner lover into a swoon, but it was seasoned enough to animate the work, especially when merged with the orchestra's inspired playing. The recording made the following week—with Schnaut's trumpet of a voice startling the musicians at her first "Ho-jo-to-ho"—went so smoothly that Decca officials said they expected the discs to be ready for release within a year, by the time the second entry, *Rheingold*, was onstage at Severance.

Their confidence wouldn't last for long. The original schedule for the Cleveland *Ring* had called for two music dramas per season over two seasons. Despite the success of *Die Walküre*, though, the project was slowed down to one music drama per season for four seasons, largely because Decca had not yet found a tenor who could sing the killing role of Siegfried in the final two works, *Siegfried* and *Götterdämmerung*.

Another impediment threatened the project: sales for classical recordings were plummeting at an alarming rate. Among the culprits were America's economic recession and changes in the distribution of compact discs. But classical recording companies also suddenly realized that the market had become glutted with product. Since the creation of the compact disc in 1980, record companies had gone crazy recording standard classical repertoire in the new digital format, which had room for up to 78 minutes of music per disc (the length of a spacious performance of Beethoven's Ninth Symphony) and—arguably, to many ears—improved the sound. At the same time, major and minor record labels had begun to release remastered versions of historic performances, including many that had been off the market for decades. The mass of recordings—literally hundreds of the Beethoven symphonies, for example—led to a sharp decrease in public demand. The news was the worst for American orchestras, which were committed to union payment scales requiring two or even three times the recording fees earned by European orchestras. The bottom was dropping out of the classical recording industry, and Cleveland would be hit hard.

A year after *Die Walküre*, despite dark clouds on the recording front, the orchestra was ready to plunge into another *Ring* entry, *Das Rheingold*. Already there was trouble. Anja Silja, Dohnányi's wife, who had sung the role of Fricka in *Die Walküre*, had decided that the same character in the prologue was not for her. As Dohnányi explained it, Fricka in *Rheingold* is "a sweet, soft-minded woman who wants always to please her husband, and that's not Anja's cup of tea." The conductor's remark seemed fraught with personal implications: Silja's subsequent absence from the city suggested that the Dohnányi marriage was on the rocks.

✿   ✿   ✿

Several other farewells touched the orchestra during the fall of 1993. In September, Erich Leinsdorf, the ensemble's third conductor, died at the age of 81. Then, in late November, longtime concertmaster Daniel Majeske died at 61 after a prolonged battle with prostate cancer. He had been in and out of the orchestra for a year and had missed the Tokyo tour in October. During his absences, associate concertmaster Martin Chalifour had assumed the post of concertmaster, with distinction, and soon was named acting concertmaster. "Danny, of all people, maintained the traditions of George Szell," said Ronald Whitaker, the orchestra's head librarian. "With his death, the Szell era has ended."

Majeske died the week before the orchestra's performances of *Das Rheingold* and two weeks before the 75th-anniversary celebration at Public Auditorium. With *Rheingold*, Dohnányi once again invested Wagner's music with unusual transparency and dramatic command. Robert Hale returned as Wotan, this time paired with the Fricka of German mezzo-soprano Hanna Schwarz. Like the performances of *Die Walküre*, the prologue was presented with the singers performing on a platform upstage, above the orchestra, giving the impression of true operatic space. In contrast to the *Walküre* performances, Dohnányi now had the strings seated in a 19th-century configuration he would make permanent: first violins to his left, second violins to his right, with cellos and violas between these sections and basses arrayed along the wall behind the first violins and cellos. The placement would cause some distress within the ensemble—the first and second violins complained that they couldn't hear one another—but the effect was striking.

The *Rheingold* concert version, if anything, confirmed the timeliness of the *Ring* project. "Only now, in its 75th-anniversary celebration, has the versatile Cleveland Orchestra come round to one of the most glorious symphonies of all: Wagner's 'Rheingold'," wrote the *New York Times*'s James R. Oestreich, the orchestra's former program annotator, after a Severance Hall performance. "Oh, sure, Wagner called it a music drama, and it functions admirably as opera. But with its incomparably rich orchestral fabric, its taut evolutionary musical logic and its epically scaled four-movement structure, it can also be viewed as a powerful oversize symphony. Hearing the fresh emphases and nuances, let alone the sheer imposing sonorities, that a great symphony orchestra can find in the score is often thrilling."

Accolades for the music director and his orchestra soon came from another source, including a catchy phrase that the institution would emblazon on promotional materials. "Under Dohnányi, the Cleveland has become the best band in the land," wrote Michael Walsh in *Time* magazine in January 1994. "No other American orchestra can rival its combination of virtuosic technique, consummate ensemble playing and rich, burnished tone, especially in the Central European repertory of Haydn, Beethoven and Brahms. It has also successfully branched out into opera: last month's dazzling concert version of Wagner's *Das Rheingold*, continuing a *Ring* cycle that is being recorded by London/Decca, was as fine a performance as one is likely to hear outside Bayreuth or the Metropolitan Opera."

The article generated not only elation in Cleveland but also controversy, especially in the opera community. "For musicians there's not much else to do," Dohnányi was quoted as saying. "There's no opera, there's no freelancing; you don't come to Cleveland to enjoy the weather. You come here to play in the Cleveland Orchestra." In fact, Cleveland did have opera—a regional company, Cleveland Opera, and a small, plucky summer troupe, Lyric Opera Cleveland. Dohnányi's point, if not particularly well articulated, was essentially correct: the musicians in the Cleveland Orchestra didn't have the musical opportunities available in some other cities with major orchestras. The Cleveland players could concentrate almost exclusively on the orchestra. "And play they do," concluded Walsh, "better than anybody."

Critics also praised the orchestra when its recording of *Das Rheingold* was released in Europe in September 1995 and in the United States the following January. Response to the conducting and singing was mixed. But "it is worth the money for the orchestral playing alone," wrote Michael Kennedy in London's *Sunday Telegraph*. "Some might find Dohnányi's interpretation on the cool side, I suppose. Tempi are fastish, and we don't get the sumptuousness of [Clemens] Krauss or [Hans] Knappertsbusch (nor ever will again, I'm sure). But we do get a marvelously incisive and penetrating view of the great score." David Patrick Stearns, in *USA Today*, found most of the singing problematic, but he was high on both Dohnányi and the orchestra. "This *Rheingold* has its own sense of excitement, with the clarion brilliance of the Cleveland Orchestra brass, the crystal clarity of the strings and a surging forward motion, unlike James Levine's Metropolitan Opera recording. Dohnányi seems almost like a revisionist: His interpretation never dallies, nor is it pulled down by obligations toward tradition."

✿   ✿   ✿

Cleveland was the most recorded orchestra in America during the 1992–93 season, with 20 works conducted by Dohnányi, Ashkenazy, Boulez, and Oliver Knussen. It was also the nation's most financially strapped orchestra. Although the annual deficit had dropped from $756,000 for the 1990–91 season to $437,000 for the 1991–92 season, the Musical Arts Association was facing a crushing accumulated deficit of more than $6 million. "That is the bad news," said board president Smith, ever dry of wit. "The good news is that the future is in our hands, and those of the community led by the Trustees and the members of the Association, and we can, in fact, secure the future of this extraordinary institution. To that end, I am happy to tell you that we are, in fact, undertaking a committed effort to attempt balancing the budget this year." As part of the push, trustees would be asked to give an average gift of $10,000.

Although Smith couldn't spread much fiscal sunshine, he could report a promising artistic development: immediately after the *Walküre* recording sessions, Dohnányi had signed another contract effective through the 1999–2000 season. Dohnányi's presence was "one of the linchpins of future artistic success," Smith said.

Dohnányi actually did less conducting than expected in both Cleveland and Vienna during the 1992–93 season. In March 1993, while preparing the new production of *Siegfried* at the Vienna State Opera, he was hospitalized with an intestinal ulcer, forcing him to withdraw from the performances. Dohnányi's illness also forced him to cancel two weeks of concerts in Cleveland, where he was replaced by resident conductor Jahja Ling (who was becoming a virtuoso at substituting for ailing conductors in Cleveland and elsewhere at the last minute) and Sylvain Cambreling.

The four months that Dohnányi was away from Severance Hall held a number of important developments, including one with ramifications that couldn't have been clear at the time. In February 1993, the orchestra welcomed Franz Welser-Möst for his Cleveland debut. The Austrian conductor had been catapulted—too early, many would say—to international attention in 1990, when he became music director of the London Philharmonic at the age of 30. He had conducted several admired EMI recordings by the time he arrived in Cleveland, where he made a favorable first impression leading Schubert's Symphony No. 3, Mozart's Piano Concerto No. 24 (with Yefim Bronfman), and Martinů's Symphony No. 5.

The major announcement of the period concerned the orchestra's upcoming 75th anniversary. It planned to celebrate with its annual Public Square concert in July under Ling. Another milestone—the 25th anniversary of Blossom Music Center—would be marked with a performance of the major work that had opened the facility in 1968, Beethoven's Ninth Symphony, led by Slatkin. And yet another Beethoven Ninth was planned for December 12, 1993—75 years and a day after the orchestra's inaugural concert in 1918—with Dohnányi on the podium at Public Auditorium. Two other endeavors would mark the 75th anniversary. The Musical Arts Association was publishing *Not Responsible for Lost Articles: Thoughts and Second Thoughts from Severance Hall*, a book of witty and probing essays by former program annotator and editor Klaus George Roy and others. The orchestra also had something tantalizing for audiophiles: a set of 10 compact discs featuring performances led by all of the orchestra's music directors and former musical advisor Boulez. Executive director Morris, English hornist Felix Kraus, and advertising and promotion manager Christopher Stager devised the compilation from out-of-print commercial recordings and unreleased broadcast performances. Cleveland's self-produced set provided a glimpse into the future of recording: American symphony orchestras soon would be forced to generate their own discs due to the collapse of the classical recording industry.

The orchestra was about to reappear on radio after a hiatus of seven months. Concerts had been broadcast by WCLV-FM from 1965 until the end of 1992, when BP America, its latest sponsor, withdrew funds for the series. Now a consortium of eight Cleveland corporate sponsors stepped forward to enable WCLV to resume the broadcasts starting in July 1993. Unlike the previous agreement, which covered 52 weeks of concerts, the new series would run for only 26 weeks and exclude concerts from Blossom Music Center. Other major American orchestras weren't having even this much luck. "We're alive, while Philadelphia, Boston and New York are dead," said WCLV's Robert Conrad.

The orchestra's touring schedule also was alive. In October 1993, Dohnányi traveled with the ensemble to Tokyo to perform a Beethoven festival of all nine symphonies and two piano concertos with Mitsuko Uchida at Suntory Hall. Soon thereafter, the conductor's international profile was further enhanced when he was named principal guest conductor of the

Philharmonia Orchestra of London, an ensemble formerly led by Herbert von Karajan and Otto Klemperer. "We're pleased," said Cleveland's executive director, Morris. "It will concentrate Christoph's European activity with the Philharmonia, and it will have no effect on his relationship with the Cleveland Orchestra."

The 1993–94 Severance Hall season had been over for only a week when the orchestra made a crucial announcement: a successor to the late concertmaster, Daniel Majeske, had been found in William Preucil, first violinist of the Cleveland Quartet. "For a music director," James R. Oestreich had observed in the *New York Times* after Majeske's death, "the choice of a concertmaster is analogous to a President's choice of a Supreme Court Justice, since the appointee may continue to shape the orchestra's style long after the music director is gone." In a rare phenomenon, two top American orchestras had offered Preucil the post of concertmaster on the same day—Philadelphia and Cleveland. "The Philadelphia Orchestra is a great orchestra," said Preucil. "I have great respect for everyone there. All that said, it's Cleveland where I need and want to be." One of his reasons was sentimental: Preucil's beloved teacher was Josef Gingold, Cleveland's concertmaster from 1947 to 1960.

❃   ❃   ❃

Two major events kept the orchestra busy during the summer of 1994. The first was the ensemble's first concert at Jacobs Field, the new, handsome home of the Cleveland Indians, where 42,000 people showed up to hear Jahja Ling conduct the *1812 Overture* and other pieces during a July Fourth weekend celebration. "It's fun," said violinist Stephen Majeske before the concert, winding up for a baseball pun. "So far, there are no errors."

The other big event was the orchestra's 10-concert European tour in August 1994, featuring appearances at four of the world's most prestigious festivals—Salzburg, Lucerne, London's BBC Proms, and Edinburgh. The orchestra had not played at the Salzburg, Lucerne, and Edinburgh festivals during a single trip since 1967. Now, with Dohnányi, the ensemble was returning to Salzburg for the third time in the 1990s. Along with music by Mahler, Dvořák, and Bach (as orchestrated by Webern), the conductor offered the conservative Salzburg audience two 20th-century works—the neoclassical Stravinsky Violin Concerto (with Christian Tetzlaff as elegant soloist) and Sir Harrison Birtwistle's *Earth Dances*. The Birtwistle was booed, which seemed to please the British composer, who flashed a "V" sign while being screamed at by the Salzburgers.

Mixed messages about the Cleveland *Ring* cycle came during the

Salzburg engagement: Decca president Roland Kommerell implied that the company had found a Siegfried (rumored to be Canadian tenor Ben Heppner), but that the last two music dramas wouldn't be performed and recorded for at least three years. Such matters couldn't mar the triumph of the orchestra's Salzburg residency, part of Morris's strategic plan to give the ensemble a more global profile. "You have to be very aggressive in the international market," he said. "That's the competitive league."

But nothing during the tour—concerts, reviews, sightseeing—generated more talk than an interview in *The Times* of London headlined "Acid words from maestro of Ohio," in which Dohnányi made candid and ungracious (and, possibly, off-the-record) remarks about conducting colleagues, both living and deceased. He said Leonard Bernstein's interpretation of Mahler was "totally wrong, and I can prove it." Dohnányi skewered Claudio Abbado's rehearsal methods. Referring to Franz Welser-Möst's recent withdrawal as music director of the London Philharmonic, Cleveland's maestro claimed that "young conductors can be overwhelmed by a famous orchestra." The interviewer, Richard Morrison, employed overheated prose of his own when discussing Cleveland's hiring of Dohnányi: "The Clevelanders knew their business. They wanted what was fondly known in the early 1980s as 'the smack of firm government': a disciplinarian with a thorough grounding in the Austro-Germanic symphonic repertoire, a central European who would whip the orchestra into shape and instill a precision so ferocious that you could set your watch by it. What they wanted, perhaps, was George Szell . . . Szell, however, was not available, being deceased."

Dohnányi faced up to the controversy days after the article appeared, quipping that "this interview was certainly something people read even twice" and then clarifying his views. He registered satisfaction that European audiences appeared to recognize that the orchestra was not the same ensemble that Szell had shaped. "Szell was a tremendous musician and a very strict musician," Dohnányi said. "The breathing and special improvisation of the players was certainly more limited than the way I like it. Szell took a breath before and after the concert. That could have been his limitation."

Chattering voices were calmed somewhat when the orchestra got down to work at the festive BBC Proms at London's Royal Albert Hall, where *Earth Dances* was cheered, as were the orchestra's three concerts soon afterward at the Edinburgh Festival. "This is a super-efficient, absolutely together, immaculate ensemble, utterly seamless violin tone, stunningly balanced, and with a responsiveness to Dohnányi's quicksilver direction that is almost miraculous," exclaimed Michael Tumelty in *The Herald*. "They're not a high gloss outfit; there's not a spare ounce of flesh on the band. They are riveting."

They also were completely solvent for the first time in years. Along with posting an $11,000 surplus for the 1993–94 season, the orchestra retired its $6.24 million accumulated deficit during the summer by withdrawing the amount from the endowment fund. The Musical Arts Association had said the previous year that the fund would never be tapped for such a purpose. But the trustees changed their mind "to stop the place from fiscally hemorrhaging," said Morris. The endowment normally supplied 5 percent of the annual budget; this season, the amount had been 8.1 percent. The endowment stood at $70 million, about $30 million below the figure board president Smith said the orchestra should have by the year 2000. The orchestra had a $23.56 million budget during the 1993–94 season, when the annual minimum scale for the musicians was $65,000, below only the New York Philharmonic ($68,120), Boston and Chicago symphonies (both $67,700), Philadelphia Orchestra ($67,080), San Francisco Symphony ($66,430), and Los Angeles Philharmonic ($66,040)—all in much larger cities. Cleveland's board knew that a major fund-raising campaign was needed to avoid the kind of fiscal worries it had endured over the last decade.

Despite encouraging finances, the orchestra's 1994–95 season was a seesaw. In late October 1994, less than the year after the death of concertmaster Daniel Majeske, the ensemble experienced another major loss when principal second violinist Bernhard Goldschmidt, an orchestra member since 1958, died suddenly of a heart attack at age 69. Now Dohnányi faced the formidable challenge of nurturing two new string principals at once. William Preucil was set to arrive as Majeske's successor in April 1995, but who could sit in the seat long occupied by the intensely devoted Goldschmidt? Dohnányi soon had an inspiration: Stephen Majeske, the late concertmaster's son and a member of the orchestra's first violin section since 1979. "I feel like I'm continuing my dad's work," said the younger Majeske upon his appointment. "More than anything else, he felt he was a servant to this orchestra."

The major works this season were big and bigger German scores—Berg's opera *Wozzeck* and Mahler's Symphony No. 8, dubbed the "Symphony of a Thousand" for the multitudes (hundreds, if not thousands) of instrumentalists and singers required. Dohnányi presided over concert performances of *Wozzeck* at Severance and Carnegie Hall in January 1995 with Franz-Josef Kapellmann and Hildegard Behrens heading the cast. After the Carnegie performance, *Newsday*'s Tim Page wrote: "Those of us who never heard Stokowski, Caruso, Heifetz, Callas and other musical legends in the flesh can console ourselves with the fact that we have heard Christoph von Dohnányi's Cleveland Orchestra. There is much talk of the 'Big Five' of American orchestras; to this taste, at this particular point in time, there is Cleveland and then there are some other fine ensembles."

In April, there was more excitement. The Mahler Eighth brought Robert Shaw back to the orchestra's podium, both at Severance and Carnegie, and reunited him with his former Atlanta Symphony concertmaster, Preucil, who had just arrived in Cleveland. Audiences in Northeast Ohio had heard the Eighth Symphony before, but only at Blossom. Severance Hall, slightly too small for the work, was packed to the rafters with 440 performers—the augmented orchestra, Cleveland Orchestra Chorus and Children's Chorus, Oberlin College Choir, and eight vocal soloists. At Carnegie, the performances were even more spectacular, bulging with almost 700 musicians. With choristers singing from boxes ringing the hall, as well as from the stage, the music literally surrounded the audience, bathing listeners in Mahlerian splendor.

At the end of the 1994–95 season, nine players hired by George Szell retired after combined service of 321 years. Their successors comprised a group of excellent young players who looked like teenagers when they arrived at the start of the 1995–96 season. But even with almost 10 percent of the ensemble new, there was no perceptible change in its musical personality, as there hardly had been for almost half a century. While Dohnányi had added warmth and breathing space, the orchestra still closely resembled the group that Szell molded.

The departure of the Szell appointees in 1995 highlighted both the ensemble's adaptability and, especially in one tragic case, the community's affection for its orchestra. Among the musicians scheduled to retire at the end of the 1995 Blossom season was Leonard Samuels, a member of the first violin section since 1957. Samuels was just another superlative Cleveland Orchestra musician until he grew a beard and ponytail after the 1970 death of Szell, who had barred such grooming from his ensemble. His distinctive appearance made the soft-spoken Samuels one of the most familiar figures on Cleveland's cultural scene. Even people who knew little about the orchestra recognized the abundantly whiskered violinist on the outside fourth stand of the first violins. So when Samuels died of a heart attack while exercising less than two weeks before his retirement, orchestra lovers and the general public alike mourned the loss. Samuels symbolized the human element in an artistic institution that celebrates communal accomplishment over individuality. "You can be creative as an orchestral musician by creating your own atmosphere, by imagining you are sitting under the conductor's nose in a leadership position, in a responsible position," Samuels said in an interview a month before his death. "You have to take advantage of that moment. I've been lucky to have had a lot of those great moments in music."

❊   ❊   ❊

By the mid-1990s, dwindling classical recording activity was affecting American ensembles, though the Decca and Deutsche Grammophon agreements with Cleveland were still in place, at least for the time being. During the 1993–94 season, only Decca made recordings in Cleveland, with both Dohnányi and Ashkenazy. By the 1995–96 season, only Deutsche Grammophon was making Cleveland recordings, with Pierre Boulez and Oliver Knussen. Except for a final recording for Decca in 1997 (Mahler's Ninth Symphony) and one for Nonesuch/Elektra in 1999 (John Adams's *Century Rolls*, with pianist Emanuel Ax as soloist), Dohnányi's commercial recording activity with the orchestra was finished.

The demise of the orchestra's relationship with Decca spelled doom for the second half of the *Ring* cycle recording. Decca, like most of its counterparts in the industry, was in dire shape financially, and it was suffering from managerial confusion. While maintaining several European relationships, the company was backing out of its American agreements, which had become too expensive.

Amid the confusion, Cleveland's second *Ring* recording, *Die Walküre*, was released in the fall of 1997. Reaction again was mixed. Some critics questioned what they perceived as Dohnányi's detached approach, while others praised him—and the orchestra, without qualification—for bringing freshness and clarity to the work. "This is a grand, satisfying performance on almost every count," wrote Alan Blyth in *Gramophone*. "Dohnányi conducts a well-paced, thought-through reading that at once creates dramatic excitement and attends to the long view." In *Stereophile*, Richard Lehnert decried the *Rheingold* recording, criticizing Dohnányi for noncommittal conducting, but generally admired the *Walküre* performance. He also sounded a hopeful note for the future: "If nothing else, Dohnányi's *Ring* may end up being the most natural-sounding yet—so far, it's a sensual feast. But sonics aside, his *Walküre* is a very pleasant surprise . . . . The completion of this *Ring* now seems very much worth the effort and—as the project has been on hold for five years until a worthy Siegfried is found—the wait."

By now, however, the wait for—and projected cost of—the last two recordings had become unbearable. Dohnányi had viewed the project as the most important of his Cleveland tenure and, indeed, of his career. Only a tiny percentage of conductors have the opportunity to record a full *Ring*. At first, Decca appeared willing to make a deal with the Musical Arts Association to jointly fund recordings of the last two music dramas, *Siegfried* and *Götterdämmerung*, with an investment of $250,000 from the association. The total cost of the final two recordings would be $1.5 million. Soon, however, Decca realized that it could not muster the money to continue, although the orchestra's board was still tentatively thinking of presenting concert performances of *Siegfried* in the 2000–2001 season and *Götterdämmerung* in 2001–2002.

The project was not entirely dead without Decca. Once it was clear that the British company was washing its hands of the second half of the Cleveland *Ring*—whose first half had sold miserably, like virtually everything else on the recent international classical market—the Musical Arts Association began investigating other options. Gary Hanson, the orchestra's associate executive director, explored the possibilities with Telarc International, the local company that had made Dohnányi's initial Cleveland recordings. Telarc declined. Then Hanson and Morris came up with an imaginative plan: Self-produce the recording of the concert performances of *Siegfried* and *Götterdämmerung* by making tapes of the radio broadcasts and then polishing them in "patch" sessions (to correct mistakes or imbalances) after the concerts. This method would cost $500,000, as opposed to $1.5 million for commercial recording. By agreement with Decca, the final two operas would be boxed with the first two.

It was not to be. At first, Dohnányi rejected the broadcast-patch system, insisting that internationally known singers might not show up for performances not released on a major label. Then he agreed on condition that the recordings feature young, unknown singers on the verge of major careers. This idea was deemed implausible, and the project was scrapped.

✻   ✻   ✻

In 1996, Dohnányi and the orchestra made two trips to Europe—the first, in March and April, to eight cities (with a final concert conducted by Boulez at Paris's modern Cité de la Musique) and the second, in August, to the Salzburg and Edinburgh festivals and concert halls in Germany and Spain. The three-week spring tour began at London's Royal Festival Hall, where Sir Georg Solti (who would make his debut with the orchestra the following season at Severance Hall) stopped by to say hello to the musicians, but not to stay for the concert. One visitor who did listen, Philip Hensher of *The Daily Telegraph*, was exhilarated by Dohnányi's performances of works by Ligeti, Wagner, Schumann, and Stravinsky. Weeks before the concert, he had ranked Cleveland third among the world's great orchestras, just behind those of Vienna and Berlin: "Under Christoph von Dohnányi, the Cleveland Orchestra has become the most characterful and perceptive of American orchestras; capable of great force and drive, but with a suavity which seems to suit its music director's glamorous, intellectual style." From London, the tour moved on to Berlin, Hamburg, Budapest (where the orchestra had last played in 1979 under Lorin Maazel), Vienna, Lucerne (Easter Festival), Amsterdam, and Paris. In many tour reviews, the word "cool" showed up referring to Dohnányi's interpretations, though one Vienna newspaper ran a headline that read, "Cleveland Took Vienna By Storm," and Klaus Geitel, critic of the Berliner *Morgenpost*, said of Dohnányi's performance of Stravinsky's *The Firebird* that "we may never hear this dance poem performed in such glowing colors again."

Between this tour and the summer tour (including the orchestra's last residency in Salzburg), Decca cancelled a proposed recording of Mahler's Symphony No. 2 under Dohnányi, weeks before the scheduled sessions. At that moment, the second half of the *Ring* recording was still up in the air. "Morally, we are committed to it," said Evans Mirages, Decca's vice president for artists and repertoire. But morals were fated to take a back seat to finances, especially at a time when the classical recording industry was in deep trouble. With U. S. production costs for one orchestra disc averaging $200,000, the American Federation of Musicians needed to rethink its stance on the funding of recordings. But it never did, and commercial orchestral recording in America was doomed.

Soon, as the Musical Arts Association moved forward with an ambitious plan to renovate Severance Hall, Dohnányi would decide that his Cleveland tenure was nearing its end.

Building for the
Millennium

*M*ore than 60 years after its opening, Severance Hall still looked and felt like a building from the 1930s. Its main concert hall was a jumble of styles. In 1996, Christoph von Dohnányi again declared that the modernist "Szell shell" should be removed and replaced by something more architecturally faithful to the auditorium and acoustically warmer. And in the process, the E. M. Skinner organ should be restored and brought down to the stage. In response, a task force led by orchestra trustee Alex Machaskee, president and publisher of *The Plain Dealer*, began to evaluate the status of the hall.

The result was a major fund-raising program that set a goal of $100 million by the year 2000 for operating support, the endowment fund, and the Severance Hall project. Richard J. Bogomolny, who had served as association fund-raising chairman and succeeded Ward Smith as board president in the fall of 1995, emphasized the need to take these crucial steps to lead the orchestra into the next century. "As an organization that is *not* in crisis, we face the serious threat of complacency," he told the trustees in January 1996. "As a long-standing community treasure, we could be overlooked in the euphoria of dynamic new civic venues. And as a team that is ranked number one, we might be tempted to rest on our laurels, inviting a successful challenge from an aggressive competitor. In every way for the Cleveland Orchestra, standing still would mean falling behind." The association's goals could be met, said Bogomolny, by raising $35 million for the Annual Fund, $15 million for special projects, $30 million for the endowment, and $20 million for Severance Hall.

The beginning of the orchestra's 1996–97 season coincided with the official kickoff of the $100 million comprehensive fund-raising campaign, now called "Our Legacy to the 21st Century: The Campaign for the Cleveland Orchestra." The Musical Arts Association had begun raising money the previous season through the Annual Fund, which netted $6.1 million. But the campaign received its major push in September 1996 when board president Bogomolny, former chairman and chief executive officer of First National Supermarkets, and his wife, Patricia Kozerefski, made an inaugural gift of $3 million. To honor the couple, the association voted to name the grand foyer at Severance Hall after them.

The most intriguing (and provocative) aspect of the campaign, from the standpoint of both the musicians and the public, was the proposed renovation, restoration, and expansion of Severance Hall. In the main auditorium, which hadn't been refurbished since opening in 1931, the work would include the removal of the "Szell shell," the transformation of the stage to conform with the rest of the Art Deco architecture, and the moving of the disused E. M. Skinner organ (from its loft above the stage). The renovation would involve inevitable but controversial changes to the admired acoustics.

The project would also include a 39,000-square-foot addition to the rear of the building. The association hired David M. Schwarz Architectural Services of Washington, D.C., and Fort Worth, Texas, for the job. Schwarz was chosen for his ability to preserve and enhance historic buildings. His collaborators would be GSI Architects and Panzica Construction, both Cleveland firms, and acousticians Christopher Jaffe and Paul Scarbrough, from the Connecticut-based acoustical firm of Jaffe, Holden, Scarbrough. Jaffe already had a close connection with the orchestra: he had worked on the acoustics of Blossom Music Center until George Szell decided to bring in his German colleague, Heinrich Keilholz, to finish the project (and, largely, draw on Jaffe's ideas).

Soon after Schwarz submitted designs, the trustees realized that a $20 million budget wouldn't meet the orchestra's needs. For $20 million, Schwarz's plan could accomplish four goals: restore the concert hall; add restrooms, especially for women (who had been forced to wait in long lines during intermission); reinstall the restored E. M. Skinner organ; and create a loading dock, a first for the hall. For $30 million, the hall could have new accommodations for patrons, spaces for public activities, a bona fide restaurant (the old hall never had a kitchen; the new one would have four), a gift shop, and a new circulation pattern that would correct the traffic-flow problem that had plagued concertgoers for decades. To replace the cramped ground-floor hallway through which most patrons entered the building, Schwarz envisioned two wide galleries leading to a spacious new lobby (where first the motor driveway and then the Keynote Restaurant had been located), which then would lead up to the grand foyer. The $30 million plan was adopted (it eventually would cost $36.7 million). Daily responsibility for the renovation was assigned to associate executive director Gary Hanson, who would win plaudits from every side for his meticulous attention to detail.

✿   ✿   ✿

Amid planning for the renovation, the orchestra continued its 1996–97 season. One of the highlights was the debut of Sir Georg Solti, the 84-year-old conductor laureate of the Chicago Symphony, who had been Dohnányi's first boss in Germany. His concerts in April 1997 at Severance Hall, which included Bartók's Concerto for Orchestra and Beethoven's Symphony No. 5, turned out to be his last with the Cleveland Orchestra: He died in Italy in late summer, though his passing was overshadowed by the death the same weekend of Princess Diana Spencer in a car crash in Paris.

Much attention was focused on Dohnányi, who had agreed to become principal conductor of the Philharmonia Orchestra of London starting in September 1997. Would he continue as Cleveland's music director beyond his current contract, which was set to end in 2000? His stock was still high. When he took the orchestra to Carnegie Hall in January 1997 for three concerts marking the 200th anniversary of Schubert's birth, he again was praised by the *New York Times*. "We were in safe hands at Carnegie Hall on Thursday, Friday and Saturday with Christoph von Dohnányi and the Cleveland Orchestra," wrote Paul Griffiths. "Schubert was in safe hands. The three concerts, celebrating his bicentenary, were beautifully prepared and beautifully accomplished; they were also beautifully programmed, around two finished symphonies and two unfinished, though with the underlying message that all symphonies are unfinished until realized in performance. Even then life goes on. But these performances, so definite, won't be forgotten."

Days before these concerts, the *Times*'s James R. Oestreich placed Dohnányi's Cleveland accomplishment in perspective in an interview, headlined "Out from Under the Shadow," that essentially said the orchestra could no longer be considered George Szell's domain:

> Throughout [Dohnányi's] tenure, the Cleveland has been cited as perhaps America's finest orchestra, more or less on a par with the august philharmonics of Vienna and Berlin. And Mr. Dohnányi has increasingly been credited with the achievement, which, despite numerous and crucial changes of personnel in recent years, seems only to have grown more impressive.

As impressive as the achievement may have been, Dohnányi sensed that the time to move on was approaching. No one was more distressed about the failure to complete the *Ring* cycle than Dohnányi himself, who had been having difficulty communicating with Morris and Bogomolny about this and other subjects. In the case of Dohnányi and Morris, it was a matter of two brilliant and stubborn men not always seeing eye to eye, especially on the subject of artistic control. In the case of Bogomolny, the problem was inexperience in dealing with a strong-willed music director. In time, these men would work out many of their differences. But the frustrations surrounding the *Ring* cycle crystallized for Dohnányi the fact that he was ready to go on to the next phase of his career. If there was to be no conclusion to the *Ring* recording in Cleveland, he would have to seek new challenges elsewhere.

The saga of the *Ring* recording had not reached its climax by the spring of 1997, when Dohnányi signed a new contract to continue as music director until 2002, with an option to remain until 2004. His decision to become principal guest conductor of the Philharmonia Orchestra of London would not affect his Cleveland duties. Still, upon signing the new agreement with Cleveland in June 1997, Dohnányi sent the Musical Arts Association a clear signal that his tenure was on the wane. "My staying has two essential motivations. First, my love of this orchestra and the way they make music. The orchestra also has to have time to find the right successor," he said. "There is an inevitable end to this. If nature does it, OK. Otherwise, I do it. . . My main concern is the continuation of my work here. I have seen institutions go down, and it's hard to build up."

But if not Dohnányi, who would keep the institution on top? The field was meager, especially if measured in terms of hallowed names. There was little likelihood that such veteran conductors as Claudio Abbado, Sir Colin Davis, Bernard Haitink, Carlos Kleiber, or Carlo Maria Giulini would consider taking over in Cleveland. They could make better money in Europe, and work less. Even in competition with American orchestras, Cleveland faced unique obstacles: a city slightly off the beaten path, with unpredictable weather and fewer perceived amenities than in larger population centers. The recording industry would be no help: a conductor with a contract in Europe was no longer assured that any orchestral recordings would be made in the United States.

Still, the conducting world did have some figures who showed potential. Among those who had stood on the Cleveland Orchestra's podium in recent seasons, Franz Welser-Möst and Christoph Eschenbach had made positive impressions. David Zinman, the Baltimore Symphony's departing music director, also was admired, but he was preparing to become music director of the Aspen Music Festival. Other names came up: Sir Simon Rattle (soon leaving the City of Birmingham Symphony Orchestra for the life of the guest conductor), Esa-Pekka Salonen (music director of the Los Angeles Philharmonic), Michael Tilson Thomas (happily ensconced at the San Francisco Symphony), and Christian Thielemann (music director of the Deutsche Oper Berlin).

The Musical Arts Association began the search process in January 1998 by forming an Artistic Direction Committee, chaired by trustee James D. Ireland III, to develop criteria for selection of a new music director and to make recommendations to the board. In addition to Ireland, the committee consisted of trustees Bogomolny, John Ong, and Ward Smith; orchestra members William Preucil, Robert Vernon, Richard King, and Ronald Bishop; and, representing the staff, Morris, Hanson, artistic administrator Edward Yim, and orchestra manager NancyBell Coe. They would review the qualifications of more than 100 conductors.

The public could soon start to speculate on the top candidates. The orchestra's 1998–99 season included fall performances led by Welser-Möst, Salonen, Eschenbach, and Thielemann. As it turned out, none of their concerts suggested, conclusively or otherwise, that a music director had been found. Whether or not they froze under the pressure, these conductors failed to make convincing cases that they were qualified to lead the orchestra into the future. Of the four, only Salonen sounded comfortable with his repertoire (works by Debussy, Nielsen, and Bartók, which could not establish his ability in the Central European music at the core of Cleveland's tradition). Welser-Möst appeared distracted and enervated, not the incisive maestro he had been during previous engagements with the orchestra. Eschenbach, a dynamo on other occasions, led a performance of Mahler's Symphony No. 5 so distorted as to render the piece almost unrecognizable. Thielemann was commanding, in his strange way: he treated Beethoven's Symphony No. 5 with perplexing and willful heaviness. The public, and the musicians, were bewildered.

To add to the confusion, the *Los Angeles Times* ran a story in early February 1999 stating that Salonen had turned down an offer from Cleveland and pledged his continuing allegiance to the Los Angeles Philharmonic. "I'm very pleased he's going to stay here," said Willem Wijnbergen, the orchestra's executive director at the time. "We want him here. He made a wise decision." The incident caused consternation in Cleveland, where no one at Severance Hall would comment (another long-standing Cleveland Orchestra tradition). Ireland soon told the trustees that no such offer had been made, but that a possible source for the story had emerged: "It was learned recently that the LA rumor actually was attributed to a comment supposedly made by a Musical Arts Association Trustee to a counterpart Trustee of the Los Angeles Philharmonic."

Then, silence for four months. On June 7, the orchestra announced that Welser-Möst, chief conductor at the Zurich Opera, would succeed Dohnányi at the start of the 2002–2003 season. The Austrian conductor came to Cleveland that day to attend a press conference and to sign a five-year contract. He had been a conductor since his teens—his repertoire was enormous, ranging from beloved symphonic literature to contemporary works—and he had served as music director of the London Philharmonic for five turbulent years. With Welser-Möst's appointment, Cleveland's board was poised to achieve something that had eluded the orchestra since the 1940s—a seamless transition between music directors. According to Bogomolny, the choice had been carefully weighed: "In selecting the seventh music director of this distinguished Orchestra, it was necessary to find a musical leader who will continue the artistic legacy of the organization as it is known throughout the world," he told the orchestra's trustees before the public announcement.

> Equally important was to find an individual who could boldly lead the Orchestra into the twenty-first century with initiative, distinction, and vision. In the search, Franz Welser-Möst stood apart. He represents a new generation of conductors . . . equally at home with the classical and Central European repertoire, . . . [and] with the innovative and unusual music of the 20th century. Most importantly, he is firmly grounded in the great musical traditions of The Cleveland Orchestra.

Welser-Möst's appointment impressed the music world for at least one other reason: Cleveland was the first of nine American orchestras looking for a new music director to complete its search.

❀   ❀   ❀

From the moment he told the board to begin searching for his successor, Dohnányi demonstrated that he had no intention of being a lame-duck music director. He proved it by continuing to be the biggest champion of the Severance Hall renovation project, by hiring superb players for the orchestra, by programming with flair, and by taking his ensemble on successful foreign tours. In the seasons before and following the announcement of his departure, Dohnányi led a bounty of world premieres in Cleveland: John Williams's Trumpet Concerto (with principal trumpet Michael Sachs),

Elliot Carter's *Allegro scorrevole*, John Adams's *Century Rolls* (with pianist Emanuel Ax), Christopher Rouse's *Der gerettete Alberich* (a percussion concerto featuring Evelyn Glennie), Paul Schoenfield's Viola Concerto (with principal violist Robert Vernon), Charles Ives's Emerson Concerto (with pianist Alan Feinberg), Magnus Lindberg's *Cantigas*, Nicholas Underhill's *Aspirant Variations* (written for the orchestra's flute section), and Jeffrey Rathbun's *Motions for Cellos*.

In May 1998, Dohnányi took the orchestra to China for the first time. In Beijing, they gave a concert at the Great Hall of the People for an audience of almost 10,000. Among the concertgoers was Chinese president Jiang Zemin, who sat with Morris and his wife, Jane, listening to Bartók's Divertimento for Strings, Strauss's *Till Eulenspiegel*, and Dvořák's "New World" Symphony. One taxi driver indicated how special the city considered their Western guests. "Oh, you Cleveland Orchestra," he told first assistant principal cellist Richard Weiss. "You big potato." Along with Beijing, the orchestra made its debut in Shanghai (in a 3,500-seat basketball arena in front of an enormous, idyllic mural), and gave five performances in Japan and two in Hong Kong.

The orchestra played for foreign audiences again in January 1999 in the Canary Islands, where Dohnányi led four concerts at the Festival de Musica de Canaris. In Las Palmas, Cleveland became the first American orchestra to play in the two-year-old Auditorio Alfredo Kraus, whose stage features an enormous window with a spectacular view of the sea. After concerts in Tenerife, the orchestra headed to Madrid and Barcelona before ending the tour in Paris with performances at the Salle Pleyel and Cité de la Musique, where they presented the European premiere of Ives's Emerson Concerto (again with Feinberg as soloist).

The orchestra was on its way to Madrid on January 25 when it learned of the sudden death of Robert Shaw, 82, who had served as director of choruses and associate conductor from 1956 to 1967. "He inspired thousands and thousands of people who have sung for him and hundreds and hundreds of choral conductors who have worked with him," said Robert Porco, who succeeded Gareth Morrell as the orchestra's director of choruses in 1998.

The chorus was still under Morrell's leadership in July 1997, when it undertook its own foreign tour to three cities in Great Britain. Morrell, who would depart the following season to become an assistant conductor at the Metropolitan Opera, led Brahms's *A German Requiem* in Oxford, England. The chorus sang the same work in Cardiff with the BBC National Orchestra and Chorus of Wales under Richard Hickox, with Norwegian soprano Solveig Kringelborn and Welsh bass-baritone Bryn Terfel as soloists. Then the Cleveland singers were off to Birmingham, England, to perform Walton's *Belshazzar's Feast* with Sir Simon Rattle and the City of Birmingham Symphony Orchestra and Chorus and to record the piece for EMI Classics. The two-day recording session, in Birmingham's acoustically lauded Symphony Hall, proved an exhilarating event for the American and British choristers, thanks in large part to the irrepressible Rattle. "I can't imagine there has been quite so much sound in this hall," he told the singers at one point. "I can't wait for the disc to come out to get letters from angry neighbors." The recording instead was nominated for a Grammy Award in 2000, the same year the chorus finally returned to Europe with the Cleveland Orchestra and Dohnányi—for the first time since 1986—to perform Berlioz's *La damnation de Faust* at the Edinburgh Festival.

✻   ✻   ✻

The year 2000 also brought the orchestra more attention at home than it had received in several decades. Over the past three years, Severance Hall had undergone the renovation, restoration, and expansion that was part of the Musical Arts Association's $100 million capital campaign. The project inspired thousands of local residents to make donations, and it involved hundreds of construction workers and artisans.

"The notion wasn't to copy the original building but to emulate it in a way that's extraordinary sympathetic but not identical," said architect David M. Schwarz.

During much of the renovation process, life in the hall went on almost as usual. To control the level of construction noise while the orchestra was still rehearsing and performing there, red, yellow, and green flags were flown on brackets throughout the building. The red flags warned workers not to make a peep and the yellow to proceed with quiet chores, such as ripping up carpet. The green flag provided the "all clear" signal to dig, rivet, and hammer as necessary.

In March 1999, the orchestra moved downtown to the restored Allen Theatre in Playhouse Square, allowing work at Severance Hall to proceed virtually around the clock. Coordinated by associate executive director Gary Hanson and overseen by the hall's maintenance chief and restoration expert, Sonya Winner-Smith, the final phase of renovation kept the musicians and the public in suspense for 10 months.

Finally, on January 8, 2000, a capacity audience of music lovers, politicians, community leaders, and other prominent local figures, as well as both American and foreign music critics, got their first taste of the hall. The gala concert presented Dohnányi and the orchestra in works by Sir Harrison

Birtwistle (Sonance Severance 2000, a dour fanfare commissioned for the occasion), Wagner, Vaughan Williams, Ligeti, Prokofiev, and Ravel. A nervous public quickly learned that the hall had received the added pinch of reverberation it long had needed, the public spaces had been vastly enlarged, and the building's architectural integrity had not only been maintained, but also gloriously enhanced.

Without actually sitting in the hall, an even wider audience could form an opinion about the new stage. The gala concert, televised by Cleveland public station WVIZ, was broadcast live throughout Ohio—with sportscast-style close-ups of the musicians and helpful information about the program's works projected on the screen—and aired nationally in an abridged version several months later by PBS. Most of the orchestra's musicians found, to their relief, that the acoustics had not been compromised, though some players weren't convinced that the new platforms for the wind, brass, and percussion sections helped balances.

All of the improvements, including the lovely restoration of the 400-seat Reinberger Chamber Hall, had made Severance capable of accommodating artistic events appealing to a wider range of tastes. With Schwarz, whose striking (and extravagant) design brought the stage into elegant accord with the rest of the Art Deco architecture, acousticians Christopher Jaffe and Paul Scarbrough had transformed one of the finest concert halls in the United States into one of the best in the world.

"Severance Hall sounds as seductive as it looks," wrote Allan Kozinn in the *New York Times*.

"The result of the renovation is wonderful, a rich, warm sound that enhances The Cleveland Orchestra's renowned clarity," raved *Musical America*. "Now it has an added bloom on its famous sound, taking the ear to new places and revealing scores in all their pulsating immediacy."

– 38 –

Coda

A renovated hall and a bright financial picture alone can't ensure that the Cleveland Orchestra will continue to hold its enviable position in the musical world. But the orchestra's history suggests that its commitment to remaining "second to none" will not waver.

The musicians of the Cleveland Orchestra enjoy an artistic stature at home and abroad that is virtually unequalled. In terms of lifestyle, they are worlds away from the players of the 1950s and earlier who had to scrape out livings after their short orchestra seasons with second jobs. In December 1999, the musicians signed their first five-year contract, which put the minimum annual salary at $85,280, a figure that will rise to $100,620 by the end of the agreement. Just as important is the pension plan, a sore spot until well into the 1970s. The pension will rise to $55,000 a year in 2004, placing Cleveland even with Philadelphia and only slightly behind Chicago and New York (all cities with much higher costs of living).

Institutional finances are currently healthy, partly as a result of the comprehensive fund-raising campaign that ended in January 2000. During the 1998–99 season, the orchestra balanced its budget for the seventh year in a row. Its budget for 1999–2000 was $30.4 million.

Many challenges lie ahead in maintaining the ensemble as a top-flight artistic force. Like every major American orchestra, Cleveland's ensemble is addressing the collapse of the classical recording industry by exploring new ways to preserve its artistry. The short-term solution is the release of self-produced archival recordings, an area in which orchestras such as the New York Philharmonic and the Philadelphia Orchestra have had major success. So, too, has Cleveland, with two superb compact disc sets—a 75th-anniversary album of performances led by each of its music directors, and a collection of previously unreleased George Szell recordings (from live concerts) to mark his centenary. The main distribution channel for music soon will be the Internet. Orchestras will have to be part of this revolution if they hope to continue documenting their music-making and reaching out to a wider audience.

International endeavors have been, and will continue to be, important to the Cleveland Orchestra. But just as vital are activities that will affect the institution at home. The orchestra—founded, after all, for educational purposes—continues to develop its admired "Learning Through Music" program, which takes members of the ensemble into public schools to make music an essential part of the curriculum. These sessions are nurturing new generations of audiences. The Cleveland Orchestra Youth Orchestra and Youth Chorus promise to do the same, as well as train musicians who might enter the field as professionals. The Martin Luther King Jr. Celebration Concert, an annual event for two decades, and the July Fourth concerts at Public Square in downtown Cleveland, are signals that the orchestra welcomes the broadest possible audience. Its Community Relations Committee is reaching out to ethnic and racial minorities, who will make vibrant contributions to the city's cultural life.

Volunteerism on behalf of the orchestra, healthy since the ensemble's founding in 1918, still thrives through groups ranging from the Women's Committee, the Junior Committee (an organization for younger women), and the Blossom Women's Committee to the three choral organizations that perform with the orchestra (Cleveland Orchestra Chorus, Cleveland Orchestra Children's Chorus, Blossom Festival Chorus), and the large core of ushers who are devoted to Severance Hall patrons. Individual and corporate philanthropy continues to keep the orchestra alive and thriving. The most recent fund-raising campaign, which raised $115.9 million, represented an outpouring of affection by the community for its stellar cultural institution.

Artistically, the Cleveland Orchestra will continue to undergo significant changes. Resident conductor Jahja Ling succeeded Leonard Slatkin as Blossom Festival Director in the summer of 2000. Franz Welser-Möst, who still looks like a graduate student on the podium, will be 42 when he succeeds Christoph von Dohnányi in September 2002 (only Szell and Dohnányi were older when they took charge in Cleveland).

In the midst of change, the orchestra will need to serve its public with continued commitment and retain the artistic excellence that has brought high honor to the institution and its city. Reflecting the "culture of a community" has become infinitely more difficult than it was a century ago, when Theodore Thomas proclaimed that a symphony orchestra could have a profound local impact. The fact that the Cleveland Orchestra has sustained a towering artistic level while enduring its share of ups and downs is a mark of the dedication and vision that have made the institution a cultural icon.

Attaining this position has been possible because the forces that built and nurtured the orchestra remained focused, without compromise, in one direction: the music. Founding manager Adella Prentiss Hughes had experience first as a musician and then as an impresario, which gave her a perspective based on artistic priorities. She promoted the symphonic medium in Cleveland for two decades until the circumstances were ripe to create a homegrown ensemble. Hughes knew that provincialism would never suffice. With Nikolai Sokoloff at her side, she pushed to draw the finest musicians and guest artists to Cleveland instead of relying on local talent. She couldn't have achieved much of anything had she not had the foresight to surround herself with intelligent and generous trustees whose love for their city was accompanied by an enthusiasm for great music.

The Cleveland Orchestra has been run by trustees, and especially by strong board presidents, who have left the artistic side of the operation to the music directors but who have also maintained an abiding interest in the institution's artistic welfare. Since the earliest days, the board of the Musical Arts Association has been kept abreast of major and minor musical developments, and not merely in the cause of keeping budgets in line: Cleveland's conductors and managers have always made it clear to its trustees that the musical product comes first. This may be one reason why Cleveland came to be known, for better or worse, as a "connoisseur's orchestra." Promotion of self has never been a major concern of this institution, which has favored tasteful, careful marketing over splashy display. Promotion of the music has meant everything.

And how could it not, considering the artistic leaders who imposed their wills on the orchestra? Sokoloff may not have been a supremely gifted maestro, but he was an adventurous and forceful leader. Artur Rodzinski deserves a higher place in the orchestra's history than is generally acknowledged. If a world war hadn't been raging at the time, Erich Leinsdorf might have had a more significant impact than he did. It was left to Szell, a master who arrived at just the right moment, to take the orchestra to the highest level and give it an international profile. His legacy in Cleveland runs so deep that his name will be forever linked with its orchestra. So, in crucial ways, will those of Lorin Maazel and Dohnányi, both of whom stretched the ensemble's artistic reach and brought new facets to its personality.

That Cleveland has deserved, and continues to deserve, its world-class orchestra cannot be questioned. The confluence of an industrial city, bold artistic and business leaders, superior musicians, and devoted audiences has brought about a remarkable musical phenomenon. Throughout its history, the Cleveland Orchestra has reflected a community's ability to sustain—as board president Thomas L. Sidlo put it so eloquently—"something fine and beautiful."

Acknowledgments

The number of people who assisted me during the writing of this book could fill a symphony orchestra.

Chief among the "players" was Carol Jacobs, peerless archivist of the Cleveland Orchestra, who pointed me to sources primary and otherwise, shared discoveries, and answered thousands of questions. Her knowledge and patience were bountiful. My thanks also to Thomas W. Morris, the orchestra's executive director, and Gary Hanson, associate executive director, for granting me permission to make use of a large portion of the archives. The treasure trove of information I found laid the foundation for the book's narrative.

I am indebted to several other archive collections and their staffs, including those at the New York Philharmonic (Barbara Haws, Michele Smith, Richard Wandel), Chicago Symphony (Brenda Nelson-Strauss), Philadelphia Orchestra (JoAnne Barry), Metropolitan Opera (Robert Tuggle and John Pennino), and Western Reserve Academy (Thomas L. Vince). Carol Bradac at the Pittsburgh Symphony and James North, who has catalogued Artur Rodzinski's New York Philharmonic recordings, made important contributions, as did Chris Krosel at the Diocese of Cleveland, Rebecca Ball in the Fine Arts Department at the Cleveland Public Library, and Richard Worthing and Jerome LaCorte at Kent State University.

The Sokoloff family graciously allowed me to quote from Nikolai Sokoloff's unpublished memoirs. Edward Brown made it possible for me to peruse the diary kept by his father, Percy W. Brown, a longtime trustee of the Musical Arts Association. Mary Wagner provided a crucial link to Cleveland's musical past by sharing her fascinating study of the city's early orchestras.

Among the valuable and delightful conversations held in preparation for this book, two stand out. Kurt Loebel, a member of the Cleveland Orchestra's first violin section for 50 years, brought his special brand of candor to the topic, making pertinent observations and digging deeply into his enormous collection of orchestra memorabilia. Klaus George Roy, the orchestra's program editor and annotator from 1958 to 1988, provided an endless flow of amusing anecdotes and crucial insights.

I can't begin to thank Richard Rodzinski enough for sharing family correspondence and photos, and stories about his father, Artur Rodzinski. Jack Saul, the guru of Cleveland classical music record collectors, never blinked when I asked him if he would share yet another mint copy from his vast collection of Cleveland Orchestra recordings. He made it possible for me to hear how the orchestra sounded from the moment it began making recordings five years after its founding. Mark Kanny, music critic of the *Pittsburgh Tribune-Review*, engaged in provocative discussions about many aspects of orchestral life and shared many Szell recordings.

Among current and former members of the Cleveland Orchestra staff, I must extend my gratitude to Charles Calmer, Julie Demorest, Amy Gill, Louis Lane, Michael Maxwell, Timothy Parkinson, Sharon Ruebsteck, Carolyn Schwartz, Eric Sellen, Rita Shapiro, Christopher Stager, Kelly Tweeddale, and Mary Yee.

I received encouragement and input from dozens of wonderful friends and colleagues, as well as help from sources who generously shared their experiences: Theodore Albrecht, John Stark Bellamy III, David Bianculli, Bette Bonder, Rose Breckenridge, Michael Charry, Robert Conrad, Paul Cox, Irene Dias, Jean Dubail, Ross Duffin, John Ferrito, Robert Finn, Annie Fullard, Betty Gilruth, Roger Gilruth, Mary Ann Griebling, Stephen T. Griebling, David Hall, Kenji Harahata, Janice Harayda, Frank Hruby, Gwen Jacobs, Keith A. Joseph, Philippa Kiraly, Cheryl Kushner, Zachary Lewis, Steven Litt, Dale Loomis, Lois Mitchell, Thomas Mitchell, Peter Nicholson, Paula Ockner, Stephen Ockner, Tim Page, Lewis Perelman, Catherine Peterson, Eunice Podis, Steven Richman, James Rosenthal, Robert Ryker, Harvey Sachs, Susan Schwartz, Beverly Simmons, Bill Wendling, Lynne Woodman, and Abe Zaidan.

Mark Dawidziak, a longtime chum and colleague, provided sage advice on subjects relating to publishing and authorship. Carolyn Jack applied keen editorial skills to the manuscript. I thank them both.

A number of photographers, or their families, granted me permission to use their work, which makes an essential contribution to the story. I am especially grateful to Stephen Landesman for the photos taken by his father, Geoffrey, and to Holly Hastings, for the photos by her father, Peter. These photographers chronicled more than 50 years of Cleveland Orchestra history. Since the 1980s, Jack Van Antwerp and Roger Mastroianni have captured the orchestra in indelible ways.

To Gray & Company, Publishers, I convey warm thanks for careful attention to literary and other matters. David Gray proved a superb editor, constantly urging me to hone the manuscript to more readable proportions. Rosalie Wieder's experience as a musician helped to make her a remarkably observant, and meticulous, copy editor. I also thank Karen Fuller, Chris Andrikanich, Frank Lavallo, Jane Lassar, and Caroline Kruse for their amiable and efficient assistance.

My parents, Lenore and Sy Rosenberg; brothers, Marc and Andy, and their families; aunt, Joan Harmon; and in-laws, Bernette and Doug Brewster, were unfailingly sympathetic during my orchestral adventure. Finally, this book wouldn't exist without the love and understanding of my wife, Kathy, and children, Seth and Emily, who endured prolonged periods of neglect and gave me the support I needed to undertake and complete the task. They deserve the biggest fanfare of all.

Photo Credits

1–21. Courtesy of The Cleveland Orchestra Archives.

22–24. Geoffrey Landesman, courtesy of The Cleveland Orchestra Archives.

25. Geoffrey Landesman, courtesy of Rodzinski.

26–28. Geoffrey Landesman, courtesy of The Cleveland Orchestra Archives.

29. Halina Rodzinski, courtesy of The Cleveland Orchestra Archives.

30–31. Geoffrey Landesman, courtesy of The Cleveland Orchestra Archives.

32. Geoffrey Landesman, courtesy of Cleveland Press Collection, Cleveland State University.

33. Courtesy of Cleveland Press Collection, Cleveland State University.

34. Geoffrey Landesman, courtesy of The Cleveland Orchestra Archives.

35. Courtesy of The Cleveland Orchestra Archives.

36. Courtesy of *The Plain Dealer*.

37. Geoffrey Landesman, courtesy of The Cleveland Orchestra Archives.

38. Löwy-Wien, courtesy of The Cleveland Orchestra Archives.

39–41. Geoffrey Landesman, courtesy of The Cleveland Orchestra Archives.

42. Robert Carman, courtesy of The Cleveland Orchestra Archives.

43–45. Geoffrey Landesman, courtesy of The Cleveland Orchestra Archives.

46. Courtesy of *The Plain Dealer*.

47. Geoffrey Landesman, courtesy of Cleveland Press Collection, Cleveland State University Library.

48–49. Courtesy of The Cleveland Orchestra Archives.

50. Susanne Faulkner Stevens, courtesy of Metropolitan Opera.

51. Robert Carman, courtesy of The Cleveland Orchestra Archives.

52. Courtesy of The Cleveland Orchestra Archives.

53–54. Bert Arenson, courtesy of The Cleveland Orchestra Archives.

55. Courtesy of The Cleveland Orchestra Archives.

56–58. Robert Carman, courtesy of The Cleveland Orchestra Archives.

59–63. Peter Hastings, courtesy of The Cleveland Orchestra Archives.

64–65. Robert Carman, courtesy of The Cleveland Orchestra Archives.

66. Robert Carman, courtesy of The Cleveland Orchestra Archives.

67. Peter Hastings, courtesy of The Cleveland Orchestra Archives.

68. Eugene Cook, courtesy of The Cleveland Orchestra Archives.

69. Peter Hastings, courtesy of The Cleveland Orchestra Archives.

70. Adrian Siegel / Philadelphia Orchestra, courtesy of The Cleveland Orchestra Archives.

71–74. Peter Hastings, courtesy of The Cleveland Orchestra Archives.

75. William G. Volpe / *The Plain Dealer*, courtesy of *The Plain Dealer*.

76–81. Peter Hastings, courtesy of The Cleveland Orchestra Archives.

82. C. H. Pete Copeland / *The Plain Dealer*, courtesy of *The Plain Dealer*.

83. Courtesy of Cleveland Orchestra Archives.

84. Peter Hastings, courtesy of The Cleveland Orchestra Archives.

85. Kurt Mutchler / *The Plain Dealer*, courtesy of The Cleveland Orchestra Archives.

86. Peter Hastings, courtesy of The Cleveland Orchestra Archives.

87. Courtesy of The Cleveland Orchestra Archives.

88. Peter Hastings, courtesy of The Cleveland Orchestra Archives.

89. Roger Mastroianni.

90. Peter Hastings, courtesy of The Cleveland Orchestra Archives.

91. Courtesy of The Cleveland Orchestra Archives.

92–93. Jack Van Antwerp, courtesy of The Cleveland Orchestra Archives.

94. Roger Mastroianni.

95. Jack Van Antwerp, courtesy of The Cleveland Orchestra Archives.

96–97. Roger Mastroianni.

98. Peter Hastings, courtesy of The Cleveland Orchestra Archives.

99–103. Roger Mastroianni.

Notes

Abbreviations

COA—Cleveland Orchestra Archives
      BT—Board of Trustees files
      C—Conductor files
      GM—General Manager files
      GE—General Manager/Executive Director files;
      M/PR—Marketing/Public Relations files
EB—Edward Brown collection
KL—Kurt Loebel collection
RR—Richard Rodzinski collection

Chapter 1: Overtures

20   *in 1840:* Grossman, p. 12.

20   *Baptiste Dreher:* Van Tassel, p. 350.

21   *"great musical highway":* Alexander, p. 19.

21   *"the finest we have ever heard":* Ibid.

21   *Austrian-born Ferdinand Puehringer:* Grossman, p. 61.

22   *"The orchestral numbers":* Alexander, p. 19.

22   *"the most supreme":* Quoted in Grossman, p. 35.

22   *Hans von Bülow:* Sadie, *New Grove*, Vol. III, p. 452.

23   *"150 performers":* Hughes, p. 42.

23   *"In the best sense":* Quoted in Schonberg, p. 215.

23   *Starting in the early 1890s:* Van Tassel, p. 925.

23   *The conductorship of the Philharmonic Orchestra:* Alexander, p. 20.

24   *"scenes are enacted there":* Van Tassel, p. 483.

24   *The conductor was Johann Beck:* Van Tassel, pp. 84–85.

25   *Beck conducted:* Wagner, p. 39.

25   *"Beck produced unexpectedly good results":* Quoted in Alexander, p. 22.

25   *"experimental Cleveland Symphony Orchestra season":* Ibid., p. 23.

25   *"success had come and come to stay":* Quoted in Wagner, p. 46.

25   *as well as works by:* Beck performed Pittsburgh composer Charles D. Carter's overture *As You Like It*; Cleveland composer Harry Lawrence Freeman's "Intermezzo and Prayer" from his music drama, *Nada*; and Cleveland composer Charles Somme's *Hero and Leander*. Grossman, p. 81.

25   *"of the story of":* Quoted in Grossman, p. 80.

26   *"knocking [down] has always been a favorite diversion":* Ibid., p. 47.
26   *a benefit concert on May 28, 1901:* Ibid., p. 47.
26   *The new institution:* Alexander, p. 24.
26   *all men, according to* Town Topics: Wagner, p. 62.
27   *"not only a 'pop' but":* Quoted in Wagner, p. 64.
27   *"if these same guarantors":* Ibid., p. 64.
27   *"inadequate rehearsals":* Ibid., p. 66.
28   *"The Sunday pops":* Hughes, p. 151.
28   *"Mr. Timmner is well remembered":* Flyer announcing Timmner recital April
     24, 1912.
28   *"new broom who can sweep":* Quoted in Wagner, p. 77.
29   *"we have local men":* Ibid., p. 81.
29   *"It is too rotten":* Cleveland News, June 16, 1913.
29   *"They practice with a long stogie":* Ibid., April 24, 1913.
29   *"People in general like music":* Cleveland Press, May 6, 1913.
30   *"on the job all the time":* Ibid., May 30, 1913.
30   *"Rehearsals are held each day":* Ibid.
30   *"If any doubt existed":* Ibid., June 16, 1913.
30   *"I cannot possibly see":* COA/M/PR, unknown source.
30   *He would be paid $2,400:* Wagner, p. 85.
31   *"There is no question":* Quoted in Wagner, p. 86.
31   *a court case against Timmner:* Wagner, p. 87.
31   *employment out of the region:* The Timmners moved to Glendale, California,
     where he served as first violinist in a string quartet from 1916 to 1918 and sub-
     sequently appeared as guest soloist with the Grauman Symphony Orchestra
     in San Francisco. Timmner was considered for the conductor's post with the
     Municipal Symphony Orchestra of San Francisco, but the job never materi-
     alized. During the 1930s, he principally played in a string quartet in southern
     California. From Wagner, pp. 91–92.
31   *"Years later, with a twinkle in his eye":* Hughes, p. 152.

CHAPTER 2: ADELLA

33   *"Why don't you bring them here?":* Hughes, p. 45.
33   *"My personal bank account":* Ibid., pp. 45–46.
33   *"The aftermath of this concert":* Ibid., p. 46.
34   *"It's good enough":* Ibid., p. 29.
34   *"a tall and handsome blonde":* Ibid., p. 30.
34   *"And there began":* Ibid.
34   *"The noise was overwhelming":* Ibid., p. 35.
35   *At Vassar, she had met:* Ibid., p. 66.
36   *"My first interest was orchestral music":* Ibid., p. 103.
36   *she managed 162 concerts by 11 orchestras:* the Boston Symphony, Chicago
     Symphony (sometimes known as the Theodore Thomas Orchestra),
     Cincinnati Symphony, Cleveland Orchestra, Detroit Symphony, Minneapolis
     Symphony, New York Philharmonic, New York Symphony, Philadelphia

Orchestra, Pittsburgh Orchestra, and Russian Symphony.

36 *Bohemian-born contralto:* The rest of the cast comprised Melanie Kurt (Brünnhilde), Johannes Sembrich (Siegfried), Clarence Whitehill (Wanderer), Frieda Hempel (Forest Bird), Carl Braun (Fafner), Otto Goritz (Alberich), and Albert Reiss (Mime).

37 *"He is all":* Hughes, p. 97.

37 *"the most interesting":* Ibid. Strauss was in the midst of work on his newest opera, *Salome,* when he came to the U.S. in 1904. The opera had its premiere on December 9, 1905, in Dresden.

37 *"Cleveland knew its Richard Strauss":* Ibid., p. 98.

37 *The 24-year-old Stokowski:* Hughes, p. 126.

37 *"young Jupiter of a conductor":* Ibid.

38 *Beginning with the 1906–07 season:* Hughes, p. 103.

38 *But this still would have paled:* During this tour, Mahler led the same program—which included the Bach-Mahler Suite for Orchestra (with Mahler playing harpsichord)—in Pittsburgh, Cleveland, Buffalo, Rochester, Syracuse, and Utica. From New York Philharmonic Historic Recordings CD compilation.

38 *"Little Mahler":* Hughes, p. 130.

38 *The school was to be modeled:* Ibid., p. 153.

39 *"Now Cleveland is recognized":* Cleveland News, March 21, 1913.

39 *"the poor things":* Hughes, p. 173.

39 *"A very successful season":* Ibid., p. 190.

40 *"fired my imagination at once":* Ibid., p. 202.

40 *"the interests of music in the community":* COA/BT, Musical Arts Association articles of incorporation, October 5, 1915.

40 *"But the music":* Hughes, p. 208.

40 *"Shut your eyes":* Ibid., pp. 208–09.

41 *"SIEGFRIED IN BOX":* Ibid., p. 211.

41 *"Sometimes a prophet":* Cleveland Leader, September 16, 1917.

CHAPTER 3: BIG NOISE AND AN ORCHESTRA

43 *"the big noise now":* Hughes, p. 254.

43 *"Is there to be an orchestra?":* Cleveland Town Topics, December 7, 1918.

44 *"I'm sorry, but I could not help overhearing":* Sokoloff, p. 127.

44 *"We recognize the difficulty":* COA/GE, first Sokoloff contract, signed September 12, 1918, by Sokoloff and D. Z. Norton.

44 *"to stimulate music":* Cleveland News, September 18, 1918.

45 *"supplied and conducted":* Sokoloff, p. 10.

45 *"Finally, and for the first time":* Ibid., p. 86.

45 *Cecelia Casserly:* Ibid., p. 91.

46 *"Sokoloff was a vivid, interesting person":* Hughes, p. 246.

47 *"So you see":* Sokoloff, p. 115.

47 *"Cleveland is sponging":* Ibid., p. 116.

47 *"to promote pupil attendance":* Hughes, p. 248.

47   *"I realized that our visiting orchestra concerts":* Ibid., p. 249.
48   *Hughes's salary figure:* COA/GE, letter from John L. Severance to Hughes, August 12, 1918.
48   *"I was equally frank":* Hughes, p. 250.
48   *not the Plaza:* COA/GE, letter from Severance to Sokoloff, June 8, 1919.
48   *"No matter how many":* Sokoloff, p. 123.
49   *$6,000 for the nine-month period:* COA/GE, first Sokoloff contract, signed September 12, 1918, by Sokoloff and D. Z. Norton. Sokoloff's annual salary continued to rise throughout his tenure—$10,000 (1919–20 season), $20,000 (1920–21), $21,000 (1921–22), $22,000 (1922–23), $23,000 (1923–24), $24,000 (1924–25), $25,000 (1925–26), $27,000 (1926–27 and 1927–28), and $30,000 (1928–1933).
49   *"a fine local orchestra":* COA/BT, minutes, September 10, 1918.
49   *She told him that the Fortnightly Musical Club:* COA/GE, Hughes letter to Severance, September 13, 1918.
49   *"in a cubbyhole":* Sokoloff, p. 123.
49   *"I interviewed many teachers":* Ibid., p. 124.
49   *"Cleveland is to have":* The Plain Dealer, September 13, 1918.
49   *"Get used to pronouncing it":* Cleveland News, September 18, 1918.
49   *"central pivot":* Ibid.
49   *"I find that Cleveland":* Ibid.
50   *Now, in the midst of a war:* COA/GE, Hughes letter to Severance, September 13, 1918.
50   *Hughes nixed the idea:* Hughes, p. 253.
50   *Sibelius's Symphony No. 1:* Sokoloff, p. 124.
50   *"to assemble fifty men":* Hughes, p. 252.
51   *The flu, which would eventually kill:* Chicago Sun-Times, January 10, 1999.
51   *"to provide music":* Cleveland Town Topics, October 19, 1918.
51   *"I would like to make":* Ibid.
51   *"Mr. Sokoloff comes to us":* The Plain Dealer, September 29, 1918.
51   *"my Man Friday":* Sokoloff, p. 125.
52   *"Sokoloff and I went":* Cleveland Press, December 10, 1928.
52   *"the first bass was":* Ibid.
52   *Clarinetist Frank:* Frank Hruby's son, also Frank, recalls going to a rehearsal of Rimsky-Korsakov's *Scheherazade* at Masonic Hall at age 2 ¼, getting excited, and making noise. Sokoloff said, "Who let that child in here?" Frank Hruby (son), interview by author, March 14, 1999.
52   *"I found another family":* Sokoloff, p. 125.
53   *On one extraordinary day:* COA/M/PR, Player bios.
53   *the Chicago Orchestra:* The Chicago Symphony has had several names throughout its history
53   *"relegated to the limbo":* The Plain Dealer, October 27, 1918.
53   *"whatever of latent talent":* Musical Leader, October 31, 1918.
54   *"to furnish the services":* COA/GE.
54   *Powers agreed:* Hughes, p. 254.
54   *"In the desert waste":* The Plain Dealer, November 3, 1918.
54   *". . . a notable attraction":* The Plain Dealer, November 10, 1918.

54   *"Most of the members this year":* Cleveland News, November 13, 1918.

55   *Hughes claims:* Hughes, p. 254.

55   *"it would be impossible to groom":* Sokoloff, p. 128.

55   *"A profitable and most agreeable time":* Cleveland News, November 20, 1918.

55   *The first piece the orchestra rehearsed:* Cleveland Press, December 10, 1928.

55   *"with highly promising results":* The Plain Dealer, November 24, 1918.

55   *"The concert at once":* Sokoloff, p. 125.

56   *"You'll be surprised":* Cleveland Leader, December 8, 1918.

56   *None of the critics:* Cleveland News, November 13, 1918.

56   *"with a list":* The Plain Dealer, December 8, 1918.

56   *"not only a faithful shepherd of his flock":* Ibid.

57   *The day of the inaugural concert:* COA/GE, Hughes letter to Winston & Livingston, December 11, 1918.

57   *Sokoloff's program:* Another major event happened the same night in New York. Modest Altschuler conducted the Russian Symphony Orchestra, of which Sokoloff had been concertmaster in 1910 when they played in Cleveland, in the American premiere of Prokofiev's "Classical" Symphony. The Plain Dealer, December 8, 1978.

57   *"By securing the Orchestra":* COA/M/PR, inaugural program book, December 11, 1918.

57   *"I presume that":* Cleveland Press, December 12, 1918.

58   *"highly intelligent musicianship":* Ibid.

58   *"Conductor Nikolai Sokoloff has succeeded":* The Plain Dealer, December 12, 1918.

58   *"I can honestly say":* COA/M/PR, Rev. A. B. Stuber letter to Hughes, December 12, 1918.

59   *"His fifty-four players":* The Plain Dealer, December 22, 1918.

CHAPTER 4: THE LUSTY INFANT

61   *"Engage oboe bassoon viola":* COA/GE, Hughes telegram to Sokoloff, late December 1918.

61   *They hadn't been paid:* COA/GE, Hughes letter to Sokoloff, April 4, 1919.

61   *"We can afford two horns":* COA/GE, Hughes telegram to Sokoloff, March 5, 1919.

62   *"most of the people":* Sokoloff, p. 137.

62   *The conversation led:* Hughes, p. 258.

62   *"It may be shown":* Ibid. p. 280.

62   *"He revealed attainments":* The Plain Dealer, January 31, 1919.

63   *"He will select movements":* Cleveland News, January 2, 1919.

63   *Stransky suggested a member:* Hughes, p. 259.

63   *"Never have three":* COA/GE, Hughes letter to John L. Severance, April 1, 1919.

63   *Another important addition:* COA/M/PR, Player bios.

64   *The orchestra would need:* Hughes, p. 253.

64   *"This orchestra a greata thing":* COA/GE, Hughes letter to Severance, March

15, 1919.

64 *"though how the marvel of hearing"*: Sokoloff, p. 138.

64 *The association agreed to come up with the $400*: COA/GE, Hughes letter to Severance, April 4, 1919.

64 *"why, you ought to go"*: *Cleveland News*, May 28, 1919.

65 *As the inaugural season came to a close*: Hughes, p. 264.

65 *"You have accomplished marvels"*: COA/GE, Severance letter to Sokoloff, June 8, 1919.

66 *Hughes was invited*: Hughes, p. 264.

66 *"an excellent drill master"*: *Cleveland News*, October 22, 1919.

66 *"What are you?"*: Ibid.

66 *"Nikolai Sokoloff's Cleveland Orchestra"*: *Chicago Evening American*, January 23, 1920.

67 *a blonde*: Sokoloff, p. 140.

67 *"had nothing to give"*: Ibid., p. 141.

67 *"I looked him"*: Ibid.

67 *"We have run"*: COA/GE, Hughes letter to Severance, March 3, 1920.

67 *"organize and rehearse"*: Ibid.

68 *at $5 to $10 a week*: COA/BT, minutes, June 1, 1920.

68 *"As a result of this teaching, a band was organized"*: Ibid.

68 *In addition to Clarke*: Grossman, p. 97.

68 *"It is most astonishing"*: COA/GE, Mischa Levitzki letter to Hughes, March 14, 1920.

69 *"I again heard"*: COA/GE, Severance letter to Hughes, March 31, 1920.

69 *Sokoloff found the experience "unnerving"*: Sokoloff, p. 142.

69 *"I want to give people"*: *Musical America*, May 1, 1920.

70 *After 162 concerts*: COA/M/PR, Summary of the Nineteen Seasons of the Symphony Orchestra Concerts, 1901–1920.

70 *"Cleveland may well"*: COA/GE, Hughes letter to Severance, March 3, 1920.

70 *"As a matter of unadulterated fact"*: *Sunday News-Leader*, September 5, 1920.

70 *"a truly great symphony orchestra"*: *Cleveland News*, October 22, 1920.

71 *"When Cleveland is exhumed"*: Ibid., February 4, 1921.

71 *After the first concert, Toscanini attended a supper party*: Ibid.

71 *"Our marriage resulted"*: Quoted in *The Plain Dealer*, December 10, 1978.

71 *"Oh, do you sing?"*: Hughes, p. 277.

72 *"the string band"*: *New York Tribune*, February 14, 1921.

72 *"As far as could be judged"*: *New York Herald*, February 14, 1921.

72 *"the quality of the band"*: *New York Times*, February 14, 1921.

72 *"with all the crudities of youth"*: *New York Evening World*, February 14, 1921.

72 *"In the Tschaikowsky sixth"*: *New York World*, February 14, 1921.

72 *"One of these days"*: COA/GE, 1920–21.

73 *"misunderstanding and discontent"*: COA/GE, minutes of Orchestra Committee Meeting with Hughes, February 9, 1921.

73 *Minimum weekly salaries for first violins*: COA/GE, orchestra salaries 1920–21.

73 *"A player cannot do"*: *The Plain Dealer*, March 25, 1921.

73   *"No member of the orchestra":* Ibid.

74   *"I adore jazz": Cleveland News,* May 20, 1921.

74   *"the rhythm of jazz":* Ibid.

74   *At the end of its first season:* COA/BT, Hughes report entitled "The Musical Arts Association Symphony Orchestra Concerts Eighteenth Season 1918–19."

74   *A year later, she assigned it to the eighth position:* COA/GM, MAA statement, 1919–20.

74   *"a good orchestra of the second class":* Sokoloff, p. 147.

74   *"I believe in ensemble, naturally":* Ibid.

75   *"The building process has been completed": The Plain Dealer,* January 1, 1922.

75   *"In my humble opinion": Cleveland Press,* October 21, 1921.

75   *The Philadelphia Orchestra had amassed:* MAA brochure, 1921–22.

76   *to raise the $200,000: Cleveland Commercial News,* March 16, 1922.

76   *"are strongly endowed":* Ibid.

76   *"The bars are down":* COA/BT, Dudley Blossom memo to Men's Committee, June 26, 1922.

76   *"over five times the number":* COA/BT, Blossom letter to donors, July 21, 1922.

76   *the final tally was 803 donors: Cleveland News,* October 20, 1922.

77   *"Under the present condition in Cleveland":* COA/BT, minutes, January 4, 1923.

77   *The Women's Committee of the Cleveland Orchestra was formed:* Hughes, p. 283.

77   *Music Memory Contest, which was inaugurated:* Ibid., p. 292.

78   *At the inaugural contest:* Ibid.

78   *"The important thing in all this":* COA/GM, transcript of Sokoloff speech to music teachers, April 9, 1923.

78   *"to cultivate a distaste for jazz": Mid-Week Review,* March 23, 1921.

78   *"By the orchestra's fifth season":* Sokoloff, p. 159.

79   *"You know I was much younger":* Document for Brunswick recording of Rachmaninoff's Second Symphony, 1928.

79   *After further performances:* The Cleveland Orchestra had made its debut at Carnegie Hall, under Sokoloff, on January 24, 1922, playing Beethoven's *Coriolanus* overture, Brahms's Symphony No. 2, Respighi's *Fountains of Rome,* and Loeffler's *A Pagan Poem.*

79   *"It was a regular love feast":* Document for Brunswick recording of Rachmaninoff's Second Symphony, 1928.

79   *"the only symphonic organization except one":* COA/GM, Henry L. Hewes to Severance, March 8, 1923.

79   *"Casella himself has conducted":* Ibid.

79   *At the end of the 1922–23 season:* COA/BT, minutes, June 26, 1923.

80   *"All the musicians of importance": The Plain Dealer,* August 1, 1923.

80   *When Janovsky died:* COA/BT, minutes, June 26, 1923.

80   *When the Cleveland ensemble: Allentown (Pa.) Chronicle-News,* July 16, 1923.

CHAPTER 5: FOR POSTERITY

81   *"The only woman manager in America": Raleigh [N.C.] Observer-Dispatch*, September 2, 1923.

81   *The orchestra comprised 16 nationalities:* COA/GE, 1923–24.

82   *"Be on time": Cleveland News*, October 1, 1923.

82   *Salesmen in piano stores:* COA/GE, Hughes letter to William E. Walter, September 28, 1923.

82   *"This will deprive the radio people":* Ibid.

83   *When Mengelberg:* COA/BT, minutes, December 15, 1923.

83   *The Brunswick agreement:* Ibid.

84   *The record company requested that the piece be edited:* COA/GE, Brophy telegram to orchestra, early January 1924.

84   *an assignment that Sokoloff:* COA/GE, Hughes telegram to Brophy, January 10, 1924.

84   *Sokoloff conducted:* COA/GE, Brophy telegram to orchestra, early January 1924.

84   *Only 47:* COA/GE, Brophy letter to Hughes, January 24, 1924.

84   *"Why we ever had the courage":* Sokoloff, p. 187.

85   *The board authorized:* COA/BT, minutes, November 13, 1923. The soloists were soprano Jeannette Vreeland, mezzo-soprano Mildred Brynars, tenor Robert Quai, and bass Norman Jolif.

85   *"In fact, one can say": Cleveland Press*, April 25, 1924.

86   *"a grand musical love-feast": Cleveland News*, February 8, 1924.

86   *"He wields the baton with infectious persuasion": Cleveland Press*, February 8, 1924.

86   *"You have no cultural roots": The Plain Dealer*, February 7, 1924.

86   *"fell down completely":* COA/GE, Hughes letter to Sokoloff, February 25, 1924.

86   *"He was a dear and charming man":* Sokoloff, p. 165.

87   *"gift of summoning orchestral sonorities": The Plain Dealer*, February 27, 1924.

87   *"a splendid musician":* Sokoloff, pp. 268–69.

87   *"We found him": Cleveland Press*, February 13, 1925.

87   *"But, I assure you": Cleveland Times*, February 12, 1925.

88   *Leopold Stokowski wrote to him:* COA/GE, Stokowski letter to Sokoloff, September 26, 1925.

88   *"Alas, all of our engagements":* COA/GE, Sokoloff letter to Stokowski, October 1, 1925.

88   *"loved the orchestra":* Sokoloff, p. 166.

88   *"Respighi got more from the players": Cleveland Press*, February 4, 1927.

89   *"In France, we are not so particular":* Sokoloff, pp. 166–67.

89   *"I saw immediately":* Ibid., p. 167.

89   *Sergei Prokofiev, who had been recommended:* COA/GE, Koussevitzky letter to Sokoloff, November 22, 1928.

89   *"falls down dead":* COA/GE, Hughes letter to Sokoloff, September 25, 1929.

89   *The composer wrote to his manager:* COA/GE, Prokofiev letter to Haensel &

Jones, September 29, 1929.

90   *"enfant terrible": Cleveland News*, January 9, 1930.

90   *"I don't want to think":* Ibid.

90   *"There is something baffling": Cleveland Press*, January 10, 1930.

90   *"quite respectable and large":* Quoted in Robinson, p. 242.

CHAPTER 6: UPBEATS AND DOWNBEATS

93   *"Before importing or endeavoring":* COA/GE, clause in union contract to members of Musical Mutual Protective Association, Local 4 of the American Federation of Musicians, December 20, 1926.

93   *The orchestra's quality certainly rose:* COA/M/PR, Player bios.

93   *by the 1924–25 season:* COA/BT, minutes, annual meetings, 1919–1925. The budgets for these years were The budgets for these years were: $31,876.08 (1918–19), $121,095.62 (1919–20), $165,268.62 (1920–21), $185,403.50 (1921–22), $223,707.34 (1922–23), $231,941.51 (1923–24), and $223,409.56 (1924-25).

93   *Blossom calmed Ginn down:* Ibid.

94   *Principal oboist Philip Kirchner was paid:* COA/GE, player salaries for 1924–25 season.

94   *"This will make six years":* COA/BT, minutes, January 27, 1926.

94   *At the end of the 1926–27 season:* COA/BT, minutes, June 22, 1927.

94   *"unbecoming a gentleman":* Quoted in COA/BT, executive committee minutes, May 7, 1926.

94   *The incident involved:* Ibid.

95   *Sokoloff wrote to Mrs. Mnuchin:* COA/GE, Sokoloff letter to Mrs. Marutha Mnuchin (misspelled Nienuchin), December 30, 1925.

96   *"scoops and wobbles": New York Herald Tribune*, December 4, 1929.

96   *"colossal outwellings": New York Evening Post*, December 4, 1929.

96   *"the new music of the evening":* Ibid.

96   *The recording was released the following September:* Brunswick advertisement of Sokoloff-Cleveland recordings, 1929.

97   *"Altogether apart":* COA/M/PR, *Phonograph Monthly Review*, September 1928.

97   *"I have decided not to announce":* COA/GE, Sokoloff letter to Hughes, September 10, 1928.

97   *"The whole symphony": New York Evening Sun*, December 5, 1928.

CHAPTER 7: HOME, SWEET SEVERANCE

99   *The place went wild:* Hughes, p. 78. The Severance donation of $1 million would be worth $10 million in the year 2000.

99   *Hughes and the public:* Ibid.

100   *"Grand Orchestra Ousted":* Ibid., p. 108.

100 *"I have personally raised"*: COA/GE, Hughes letter to Andrew Carnegie, March 10, 1905.

100 *Two years later, Hughes made her plea:* Hughes, p. 75.

101 *"was never driven to occupy"*: Quoted in *The Gamut*, Number 18, Spring/Summer, 1986.

101 *"John Royal made us welcome"*: Hughes, p. 75.

101 *"When the time comes"*: Hughes, p.76 (Rockefeller letter to Hughes, November 28, 1922).

101 *She even commissioned drawings:* Ibid.

101 *a subcommittee:* COA/BT, executive committee, minutes, January 7, 1926. Subcommittee consisted of Mrs. A. A. Brewster (chairman), Mrs. Newton D. Baker, Mrs. Myron Wick, Mrs. F. F. Prentiss (ex-officio, as current president of the Women's Committee), and Mrs. Dudley S. Blossom.

101 *The orchestra's Executive Committee, except:* Ibid.

101 *shouldn't necessarily be located:* Hughes, pp. 77–78.

101 *an oasis of parks: The Gamut*, Number 18, Spring/Summer, 1986.

102 *When Robert E. Vinson:* Hughes, p. 77.

102 *In February, board members received preliminary sketches:* Klassen, p. 26.

102 *"During the period from 1921 when the first"*: Ibid.

102 *"Will there not be occasion"*: COA/GE, Severance letter to Hughes, February 13, 1928.

103 *"that he was not willing"*: COA/GE, Hughes notations of conferences with John L. Severance, July 13, 1928.

103 *In June 1928: The Gamut*, Number 18, Spring/Summer, 1986.

103 *Hughes and McCornack:* COA/GE, McCornack statement included in Hughes letter to Frank Ginn, January 29, 1929.

103 *provided a specific dollar figure:* COA/GE, 1929–30.

103 *the 161-acre Severance estate in Cleveland Heights:* Now the site of the commercial development known as Severance Town Center at the corner of Mayfield and Taylor roads.

103 *"The two butlers"*: Hughes, p. 80.

103 *donating $750,000:* COA/GE, original Pledge of Donation agreements signed by Mr. and Mrs. Blossom on February 1, 1929.

103 *a motion to engage Walter McCornack:* COA/BT, executive committee, minutes, December 20, 1928.

104 *an annual rental fee of one dollar:* COA/GE, Indenture of Lease between Western Reserve University and Musical Arts Association signed April 3, 1930.

104 *"a personally conducted quiet campaign"*: COA/BT, executive committee, minutes, December 20, 1928.

104 *"important and reliable information"*: COA/GE, Ginn telegram to Severance, January 4, 1929.

104 *Severance would come to agree:* COA/GE, Severance letter to Ginn, January 15, 1928. In the same letter, Severance agreed with Ginn on an issue that would have long-term ramifications for the musicians" "I do not think the time has arrived when we can consider pensioning employees. This hardly seems an appropriate thing for us to do when we are dependent upon the generos-

ity of so many people to keep the Orchestra going."

104   *suddenly, and mysteriously, resigned:* COA/GE, Warner, McCornack & Mitchell letter, October 15, 1928.

104   *accused McCornack:* COA/GE, Ginn letter to Severance, February 7, 1929.

104   *"I have a very distinct feeling":* COA/GE, McCornack letter to Hughes, January, 24, 1929.

104   *Mrs. Severance's death:* The orchestra gave concerts in Mrs. Severance's memory on January 31 and February 1, 1929, at which 12-year-old violinist Yehudi Menuhin made his debut with the ensemble.

104   *whatever amount was needed:* COA/GE, Severance letter to Ginn, March 25, 1929.

105   *"I hope that by the time":* Ibid.

105   *The board president proposed:* COA/GE, Severance letter to Ginn, February 14, 1929.

105   *McCornack was removed:* Despite his unhappy experience with the Musical Arts Association, McCornack (1877–1961) became a pioneer in the field of public housing and served as dean of the School of Architecture and Regional and City Planning at MIT from 1939–45.

105   *a contract with Walker and Weeks:* COA/BT, contract, May 18, 1929.

105   *"ever-ready wit":* Hughes, p. 79.

105   *"Cleveland Habit":* *Cleveland News*, April 7, 1929.

105   *"While my active interest":* Hughes, p. 79.

106   *"Of course," their letter said:* COA/GE, Cleveland Boy's Farm letter to Blossom, April 16, 1929.

106   *"the financial emancipation": Time,* May 6, 1929. The campaign raised $4,970,195, equivalent to $49,701,950 in the year 2000.

107   *"I do not wish to interfere":* COA/GE, Severance letter to Ginn, May 23, 1929.

107   *"because I know":* COA/GE, Stokowski letter to Sokoloff, July 24, 1929.

107   *The spacious mansion on their estate:* A piece of the linen-fold paneling from the dining room at Longwood was installed in the organ gallery of the renovated Severance Hall in 2000.

107   *"Please see that the seats":* Quoted by Hughes in *Cleveland Town Topics,* February 2, 1929.

107   *The architects were renowned: The Gamut,* Number 18, Spring/Summer, 1986.

108   *"The architects have much improved":* COA/GE, Hughes letter to Sokoloff, August 20, 1929.

108   *The size of the main auditorium: The Gamut,* Number 18, Spring/Summer, 1986.

108   *"Even the fifty-cent seat holders":* Ibid.

109   *"Mr. Severance called me in":* COA/GE, Vosburgh letter to Hughes, August 9, 1929.

109   *"I must say I never imagined":* COA/GE, Sokoloff letter to Severance, April 21, 1920.

109   *"This was the most ghastly thing imaginable":* Sokoloff, p. 209.

110   *Severance would lose: The Gamut,* Number 18, Spring/Summer, 1986.

110   *"any and all funds":* COA/GE, Severance memo to Musical Arts Association,

November 27, 1929.

110   *The orchestra hoped to inhabit its new home:* A much larger building was under construction in New York City during the same period Severance Hall was rising—the Empire State Building.

110   *"I think we would regret it":* COA/GE, Severance letter to Ginn, March 31, 1930.

110   *"Erecting steel":* COA/GE, Ginn telegram to Severance, January 20, 1930.

110   *"the steel work":* COA/GE, Ginn letter to Severance, March 28, 1930.

111   *"We do not want":* COA/GE, Ginn letter to Loeffler, May 7, 1930.

111   *"I am feeling very fit":* COA/GE, Sokoloff letter to Hughes, June 13, 1930.

111   *"will be directly over the orchestra":* Cleveland Press, September 20, 1930.

111   *"The orchestra this year has given me the greatest joy":* COA/GE, Sokoloff letter to Gilman, October 29, 1930.

112   *"increasing tendency to speechify":* Cleveland News, December 19, 1930.

112   *To test out the new hall's acoustics:* The Plain Dealer, February 2, 1931.

112   *"for congregations, commencements":* The Plain Dealer, February 6, 1931.

112   *"When the pledge":* Ibid.

112   *"is in the last analysis":* Ibid.

113   *"contribute to the organized life":* Ibid.

113   *Among the opening-night audience:* Hughes, p. 81.

113   The Plain Dealer's *banner headline:* The Plain Dealer, February 6, 1931.

113   *"One sees many premieres":* Ibid.

113   *"We hope that 'society'":* Cleveland Press, February 6, 1931.

114   *"My heart is full of joy":* COA/GE, Hughes note to orchestra, February 7, 1931.

114   *"When we held our first rehearsal there":* Sokoloff, p. 210.

115   *Writing to Severance:* COA/GE, Ginn letter to Severance, February 27, 1931.

115   *E. M. Skinner, in town soon afterward:* COA/GE, Ginn letter to Severance, April 10, 1931.

115   *"if the audience":* COA/GE, Alice C. Hickox letter to Hughes, March 3, 1931.

115   *"Mrs. Hickox's":* COA/GE, Hughes letter to Ginn, March 9, 1931.

CHAPTER 8: EDUCATION AND TRANSITION

117   *"for the purpose of furthering":* COA/BT, Musical Arts Association Articles of Incorporation, October 5, 1915.

117   *she helped Almeda Adams:* Hughes, p. 153.

117   *"The heart of the matter is what we do for the children":* COA/GE, Sokoloff speech to music teachers, April 9, 1923.

118   *"Our children are learning":* Ibid.

118   *33 members of the orchestra:* Massmann, p. 22.

118   *Daniel Gregory Mason:* Hughes, p. 293.

119   *Theodore Thomas had started:* Massmann, pp. 4–9.

119   *"The idea of musical literacy":* Ibid., p. 11.

119   *"For learning that lasts":* Ibid., p. 34.

120   *Little Folks' Programs:* Ibid., pp. 44–5.

120 *"Musicianly listeners"*: Ibid., p. 39.

120 *"And I said to my wife"*: Hughes, p. 295.

121 *"My dear Adella"*: COA/GE, Sokoloff letter to Hughes, May 2, 1930.

121 *"There were moments of a fine realization"*: Cleveland Press, March 2, 1927.

121 *"Its reading was sadly lacking"*: Cleveland Press, October 21, 1927.

121 *"first time given in a stage presentation"*: Program, Manhattan Opera House, April 26–30, 1929.

121 *"Musically, the occasion"*: New York Telegram, April 27, 1929.

122 *"No matter how kindly"*: New York Times, February 21, 1930.

122 *"The playing of the Cleveland Orchestra"*: New York Evening World, February 21, 1930.

122 *"Rehearsal drill"*: Norwalk [Conn.] Hour, February 5, 1931.

122 *"Sokoloff would sometimes"*: Cleveland Press, April 23, 1982.

123 *"That crowd, that throng of people"*: COA/GE, Blossom speech at Women's Auxiliary Luncheon, University Club, January 11, 1928.

123 *he asked city officials*: COA/GE, Blossom letter to D. E. Morgan, City Manager, and Samuel Newman, Director, Department of Parks and Public Property, May 28, 1930.

124 *"If the wage which we pay"*: COA/GE, Ginn letter to Severance, April 18, 1931.

124 *principal oboist Philip Kirchner protested*: COA/GE, Kirchner letter to A. A. Brewster, August 12, 1933.

124 *The situation was so drastic*: COA/BT, minutes, December 31, 1931.

124 *"It was the sense"*: COA/BT, minutes, April 16, 1932.

124 *"the devoted and skillful guidance"*: COA/BT, resolution, July 27, 1932.

124 *"the orchestra had sort of outgrown him"*: Alice Chalifoux, interview by author, Cleveland Heights, Oh., November 15, 1998.

124 *"agreed with the management"*: The Plain Dealer, August 4, 1932.

125 *His emphasis is slightly different*: Sokoloff, p. 215.

125 *"Public attitude"*: Cleveland Press, July 28, 1932.

125 *"have excused shortness of temper"*: Reprinted in The Pittsburgh Press, August 7, 1932.

125 *"lonely figure"*: Associated Press article reprinted in Akron Beacon Journal, August 2, 1932.

125 *Ringwall, Eugene Ormandy, and Sir Hamilton Harty*: Cleveland Press, July 28, 1932.

125 *Blossom and Hughes*: Ibid.

125 *"caused a veritable riot"*: William E. Walter letter to Florence Sherwin, August 15, 1932.

125 *"Racially he is a Hungarian"*: Ibid.

126 *"Szell is now in his mid-thirties"*: Ibid.

126 *"I happened to have heard"*: Hughes letter to Walter, August 27, 1932.

126 *the press mentioned Artur Rodzinski*: Parade, August 18, 1932.

126 *"The Cleveland Orchestra management refuses to say"*: Cleveland Press, September 26, 1932.

127 *"Do not think that your future"*: COA/GE, Stokowski letter to Rodzinski, October 4, 1932.

127   *"Cleveland has one"*: *Cleveland News*, October 14, 1932.
127   *One person prominent in the music business*: Rodzinski, pp. 279–80.
127   *"Severance Hall is the most beautiful hall"*: *Cleveland Press*, December 29, 1932.
127   *"What a fine orchestra!"*: *Cleveland News*, December 29, 1932.
128   *"My private tip to the powers that be"*: Ibid., December 30, 1932.
128   *"to outline an agreement"*: COA/BT, minutes, December 28, 1932.
128   *upped to $30,000 when finances improved*: Rodzinski's annual Cleveland salary rose to $28,500 for the 1935–36 season and to $30,000 annually for the rest of his tenure.
128   *"It is understood that you will be accorded"*: COA/BT, minutes, January 9, 1933.
128   *Announcement of the appointment*: At the same meeting, results of negotiations on pay cuts for orchestra members were announced, with the players "agreeing to a contribution schedule on weekly salary of 10–15% up to $76.50 per week and 15% on wage of $80.00 or more." COA/BT, minutes, January 9, 1933.
128   *"The world has been too much for me"*: Hughes letter to Mrs. Archibald [Kathie] Diack , January 3, 1933.
129   *"is definitely settled"*: Hughes letter to Miss Cora A. Start, January 7, 1933.
129   *"We had a very exciting week"*: Hughes letter to Sokoloff, January 9, 1933.
129   *"can stand on his own merits"*: *Cleveland News*, February 20, 1933.
129   *"In many ways [Rodzinski] is an entirely different person"*: Hughes letter to Mrs. Forrest [Althea] Rutherford, January 24, 1933.
130   *"losing dignity fast"*: Vosburgh letter to Hughes, February 18, 1933.
130   *"gave parties mornings, noons and nights"*: United Press International article reprinted in *Poughkeepsie Sunday Courier*, February 5, 1933.
130   *"His work is so well known"*: *The Plain Dealer*, April 2, 1933. In the first of would become a long series of conflicts of interest, Elwell conducted the Cleveland Orchestra in the Overture and Finale to his own composition, *The Happy Hypocrite*, on April 3 and 5, 1930, at Masonic Hall, with Sokoloff conducting the rest of program.
130   *By the end of Sokoloff's tenure*: *Cleveland Press*, October 24, 1933.
130   *"Tell them good luck"*: *The Plain Dealer*, April 9, 1933.

Chapter 9: A New Level

133   *"He came out of the West"*: *Cleveland Press*, December 6, 1958.
133   *"people might think"*: COA/BT, annual meeting, June 28, 1933.
134   *"a lousy pianist"*: *New York Post*, November 18, 1938.
134   *for a salary of $100 a week*: RR, Stokowski letter to Rodzinski, May 19, 1926.
134   *Late in life*: Richard Rodzinski, interview by author, Shaker Hts., Oh., August 13, 1999.
135   *pinch his left arm*: Rodzinski, p. 112.
135   *A number of Cleveland players*: They were trombonist Guy Boswell, harpist Alice Chalifoux, flutist George Drexler, violinist Paul Gershman, violist

Samuel Goldblum, bassoonist William Polisi, violinist Fred Rosenberg, hornist Theodore Seder, and flutist Maurice Sharp. They posed with Rodzinski for a Geoffrey Landesman photo that appeared in *Cleveland Weekly* during the conductor's first week.

135 *"Black Monday"*: Alice Chalifoux, interview by author, Cleveland Heights, Oh., November 15, 1998.

135 *"The orchestra is a splendid one"*: COA/GE, Rodzinski address to members of the Women's Committee, September 29, 1933.

135 *Rodzinski told the women:* Ibid.

136 *"I believe that George Bernard Shaw":* Ibid.

136 *"With all the rich offerings":* COA/GE, Rodzinski remarks on WTAM radio, September 30, 1933.

136 *"You've got the best climate": Cleveland News*, September 27, 1933.

136 *"in three days of rehearsing": The Plain Dealer*, October 27, 1933.

137 *"I am very happy over the way the orchestra played":* RR, Rodzinski letter to Severance, October 27, 1933.

137 *"You are a blessing to us all!":* RR, Hayden letter to Rodzinski, November 7, 1933.

137 *"his sepia valet-chauffeur-butler": Cleveland News*, October 27, 1933.

137 *Severin Eisenberger, who was teaching:* Eisenberger (1879–1945), who heard Johannes Brahms, Hans von Bülow, and Anton Rubinstein in concert, studied with Theodor Leschetizky. He came to the U.S. in 1928 to teach in Cleveland.

137 *"I found that Clevelanders":* Rodzinski, pp. 90–91.

138 *Rodney C. Sutton's article: The Plain Dealer*, November 19, 1933.

138 *Denoe Leedy, in the Press: Cleveland Press*, November 25, 1933.

139 *"Musical History was made": Cleveland News*, December 1, 1933.

139 *47 minutes: Cleveland Press*, December 2, 1933.

139 *"one of the things for which people love you":* RR, Lake letter to Rodzinski, late 1933.

139 *"Rodzinski is a great conductor": The Plain Dealer*, December 3, 1933.

139 *"Mr. Rodzinski's programs":* COA/GE, Sowers letter to Blossom, November 24, 1933.

140 *"Jazz Invades Sacred Precincts": Cleveland Press*, January 23, 1934.

140 *Ermanno Wolf-Ferrari's one-act comic opera:* Rodzinski recorded the overture with the New York Philharmonic in February 1945.

140 *"I realize also":* COA/GE, Quimby letter to Rodzinski, March 6, 1934.

140 *"There should be a department of fine arts": Cleveland Press*, January 26, 1934.

140 *"There is a great deal of truth":* RR, Blossom letter to Rodzinski, February 12, 1934.

141 *"There are no vintage years in music": The Clevelander*, February 1934.

141 *"it had been suggested that we give": Cleveland News*, April 11, 1934.

141 *"Why not let him play": Cleveland Press*, April 14, 1934.

142 *The first list of possibilities:* COA/BT, minutes, January 26, 1934.

142 *Feodor Chaliapin:* COA/GE, Vosburgh letter to Rodzinski, April 12, 1934.

142 *Leedy told readers: Cleveland Press*, April 14, 1934.

142 *Lauritz Melchior, the reigning heroic tenor of the day: Cleveland News*, April

11, 1934.
142 *"just before intermission"*: The Plain Dealer, March 18, 1971.
142 *"Probably the only thing"*: Ibid., December 30, 1933.
143 *Ringwall and the orchestra*: COA/BT, minutes, January 26, 1934.
143 *"Now, for my usual plea!"*: COA/GE, Vosburgh letter to Rodzinski, June 21, 1934.
143 *"Not Indian tomtom beating"*: Cleveland News, June 6, 1934.
143 *he negotiated a deal*: COA/GE, Vosburgh letter to Phillips Carlin at the National Broadcasting Company, June 21, 1934.
144 *"So Dear Mr. Vosburgh"*: COA/GE, Rodzinski letter to Vosburgh, August 14, 1934.
144 *"I spent nearly three weeks in Russia"*: COA/GE, Rodzinski letter to Vosburgh, June 28, 1934.

Chapter 10: Nights at the Opera

145 *full-scale productions in 1899*: The Barber of Seville, Carmen, La Traviata, and *Faust*.
145 *"your service would include"*: COA/BT, minutes, January 9, 1933.
146 *"Believe me, this opera business is some job"*: COA/GE, Vosburgh letter to Rodzinski, May 15, 1934.
146 *"an absolute impossibility"*: COA/GE, Vosburgh letter to Wilhelm von Wymetal, April 10, 1934.
146 *Pinza informed his agent*: COA/GE, Alexander F. Haas, from NBC Artists Service, letter to Vosburgh, July 3, 1934.
146 *Edward Ziegler, the company's assistant manager,*: COA/GE, Ziegler letter to Vosburgh, May 14, 1934.
146 *Cleveland's manager*: COA/GE, Vosburgh letter to Judson, May 15, 1934.
146 *"We might just as well"*: Cleveland Press, July 21, 1934.
147 *"These young Ohio artists"*: COA/GE, Rodzinski interview on WTAM radio with Walter Logan, October 10, 1934.
147 *"fiery zeal"*: Musical America, November 10, 1934.
147 *"I defy anyone"*: Cleveland Press, November 2, 1934.
147 *"The dignity and sincerity"*: RR, King letter to Rodzinski, November 5, 1934. An idea of Rodzinski's Wagner conducting can gained from the New York Philharmonic recordings of excerpts from *Die Walküre, Tristan und Isolde,* and *Lohengrin* he made in May 1945 with soloists Helen Traubel and Herbert Janssen.
148 *"Somehow, the conceit of Strauss"*: Rodzinski, p. 111.
148 *"achieved a degree of perfection"*: Quoted in Rodzinski, p. 114.
148 *"They seemed, on the contrary"*: The Plain Dealer, November 9, 1934.
148 *"That its conductor can turn"*: Cleveland Press, December 14, 1934.
149 *"is as much at home"*: The Plain Dealer, January 4, 1935.
149 *Rodzinski, deeming it "the best opera written in this century"*: COA/GE, Rodzinski letter to Vosburgh, June 28, 1934.
149 *The directors listened*: Rodzinski, p. 97.

149 *"It was fortunate":* COA/GE, Rodzinski interview on WTAM radio with Walter Logan, October 10, 1934.

150 *Early in October:* COA/BT, minutes, October 4, 1934.

150 *Claire Reis:* Rodzinski, p. 117.

150 *The two Cleveland performances (January 31, February 2):* COA/BT, minutes, October 16, 1934.

150 *"Wymie":* Richard Rodzinski, interview by author, Shaker Heights., Oh., August 13, 1999.

150 *"Shostakovich's patterns and tempi":* Rodzinski, pp. 116–17.

151 *"pornophony":* Lebrecht, p. 263.

151 *"When you see the Cleveland Orchestra's presentation":* The Clevelander, January 1935.

151 *"has led to the erroneous assumption":* The Plain Dealer, January 31, 1935.

151 *"could have been younger":* Rodzinski, p. 118.

151 *Among the VIPs:* Ibid., pp. 118–19.

152 *"Shocked, Amused":* Ibid, p. 119.

152 *"The Lady Macbeth premiere":* Cleveland News, February 1, 1935.

152 *"Young Shostakovich":* Cleveland Press, February 1, 1935.

152 *"Packed House":* COA/GE, Rodzinski telegram to Shostakovich, February 2, 1935.

152 *The audience included Toscanini:* Rodzinski, p. 120.

152 *"performed magnificently":* New York Times, June 6, 1935.

153 *"Bravo, bravo, Rodzinski":* Rodzinski, p. 121.

153 *$1,900, which was applied to the tour fund:* COA/BT, annual meeting, minutes, June 26, 1935.

153 *But problems with materials:* COA/BT, minutes, March 25, 1935.

153 *Nelson Eddy as Figaro:* COA/GE, Vosburgh letter to Rodzinski, November 23, 1934.

153 *"Dr. Rodzinski, following tradition":* Cleveland Press, March 8, 1935.

154 *on the same program with his* An American in Paris: The Gershwin work was the first piece Rodzinski recorded with the New York Philharmonic, on December 11, 1944.

154 *"most accomplished performance":* Levant, p. 233.

154 *"From what I have heard":* COA/GE, Vosburgh letter to Severance, March 11, 1935.

154 *"It remains an incomparable masterpiece":* Cleveland Press, March 15, 1935.

154 *"management of the orchestra":* The Plain Dealer, April 12, 1935.

154 *"Porgy and Bess will be a fantastic hit":* Rodzinski, p. 125.

154 *"Received word from":* RR, Gershwin letter to Rodzinski, March 1935.

155 *"It would give me the greatest pleasure":* RR, Rodzinski letter to Gershwin, March 19, 1935.

155 *How the work would have been perceived:* There is an odd postscript to the Gershwin story, a Rodzinski memo to Vosburgh about upcoming orchestra concerts, including a Gershwin program: "However, if our Board decides to engage John Charles Thomas (for a downtown concert of popular music) and go ahead with plans for the Gershwin memorial, I recommend that Mr. Ringwall conduct the former, and Mr. [Alexander] Smallens be considered as

a conductor for the latter since he has conducted 'Porgy' and is acquainted with that type of music, which is entirely unknown to me." COA/GE, February 25, 1939.

155 *He requested that the board consider:* COA/BT, minutes, March 25, 1935.

155 *When Lulu didn't strike the board's fancy:* COA/BT, minutes, April 30, 1935.

155 *By the end of 1934–35:* Ibid.

156 *"During the second act":* Rodzinski, p. 138.

156 *"This reviewer has seen":* The Plain Dealer, November 1, 1935.

156 *"that conquering women":* Rodzinski, p. 138.

157 *"with world famous cast":* Ibid., p. 140.

157 *"The performance was a sensation":* Ibid., p. 141.

157 *"I have once again lost my father":* Ibid., p. 142.

157 *"Mr. Severance provided Artur":* Ibid., p. 137.

157 *"In a thousand ways":* Ibid., p. 142.

158 *"placed a microphone":* COA/GE, Vosburgh letter to Blossom, February 29, 1936.

158 *"that he was 100%":* COA/BT, executive committee, minutes, March 21, 1936.

158 *There was talk of abandoning the opera season:* Ibid.

159 *"The performance was exhilarating":* New York Times, November 1, 1936.

159 *"on the present basis":* COA/BT, executive committee, minutes, March 21, 1936.

159 *Whether 100 or more players:* Alice Chalifoux, interview by author, Cleveland Heights, Oh., November 15, 1998.

160 *"incomparably magnificent":* RR, Fuldheim letter to Rodzinski, December 5, 1936.

160 *"Though it makes extraordinary demands":* The Plain Dealer, December 4, 1936.

CHAPTER 11: AMAZED BY ARTUR

161 *"We only hear your criticism":* Rodzinski, p. 154.

161 *"a bundle of contradictions":* New York Post, November 18, 1938.

162 *Perhaps he landed in music:* RR, Scarlini letter to Richard Rodzinski, October 4, 1999.

162 *When management tried to engage:* The Plain Dealer, October 14, 1937.

162 *Albert Stoessel, a composer and conductor:* Cleveland Press, December 4, 1937.

162 *These were the same players:* Leon Zawisza, David Schwartz, Jac Gorodetzky, Theron McClure, and Tom Brennand.

162 *"There may be a hundred":* The Plain Dealer, October 15, 1937.

162 *"Artur had an uncanny feel":* Rodzinski, p. 160.

163 *"of their own accord":* COA/BT, minutes, September 16, 1937.

163 *"a great guy":* Alice Chalifoux, interview by author, Cleveland Heights, Oh., November 15, 1998.

163 *"let's say the strings botched":* Quoted in Trotter, pp. 384–85.

163　*"At the beginning of next season"*: COA/GE, Rodzinski memo "To the Members of all String Sections", April 16, 1941.

163　*"Good orchestras are not made"*: COA/GE, Mary Shuldiner letter to Cleveland Orchestra management, March 27, 1936.

164　*"With an orchestra of eighty"*: *Boston Transcript*, November 27, 1937.

164　*Vosburgh, always the voice of conscience*: COA/BT, minutes, February 25, 1935.

164　*"Why I should be expected"*: COA/GE, Fiore letter to Rodzinski, April 10, 1936.

165　*"How can I trust such a manager"*: COA/GE, Rodzinski letter to Vosburgh, May 30, 1936.

165　*"I understand—you all including"*: Ibid.

165　*"I am amazed, astonished"*: COA/GE, Vosburgh letter to Rodzinski, June 14, 1936.

166　*"the volume of sound"*: *Cleveland Press*, January 3, 1936.

166　*Frances Payne Bolton*: Bolton (1885–1977) was a member of Congress from 1939 to 1968 and an orchestra trustee from 1925 to 1938.

166　*"It took courage"*: RR, Bolton letter to Rodzinski, January 4, 1936.

166　*"This being Cleveland's first exposure"*: *The Plain Dealer*, December 13, 1940.

166　*"crazy radical"*: *Cleveland Press*, September 15, 1934.

167　*"Would you be so kind"*: COA/GE, Schoenberg letter to Vosburgh, January 16, 1939.

167　*"The plain truth of the matter"*: *Cleveland News*, August 24, 1941.

167　*"Maybe European audiences"*: COA/GE, Smith letter to Rodzinski, September 13, 1941.

167　*"discover your own form"*: RR, Downes letter to Kern, August 13, 1941.

167　*"not add a single note"*: RR, Kern letter to Rodzinski, August 18, 1941.

167　*"The panicky apprehension of being a cobbler"*: RR, Kern letter to Rodzinski, August 13, 1941.

167　*the very humble sum of $940*: COA/GE, 1941.

168　*October 23 and 25, 1941*: The program included Hindemith's *Mathis der Maler*, Beethoven's First Symphony, and Mendelssohn's incidental music to *A Midsummer Night's Dream*, with the orchestra's new first horn, Philip Farkas, making his debut playing the famous "Nocturne."

168　*Kern, grieving over the death*: RR, Kern telegram to Rodzinski, October 24, 1941.

168　*"They used to call it a medley"*: *The Plain Dealer*, October 24, 1941.

168　*"If your sister came out"*: Quoted in Bordman, p. 389.

168　*Kern was overwhelmed*: COA/GE, Smith letter to Vosburgh, November 21, 1941.

168　*The board opted*: COA/BT, minutes, January 11, 1938.

168　*the cost would be prohibitive*: Ibid., March 22, 1940.

169　*Vosburgh received the go-ahead*: Ibid., minutes, January 11, 1938.

169　*But Rodzinski later rescinded the offer*: Ibid., executive committee, minutes, March 2, 1938.

169　*"a full-fledged member of the landed gentry"*: *Albany Times-Union*, September 4, 1938.

169   *"Would like to have photos":* RR, Vosburgh letter to Rodzinski, May 27, 1938.
169   *"I don't know how to milk": Cleveland News,* May 28, 1938.
169   *"All along I've known":* COA/GE, de Gomez letter to Vosburgh, May 4, 1937.
170   *"a young Negro woman":* 1932 press release by Ernestine Alderson, who worked at Severance Hall.
170   *the Shubert brothers:* Percy Brown's history of orchestra in the 40th-anniversary booklet, 1958.
170   *"the Aquastage was abandoned": Cleveland Press,* June 13, 1939.
171   *"I have given more than five years":* RR, Rodzinski memo to Vosburgh, February 22, 1939.
171   *"Such a great audience": Cleveland News,* November 21, 1938.
172   *"What do you mean 'modern?'": Cleveland Press,* February 20, 1937.
172   *"This reviewer begs liberty":* Ibid., February 26, 1937.
172   *"Let it be 'Hats Off' to Igor Stravinsky: The Plain Dealer,* February 26, 1937.
172   *"At first I was not interested": Cleveland News,* February 2, 1939.
173   *"It means a great deal":* COA/GE, Hughes letter to Vosburgh, April 23, 1935.
173   *"nasty" and "uninspiring": The Plain Dealer,* December 5, 1940.
173   *"modern music of the mathematical sort": Cleveland News,* December 6, 1940.
173   *"elemental, barbaric": Cleveland Press,* December 6, 1940.
174   *"Poland's music springs from its soil": Portsmouth [Oh.] Times,* November, 2, 1939.
174   *"I cannot tell you":* RR, Elisabeth Prentiss letter to the Rodzinskis, September 25, 1939.
174   *"Nazi gang":* Associated Press, April 17, 1942.
174   *"proved to be such abominable music": The Plain Dealer,* April 17, 1942.
174   *Rodzinski immediately led:* Rodzinski, p. 212.
175   *"Expense we shall be able to control":* COA/BT, minutes, July 3, 1940.
175   *"Despite the general uncertainty":* Ibid., annual meeting, minutes, June 24, 1942.
175   *"I don't look for it": The Plain Dealer,* October 5, 1942.
175   *"It is a blessing":* RR, Hughes letter to Halina Rodzinski, October 1, 1939.
175   *"It is one of the very great symphony orchestras": Cleveland Press,* January 10, 1942.
176   *"insight and skill":* RR, Elwell letter to Rodzinski, October 26, 1942.
176   *"you could give some anesthetic":* RR, Rodzinski letter to Elwell, November 7, 1942.
176   *"presented a skillful": Cleveland News,* December 4, 1942.
176   *"I used to feel": The Plain Dealer,* December 11, 1942.

CHAPTER 12: RECORDING WITH RODZINSKI

177   *Costs for the musicians' services:* COA/BT, minutes, January 23, 1935.
177   *The next firm:* Ibid., December 12, 1935.
177   *RCA again came knocking:* Ibid., May 7, 1937.
177   *RCA's Charles O'Connell:* COA/GE, Vosburgh letter to Rodzinski, May 28,

1937.

178 *The board voted to make no recordings:* COA/BT, minutes, June 18, 1937.

178 *William S. Paley:* Trotter, p. 173.

178 *The terms called for:* COA/BT, executive committee, minutes, November 3, 1939.

178 *"the high spots" (only a test): Cleveland Press,* December 12, 1939.

178 *"After some suggested changes":* Ibid.

178 *"The line of a piece":* Rodzinski, p. 202.

178 *"HAVE JUST HEARD SHEHERAZADE":* COA/GE, Rodzinski telegram to Vosburgh, late December 1939.

180 *"The performance leaves nothing to be desired": Cleveland Press,* February 15, 1940.

180 *"The play-backs on this were so extraordinarily fine":* COA/GE, Rodzinski letter to Smith, March 15, 1940.

180 *"You tout Barbirolli":* COA/GE, Vosburgh letter to Smith, November 29, 1940.

182 *"I think that your conducting":* Ibid., Smith letter to Rodzinski, March 24, 1941.

182 *The board of the Musical Arts Association at first looked skeptically:* COA/BT, executive committee, minutes, May 8, 1941.

182 *"There was discipline":* Marsh, p. 83.

183 *ban on all recording activity:* The ban was lifted in November 1944. A month later, Rodzinski began recording with the New York Philharmonic, with which he made recordings of 32 works for Columbia, none of them duplicating repertoire he had recorded in Cleveland. He recorded with the Philharmonic until October 1946.

CHAPTER 13: NEW YORK BECKONS

185 *"Eighty of Us":* COA/GE, Cleveland Orchestra musicians' telegram to Rodzinski, November 22, 1934.

185 *"WE THE PHILHARMONIC":* Ibid., New York Philharmonic musicians' telegram to Vosburgh, November 1934.

185 *"Cheerio for now":* RR, Vosburgh letter to Rodzinski, November 23, 1934.

186 *He once helped Rodzinski:* Rodzinski, p. 74.

186 *"a master of economy": Salzburger Volksblatt,* summer 1936.

186 *Seated in the audience was Musical Arts Association president:* COA/GE, Blossom telegram to orchestra management, summer 1936.

186 *"I have heard nothing of any such move": Cleveland News,* March 10, 1936.

186 *Rodzinski, answering a testy group of trustees:* COA/BT, executive committee, minutes, March 21, 1936.

187 *"but may we insert":* RR, Waltz letter to Rodzinski, April 17, 1936.

187 *"formally requested":* COA/BT, executive committee, minutes, April 11, 1936.

187 *"PLEASE URGE POSSIBLY":* COA/GE, Kathryn Tifft telegram to Vosburgh, April 23, 1936.

187   *"a distinctly likely successor"*: COA/BT, minutes, April 5, 1937.

187   *"Plot!" he exclaimed when he heard of the Barbirolli appointment*: Rodzinski, p. 152.

187   *"Thus, in accepting an offer"*: Ibid., p. 159.

188   *"I am thoroughly convinced"*: RR, Blossom letter to Rodzinski, June 11, 1937.

188   *"My work in Cleveland"*: *Cleveland Press*, October 1, 1937.

188   *NBC contractor H. Leopold Spitalny*: COA/BT, executive committee, minutes, March 30, 1937.

188   *"hears about 60 or 70 applicants"*: *Cleveland Press*, May 1, 1937.

189   *Frank Ginn*: COA/BT, minutes, May 8, 1925.

189   *Blossom's death in October*: A major contributor to many Cleveland organizations, Blossom had abandoned the lucrative business world to serve as the city's public health and welfare director. He had played violin (more than ably) until he was stranded one night in 1924 in a snowstorm that left his hands frozen, requiring the amputation of two fingers on each hand. Nevertheless, he continued to play the pipe organ in the living room of his home on Cedar Road in South Euclid. In 1932, Arthur Shepherd composed a 12-minute piece for Dudley S. Blossom and Elizabeth Blossom, *Sinfonia Domestica de Famiglia Blossom*, to be played in their home. Scored for small orchestra, it was based on a series of bizarre accidents—falling ceiling, squirrels, the family cat making a home in the pipe organ in the living room—at the Blossom mansion. The work possibly was performed on Blossom's 55th birthday, October 10, 1934. The Blossom mansion was torn down in 1940. This story from *The Plain Dealer*, May 21, 1972.

189   *When the trustees arrived*: Alice Chalifoux, interview by author, Cleveland Heights, Oh., November 15, 1998.

189   *For Hugo Kolberg*: *Cleveland News*, May 4, 1942.

190   *"Although we don't really know each other"*: RR, Szell letter to Rodzinski, December 29, 1942.

190   *"When the New York Philharmonic announced"*: COA, Mary Vosburgh Bohannon, oral history transcript.

190   *"I think he did a swell job here"*: *The Plain Dealer*, December 29, 1942.

190   *"as they did in the case"*: *Cleveland Press*, December 29, 1942.

190   *His list bulged*: Ibid.

191   *"labor-pirating"*: *Cleveland Press*, January 22, 1943.

191   *"very happy to leave"*: *The Plain Dealer*, January 23, 1943.

191   *It is no wonder*: Rodzinski, p. 224.

191   *featuring Kirsten Flagstad, Rose Bampton*: Leinsdorf conducted the Metropolitan Opera broadcast, on February 8, 1941, of Wagner's *Tristan und Isolde* with almost the same cast—Flagstad, Thorborg, Melchior, Huehn, Alexander Kipnis. The performance was released on long-playing records in the Met's Historic Broadcast series.

191   *"I know that it is not without precedent"*: COA/GE, Sokoloff letter to Higgins, December 30, 1942.

192   *"I would take the choice"*: *Cleveland Press*, January 23, 1943.

192   *"The number of available American conductors"*: *Newport [R.I.] News*, January 28, 1943.

192 *"one of the great Orchestras of the world"*: COA/BT, minutes, January 6, 1943.

192 *"even takes fire"*: *Newport [R.I.] News*, January 28, 1943.

192 *"conductorship committee"*: Percy W. Brown, A.C. Ernst, Paul L. Feiss, Edgar A. Hahn, Grover Higgins, Frank G. James, E. J. Kulas, Charles B. Merrill, Thomas L. Sidlo, M.L. Sloan, and Lewis B. Williams. "In addition, Messrs. A.A. Brewster and C. J. Vosburgh were requested to act as consultants." COA/BT, February 19, 1943.

192 *Howard Barlow, Musical Director of Columbia Broadcasting Company*: Ibid.

193 *"Do we wish to be Little Clevelanders"*: Ibid.

193 *"a normal human being"*: Ibid.

193 *The five-member committee*: Ibid.

193 *"open civil war"*: *The Plain Dealer*, March 6, 1943.

193 *even receiving a message of sympathy*: *The Plain Dealer*, March 1, 1943.

193 *a gentle rebuke from First Lady Eleanor Roosevelt*: RR, Eleanor Roosevelt: "Someone sent me some literature about the Philharmonic Controversy and I do hope that what is right will be done. It does seem the men should not have been dismissed without proper consideration." RR, Rodzinski letter to Eleanor Roosevelt, April 16, 1943: "I was very happy to receive your letter indicating your great interest in the musical cause of this country. Unfortunately, there is another side to this story, too. I would be so happy if you would give me an opportunity to see you some time in the near future to talk over all those things which might interest you greatly, and to discuss many problems connected with the uncertain future of the great symphony organizations of this country."

193 *"I had plenty of troubles"*: RR, Rodzinski letter to Gorodetsky, March 13, 1943.

194 *Elmore Bacon proclaimed six conductors*: *Cleveland News*, February 27, 1943.

194 *In March 1943*: EB, Percy W. Brown notebook. March 12, 1943

194 *"the prodigy of the century"*: United Press International article in *Cleveland Press*, January 13, 1943.

194 *"The Cleveland Orchestra will have a new conductor"*: *Cleveland News*, March 12, 1943.

194 *"The orchestra played well"*: *The Plain Dealer*, March 15, 1943.

195 *"a real conductor," wrote Arthur Loesser*: *Cleveland Press*, March 15, 1943.

195 *"Before the Adelian era"*: *The Plain Dealer*, March 30, 1943.

195 *"He has given such outstanding proof"*: COA/BT, minutes, March 31, 1943.

195 *Sidlo revealed that*: Ibid.

195 *"The principal defect in the performance"*: *New York Times*, December 4, 1942.

196 *"Our Orchestra is now mature"*: COA/BT, minutes, March 31, 1943.

196 *"a greater center of music"*: Ibid.

196 *"the Dudley Blossoms"*: Leinsdorf, p. 118.

196 *After much discussion, pro and con*: COA/BT, minutes, March 31, 1943.

196 *Sokoloff's salary*: Ibid., music director contracts.

196 *$18,000 per season*: Ibid., Leinsdorf contract, July 2, 1943.

197 *"A musician's job today"*: *Cleveland Press*, April 1, 1943.

197 *"In choosing Erich Leinsdorf"*: Ibid.
197 *"trustees pointed out"*: Ibid.
197 *"You have to know your orchestra"*: Cleveland News, April 1, 1943.
197 *"I never heard him conduct"*: Ibid.
197 *instigated smear campaigns:* EB, Percy W. Brown notebook, April 1, 1943.
197 *"Adella, friend of music"*: Ibid.
198 *husbands' first names, the letter was signed:* COA/GE, Board members' letter to Sidlo, April 3, 1943.
198 *"She acted as if she were the Cleveland Orchestra"*: Leinsdorf, p. 118.
198 *"downright drunk"*: Rodzinski, p. 228.
198 *"My husband was spoiled"*: Ibid, p. 280.
199 *"Dr. Rodzinski's sojourn"*: Cleveland Press, April 17, 1943.
199 *No one yet knew:* There was an eerie postscript to the appointment of Leinsdorf and the departure of Rodzinski in the spring of 1943: On May 12, Albert Stoessel, aged 49, dropped dead while conducting Walter Damrosch's *Dunkirk* at the American Academy of Arts and Sciences in New York. The orchestra was the New York Philharmonic.

Chapter 14: Luckless Leinsdorf

201 *Two previous young conductors:* Kolodin, p. 409.
201 *"would sneak Leinsdorf in"*: Levant, p. 230.
202 *"The highest excellence in quality"*: COA/BT, annual meeting, June 23, 1943.
202 *"Then will be the moment"*: Ibid.
202 *Cleveland still couldn't muster:* COA/BT, executive committee, minutes, June 1, 1943.
203 *His new principal bassoon was George Goslee; his new principal viola, Marcel Dick:* Dick (1898–1991) would become one of the most distinguished contributors to Cleveland's artistic life. Dick was born in Hungary, where he played violin in the Budapest Philharmonic and studied with Kodály. In Vienna, he served as principal viola of the Vienna Symphony, played in the Kolisch String Quartet, and became a friend of Arnold Schoenberg, performing in the world premiere of one of the composer's first serial works, the Serenade, Op. 24. In 1934, the political situation in Europe prompted Dick to immigrate to the United States, where he worked in New York before joining to the Detroit Symphony and then the Cleveland Orchestra as principal viola. Dick composed numerous works, several heard at Severance Hall, and headed the theory and composition departments at the Cleveland Institute of Music starting in 1946. He left the Cleveland Orchestra in 1949 to devote himself to teaching and composition.
203 *Frank Sinatra:* He sang Morton Gould's arrangement of "Dark Eyes," Kern's "The Song Is You," Gershwin's "Summertime," and Porter's "Night and Day."
203 *"Better get a tight rein"*: Cleveland News, July 5, 1943.
203 *"No. 1 boudoir voice"*: Ibid., July 14, 1943.
203 *"As a mere musician"*: Cleveland Press, July 15, 1943.
203 *"No greater honor"*: COA/GE, Sidlo telegram to Toscanini, December 31,

1942.

203 *Toscanini's son:* Ibid., Walter Toscanini letter to Vosburgh, February 22, 1943.

203 *Vosburgh successfully negotiated:* COA/BT, executive committee, minutes, August 24, 1943.

204 *Leinsdorf encouraged the orchestra:* Ibid.

204 *"Neither of the former conductors":* The Plain Dealer, September 5, 1943.

204 *On the phone from Maine:* COA/C, Leinsdorf letter to Arthur Judson, September 21, 1943.

204 *"The neighbors on both sides of us":* Cleveland Press, November 23, 1943.

205 *"If there were any doubts":* Cleveland Press, October 8, 1943.

205 *"There are 15 new members":* The Plain Dealer, October 8, 1943.

205 *Goddard Lieberson, director of the Masterworks Department:* COA/C, Lieberson letter to Leinsdorf, October 11, 1943.

205 *"and murmured":* Ibid., Ziegler letter to Leinsdorf, October 12, 1943.

205 *Days before his second subscription concerts:* Ibid., Leinsdorf letter to Brown, October 12, 1943.

205 *"bringing me":* Leinsdorf, p. 120.

205 *"All my life":* Ibid.

206 *"When he came here":* Alice Chalifoux, interview by author, Cleveland Heights, Oh., November 15, 1998.

206 *"laudable effort":* The Plain Dealer, October 22, 1943.

206 *"I feel that it is almost an impossible task":* COA/C, Leinsdorf letter to Elwell (copies to Bacon, Blodgett, Smith), October 22, 1943.

206 *"real propaganda for the music":* Ibid., Leinsdorf letter to Elwell, October 28, 1943.

206 *"Much of his interpretation":* The Plain Dealer, October 29, 1943.

207 *"I intend to abide":* Cleveland News, October 29, 1943.

207 *Mary Vosburgh Bohannon:* COA, Mary Vosburgh Bohannon, oral history transcript.

207 *"best work":* The Plain Dealer, November 5, 1943.

207 *"I had, as you probably know":* COA/C, Leinsdorf letter to Levant, November 15, 1943.

207 *"it would undoubtedly please you":* Ibid., Leinsdorf letter to Johnson, November 16, 1943.

208 *Johnson wrote back:* Ibid., Johnson letter to Leinsdorf, November 20, 1943.

208 *"I praise without further analysis":* Ibid., Korngold letter to Leinsdorf, November 15, 1943.

208 *"from such an authoritative source":* Ibid., Leinsdorf letter to Korngold, November 22, 1943.

208 *But in September:* COA/GE, Walter Toscanini letter to Vosburgh, September 28, 1943.

208 *"Not only does it promise to be":* Ibid., Vosburgh letter to Walter Toscanini, October 4, 1943.

208 *Even requests for help:* Ibid., Sarnoff letter to Thomas L. Sidlo, October 7, 1943.

208 *"the distinguished Negro soprano":* COA/M/PR, orchestra press release, November 19, 1943.

208   *"I have always been eager":* The Plain Dealer, December 15, 1943.

208   *Two days later, Leinsdorf informed:* COA/C, Leinsdorf letter to Hope, December 17, 1943.

209   *"The trouble with our modern life":* Ibid., Leinsdorf letter to Herbert F. Aldrich, Cleveland Heights, December 27, 1943.

209   *"anything around your working orbit":* Ibid., Leinsdorf letter to Spivacke, December 24, 1943.

209   *"Leinsdorf Is Accepted":* Cleveland News, December 31, 1943.

209   *In his memoirs, Leinsdorf took a different view:* Leinsdorf, p. 121.

209   *He told the board that he could secure Frank Black:* COA/BT, minutes, January 3, 1944.

210   *Otto Klemperer, conductor of the Los Angeles Philharmonic:* COA/C, Klemperer telegram to Leinsdorf, January 8, 1944.

210   *"the most vital artistic manifestations":* Ibid., Barrows letter to Leinsdorf, January 10, 1944.

210   *"rousing farewell":* Cleveland News, January 17, 1944.

210   *"selfish considerations behind":* COA/C, Leinsdorf letter to Charles McBride, January 17, 1944.

210   *The main work on the January 18 program:* Heard more than half a century later, the performance of Brahms's *A German Requiem* finds Leinsdorf thoroughly committed to his duties. The reading is keenly paced and dramatic without sounding operatic. The orchestra plays warmly—only Philip Kirchner's squeezed oboe sound sticks out from textures—and responds with subtle vibrancy to its departing conductor's thoughtful approach. The soloists are variable—soprano Mary Marting, from Baldwin-Wallace College, is tender if thin sounding, while Chicago baritone Bruce Foote brings noble declamation to his lines. The St. James Choir, a local church ensemble, struggles valiantly with the difficult choral part and is challenged to stay in tune.

211   *the orchestra received $869,938:* COA/BT, minutes, January 22, 1945.

211   *Leinsdorf agreed that plans:* COA/C, Leinsdorf letter to Sidlo, January 19, 1944.

211   *the go-ahead to clean house:* On Szell's impact at the Metropolitan Opera

211   *"Since replacements are hard to find":* COA/GE, Leinsdorf letter to Vosburgh, March 12, 1944.

211   *He told Sidlo:* Ibid., Vosburgh letter to Sidlo, March 13, 1944.

212   *"I am always very elated":* Ibid., Leinsdorf letter to Vosburgh, March 3, 1944.

212   *"from top to bottom":* COA/BT, minutes, March 30, 1944.

212   *The result was a resolution stating:* Ibid.

212   *"How are you getting along":* COA/GE, Vosburgh letter to Leinsdorf, April 7, 1944.

212   *"I am certain that if we had":* COA/BT, annual meeting, minutes, June 28, 1944.

212   *"Otherwise I avoided the live gossip-columns":* Ibid.

213   *for flat feet:* Cleveland News, September 13, 1944.

213   *Sidlo told the press:* Ibid.

213   *"If the army had got":* Cleveland Press, September 14, 1944.

213   *"With only the courtesy":* The Plain Dealer, October 13, 1944.

213 *"Under the circumstances":* COA/BT, minutes, October 13, 1944.
214 *"if by chance we made a mistake":* Ibid.
214 *"We are the custodians":* Ibid.
214 *"looking forward to working":* The Plain Dealer, October 30, 1944.
214 *"In his debut as guest conductor":* The Plain Dealer, November 3, 1944.
215 *"George Szell is a great conductor":* Cleveland Press, November 3, 1944.
215 *"Perfect party":* EB, Percy Brown notebook, November 10, 1944.
216 *"Unprecedented interest":* The Plain Dealer, November 10, 1944.
216 *more succinctly: "Thrilling":* EB, Percy Brown notebook, November 11, 1944.
216 *"We join in the opinion":* Cleveland News, November 11, 1944.
216 *lobbying for Leinsdorf to record:* COA/GE, Judson letter to Vosburgh, November 27, 1944.
216 *"If a poll of the Board":* COA/BT, minutes, December 11, 1944.
216 *"it being the opinion":* Ibid.
217 *Columbia Records was extending:* Ibid.
217 *"I am delighted":* The Plain Dealer, December 13, 1944.
217 *"Had it degenerated":* Ibid., December 24, 1944.
217 *"Koussevitzky could conduct":* Ibid.
218 *"Great triumph":* EB, Percy Brown notebook, January 12, 1945.
218 *"I am very happy about this":* COA/GE, Szell letter to Vosburgh, January 17, 1945.
218 *"I enjoyed every split-second of it":* COA/C, Szell letter to Rodzinski, December 15, 1944.
218 *The board voted to pay:* COA/BT, executive committee, minutes, January 22, 1945.
218 *Columbia Records now suggested:* Ibid.
218 *When Leinsdorf demanded:* Ibid.
218 *"Since it is not customary":* COA/GE, Leinsdorf letter to Vosburgh, January 23, 1945.
218 *"I had little time to prove":* Ibid.
219 *"Let's work toward the goal":* COA/BT, executive committee, minutes, January 22, 1945.
219 *"I gave her a complete bawling out":* EB, Percy Brown notebook, January 31, 1945.
219 *"the big money":* COA/GE, Leinsdorf telegram to Vosburgh, February 25, 1945.
219 *"As far as maintenance and improvement":* Ibid., Leinsdorf memo on policy for the orchestra, spring 1945.
220 *the three recording sessions:* COA/BT, executive committee, minutes, April 9, 1945.
220 *The Cleveland Orchestra Pension Institute:* Ibid.
220 *"As it was, the constellation":* Leinsdorf, p. 125.
220 *"As the broad lines":* Cleveland Press, April 13, 1945.
220 *"somewhat blatant and coarse":* Ibid.
220 *"I am afraid that the reception":* COA/C, Leinsdorf letter to Heinsheimer, April 14, 1945.
221 *"a note of farewell":* Cleveland News, April 13, 1945.

221   *The board voted to continue:* COA/BT, minutes, July 6, 1945.
221   *"I am asking today":* Ibid.
221   *"It took 5 or 6 big strong men":* EB, Percy Brown notebook, July 6, 1945.

CHAPTER 15: SOMETHING FINE AND BEAUTIFUL

223   *"I couldn't find a weak spot":* Cleveland News, October 10, 1945.
223   *He can be heard swooping up:* Upon leaving Cleveland, James Stagliano switched places with Philip Farkas in the Boston Symphony and later, coincidentally (but none too happily), was reunited with Erich Leinsdorf when the conductor served as the Boston Symphony's music director from 1962 to 1969.
224   *"the first postwar symphony concert":* The Plain Dealer, October 12, 1945.
224   *a proposal to record Antheil's Fourth Symphony:* COA/C, Lieberson letter to Leinsdorf, October 31, 1945.
224   *"this 'enfant terrible' of the '20s":* The Plain Dealer, November 2, 1945.
225   *"a young and ambitious conductor":* Ibid.
225   *"This was surely not the same orchestra":* The Plain Dealer, December 21, 1945.
224   *The Antheil recording:* COA/C, Leinsdorf letter to Lieberson, November 5, 1945.
225   *"the whole orchestra, in fact, sounded better":* The Plain Dealer, December 7, 1945.
225   *"this city's Number One civic asset":* Cleveland Press, November 23, 1945.
226   *"The massive tranquility of Severance Hall":* Cleveland Press, December 27, 1945.
226   *Telling Leinsdorf:* Leinsdorf, p. 127.
226   *"All those difficulties":* COA/C, Leinsdorf letter to Sidlo, January 12, 1946.
227   *Szell engaged in a shrewd negotiating game:* EB, Percy Brown notebook, January 15, 1946.
227   *"Dr. Szell is no easy-going person":* COA/BT, minutes, January 24, 1946.
227   *"You have requested":* Ibid., Szell contract, January 15, 1946.
227   *The salary Szell demanded:* Ibid.
227   *a slap in the face for Leinsdorf:* If their salaries were calculated for the year 2000, Leinsdorf made $157,846.15 during his last year as conductor and Szell made $306,726.46 for his first year. The situation is even odder in the cases of Sokoloff and Rodzinski, both of whom were paid $30,000 for their final seasons (10 years apart). Since Sokoloff made the equivalent of $394,615.38 for his last year in 1933, Rodzinski was paid far less in 1943 ($296,531.79). Another oddity: based on what their relative value would be today, Sokoloff's figure of $394,615.38 is higher than any Szell salary, except for the latter's final season (1969–70), when he made $440,721.65.
227   *"Musical Director and Conductor" to reflect :* COA/C, Sidlo letter to Szell, January 21, 1946.
227   *"For the first time":* COA/BT, minutes, January 24, 1946.
228   *"the work involved":* Ibid.
228   *the budget would be $480,000:* COA/BT, minutes, March 7, 1946.

228 *"a worker, a terrific worker"*: COA/BT, minutes, January 24, 1946.
228 *despite premeeting lobbying:* EB, Percy Brown notebook, February 1, 1948.
229 *"I shall do my best"*: *Cleveland News* dummy paper, January 25, 1946.
229 *"the anteroom for the Philharmonic"*: *New York Sun*, February 2, 1946.
229 *"a tall, near-bald, thick-spectacled Czech-Hungarian"*: *Time*, February 4, 1946.
229 *Widder finally chimed in:* *Cleveland Press*, February 6, 1946.
229 *I had to reaudition :* Evelyn Botnick, interview by author, April 16, 1999.
230 *"Erich Leinsdorf deserves better"*: *Cleveland Press*, February 7, 1946.
230 *"There is justification"*: Ibid., February 8, 1946.
231 *"We musicians are very fortunate"*: *The Plain Dealer*, February 23, 1946.
232 *"But let the Orchestra strike fire"*: COA/BT, minutes, March 7, 1946.
232 *doubling his contribution:* Ibid.
232 *Szell was beginning to reveal his compulsion to control:* COA/GE, Szell letter to Smith, March 11, 1946.
233 *"sourpuss"*: COA, Louis Lane, oral history transcript.
233 *"as happy and gratifying an evening as I can recall"*: Leinsdorf, pp. 128–29.
233 *One of his first major announcements:* *New York Times*, June 2, 1946.
233 *The Kulas Foundation:* COA/BT, executive committee, minutes, June 13, 1946.
234 *"so insulted"*: COA/GE, Szell letter to George H. L. Smith, August 22, 1946.
234 *"You return to the task"*: COA/BT, annual meeting, minutes, June 26, 1946.

CHAPTER 16: GENIUS GEORGE

237 *"a private door-shaking police force"*: *Time*, February 22, 1963.
238 *Through the doctor:* *The New Yorker*, November 6, 1965.
238 *with the Wiener Tonkünstler:* Ibid., November 6, 1965.
238 *"the new Mozart"*: *London Daily Mail*, November 14, 1908.
238 *"Is this for piano only"*: Ibid.
238 *"I got a lot out of Vienna"*: *The New Yorker*, November 6, 1965.
238 *"Serkin! How can you play such trash?"*: Fisher, pp. 83–84.
239 *hit in the groin by a tennis ball:* *Time*, February 22, 1963.
239 *cascading about the keyboard with his cufflinks:* *The New Yorker*, November 6, 1965.
239 *"Well, in this case one can cheerfully bite the dust"*: Szell interview with John Culshaw for BBC, April 8, 1969.
239 *"Now I can die happy"*: *The New Yorker*, November 6, 1965.
239 *Szell played the prominent piano part:* Heyworth, p. 115.
239 *Among those in the audience:* Ibid.
240 *He gained more operatic experience:* Berlin was an important, and stormy, destination for Szell during this period for another reason: Berlin was an important, and stormy, destination for Szell during this period for another reason: In 1920, he married Olga Band, who later fell in love with the concertmaster of the Berlin Philharmonic. The Szells were divorced around 1926, after which Band married the violinist. (Information courtesy of Michael

Charry.)

240 *"The clarity of texture"*: *New York Times*, July 30, 1935.

240 *"From the musicians he conducted"*: *The New Yorker*, November 6, 1965.

240 *"But how stern and harsh he was with me"*: Biancolli, p. 70.

241 *"Pussi Teddybear"*: COA/C, Szell letters to Helene Szell.

241 *he took Helene to New York City:* Helene's two sons remained in Europe with their father. "One disappeared during the occupation of France as did Szell's parents, who were presumed to have died in a Nazi concentration camp. The other son [John Teltsch] rejoined his family in 1945 on the first postwar immigration visa issued in France—a sign that Szell was already in string-pulling position in his new country," according to *Time* magazine, February 22, 1963. Teltsch was raised by his mother and Szell in Cleveland and became a prominent builder in Atlanta.

241 *He also studied the top American orchestras:* *The New Yorker*, November 6, 1965. Szell played chamber music during this period with Paul Hindemith, Erica Morini, Emanuel Feuermann, Adolf Busch, Zino Francescatti, Lillian Fuchs, Leonard Rose, and Rudolf Serkin.

241 *"It was Beethoven's Second Symphony"*: Levant, p. 211.

242 *Szell made his Met debut:* Since *Salome* is short, it was not the only work on the bill that night. Pergolesi's *La Serva Padrona* (with Bidu Sayao and Salvatore Baccaloni) preceded the Strauss at the first and third performances; at the second, due to Sayao's illness, Act II of Verdi's *La Traviata* was performed with what today looks like a dream cast—Licia Albanese, Leonard Warren, and James Melton. Szell conducted only the Strauss. Paul Breisach led the Pergolesi and Verdi. Kolodin, p. 440.

242 *"a virtuoso job"*: Quoted in Kolodin, pp. 434–40.

242 *"the score glowed and pulsated"*: Ibid., p. 440.

242 *also conducting Wagner's Tannhäuser:* Cast of the Wagner included Helen Traubel, Lauritz Melchior, Herbert Janssen, and Kerstin Thorborg; for the Mussorgsky, various casts included Ezio Pinza, René Maison, Thorborg, Salvatore Baccaloni, Nicola Moscona, Alexander Kipnis, and Norman Cordon. Ibid., p. 440.

Chapter 17: Raves and Raids

243 *"Second to none." They sounded like fighting words.*: Szell statement upon announcement of his appointment as the Cleveland Orchestra's musical director and conductor, January 24, 1946

243 *Holding nine preseason rehearsals:* COA, Vosburgh date book, 1946–47 season.

243 *"Rehearsals were a matter of life and death"*: *Beacon Magazine*, July 27, 1980.

243 *Szell viewed the ideal orchestra:* Schonberg, p. 337.

244 *"I personally like complete homogeneity of sound"*: Quoted in Schonberg, p. 337.

244 *"which is so much more important"*: Szell interview with Paul Myers for CBS, March 25, 1966.

244 *"He wouldn't allow you to think for yourself"*: Beacon Magazine, July 27, 1980.

244 *"Well, that went so well"*: COA, Klaus G. Roy quoted in Louis Lane oral history transcript.

244 *"It was just like at the dentist's"*: Ibid.

244 *"That was a real weakness"*: Beacon Magazine, July 27, 1980.

244 *"He was prepared to sacrifice"*: COA, Louis Lane, oral history transcript.

244 *"I want this phrase to sound"*: Beacon Magazine, July 27, 1980.

244 *Cloyd Duff, the orchestra's principal timpanist*: Duff, the orchestra's principal timpanist from 1942 to 1981, died on March 12, 2000, at age 84.

245 *"He never took a chance on things"*: Beacon Magazine, July 27, 1980.

245 *"This is it, the kind of Cleveland Orchestra we have been waiting for"*: The Plain Dealer, October 18, 1946.

245 *"The ensemble hasn't had"*: Akron Beacon Journal, October 18, 1946.

246 *"The opening night went splendidly"*: New York Philharmonic Archives, Szell letter to Zirato, October 19, 1946.

246 *The 18-year-old Fleisher*: In 1965, Fleisher was preparing to travel with Szell and the Cleveland Orchestra to the Soviet Union and Europe when his playing began to go awry. The condition, a cramping of the right hand, was to put the pianist's performing career on extended hold and ultimately change its direction.

246 *"Gave him long lecture"*: EB, Percy Brown notebook, January 29, 1947.

247 *Szell had been so intent*: COA, Louis Lane, oral history transcript.

247 *Szell led a program*: The remainder of these concerts included Sibelius's Symphony No. 3 and Brahms's Double Concerto, with Adolf and Hermann Busch as violin and cello soloists, respectively.

247 *"I wouldn't," Szell cautioned*: COA, Louis Lane, oral history transcript.

247 *"under-handed"*: Ibid.

247 *A contract was signed*: Detroit Times, February 21, 1947.

247 *Their Saturday night radio broadcasts*: COA/BT, minutes, January 14, 1947. Szell made his debut with the Philadelphia Orchestra in early January 1947.

248 *"absolute equality with the Big Four"*: Ibid.

248 *Thaviu would leave*: The Plain Dealer, January 30, 1947.

248 *"wave of resignations of principal players."*: Cleveland Press, February 15, 1947.

248 *"Is it absolutely necessary to rip"*: Ibid., February 18, 1947.

248 *"a delicate matter"*: RR, Rodzinski letter to Szell, January 9, 1947.

248 *Upon signing in Chicago*: Cleveland News, February 19, 1947.

248 *Karl Krueger*: Cleveland Press, February 20, 1947.

249 *"Any organization is entitled"*: Detroit Times, February 21, 1947.

249 *"I cannot for a moment"*: COA/GE, Krueger letter to Szell, February 20, 1947.

249 *"Sympho Slugfests"*: Downbeat, March 12, 1947.

249 *The city's music critics were divided*: Cleveland Press, March 21, 1947; The Plain Dealer, March 21, 1947.

249 *"forced 'resignations' and general bad feelings"*: Charles P. Walter letter to the editor, Cleveland Press, March 27, 1947.

249 *"stalked out of the room"*: Cleveland Press, March 27, 1947.

249 *Vosburgh defended Szell's methods*: Ibid.

249 *"Szell has shown apparent coldness":* Carlton K. Matson letter to the editor, *Cleveland Press*, March 29, 1947.

250 *87 of the orchestra's 92 players: The Plain Dealer*, March 31, 1947.

250 *"The two oldest cronies": Cleveland News*, April 3, 1947.

250 *"George Szell's conducting": The Plain Dealer*, April 18, 1947.

251 *"male or female":* COA/GE, Szell letter to Vosburgh, May 22, 1947.

252 *His scheduled operatic engagements:* Ibid., Szell letter to Vosburgh, August 12, 1947.

252 *"a nasty man, God rest his soul":* Bing, p. 121.

252 *"it would not be the last time":* Ibid.

CHAPTER 18: HONING THE INSTRUMENT

253 *"decent bow": The New Yorker*, February 4, 1991.

254 *"First, never take your eyes off the baton":* Ibid.

254 *"nine words out of ten":* Ibid.

254 *"More salt":* Ibid.

254 *"Musically, Joe made up for Szell's limitations":* Ibid.

255 *"Mr. Loebel, take it or leave it": The Plain Dealer*, August 24, 1997.

255 *"To come to Cleveland was not to come to Cleveland":* Ibid.

255 *"Thank you very much":* COA, Louis Lane, oral history transcript.

256 *"It came, I think": Beacon Magazine*, July 27, 1980.

256 *"Dr. Cyclops": The New Yorker*, February 4, 1991.

256 *"Look out":* Ibid.

256 *he informed mezzo-soprano Janet Baker:* COA/C, Szell letter to Baker, January 29, 1970.

256 *He personally negotiated:* David Zauder interview by author, Cleveland Heights, Oh., February 18, 1999.

257 *"The hernias in the Orchestra":* COA/GE, Szell letter to Barksdale, December 19, 1964.

257 *"Thank you, very well driven": Beacon Magazine*, July 27, 1980.

257 *"Every Monday-morning rehearsal": Plain Dealer Sunday Magazine*, May 4, 1997.

257 *"about forty percent of the musicians":* Maxwell fax to the author, January 11, 1999.

258 *"emerged from the bathroom":* Steinhardt, p. 58.

258 *"I thought you might not know it so well":* COA, Louis Lane, oral history transcript.

258 *a full extra week of rehearsals:* Ibid., Vosburgh date book, 1947–48 season.

258 *The first five weeks of Szell programs:* Szell opened the 1947–48 season on October 9 and 11 with Weber's *Euryanthe* overture, two of Debussy's *Nocturnes*, Smetana's *Vltava*, and Brahms's First Symphony.

259 *"if you think I chew nails for breakfast": The Plain Dealer*, December 3, 1947.

259 *"manly, direct and terse": Cleveland Press*, December 4, 1947.

259 *"The Cleveland Orchestra is a highly satisfactory musical instrument":* New York Herald Tribune, February 10, 1948.

259 *"The borderline is very thin":* The New Yorker, November 6, 1965.

260 *"This is an admirable orchestra":* New York Times, February 10, 1948.

260 *"beautiful, big warm fiddle tone":* Quoted in Hart, *Conductors: A New Generation,* p. 252.

260 *"deathly afraid":* COA, Louis Lane, oral history transcript.

261 *Many of the orchestra's musicians were big Indians fans: Cleveland Press,* November 1, 1948. This rehearsal incident has often been recounted inaccurately—even in Szell's obituary in the *New York Times*—as having occurred in 1954, when the Indians lost the World Series to the New York Giants.

261 *"The Cleveland Orchestra, which Mr. Szell is training":* New York Times, February 15, 1949. The program comprised Smetana's *The Bartered Bride* overture, Strauss's *Till Eulenspiegel*, Schumann's First Symphony, and Brahms's Piano Concerto No. 1, with Rudolf Firkusny as soloist.

262 *"Let us remind ourselves":* COA/BT, annual meeting, minutes, June 22, 1949.

263 *two weeks of purely orchestral programs:* Beethoven's "Eroica," Stravinsky's *Firebird* suite, Strauss's *Till Eulenspiegel*, Bartók's Concerto for Orchestra, Tchaikovsky's Sixth Symphony. In addition, he scheduled a series of Cleveland (or Cleveland Orchestra) premieres, including Poulenc's Sinfonietta (first in America), Mozart's Piano Concerto No. 18 (with Leonard Shure), Norman Dello Joio's Serenade for Orchestra, Delius's *Brigg Fair*, David Diamond's *The Enormous Room*, Hindemith's Concert Music for String Orchestra and Brass Instruments, Alvin Etler's Passacaglia and Fugue, and, perhaps surprisingly (considering how old they were by this time), Schubert's Symphony No. 5, and Wagner's *Rienzi* overture.

263 *"The orchestras in Vienna and Amsterdam":* Associated Press, December 14, 1949.

264 *to make disruptive breathing sounds:* COA, Louis Lane, oral history transcript.

264 *"We would have engaged you":* Ibid.

264 *"Best in U.S.A!":* EB, Percy Brown notebook, March 2, 1950.

264 *"Let me congratulate you":* COA/GE, Walter letter to Sidlo, March 15, 1950.

264 *"Cleve. Orch. now second to none in U.S.A.":* EB, Percy Brown notebook, March 13, 1950.

264 *"I really honestly believe":* COA/GE, Mitropoulos letter to Sidlo, April 4, 1950.

265 *Radio listening plunged:* Bianculli, p. 57.

265 *"it was like a bomb had dropped":* COA, Louis Lane, oral history transcript.

265 *Sidlo wrote to Margaret Truman:* COA/GE, Sidlo letter to Margaret Truman, January 12, 1949.

265 *"I don't know if there is anything I can do":* Ibid., Margaret Truman letter to Sidlo, January 24, 1949.

265 *"persuade even the hard-boiled ticket subscriber":* Ibid., Sidlo letter to Szell, May 12, 1950.

265 *Given the effects of television and the admissions tax:* Congress finally passed a bill in October 1951 restoring to symphony orchestras an exemption from the federal admissions tax.

265 *"Henry thinks we should":* EB, Percy Brown notebook, June 2, 1950.

265   *"The orchestra board is in a mess"*: Ibid., June 3, 1950.

266   *"She did so many things herself"*: COA/BT, minutes, September 8, 1950.

266   *"I have never heard such an exhausting audition"*: COA, Louis Lane, oral history transcript.

267   *"Tom and I have had many questions"*: COA/GE, Vosburgh letter to Szell, January 2, 1951.

267   *not asking Mitropoulos back:* Ibid.

267   *"Taking all things into consideration"*: *Cleveland Press*, January 20, 1951.

267   *"Stokowski did nothing"*: COA, Louis Lane, oral history transcript.

267   *"Your orchestra is superb"*: COA/GE, Stokowski telegram to Szell, December 17, 1951.

267   *"The manner in which both the orchestra and the Severance Hall audiences"*: *Cleveland News*, December 29, 1951.

268   *"The Orchestra is really TOPS"*: Quoted in Sachs, p. 252.

268   *"As the weeks go by"*: The Plain Dealer, January 25, 1952.

Chapter 19: Orchestra Ascending

269   *"I was in my 20s"*: COA, Louis Lane, oral history transcript.

269   *"I could do nothing"*: Kurt Loebel, interview by author, Cleveland Heights, Oh., June 27, 1998.

269   *groceries cost the same:* Ibid.

269   *"We have a first-rate Orchestra"*: COA/BT, minutes, March 7, 1949.

270   *"They feel that they are"*: Ibid.

270   *"arouse feelings of astonishment"*: Ibid.

270   *Of the ensemble's 95 members:* Cleveland Press, July 26, 1952.

270   *annual compensation of $3,240:* Ibid. The figure in the year 2000 would be $20,907.17.

270   *"the borderline of poverty"*: COA, Cleveland Orchestra Committee document, December 26, 1962.

270   *Szell was being paid $48,000 a year:* COA/BT, Szell contract, March 25, 1950. The figure in the year 2000 would be $309,735.85.

271   *"drill press operator"*: Cleveland Press, July 26, 1952.

271   *"as good as any conductor could wish for"*: Time, January 12, 1953.

271   *The endowment was up to $5 million:* Ibid.

271   *the summer season would resume only in 1954:* Cleveland News, March 4, 1953.

271   *"Not only for the sake of continuity"*: Cleveland Press, March 27, 1953.

271   *"The orchestra of 70 men"*: Cleveland News, April 2, 1953.

271   *"Louis Lane, conductor of the Cleveland Summer Orchestra"*: Ibid., April 4, 1953.

272   *Indipops:* Ibid., June 2, 1953.

272   *"Beethoven Up"*: Ibid.

272   *"Acoustics, Orchestra Excellent at Stadium"*: Cleveland Press, June 3, 1953.

272   *"It was quite an effort"*: COA, Louis Lane, oral history transcript.

272   *"Your auditorium is beautiful and luxurious"*: COA/GE, Swan letter to

Musical Arts Association, December 30, 1947.

272 *The price tag for the project: $25,000:* Ibid.

272 *"I only wish you had a hall":* COA/GE, Stokowski letter to Szell, April 10, 1953.

273 *greater use of plywood:* COA/BT, minutes, April 24, 1953.

273 *removing the heavy carpeting and drapes:* Shankland, pp. 868–69.

273 *"This would completely offset":* COA/GE, Szell letter to Vosburgh, July 7, 1953.

273 *Vosburgh wrote back:* COA/GE, Vosburgh letter to Szell, July 14, 1953.

274 *"an ideal esthetic marriage":* The Plain Dealer, October 19, 1951.

274 *"Szell proved emphatically":* Cleveland Press, October 19, 1951.

274 *"This certainly was one of the high spots":* COA/GE, Vosburgh letter to Gilbert, October 22, 1951.

274 *Gilbert wrote back:* Ibid., Gilbert letter to Vosburgh, October 26, 1951.

274 *"George, I feel we have one of the great orchestras":* COA/BT, Presidents' Office Files (Percy Brown), Vosburgh letter to Szell, July 1, 1954.

274 *"The present contract with Columbia":* Cleveland Press, August 6, 1954.

275 *"Now Szell is in competition with himself":* Ibid., September 7, 1954.

275 *"It is an orchestra":* Saturday Review article quoted in the Cleveland Press, February 21, 1953.

276 *"the establishment of a permanent Cleveland Orchestra chorus":* The Plain Dealer, February 19, 1952.

276 *"The joy and emotional satisfaction":* Ibid.

276 *"responded wonderfully":* The Plain Dealer, May 1, 1953.

276 *"responded to every Szell demand":* Cleveland News, May 1, 1953.

276 *his beloved Cadillac:* COA/GE, Szell letter to Vosburgh, June 24, 1953.

276 *"Your paragraph regarding the migraines":* COA/GE, Vosburgh letter to Szell, June 12, 1953.

277 *"I'm going to have a team":* Cleveland Press, June 25, 1953.

277 *"If you want a top-flight musician":* Ibid., October 3, 1953.

277 *"A $6,000,000 endowment":* Ibid.

277 *"Cleveland's most accomplished and effective worrier":* Joseph obituary, The Plain Dealer, July 1, 1995.

278 *"I'm still polite from Europe":* Cleveland Press, September 26, 1953.

278 *"Each year I await":* Ibid., September 29, 1953.

278 *"sorry they were subjected":* Ibid., October 10, 1953.

278 *"George Szell now has":* The Plain Dealer, October 9, 1953.

278 *"Your orchestra is as fine":* Quoted in The Plain Dealer, January 31, 1954. Ansermet's program comprised Beethoven's Symphony No. 2, his own orchestration of Debussy's *Six épigraphes antiques*, and Bartók's Music for Strings, Percussion, and Celesta.

279 *"we both, alas":* COA/GE, Bing letter to Szell, January 14, 1954.

279 *"forty years":* Ibid., Szell letter to Bing, January 18, 1954.

279 *"scandalous mechanical breakdown":* Ibid. The cast included Margaret Harshaw, Astrid Varnay, Ramon Vinay, George London, and Jerome Hines.

279 *"Not while I'm alive":* Quoted in Schonberg, p. 339.

279 *At the end of January 1954:* Szell held two more conductors' workshops, in

March 1955 and September/October 1956.

279 *These performances would have revealed:* Beethoven's *Leonore* Overture No. 3 and Symphony No. 8, Tchaikovsky's Symphony No. 6, three Brahms scores (*Academic Festival Overture*; Violin Concerto, with Erica Morini; and Fourth Symphony), Sibelius's *En Saga*, Mozart's *Exsultate, Jubilate* (with soprano Maria Stader), Bach's Wedding Cantata, and Strauss's *Death and Transfiguration*.

279 *"In a physical sense": Beacon Magazine*, July 27, 1980.

279 *"Sometimes when he used a casual beat":* Ibid.

279 *"Cut down on Tchaikovsky and Beethoven": Cleveland Press*, June 19, 1954.

280 *"If we were to reduce the size":* COA/BT, annual meeting, minutes, June 23, 1954.

280 *"Frankly, I am beginning to believe":* COA/GE, Vosburgh letter to Gingold, July 12, 1954.

280 *As guest conductor of the Philharmonic:* Myron Bloom, interview by author, Cleveland Heights, Oh., December 24, 1999.

280 *"I went to Szell immediately":* Ibid.

281 *"a mind and a heart":* Ibid.

281 *"Before I could say a word":* Myron Bloom interview with Michael Charry in Sony Classical rerelease of Strauss's Horn Concerto No. 1.

281 *"I did this not only because":* COA/GE, Szell letter to Brown, November 22, 1954.

282 *"May I say":* COA/GE, Taylor letter to Vosburgh, March 19, 1955.

283 *assistant manager of the Los Angeles Philharmonic:* While in Los Angeles in 1938, McKelvy had corresponded with Vosburgh about Schoenberg's orchestration of the Brahms Quartet in G Minor, which Rodzinski later conducted in Cleveland and on tour. COA/GE, McKelvy letter to Vosburgh, February 1939.

283 *"This is what I want. Let's get him":* Quoted by Louis Lane in COA, Lane, oral history transcript.

283 *The musicians were guaranteed: Cleveland Press*, May 4, 1955.

283 *"he did not have the urge for power":* Edward Brown interview with the author, July 17, 1999.

CHAPTER 20: PEAK PERFORMANCE

285 *"Pretty soon the Cleveland Orchestra":* COA/BT, Presidents' Office Files (Frank Taplin), Szell letter to Taplin, January 23, 1956.

286 *The trip would probably occur:* Ibid.

286 *"As to the Orchestra's fees in Europe":* COA/BT, Presidents' Office Files (Frank Taplin), Charlotte Flatow letter to Szell, September 2, 1955.

286 *"I think that I should emphasize":* Ibid., Presidents' Office Files (Frank Taplin), Szell letter to Flatow, October 25, 1955.

286 *"Retirements and jobs": Cleveland Press*, September 17, 1955.

286 *"the orchestra today":* Ibid., September 24, 1955.

286 *"While all this is gratifying":* Ibid.

287 *"Szell Starts 11th Year Here": Cleveland News*, October 26, 1955.

287 *"was given an exemplary performance": Cleveland Press*, November 4, 1955.

287 *"must be better than this": The Plain Dealer*, November 4, 1955.

287 *"Let no one cast any asparagus":* Ibid., November 18, 1955.

287 *voted not to renew Rudolph Ringwall's contract:* COA/BT, executive committee, minutes, December 16, 1955.

288 *"Why do you play trash for our children?":* Quoted by Baldwin in *Cleveland Press*, March 8, 1956.

288 *And, curiously, the program he objected to:* The program comprised Wolf-Ferrari's *The Secret of Suzanne* overture, Vaughan Williams's *Fantasia on 'Greensleeves*,' Eric Coates's *Three Bears*, Percy Grainger's *Country Gardens*, Sibelius's *Valse Triste*, Ernesto Lecuona's *Malagueña*, and Victor Herbert's *March of the Toys*. If Szell had considered such works as the Lecuona trashy, why did he allow Louis Lane to record the piece with the Cleveland Pops Orchestra in July 1959?

288 *"When Szell came":* Alice Chalifoux, interview by author, Cleveland Heights, Oh., November 15, 1998.

288 *"The conferences convinced me":* COA/GE, Baldwin letter to Taplin, January 19, 1956.

288 *"We all love the Orchestra":* COA/GE, Taplin letter to Baldwin, January 23, 1956.

289 *"only a violinist":* Quoted in *The Plain Dealer*, March 28, 1956.

289 *"like Truman and Liberace":* Ibid.

289 *"Some people seem to regard":* Mussulman, p. 132.

289 *"The first year I was there": Symphony Magazine*, February/March 1984.

289 *"is the best thing to happen to the Cleveland Orchestra since the resignation of Rodzinski":* COA/GE, Donald F. Wilson letter to Taplin, December 17, 1955.

289 *"I'd like to audition 600 singers": Cleveland Press*, January 9, 1956.

289 *"I'm sorry," Shaw told the rejected singers:* Quoted by Louis Lane in COA, Lane, oral history transcript.

290 *"It is astonishing":* Mussulman, p. 138.

290 *The board president's Band-Aid solution:* COA/BT, minutes, March 16, 1956.

290 *"Will be with you in spirit":* COA/GE, Sokoloff telegram to Taplin, February 2, 1956.

290 *"had one gift that has not been equaled": The Plain Dealer*, February 12, 1956.

291 *"At various times":* COA/BT, annual meeting, minutes, June 20, 1956.

291 *"peach of a [Mozart] performance":* COA/GE, Szell letter to Smith, August 18, 1956.

291 *"Perhaps you save":* Ibid.

291 *Writing to Anatole Heller:* COA/GE, Szell letter to Heller, September 18, 1956.

292 *"he cannot have me conduct":* Ibid.

292 *during the concert on November 1:* On the same day, the orchestra's first pension plan went into effect, making it one of only four U.S. orchestras to have such a plan. COA/BT, annual meeting, minutes, June 26, 1957.

292 *He taped Szell:* The players objected to Heller's tape recordings, which he had

been making for two years during every Saturday concert at Szell's request, because they weren't paid and because Heller had never received permission from the American Federation of Musicians to make the tapes. "Szell has used these tapes to study (at an octave lower) his men in close detail," reported Jim Frankel in the *Press* on December 16, 1956. The musicians were "irked that Szell has used these tapes as a kind of police club to hold over their heads." They threatened a strike if Szell didn't desist from the practice.

292   *"His playing was almost shy"*: The Plain Dealer, March 29, 1957.

293   *"Perhaps if we were to slice"*: Quoted in Ostwald, p. 148.

293   *"His habits annoy me"*: COA, Louis Lane, oral history transcript.

293   *"That nut is a genius"*: Ibid.

293   *A. Beverly Barksdale, a tall, soft-spoken Southerner:* Appointment announced May 2, 1957.

293   *During their 1957 European debut:* The soloists' repertoire comprised Mozart's Piano Concerto in C Minor, K. 491 (Robert Casadesus); Beethoven's "Emperor" Concerto (Leon Fleisher); Mozart's Piano Concerto in D Minor, K. 466 (Rudolf Serkin); Brahms's Violin Concerto (Wolfgang Schneiderhan); three Mozart arias, including one, "Ch'io mi scordi di te," K. 505, with Louis Lane playing the piano obbligato (Elisabeth Schwarzkopf); and three Strauss songs (Schwarzkopf).

293   *"Only a few hotels"*: The Plain Dealer, June 30, 1957.

293   *"You have changed my life"*: The Polish trumpeter was Fransicek Stockfiscz. *Hi-Fi Music at Home*, September 1957.

294   *"In a scant six weeks"*: Eleanor Morrison in *Hi-Fi Music at Home*, September 1957.

294   *"A prodigious orchestra"*: Brussels review (unknown paper) of May 8, 1957, concert.

294   *"I hardly recognized Berlin"*: Associated Press, May 27, 1957.

294   *"Is this the initial break"*: Cleveland Press, June 1, 1957.

295   *"because of intolerable treatment"*: Cleveland News, June 3, 1957.

295   *"Have today released George Smith"*: Ibid.

295   *"non-performance"*: Quoted in *Cleveland News*, June 3, 1957.

295   *losing the orchestra's payroll:* David Zauder, interview by author, Cleveland Heights, Oh., February 18, 1999.

295   *"suddenly turned on me"*: Quoted in *Cleveland News*, June 3, 1957.

295   *"was magnified due to the strenuousness"*: Cleveland News, June 12, 1957.

295   *"the other woman in an alleged triangle"*: Cleveland Press, June 18, 1957.

295   *"Mrs. Smith is a fool"*: Ibid.

295   *"we returned home"*: Beacon Magazine, July 27, 1980.

295   *"No finer orchestra playing"*: The New Statesman and Nation, June 1957.

296   *"magnificent sonority"*: United Press International, June 6, 1957.

296   *"an India rubber jumping jack"*: Ibid.

296   *"In these excellent [European] halls"*: The Plain Dealer, June 30, 1957.

296   *"The Cleveland Orchestra may well be entering"*: Ibid.

296   *"Exploit to the utmost"*: COA/BT, Presidents' Office Files (Frank E. Joseph), Quoted in Joseph letter to Barksdale, July 15, 1957.

Chapter 21: Resounding Success

297 *"That European trip": The Plain Dealer,* October 10, 1957.

297 *Twenty one-hour programs: Cleveland News,* October 8, 1957.

297 *"As I am to have the privilege":* COA/GE, Lindsay letter to Szell, October 18, 1957.

298 *"Orchestra Here Signs First Negro": The Plain Dealer,* October 3, 1957.

298 *"We heard a group of cellists":* COA, Louis Lane, oral history transcript.

298 *"My initial reaction":* COA/GE, Szell letter to Barksdale, December 11, 1957.

298 *"The dates for 2 weeks":* RR, Rodzinski letter to Szell, November 8, 1957.

298 *be $2,000 per week:* COA/C, George Szell, correspondence and subject files, Barksdale letter to Rodzinski, November 26, 1957.

299 *an "exorbitant fee":* Rodzinski, p. 365.

299 *"Right now I have a small complication":* COA/C, George Szell, correspondence and subject files, Rodzinski letter to Barksdale, December 21, 1957.

299 *"and had then found":* Ibid., Barksdale letter to Rodzinski, January 16, 1958.

299 *and asked Heinrich Keilholz:* Shankland, p. 869.

299 *"everything he had": The Plain Dealer,* November 28, 1958.

299 *"If Rodzinski left turbulence": New York Times,* December 7, 1958.

299 *The renovation, estimated at $300,000: Cleveland Press,* October 8, 1958.

300 *"The brassiness is due precisely":* COA/GE, Szell letter to Barksdale, December 11, 1957.

300 *"to permit the Cleveland Orchestra": The Plain Dealer,* July 1, 1958.

300 *"We not only want to hear a pin drop":* Ibid.

300 *"With our new setup":* Ibid.

300 *"unbearably loud and raucous":* David Zauder interview by author, Cleveland Heights, Oh., February 18, 1999.

300 *"I am as pleased as punch":* COA/GE, Szell letter to Barksdale, July 14, 1958.

301 *popular repertoire:* The repertoire for the recordings made on August 21 and 22, 1958, comprised Gould's *American Salute,* Anderson's Serenata, Copland's Three Dance Episodes from *Rodeo,* Bernstein's *Candide* overture, and Piston's *The Incredible Flutist* suite.

301 *"It must have been a real shock":* COA/GE, Szell letter to Barksdale, August 25, 1958.

301 *"Two main considerations":* Ibid., Szell letter to Barksdale, August 28, 1958.

301 *From Hamburg:* Ibid., Keilholz letter to Barksdale, September 2, 1958.

301 *"Pappy objects":* Ibid., Szell letter to Barksdale, September 12, 1958.

301 *Barksdale soothed him:* Ibid., Barksdale letter to Szell, September 15, 1958.

301 *"Heavens, NO, NO":* Ibid., Szell letter to Barksdale, September 11, 1958.

301 *"along the balcony":* COA, Louis Lane, oral history transcript.

302 *"Achtung, Schuss!":* Ibid.

302 *"In very simple terms": The Plain Dealer,* October 8, 1958.

302 *"Tomorrow night for the first time": Cleveland Press,* October 8, 1958.

302 *recounted years later by violinist Bernhard Goldschmidt:* Goldschmidt replaced Salvatore Fiore, who retired in the spring of 1958 from the violin section after 40 years. Fiore was the only remaining member who had been with the orchestra since its formation in 1918 under Nikolai Sokoloff.

302   *"Is this really an orchestra?": The Plain Dealer*, September 29, 1994.

302   *"From the opening heraldry"*: Ibid., October 10, 1958. During the 1957–58 season, Szell kept his promise to offer contemporary music for the 40th anniversary by conducting 9 of the 10 commissioned works (Henri Dutilleux's entry wouldn't show up until 1965). Two outstanding Cleveland pianists impressed audiences this season: Marianne Mastics, as comfortable in jazz as in classics, made her debut under Szell playing Rachmaninoff's Piano Concerto No. 2 in Lakewood; and Eunice Podis made her 50th solo appearance with the orchestra at Carnegie Hall in Peter Mennin's Piano Concerto, whose world premiere she had recently given with Szell at Severance Hall.

303   *"Cleveland can be proud": New York Herald Tribune*, February 6, 1958.

303   *"Such a step"*: COA/BT, annual meeting, minutes, June 25, 1958.

303   *"The Cleveland Orchestra behaves": New York Times*, February 5, 1959.

303   *"the true revelation": New York World-Telegram*, February 5, 1959.

303   *"Its playing is everywhere solid": New York Herald Tribune*, February 5, 1959.

303   *"Orchestra Slowly Thwarts": New York Times*, February 5, 1959.

303   *"The Cleveland Orchestra, one of the best-disciplined groups"*: Ibid.

304   *"This is the kind of blackmail"*: COA/GE, Barksdale letter to Szell, December 12, 1957.

304   *"Consequently, we have changed"*: Ibid., Szell letter to Fleisher, April 26, 1958.

305   *"We brought Schwarzkopf": Cleveland News*, October 8, 1958.

305   *"That's what they always ask!": The Plain Dealer*, November 15, 1958.

305   *"If Frank + Seelbach are opposed"*: COA/GE, Szell letter to Barksdale, May 25, 1958.

305   *"For the many Benny fans": Cleveland Press*, November 5, 1958.

306   *$42,000 went to the pension fund*: COA/GE, Blossom letter to Benny, February 2, 1961.

306   *Cox had learned*: Ibid., Cox letter to Barksdale, November 14, 1958.

306   *Szell gave the idea his blessing*: Ibid., Barksdale letter to Cox, November 18, 1958.

306   *"I probably do not need to point out"*: Ibid., Barksdale letter to Charles S. Boren, February 24, 1959.

306   *Boren wasn't interested*: Ibid., Boren letter to Barksdale, March 3, 1959. The Cleveland Orchestra has had two brushes with the movies. In 1968, it played a score for the *Double-Step*, a fictitious tragedy about the family of a Cleveland Orchestra cellist. The exterior of Severance Hall was used in the opening sequence of *Air Force One*, a film starring Harrison Ford that was released in 1997.

306   *"As I have not heard from you"*: Ibid., Szell letter to Barksdale, December 24, 1957.

307   *"It is our belief"*: Ibid., Cleveland Orchestra resolution to the Musical Arts Association, January 5, 1959.

307   *"I don't think I would accept": Columbus Citizen*, May 17, 1958.

307   *In 1958, Szell's new contract*: COA/BT, Szell contract, April 21, 1958. In the year 2000, the total amount for this period would come to $1,065,918.87. Szell's salary reverted to normal annual compensation for his last five seasons

308   *"It's tremendous": Cleveland Press*, October 23, 1958.

308   *Schumann symphonies:* Szell had recorded Schumann's Second Symphony in 1952 for Columbia, but this performance was a monaural recording.

308   *"orchestral retouches": New York Times*, March 13, 1960.

308   *"I shall not even try":* COA/GE, Szell letter to Barksdale, December 11, 1958.

308   *"Perhaps it is only in the imagination": Cleveland Press*, January 30, 1959.

309   *scheduled to begin an all-Tchaikovsky program:* The program included the Violin Concerto, with Nathan Milstein as soloist, and the Fourth Symphony.

309   *"I'll give you five minutes to clear your throats": The Plain Dealer*, April 10, 1959.

309   *"The orchestra was driven unmercifully":* Ibid.

309   *"This is the first time": Cleveland Press*, April 10, 1959.

309   *"George Szell should understand":* Ibid.

309   *"the audience, duly chastened":* Klaus G. Roy, interview by author, Cleveland Heights, Oh., January 14, 2000.

309   *"I think that New Yorkers":* Associated Press, April 24, 1959.

310   *"I think that that is part of an orchestra's job": New York World-Telegram*, March 26, 1959.

310   *"While in Zurich":* COA/GE, Szell letter to Barksdale, July 2, 1959.

310   *"One day in his office":* COA, Louis Lane, oral history transcript.

CHAPTER 22: ARTISTIC MORALITY

311   *"Good orchestras are common": Saturday Review*, March 10, 1962.

311   *"Szell is one of the world's great musicians": Time*, February 22, 1963.

311   *"For all its glorious sound":* Steinhardt, p. 87.

312   *"What was underneath was pure gold":* Myron Bloom, interview by author, Cleveland Heights, Oh., December 24, 1999.

312   *"It's ironic": Time*, February 22, 1963.

312   *"Rights of Conductor":* COA/GE, trade agreement draft, February 11, 1961.

313   *"Mr. Szell's inspired leadership":* Ibid., Lifschey letter to Barksdale, March 21, 1959.

313   *"He has a beautiful tone": The Plain Dealer*, February 26, 1960.

313   *"This exchange was arranged":* Ibid., March 3, 1960.

313   *"I had no desire to leave Cleveland": Cleveland Press*, March 8, 1960.

314   *"For the first time in fourteen years": The New Yorker*, February 4, 1991.

314   *Among the names Szell and Gingold suggested:* COA/GE, Szell letter to Barksdale, July 24, 1959; Barksdale letter to Szell, July 29, 1959.

314   *"are positively ingenious":* COA/GE, Gingold letter to Druian, December 17, 1959.

315   *The most promising prospect was RCA:* Ibid., Szell letter to Barksdale, August 17, 1962.

315   *about the possibility of succeeding Reiner:* Ibid., Szell letter to Barksdale, June 9, 1961.

315   *"He should intimate to Kayes":* Ibid.

315   *Szell agreed to serve as pianist:* Ibid., Friedmann letter to Barksdale, March

6, 1961.

315   *Another unrealized ambition:* Ibid., Friedmann letter to Barksdale, October 5, 1962.

315   *Barksdale did prove his mettle:* COA/BT, minutes, May 25, 1960.

316   *"Well, let's go through the piece":* Bookspan and Yockey, pp. 176–77.

316   *"I have never had any special yearning":* San Diego Union, May 10, 1960.

317   *"You need money":* San Francisco Examiner, May 14, 1960.

317   *deficits of nearly $900,000:* The Plain Dealer, April 6, 1960.

317   *"When our major athletic teams":* Ibid.

317   *the committee's first major fund-raiser:* Cleveland Press, May 17, 1961.

318   *The judge had agreed:* Associated Press, April 28, 1961.

318   *"None of the major objectives":* The Plain Dealer, June 3, 1961.

318   *"promoting disunity":* Cleveland Press, October 7, 1961. The 16 players were Lawrence Angell, Bert Arenson, William Brown, Warren F. Downs, Felix Freilich, Elden Gatwood, Thomas Liberti, Kurt Loebel, Richard Mackey, Philipp Naegele, Edward Ormond, Gino Raffaelli, Leonard Samuels, George Silfies, Walter Stummer, and Roy Waas.

318   *"I fear that you may lend":* COA/GE, Szell letter to Barksdale, December 5, 1960.

319   *"I hope and pray":* Ibid., Barksdale letter to Szell, December 12, 1960.

319   *"We can not understand":* Ibid., Raffaelli letter to Barksdale, January 15, 1961.

319   *An AFM study:* Bowling Green Daily Sentinel Tribune, July 6, 1961.

319   *"In fact, the average annual wage":* Ibid.

319   *"Yesterday I had my first session":* COA/GE, Barksdale letter to Szell, December 1, 1960.

320   *"If you work to drive me out":* Ibid., Szell letter to Barksdale, undated, late 1960 or early 1961.

320   *"for a fine and difficult season":* Ibid., Szell letter to Barksdale, May 22, 1961.

320   *"Many of our supporters":* Chicago Daily News, March 6, 1963.

320   *A season earlier:* Cleveland Press, October 2, 1961.

320   *"We start rehearsing":* New York Times, February 2, 1964.

320   *"I recall very clearly":* Quoted in COA, Louis Lane, oral history transcript.

321   *"And at the end he started to cry":* COA, Louis Lane, oral history transcript.

321   *"a frightening experience":* New York Times, February 2, 1964.

321   *"Sometimes, but rarely":* Klaus G. Roy, interview by author, Cleveland Heights, Oh., January 14, 2000.

321   *"It was useless":* The Plain Dealer, February 17, 1961.

321   *"It was an extremely brilliant":* Ibid.

321   *"Charming man in his own way":* COA, Louis Lane, oral history transcript.

322   *When Milstein and Szell disagreed:* Ibid.

322   *"At the time of this tour":* COA/GE, Barksdale memo to Szell, October 20, 1969.

322   *"At the end of the concert, several people came backstage":* Ibid.

322   *"tired and was forced to withdraw":* San Francisco Examiner, March 18, 1962.

322   *"It would therefore be a just":* COA/GE, Frankenstein letter to Szell, March 24, 1962.

322   *"It is entirely out of order":* Ibid., Szell letter to Frankenstein, March 26, 1962.

323 *"the airy vagueness"*: San Francisco Examiner, March 29, 1962.

323 *"The secret of this phenomenal symphonic development"*: New York Herald Tribune, February 11, 1962.

323 *"It is a matter of artistic morality"*: Ibid.

323 *"Mr. Szell has lifted the Cleveland Orchestra"*: The New Yorker, Feb. 24, 1962.

323 *"In contrast to the crystalline clarity"*: Cleveland Press, November 2, 1961.

324 *"It was fine except"*: COA, Louis Lane, oral history transcript.

324 *"Topsy-turvy"*: RR, Szell letter to Bruno Zirato, September 7, 1944.

324 *"I have asked the intellectuals"*: Cleveland Press, March 6, 1962.

324 *"It isn't everyone"*: Kathleen Shamp letter to the author, February 2, 1999.

324 *"It was truly heavenly"*: Ibid.

325 *"Trust Beranek"*: COA/GE, Szell letter to Barksdale, June 5, 1962.

325 *"Stokowski was invited to attend"*: Ibid., Barksdale letter to Szell, September 5, 1962.

325 *"In the Lincoln Center parade"*: New York Journal-American, September 28, 1962.

325 *"I agree a hundred percent"*: COA/GE, Szell letter to Barksdale, August 5, 1960.

326 *"an acoustic failure"*: New York Times, April 4, 1963.

326 *"Let me give you a little simile"*: Ibid., July 31, 1970.

326 *"Tear the place down"*: Ibid., February 2, 1964.

326 *"The program is already fixed"*: COA/GE, Szell letter to Barksdale, December 12, 1962.

326 *"cold squire of Severance"*: Cleveland Press, September 20, 1960.

326 *"particularly those of which"*: COA/GE, Szell letter to Barksdale, December 12, 1962.

326 *One of the commemorative articles*: Time, February 2, 1963.

327 *The consul responded*: COA/M/PR, Program Production Files (Klaus Roy), Deutz letter to Barksdale, December 5, 1962.

327 *"a still very young piano virtuoso"*: Ibid.

327 *"in a concert together"*: Ibid.

327 *"Roy Hide this away"*: Ibid.

327 *"It's official!"*: Graffman, p. 152.

CHAPTER 23: DREAMING BIG

329 *Barksdale had mentioned the subject*: COA/GE, Barksdale letter to Szell, July 17, 1959.

329 *"two of the top U.S. symphonies"*: Ibid., Szell letter to Glenn G. Wolfe, director, Office of Cultural Presentations, Department of State, Washington, D.C., July 31, 1963.

329 *the Pittsburgh Symphony drew the plum assignment*: This scenario would turn out to be only partly correct: Pittsburgh and music director William Steinberg *would* beat Cleveland out of the starting gate in 1964 with an 11-week trip to the Middle East and Europe, but they would not appear in Salzburg. Information courtesy of the Pittsburgh Symphony.

329   *"There are only two members"*: COA/GE, Szell letter to Wolfe, July 31, 1963.
Szell discussed his linguistic facility with Doris O'Donnell in a *Plain Dealer*
interview September 29, 1963, previewing his 18th season in Cleveland.
Asked in what language he conducts, Szell answered, "In Switzerland, it's
German, in Prague, it's Czech, in France, French, and Italian in Italy." And in
what language does he swear? "IN ENGLISH."

330   *"expressed keen interest"*: COA/GE, Szell letter to Wolfe, July 31, 1963.

330   *When RCA again pursued:* Ibid., Barksdale letter to Roger G. Hall at RCA,
February 25, 1964.

330   *"Is this not the time"*: Ibid., Barksdale letter to John McClure at Columbia,
June 8, 1964.

331   *"To castigate the moronic qualities"*: Ibid., Szell letter to Burkat, September
11, 1964.

331   *the union adopted a resolution: The Plain Dealer*, December 10, 1963.

331   *only after Szell had stepped down:* COA/GE, Robert L. Larson, lawyer with
Thompson, Hine and Flory, letter to Barksdale, March 1, 1964.

331   *"He should be equipped": Ann Arbor (Mich.) Daily*, November 10, 1963.

332   *"the world seemed a cold":* All quotes from this paragraph from COA/M/PR,
player bios, Harrell interview with Carroll Moore for National Public Radio's
Performance Today, 1997.

332   *"took a great dislike"*: COA, Louis Lane, oral history transcript.

332   *"While Cleveland can attract": The Plain Dealer*, January 28, 1964.

333   *the orchestra's deficit for the previous season: The Plain Dealer*, October 21,
1963.

333   *"When Severance Hall was originally built": Fine Arts*, September 26, 1963.

334   *"Stravinsky had the habit":* Quoted in Roy, p. 166.

334   *"the wonderful atmosphere": The Plain Dealer*, January 1, 1964.

334   *impending retirement in May 1964:* Frank E. Joseph addressed the issue of
Elwell's retirement in a letter to *Plain Dealer* publisher Thomas Vail in a letter on June 3, 1964: "All of us are shocked, if not surprised, at Herbert Elwell's
retirement because he was such a qualified person. The purpose of this letter
is to urge that he be replaced with a music critic of equal standing and stature
who has a broad musical background . . . . The best way to encourage our musical institutions and make *The Plain Dealer* a rallying point of our cultural
world would be to have a music critic on your staff who is really outstanding."
Elwell's successor was Robert Finn, formerly a reporter with the *Akron
Beacon Journal*.

334   *"Mahler's music sounds insufferably old-fashioned": The Plain Dealer*,
February 1, 1964. The so-called "lost cause" ended a program that included
Mozart's *Marriage of Figaro* overture and Beethoven's Piano Concerto No. 4,
with Ivan Moravec in his American debut.

334   *"The orchestra was magnificent in its struggle":* This was yet another instance
of Elwell damning a work that has come to be regarded as a masterpiece. In
December 1940, he used the same words to describe the Berg Violin
Concerto.

334   *"A magician conducted": New York World-Telegram & Sun*, February 4, 1964.

334   *"Mr. Szell and his men": New York Times*, February 4, 1964.

335 *"One must remember":* Columbia Daily Spectator, February 6, 1964.

335 *"at this time unequaled":* Boston Sunday Globe, February 9, 1964.

335 *"The next day in Boston":* The orchestra's program at Boston's Symphony Hall on February 10, 1964, comprised Berlioz's *Roman Carnival Overture*, Mozart's Symphony No. 34, Walton's Variations on a Theme by Hindemith, in its first Boston performance, and Beethoven's Fifth Symphony. The quote appears in a Bloom interview with Michael Charry in the notes accompanying a Sony Classical rerelease of Strauss works performed by the orchestra under Szell.

335 *"That kind of playing":* Myron Bloom, interview by author, Cleveland Heights, Oh., December 24, 1999.

335 *"It was interesting, in fact, how much the Cleveland":* New York Herald Tribune, February 11, 1964. Two weeks later, Clevelanders could discover just how un-American their orchestra had become

336 *"symphony musicians as a group":* COA/GE, Raffaelli letter to Barksdale, March 26, 1964.

336 *Negotiations for a new three-year agreement:* The Plain Dealer, May 5, 1964.

336 *"a dangerous atmosphere":* COA/GE, Szell statement, undated, but early May 1964.

336 *"Rudi Serkin":* Ibid.

337 *A few days later, the musicians, by a vote of 85 to 12:* Cleveland Press, May 11, 1964.

337 *"These are great gains":* Ibid.

337 *"Let's try to find out more":* COA/GE, Szell letter to Barksdale, August 5, 1964.

337 *"very tentative drawings":* Ibid., Barksdale letter to Szell, August 6, 1964.

337 *Officials in University Circle:* Ibid.

338 *"but preferably 200":* Cleveland Press, November 21, 1964.

338 *"We're sensitive to the fact":* Ibid.

338 *"this is what they criticize us for":* The Plain Dealer, September 13, 1964.

338 *Szell asked Levine:* Matheopoulos, p. 280.

338 *On the third program:* The rest of program on October 1 and 3, 1964, was conducted by Szell

339 *Szell devoted many private coaching sessions:* Matheopoulos, pp. 280–81.

339 *Cleveland Concert Associates:* James Levine and general manager John Gidwitz put together remarkable casts for their concert performances at Severance Hall: Mozart's *Don Giovanni* (March 22, 1969)—Ezio Flagello, Franco Iglesias, Lorna Haywood, Ramon Vinay, Jan Peerce, Saramae Endich, Evelyn Mandac, and Italo Tajo; Verdi's *Simon Boccanegra* (December 13, 1969)—Cornell MacNeil, Renata Tebaldi, Richard Tucker, Flagello, Iglesias, Ara Berberian, Rod MacWherter, Penelope Jensen; Beethoven's *Fidelio* (December 16, 1970, the 200th anniversary of Beethoven's birth)—Marion Lippert, Seth McCoy, Vinay, Berberian, Donald Gramm, Mandac, John McCollum, John Walker, Arthur Thompson; Verdi's *Don Carlo* (March 6, 1971)—Berberian, Tucker, MacNeil, Flagello, Gabriella Tucci, Maria Ewing, Janet Coster, MacWherter, Mandac, Vinay.

339 *Lane talked Szell out of making the call:* COA, Louis Lane, oral history tran-

script.

339   *"I find that forcing an orchestra shuts it down"*: Matheopoulos, p. 251.

340   *The reason, according to longtime violinist Evelyn Botnick:* Evelyn Botnick, telephone interview by author, April 16, 1999.

340   *"What do you mean?" he said to the happy father:* Catherine and Stephane Dalschaert, telephone interviews by author, January 20, 2000.

340   *"The lot of the musician": Lorain Journal*, October 31, 1964.

341   *"Both Mr. Szell and I":* COA/GE, Barksdale letter to the men of the orchestra, October 19, 1964.

341   *"We are told":* Ibid., Joseph letter to Warren, November 30, 1964.

341   *"Now Marc, what's wrong?":* Associated Press, January 7, 1965.

341   *"That's the way I play it": The Plain Dealer*, January 7, 1965.

341   *The Lifschey incident:* Henri Dutilleux's *Cinq Métaboles*, the last of the 40th-anniversary commissions, received its world premiere performances on January 14 and 16, 1965, under Szell. The program, the first without Lifschey, also included Prokofiev's Piano Concerto No. 3, with Gina Bachauer as soloist, and Bartók's Concerto for Orchestra.

341   *The obstruction in his urinary tract:* Szell underwent surgery at University Hospitals on February 26, 1965.

342   *"Boulez Bowls 'Em Over": The Plain Dealer*, March 12, 1965.

342   *terminating individual contracts:* COA/BT, Szell contract, February 6, 1965.

342   *a clause to his own new contract:* Ibid.

342   *Initially, Fleisher thought: The Plain Dealer*, April 6, 1965. Fleisher's replacement on the tour was Grant Johannesen.

343   *"We lost contact":* United Press International story printed in *Cleveland Press*, April 16, 1965.

343   *Following the concert:* Associated Press story printed in *Buffalo Courier-Express*, April 17, 1965.

343   *In Moscow, Lane conducted a program:* The American fare comprised Gershwin's Concerto in F, with John Browning as piano soloist, and *Porgy and Bess* suite; Bernstein's *Candide* overture; and Cleveland composer-critic Herbert Elwell's *The Happy Hypocrite* suite; the European repertoire consisted of Sibelius's Symphony No. 5 and Stravinsky's *Firebird* suite.

343   *"What a marvelous interpretation!": The Plain Dealer*, April 21, 1965.

343   *"We consider to be asked to play":* United Press International story printed in *Cleveland Press*, April 23, 1965.

343   *The goodwill gesture:* Ibid.

344   *"The reception we are getting here":* United Press International story printed in *Cleveland Press*, April 30, 1965.

344   *"Armenians Won't Let Szell Stop":* Associated Press story printed in *The Plain Dealer*, May 8, 1965.

344   *"When violinist Gino Raffaelli":* United Press International story printed in *Cleveland Press*, May 10, 1965.

344   *"hundreds of fans attempted": Time*, May 28, 1965.

344   *"It is the only contact":* Associated Press story printed in many newspapers, May 18, 1965.

344   *"Since Mrs. Sibelius is 93":* COA/BT, minutes, July 15, 1965.

344 *"was the greatest lesson"*: Associated Press story printed in *The Plain Dealer*, May 28, 1965.

344 *"I have been a little frightened"*: Ibid.

344 *"In the afternoon we took a taxi"*: COA/BT, minutes, July 15, 1965.

345 *"Wizards from Cleveland"*: Polish Communist Party newspaper *Trybuna Ludu*, May 29, 1965.

345 *"Cleveland Conquered Paris"*: *Paris-Press*, June 1, 1965.

345 *"He was scared and neurotic"*: Kurt Loebel interview by author, Cleveland Heights, Oh., January 28, 1999.

345 *"From that point on"*: Ibid.

345 *"Our Szell"*: United Press International story printed in *Cleveland Press*, June 11, 1965.

345 *"This orchestra does not need to improve"*: *The Plain Dealer*, June 15, 1965.

345 *"The Cleveland players show"*: *Financial Times*, June 22, 1965.

346 *"To your loved ones at home"*: COA/BT, minutes, July 15, 1965.

CHAPTER 24: SUMMER MUSIC

347 *Eleven parcels of land*: *Akron Beacon Journal*, October 9, 1966.

347 *"Our site developers studied"*: COA/BT, Advisory Council to the Public Relations Committee of the Musical Arts Association Report of Meeting, June 6, 1981.

348 *"If we ever get"*: RF, Joseph letter to Finn, May 10, 1965. Courtesy of Robert Finn.

348 *a 200-acre site in Peninsula*: *Akron Beacon Journal*, July 6, 1965.

348 *"The Cleveland Orchestra has become the best"*: *Cleveland Press*, July 10, 1965.

348 *"While it is of course IMPERATIVE"*: COA/GE, Szell letter to Barksdale, July 13, 1965.

348 *"I hope that we can actually acquire"*: COA/GE, Barksdale letter to Szell, July 19, 1965.

349 *"This comparison with Detroit"*: COA/BT, minutes, April 1, 1966.

349 *He chose the phrase*: 1966 and 1967 were peak years for orchestra personnel at 111, including five on the conducting staff during the 1965–66 season and six during the 1966–67 season.

349 *"a step closer to year-round employment"*: *Cleveland Press*, April 8, 1966.

349 *"We considered that site"*: COA, Louis Lane, oral history transcript.

350 *"We have had meetings"*: COA/GE, Barksdale letter to Szell, June 21, 1966.

350 *"described as having"*: *Cleveland Press*, June 25, 1966.

350 *"the largest ever to be developed"*: Ibid.

350 *"Please do not attempt"*: COA/GE, Barksdale memo to the orchestra, June 30, 1966.

350 *site committee chairman Reed*: The committee also included James D. Ireland and R. Henry Norweb Jr.

350 *the Musical Arts Association was buying 571 acres*: COA/BT, minutes, July 28, 1966.

350   *Christopher Jaffe, an acoustician from Connecticut:* Jaffe would be the acoustical consultant for the Severance Hall renovation in the late 1990s.

350   *"Why don't we build":* Christopher Jaffe, interview by author, Cleveland, Oh., January 7, 2000.

351   *naming the facility Blossom Music Center:* COA/BT, minutes, July 28, 1966.

351   *"weren't sure people would understand":* COA, Michael Maxwell, oral history transcript.

351   *"I do hope that the tickets":* COA/BT, minutes, 1966, Emily Blossom letter to Musical Arts Association board, September 14, 1966.

351   *"The crises have been frequent":* Ibid., Joseph letter to Emily Blossom, September 26, 1966.

351   *"big name" architects hadn't been hired:* COA/GE, Barksdale letter to Szell, August 18, 1966.

351   *"the most brilliant young architect":* Ibid., Barksdale letter to Szell, August 29, 1966.

351   *Walter Gropius:* Ibid.

351   *Robert C. Marsh, the Chicago Sun-Times critic:* The critic of the *Chicago Sun-Times* had written a laudatory article about the Cleveland Orchestra, inaccurately titled "One Hundred Men and a Perfectionist," for the February 1961 issue of *High Fidelity* magazine. In 1966, he was the third choice—after Paul Henry Lang and Winthrop Sargent—to write a book about the orchestra for its 50th anniversary. COA/GE, Barksdale letter to Szell, August 20, 1965.

351   *"Wags are already referring to it as the Szellsburg Festival":* Chicago Sun-Times, September 8, 1966.

352   *Even after four wells were dug:* The Plain Dealer, January 9, 1968.

352   *"The only reason":* Ibid.

352   *"build now a fire":* COA/GE, Szell letter to Barksdale, November 16, 1966.

352   *"It is quite possible":* Ibid.

352   *Szell convinced the board:* COA, Louis Lane, oral history transcript.

353   *had begun to build an airstrip:* COA/BT, minutes, January 13, 1967.

353   *the Court of Appeals:* Ibid., October 27, 1967.

353   *"The Cleveland Symphony should not settle":* COA/GE, Mills letter to Barksdale, September 20, 1966.

353   *"Such a facility":* COA/BT, minutes, press release, November 15, 1966.

353   *"future costs of area maintenance":* Ibid., January 13, 1967.

353   *$6.6 million:* Ibid.

353   *"This is the first capital fund effort":* The Plain Dealer, March 26, 1967.

354   *building an annex onto Severance Hall:* COA/BT, minutes, October 27, 1967.

354   *Although the orchestra had balanced:* Ibid., annual meeting, minutes, October 22, 1967.

354   *Reed told him:* Ibid., minutes, October 27, 1967.

354   *He had insisted:* COA/GE, Szell letter to Barksdale, August 17, 1968.

354   *When Barksdale and trustees:* Ibid., Barksdale letter to Szell, November 16, 1967.

354   *"I am writing to you":* Ibid., Szell letter to Stokowski, September 26, 1967.

354   *"As you can possibly imagine":* Ibid., Copland letter to Szell, November 1, 1967.

355 *"Ah, but we hope our acoustics": Plain Dealer Sunday Magazine*, June 9, 1968.

355 *"[Every] time we have mentioned"*: Ibid.

356 *"The Cleveland Orchestra has a record": Chicago Sun-Times*, July 14, 1968.

356 *"The whole idea of the Blossom Festival": Akron Beacon Journal*, July 18, 1968.

356 *"I believe that Blossom Music Center": Cleveland Press*, July 19, 1968.

356 *"For a while it appeared": New York Times*, July 20, 1968.

357 *"there is something of Saarinen"*: Ibid., July 28, 1968.

357 *"Mr. Keilholz has done an impressive job"*: Ibid., July 20, 1968.

357 *"Don't waste time": Chicago Tribune*, July 20, 1970.

357 *"It is obvious no one did"*: Ibid.

357 *"Perhaps only in the name of a family": Saturday Review*, August 3, 1968.

357 *"The verdict on Blossom Music Center": The Plain Dealer*, July 20, 1968.

358 *"In one jump": Cleveland Press*, July 20, 1968.

358 *"The music received": New York Times*, July 20, 1968.

358 *Peinemann played:* Two months later, in September 1968, the violinist was the soloist when Szell recorded Strauss's "Morgen" with soprano Elisabeth Schwarzkopf and the London Symphony for EMI.

358 *Mahler Fourth Symphony:* Reviewing the Mahler Fourth in *The Plain Dealer* on July 27, 1968, Finn dreamed about other Mahler at Blossom: "How the great Second, Third or Eighth Mahler Symphonies would resound in this grand setting! I'll put a wish in my Christmas stocking." Eventually, he would get all of these wishes. Elisabeth Schwarzkopf had sung with Szell and the orchestra during their first European tour in 1957 and recorded the *Four Last Songs* with Szell and the Berlin Radio Symphony Orchestra in 1965 (and almost made a recording with Szell in Cleveland in April 1966 for Columbia Records). The soprano's husband, Walter Legge, produced the 1965 Strauss recording on EMI. "Walter and I began to work rather late in my career with Maestro Szell—a concert with the incomparable Cleveland Orchestra and three records," Schwarzkopf wrote in her memoirs. "But they were some of the most rewarding music-making experiences we had." Schwarzkopf, p. 75.

358 *Herb Alpert and the Tijuana Brass: The Plain Dealer*, August 6, 1968.

359 *"At least once during each concert"*: Ibid., August 14, 1968.

359 *The "Blossom boom:* COA/BT, minutes, July 18, 1969.

359 *"Even if the term"*: COA/GE, Szell letter to Barksdale, September 3, 1968.

360 *Although operating expenses: Cleveland Press*, November 26, 1968.

360 *"exercise complete artistic control": New York Times*, July 28, 1968.

360 *"If I were you"*: COA/GE, Szell letter to Barksdale, November 10, 1968.

360 *"Along with every other orchestra"*: COA/BT, annual meeting, minutes, October 13, 1968.

CHAPTER 25: MUSICIANS AND MIRACLES

361 *"I am herewith giving notice"*: COA/GE, Szell letter to Frank E. Joseph, October 4, 1965.

362 *"If you were a player": Beacon Magazine*, July 28, 1980.

363   "He wanted more string sound": Robert Conrad, interview by author, Warrensville Heights, Oh., September 9, 1999.

363   "and this is what I want to fix": Ibid.

364   "Violin players set up a betting pool": Cleveland Press, February 1, 1966.

364   "Resolved, that the Orchestra membership": COA/GE, Martin Morris letter to Barksdale, February 5, 1966.

364   "This will be a grand tour": The Plain Dealer, February 6, 1966.

364   "In cities having major symphony orchestras": COA/GE, Joseph letter to Stanton, February 21, 1966.

365   "Year by year": New York Herald Tribune, February 22, 1966.

365   invited Maxwell: COA, Michael Maxwell, oral history transcript.

366   "Anyone reading the entire article": The Plain Dealer, April 13, 1966.

366   "A man presently retiring": Ibid.

366   "an angry Cleveland Orchestra": Ibid.

366   the musicians had been displeased: Cleveland Heights Sun Messenger, May 19, 1966.

367   "In the 20 years": Los Angeles Times, May 1, 1966.

367   "You can't be a 'good guy' and whip an orchestra into shape": San Francisco Examiner, May 2, 1966.

367   "RE his programs with the C.O.": COA/GE, Szell letter to Barksdale, June 21, 1966.

367   "Hitler's Conductor": Sun Press, August 18, 1866.

368   "One Cleveland musician": Ibid.

368   "I must say that the almost embarrassingly fine reputation": Cleveland Press, September 16, 1966.

368   "a marked decline": COA/GE, Barksdale letter to the orchestra, September 1966.

368   "This could be of great help": COA/GE, Barksdale memo to the orchestra, September 12, 1966.

368   Months after the program aired: The orchestra received some unwanted publicity in November 1966. Between concerts featuring Mozart's C Minor Mass and Stravinsky's Symphony of Psalms under Robert Shaw, Marjorie A. Winbigler, an assistant librarian at the Cleveland Public Library who had sung alto in the Cleveland Orchestra Chorus for 10 years, was beaten, raped, and stabbed to death in the Fine Arts Garden about 100 yards from Severance Hall. She was walking toward the hall when she was attacked. "She was outstanding both vocally and musically," Shaw told The Plain Dealer on November 10. "But even more than that, it was her personality and dedication that made her so remarkable." The case was never solved.

369   "the atmosphere is bleak": COA/BT, minutes, January 13, 1967.

369   Szell and the orchestra largely kept their heads: Several Szell programs during the 1966–67 season contained unusual fare, such as Easley Blackwood's Symphony Fantasy (Cleveland premiere), Carlos Chávez's Resonances (U.S. premiere), and Benjamin Lees's Concerto for String Quartet and Orchestra (Cleveland premiere, with violinists Rafael Druian and Bernhard Goldschmidt, violist Abraham Skernick, and cellist Lynn Harrell as soloists). But most of Szell's programs again stood firmly in mainstream territory, as can

be heard on the vibrant Columbia recordings that were made surrounding these performances. Szell and the orchestra this season recorded works by Brahms (Symphonies nos. 1 and 2, *Academic Festival Overture, Tragic Overture*) and Beethoven (*Egmont, Leonore No. 2, King Stephen*, and *Coriolan* overtures), excerpts from Schubert's *Rosamunde* and Mendelssohn's *A Midsummer Night's Dream* incidental music, Haydn's "Surprise" Symphony, and Rossini overtures (*La gazza ladra, L'italiana in Algeri, Il viaggio a Reims, La scala di seta, Il turco in Italia*).

369   *"One must go back to Toscanini"*: New York Times, May 7, 1967.

369   *"There was a cough"*: United Press International, February 4, 1967.

370   *"As a great conductor"*: COA/GE, Granata letter to Szell, February 3, 1967.

370   *"A businessman who did not have legal counsel"*: Quoted in *Cleveland Press*, March 31, 1967.

370   *go out on strike*: Ibid.

370   *"the highest paid"*: Cleveland Press, May 11, 1967.

370   *Union president Granata*: Ibid.

370   *"callous disregard for minimal standards"*: The Plain Dealer, May 13, 1967.

370   *"as high wage rates as the plumbers"*: Ibid.

371   *"We hope last night's massive strike vote"*: Cleveland Press, May 19, 1867.

371   *"Under the present contract"*: Sun Press, May 25, 1967.

371   *Adams told the trustees*: COA/BT, minutes, May 26, 1967.

371   *"May 70 for Japan"*: COA/GE, Szell letter to Barksdale, July 11, 1967.

371   *Granata said he had received*: Cleveland Press, July 19, 1967.

371   *"the orchestra will strike"*: Ibid.

372   *"it's so good"*: New York Times, August 2, 1967.

372   *"we shall find the international audience"*: Chicago Sun-Times story printed in *Washington Post*, August 19, 1967.

372   *"audiences cheered and critics lyricized"*: The Plain Dealer, August 15, 1967. The program comprised Weber's *Oberon* overture, Strauss's *Don Juan*, and Beethoven's "Eroica".

372   *"a fascinating performance"*: Ibid.

372   *"Precision and Virtuosity"*: Die Presse (Vienna), August 16, 1967. The program comprised Brahms's Symphony No. 2, Mozart's Symphony No. 40, and Ravel's *Daphnis et Chloé* Suite No. 2.

372   *"I just decided to try my comeback"*: United Press International, August 16, 1967.

372   *"In the interval of the rehearsal"*: Gramophone, April 1988.

373   *"Half an hour"*: Karajan, p. 77.

373   *"The Salzburg audience"*: Die Kurier (Vienna), August 1967.

373   *"Karajan liked to conduct"*: COA, Louis Lane, oral history transcript.

373   *"Really, now, no orchestra can be that good"*: United Press International story printed in *Cleveland Press*, August 21, 1967.

373   *"What an orchestra it is! Is there any other that combines"*: Financial Times, August 21, 1967.

374   *"During the third suite of Bach"*: The Guardian, August 22, 1967.

374   *"a very run of the mill concert"*: Scottish Daily Express, August 21, 1967.

374   *"disappointingly unadventurous"*: Scottish Daily Mail, August 23, 1967.

374   "began with a performance": The Scotsman, August 22, 1967.

374   "that I cannot read without blushing": The Plain Dealer, September 24, 1967.

374   "Here I must call on the muse of caution": The Guardian, August 23, 1967.

375   Cleveland became the first major American orchestra to record in Britain:
       Gramophone, October 1967.

375   "indisputably the best": Associated Press story reprinted in Toledo Times,
       September 1, 1967.

375   "tremendous fund-raising efforts": COA/GE, Cleveland Orchestra
       Committee letter to subscribers, August 30, 1967.

375   "We earnestly hope": The Plain Dealer, August 31, 1967.

375   "We played at our best": United Press International story printed in Cleveland
       Press, September 1, 1967.

375   "The orchestra members are seeking": New York Times, September 11, 1967.

376   "Why were we not kept informed": COA/GE, Cleveland Orchestra
       Committee letter to subscribers, September 13, 1967.

376   their union squeezed through a new three-year contract: The Plain Dealer,
       September 18, 1967.

376   "instructed me to institute legal action": Ibid., September 19, 1967.

376   The orchestra countered: Ibid., March 30, 1967.

377   Szell was being named senior guest conductor: Cleveland Press, October 8,
       1967.

377   "I can't tell you how pleased I am": COA/GE, Bernstein letter to Szell,
       November 22, 1967.

377   "No other kind of long-range commitment": New York Times, March 21, 1968.

377   Boulez later confirmed: Pierre Boulez, interview by author, Cleveland, Oh.,
       April 29, 1999.

377   "Everything is going extremely well": COA/GE, Barksdale letter to Szell,
       November 16, 1967.

378   management announced that the ensemble: Cleveland Press, November 14,
       1967.

378   "How is it possible that this could be done": COA/GE, Barksdale memo to
       Szell, December 14, 1967.

378   "It is in behalf of the musicians": Ibid., Barksdale letter to Davis, November
       24, 1967.

379   The recording sessions with Gilels: Gilels was the second eminent pianist to
       record with Cleveland at this time

379   "Shostakovich Tenth Long Crap": COA/GE, Szell telegram to Barksdale,
       November 2, 1967.

379   Triple Concerto, with Rostropovich and pianist Sviatoslav Richter: EMI in-
       stead made the Beethoven Triple Concerto recording with violinist David
       Oistrakh, cellist Mstislav Rostropovich, and pianist Sviatoslav Richter with
       Herbert von Karajan and the Berlin Philharmonic.

379   and pianist Sviatoslav Richter: Other Cleveland projects on the drawing
       board at EMI at this time but never realized were Karajan and Szell per-
       formances of the Tchaikovsky and Mendelssohn violin concertos, again with
       Oistrakh, and the Brahms and Verdi requiems. COA/GE, Summary of
       Meeting with CBS Records and EMI in New York, August 13, 1968.

379 *"George Szell conducted"*: New York Times, February, 1968.

379 *"be prepared at all times"*: COA/C, Szell letter to U.S. Selective Service Board No. 50 in Cincinnati, April 4, 1968.

380 *"This seems to be the case of the 2 herons"*: COA/GE, Maazel letter to Szell, April 30, 1968.

380 *"I share your wish"*: Ibid., Szell letter to Maazel, May 7, 1968.

CHAPTER 26: DEPARTURE

381 *"Should death intervene"*: COA, Music Director Contracts, Szell contract, February 6, 1965.

382 *"If there has to be chaos"*: The New Yorker, May 30, 1970.

382 *A study commissioned:* COA/GE, Barksdale letter to the orchestra, November 27, 1968.

382 *Columbia agreed to record:* Ibid., CBS Records agreement with Musical Arts Association, October 1, 1968.

383 *"If I see a single one"*: Ibid., Szell note to Barksdale scribbled on page 63 of Time magazine, November 15, 1968 issue.

383 *He did so, and later would show Cleveland:* The week Eschenbach was at Severance Hall for his debut as piano soloist, Maxwell heard from another young man who would have an impact on the orchestra. Thomas W. Morris, a former musician who had tried his hand at arts management, wanted to know if Cleveland had any openings. "If I do go back into orchestra management, which at present I intend to do, I have decided that I would rather start out as an assistant in a big orchestra rather than top man in a little one," wrote Morris, whose father had been board president of the Rochester Philharmonic when Erich Leinsdorf was conductor. (COA/GE, Morris letter to Maxwell, January 12, 1969.) Maxwell advised Morris not to consider a British orchestra and instead to pursue leads in the United States. (COA/GE, Maxwell letter to Morris, January 19, 1969.) Two months later, Maxwell again heard from Morris, who told him he had accepted a job in the business office of the Boston Symphony Orchestra, which he later would lead as general manager before assuming the same post (renamed executive director) in Cleveland in 1987. (COA/GE, Morris letter to Maxwell, March 1, 1969.)

383 *Barksdale already was negotiating:* He hoped that Boulez would make recordings of works by Stravinsky, Ravel, Bartók, Schubert, Ives, Berlioz, and Haydn with the Cleveland Orchestra. Boulez would later make most of them with the New York Philharmonic. COA/GE, Barksdale letter to Thomas Frost at CBS Records, January 23, 1969.

384 *"I remember the date"*: Pierre Boulez, interview by author, Cleveland, Oh., April 29, 1999.

384 *"You will agree with me"*: COA/C, Boulez letter to Szell, May 28, 1969.

384 *"The Frenchman's escalating guest conducting arrangements"*: The Plain Dealer, June 11, 1969.

384 *Szell and Barksdale began talks:* COA/GE, Szell letter to Barksdale, February 21, 1969.

384   *"I'm not apologizing":* COA, Michael Maxwell, oral history transcript.

384   *associate concertmaster Daniel Majeske moved over:* Majeske played his first
concerts as concertmaster on May 15, and 17, 1969. The program, led by Szell,
comprised Weber's *Oberon* Overture, Mendelssohn's Violin Concerto (with
Erica Morini as soloist), and Brahms's Symphony No. 2.

385   *"The orchestra may face death":* Associated Press, May 19, 1969.

385   *"disband or face bankruptcy":* Ibid.

385   *"Meeting in New York City":* The Plain Dealer, November 26, 1969.

385   *By mid-July 1969:* COA/BT, minutes, July 18, 1969.

385   *"negative press":* Ibid.

385   *Szell had cut back his 1969 Blossom schedule:* Blossom audiences in 1969
heard Szell conduct Prokofiev's "Classical" Symphony, Mozart's Piano
Concerto No. 27 (with Robert Casadesus), Franck's Symphony in D Minor,
Mendelssohn's Violin Concerto (James Oliver Buswell IV), Tchaikovsky's
Sixth Symphony, Mozart's *Figaro* overture and Piano Concerto No. 21 (Geza
Anda), and Brahms's Fourth Symphony.

386   *"success has brought with it":* COA/C, Barksdale letter to Joseph and Rankin,
September 22, 1969.

386   *When Maxwell received an invitation:* COA, Michael Maxwell, oral history
transcript.

386   *Haber said:* Haber, interview by author, Shaker Heights, Oh., September 9,
1999.

387   *"I already saw a change in him":* COA, Michael Maxwell, oral history transcript.

387   *A solution seemed to arrive:* COA/GE, Barksdale memo, May 19, 1969.

387   *Then a sticky technicality emerged:* Ibid.

387   *Szell, not unreasonably, insisted:* COA/GE, Andrew Kazdin (Columbia
Records) letter to Robert Crothers (American Federation of Musicians, New
York), August 22, 1969.

387   *"I am really heartsick":* Ibid., Barksdale letter to Kazdin, October 21, 1969.

387   *Baker's searching artistry:* In the July 1977 issue of *Opera News*, Baker discussed Mahler's music with Stephen Wadsworth" "I also did a lot of Mahler
with Szell. I wish he'd lived longer. He was a frightening man, but if one survived the initial impact of the personality, one learned a great deal. He was a
superb musician who demanded absolute excellence and preparedness."

387   *"George Szell, looking trim and fit":* New York Times, February 10, 1970.

388   *he solidified plans:* COA/GE, Carlos Moseley (managing director, New York
Philharmonic) letter to Barksdale, September 15, 1969.

388   *"We would be honored beyond measure":* COA/C, Shaw letter to Szell,
October 31, 1969.

388   *Yet another request:* Ibid., Ormandy letter to Szell, November 8, 1969.

388   *"There is nothing at all subtle":* The Plain Dealer, November 7, 1969.

388   *One project that had been in the works:* COA/GE, John Coveney (Angel in
New York) letter to Peter Andry (EMI in London), November 21, 1969.

388   *"Dr. Szell is quite willing":* Ibid., Coveney memo to Meggs, November 25,
1969. One conductor EMI was eyeing for Cleveland recordings was Herbert
von Karajan, who had been so impressed when he led the ensemble at the

1967 Salzburg and Lucerne festivals. Maxwell was holding the first week of November 1971 for a Karajan engagement in Cleveland in case the deal worked out. (It wouldn't.) A conductor who was becoming increasingly popular in Cleveland, with the musicians as well as audiences, was back in late November and early December 1969 for two weeks of concerts: Istvan Kertész, who led a Mozart-Dvorak program the first week and works by Brahms, Mahler, and Bartók the second week.

389 *"if the orchestra as we know it":* The Plain Dealer, October 15, 1969.

389 *The players were asking:* COA/GE, Cleveland Orchestra contract proposal, December 1969.

389 *"A voice in the selection of the Musical Director":* Ibid.

389 *He had commitments:* COA/C, Mrs. Margaret Glove (special assistant to Szell) letter to Susan J. Rogan (at EMI in London), December 2, 1969.

389 *"This is to certify":* COA/GE, Dr. Kurt Altman (New York Medical College) note regarding Szell, February 16, 1970.

390 *"Lane, although he had had only one rehearsal":* New York Times, February 22, 1970.

390 *Leighton Kerner:* Women's Wear Daily, February 24, 1970.

390 *"with the score":* Barenboim, p. 122.

390 *"The Cleveland Orchestra is in trouble":* Orchestra advertisement in local newspapers, April 3, 1970.

391 *"He was just worried about the state of the world":* COA, Michael Maxwell, oral history transcript.

391 *"Ladies and gentlemen, my gratitude for your warm reception":* Tape of Szell introduction to concert, May 7, 1970, courtesy of WCLV.

391 *"The orchestra's final concert":* Sun Press, May 14, 1970.

392 *"In the past 24 years":* Oregon Journal, May 11, 1970.

392 *"This is the finest symphony orchestra":* Seattle Post-Intelligencer, May 12, 1970.

392 *"He shook as many hands":* Sun Press, May 28, 1970.

392 *"Oh, yes, Dr. Szell":* COA, Louis Lane, oral history transcript.

393 *"I won't be here":* Humel quoting Szell in COA, Louis Lane, oral history transcript.

393 *"who fed us at the table":* COA, Louis Lane, oral history transcript.

393 *"Did he have some premonition":* The Plain Dealer, August 22, 1971.

393 *"I felt a chill through my body":* Michael Haber, interview by author, Shaker Heights, Oh., September 9, 1999.

393 *"He looked like the wrath of God":* Beacon Magazine, July 27, 1980.

393 *"With the memories of the recent tour":* COA/C, Loebel letter to Szell, June 2, 1970.

394 *"Your kind letter":* Ibid., Szell letter to Loebel, June 5, 1970.

394 *"Bring your score over":* COA, Louis Lane, oral history transcript.

394 *"Please set the tempo":* COA/C, Kazdin letter to Szell, July 2, 1970. For Columbia, Kazdin and Szell were planning to record the Prelude and "Good Friday Spell" from Wagner's *Parsifal* and Mozart piano concertos nos. 20 and 25 with Robert Casadesus in January 1971; and excerpts from Wagner's *Lohengrin* and *Meistersinger* and Tchaikovsky's Fourth Symphony in May

1971.

394 *beards and mustaches:* COA/GE, Gino Raffaelli letter to Maxwell, June 27, 1970.

395 *"You guys are so fucking good":* Several former members of the orchestra confirmed the essential accuracy of the phrase.

395 *"I gave them so much":* COA, Louis Lane, oral history transcript.

395 *"was crestfallen":* Ibid., Michael Maxwell, oral history transcript.

395 *"He looked like a white cupcake":* Ingrid Loebel, interview by author, Cleveland Heights, Oh., June 27, 1998.

395 *"quite simply, one of the greatest occasions":* Ibid., July 10, 1970.

395 *Local newspapers carried stories:* Announcement in newspapers, July 16, 1970.

395 *"any economic agreement":* COA/BT, Rankin statement to orchestra and union representatives, July 16, 1970.

395 *"in terms not of compensation increases":* Ibid.

396 *"an audition committee for new members":* COA/GE, Cleveland Orchestra contract proposal, July 22, 1970.

396 *"They were like father and daughter":* COA, Michael Maxwell, oral history transcript.

396 *a doctor wrote a note:* COA/BT, Presidents' Office Files (Frank E. Joseph), Dr. Gerald T. Kent note, July 24, 1970.

396 *"Some of the artists":* Cleveland Press, July 24, 1970.

396 *"A number of guest conductors":* COA/BT, Presidents' Office Files (Alfred M. Rankin), Rankin letter to Mrs. George Szell, July 28, 1970.

397 *the association agreed to a compromise:* Ibid., Musical Arts Association additions to proposal for three-year trade agreement, July 28, 1970.

397 *"like the Chicago Symphony":* Chicago Sun-Times, July 29, 1970.

397 *"by relaxing present humiliating and punitive measures":* COA/GE, Cleveland Orchestra Committee newsletter, July 30, 1970.

397 *"It is not our intention":* COA/GE, Cleveland Orchestra Committee newsletter, August 16, 1970.

398 *Lane claims Barksdale:* COA, Louis Lane, oral history transcript.

398 *"the shock of the news":* The Plain Dealer, July 31, 1970.

398 *"For me it was like a pupil and teacher":* Ibid.

398 *"Few men did more":* Ibid.

CHAPTER 27: DISCORD

401 *"The board left me":* Maxwell fax to the author, January 7, 1999.

401 *"My principal concern":* Ibid.

401 *the conductor lay dying:* COA, Louis Lane, oral history transcript.

402 *His input during the two years:* Pierre Boulez interview with the author, April 29, 1999.

402 *"Obviously the repertoire":* The Plain Dealer, August 19, 1970.

402 *a vote of 84 to 14:* Cleveland Press, August 4, 1970.

403 *"absolutely refuse any change":* COA/BT, minutes, August 14, 1970.

403   *messages from István Kertész and Robert Shaw:* COA/GE, Kertész telegram to Maxwell, August 2, 1970; Shaw phone call to Frank E. Joseph, COA/BT, minutes, August 14, 1970.

403   *formation of a search committee:* COA/BT, minutes, August 14, 1970.

403   *"We have some horrendous financial and other problems":* COA/GE, Joseph letter to cellist Diane Mather, August 25, 1970.

403   *Recording might resume: The Plain Dealer,* August 14, 1970.

404   *At 12:01 a.m. on September 7:* Ibid., September 7, 1970.

404   *"They're afraid that a new conductor": Columbus Citizen-Journal,* September 10, 1970.

404   *"The passing of George Szell": The Plain Dealer,* September 13, 1970.

404   *"with your help":* COA/GE, Maxwell letter to orchestra members, September 18, 1970.

404   *"The Cleveland Orchestra's 1970–71 season": The Plain Dealer,* September 19, 1970.

405   *"very foreign to our nature": Cleveland Press,* September 23, 1970.

405   *The new Cleveland proposal:* Cleveland Orchestra Committee and Cleveland Federation of Musicians advertisement in Cleveland newspapers, September 26, 1970.

405   *"We have repeatedly informed the members":* COA/BT, annual meeting, minutes, September 27, 1970.

405   *"It is a testing time for us all":* Ibid.

405   *The orchestra committee addressed their grievances:* COA/BT, Presidents' Office Files (Alfred M. Rankin), Cleveland Orchestra Committee letter to trustees, October 9, 1970.

406   *The board briefly took up:* Ibid., minutes, October 13, 1970.

406   *The season was saved:* COA/GE, Maxwell telegram to Thomas Perry (Boston Symphony), October 16, 1970.

406   *"I really feel": The Plain Dealer,* October 17, 1970.

406   *"major victory":* COA/BT, minutes, October 21, 1970.

406   *"somewhat bitter":* Ibid.

407   *The board had appointed a search committee:* COA/BT, minutes, January 15, 1971.

407   *he suggested to colleagues:* Ibid., Presidents' Office Files (Alfred M. Rankin), Maxwell memo to Rankin, Joseph, Adams, Vignos, and Lane, October 14, 1970.

407   *Beethoven programs:* Eugene Ormandy began the 1970–71 season on October 22 and 24 with Beethoven concerts comprising the first and ninth symphonies, with soprano Heather Harper, mezzo-soprano Helen Vanni, tenor Stuart Burrows, bass-baritone Tom Krause, and the Cleveland Orchestra Chorus. On October 25, the Ninth was preceded by the composer's Quintet for Piano and Winds with pianist Victor Babin and orchestra principals John Mack (oboe), Robert Marcellus (clarinet), George Goslee (bassoon), and Myron Bloom (horn).

407   *"inflexible perfectionist": The Plain Dealer,* October 20, 1970.

407   *Few of the names:* COA/BT, Presidents' Office Files (Alfred M. Rankin), Musical Arts Association list of possible conductor candidates, 1970–71:

Young conductors of established international reputation: Abbado, Barenboim, Boulez, C. Davis, Frühbeck de Burgos, Haitink, Kertész, Maazel, Mehta, Ozawa, Prêtre, Previn, Sawallisch, Schippers; Young conductors of national reputation: Almeida, Commissiona, Foster, Johanos, Lombard, Lewis, Mester, Schermerhorn, Torkanowsky; Young conductors of growing reputation: Atzmon, Ceccato, Dohnányi, Gibson, Gielen, Tilson Thomas, Varviso, Zinman; Senior conductors of established international reputation: Bernstein, Karajan, Krips, Kubelik, Kletzki, Leinsdorf, Martinon, Schmidt-Isserstedt, Solti; Senior conductors of national reputation: Ehrling, Katims, Shaw, Skrowaczewski, Solomon, Susskind.

407   *"to decide the qualifications"*: Ibid., Presidents' Office Files (Frank E. Joseph), Joseph letter to Maxwell, October 21, 1970.

407   *"When the musical rumor mills start grinding"*: *The Plain Dealer*, October 26, 1970.

408   *But Maazel actually had known:* Maazel's Royal Festival Hall program in May 1961 with the Philharmonia Orchestra of London consisted of Bartók's Concerto for Orchestra and Berlioz's *Symphonie fantastique*. A year later, Maazel and the Philharmonia were supposed to record Puccini's *Tosca* with Maria Callas in the title role, but she cancelled. Since the EMI sessions were already scheduled, Maazel and the Philharmonia instead recorded Mussorgsky's *Pictures at an Exhibition*, Debussy's *Afternoon of a Faun*, and Strauss's *Till Eulenspiegel* and *Also sprach Zarathustra*, with Maxwell turning pages for string players in the last work. Preceding information from Maxwell fax to the author, January 27, 1999. (Maazel finally made a *Tosca* recording in 1966 for Decca/London, with Birgit Nilsson, Franco Corelli, Dietrich Fischer-Dieskau, and the Chorus and Orchestra of the Accademia di Santa Cecilia, Rome.)

408   *"This question is not official"*: Ibid.

408   *Mehta, without giving a reason: The Plain Dealer*, November 10, 1970.

408   *"It becomes a contest"*: Ibid., November 4, 1970.

408   *Abbado's two weeks of concerts:* Abbado's program on November 5 and 7, 1970, comprised Mozart's "Vorrei spiegarvi, O dio" and Berg's *Lulu* suite, both with soprano Margaret Price, and Bruckner's Symphony No. 1. On November 11, 12, and 14, he conducted Webern's Five Pieces for Orchestra, Bartók's Piano Concerto No. 2, with Maurizio Pollini, and Brahms's Symphony No. 1.

408   *"His Cleveland debut on the Severance podium"*: *Sun Press*, November 19, 1970.

409   *"I think this could be quite disastrous"*: COA/BT, Presidents' Office Files (Alfred M. Rankin), Majeske letter to Rankin, November 20, 1970.

409   *the names of five candidates:* Ibid., Presidents' Office Files (Alfred M. Rankin), Minutes of Meeting of Search Committee, December 9, 1970.

409   *Among those "discarded"*: Ibid.

409   *"the new Musical Director should be a younger man"*: COA/BT, minutes, January 15, 1971.

409   *a preposterous number of conductors:* Ibid. Pierre Boulez, Louis Lane, Karel Ancerl, Daniel Barenboim, Aldo Ceccato, Rafael Frühbeck de Burgos, Bernard Haitink, István Kertész, Paul Kletzki, Rafael Kubelik, Erich

Leinsdorf, Lorin Maazel, Eugene Ormandy, André Previn and Sir William Walton (the latter two sharing one program; Walton cancelled and was replaced by Charry).

409 *Leinsdorf walked into Severance Hall:* His first Severance Hall concerts since 1946 were on March 11 and 13, 1971, when he conducted Schubert's Symphony No. 5 and Mahler's Symphony No. 4 and served as pianist in Schubert's *The Shepherd on the Rock* with clarinetist Robert Marcellus and soprano Benita Valente.

410 *"the great Cleveland Orchestra played well for Mr. Kubelik":* New York Times, February 24, 1971.

410 *"After Philadelphia, I think that is the best orchestra":* Philadelphia Inquirer, February 14, 1971.

410 *"that Mr. Boulez' recent programs":* COA/BT, minutes, April 9, 1971.

410 *exploring the possibilities for recording, which looked bleak:* The major recording companies were leaning toward European orchestras, which cost about a third of the scale paid to American orchestras. RCA, Angel, and London were not renewing contracts with American ensembles, although Columbia was showing interest in making Cleveland recordings during the summer of 1971 with violinist Pinchas Zukerman and conductor Daniel Barenboim, who was set to make his debut with the orchestra at Blossom Music Center, and in September with conductors Karel Ančerl and Morton Gould. None of these projects would happen.

410 *a visit with Maazel:* COA/GE, Maxwell letter to Maazel, March 8, 1971.

411 *final concerts with the orchestra:* Stokowski program on May 13 and 15, 1971, comprised Bach's Toccata and Fugue in D Minor (arranged by Stokowski), Beethoven's Symphony No. 7, Sibelius's *The Swan of Tuonela*, and Glière's Symphony No. 3 ("Ilya Mourometz").

411 *"No, I am not a candidate":* Cleveland Press, May 11, 1971.

411 *Maxwell proceeded to give him:* Maxwell fax to the author, January 26, 1999.

411 *"There is no doubt in my mind":* Ibid., February 4, 1999.

411 *"for quite specific reasons":* Ibid., January 7, 1999.

411 *"Maazel's situation at Blossom":* The Plain Dealer, June 6, 1971.

412 *"This is simply to confirm":* COA/BT, Presidents' Office Files (Alfred M. Rankin), Maazel letter to Maxwell, June 12, 1971.

412 *No other guest artist:* COA/GE, concert files/guest artist files.

412 *Maazel's conducting dates for July 1971:* COA/BT, Presidents' Office Files (Alfred M. Rankin), Maxwell memo to Rankin, June 30, 1971.

412 *"Further to our conversation":* Ibid. The fee structure for Maazel for these concerts is listed on an attachment to this memo, as follows

412 *"At the invitation of your manager":* Cleveland Press, July 2, 1971.

412 *"It is doubtful":* The Plain Dealer, July 4, 1971.

413 *"For those able to shut out of their minds":* Ibid., July 11, 1971. The performance of the *Roman Carnival Overture* from Maazel's first Blossom concert is available on a Columbia Records album produced for a Cleveland Orchestra Marathon. It includes Brahms's *Academic Festival Overture* and Barber's *The School for Scandal* overture under Maazel from the Blossom concerts of July 14 and 15, 1972.

413   *"Whether he has his eye"*: Akron Beacon Journal, July 10, 1971.
413   *"The Cleveland Orchestra could do a lot worse"*: Toledo Blade, July 11, 1971.
413   *"glib, superficial"*: Sun Press, July 15, 1971.
413   *"Maazel's attitude seemed to be"*: The Plain Dealer, July 12, 1971.
414   *"I hear we're losing you"*: KL, notes from Maazel's first rehearsal as music director, November 21, 1972.
414   *"That's not according to the text"*: Myron Bloom, interview by author, Cleveland Heights, Oh., December 24, 1999.
414   *"Mr. Bloom to you"*: Ibid.
414   *When the search committee met:* COA/BT, minutes, August 13, 1971.
414   *Skernick quickly discussed the developments:* Ibid.
414   *"I feel closer to you"*: COA/BT, Presidents' Office Files (Alfred M. Rankin), Brown letter to Joseph, July 13, 1971.
414   *"How much better it is"*: Ibid., Brown letter to Rankin, July 18, 1971.
414   *"If we go too long"*: Ibid., Joseph letter to Brown, July 14, 1971.
415   *Rankin drew up an agreement:* COA/BT, Presidents' Office Files (Frank E. Joseph), Joseph letter to Maxwell, July 22, 1971.
415   *Meanwhile, rumors continued to fly:* Cleveland Press, July 27, 1971.
415   *"the most satisfying performance"*: The Plain Dealer, August 2, 1971. Kertész's program on July 31, 1971, included Schubert's *Rosamunde* overture, Sibelius's Violin Concerto, with Itzhak Perlman, and Dvořák's "New World" Symphony.
415   *"A musician of mystique"*: Ibid.
415   *"There have been persistent rumors"*: Ibid., August 5, 1971.
415   *"This letter constitutes an Agreement"*: COA/BT, Presidents' Office Files (Alfred M. Rankin), Maazel agreement to become musical director of the Cleveland Orchestra signed by Maazel and Rankin in London, August 7, 1971.
416   *"If he should be chosen"*: The Plain Dealer, August 7, 1971.
416   *"[He] jabbed at the ensemble"*: Ibid., August 9, 1971. Frühbeck de Burgos and Barenboim both made their Severance Hall debuts in early 1972—Frühbeck de Burgos on January 13 and 15, and Barenboim on February 3 and 5.
416   *When the votes of the 98 players:* Cleveland Press, August 9, 1971.
417   *"We have it from good sources"*: Ibid.
417   *"This expression of preference"*: The Plain Dealer, August 10, 1971.
417   *The day the orchestra poll:* Ibid.
417   *Joseph told the trustees:* COA/BT, minutes, August 13, 1971.
417   *Skernick later pinpointed the statement:* Ibid.
417   *"embarrassing to the guest conductors"*: Ibid.
417   *"reconsider his candidacy"*: Ibid.
417   *Kertész told Maxwell:* Ibid.
417   *News of Kertész's cancellation:* The Plain Dealer, August 11, 1971.
417   *"I've never made a secret of it"*: Ibid., August 20, 1971.
418   *"the recommendations of the orchestra"*: Ibid.
418   *"I know you agree with me"*: Ibid., Presidents' Office Files (Alfred M. Rankin), Joseph note to Rankin, August 16, 1971.
418   *"I just don't think"*: Ibid., Joseph letter to Rankin, August 30, 1971.
418   *"I feel very strongly"*: Ibid., Griesinger letter to Vignos, September 1, 1971.
418   *"inquisition"*: Ibid., Rankin memorandum summarizing his conversation with

Ernest Fleischmann, September 8, 1971.

419   *"Do you think":* Ibid., Boulez letter to Rankin, September 25, 1971.

419   *The board's executive committee was not informed:* COA/BT, executive committee, minutes, September 13, 1971.

419   *One trustee, Peter Reed:* Ibid., Presidents' Office Files (Alfred M. Rankin), Rankin memorandum about meeting of executive committee, September 13, 1971.

419   *"Cleveland was and still is my dream": The Plain Dealer,* September 18, 1971.

419   *"I greatly admire Szell": Cleveland Press,* September 23, 1971.

419   *"selflessness, dignity": The Plain Dealer,* September 30, 1971.

419   *Three days later, the search committee:* COA/BT, executive committee, minutes, October 1, 1971.

419   *"the unanimous recommendation":* Ibid., minutes, October 1, 1971.

420   *concerned his reputation as "a disciplinarian":* Ibid.

420   *"is indeed a source of great concern":* Ibid.

421   *"twelve of the 36": Sun Press,* October 14, 1971.

421   *"We have, of course, been mindful of the differing views":* COA/BT, Presidents' Office Files (Alfred M. Rankin), Rankin and Joseph letter to Ladies and Gentlemen of the Orchestra announcing Maazel appointment, October 1, 1971.

421   *"Maazel Named by Orchestra": Cleveland Press,* October 1, 1971.

421   *"were angry and upset":* Ibid., October 2, 1971.

421   *"The search committee was a sham":* Ibid.

421   *"the most important musical position": Cleveland Press,* October 2, 1971. Maazel sent a telegram to the orchestra on October 5, 1971, that said, in part

421   *"day of great sadness":* Associated Press, October 2, 1971.

421   *"Whatever their personal reactions": The Plain Dealer,* October 2, 1971.

421   *"We emphasize that the orchestra":* COA/BT, Presidents' Office Files (Alfred M. Rankin), Bert Siegel letter from Cleveland Orchestra Committee to Maxwell, October 7, 1971.

422   *The other was second bassoonist Vaclav Laksar:* Robert Finn e-mail to author, December 15, 1999, about his column in *The Plain Dealer,* November 14, 1971, that contained the sentence: "The view from the boardroom is quite different from that from the second bassoonist's chair." The sentence, e-mailed Finn, "brought a plaintive call from Vaclav Laksar," who admitted he was the other musician who had voted for Maazel in the August 1971 poll.

422   *"the young Szell's equal": The Plain Dealer,* October 24, 1971.

422   *"dare to compare [Maazel]":* Ibid.

422   *"You can well imagine":* COA/BT, Presidents' Office Files (Alfred M. Rankin), Maazel letter to Rankin, October 25, 1971.

CHAPTER 28: FOLLOWING A GIANT

423   *the orchestra's new music director :* Maazel was the first conductor of the Cleveland Orchestra to be known simply as music director. Nikolai Sokoloff, Artur Rodzinski, and Erich Leinsdorf had been called "conductor"; George

Szell had the title "Musical Director and Conductor."

423   "That's A-flat": Beacon Magazine, September 20, 1981.

424   "the most disconcerting": Ibid. At his first concert with the National Music
       Camp Orchestra at the World's Fair, Maazel led Tchaikovsky's Marche slav; at
       the second, Schubert's Rosamunde overture, Dika Newlin's Cradle Song, and
       the first movement from Mendelssohn's "Italian" Symphony.

424   "He was a high-class carnival act": People, January 12, 1976.

424   Among his high-profile concerts: Maazel conducted the NBC Symphony in a
       program that included Wagner's Rienzi overture and Mendelssohn's entire
       "Italian" Symphony.

424   "I was dropped": People, January 12, 1976.

424   he married Miriam Sandbank: The couple had two daughters, Lorian, born
       1962, and Daria, born 1967.

425   "Nostalgia recedes into nothingness": Jackson, Sign-Off for the Old Met: The
       Metropolitan Opera Broadcasts 1950–1966, p. 307. The Rosenkavalier cast
       included Régine Crespin, Anneliese Rothenberger, Hertha Töpper, Otto
       Edelmann, Ralph Herbert, and Sándor Kónya.

425   "I'm starting this position": Associated Press, December 5, 1971.

425   "Personally I have not the slightest reservation": COA/BT, Presidents' Office
       Files (Alfred M. Rankin), Joseph letter to Marjorie McDonald, October 28,
       1971.

425   "And I don't believe": New York Times, October 2, 1971.

426   "My first aim": Philadelphia Inquirer, November 7, 1971.

426   "I'm a strong personality": Associated Press, December 5, 1971.

426   "I don't believe in the mechanical reproduction": Ibid.

427   "I hope it keeps up": The Plain Dealer, December 15, 1971.

427   "Twenty-five years ago": Ibid., December 18, 1971.

427   "It is Maazel's kind of piece": Ibid.

428   "The audience rated a higher score": Cleveland Press, December 17, 1971.

428   This review, and a follow-up column: Hruby's column in the Press on
       December 12, 1971, was headlined, "Orchestra was childish in rudeness to
       Maazel." The Cleveland Orchestra Committee answered in a letter to the ed-
       itor in the Press headlined, "Musicians Assail Hruby on Maazel concert,"
       January 1, 1972.

428   "We are in for a heart-on-the-sleeve": Sun Press, December 23, 1971.

428   "absolutely dreadful": Cleveland Press, January 13, 1972.

429   "stirred a mild tremor or two": New York Times, February 9, 1972. The en-
       semble's concert at Carnegie Hall on February 7, 1972, under Barenboim was
       the first time the author heard the orchestra.

429   "Barenboim Lays Egg With Great Orchestra": Washington Star, February 14,
       1972.

429   "With Erich Leinsdorf on the podium": Ibid., February 21, 1972.

429   Some accounts claimed: The Plain Dealer, March 3, 1972.

429   Management countered: Maazel's resignation was the second blow to the New
       Philharmonia in a month: Otto Klemperer, the orchestra's 87-year-old princi-
       pal conductor, had just announced that he was leaving the podium for good.
       Klemperer wasn't the only conductor to reach a milestone this season. Louis

Lane, who had joined the Cleveland Orchestra in 1947, was completing 25 years at Severance Hall. Typically, he led an eclectic program to mark the occasion—works by Easley Blackwood, Franz Berwald, and Richard Strauss – and was surprised after one concert to receive the $1,000 Alice M. Ditson conductor's award from Columbia University for his commitment to American composers.

430   *"Our job is to make it fun": The Plain Dealer*, May 9, 1972.

430   *"Years ago, Alfred Frankenstein": San Francisco Chronicle*, June 4, 1972.

430   *"orchestra made a fat, rumbly sound": The Plain Dealer*, July 15, 1972.

430   *"plays on the Cleveland Orchestra":* Ibid., July 17, 1972.

430   *first Northeast Ohio performance of Mahler's Symphony No. 8:* The performance on July 22, 1972, featured the Blossom Festival Chorus and Children's Chorus, sopranos Phyllis Curtin, Johanna Meier, and Lynn Griebling, contraltos Grace Reginald and Birgit Finnila, tenor Seth McCoy, baritone Morley Meredith, and bass Yi-Kwei Sze.

430   *In a biting parody: The Plain Dealer*, August 20, 1972.

431   *"In short, I need trust in my critic":* COA/M/PR, Maxwell essay in second program book of the 1972–73 season, September 28, 29, and 30, 1972.

431   *"We who love music":* COA/BT, Presidents' Office Files (Alfred M. Rankin), Katherine B. Baker letter to Rankin, September 6, 1972.

432   *"The real significance of 1972–73": The Plain Dealer*, September 17, 1972.

432   *"There is a great similarity":* Ibid., November 4, 1972.

432   *"Oh, he's wonderful":* COA, Michael Maxwell, oral history transcript.

433   *"the longest speech ever given":* KL, Loebel record of Maazel's first rehearsal as music director, November 21, 1972.

433   *"instituting a regime": New York Times*, November 26, 1972.

433   *"His ideas were completely different from":* Ibid., November 29, 1972.

433   *"unsettled"* and *"too theatrical": New York Post*, November 29, 1972.

434   *"Gone was the crisp, transparent elegance": The Plain Dealer*, December 2, 1972.

434   *Maazel tried to change Karajan's mind:* COA/GE, Maazel letter to Glotz, January 1, 1973.

434   *"was simply too exaggerated": The Plain Dealer*, January 6, 1973.

434   *played the Lalo concerto:* A recording of the du Pré/Barenboim performance of the Lalo concerto with the Cleveland Orchestra from the concerts of January 4 and 6, 1973, was issued in 1995 on an EMI disc also containing Strauss's *Don Quixote* featuring the cellist with Sir Adrian Boult and the New Philharmonia Orchestra.

434   *The early months of 1973:* Not long after Maazel's appointment, Frank E. Joseph and others expressed concern about István Kertész returning to conduct, as he wrote in a letter to Maxwell: "Some people seem worried that there may be embarrassing situations when Kertész comes to conduct. You, of course, mustn't cancel his appearances as the reaction to that would be really bad. However, there perhaps is some way you can slip out gracefully." COA/GE, Joseph letter to Maxwell, February 24, 1972.

435   *"Wednesday's performance was vintage Cleveland": Boston Globe*, February 7, 1973.

435   *"I think the jackets"*: COA/GE, Joseph letter to Maxwell, March 2, 1973.

435   *the "Ode to Joy" from Beethoven's Ninth:* The vocal soloists were soprano
Veronica Tyler, mezzo-soprano Joanna Simon (replacing Betty Allen), tenor
Mallory Walker, and bass-baritone Simon Estes.

436   *"Maazel's performance was grossly overinterpreted"*: The Plain Dealer,
March 17, 1973.

436   *"Loud, Louder"*: Ibid., April 14, 1973. The performances of Beethoven's
Missa Solemnis on April 12, 13, and 14, 1973, featured soprano Margaret
Price, alto Anna Reynolds, tenor Werner Hollweg, bass Martti Talvela, and
the Cleveland Orchestra Chorus, prepared by Robert Page.

436   *an analysis of the conductor's inaugural season:* Maazel didn't conduct the
final subscription concerts of the 1972–73 season. William Steinberg was on
the podium May 10 and 11, 1973, for performances of Beethoven's "Eroica"
Symphony, Copland's *Appalachian Spring* suite, and orchestral excerpts from
Wagner's *Die Meistersinger*. But Maazel led a special nonsubscription concert
May 12 comprising Prokofiev's complete *Romeo and Juliet*, in preparation for
his first recording with the orchestra for Decca/London in early June.

436   *"The players, I think"*: The Plain Dealer, April 22, 1973.

CHAPTER 29: MAAZEL IN CHARGE

437   *"There's a certain reticence"*: Washington Post, May 20, 1973.

438   *Even if there were slight flaws:* Maazel would later deny that his Cleveland
recordings for Columbia and London were splice jobs

438   *"Not in many years"*: Washington Post, May 23, 1973.

438   *"Had the soloists"*: Ibid., May 24, 1973. The soloists were soprano Pilar
Lorengar, mezzo-soprano Shirley Verrett, tenor Enrico di Giuseppe, and bass
Bonaldo Giaotti.

438   *"struck me as excellent"*: Ibid., May 27, 1973. The soloists in Beethoven's
Ninth Symphony were soprano Veronica Tyler, mezzo-soprano Betty Allen,
tenor Kenneth Riegel, and bass-baritone Simon Estes.

439   *a slight drop in attendance:* The Plain Dealer, September 5, 1973.

439   *"The top internationally famous Cleveland Orchestra"*: The Evening Post
(Wellington, New Zealand), September 18, 1973.

440   *"whirlwind from Cleveland"*: The Australian, September 22, 1973.

440   *"opera auditorium seating 1,400"*: Leinsdorf, p. 290.

440   *the ensemble might have been created:* Sydney Morning Herald, October 2,
1973.

440   *"Under its present incumbent"*: Sydney Sun, October 3, 1973.

440   *"the European memories"*: Melbourne Age, September 15, 1973.

441   *"Lorin Maazel, the controversial heir"*: Los Angeles Times, October 4, 1973.

441   *"with regret that the Cleveland Orchestra"*: Financial Times, October 22,
1973.

441   *"You came through magnificently"*: The Plain Dealer, October 11, 1973.

441   *The musicians shuffled:* There was another reason Maazel might have been
happy at this time: he finally signed a four-year contract on October 8, 1973,

calling for the following salaries—1973–74 season: $100,000; 1974–75: $130,000; 1975–76: $140,000; 1976–77: $150,000; plus Deferred Compensation for period October 1, 1973, to May 31, 1976, of $166,000.

442 *"I've been wanting to tell"*: The Plain Dealer, October 11, 1973.

442 *which the Sun Press's Bain Murray termed "a disaster"*: Sun Press, October 25, 1973.

442 *Observers may have known that something was wrong:* The orchestra soon announced that David Shifrin, a former Marcellus student who was serving as principal clarinetist of the Dallas Symphony (where Lane was resident conductor), would succeed his teacher later in the season.

443 *more money than any orchestra but the Chicago Symphony:* United Press International article in many newspapers, late June 1973.

443 *"Let's examine the logic of the position":* COA/GE, An Urgent Message from the Members of the Cleveland Orchestra, December 1973.

443 *A few trustees:* Robert C. Weiskopf often collaborated in concert with his wife, pianist Eunice Podis.

443 *"to empower the negotiating team":* COA/BT, minutes, November 28, 1973.

443 *"live dangerously":* Ibid.

443 *the players voted 83 to 2 to strike:* The Plain Dealer, January 25, 1974.

443 *It came a few days later:* Ibid., January 28, 1974.

444 *"It was on all counts":* Cleveland Press, February 1, 1974.

444 *"The orchestra played with tremendous sweep":* Sun Press, February 7, 1974.

444 *"It was an exciting evening":* New York Times, February 6, 1974.

444 *"Lorin Maazel's appointment as conductor":* New York magazine, February 25, 1974.

445 *"Members of the orchestra reported yesterday":* The Plain Dealer, April 2, 1974.

445 *"The performance of the punks":* Ibid., April 3, 1974.

445 *"We had the honor of hearing":* Cleveland Press, May 21, 1974.

446 *"Let it be said":* Daily Yomiura, June 6, 1974.

446 *the British firm signed a three-year deal:* The Plain Dealer, July 30, 1974.

446 *Carl Orff's orgiastic cantata:* Tilson Thomas made his Cleveland Orchestra debut conducting two programs at Blossom. On August 2, 1974, he led Balakirev's Overture on Three Russian Themes, Tchaikovsky's Violin Concerto (with Pinchas Zukerman), and the Brahms/Schoenberg Quartet in G minor. His program on August 3 consisted of Beethoven's Symphony No. 8, Debussy's *Afternoon of a Faun*, and Orff's *Carmina Burana*.

446 *Maazel resented the recording:* Michael Maxwell, fax to author, January 11, 1999.

447 *a significant drop in the annual deficit:* The Plain Dealer, July 27, 1974.

447 *"Ah, the irony of it all!":* Akron Beacon Journal, September 8, 1974.

447 *Blossom set an attendance record:* The Plain Dealer, September 13, 1974.

447 *"at the corner of Courtland and Shaker":* Plain Dealer Sunday Magazine, May 4, 1997.

447 *"The boys said if they got up a petition":* Alice Chalifoux, interview by author, Cleveland Heights, Oh., November 15, 1998.

448 *"Maazel's performance of the Mahler Fifth":* The Plain Dealer, September 28,

1974.

448   *"He gave the orchestra a chance to play"*: David Zauder, interview by author, Cleveland Heights, Oh., February 18, 1999.

448   *"has not sounded so well"*: COA/BT, minutes, October 1, 1974.

CHAPTER 30: IMAGE MAKING

449   *"The Cleveland Orchestra used to be a jewel"*: New York Times, February 2, 1975.

450   *"They play wonderfully, but they are so inflexible"*: COA, Michael Maxwell, oral history transcript.

451   *"I'm recently back"*: COA/C, Copland letter to Maazel, November 12, 1974.

451   *Maazel was talking about a cast:* COA/GE, Maazel letter to Maxwell, November 7, 1974.

451   *It didn't seem to matter to Maazel:* Even so, white artists had performed *Porgy* before, at least in concert and on recordings. Robert Merrill, a stalwart at the Metropolitan Opera, had recorded an all-white *Porgy* in the 1950s for RCA with another Met star, mezzo-soprano Rise Stevens, as Bess.

451   *"It is a thrill to work"*: Cleveland Press, January 1, 1975.

452   *"inspirational under your direction"*: COA/C, Ringwall letter to Maazel, February 25, 1975.

452   *"Ever heard of Benjamin Britten?"*: Cleveland Press, January 16, 1975.

452   *"Only now am I really doing"*: The Plain Dealer, January 10, 1975.

453   *The orchestras of Boston, Chicago, Cleveland, Los Angeles, New York, and Philadelphia:* COA/M/PR, Musical Arts Association press release, January 27, 1975.

453   *The German recording company had come up with a novel idea:* Aside from the Cleveland Orchestra (in its first recording for Deutsche Grammophon), the ensembles were the London Symphony (Symphony No. 1), Concertgebouw Orchestra of Amsterdam (2), Berlin Philharmonic (3), Israel Philharmonic (4), Boston Symphony (5), Orchestre de Paris (6), Vienna Philharmonic (7), and Bavarian Radio Symphony Orchestra (9; with Helen Donath, Teresa Berganza, Wieslaw Ochman, Thomas Stewart, and the Bavarian Radio Chorus). Some of the recordings were made after performances. Others, like the Cleveland recording, were done in the studio.

453   *"Many recordings of this kind"*: COA/BT, minutes, February 27, 1975.

453   *"a finely scaled, musically satisfying account"*: Gramophone, October 1976.

454   *In Rio, Maazel spoke to reporters:* The Plain Dealer, April 24, 1975.

454   *"still fighting the memory of George Szell"*: Ibid., April 20, 1975.

454   *"It is not an operetta"*: Maazel liner note in libretto of *Porgy* recording.

454   *"Alas, I shall not be able"*: COA/C, Ira Gershwin letter to Maazel, July 30, 1975.

455   *Maazel, originally unopposed to the idea:* New York Times, August 24, 1975.

455   *"There's a stipulation in the score"*: Gramophone, February 1976.

455   *"FIRST OPPORTUNITY SATURDAY NIGHT"*: COA/C, McEwan telegram to Maazel, November 3, 1975.

455 *"I had to listen to the tapes critically":* Ibid., Maazel letter to McEwen, November 5, 1975.

455 *"Fortunately, for this excellent recording":* Tribune (London), April 9, 1976.

456 *"For all its passing flaws":* New York Times, April 25, 1976.

456 *As I was a close friend of George Gershwin:* COA/C, Swift letter to Maazel, March 21, 1976.

456 *"The recording, finally, says a lot about Maazel":* Cleveland Magazine, May 1976.

457 *"absolutely unacceptable":* COA/C, Maazel memo to Maxwell, October 28, 1975.

457 *"My one worry":* The Daily Telegraph, September 10, 1975.

457 *"extremely pompous":* The Times, September 10, 1975.

458 *"I feel very much like the President of the United States":* Associated Press story printed in many newspapers, September 13, 1975.

458 *"The Cleveland Orchestra has not been talked about much":* The Plain Dealer, September 18, 1975.

458 *"I saw these robots come alive":* France-Soir (Paris), October 1975.

458 *"Maazel is seen by his critics":* Plain Dealer Sunday Magazine, September 28, 1975.

458 *"Its success has been truly gratifying":* COA/C, Maazel letter to McEwan, early October 1975.

459 *"The success of Porgy":* Ibid., McEwan letter to Maazel, October 14, 1975.

459 *"What do you do":* Cleveland Press, December 27, 1975.

459 *Maxwell had noticed changes in Maazel:* Michael Maxwell, fax to author, January 28, 1999.

459 *"These aberrations":* COA, Michael Maxwell, oral history transcript.

459 *dressing the entire Cleveland Orchestra:* Ibid.

460 *installing a canvas tent:* Ibid.

460 *he would have to go:* Michael Maxwell, fax to author, January 28, 1999.

460 *"acquired a host of friends in Cleveland":* Cleveland Press, March 10, 1976.

460 *"no longer be Maxwell House":* Ibid., March 3, 1976.

460 *Thirty-three-year-old Kenneth Haas:* Michael Maxwell's next post was as managing director of the Opera Company of Boston.

460 *"Sour notes in Orchestra":* The Plain Dealer, March 23, 1976.

460 *"I'm leaving in concern":* Detroit News, April 18, 1976.

461 *"He didn't resign, he was fired":* Lorain Journal, May 2, 1976. Shifrin went on to a distinguished career as a soloist, chamber musician, and artistic director of the Chamber Music Society of Lincoln Center.

461 *"the worst orchestra that ever existed":* Myron Bloom, interview by author, Cleveland Heights, Oh., December 24, 1999.

461 *another plane was summoned:* Ibid. According to Bloom, the Concorde passengers that day included writer Jimmy Breslin and arts patron Alice Tully.

461 *Bloom returned to Paris without calling Cleveland:* Ibid. Bloom did return to Cleveland briefly in May 1976 to appear as soloist in Mozart's Horn Concerto No. 4 (under Maazel, oddly enough).

461 *After an audition:* COA/BT, minutes, November 15, 1977.

461 *"Suddenly the relative serenity":* Sunday Plain Dealer, May 16, 1976.

CHAPTER 31: ROLLER COASTER

463   *"one of the world's finest festivals of music":* Cleveland Press, September 22, 1976.

463   *"You have a great symphony orchestra":* The Plain Dealer, August 9, 1976.

464   *"Oh, I've worked with him":* Cleveland Press, August 6, 1976.

464   *"Martin, I'm glad you called":* Ibid., September 29, 1976.

464   *"I have never done anything like this":* Ibid.

464   *"By the second act":* Washington Post, September 29, 1976.

465   *Bartók, Shostakovich, and Falla:* The program on September 30, 1976, contained Bartók's *Deux Images*, Shostakovich's Cello Concerto No. 1 (with principal cellist Stephen Geber), and Falla's complete *Three-Cornered Hat* ballet (with mezzo-soprano Barbara Conrad).

465   *"I stand on my record":* COA/GE, Maazel letter to Haas, October 20, 1976.

466   *"The result is in effect a live performance":* The Plain Dealer, December 21, 1976.

466   *Maazel and the orchestra made their first direct-to-disc recording:* The repertoire comprised Berlioz's *Le Corsaire* overture and *Rakoczy March*, the "Jota" from Falla's *The Three-Cornered Hat*, the "Farandole" from Bizet's *L'Arlésienne* Suite No. 2, and the "Polonaise" from Tchaikovsky's *Eugen Onegin*.

466   *"I was knocked into the middle of next week":* Washington Star, September 18, 1977.

466   *"contradictory, sometimes infuriating affair":* New York Times, December 22, 1977.

466   *"There is really no point":* Gramophone, November 1977.

467   *Sir Michael Tippett:* The British composer came to Cleveland in October 1977 to conduct his *Fantasia Concertante on the Theme of Corelli* and Second Symphony on a program during which Maazel also led Tippett's oratorio, *A Child of Our Time.* No one seemed to mind that another admired Englishman briefly upstaged the composer and company: Prince Charles. The heir to the British throne attended the first Tippett concert at Severance Hall and generated much hoopla in the print and broadcast media. "Charlie's our darling," announced a sizable front-page headline in *The Plain Dealer* on October 22.

467   *"Regarding our Boheme":* COA/GE, Haas memo to Maazel, April 14, 1978.

467   *"one of Blossom Center's":* Cleveland Press, July 11, 1977.

467   *"When a musician of exceptional integrity":* The Plain Dealer, July 25, 1977.

467   *The deficit for fiscal year 1975–76:* Ibid., August 20, 1976.

468   *Although the accumulated deficit would rise:* The Plain Dealer, September 19, 1977.

468   *"As a start of Maazel's complete Cleveland Beethoven cycle":* Gramophone, February 1978.

468   *"I never stop wondering":* New York magazine, February 27, 1978.

468   *"I wish to say that your orchestra":* COA/C, Steinberg letter to Maazel, March 20, 1978.

469   *"I do it all by ear":* The Plain Dealer, May 5, 1978.

469   *Kaye called the Cleveland Orchestra:* COA/BT, minutes, June 14, 1978.

469 *ended the previous fiscal year in the black:* Akron Beacon Journal, September 1, 1978.

470 *royalties were up:* Ibid., November 6, 1978.

470 *"At all times, even during trying union negotiations":* Ibid.

470 *former staff conductor Louis Lane:* Lane's program on December 14, 15, and 16, 1978, comprised Walton's Partita, Babin's Concerto No. 2 for Two Pianos (with Richard and John Contiguglia as soloists), Bloch's Sinfonia Breve, and Hindemith's Symphonic Metamorphosis. All of these works had received their local premieres by the Cleveland Orchestra under Szell and others.

470 *"Mention Cleveland these days":* Associated Press, March 27, 1979.

471 *"an annual Beethoven festival":* COA/BT, minutes, December 14, 1978.

471 *"Lorin Maazel remains one of the most fascinating enigmas":* New York Times, March 25, 1979.

471 *"The music-making is full-bodied":* Ibid.

472 *an AT&T program:* Announced in many newspapers, March 23, 1979.

472 *The 1978–79 season ended:* The Plain Dealer, August 30, 1979.

472 *"When I took over in 1972":* Cleveland Press, August 30, 1979.

CHAPTER 32: LONGTIME LAME DUCK

473 *Repertoire weighty enough:* Lorin Maazel chose his principal clarinetist, Franklin Cohen, to be the tour soloist in Mozart's Clarinet Concerto in Oslo, Munich, and Bonn. After the concerto, Cohen was expected to play in either Brahms's Second Symphony, Bruckner's Eighth Symphony, or Strauss's *Ein Heldenleben*. And he had to perform these feats knowing that his wife, bassoonist Lynette Diers, was at home in Cleveland preparing to give birth to their first child. Four days (and three concerts) before the end of the tour, Diers went into labor, and Cohen made the mad dash home, arriving just in time to welcome daughter Diana into the world.

473 *"Most speculation assumes":* The Plain Dealer, September 19, 1979.

473 *"I do not expect that any commitment":* Ibid.

474 *"A press conference is being held today":* COA/C, Maazel memo to the orchestra, September 21, 1979.

474 *"we believe it would be a mistake":* The Plain Dealer, September 20, 1979.

474 *"to extend [Maazel's] music directorship":* Ibid., October 11, 1979.

474 *"complementary":* Ibid.

474 *Maazel had intended:* COA/BT, minutes, October 10, 1979.

475 *"I did not mean to give that impression":* The Plain Dealer, October 11, 1979.

475 *As conductor emeritus:* Ibid.

475 *"contract for services as Conductor Emeritus":* COA/BT, minutes, October 10, 1979.

475 *"Tennstedt groupies":* The Plain Dealer, October 21, 1979.

476 *general manager Kenneth Haas and board member Thomas J. Quigley:* COA/BT, minutes, November 21, 1979.

476 *He devised a list of former candidates:* The Plain Dealer, November 25, 1979.

476 *"This being the Important Season":* Cleveland Press, December 14, 1979.

476 *"a musician selected by the Orchestra":* COA/BT, minutes, January 23, 1980.

477 *"The Cleveland Orchestra remains one of the top groups in the world":* New York Times, February 14, 1980.

477 *"an inappropriate style":* The Times (London), February 23, 1980.

477 *In early March, the Chicago Tribune reported:* Reported in The Plain Dealer, March 4, 1980.

477 *"The position has not been discussed":* Ibid.

477 *it hoped the Ad Hoc Committee:* Ibid., March 21, 1980.

478 *"It is clear that the necessity":* COA/BT, minutes, May 21, 1980.

478 *On July 1, the musicians announced:* The Plain Dealer, July 2, 1980.

478 *"wage scales, workload, pension plan":* Ibid.

478 *"We joined the orchestra":* Akron Beacon Journal, July 13, 1980.

479 *"This kind of erosion of talent pool":* Ibid.

479 *eleventh in pay to fifth place:* Associated Press, July 18, 1980.

479 *"largest salary increase":* COA/M/PR, Musical Arts Association news release, July 18, 1980.

480 *a small surplus:* The Plain Dealer, September 24, 1980.

480 *"You may be confident":* COA/BT, minutes, November 3, 1980.

481 *"The Cleveland Orchestra responded superbly":* The Plain Dealer, August 22, 1981.

481 *Sir Colin's two Blossom concerts:* On August 21, 1981, Sir Colin Davis conducted Dvořák's Cello Concerto, with Heinrich Schiff as soloist, and Sibelius's Symphony No. 2. His program on August 22 comprised Mozart's Minuet in G, K. 409, and Piano Concerto No. 24, K. 491, with Clive Lythgoe as soloist, and Walton's Symphony No. 1.

481 *"We are pleased to propose":* COA/BT, Presidents' Office Files (Alfred M. Rankin), Rankin/Haas letter to Davis, September 8, 1981.

481 *"You may be sure that our negotiations":* Ibid., minutes, November 2, 1981.

481 *"Help Wanted":* New York Times, November 15, 1981.

CHAPTER 33: CHRISTOPH VON WHO?

483 *Instead, the program included:* Christoph von Dohnányi had two soloists in the Bartók pieces at his Cleveland debut: the orchestra's concertmaster, Daniel Majeske (in Two Portraits, Op. 9), and cellist Janos Starker (in the Cleveland premiere of a transcription of the Viola Concerto).

483 *"The intelligence reports out of Severance Hall rehearsals":* The Plain Dealer, December 4, 1981.

483 *"The Dvořák Eighth was given":* Cleveland Press, December 4, 1981.

484 *"the usual suspects":* The Plain Dealer, September 29, 1998.

484 *the musicians on the Ad Hoc Committee on Artistic Direction:* Northern Ohio Live, May 1982. The musicians were Ronald Bishop, Stephen Geber, George Goslee, Ronald Phillips, Joan Siegel, and Robert Vernon.

484 *Haas phoned Dohnányi:* Ibid.

484 *The decision to offer Dohnányi the post was made on January 25:* Ibid.

484 *On the morning of March 12:* In an odd coincidence, news of former resident

conductor Louis Lane's retirement as music director of the Akron Symphony, after 23 seasons, was announced the same week.

484   *"Those audience members and ushers": Northern Ohio Live,* May 1982.

485   *a guest conductor with the St. Louis Symphony:* Three music directors of the Cleveland Orchestra made their U.S. debuts with the St. Louis Symphony— Szell, Dohnányi, and Franz Welser-Möst, who becomes music director in September 2002.

486   *"I was very young at 13":* All quotes from this paragraph from *Beacon Magazine,* May 23, 1982.

487   *ran the wind machine: Opera,* January 1984.

487   *"It's very funny": Beacon Magazine,* May 23, 1982.

487   *In the summer of 1952:* Among Dohnányi's classmates at Tanglewood was a young American named Lorin Maazel, who spent several days that summer conducting the Cleveland Summer Orchestra.

487   *"You may do whatever you like!": Beacon Magazine,* May 23, 1982.

488   *"Now we know why Toscanini":* Ibid.

489   *"I would have left":* Ibid.

489   *he told management:* COA/BT, minutes, May 12, 1982.

489   *"It was not a happy marriage": The Plain Dealer,* May 9, 1982.

489   *Maazel's "greatest pride as he leaves":* Ibid.

489   *Maazel's final concert:* The soloists for the Verdi Requiem at Carnegie Hall on May 22, 1982, were soprano Hildegard Behrens, mezzo-soprano Dunja Vejzovic, tenor Peter Dvorsky, and bass John Paul Bogart. The soprano for the Cleveland performances was Mariana Niculescu.

489   *"The showmanship and baton techniques": New York Times,* May 19, 1982.

490   *"four impeccably groomed": New York* magazine, June 7, 1982.

490   *"He leaves his successor": Christian Science Monitor,* May 26, 1982.

491   *"I'll miss out on music director No. 6": Cleveland Press,* April 23, 1982.

491   *"I am the bridge": The Plain Dealer,* October 6, 1982.

491   *"In looking back 40 years": Akron Beacon Journal,* October 7, 1982.

491   *A new orchestra contract would raise the minimum:* Ibid., August 30, 1982.

491   *"It is a tremendous pleasure":* COA/BT, annual meeting, November 8, 1982.

492   *"This looks like an extraordinary love affair": Dayton Daily News,* February 8, 1983.

492   *"did wonders for the Orchestra's esprit":* COA/BT, annual meeting, minutes, October 31, 1983.

492   *appearing with the Detroit Symphony, Pittsburgh Symphony, and New York Philharmonic:* Dohnányi conducted 11 concerts with Philharmonic in March 1983 of works by Beethoven, Schubert, Strauss, Mozart, Haydn, Dvořák, and Henze, as well as the U.S. premiere of Manfred Trojahn's *First Sea Picture.*

492   *"As leader of the censure faction": The Plain Dealer,* February 21, 1983.

492   *"Under the late George Szell": Time,* April 25, 1983.

493   *"There is no record":* COA/BT, minutes, April 20, 1983.

493   *"The recording sessions went extraordinarily well":* COA/BT, minutes, November 2, 1983.

493   *"Dohnányi is a conductor":* Quoted in COA/BT, minutes, June 27, 1984.

493   *"The curtain has gone up":* Ibid.

494 *Stravinsky's opera-oratorio, Oedipus Rex:* The cast for Stravinsky's oratorio in April 1984 comprised tenor Kenneth Riegel, mezzo-soprano Tatiana Troyanos, bass Robert Lloyd, baritone Oskar Hillebrandt, narrator James Earl Jones, and men of the Cleveland Orchestra Chorus.

494 *"is clearly well on his way":* COA/BT, annual meeting, minutes, October 31, 1983.

494 *The broadcasts promised to net:* Ibid.

CHAPTER 34: UPWARDS AGAIN

495 *later shown on PBS:* The program was a co-production of the Musical Arts Association and Hamburg-based Polyphon Film und Fernseh Gesellschaft. John Goberman was producer and Kirk Browning was director.

496 *an exceptional roster of singers:* The cast for *Die Jakobsleiter* included Julian Patrick (Gabriel), William Johns (The Called One), Jaroslav Kachel (The Rebellious One), Andrew Foldi (The Struggling One), Oskar Hillebrandt (The Chosen One), Ernst Haefliger (The Monk), Richard Brunner (The Noble One), Helga Pilarczyk (The Dying One), and Celina Lindsley (The Soul).

496 *"a remarkable performance":* The New Yorker, November 26, 1984.

496 *a contract to make 10 compact discs:* COA/BT, minutes, September 19, 1984.

497 *"The orchestra is in a fortunate position":* Ibid.

497 *"I think good orchestras":* New York Times, October 14, 1984.

497 *"Dohnányi is a real musical firecracker":* Quoted in COA/BT, annual meeting, minutes, October 29, 1984.

497 *"the Cleveland sounded in every important respect":* Chicago Tribune, October 15, 1984.

497 *"The Clevelanders appear":* Opus, December 1984.

497 *"the Cleveland is one of America's unique orchestras":* Christian Science Monitor, May 22, 1985.

498 *"has become an overnight sensation":* Quoted in COA/BT, minutes, May 29, 1985.

498 *"The Cleveland under Dohnányi":* The New Yorker, June 10, 1985.

498 *"The first season with Mr. Dohnányi":* COA/BT, minutes, May 29, 1985.

499 *"Christoph von Dohnányi's imaginative production":* The Plain Dealer, September 1, 1985.

499 *"the Ohio musical event of the summer":* Columbus Dispatch, September 2, 1985.

499 *other sponsors:* The Magic Flute production was also sponsored by the National Endowment for the Arts, Chessie System Railroads, Eaton Corporation, Midland-Ross Corporation, Ohio Edison, and the Stouffer Corporation.

500 *"the future of opera in the Cleveland area":* COA/BT, minutes, September 18, 1985.

500 *He came up with the idea of having Dohnányi conduct:* Ibid.

501 *David Bamberger, general director of Cleveland Opera:* Ibid.

501 *"an anti-Merry Widow Merry Widow":* David Bamberger, interview by author, Cleveland, Oh., February 2, 2000.

501 *"With each succeeding visit to New York":* New York Times, December 16, 1985.

501 *"It was a real performance":* Ibid., December 19, 1985.

502 *21 concerts in 17 European cities:* The February 1986 tour itinerary comprised London, Antwerp, Brussels, Bern, Warsaw, Vienna, Linz, Munich, Zurich, Paris, Düsseldorf, Bonn, Stuttgart, West Berlin, Hamburg, Höchst, and Frankfurt.

502 *Dohnányi opted to tour with only 12:* Repertoire for the 1986 European tour comprised six symphonies (Beethoven's Ninth, Bruckner's Third, Dvořák's Seventh, Mendelssohn's Fourth, Schumann's Second, Tchaikovsky's Sixth), Ives's *The Unanswered Question* (the only American work), Mozart's Oboe Concerto (with principal oboist John Mack), Ravel's *Daphnis et Chloé* Suite No. 2, Schoenberg's *A Survivor from Warsaw* (featuring Gunther Reich and the men of the Cleveland Orchestra Chorus), Strauss's *Burleske* (with principal keyboardist Joela Jones), and Zemlinsky's Sinfonietta.

502 *"In full charge for little over a year":* Quoted in *Akron Beacon Journal,* February 7, 1986.

502 *"Unfortunately, London is not the best place":* Quoted in *Akron Beacon Journal,* February 10, 1986.

502 *"perfection of unity":* Quoted in *Akron Beacon Journal,* February 13, 1986.

502 *"an American orchestra that plays in a European way":* De Standaard (Brussels), February 10, 1986.

503 *"If the Cleveland Orchestra didn't exist":* Quoted in *Akron Beacon Journal,* March 2, 1986.

503 *"when he was in Hamburg":* Hamburger Abendblatt, February 27, 1986.

503 *"I think the Cleveland Orchestra":* Akron Beacon Journal, March 2, 1986.

503 *Sales of Telarc recordings:* COA/BT, minutes, June 18, 1986.

503 *"the Brussels Opera":* Ibid.

504 *"the Garbo of opera":* Ibid.

505 *"In addition to his significance":* Pittsburgh Post-Gazette, November 24, 1986.

505 *Haas had hired architect Peter van Dijk:* COA/BT, minutes, December 12, 1984.

505 *Cleveland Orchestra Youth Orchestra, with Jahja Ling as music director:* COA/BT, minutes, November 6, 1985.

505 *"The performance was astonishingly good":* The Plain Dealer, February 3, 1987.

506 *"always struck one":* New York Times, March 12, 1987.

506 *"Rich, detailed and burnished":* Time, March 2, 1987.

CHAPTER 35: A VERITABLE EXPLOSION

507 *Morris had initially stepped down:* Akron Beacon Journal, September 20, 1987.

507   *"six or seven records annually with our Music Director":* COA/BT, minutes, September 16, 1987.

508   *"My interest is in the creative side": The Plain Dealer,* September 20, 1987.

508   *"We have to understand each other":* Akron Beacon Journal, September 20, 1987.

508   *"One of the prime thrusts":* COA/BT, minutes, November 18, 1987.

508   *"This whole picture": Cleveland Edition,* September 1987.

508   *"There is a veritable explosion":* COA/BT, April 27, 1988.

509   *"My approach is": Gramophone,* June 1989.

509   *The 13-concert tour:* The orchestra played concerts in Yokkaichi, Amagasaki, Hiroshima, Fukuoka, Osaka, Nagoya, Shizuoka, Matsudo, and Tokyo, Japan; and at Tapei's National Concert Hall.

509   *"If the orchestra comes back": Akron Beacon Journal,* October 6, 1987.

510   *"As London is the most competitive musical environment":* Quoted in COA, Gary Hanson memo to Robert Finn (*The Plain Dealer*) and Donald Rosenberg (*Akron Beacon Journal*), May 18, 1989.

510   *"The Ferrari of orchestras":* Quoted in *Akron Beacon Journal,* May 25, 1989.

510   *"Disciplined, technically perfect": Lideva Denekracie* (Prague), May 31, 1989.

510   *"Were we not so happily married": Die Kurier* (Vienna), June 2, 1989.

511   *"George Szell gave the Cleveland Orchestra": The Times* (London), June 15, 1989.

512   *"In four years of working with Bob":* Statement quoted in *Akron Beacon Journal,* October 5, 1988.

513   *"For all his virtuosity and seriousness": New York Times,* February 6, 1988.

513   *"Vladimir Ashkenazy's musicality": New York Post,* February 5, 1988.

514   *"The conductor most sought-after":* Quoted in *Akron Beacon Journal,* January 31, 1988.

514   *"a hot property":* As hot as Dohnányi may have been, the *Financial Times* was right: he *was* happily placed in Cleveland, and not only for artistic reasons. Internal Revenue Service records show for the period that Dohnányi was making an eminently handsome living in Cleveland ($331,778 in 1986, not including fees from European orchestral and operatic engagements).

514   *"What an orchestra this is": Newsday,* February 8, 1988.

514   *"Mr. Dohnányi and his orchestra": The New Yorker,* February 22, 1988.

515   *"Dohnányi and the Cleveland Orchestra almost immediately forged": Boston Globe,* February 10, 1989. The Boston Symphony's principal oboe at this time was Alfred Genovese, who had served as principal in the Cleveland Orchestra during the 1959–60 season under Szell. See the chapter, Artistic Morality.

515   *"He had very hard working rehearsals":* Ibid., February 13, 1989. Haas's career came to a tragic end when he suffered cardiac arrest on resulting in serious brain damage, October 8, 1996. On April 13, 1998, members of the Cleveland Orchestra, Boston Symphony, Cincinnati Symphony, and New York Philharmonic gave a benefit concert at Symphony Hall in Boston led by Pierre Boulez, Christoph von Dohnányi, Kurt Masur and Seiji Ozawa, and featuring violinist Itzhak Perlman. The concert raised $850,000—or $350,000 more than expected—to support Haas's long-term medical care. Thomas Morris, the Cleveland Orchestra's executive director, was one of the concert

organizers. From the *New York Times*, February 15,1998.

515   *"A genuine festive spirit"*: *New York* magazine, February 13, 1989.

515   *"imaginatively planned"*: Ibid.

516   *"giving the public 'safe' programming is dangerous"*: Ibid.

516   *announced that the orchestra had a deficit*: *The Plain Dealer*, August 28, 1989.

516   *"treating this as a crisis"*: Ibid.

516   *"The primary reason for the Cleveland Orchestra's outstanding quality"*: COA/BT, minutes, September 16, 1989.

517   *They could get rid of*: Ibid.

517   *"go down fairly markedly"*: *The Plain Dealer*, January 10, 1990.

517   *"Besides helping in a long-term solution"*: Ibid., January 28, 1990.

517   *"an Orchestra-only approach"*: COA/BT, minutes, December 18, 1989.

517   *The company planned to build a temporary stage*: The first work recorded in the new arrangement was Bruckner's Symphony No. 7 under Dohnányi.

518   *Recalling his experience*: *Diversion*, September 1993.

518   *"Salzburg is really THE festival"*: *The Plain Dealer*, August 19, 1990.

518   *"Together they are virtually unbeatable"*: *Die Kurier* (Vienna), September 9, 1990.

518   *"intelligence, honesty and rigorous musicianship"*: Quoted in *The Plain Dealer*, September 30, 1990.

518   *"I am committed to presenting"*: *The Plain Dealer*, January 14, 1991.

CHAPTER 36: MUSIC DRAMAS

521   *"the results reach a pinnacle"*: *Artspace*, Vol. 12, No. 4, April/May/June 1990.

521   *from $2.2 million to $1.1 million*: *The Plain Dealer*, December 2, 1990.

521   *the Cleveland Foundation announced*: *The Plain Dealer*, November 22, 1990.

521   *average attendance at orchestra concerts*: COA/BT, minutes, October 3, 1990.

522   *"Americans love their Best Games"*: *Los Angeles Times*, October 24, 1991.

522   *To keep the orchestra there*: The orchestra's finances would be helped by victory in a lawsuit filed by the Musical Arts Association against pop singer Michael Jackson and Sony Music Entertainment for copyright infringement. In the fall of 1991, Dohnányi's teenaged daughter, Julia, had noticed that "Will You Be There," a song on Jackson's *Dangerous* album, included a snippet from Beethoven's Ninth Symphony. Listening to the recording, Dohnanyi instantly recognized the ensemble: the Cleveland Orchestra. It wasn't *his* 1987 recording, but George Szell's 1961 performance. Jackson and his recording company, Sony, had incorporated a 67-second excerpt from Szell's Beethoven Ninth (originally on Columbia, which was purchased by Sony in 1988) without permission from the Cleveland Orchestra. By spring 1992, when the Musical Arts Association filed a complaint in United States District Court in Manhattan asking for $7 million in damages, the Jackson album had sold 14 million copies (*New York Daily News*, April 25, 1992). The orchestra later won the case, receiving an undisclosed amount.

523   *"We are once more at the peak"*: COA/BT, annual meeting, minutes, December 1, 1991.

523   *"at the center of the community's self-esteem"*: Ibid.

523   *For Dohnányi, the residency at the Salzburg Festival:* Before heading to Salzburg with his orchestra in August 1992, Dohnányi participated in an event of great personal significance

523   *"If there is a problem with Cleveland"*: Symphony Magazine, March/April 1991.

523   *"something like the Olympics of classical music"*: The Plain Dealer, July 19, 1992.

523   *"London critics have accused Dohnányi"*: Akron Beacon Journal, July 27, 1992.

524   *"Distinctly short on passion"*: The Times (London), July 28, 1992.

524   *"the underlying rhythmic impulse"*: The Daily Telegraph (London), July 27, 1992.

524   *"Dohnányi needs to let himself go more"*: Financial Times, July 27, 1992.

524   *"What they're saying is a cliché"*: The Plain Dealer, August 1, 1992.

524   *"There were 10 years of [Lorin] Maazel"*: Ibid., August 3, 1992.

525   *Decca officials said they expected the discs:* COA/BT, annual meeting, minutes, November 23, 1992.

526   *"a sweet, soft-minded woman"*: The Plain Dealer, November 5, 1993.

526   *"Danny, of all people"*: New York Times, December 11, 1993.

527   *"Under Dohnányi, the Cleveland has become the best band in the land"*: Time, January 10, 1994.

527   *"it is worth the money"*: Quoted in The Plain Dealer, January 21, 1996.

528   *"That is the bad news"*: COA/BT, annual meeting, minutes, November 23, 1992.

528   *"This Rheingold has its own sense of excitement"*: USA Today, February 6, 1996.

528   *"one of the linchpins of future artistic success"*: Ibid.

529   *"We're alive"*: The Plain Dealer, June 3, 1993.

530   *"It will concentrate Christoph's European activity"*: The Plain Dealer, March 23, 1994.

530   *"For a music director," James R. Oestreich had observed:* New York Times, December 11, 1993.

530   *"The Philadelphia Orchestra is a great orchestra"*: The Plain Dealer, June 3, 1994.

530   *"It's fun"*: Ibid., July 6, 1994.

531   *Decca president Roland Kommerell:* The Plain Dealer, August 21, 1994.

531   *"You have to be very aggressive"*: Ibid., August 4, 1994.

531   *"totally wrong, and I can prove it"*: All quotes from this paragraph from The Plain Dealer, August 28, 1994.

531   *"this interview was certainly something people read even twice"*: The Plain Dealer, September 2, 1994.

531   *"This is a super-efficient, absolutely together"*: Quoted in The Plain Dealer, September 5, 1994.

532   *"to stop the place from fiscally hemorrhaging"*: The Plain Dealer, October 10, 1994.

532   *"I feel like I'm continuing my dad's work"*: Ibid., February 4, 1995.

532   *"Those of us who never heard Stokowski":* Newsday, January 30, 1995.

533   *nine players hired by George Szell:* The Plain Dealer, April 8, 1995.

533   *"You can be creative as an orchestral musician":* Ibid., July 21, 1995.

534   *While maintaining several European relationships:* Decca had planned to make two opera recordings in Cleveland under Dohnányi: a disc of Strauss scenes with soprano Renée Fleming in January 1998, and a complete performance of Strauss's opera, *Ariadne auf Naxos,* with Deborah Voigt (Ariadne), Ben Heppner (Bacchus), Anne Sofie von Otter (Composer), and Natalie Dessay (Zerbinetta) in April 1999. Both projects were scrapped. (Fleming instead made the Strauss recording, for Decca, with the Vienna Philharmonic under Christoph Eschenbach.) COA/BT, minutes, December 18, 1997.

534   *"this is a grand, satisfying performance":* Gramophone, October 1997.

534   *"if nothing else":* Stereophile, December 1997.

534   *At first, Decca appeared willing:* COA/BT, minutes, March 6, 1998.

535   *Telarc declined:* Ibid.

536   *"Under Christoph von Dohnányi, the Cleveland Orchestra has become the most characterful":* The Daily Telegraph, March 2, 1996.

536   *"Cleveland Took Vienna By Storm":* Quoted in *The Plain Dealer,* April 14, 1996.

536   *"we may never hear this dance poem":* Berliner Morgenpost, March 25, 1996.

536   *Between this tour and the summer tour:* Even before the orchestra set off for its second tour of 1996, other major changes were in store. Two out of 11 new players this season decided to leave the orchestra at the end of the summer. Christopher Hanulik, a superb bass player who had succeeded Lawrence Angell as principal, decided to return to his post as co-principal bass of the Los Angeles Philharmonic due to family considerations and unsuccessful negotiations with Cleveland management. Elisa Barston, a member of the first violin section, had won the post of associate concertmaster of the St. Louis Symphony. The following year, Cleveland would suffer another blow when David McGill, the orchestra's principal bassoonist, would leave for the Chicago Symphony. (His successor, John Clouser, has proved to be a sensitive, elegant player ideally suited to the Cleveland tradition.)

536   *"Morally, we are committed to it":* The Plain Dealer, June 2, 1996.

CHAPTER 37: BUILDING FOR THE MILLENNIUM

537   *began to evaluate the status of the hall:* COA/BT, minutes, April 26, 1995.

537   *"As an organization that is not in crisis":* COA/BT, minutes, January 26, 1996.

538   *made an inaugural gift of $3 million:* The Plain Dealer, September 17, 1996.

538   *The association hired David M. Schwarz Architectural Services:* The Plain Dealer, July 25, 1996.

538   *Soon after Schwarz submitted designs:* COA/BT, minutes, January 24, 1997.

539   *"We were in safe hands":* New York Times, February 3, 1997.

539   *"Throughout [Dohnányi's] tenure":* Ibid., January 26, 1997.

540   *"My staying has two essential motivations":* The Plain Dealer, June 1, 1997.

541   *Other names came up: Sir Simon Rattle:* He later was named conductor of the Berlin Philharmonic, starting in 2002.

541   *by forming an Artistic Direction Committee:* COA/BT, minutes, January 22, 1998.

541   *"I'm very pleased he's going to stay here":* The Plain Dealer, February 4, 1999.

542   *"It was learned recently":* COA/BT, minutes, February 12, 1999.

542   *"In selecting the seventh music director":* Ibid., June 4, 1999.

543   *"Oh, you Cleveland Orchestra":* The Plain Dealer, May 31, 1998.

543   *"He inspired thousands and thousands":* Ibid., January 26, 1999.

544   *"I can't imagine there has been quite so much sound":* Ibid., July 8, 1997.

544   *"The notion wasn't to copy":* The Plain Dealer, January 2, 2000.

545   *All of the improvements:* The final aspect of the renovation is the installation of the restored E. M. Skinner organ, to be heard by the public for the first time in January 2001.

544   *"Severance Hall sounds":* New York Times, January 10, 2000.

545   *"The result of the renovation":* Musical America, January 10, 2000.

Bibliography

Alexander, J. Heywood. *It Must Be Heard: A Survey of the Musical Life of Cleveland, 1836–1918*. Cleveland: Western Reserve Historical Society, 1981.

Badal, James. "Cleveland's Christoph von Dohnányi." *Symphony,* June/July 1984.

Barenboim, Daniel. *A Life in Music.* New York: Charles Scribner's Sons, 1991.

Beranek, Leo. *Concert and Opera Halls: How They Sound.* Woodbury, N.Y.: Acoustical Society of America, 1996.

Biancolli, Louis. *The Flagstad Manuscript.* New York: G. P. Putnam's Sons, 1952.

Bianculli, David. *Teleliteracy: Taking Television Seriously.* New York: Continuum, 1992.

Bing, Rudolf. *5000 Nights at the Opera.* Garden City, N.Y.: Doubleday, 1972.

Bispham, David. *A Quaker Singer's Recollections.* New York: Macmillan, 1920.

Blum, David. "Profiles: A Gold Coin." *The New Yorker,* February 4, 1991.

Bookspan, Martin, and Ross Yockey. *André Previn.* New York: Doubleday, 1981.

Bordman, Gerald. *Jerome Kern: His Life and Music.* New York: Oxford University Press, 1980.

Craven, Robert R. *Symphony Orchestras of the United States: Selected Profiles.* New York: Greenwood Press, 1986.

Davis, Peter G. *The American Opera Singer.* New York: Doubleday, 1997.

Dooley, Dennis. "We Have a Maestro!" *Northern Ohio Live,* May 1982.

Erskine, John. *The Philharmonic-Symphony Society of New York: Its First Hundred Years.* New York: Macmillan, 1943.

Faulkner, Maurice. "The Cleveland Orchestra at the Salzburg Festival." *Instrumentalist,* August 1968.

Fellers, Frederick P., and Betty Meyers. *Discographies of Commercial Recordings of The Cleveland Orchestra (1924–1977) and The Cincinnati Symphony Orchestra (1917–1977).* Westport, Conn.: Greenwood Press, 1978.

Fisher, Renee B. *Musical Prodigies: Masters at an Early Age.* New York: Association Press, 1973.

Furlong, William Barry. *Season with Solti.* New York: Macmillan, 1974.

Geleng, Ingvelde. *Monographie eines Musikers.* Berlin: Rembrandt Verlag, 1971.

Gilman, Lawrence. *Toscanini and Great Music.* New York: Farrar & Rinehart, 1938.

Goulder, Grace. *John D. Rockefeller: The Cleveland Years.* Cleveland: Western Reserve Historical Society, 1972.

Graffman, Gary. *I Really Should Be Practicing*. New York: Doubleday, 1981.

Gruber, Paul, ed. *The Metropolitan Opera Guide to Recorded Opera*. New York: Norton, 1993.

Grossman, F. Karl. *A History of Music in Cleveland*. Cleveland: Case Western Reserve University Press, 1972.

Hamilton, David, ed. *The Metropolitan Opera Encyclopedia: A Comprehensive Guide to the World of Opera*. New York: Simon and Schuster, 1987.

Hart, Philip. *Conductors: A New Generation*. New York: Charles Scribner's Sons, 1979.

——— . *Orpheus in the New World*. New York: Norton, 1973.

Heyworth, Peter. *Otto Klemperer: His Life and Times (Volume I: 1885–1933)*. Cambridge: Cambridge University Press, 1983.

Holoman, D. Kern. *Evenings with the Orchestra*. New York: Norton, 1992.

Horowitz, Joseph. *Understanding Toscanini*. New York: Knopf, 1987.

Hughes, Adella Prentiss. *Music Is My Life*. Cleveland: World Publishing Company, 1947.

Jablonsky, Edward. *Gershwin: A Biography*. New York: Doubleday, 1987.

Jackson, Paul. *Saturday Afternoons at the Old Met: The Metropolitan Opera Broadcasts 1931–1950*. Portland, Ore.: Amadeus Press, 1992.

——— . *Sign-Off for the Old Met: The Metropolitan Opera Broadcasts 1950–1966*. Portland, Ore.: Amadeus Press, 1997.

Johannesen, Eric. *A Cleveland Legacy: The Architecture of Walker and Weeks*. Kent, Oh.: Kent State University Press, 1999.

Karajan, Herbert von. *Herbert von Karajan: My Autobiography*. London: Sidgwick & Jackson, 1989.

Kirk, Elizabeth P. "Severance Hall, Cleveland's Temple of Music." *The Gamut* 18 (Spring/Summer 1986).

Klassen, Hope M. "Maestros and Management: The Cleveland Orchestra, 1918–1994." Master's thesis, University of Akron , 1995.

Kolodin, Irving. *The Metropolitan Opera, 1883–1966: A Candid History*. New York: Knopf, 1966.

Krause, Ernst. *Richard Strauss: The Man and His Work*. Boston: Crescendo Publishing, 1969.

Lebrecht, Norman. *The Companion to 20th Century Music*. New York: Simon & Schuster, 1992.

Lehmann, Lotte. *My Many Lives*. New York: Boosey & Hawkes, 1948.

Leinsdorf, Erich. *Cadenza: A Musical Career*. Boston: Houghton Mifflin, 1976.

Levant, Oscar. *The Memoirs of an Amnesiac*. New York: G. P. Putnam's Sons, 1965.

Levine, Lawrence W. *Highbrow/Lowbrow: The Emergence of Cultural Hierarchy in America*. Cambridge: Harvard University Press, 1988.

Marsh, Robert C. *The Cleveland Orchestra*. Cleveland: World Publishing Company, 1967.

Massmann, Richard Lee. *Lillian Baldwin and the Cleveland Plan for Educational Concerts*. Ann Arbor, Mich.: University Microfilms, 1972.

Matheopoulos, Helena. *Maestro: Encounters with Conductors of Today.* New York: Harper & Row, 1982.

Mayer, Martin. "Szell, Still Storming After 50 Years." *New York Times*, February 2, 1964.

Menuhin, Yehudi. *Unfinished Journey*. New York: Knopf, 1977.

Mueller, Kate Hevner. *Twenty-Seven Major American Symphony Orchestras: A History and Analysis of Their Repertoires, Seasons 1842–43 Through 1969–70.* Bloomington: Indiana University Press, 1973.

Mussulman, Joseph A. *Dear People . . . Robert Shaw: A Biography*. Bloomington: Indiana University Press, 1979.

Osborne, Richard. *Conversations with Karajan*. New York: Harper & Row, 1989.

Ostwald, Peter. *Glenn Gould: The Ecstasy and Tragedy of Genius.* New York: Norton, 1997.

Porter, Andrew. *Musical Events: A Chronicle, 1983–1986.* New York: Summit Books, 1989.

Raynor, Henry. *The Orchestra*. New York: Charles Scribner's Sons, 1978.

Renehan, Edward J., Jr. *The Lion's Pride: Theodore Roosevelt and His Family in Peace and War*. New York: Oxford University Press, 1998.

Robinson, Harlow. *Sergei Prokofiev: A Biography*. New York: Viking Penguin, 1987.

Rodzinski, Halina. *Our Two Lives.* New York: Charles Scribner's Sons, 1976.

Rose, William Ganson. *Cleveland: The Making of a City*. Cleveland: World Publishing Company, 1950.

Roy, Klaus George. *Not Responsible for Lost Articles*. Cleveland: Musical Arts Association, 1993.

Rubinstein, Arthur. *My Many Years*. New York: Knopf, 1980.

Sachs, Harvey. *Rubinstein: A Life*. New York: Grove Press, 1995.

——— . *Toscanini*. Philadelphia: J. B. Lippincott, 1978.

Sadie, Stanley, ed. *The New Grove Dictionary of Music and Musicians.* London: Macmillan Publishers, 1980.

Schonberg, Harold C. *The Great Conductors*. New York: Simon and Schuster, 1967.

Schwarzkopf, Elisabeth. *On and Off the Record: A Memoir of Walter Legge*. New York: Charles Scribner's Sons, 1982.

Shanet, Howard. *Philharmonic: A History of New York's Orchestra*. Garden City, N.Y.: Doubleday, 1975.

Shankland, Robert S., and Edward A. Flynn. "Acoustics of Severance Hall." *Journal of the Acoustical Society of America* 31, no. 7 (July 1959).

Smith, Cecil. *Worlds of Music*. Philadelphia: J. B. Lippincott, 1952.

Sokoloff, Nikolai. "Reminiscences." (Unpublished). Copyright held by Eleanor Sokoloff, 1977.

Steinhardt, Arnold. *Indivisible by Four: A String Quartet in Pursuit of Harmony*. New York: Farrar Straus Giroux, 1998.

Trotter, William R. *Priest of Music: The Life of Dimitri Mitropoulos*. Portland, Ore.: Amadeus Press, 1995.

Vacha, John. "The Selling of Szell: The Cleveland Orchestra Meets Its Maestro." *Timeline* 15, no. 6 (December 1998).

Van Tassel, David D., and John J. Grabowski, eds. *The Encyclopedia of Cleveland History*. Bloomington: Indiana University Press, 1987.

Wagner, Mary Cleveland. "Early Orchestras in Cleveland (1900–1915)." Graduate thesis, Kent State University, 1998.

Wechsberg, Joseph. "Profiles: The Grace of the Moment." *The New Yorker*, November 6, 1965.

———. "Profiles: Orchestra." *The New Yorker*, May 30, 1970.

Yancich, Milan. *An Orchestra Musician's Odyssey: A View from the Rear*. Rochester, N.Y.: Wind Music, 1995.

Cleveland Orchestra Personnel 1918-2000

The Cleveland Orchestra has had almost 1,000 members since its inaugural season (1918–19). The musicians who have had contracts are listed below alphabetically by section. In some cases, a player moved from one section to another, from one position to another, or performed on more than one instrument. The entries give the years the musician joined and left the orchestra, not necessarily the beginning or ending concert seasons.

Much of the information included here appears, in a different form, in *Fanfare: Portraits of The Cleveland Orchestra*, whose most recent edition was published in January 1995 by the Musical Arts Association.

First Violin

Abbott, Muriel (1918–19); **Altschuler, Eugene** (assistant concertmaster: 1980–82; associate concertmaster: 1982–87; first violin: 1987–2000); **Antal, Jeno** (1949–61); **Arbeitman, Haim** (1955–57); **Arben, David** (1956–59); **Armin, Otto** (1964–65); **Arzewski, Cecylia** (associate concertmaster: 1987–90); **Barozzi, Socrate** (second concertmaster: 1929–30); **Barrett, James** (assistant concertmaster: 1949–59; first violin: 1959–1979); **Beckwith, Arthur** (concertmaster: 1923–26); **Bergen, Eugene** (1938–43); **Berger, Raoul** (third concertmaster: 1927–28); **Berman, Louis** (1931–40; 1942–45); **Berv, Henry** (1928–33); **Besrodny, Jack** (1942–45); **Bognar, Arpad** (1924–38); **Booth, Guy** (1918–19); **Bornstein, Milton L.** (1920–21); **Bottero, Alessandro** (1959–61); **Brenner, Joseph** (1923–29); **Bridgeman, Harold C.** (1919–20); **Brown, Walberg L.** (1924–28; 1933–37); **Brushilow, Anshel** (assistant concertmaster: 1955–57; associate concertmaster: 1957–59); **Caillon, Liliane** (1964–65); **Carabo, Madeleine** (1943–44); **Carhart, Margaret** (1918–19); **Carmell, Samuel** (1940–43); **Casabona, Alberto** (1947–54); **Ceasar, James** (1948–49); **Chalifour, Martin** (acting associate concertmaster: 1989–90; associate concertmaster: 1990–95; acting concertmaster 1993–95); **Chusid, Boris** (1979–); **Colove, Sam** (1942–47); **Cooley, Carlton** (assistant concertmaster: 1921–23); **Dalschaert, Cathleen** (1962–67); **Dalschaert, Stephane** (1961–67); **d'Auberge, Alfred** (1924–27; 1928–29); **deGranda, Alvaro** (first violin:

1966–68; assistant concertmaster: 1968–1999; first violin: 1999–); **dePasquale, Ellen** (1999– : associate concertmaster); **Dembinsky, William** (1929–32); **Demuth, Fred** (1919–20); **Denoff, Avrum** (1945–46); **Dosch, William M.** (1923–38); **Dreskell, Miles A.** (1919–20); **Drucker, Ernest** (1942–43); **Druian, Rafael** (concertmaster: 1960–69); **Dumm, Mark** (1990–93); **Edelman, Albert** (1936–42); **Edelman, Isadore** (1929–36); **Edlin, Louis** (concertmaster: 1918–23); **Eichhorn, Erich** (1969–); **Erdely, Stephen** (1951–66); **Eyle, Felix** (second concertmaster: 1933–43; assistant concertmaster: 1943–44;second concertmaster: 1944–45); **Faber, Clemens** (1945–65); **Farrar, Mabelle** (1918–22); **Fein, Israel** (1927–28); **Ferrara, Antonio** (1920–21); **Fichtenova, Eugenia** (1947–48); **Fiore, Salvatore E.** (1918–23); **Friedman, Sam** (1927–31); **Freudemann, William** (1918–19); **Fuchs, Josef** (concertmaster: 1926–41); **Furiyoshi, Keiko** (1972–); **Gallo, Joseph** (1946–47); **Gelbloom, Gerald** (1947–48); **Gellert, Max** (1921–27); **Gershman, Paul** (second concertmaster: 1932–33; first violin: 1933–43; assistant concertmaster: 1943–44); **Gingold, Josef** (concertmaster: 1947–60); **Gomez, Kim** (1995–); **Goodman, Bernard** (1938–46); **Gorodetzky, Jac** (1937–43); **Granat, Endre** (assistant concertmaster: 1965–66); **Grau, Gideon** (1954–55); **Greicius, Vincent** (1944–47); **Gu, Wei–Fang** (1993–); **Hagstrom, George C.** (1918–19); **Han–Gorski, Adam** (1967–70); **Hashizume, Miho** (1995–); **Helfand, Maurice** (1919–20); **Hobart, Max** (1961–65); **Hochberg, Morris** (1948–52); **Hon, Ma Si** (1952–57); **Hruby, John J.** (1919–26); **Hunneman, Edmund** (1919–21); **Kardos, Ernest** (1936–42, 1946–47; assistant concertmaster: 1947–84); **Katz, Paul** (1928–33); **Keene, James** (1967–69); **King, Erwin** (1934–36); **Klinger, David** (1927–44); **Knitzer, Joseph** (concertmaster: 1945–46); **Kobler, Raymond** (assistant concertmaster: 1973–77; associate concertmaster: 1976–80); **Koch, Joseph** (1943–85); **Kohon, Isador** (1919–24); **Kojian, Miran** (1966–67); **Kolberg, Hugo** (concertmaster: 1941–42); **Krachmalnick, Jacob** (assistant concertmaster: 1946–51, 1960–61); **Krasner, Louis** (1942–43); **Kurkdjie, L. Nazar** (1920–22); **Latzke, Edwin** (1918–19); **Levy, Louis** (1926–28); **Leysens, Maurice** (1945–48); **Lindstrom, Benjamin** (1918–20); **Loebel, Kurt** (1947–97); **Logan, Walter** (1918–23); **Madden, William** (1923–26); **Majeske, Daniel** (1955–59; assistant concertmaster: 1959–67; associate concertmaster: 1967–69; concertmaster: 1969–93); **Majeske, Stephen** (1979–95); **Marano, Raymond** (1946–47); **Marcosson, Sol** (concertmaster: 1918–19); **Martonne, Herman** (1929–37); **Masame, Takako** (1984–); **Matey, Edward** (1944–47, 1952–82); **Matthews, Eli** (1997–); **Menga, Robert** (1967–68); **Millrood, George** (1943–55); **Moore, Yoko** (assistant concertmaster: 1981–); **Morovitsky, Morris** (1929–42); **Morris, Abe** (1920–24); **Moses, Emanuel** (1930–34); **Moss, Leonard** (1949–53); **Naegele, Philipp** (1956–64); **Nowinski, David** (1922–24); **Nussbaum, Irving** (1949–51); **Offner, Herbert** (1928–36); **Park, Chul–In** (1995–); **Perutz, Robert** (1921–22); **Polyakin, Lev** (first violin: 1981–1999; assistant concertmaster: 1999–); **Poteet, Ewing** (1946–47); **Preucil, William** (concertmaster: 1995–); **Proto, Dino** (assistant concertmaster: 1946–47); **Pugatsky, William** (1920–21); **Raffaelli, Gino** (1957–68, 1969–74); **Rautenberg, Theodore** (1927–29, 1944–61); **Reve, Kalman** (second concertmaster: 1930–32); **Ringwall, Rudolph** (1926–33); **Roberts, Richard** (assistant concertmaster:

1974–82); **Roman, Isadore** (1926–29); **Rose, Jeanne Preucil** (1999–); **Rose, Stephen** (1997–); **Rosen, Jerome** (1964–67); **Rychlik, Charles V.** (1918–19); **Salkin, Samuel** (1920–62); **Sampliner, Sidney** (1918–19); **Samuels, Leonard** (1957–95); **Scharf, Philip** (1929–30); **Schmitt, Homer** (1938–46); **Schweyda, Willy** (1951–52); **Senofsky, Berl** (assistant concertmaster: 1951–55); **Setzer, Marie** (1961–90); **Shaftel, Josef** (1943–45); **Shapiro, Aaron** (1922–26); **Shapiro, Stanislaw** (1922–23); **Shiller, Ralph** (1947–52); **Shipps, Stephen** (1973–75); **Siegel, Bert** (1965–68, 1968–1995); **Silavin, Theodore** (1946–48); **Silverberg, Ben** (1923–29, 1933–45; second concertmaster: 1945–46); **Silverman, Ralph** (1923–26); **Simons, Ben** (1918–19); **Sird, Raymond** (1952–55); **Snader, Nathan** (1967–96); **Sorkin, Herbert** (1949–51); **Spielberg, Herman** (1919–27); **Spitalny, Maurice J.** (1918–20); **Spivakovksy, Tossy** (concertmaster: 1942–45); **Sroubek, Otakar** (1954–56); **Staples, Sheryl** (associate concertmaster: 1996–1998); **Steck, William** (1968–69; assistant concertmaster: 1969–74); **Stein, Sidney L.** (1918–19); **Steinhardt, Arnold** (assistant concertmaster: 1959–64); **Straka, Herman** (1948–49); **Straumann, Bruno** (1955–56); **Taub, Harry** (1948–52); **Taylor, David** (1975–79); **Terlitzky, Joseph** (1924–28); **Thaviu, Samuel** (concertmaster: 1946–47); **Tishkoff, Gary** (1966–); **Toth, Andor** (assistant concertmaster: 1948–49); **Trautwein, George** (1921–33); **van Haam, Harry** (1945–49); **Veissi, Jascha** (1921–23; assistant concertmaster: 1923–27; second concertmaster: 1927–29); **Vignetti, Georges** (1920–22); **Voldrich, Halina** (1967–72); **Vollmer, Henry** (1922–24, 1926–27); **Weicher, John** (1921–23); **Weismann, Joseph** (1921–22); **Weiss, Howard** (1965–67); **Weiss, Sidney** (1956–66); **Whittier, Fred** (1920–21); **Winder, Max** (1948–49); **Wolfson, Maurice** (1945–46); **Yerke, Kenneth** (1968–70); **Zawisza, Leon** (1937–38); **Zimmer, Robert** (1967–); **Ziska, John** (1918–19); **Zvinitzky, Gregory** (1918–20); **Zwilich, Joseph** (1943–45)

Second Violin

Adams, Eugene (1924–26, 1945–47); **Antal, Jeno** (1942–47, 1961–62); **Arenson, Bert** (1950–65); **Bandy, Albert** (1944–45); **Baron, James** (1945–46); **Benkoe, E.** (principal: 1918–19); **Benkovic, Vaclav** (1975–); **Bergen, Eugene** (1936–38); **Berman, Judy** (1980–); **Berman, Louis** (1930–31, 1940–42); **Blabolil, Charles** (1924–38, 1945–69); **Bognar, Arpad** (1922–24, 1938–40, 1942–60); **Boisvert, Emmanuelle** (1986–89); **Booth, Guy** (1919–22); **Botnick, Evelyn** (1943–75); **Bracken, Nancy** (1977–79); **Brown, William** (1946–84); **Callot, Andre** (1934–40); **Cayting, Stanley** (1920–22); **Ceasar, James** (1940–43, 1946–48); **Christopherson, Robert** (1947–49); **Chusid, Boris** (1974–79); **Clendenning, Elizabeth** (1959–61, 1963–67); **Collins, Kathleen** (1995–); **Combel, Armand** (1922–24); **Dalschaert, Cathleen** (1960–62); **Dalschaert, Stephane** (1960–61); **Deninzon, Vladimir** (1979–); **Dolnick, Samuel M.** (1921–22); **Dosch, William M.** (1938–54); **Dresskell, Miles A.** (1920–21); **Drucker, Ernest** (1942–43); **Dumm, Mark** (1985–90; first assistant principal: 1992– ; acting principal: 1994–96); **Edelman, Isadore** (1928–29); **Eichhorn, Erich** (1967–70); **Epstein, Samuel** (1949–1985); **Faber, Clemens** (1931–36, 1965–68); **Fink, Irving** (1938–42); **Fiore, Salvatore E.** (1923–29, 1930–58); **Fontana, Ido** (1921–23); **Freed, Jacob** (1924–26); **Freilich, Felix**

(1955–2000); **Fridkowsky, Simeon** (1918–22); **Friedel, Albert** (1919–34); **Friedman, Sam** (1918–27); **Fulkerson, Gregory** (1971–74); **Funakoshi, Kozue** (1998–); **Furiyoshi, Keiko** (1971–72); **Gelbloom, Gerald** (1948–49); **Goldman, Michael** (1962–65, 1969–73); **Goldschmidt, Bernhard** (1958–64; principal: 1964–95); **Gomez, Kim Nolan** (1990–1995); **Goodall, John B.** (1919–38); **Goodman, Bernard** (1936–38); **Green, William** (1918–19); **Greicius, Vincent** (1940–44); **Grunwald, Ernst G.** (1919–20); **Gu, Wei–Fang** (1990–93); **Han–Gorski, Adam** (1969–70); **Hellman, Leo** (principal: 1919–21); **Holmes, Harley** (1923–40); **Hruby, John J.** (1918–19); **Jordan, Ray** (1920–27); **Juergensen, Anton** (1919–20); **Kaminker, Harry** (1920–24, 1926–28, 1929–36); **Kaplan, Burton** (1961–63); **Kardos, Ernest** (1934–36); **Kaston, Henryk** (1942–44); **Kaufer, Alfred** (1924–60); **King, Erwin** (1926–34, 1936–43); **Kitain, Boris** (1944–45); **Klinger, David** (1926–28); **Knox, James** (1945–68); **Koch, Joseph** (1938–43); **Kojian, Miran** (1965–66); **Kornfeld, Camille** (1918–19); **Krushinski, William** (1918–19); **Latzke, Edward** (1918–20); **Lazarev, Leon** (1985–); **Lindstrom, William** (1920–21); **Llinas, Emilio** (1968–77; assistant principal: 1977– ; acting first assistant principal: 1992–93); **Logan, Walter** (acting principal second: 1918–19); **Madden, William** (1920–23); **Majeske, Stephen** (principal: 1995–); **Matey, Edward** (1938–42); **Matson, Ralph** (1976–77); **Metzdorf, Alfred** (1928–29); **Meyer, Audrey** (1966–79); **Moran, Howard** (1918–19); **Moses, Emanuel** (1927–30); **Ochsner, A.** (1918–19); **Offner, Herbert** (1925–28); **Parmelee, Dan** (1920–21); **Patti, Kenneth** (1974–79); **Pikler, Charles** (1973–76); **Pittenger, Raymond** (1929–34); **Raffaelli, Gino** (1968–69, 1974–); **Rafferty, Patrick** (1972–74); **Rautenberg, Theodore** (1942–44); **Reinhardt, Willis** (1929–70); **Roman, Isadore** (1922–26); **Rosen, Jerome** (1959–62); **Salkin, Samuel** (1962–68); **Sant'Ambrogio, Stephanie** (1984–90; first assistant principal: 1990–92); **Schandler, Hyman** (1927–33; principal: 1933–64; second violin: 1964–75); **Schmitt, Homer** (1936–38); **Schuller, Arthur** (1965–66); **Setzer, Elmer** (1949–77; first assistant principal: 1977–90); **Shapiro, Aaron** (1920–21); **Shaw, Carl** (1947–50); **Sholle, Emil** (1924–69); **Siegel, Bert** (1968–69); **Siegel, Joan** (1965–1995); **Silverberg, Ben** (1921–23); **Simons, Ben** (1918–19); **Straumann, Bruno** (1954–55); **Strawn, Roberta** (1962–84); **Taylor, David** (1973–75); **Terlitzky, Joseph** (1923–24); **Tierney, John Joseph** (1918–20); **Traupe, William** (principal: 1921–33); **Ungar, Bert** (1918–19); **Ungar, Irwin** (1923–24); **Ungar, Maurice** (1918–19); **VanAiken, Hal** (1918–19); **van Haam, Harry** (1944–45); **Veissi, Harold** (1927–30); **Vernon, Paul** (1921–23); **Vietri, Scipione** (1922–25); **Voldrich, Richard** (1967–); **Warner, Carolyn Gadiel** (1979–); **Warner, Stephen** (1978–); **Weber, Scott** (1989–); **Wolfson, Maurice** (1946–85); **Woodside, Beth** (1994–); **Zimmer, Robert** (1966–67)

Viola

Beck, Benjamin (1918–19); **Berman, Louis** (1928–30); **Blackman, Alexander** (1920–21); **Boyko, Lisa** (1991–); **Braunstein, Mark** (assistant principal: 1984–93); **Brennand, Tom** (1937–39; principal: 1939–41; viola: 1941–42; principal: 1941–42; viola: 1942–65); **Brown, Marian** (1953–55); **Burnau, Sally** (1960–61); **Cahill, Vaughn D.** (1918–19); **Carhart, Margaret** (1919–20);

Carmen, Muriel (1951–94); Chapin, Clifford M. (1920–22); Cheifetz, Sussman (1919–21); Collins, LeRoy (1937–45); Connolly, Patrick (1988–); Cooley, Carlton (principal: 1920–21, 1923–37); Coonley, Vladimir (1924–25, 1929–40); Cox, John (1956–59, 1965–66); Czapko, Julius (1924–34); Demuth, Fred (1920–21, 1922–23); Dick, Marcel (principal: 1943–49); Dumm, Thomas (1961–67); Elkind, Samuel W. (1919–20); Faden, Yarden (1966–); Fleitman, Leo (1921–27); Frederick, Walter (1918–19); Freed, Jacob (1921–24, 1926–29); Frengut, Leon (principal: 1937–39); Freund, Arnold (1925–26); Funkhouser, Frederick (1929–84); Gans, Isaac (1944–60); Goldblum, Samuel (1925–29, 1931–47); Goldsmith, Rosemary (1967–81); Gray, William (1920–25); Green, Louis (1919–20); Gruber, Gabriel (1949–51); Harris, Stanley (1941–43); Hedberg, Earl (1955–56); Hoech, Robert (1919–20); Jackobs, Mark (1993–); Janovsky, Ernest K. (1922–23); Jilovec, Otto (1918–24); Joel, Lucien (1969–2000); Johnston, James D. (principal: 1918–19); Kahlson, Erik (1927–31, 1932–37); Kiraly, William (1947–49, 1953–88); Klima, Arthur (1977–); Kolodkin, Herman M. (principal: 1919–20); Konopka, Stanley (1991–93; assistant principal: 1992–); Krausslich, Alvin (1919–20); Krausz, Laszlo (1947–69); Kushleika, Vitold (1944–88); Layefsky, Godfrey (1939–41); Levin, Louis (1920–21); Lifschey, Samuel (principal: 1921–23); Lincer, William (principal: 1942–43); Logan, Walter (1923–29); Manson, Robert G. (1923–25); Marcosson, Sol (1928–31); Mark, Malcolm (1945–69); Mende, Paul (1920–24); Miller, Harry (1944–48); Ormond, Edward (1959–71; first assistant principal: 1971–89; acting principal: 1976–77; assistant principal: 1988–1997)[check status at retirement]/Paananen, Ernest (1923–32); Paeff, Spinoza (1943–44); Ramsey, Lynne (first assistant principal: 1988–); Reichman, Aaron (1921–22); Rennert, Bruno (1919–20); Ressler, Julius (1924–27); Rosenberg, Fred (1933–43); Schaffer, Max (1930–37); Schwartz, David (1937–41; principal: 1941–42); Selcer, Ben (1934–77); Senyak, Joseph (1923–49); Sicre, Ursula Urbaniak (1981–91); Skernick, Abraham (principal: 1949–76); Spitalny, J. (1918–19); Steinbach, Paul (1918–19); Stummer, Walter (1953–91); Sweet, Myron (1921–23, 1925–28); Thomas, Milton (1940–44); Vernon, Robert (principal: 1976–); Veskimets, Lembi (1997–); Victors, Harry (1919–20); Wallfisch, Ernst (1949–53); Waugh, Richard (1994–); Williams, Caroline Harter (1918–19); Woodward, Olive (1920–23, 1930–33); Zaslav, Bernard (1947–49)

Cello

Albers, Fred (1918–19); Appleman, Gerald (principal: 1964–65; alternating principal: 1965–66); Arenstein, Michael (1927–31); Baar, Theodore (1944–45, 1948–74); Baer, Armand (1929–31); Bandy, John (1944–49); Barab, Seymour (1941–42); Bernard, Charles (1991–); Birnn, Edward (1947–49); Bodenhorn, Aaron (1923–24, 1927–28); Brennand, Charles (1955–56); Brey, Carter (1979–81); Bush, Dudley (1926–27); Chaikin, Nathan (1940–41); Collins, Alan (1945–47); Curry, Ralph (1978–); de Gomez, Victor (principal: 1919–39); Dinger, Nahoun J. (1921–24); Domb, Daniel (first assistant principal: 1971–73); Downs, Warren (1956–71); Drossin, Julius (1948–57); Dufrasne, Maurice (1922–26); Dumm, Bryan (1986–);

Eiler, Oscar (principal: 1918–19; cello: 1918–21); **Elliot, Harry R.** (1921–23); **Emelianoff, Andre** (1967–72); **Eskin, Jules** (principal: 1961–64); **Evans, Louis** (1921–22); **Feidelholtz, Israel** (1920–21); **Frezin, Adolphe** (co–principal: 1959–60; principal: 1960–61); **Fuchs, Harry** (1937–43; principal: 1943–47; cello: 1949–79); **Geber, Stephen** (principal: 1973–); **Gelfand, Michael** (1972–74); **Gelzayd, Mitchell** (1932–37); **Gerkowski, Raymond** (1926–40); **Gershman, Nathan** (1941–48); **Goetsch, Erwin F.** (1919–26); **Gordon, Isadore** (1919–20, 1921–22, 1934–44); **Grant, Frank** (1925–42); **Grebanier, Michael** (1959–63); **Greenbaum, David** (1941–44); **Haber, Michael** (1969–71); **Hamer, Charles F.** (1923–27); **Hamer, Sydney** (1922–29); **Hampel, Alford** (1927–40); **Harrell, David Alan** (1995–); **Harrell, Lynn** (1963–65; alternating principal: 1965–66; principal: 1966–71); **Hazlett, George** (1918–19); **Hensel, Harry** (1924–40); **Hollander, Norman** (1946–48); **Howard, Arthur** (1957–58); **Hruby, Alois** (1918–26); **Hruby, Mamie** (1918–19); **Hunkins, Nella** (first assistant principal: 1973–78); **Joachim, Heinrich** (1946–47); **Kapuscinski, Richard** (1943–48); **Kayaloff, Jean** (1924–25); **Kellert, Gabriel** (1943–44); **Krausslich, Al (Jr.)** (1919–20); **Kushious, Paul** (1995–); **Lamp, Karl** (1944–46); **Landshoff, Werner** (1944–47); **Laut, Edward** (1973–77); **Lavin, Avram** (1948–49); **Leonard, Ronald** (1955–57); **Levenson, David** (1944–48); **Levine, David** (1966–67); **Lewin, Morris** (1920–27); **Liberti, Thomas** (1948–66); **Lingeman, Johan F.** (1919–20); **Mansbacher, Thomas** (1977–); **Mather, Diane** (1963–67; first assistant principal: 1967–69; assistant principal: 1969–); **McBride, Charles** (1926–44); **Meints, Catharina** (1971–); **Michelson, Albert** (1947–69); **Munroe, Lorne** (1949–50); **Musgrave, C. Philip** (1918–19); **Narovec, Edward** (1918–19); **Nimz, Arthur** (1918–19); **Paskewitz, Morris** (1920–22); **Perry, Robert** (1968–94); **Phillips, Bert** (1958–59); **Ripley, Robert** (1942–43, 1946–55); **Robbins, Channing** (1940–41); **Rose, Leonard** (principal: 1939–43); **Sayre, Robert** (1949–52); **Schmitt, Max** (1921–26, 1928–32); **Schones, Maurice** (1920–21); **See, William J.** (1920–21); **Sicre, Jorge** (1961–91); **Silberstein, Ernst** (principal: 1947–59; co–principal: 1959–67); **Simon, Martin** (1947–95); **Sims, Rudolph** (1966–67); **Sophos, Anthony** (1942–44); **Steingraber, Harvey** (1918–19); **Stokking, William (Jr.)** (1958–60; principal: 1971–73); **Störseth, Rolf** (1950–63); **Stucka, Gary** (1981–86); **Stutch, Nathan** (1940–42); **Swenson, Robert** (1931–46); **Thornton, Brian** (1994–); **Trepel, Shirley** (1952–55); **Troostwyk, Leo** (1919–20); **Tucker, Irwin B.** (1920–21); **Weiss, Richard** (1974–78; acting assistant principal: 1977–78; first assistant principal: 1977–); **White, Donald** (1957–1996); **Wolfe, Harvey** (1967–); **Zeise, Karl** (1926–27)

BASS

Angell, Lawrence (1955–61; assistant principal: 1961–76; first assistant principal: 1975–81; acting principal: 1981–82; principal: 1981–95); **Aradi, George P.** (1918–19); **Atherton, Mark** (1983–); **Barnoff, Harry** (1953–97); **Benner, Raymond** (1956–62); **Bernhart, Arnold** (1948–50); **Bortolamasi, Albert** (1923–24, 1929–36); **Bulik, John** (1943–49); **Carbone, John** (1969–70); **Chassagne, Louis** (1920–21); **Civiletti, Charles** (1918–28); **Clair, Nathalie**

(1943–47); **Clarke, Harry F.** (1918–22); **Connor, Ethan** (1978–); **Dimoff, Maximilian** (principal: 1997–); **Dvořák, Anton** (1918–19); **Fiedelholz, Nathan** (1919–26); **Fiore, Gerald F.** (principal: 1918–36); **Flowerman, Martin** (1967–); **Garratt, Harold** (1943–46); **Gennert, Albert** (1918–19); **Glassman, Joseph** (1919–20); **Goldin, Hyman** (1920–21, 1926–43); **Goldlust, Marvin** (1942–43, 1946–50); **Gould, Howard J.** (1926–29); **Guia, L. Perez** (1922–26); **Haigh, Scott** (1978–80; assistant principal: 1980–82; first assistant principal: 1981– ; acting principal: 1996–97); **Hanulik, Christopher** (principal: 1995–96); **Harnach, Fred** (1943–46); **Harnett, James** (1950–55); **Jennings, Fay** (1949–78); **Knight, Anthony** (1974–82; assistant principal: 1982–91); **Krausslich, Alvin** (1918–19); **Lamagna, Michael** (1924–37; principal: 1937–39; bass: 1939–44); **Lapenna, Angelo** (1950–51); **LaRusso, Thomas** (1959–67); **Maresh, Ferdinand** (1941–42, 1945–48); **May, Frank** (1937–42, 1945–74); **McAllister, J.R.** (1918–19); **McClure, Theron** (1937–43); **McGibeny, Fred** (1918–1919); **Murphy, Alfred** (1918–1919, 1928–34); **Nadelson, Meyer** (1920–21); **Nathanson, Irving** (1947–84); **Perlman, David** (principal: 1966–81); **Peyrebrune, Henry** (1997–); **Pitts, Timothy** (1985–92); **Pivonka, Thomas** (1918–19, 1920–57); **Posell, Jacques** (1936–39; principal: 1939–66; co–principal: 1966–78; bass: 1978–85); **Prohaska, Paul** (1921–23); **Ravagnani, Albert** (1926–37); **Salkowski, John** (1962–66); **Salvatore, Fred** (1921–23); **Schettler, Theodore** (1942–56); **Sepulveda, Thomas** (1966–67, 1970–79, 1981–); **Shmuklovsky, Dmitri** (1934–36; principal: 1936–37); **Sperl, Thomas** (1991–); **Steelman, Ronald** (1951–53); **Stein, William** (1920–27); **Switalski, Kevin** (assistant principal: 1991–); **Totten, Clarence** (1935–41); **Trogdon, Olin** (1937–69); **Van Sickle, Rodney** (1957–59); **Yirberg, Charles** (1923–37); **Ziporkin, Leon** (1919–20)

HARP

Chalifoux, Alice (principal: 1931–74); **Chiostergi, Carmela Cafarelli** (principal: 1918–19; harp: 1919–21); **Dalton, Martha** (1947–51, 1952–81); **de Bona, Francisco** (principal: 1919–20); **De Lone, Loretta** (1922–23); **Hopka, Dorothy** (1921–22); **Mills, Verlye Arlyn** (principal: 1930–31); **Morscher, Sepp** (principal: 1920–22); **Okuniewski, Laura** (1980–81; assistant principal: 1980–92); **Pedicord, Charles** (1947–49); **Pizzo, Joseph** (principal: 1928–29); **Steck, Nell** (1923–35); **Struble, Trina** (assistant principal: 1991–); **Veissi, Laura Newell** (principal: 1922–26); **Vitale, Valerie** (1945–46); **Vito, Edward** (principal: 1926–28); **Wellbaum, Lisa** (principal: 1974–); **Wightman, Florence** (principal: 1929–30)

FLUTE

Aarons, Martha (1981–); **Baker, Julius** (1937–41); **Bernthaler, Otto** (1920–21); **Bladet, Robert** (1928–29); **Brewer, Florence McGibeny** (1918–26); **Caratelli, Sebastian** (1942–43); **Chapoff, S.** (1918–19); **Clappe, Costa** (principal: 1918–19); **Drexler, George** (1932–37); **Fiedelman, I.** (1925–26); **Fink, Mary Kay** (1989–); **Fiore, Joseph S.** (1918–19; principal: 1918–19; flute: 1919–21); **Gaskins, Benjamin A.** (1921–25, 1926–29); **Goldberg, Bernard** (1934–45; principal: 1945–46); **Hambrecht, George** (1955–61); **Heylman, Martin** (1941–42; principal: 1946–47; flute: 1946–81);

Khaner, Jeffrey (principal: 1982–90); Lane, Timothy (1980–81); MacKnight, John (1922–25); Mayhall, Walter (1945–46); Mendoza, A. (1918–19); Moor, Bartley C. (1925–26); Moor, Weyert A. (principal: 1919–31); Morris, Robert (1942–47); Pagano, Emil (1928–42); Rautenberg, John (1961–81; associate principal: 1980– ; acting principal: 1982–83); Sharp, Maurice (principal: 1931–45; flute: 1946–47; principal: 1946–82); Smith, Joshua (principal: 1990–); Sulanchek, Vincent (1921–22); Sylvester, Louis (1926–28); Torno, Laurent (1926–32); Willoughby, Robert (1946–55)

PICCOLO

Baker, Julius (1937–41); Caratelli, Sebastian (principal: 1942–43); Drexler, George (1932–37); Fiedelman, I. (1925–26); Fink, Mary Kay (principal: 1989–); Fiore, Joseph S. (principal: 1919–21); Gaskins, Benjamin S. (1921–25; principal: 1926–28; piccolo: 1928–29); Goldberg, Bernard (1943–45); Hebert, William (principal: 1947–88); Heylman, Martin (1941–43); Mayhall, Walter (1945–46); Moor, Bartley C. (principal: 1925–26); Morris, Robert (1942–27); Pagano, Emil (principal: 1928–42); Robertello, Thomas (principal: 1988–89); Sulanchek, Vincent (principal: 1921–22); Torno, Laurent (1926–32)

OBOE

Aldi, Dominic (principal: 1918–19; oboe: 1918–20); Andraud, Albert (1926–29); Brenner, Engelbert (1928–31); Camus, Elizabeth (1979–); Gassman, Bert (1930–44; principal: 1947–49); Gatwood, Elden (1953–63); Genovese, Alfred (principal: 1959–60); Gnam, Adrian (1964–66; acting co–principal: 1964–65); Goldblum, Isadore (1929–30); Hoffman, Owen W. (1920–21); Kirchner, Philip (principal: 1919–47); Kirkpatrick, Vernon (1945–46); Kraus, Felix (1963–); Leoncavallo, John (1924–26); Lifschey, Marc (principal: 1950–59; principal: 1960–65); Lym, William R. (1921–24); Mack, John (principal: 1965–); Marsh, Albert (principal: 1918–19); McGuire, Harvey (1944–46); Paolucci, Italo (1931–32); Rathbun, Jeffrey (assistant principal: 1989–); Reger, Vance (1977–78); Rey, Albert (1919–22); Ruckle, Albert (1919–20); Ruckle, Leo E. (1918–20); Serpentini, Ernest (1923–24, 1932–45, 1946–53); Stefano, Arthur (1922–27); Tivin, Emanuel (principal: 1949–50); Wolfe, Joseph (1927–28); Woods, Pamela Pecha (1978–81; assistant principal: 1980–90); Zupnik, Robert (1946–77; acting co–principal: 1964–65)

ENGLISH HORN

Andraud, Albert (1926–1929); Brenner, Engelbert (1929–31); Gassman, Bert (1931–44); Kirchner, Philip (1919–20, 1926–27); Kraus, Felix (1979–); Kirkpatrick, Vernon 1945–46); Leoncavallo, John (1924–26); Lym, William R. (1921–24); Marsh, Albert (1918–19); McGuire, Harvey (1944–79); Rey, Albert (1919–22); Ruckle, Leo E. (1918–19); Serpentini, Ernest (1933–45); Wolfe, Joseph (1927–28)

CLARINET

Bonade, Daniel (principal: 1933–41); Both, Emerson (principal: 1944–45); Cherlin, Johan (1920–24); Ciccarelli, Anthony (1951–54); Cioffi, Gino (principal: 1942–44); **Cohen, Franklin** (principal: 1976–); **de Santis, Louis** (principal: 1926–29); **Fatt, Philip** (1954–56); **Frederick, Walter** (1918–19); **Gilbert, Daniel** (1995–); **Glazer, David** (1946–51); **Gorodner, Aaron** (principal: 1930–31); **Green, Louis** (principal: 1920–25); **Hamm, Harry** (1918–19); **Hasty, D. Stanley** (1945–46); **Hruby, Frank** (1918–26); **Johnson, Theodore** (1959–95); **Kuhlmann, Carl** (1934–46); **LeRoy, Henry** (principal: 1929–30); **Lucas, Frank** (1927–34); **Marcellus, Robert** (principal: 1953–73); **McGibeny, Charles G.** (principal: 1918–20); **McGinnis, Robert** (principal: 1941–42, 1946–47); **McKelway, Daniel** (assistant principal: 1995–); **Nereim, Linnea** (1984–); **Peterson, Thomas** (1963–81; assistant principal: 1980–95); **Portnoy, Bernard** (principal: 1947–53); **Powelson, Frank** (1918–19); **Pripadcheff, Alexander** (principal: 1931–33); **Rettew, James** (1944–59); **Rowe, George** (1924–44); **Schreiber, Otto** (1926–27); **Shifrin, David** (principal: 1974–76); **Silfies, George** (1956–63); **Thalin, Walter R.** (principal: 1925–26)

E–Flat Clarinet

Caputo, John (1925–26); **Cherlin, Johan** (1923–24); **Hlavin, Anthony** (1924–25); **Hlavin, William** (1922–23); **Hruby, Frank** (1922–24); **Johnson, Theodore** (1959–95); **McKelway, Daniel** (1995–); **Rettew, James** (1944–59); **Rowe, George** (1925–27, 1930–44)

Bass Clarinet

Green, Louis (1919–20); **Hruby, Frank** (1920–26); **Kuhlmann, Carl** (1934–50); **Lucas, Frank** (1928–34); **Nereim, Linnea** (1984–); **Rowe, George** (1927–28); **Schreiber, Otto** (1926–27); **Zetzer, Alfred** (1950–85)

Saxophone

Avellone, Charles (1941–42); **Coonley, Vladimir** (1931–35); **Lucas, Frank** (1929–30); **Peterson, Thomas** (1963–95); **Silfies, George** (1958–63)

Bassoon

Austin, Phillip (1981–); **Bucci, Marcello** (1936–52); **Carmen, Elias** (principal: 1942–43); **Clouser, John** (principal: 1997–); **Duhamel, Gaston** (principal: 1929–30); **Eifert, Otto** (1952–53); **Goslee, George** (principal: 1943–45, 1946–88); **Griffith, R.J.** (principal: 1918–19; bassoon: 1919–20); **Henker, Walter** (1953–60); **Janovsky, Ernest K.** (1921–23); **Kayser, Charles** (1925–36); **Kennedy, Raymond** (1923–25); **Kirchner, Morris** (1919–20; principal: 1920–29, 1930–33); **Kohon, Markus** (1919–21); **Kubitschek, Ernest** (principal: 1935–36); **Laksar, Vaclav** (1955–81); **MacRitchie, R.** (1925–26); **McGill, David** (principal: 1988–1997); **Phillips, Ronald** (1960–75, 1978–81; assistant principal: 1980–); **Polisi, William** (principal: 1933–35, 1936–37); **Reines, Abraham** (principal: 1918–20; bassoon: 1922–23); **Rickert, August B.** (1920–52); **Ruggieri, Frank** (principal: 1937–43, 1945–46); **Sherwin, Jonathan** (1997–); **Shubin, Matthew** (1974–78); **Van Hoesen, David** (1952–54); **Weisberg, Arthur** (1954–55)

CONTRABASSOON

Bucci, Marcello (1936–60); **Henker, Walter** (1960–62); **Janovsky, Ernest K.** (1921–23); **Kayser, Charles** (1925–36); **Kennedy, Raymond** (1923–25); **Kohon, Markus** (1919–21); **Maret, Stanley** (1962–1997); **Reines, Abraham** (1922–23); **Sherwin, Jonathan** (1997–)

HORN

Amor, Frank F. (1918–20); **Andru, Alexander** (1929–41); **Angelucci, Ernani** (1937–44, 1946–80); **Berv, Isadore** (principal: 1928–30); **Blabolil, Charles** (1941–64); **Bloom, Myron** (1954–55; principal: 1955–77); **Bloomfield, Theodore** (1946–47); **Brain, Alfred** (principal: 1934–36); **Brouk, Frank** (1946–47; principal: 1947–50); **Brown, Robert H.** (1920–25); **Cerino, Arthur** (principal: 1919–20, 1925–27); **Clebsch, Hans** (1996–); **Cras, Roman** (1922–23, 1926–29); **DeMattia, Alan** (1984–); **dePolis, Frank** (1921–24); **Deunk, Norman** (1918–19); **d'Orio, John** (1920–21); **Dufrasne, Louis** (principal: 1922–25); **Epstein, Eli** (1986–); **Farkas, Philip** (principal: 1941–45, 1946–47); **Ferrazza, Michele** (1925–27); **Fischer, Fritz** (principal: 1918–19); **Freudemann, William** (1918–19); **Geithe, Arthur** (principal: 1920–21); **Glasser, David** (1977–81; assistant principal: 1981–85; horn: 1984–1996); **Goederteir, Fred** (1924–26); **Graas, John** (1945–46); **Grant, Edward E.** (1926–29); **Grossman, Andrew** (1967–69); **Haigh, Bertram** (1926–27); **Hale, Leonard** (1952–54); **Hoss, Wendell** (principal: 1921–22, 1930–33); **Kec, Vaclav** (1926–27); **Kenny, Thomas** (1951–53); **King, Richard** (associate principal: 1988–95; co-principal: 1995–97; principal: 1997–); **Krivicek, Joseph J.** (1918–20); **Linder, Waldemar** (1929–33); **Lockwood, Ralph** (1975–76); **Macdonald Walter G.** (1926–27; principal: 1926–27; horn: 1927–28); **Mackey, Richard** (1955–63); **Mayhew, Michael** (associate principal: 1997–); **McDonald, Charles** (1966–68, 1969–71); **Miersch, Erwin** (1924–26, 1936–51); **Morris, Martin** (1941–42, 1945–81); **Morris, Walter** (1923–24); **Namen, William** (1927–45); **Nava, Lucino** (principal: 1927–28); **Paananen, Ernest** (1923–32); **Pelletier, Alphonse J.** (principal: 1919; horn: 1919–26); **Petersen, Ralph** (1944–48); **Powers, Jeffrey** (1980–85); **Puletz, Rudolph (Jr.)** (principal: 1937–41); **Rosevear, Lloyd** (1965–66); **Ruske, Eric** (associate principal: 1984–88); **Schinner, Karl** (1927–34); **Schmitter, Albert** (1963–65, 1968–95); **Seder, Theodore** (principal: 1933–34; horn: 1934–37); **Showers, Shelley** (acting principal horn: 1995–97)**Slocum, William** (1966–68); **Solis, Richard** (1971–77; acting principal: 1976–78; principal: 1977–95; horn: 1995–); **Speinson, Morris** (1920–21); **Stagliano, Albert** (principal: 1936–37); **Stagliano, James** (principal: 1945–46); **Stango, Emil** (1921–22); **Taylor, Ross** (principal: 1950–55); **Waas, Roy** (1948–51; 1953–66); **Wagnitz, Ralph** (1977–84); **Yancich, Milan** (1951–52)

TRUMPET

Adelstein, Bernard (principal: 1960–88); **Barnes, Clifford** (principal: 1918–19); **Barnes, William E.** (principal: 1918–19); **Barton, Leland S.** (principal: 1924–25); **Boos, Frank O.** (1918–19); **Collins, Philip** (1970–72); **Couch, Charles** (1972–81; assistant principal: 1980–); **Darling, James** (1973–);

Davidson, Louis (principal: 1935–58); De Gangi, Dominick (1958–60); Drucker, Vladimir (principal: 1934–35); Einhorn, Nathan (1921–22); Glickstein, David (principal: 1921–22); Hardcastle, Geoffrey (1997–98); Heim, Gustav (principal: 1923–24); Herforth, Harry (1951–58); Hering, Sigmund (principal: 1922–24); Hois, Charles (1955–60); Hoose, Clarence F. (1918–19); Hruby, Alois (1919–26; principal: 1927–34; trumpet: 1934–55); Hruby, Charles (1920–21, 1925–26); Hruby, John J. (1918–26); Hruby, William (1925–26, 1927–56); Jandorf, David (1953–55); Katz, Irwin (1955–57); Kaufer, Alfred (1926–60); Klass, Sol (1926–28); Landholt, Robert (1948–51); Miller, Samuel (1920–21); Prager, Nathan (1928–29); Rozanel, E. (principal: 1918–20); Sachs, Michael (principal: 1988–); Schiller, Steven (1972–73); Schlueter, Charles (1967–72); Schwartz, Bernard (1919–21, 1922–25); Smith, Richard (1956–58; principal: 1958–60; trumpet: 1960–67); Snyder, E.C. (1920–21); Sutphen, Albert (1926–27); Sutte, Jack (1999–); Venezia [Venezie], Frank (principal: 1925–27)[dismissed May 1926]/Wohlwender, Thomas (1960–71); Woodbury, Max (1929–34); Zauder, David (1958–97)

CORNET

Darling, James (1973–81; assistant principal: 1980–82; cornet: 1982–); De Gangi, Dominick (principal: 1958–60); Herforth, Harry (principal: 1951–58); Hruby, Alois (1953–55); Hruby, William (1950–53); Katz, Irwin (1955–57); Landholt, Robert (principal: 1850–51); Sachs, Michael (principal: 1997–); Schiller, Steven (1972–73); Schlueter, Charles (principal: 1967–69; cornet: 1968–72); Smith, Richard (principal: 1960–67); Zauder, David (1958–68; principal: 1968–97)

TROMBONE

Anderson, Edwin (1964–79); Bassett, Frank (1934–37); Belgiorgno, Simone (principal: 1926–28); Blumenthal, Jerome (1943–46); Boswell, Guy (1932–35); Boyd, Robert (principal: 1948–89); Brabenec, James F. (1918–19); Burkhart, Warren (1935–43, 1946–64); Chomet, Claude (1920–21); Clarke, Albert E. (principal: 1920–26); Coffey, John (1937–41); DeSano, James (1970–81; assistant principal: 1980–89; principal: 1989–); Dittert, Merritt (principal: 1937–48; trombone: 1948–68); Fetter, David (1968–70); Gusikoff, Charles (principal: 1919–20); Haines, Roy (1936–37); Heidenreich, Joseph (1918–19); Hensel, Harry (1927–33); Kofsky, Allen (1961–2000); Lilleback, Valdemar (1941–48); McGibeny, Fred (1918–19); Nabokin, Philip (1930–32); Nemkovsky, Philip (1921–22); Osbun, Mark T. (1918–20); Polak, Anton (1918–19); Ronka, Elmer (1928–30); Rozanel, David (1919–20); Ruta, Armand (1925–28; principal: 1927–34); Simons, Gardell (principal: 1934–37); Siroto, John (1920–34); Siroto, Joseph (1922–25, 1927–28); Warrick, Elmer E. (principal: 1918–19); Witser, Steven (assistant principal: 1989–)

BASS TROMBONE

Anderson, Edwin (principal: 1978–85); Klaber, Thomas (principal: 1985–)

EUPHONIUM AND BASS TRUMPET

Hruby, John J. (bass trumpet: 1925–26); **Kofsky, Allen** (1974–2000); **Ruta, Armand** (euphonium: 1931–34)

TUBA

Bishop, Ronald (principal: 1967–); **Burant, Edward** (principal: 1918–20); **Cesky, Mathias** (1921–22); **Chassagne, Louis** (principal: 1920–21); **Meyer, Herman** (principal: 1921–28); **Moser, Adolf** (principal: 1928–50); **Murphy, Alfred** (1928–34); **Roberts, Chester** (principal: 1950–67); **Teska, Joseph** (principal: 1918–19)

TIMPANI

Burnham, Jay (1988–91); **Denecke, Henry** (principal: 1936–37); **Duff, Cloyd** (principal: 1942–81); **Freer, Tom** (assistant principal: 1991–); **Kalinovsky, Wolf** (principal: 1937–41); **Kerr, Ian** (principal: 1941–42); **Matson, Robert** (1968–81; assistant principal: 1980–89); **Miller, Harry** (principal: 1918–31, 1933–35); **Perrin, Joseph** (principal: (1931–33); **Wagner, Roland** (principal: 1935–36); **Yancich, Paul** (principal: 1981–)

PERCUSSION

Adato, Joseph (1962–); **Bernthaler, Otto** (1920–21); **Burnham, Jay** (1988–91); **Clapsaddle, H.** (1918–20); **du Rocher, Harry** (1918–20; principal: 1920–22); **Freer, Tom** (1991–); **Gusikoff, David** (principal: 1919–20); **Hruby, William** (1953–56); **Jordan, Ray** (1921–27); **Klinger, David** (1927–44); **Kogan, Peter** (1969–72); **Lane, Louis** (1948–55); **Matey, Edward** (1944–47, 1955–70); **Matson, Robert** (1952–89); **Miller, Donald** (1972–); **Miller, Harry** (1948–52); **Omers, Constant** (1922–24; principal: 1924–44); **Pangborn, Robert** (1957–63); **Sartorius, A.** (1921–22); **Schultz, George** (principal: 1918–19); **Sholle, Emil** (1924–57; principal: 1957–68; percussion: 1968–69); **Sholle, Frank** (1920–21; principal: 1921–24; percussion: 1924–44; principal: 1944–57; percussion: 1957–60); **Sholle, James (Jr.)** (1922–23); **Weiner, Richard** (1963–68; principal: 1968–); **Wodicka, Herman** (1918–19)

KEYBOARD INSTRUMENTS

Barr, Theodore (piano and celesta: 1954–58; keyboard instruments: 1958–74); **Bloomfield, Theodore** (principal piano, celesta: 1946–47); **Boda, John** (piano, celesta: 1946–47); **Chalifoux, Alice** (principal piano: 1931–32); **Charry, Michael** (1961–63; principal keyboard instruments: 1963–72); **Gooding, David** (keyboard instruments, organ: 1970–73); **Jones, Joela** (1968–72; principal keyboard instruments: 1972–); **Königsberg, Saralee** (piano, celesta: 1945–46); **Lane, Louis** (piano, celesta: 1947–54; principal piano, celesta: 1954–59; principal keyboard instruments: 1958–61); **Levine, James** (1964–70); **Lingeman, Johan F.** (celesta: 1919–20); **Lipkin, Seymour** (principal piano, celesta: 1947–48); **Logan, Walter** (celesta: 1919–20); **Machan, Leon** (principal piano: 1932–45; celesta: 1941–45); **Martonne, Herman** (celesta: 1933–37); **Mills, Verlye Arlyn** (principal piano: 1930–31); **Pearlstein, Jeanette** (celesta: 1940–41); **Percy, Vincent** (principal organ: 1939–44); **Rosen, Jerome** (1959–62, 1963–64); **Shepherd, Arthur**

(piano, celesta: 1920–22; piano: 1922–23; principal piano, celesta: 1923–26); **Silfies, George** (piano, celesta: 1957–59; keyboard instruments: 1959–63); **Smith, Melville** (principal organ: 1933–40); **Steck, Nell** (celesta: 1929–33); **Veissi, Jascha** (celesta: 1922–29; principal piano: 1926–29); **Warner, Carolyn Gadiel** (1988–); **Wightman, Florence** (principal piano, celesta: 1929–30); **Young, Karl** (piano: 1929–30)

LIBRARIANS

Brennand, Tom (1944–54; head: 1954–71; librarian: 1970–71); **Bryce, Nikolas** (head: 1970–75); **Dosch, William M.** (1927–44; head: 1944–54); **du Rocher, Harry** (1919–22); **Griffith, R.J.** (head: 1918–19); **Janovsky, Ernest K.** (head: 1921–22); **Jordan, Ray** (1921–27); **Kilinski, Eugene** (1968–85); **Koch, Joseph** (1968–85); **Miller, Donald** (1985–); **Omers, Constant** (head: 1922–44); **Phillips, Ronald** (1966–69); **Whitaker, Ronald** (head: 1975–); **White, Donald** (1971–72); **Zimmer, Robert** (1971–)

PERSONNEL MANAGERS

Curry, Ralph (1997–); **Dosch, William M.** (1930–54); **Kofsky, Allen** (assistant: 1974–94); **Logan, Walter** (1918–19); **Moore, Weyert A.** (1919–31); **Phillips, Ronald** (assistant: 1970–75); **Trogdon, Olin** (1953–71); **Witser, Steven** (assistant: 1994–); **Zauder, David** (assistant: 1962–1970; 1970–96)

STAFF CONDUCTORS

Ashkenazy, Vladimir (principal guest: 1987–94); **Bamert, Matthias** (conducting fellow: 1969–70; conducting assistant: 1971–72; assistant conductor: 1972–76; resident conductor: 1976–78); **Becker, Carol Newhouse** (director, Children's Chorus: 1967–70); **Benic, Vladimir** (conducting fellow: 1960–61); **Berkovits, Tiberius** (conducting fellow: 1978–80); **Bloomfield, Theodore** (apprentice conductor: 1946–47); **Boda, John** (apprentice conductor: 1946–47); **Boulez, Pierre** (principal guest: 1968–72; musical advisor: 1970–72; artistic advisor, Blossom Music Center: 1969–71); **Burleigh, Betsy** (assistant director of choruses: 1998–); **Carr, Charles M.** (apprentice director of choruses: 1969–72; assistant to the director of choruses: 1972–76); **Charry, Michael** (apprentice conductor: 1961–65; conducting assistant: 1965–67; assistant conductor: 1967–72; assistant director of choruses: 1969–70; associate director of choruses: 1970–71; associate conductor of Summer Pops: 1969–72); **Cleve, George** (conducting fellow: 1964–65); **Cooper, Nancy** (director, Children's Chorus: 1990–91); **Darden, Charles** (conducting assistant: 1975–76); **Davidson, Harry** (conductor, Cleveland Orchestra Youth Orchestra: 1997); **Dawe, Charles D.** (chorus director: 1941–42); **Dohnányi, Christoph von** (music director designate: 1982–84; music director: 1984–); **Dulack, Mathis** (conducting assistant: 1992–94); **Epstein, David** (conducting fellow: 1960–61); **Erös, Peter** (conducting fellow: 1962–63); **Gee, Russell L.** (chorus director: 1951–56); **George, Vance** (assistant chorus director: 1977–83); **Gilbert, Alan** (conducting assistant: 1994–95; assistant conductor: 1995–97); **Goldovsky, Boris** (chorus director: 1936–41); **Goodman, Bernard** (conducting fellow: 1959–60); **Haller, Michael** (conducting fellow: 1961–62); **Hillis, Margaret** (director of choruses: 1969–71); **Huybrechts, François** (conducting fellow: 1969–70; conducting assistant: 1969–71); **Jean, Kenneth** (conducting assistant: 1975–78); **Jones, Frederick** (assistant to the director of choruses: 1976–77); **Jones, Griffith J.** (chorus director: 1933–36); **Judd, James** (conducting assistant: 1973–75); **Krehbiel, Clayton H.** (director of choruses: 1967–69; director, Blossom Festival Chorus: 1969–72); **Kwak, Sung** (assistant conductor: 1980–83); **Lane, Louis** (apprentice conductor: 1947–49; assistant conductor: 1956–60; associate conductor: 1960–70; resident conductor: 1970–74; conductor, Summer Pops: 1954–73); **Lee, Ella W.** (acting director, Children's Chorus: 1992–93; director, Children's Chorus: 1992–); **Leinsdorf, Erich** (music director: 1943–46); **Levi, Yoel** (conducting assistant: 1978–80; resident conductor: 1980–84); **Levine, James** (apprentice conductor: 1964–67; assistant conductor: 1967–70); **Ling, Jahja** (associate conductor: 1984–85; resident conductor: 1985– ; music directors, Cleveland Orchestra Youth Orchestra: 1986–93; Blossom Festival Director: 2000–); **Lipkin, Seymour** (apprentice conductor: 1947–48); **Maazel, Lorin** (music director designate: 1971–72; music director: 1972–82); **MacDonald, John** (assistant director, Blossom Festival Chorus: 1971–74); **Massey, Andrew** (assistant conductor: 1978–80); **Morrell, Gareth** (director of choruses: 1989–1998; director, Cleveland Orchestra Youth Chorus: 1991–97; music director, Cleveland Orchestra Youth Orchestra: 1993–1997); **Morse, Sevilla B.** (director, Children's Chorus: 1970–75, 1991–92); **Page, Robert** (director of choruses: 1972–89; assistant conductor: 1979–89); **Pearlstein, Jeanette** (assistant chorus director: 1936–37); **Porco, Robert** (director of choruses: 1998–); **Portman, Stephen** (conducting fellow: 1966–67); **Ringwall, Rudolph** (assistant conductor: 1926–34; associate conductor: 1934–56; conductor, Summer Pops: 1938–51); **Rodzinski, Artur** (music director: 1933–43); **Rosen, Jerome** (apprentice conductor: 1959–62); **Serebrier, Jose** (composer–in–residence: 1968–70); **Seredick, Becky** (director, Children's Chorus: 1975–90); **Seredick, Michael** (assistant director of choruses: 1983–90); **Shaw, Robert** (associate conductor, director of choruses: 1956–67); **Shepherd, Arthur** (assistant conductor, chorus master: 1920–21; assistant conductor: 1921–26; conductor, children's concerts: 1926–28); **Sillem, Maurits** (conducting fellow: 1959–60); **Slatkin, Leonard** (Blossom Festival director: 1990–99); **Smith, Russell** (composer–in–residence: 1965–66); **Smith, Steven** (assistant conductor: 1997–); **Sokoloff, Nikolai** (music director: 1918–33); **Spandoni, Giacomo** (chorus director: 1934–35); **Stern, Michael** (conducting assistant: 1986–87; assistant conductor: 1987–91); **Stofer, Robert M.** (chorus director: 1951–56); **Szell, George** (music director: 1946–70); **Takeda, Yoshimi** (conducting fellow: 1962–64); **Whallon, Evan** (conducting fellow: 1959–60); **Wilkins, Christopher** (conducting assistant: 1983–85; assistant conductor: 1985–86)

Cleveland Orchestra
Discography 1924–2000

The Cleveland Orchestra has made recordings throughout most of its history. All of the recordings through May 2000 are listed below by composer. The following information is provided for each recorded version of a given work: the names of soloists, chorus (if any), and conductor; dates of recording sessions; and record label of the first release. The record labels are noted by abbreviations: Angel/EMI (A); Argo, a subsidiary of Decca/London (AR); Book-of-the-Month Club (BMC); Columbia (C); Decca/London (D); Deutsche Grammophon (DG); Elektra-Nonesuch (EL); Epic, a subsidiary of Columbia (E); Erato (ER); RCA Victor (RCA); Telarc (T); and Teldec (TD). Nikolai Sokoloff and the orchestra made their recordings for Brunswick Records. All recordings by Artur Rodzinski and Erich Leinsdorf were made for Columbia. Many Szell recordings originally released on Epic were subsequently released on the Columbia label and later on compact discs on Sony Classical, which bought Columbia in the late 1980s.

ADAMS, JOHN
Century Rolls, Concerto for Piano and Orchestra—Emanuel Ax, piano; Christoph von Dohnányi (October 3, 1999/EL)

ALFORD, KENNETH
Bridge Over the River Kwai: "Colonel Bogey March"—Louis Lane; Cleveland Pops Orchestra (July 12/13, 1961/E)

ALFVEN, HUGO
Midsommarvarka, Op. 19 (Swedish Rhapsody No. 1)—Lane; Cleveland Pops Orchestra (August 13, 1963/E)

ANDERSON, LEROY
Serenata—Lane; Cleveland Pops Orchestra (August 21/22, 1958/E)

AUBER, DANIEL FRANÇOIS
Fra Diavola overture—George Szell (November 2, 1957/E)

BACH, J. S.
Concerto for Violin No. 2 in E major, S. 1042—Zino Francescatti, violin; Szell;

Columbia Symphony Orchestra (January 6, 1953/C)
Concerto for Violin in G minor (Szigeti arrangement of Concerto for Harpsichord
    in F minor, S. 1056/C)—Joseph Szigeti, violin; Szell; Columbia Symphony
    Orchestra (January 13, 1954)
Ricercare (arr. Webern)—Dohnányi (June 1, 1993/D)
St. Matthew Passion, S. 244: "Rest Well"—Robert Shaw (September 26,
    1961/RCA)
Suite for Orchestra No. 3 in D major, S. 1068—Szell; Music Appreciation
    Orchestra (December 24, 1954/BMC)

BARBER, SAMUEL
Concerto for Piano, Op. 38—John Browning, piano; Szell (January 3, 1964/C)
The School for Scandal overture, Op. 5—Lorin Maazel (July 15, 1972; live for
    marathon recording)

BARTÓK, BÉLA
Concerto for Orchestra—Szell (January 15/16, 1965/C) / Dohnányi (August 1,
    1988/D)
Concerto No. 1 for Piano in A major—Rudolph Serkin, piano; Szell; Columbia
    Symphony Orchestra (April 20/21, 1962/C)
Music for Strings, Percussion, and Celesta—Dohnányi (January 26, 1992/D)

BEETHOVEN, LUDWIG VAN
Choral Fantasy—Vladimir Ashkenazy, piano and conductor; Cleveland Orchestra
    Chorus (November 14, 1987/D)
Concerto No. 1 for Piano in C major, Op. 15—Leon Fleisher, piano; Szell
    (February 25, 1961/E) / Emil Gilels, piano; Szell (April 29–May 4, 1968/A)
    / Ashkenazy, pianist and conductor (November 13, 1987/D)
Concerto No. 2 for Piano in B-flat major, Op. 19—Fleisher; Szell (April 16,
    1961/E) / Gilels; Szell (April 29–May 4, 1968/A) / Ashkenazy (March 16,
    1987/D)
Concerto No. 3 for Piano in C minor, Op. 37—Fleisher; Szell (April 14, 1961/E) /
    Gilels; Szell (April 29–May 4, 1968/A) / Ashkenazy (April 12, 1986/D)
Concerto No. 4 for Piano in G major, Op. 58—Fleisher; Szell (January 10,
    1959/E) / Gilels; Szell (April 29–May 4, 1968/A) / Ashkenazy (April 26,
    1987/D)
Concerto No. 5 for Piano in E-flat major, Op. 73 ("Emperor")—Fleisher; Szell
    (March 3, 1961/E) / Gilels; Szell (April 29–May 4, 1968/A) / Ashkenazy
    (April 11/12, 1986/D)
Coriolan overture, Op. 62—Szell (October 29, 1966/C)
Egmont overture, Op. 84—Szell (October 8, 1966/C) / Maazel (October 24,
    1977/C)
Fidelio overture—Szell (August 25, 1967/C) / Maazel (February 24, 1978/C)
The Creatures of Prometheus, Op. 43—Lane (April 7, 1967/C)
The Creatures of Prometheus, Op. 43: Overture—Maazel (August 25, 1975/C)
King Stephan overture, Op. 117—Szell (October 29, 1966/C)
Leonore Overture No. 1—Szell (August 25, 1967/C) / Dohnányi (December 12,
    1988/T)

Leonore Overture No. 2—Szell (October 8, 1966/C)

Leonore Overture No. 3—Szell (April 5, 1963/E) / Szell (August 25, 1967/C) / Maazel (October 13/14/15, 1978/C) / Dohnányi (December 15, 1986/T)

Missa Solemnis, Op. 123 (Kyrie)—Saramae Endich, soprano; Florence Kopleff, alto; Jon Humphrey, tenor; Thomas Paul, bass; Cleveland Orchestra Chorus; Robert Shaw, conductor (September 26, 1961/RCA)

Symphony No. 1 in C major, Op. 21—Artur Rodzinski (December 28, 1941) / Szell (October 2, 1964/E) / Maazel (April 28/29, 1978/C) / Dohnányi (December 12, 1988/T)

Symphony No. 2 in D major, Op. 36—Szell (October 23, 1964/E) / Maazel (April 29, 1978/C) / Dohnányi (October 8, 1988/T)

Symphony No. 3 in E-flat major, Op. 55 ("Eroica")—Szell (February 22/23, 1957/E) / Maazel (October 24, 1977/C) / Dohnányi (October 23, 1983/T)

Symphony No. 4 in B-flat major, op. 60—Szell (April 22, 1947/C) / Szell (April 5, 1963/E) / Maazel (October 25, 1977/C) / Dohnányi (October 9, 1988/T)

Symphony No. 5 in C minor, Op. 67—Szell (November 26, 1955) / Szell (October 11/25, 1963) / Maazel (October 25, 1977/C) / Dohnányi (September 20, 1987/T)

Symphony No. 6 in F major, Op. 68—Szell (January 19/21, 1962/E) / Maazel (February 23/24, 1978/C) / Dohnányi (December 15, 1986/T)

Symphony No. 7 in A major, Op. 92—Szell (October 30/31, 1959/E) / Maazel (February 23/24, 1978/C) / Dohnányi (September 20, 1987/T)

Symphony No. 8 in F major, Op. 93—Szell (April 15, 1961/E) / Rafael Kubelik (March 3/4, 1975/DG) / Maazel (April 28, 1978/C) / Dohnányi (October 23, 1983/T)

Symphony No. 9 in D minor, Op. 125—Adele Addison, soprano; Jane Hobson, mezzo-soprano; Richard Lewis, tenor; Donald Bell, bass; Cleveland Orchestra Chorus; Szell (April 15/21/22, 1961/E) / Lucia Popp, soprano; Elena Obratzsova, mezzo-soprano; Jon Vickers, tenor; Martti Talvela, bass; Cleveland Orchestra Chorus; Maazel (October 13/14/15, 1978/C) / Carol Vaness, soprano; Janis Taylor, contralto; Siegfried Jerusalem, tenor; Robert Lloyd, bass; Cleveland Orchestra Chorus; Dohnányi (October 18/19, 1985/T)

BENJAMIN, ARTHUR

From San Domingo—Lane; Cleveland Pops Orchestra (July 22/23, 1959/E)

Two Jamaican Pieces: Jamaica Rumba—Lane; Cleveland Pops Orchestra (July 22/23, 1959/E)

BERG, ALBAN

Concerto for Violin—Louis Krasner, violin; Rodzinski (December 15, 1940)

BERLIOZ, HECTOR

Le Corsaire overture, Op. 21—Maazel (January 16, 1977/T)

La damnation de Faust: Rakoczy March—Lane; Cleveland Pops Orchestra (July 7, 1960/E) / Maazel (January 16, 1977/T)

Harold in Italy—Robert Vernon, viola; Maazel (October 7, 1977/D)

Les nuits d'été, Op. 7—Melanie Diener, soprano; Kenneth Tarver, tenor; Denis

Sedov, bass; Pierre Boulez (May 15, 2000/DG)

Requiem—Kenneth Riegel, tenor ; Cleveland Orchestra Chorus; Maazel (August 21/22/23, 1978/D)

Roman Carnival overture, Op. 9—Szell (March 15, 1958/E) / Maazel (July 9, 1971; live for marathon recording) / Maazel (August 26, 1975/D)

Romeo et Juliette, Op. 17—Diener, soprano; Tarver, tenor; Sedov, bass; Cleveland Orchestra Chorus; Boulez (May 14/15, 2000/DG)

Symphonie fantastique, Op. 14—Rodzinski (April 12/14, 1941) / Maazel (January 11, 1977/D) / Maazel (May 10, 1982/T) / Dohnányi (October 29, 1989/D) / Pierre Boulez (March 4, 1996/DG)

Tristia—Cleveland Orchestra Chorus; Boulez (March 3, 1996/DG)

BERNSTEIN, LEONARD

Candide overture—Lane; Cleveland Pops Orchestra (August 21/22, 1958/E) / Maazel (January 11, 1976; live, noncommercial release)

Fancy Free: Danzon—Lane; Cleveland Pops Orchestra (July 22/23, 1959/E)

On the Town: The Great Lover, Lonely Town, Times Square—Lane; Cleveland Pops Orchestra (July 7, 1960/E)

BIRTWISTLE, HARRISON

Earth Dances—Dohnányi (April 17, 1995/D)

BIZET, GEORGES

L'Arlésienne Suite No. 1—Maazel (May 5, 1978/C)

L'Arlésienne Suite No. 2—Szell (March 25, 1966/C) / Maazel (May 5, 1978/C)

L'Arlésienne Suite No. 2: Farandole—Maazel (January 17, 1977/T)

Suite from Children's Games—Maazel (October 19/23, 1979/D)

BORODIN, ALEXANDER

Prince Igor: Polovetsian Dances—Sokoloff (May 14, 1928) / Szell (February 28, 1958/March 1/14, 1958/E)

BRAHMS, JOHANNES

Academic Festival Overture, Op. 80—Szell; Music Appreciation Orchestra (October 19/20/21, 1955/BMC) / Szell (October 28, 1966/C) / Maazel (July 14, 1972; live for marathon recording) / Maazel (August 25, 1975/C) / Dohnányi (October 1, 1989/T)

Chorale Prelude No. 7, Op. 122 ("O Gott, du frommer Gott")—Erich Leinsdorf (February 22, 1946)

Chorale Prelude No. 8, Op. 122 ("Es ist ein Ros' entsprungen")—Leinsdorf (February 25, 1946)

Concerto No. 1 for Piano in D minor, Op. 15—Serkin, piano; Szell (November 30, 1952/E) / Fleisher; Szell (February 21/22, 1958/E) / Serkin; Szell (April 19/20, 1968/C)

Concerto No. 2 for Piano in B-flat major, Op. 83—Fleisher; Szell (October 19/20, 1962/E) / Serkin; Szell (January 21/22, 1966/C)

Concerto for Violin in D major, Op. 77—David Oistrakh, violin; Szell (May 16, 1969/A) / Thomas Zehetmair, violin; Dohnányi (October 1, 1989/TD) /

Joshua Bell, violin; Dohnányi (May 29, 1994/D)

Concerto for Violin and Cello in A minor, Op. 102—Oistrakh; Mstislav
Rostropovich, cello; Szell (May 9/12/13, 1969/A)

A *German Requiem*, Op. 45: How Lovely is Thy Dwelling Place—Cleveland
Orchestra Chorus; Shaw (September 26, 1961/RCA)

Hungarian Dance No. 5—Sokoloff (October 1924)

Symphony No. 1 in C minor, Op. 68—Szell (March 1/2, 1957/E) / Szell (October
7, 1966/C) / Maazel (October 4, 1973; Sydney Opera House live "in-
house" recording) / Maazel (August 25/26, 1975/D) / Dohnányi (October
31, 1986/TD) / Ashkenazy (November 24, 1991/July 12, 1992/D)

Symphony No. 2 in D major, Op. 73—Szell (January 6, 1967/C) / Maazel
(October 4, 1976/D) / Dohnányi (December 7, 1987/TD) / Ashkenazy
(March 5, 1990/March 21, 1993/D)

Symphony No. 2 in D major, Op. 73: Third Movement—Sokoloff (October 1924)

Symphony No. 3 in F major, Op. 90—Szell (October 16/17, 1964/C) / Maazel
(October 4/5, 1976/D) / Dohnányi (May 16, 1988/TD) / Ashkenazy (March
24, 1991/D)

Symphony No. 4 in E minor, Op. 98—Szell (April 8/9, 1966/C) / Maazel (October
4/8, 1976/D) / Dohnányi (May 22, 1987/TD) / Ashkenazy (July 12, 1992/D)

Tragic Overture, Op. 81—Szell (October 28, 1966/C) / Maazel (October 4,
1976/D) / Dohnányi (May 16, 1988/TD)

Variations on a Theme by Haydn in B-flat major, Op. 56a—Szell; Music
Appreciation Orchestra (October 19/20/21, 1955/BMC) / Szell (October
24, 1964/C) / Maazel (October 4, 1976/C) / Dohnányi (December 7,
1987/TD) / Ashkenazy (March 24, 1991/D) Variations & Fugue on a
Theme of Handel (orch. Rubbra)—Ashkenazy (July 12, 1992/D)

BRUCKNER, ANTON

Symphony No. 3 in D minor—Szell (January 28/29, 1966/C) / Dohnányi (May 30,
1993/D)

Symphony No. 4 in E-flat major—Dohnányi (October 8/10, 1989/D)

Symphony No. 5 in B-flat major—Dohnányi (January 20, 1991/D)

Symphony No. 6 in A major—Dohnányi (October 7, 1991/D)

Symphony No. 7 in E major—Dohnányi (August 20/21, 1990)

Symphony No. 8 in C minor—Szell (October 10/13, 1969/C) / Dohnányi
(February 6, 1994/D)

Symphony No. 9 in D minor—Dohnányi (October 3, 1988/D)

BUSONI, FERRUCCIO

Concerto for Piano—Garrick Ohlsson, piano; Men of the Cleveland Orchestra
Chorus; Dohnányi (February 4, 1989/T)

CHABRIER, EMMANUEL

Espana—Lane; Cleveland Pops Orchestra (August 13, 1963/E)

COPLAND, AARON

Appalachian Spring: Variations on a Shaker Theme—Maazel (January 13, 1976;
live noncommercial release)

Grohg—Oliver Knussen (May 3, 1993/AR)
An Outdoor Overture—Lane; Cleveland Pops Orchestra (July 14, 1961/E)
Rodeo: Three Dances—Lane; Cleveland Pops Orchestra (August 21/22, 1958/E)

CRAWFORD, RUTH SEEGER
Andante for Strings—Dohnányi (October 16, 1994/D)

DEBUSSY, CLAUDE
Danse sacrée et danse profane—Alice Chalifoux, harp; Boulez (November 17, 1967/C) / Lisa Wellbaum, harp; Boulez (April 25, 1999/DG)
Fêtes—Maazel (May 5, 1978/D)
Images pour orchestre—Boulez (November 17, 1967/C) / Boulez (March 4, 1991/DG)
Images: Iberia—Maazel (May 10, 1978/D) / Boulez (March 4, 1991/DG)
Le jet d'eau—Boulez (April 25, 1999/DG)
Jeux—Maazel (May 8, 1978/D) / Boulez (March 7, 1993/DG)
La Mer—Rodzinski (January 11, 1940; not released) / Rodzinski (December 29, 1941) / Szell (January 11, 1963/E) / Maazel (October 4, 1977/D) / Ashkenazy (April 6, 1986/D) / Boulez (March 7, 1993/DG)
Nocturnes—Ashkenazy (April 6, 1986/D) / Boulez (March 7, 1993/DG)
Nuages—Maazel (May 5, 1978/D)
Pelléas et Mélisande: Preludes and Interludes—Leinsdorf (February 22/24, 1946)
Prélude à "L'après-midi d'un faune"—Ashkenazy (April 6, 1986/D) / Boulez (March 11, 1991/DG)
Première rapsodie—Franklin Cohen, clarinet; Boulez (March 4,1991/DG)
Printemps—Boulez (March 11, 1991/DG)
Sirènes—Maazel (May 8, 1978/D)
Three Ballads of François Villon—Alison Hagley, soprano; Boulez (April 25, 1999/DG)

DELIBES, LÉO
Coppélia: Entr'acte and valse—Sokoloff (May 14, 1928)

DELIUS, FREDERICK
Hassan: Serenade (arr. Sir Thomas Beecham)—Rafael Druian, violin; Chalifoux, harp; Lane; Cleveland Sinfonietta (August 12, 1963/E)
Irmelin: Prelude—Szell (October 28, 1956/E)

DVOŘÁK, ANTONIN
Carnival overture, Op. 92—Szell (July 19, 1962/January 4/5, 1963/E) / Ashkenazy (March 24, 1991/D)
Concerto for Piano in G minor, Op. 33—Rudolf Firkusny, piano; Szell (April 9/11, 1954/C)
Scherzo—Dohnányi (October 26/27, 1984/D)
Slavonic Dances, Op. 46 (complete)—Szell (February 24/26, 1956/C) / Dohnányi (August 27, 1989/D)
Slavonic Dances, Op. 46, No. 1—Szell (April 21, 1947/C) / Szell (July 19, 1962; August 2, 1962; January 4/5, 1963/E)

Slavonic Dances, Op. 46, No. 2—Szell (January 22, 1965/E)

Slavonic Dances, Op. 46, No. 3—Sokoloff (October 1924) / Szell April 21–23, 1947) / Szell (July 19, 1962; August 2, 1962; January 4/5, 1963/E) / Szell (April 29, 1970/A)

Slavonic Dances, Op. 46, No. 4—Szell (April 21–23, 1947/C) / Szell (January 22, 1965/C)

Slavonic Dances, Op. 46, No. 5—Szell (January 22, 1965/E)

Slavonic Dances, Op. 46, No. 6—Szell (October 17/24, 1964/C)

Slavonic Dances, Op. 46, No. 7—Szell (January 22, 1965/C)

Slavonic Dances, Op. 46, No. 8—Szell (April 21–23, 1947/C) / Szell (October 17/24, 1964; February 11, 1965/C)

Slavonic Dances, Op. 72 (complete)—Szell (March 16/17, 1956/E) / Dohnányi (August 21, 1989/D)

Slavonic Dances, Op. 72, No. 1—Szell (October 17/24, 1964; January 29, 1965/C)

Slavonic Dances, Op. 72, No. 2—Szell (April 21–23, 1947/C) / Szell (July 29, 1962; August 2, 1962; January 4/5, 1963/E) / Szell (April 29, 1970/A)

Slavonic Dances, Op. 72, No. 3—Szell (January 22/29, 1965/C)

Slavonic Dances, Op. 72, No. 4—Szell (January 22/29, 1965/C)

Slavonic Dances, Op. 72, No. 5—Szell (October 17/24, 1964; February 11, 1965/C)

Slavonic Dances, Op. 72, No. 6—Szell (January 22/29, 1965/C)

Slavonic Dances, Op. 72, No. 7—Szell (April 21–23, 1947/C) / Szell (July 29, 1962; August 2, 1962; January 4/5, 1963/E)

Slavonic Dances, Op. 72, No. 8—Szell (January 22/29, 1965/C)

Symphony No. 6 in D major, Op. 60—Leinsdorf (February 24, 1946) / Dohnányi (March 13, 1989/D)

Symphony No. 7 in D minor, Op. 70—Szell (March 18/19, 1960/E) / Dohnányi (October 28, 1985/D)

Symphony No. 8 in G major, Op. 88—Szell (October 25/31, 1958; November 1, 1958/E) / Szell (April 28/29, 1970/A) / Dohnányi (October 26, 1984/D)

Symphony No. 9 in E minor, Op. 95 ("From the New World")—Szell (January 18, 1952/C) / Szell (March 20/21, 1959/E) / Dohnányi (October 27, 1984/D)

Symphony No. 9 in E minor, Op. 95: Largo—Maazel (January 11,1976; live non-commercial release)

ELGAR, EDWARD

Concerto for Cello in E minor, Op. 85—Lynn Harrell, cello; Maazel (October 22, 1979/C)

Pomp and Circumstance, Op. 39: March No. 1 in D major—Lane; Cleveland Pops Orchestra (July 7, 1960/E)

ELLINGTON, DUKE

Solitude (arr. Morton Gould)—Maazel (January 11, 1976; live noncommercial release)

ELWELL, HERBERT

The Happy Hypocrite suite—Lane; Cleveland Pops Orchestra (July 14, 1961/E)

ENESCO, GEORGES
Rumanian Rhapsody No. 1—Lane; Cleveland Pops Orchestra (August 13, 1963/E)

ERB, DONALD
Music for a Festive Occasion—Maazel (January 11, 1976; live noncommercial release)

FALLA, MANUEL DE
The Three-Cornered Hat: Jota—Maazel (January 17, 1977/T)

FOOTE, ARTHUR
A Night Piece—Maurice Sharp, flute; Lane; Cleveland Sinfonietta (July 7/8, 1960/E)

FRANÇAIX, JEAN
Serenade for Small Orchestra—Lane; Cleveland Sinfonietta (August 12, 1963/E)

FRANCK, CÉSAR
Symphony in D minor—Maazel (May 11, 1976/D)
Variations symphoniques—Fleisher, piano; Szell (October 28, 1956/E) / Pascal Rogé; Maazel (May 14, 1976/D)

GABRIELI, GIOVANNI
Works for Brass—Chicago Brass Ensemble; Cleveland Brass Ensemble; Philadelphia Brass Ensemble (April 12/13, 1968/)

GALINDO DIMAS, BLAS
Sones mariachi—Lane; Cleveland Pops Orchestra (July 22/23, 1959/)

GERSHWIN, GEORGE
An American in Paris—Maazel (July 15/16/17, 1974/D) / Riccardo Chailly (November 17, 1985/D)
Cuban Overture—Lane; Cleveland Pops Orchestra (July 22/23, 1959/E) / Chailly (November 17, 1985/D)
Lullaby—Chailly (November 17, 1985/D)
Porgy and Bess (complete)—Willard White; Leona Mitchell; McHenry Boatwright; Florence Quivar; Barbara Hendricks; Barbara Conrad; Arthur Thompson; François Clemmons; James Vincent Pickens; Samuel Hagan; William Brown; Christopher Deane; Alpha Floyd; Isola Jones; John Buck; Robert Snook; Ralph Neeley; Alan Leatherman; Donald Zucca; Cleveland Orchestra Chorus; Cleveland Orchestra Children's Chorus; Joela Jones, piano; Maazel (August 18/19/20/21, 1975/D)
Porgy and Bess (arr. Robert Russell Bennett): Excerpts—Maazel (January 11, 1976; live noncommercial release)
Rhapsody in Blue—Ivan Davis, piano; Maazel (July 15/16/17, 1974/D) / Katia and Marielle Labèque, pianos; Chailly (November 17, 1985/D)

GLINKA, MIKHAIL
Russlan and Ludmilla overture—Maazel (August 26, 1975/D)

GOLD, ERNEST
Exodus—Lane; Cleveland Pops Orchestra (July 12/13, 1961/E)

GOULD, MORTON
American Salute—Lane; Cleveland Pops Orchestra (August 21/22, 1958/E) /
    Maazel (January 11, 1976; live noncommercial release)
Latin American Symphonette: Guaracha, Sones mariachi—Lane; Cleveland Pops
    Orchestra (July 22/23, 1959/E)

GRAINGER, PERCY
Shepherd's Hay—Sokoloff (May 14, 1928)

GRIEG, EDVARD
Concerto for Piano in A minor, Op. 16—Fleisher; Szell (January 8, 1960/E)
Peer Gynt Suite No. 1, Op. 46—Szell (January 21, 1966/C)

GRIFFES, CHARLES TOMLINSON
Poem for Flute and Orchestra—Sharp; Lane; Cleveland Sinfonietta (July 7/8,
    1960/E)

GUARNIERI, CAMARGO
Brazilian Dance—Lane; Cleveland Pops Orchestra (July 22,23, 1959/E)

HALVORSEN, JOHAN
Bojarnese Indtog (Entrance of the Boyards)—Sokoloff (May 1927)

HANDEL, GEORGE FRIDERIC
Messiah: Hallelujah Chorus—Cleveland Orchestra Chorus; Shaw (September 26,
    1961/RCA)

HANSON, HOWARD
Serenade for Flute, Harp and Strings—Sharp; Chalifoux; Lane; Cleveland
    Sinfonietta (July 7/8, 1960/E)

HARTMANN, KARL AMADEUS
Adagio (Symphony No. 2)—Dohnányi (February 7, 1994/D)

HAYDN, FRANZ JOSEPH
The Creation: The Heavens Are Telling—Cleveland Orchestra Chorus; Shaw
    (September 26, 1961/RCA)
Symphony No. 88 in G minor—Szell (April 9, 1954/E)
Symphony No. 92 in G major—Szell (April 27, 1949/C) / Szell (October 20,
    1961/E)
Symphony No. 93 in D major—Szell (April 19, 1968/C)
Symphony No. 94 in G major—Szell (May 5, 1967/C)

Symphony No. 95 in C minor—Szell (January 17, 1969/C)
Symphony No. 96 in D major—Szell (October 11, 1968/C)
Symphony No. 97 in C major—Szell (October 25, 195/E7) / Szell (October
    3/6/10, 1969/C)
Symphony No. 98 in B-flat major—Szell (October 3/6/10, 1969/C)
Symphony No. 99 in E-flat major—Szell (October 26, 1957/E)
Symphony No. 104 in D major—Szell (April 9, 1954/E)

HERBERT, VICTOR
Irish Rhapsody—Lane; Cleveland Pops Orchestra (August 13, 1963/E)

HINDEMITH, PAUL
Symphonic Metamorphosis of Themes by Weber—Szell (November 25, 1947/C) /
    Szell (October 10, 1964/C)
Symphonic Metamorphosis of Themes by Weber: March—Lane; Cleveland Pops
    Orchestra (July 7, 1960/E)

HONEGGER, ARTHUR
Concerto da Camera for Flute, English Horn and Strings—Sharp; Harvey
    McGuire, English horn; Lane; Cleveland Sinfonietta (July 7/8, 1960/E)

IPPOLOTOV-IVANOV, MICHAEL
Caucasian Sketches: Procession of the Sardar—Lane; Cleveland Sinfonietta (July
    7, 1960/E)

IVES, CHARLES
Orchestra Set No. 2—Dohnányi (January 23, 1994/D)
Symphony No. 4—Dohnányi (May 3, 1992/D)
Three Places in New England—Dohnányi (June 1, 1993/D)
Three Places in New England: Redding Center, Conn.—Maazel (January 11,
    1976; live noncommercial release)
The Unanswered Question—Dohnányi (June 1, 1993/February 7, 1994/D)

JANÁCEK, LEOS
Capriccio for Piano and Wind Instruments—Jones, piano; Dohnányi (May 31,
    1993/D)
Sinfonietta, Op. 60—Szell (January 15, 1965/C)
Taras Bulba—Dohnányi (October 30, 1989/D)

JARNEFELT, ARMAS
Praeludium—Rodzinski (December 28, 1941)

JOPLIN, SCOTT
The Entertainer (orch. Gunther Schuller)—Maazel (January 11, 1976; live non-
    commercial release)

KERN, JEROME
Show Boat: A Scenario for Orchestra—Rodzinski (December 29, 1941)

KODÁLY, ZOLTÁN
Háry János suite—Szell (January 10/11, 1969/C)

LECUONA, ERNESTO
Andalucia: Andalucia, Malaguena—Lane; Cleveland Pops Orchestra (July 22/23, 1959/E)

LIADOV, ANTON
The Enchanted Lake, Op. 62—Szell (October 30, 1963/E)

LIEBERSON, PETER
Drala—Knussen (November 12/13, 1995/DG)
Fire—Knussen (November 10, 1996/DG)

LISZT, FRANZ
Concerto for Piano No. 2 in A major—Robert Casadesus, piano; Szell (January 20, 1952/C)
Hungarian Rhapsody No. 2—Lane; Cleveland Pops Orchestra (August 13, 1963/E)

LOEWE, FREDERICK
Gigi suite—Lane; Cleveland Pops Orchestra (July 12/13, 1961/E)
My Fair Lady: Embassy Waltz, Ascot Gavotte—Lane; Cleveland Pops Orchestra (July 7, 1960/E)

LUTOSLAWSKI, WITOLD
Concerto for Orchestra—Dohnányi (March 13, 1989/D)

MAHLER, GUSTAV
Symphony No. 1 in D major—Dohnányi (March 19, 1989/D)
Symphony No. 4 in G major—Judith Raskin, soprano; Szell (October 1/2, 1965/D) / Dawn Upshaw; Dohnányi (May 10, 1992/D) / Julianne Banse; Boulez (April 19/20, 1998/DG)
Symphony No. 5 in C-sharp minor—Dohnányi (July 25, 1988/D)
Symphony No. 6 in A major—Szell (October 9, 1967 concert; released March 1972/C) / Dohnányi (May 20, 1991/D)
Symphony No. 7 in E minor—Boulez (November 6/7, 1994/DG)
Symphony No. 9 in D major—Dohnányi (May 18/19, 1997/D)
Symphony No. 10 in F-sharp minor: Andante; Allegretto—Szell (November 1, 1958/E)

MARTINŮ, BOHUSLAV
Concerto for String Quartet—Daniel Majeske, violin; Bernhard Goldschmidt, violin; Robert Vernon, viola; Stephen Geber, cello; Dohnányi (May 3, 1992/D)

MENDELSSOHN, FELIX

Concerto for Violin in E minor, Op. 64—Francescatti, violin; Szell; Columbia
Symphony Orchestra (December 1, 1961/E)

Elijah: "He Watching Over Israel"—Cleveland Orchestra Chorus; Shaw
(September 26, 1961/RCA)

Die erste Walpurgisnacht—Jon Garrison, tenor; Cleveland Orchestra Chorus;
Dohnányi (May 22, 1988/T)

The Hebrides overture, Op. 26—Szell (October 26, 1962/E)

A Midsummer Night's Dream: Incidental Music—Rodzinski (December 28, 1941;
February 22, 1942) / Szell (January 13, 1967/C)

Symphony No. 1 in C minor, Op. 11—Lane (October 29, 1966/C)

Symphony No. 3 in A minor, Op. 56 ("Scottish")—Dohnányi (May 22, 1988/T)

Symphony No. 4 in A major, Op. 90 ("Italian")—Szell (November 26, 1947/C) /
Szell (October 26, 1962/E)

Symphony No. 4 in A major, Op. 90: First and second movements—Szell
(December 17, 1951/C)

MENOTTI, GIAN CARLO

Amahl and the Night Visitors: Suite—Lane; Cleveland Pops Orchestra (July 14,
1961/E)

MESSIAEN, OLIVIER

Chronochromie—Boulez (March 8, 1993/DG)

Et exspecto resurrectionem mortuorum—Boulez (March 8, 1993/DG)

La ville d'en-haut—Boulez (March 8, 1993/DG)

Poèmes pour Mi—Françoise Pollet, soprano; Boulez (November 14, 1994/DG)

Réveil des oiseaux—Pierre-Laurent Aimard, piano; Boulez (February 25,
1996/DG)

Sept Haikai—Jones, piano; Boulez (February 26, 1996/DG)

MOZART, WOLFGANG AMADEUS

Concerto for Bassoon in B-flat major, K. 191—David McGill, bassoon; Dohnányi
(June 1, 1993/DG)

Concerto for Clarinet in A major, K. 622—Robert Marcellus, clarinet; Szell
(October 21, 1961/E) / Franklin Cohen; Dohnányi (January 26, 1992/D)

Concerto for Flute and Harp in C major, K. 299—Joshua Smith, flute; Wellbaum,
harp; Dohnányi (June 6, 1993/D)

Concerto for Oboe in C major, K. 314—John Mack, oboe; Dohnányi (October 6,
1991/D)

Concerto No. 10 for Two Pianos in E-flat major, K. 316a—Robert Casadesus,
piano; Gaby Casadesus, piano; Szell; Columbia Symphony Orchestra
(December 19/21, 1955/C)

Concerto No. 12 for Piano in A major, K. 414—Casadesus; Szell; Columbia
Symphony Orchestra (December 19/21, 1955/C)

Concerto No. 15 for Piano in B-flat major, K. 450—Casadesus; Szell (October 18,
1968/C)

Concerto No. 17 for Piano in G major, K. 453—Serkin; Szell; Columbia
Symphony Orchestra (November 20/21, 1955/C) / Casadesus; Szell

(October 18, 1968/C)

Concerto No. 18 for Piano in B-flat major, K. 456—Casadesus; Szell; Columbia Symphony Orchestra (November 11, 1956/C)

Concerto No. 19 for Piano in F major, K. 459—Serkin; Szell; Columbia Symphony Orchestra (April 28, 1961/C)

Concerto No. 20 for Piano in D minor, K. 466—Casadesus; Szell; Columbia Symphony Orchestra (November 10, 1956/C) / Serkin; Szell; Columbia Symphony Orchestra (April 26/27, (1961/C)

Concerto No. 21 for Piano in C major, K. 467—Casadesus; Szell (November 5, 1961/C)

Concerto No. 22 for Piano in E-flat major, K. 482—Casadesus; Szell; Columbia Symphony Orchestra (November 13, 1959/C)

Concerto No. 23 for Piano in A major, K. 488—Casadesus; Szell; Columbia Symphony Orchestra (November 14/15, 1959/C)

Concerto No. 24 for Piano in C minor, K. 491—Casadesus; Szell; Columbia Symphony Orchestra (January 12/15, 1954/C) / Casadesus; Szell (November 3/4, 1961/C)

Concerto No. 25 for Piano in C major, K. 503—Serkin; Szell; Columbia Symphony Orchestra (November 20/21, 1955/C) / Fleisher; Szell (January 9, 1959/E)

Concerto No. 26 for Piano in D major, K. 537—Casadesus; Szell; Columbia Symphony Orchestra (January 12/15, 1954/C) / Casadesus; Szell; Columbia Symphony Orchestra (November 2, 1962/C)

Concerto No. 27 for Piano in B-flat major—Casadesus; Szell; Columbia Symphony Orchestra (November 3/4, 1962/C)

Concerto No. 1 for Violin in B-flat major, K. 207—Isaac Stern, violin; Szell; Columbia Symphony Orchestra (January 22, 1961/C)

Concerto No. 3 for Violin in G major, K. 216—Stern; Szell; Columbia Symphony Orchestra (January 21/22, 1961/C)

Concerto No. 5 for Violin in A major, K. 219—Stern; Szell; Columbia Symphony Orchestra (April 19, 1963/)

Divertimento No. 2 in D major, K. 131—Szell (April 20, 1963/E)

Divertimento No. 17 in D major, K. 320b—Szell (December 10, 1965/C)

Exsultate, Jubilate, K. 158a—Raskin, soprano; Szell (May 11, 1964/C)

Eine kleine Nachtmusik, K. 525—Szell (October 7, 1968/C)

Minuet in C major, K. 383f—Leinsdorf (February 25, 1946)

Le Nozze di Figaro overture—Szell (October 25, 1957/E)

Requiem, K. 626: Lacrimosa—Cleveland Orchestra Chorus; Shaw (September 26, 1961/RCA)

Der Schauspieldirektor overture—Szell (January 28/29, 1966/C)

Serenade No. 9 in D major, K. 320 ("Posthorn")—Bernard Adelstein, posthorn; Szell (January 10/18/24, 1969/C)

Sinfonia concertante in E-flat major, K. 364—Druian, violin; Abraham Skernick, viola; Szell (December 28, 1963/E) / Majeske, violin; Vernon, viola; Dohnányi (May 19, 1991/D)

Symphony No. 28 in C major, K. 200—Szell (October 1/2, 1965/C)

Symphony No. 33 in B-flat major, K. 319—Szell (October 26, 1962/E)

Symphony No. 35 in D major, K. 385 ("Haffner")—Szell (January 8/10, 1960;
    March 11, 1960/E) / Dohnányi (October 21, 1990/D)
Symphony No. 36 in C major, K. 425—Dohnányi (October 22, 1990/D)
Symphony No. 38 in D major, K. 504—Dohnányi (February 11, 1990/D)
Symphony No. 39 in E-flat major, K. 543—Szell (April 23, 1947/C) / Szell; Music
    Appreciation Orchestra (October 19/20/21, 1955/BMC) / Szell (March
    11/12, 1960/E) / Dohnányi (October22, 1990/D)
Symphony No. 40 in G minor, K. 550—Szell (November 18, 1955/E) / Szell
    (August 25, 1967/C) / Dohnányi (February 11, 1990/D)
Symphony No. 41 in C major, K. 551 ("Jupiter")—Szell (November 18, 1955/E) /
    Szell (October 11/25, 1963/E) / Dohnányi (February 17, 1990/D)

MUSSORGSKY, MODESTE
Boris Godunov: Symphonic Excerpts (arr. Stokowski)—Knussen (November 11,
    1996/DG)
Khovantchina: Prelude—Rodzinski (December 20, 1939; not released) /
    Rodzinski (December 26, 1940) / Szell (March 14, 1958/E)
Khovantchina: Entr'acte from Act IV (arr. Stokowski)—Knussen (November 10
    1996/DG)
A Night on Bare Mountain (arr. Rimsky-Korsakov)—Maazel (October 20, 1978/T)
    / Dohnányi (May 16, 1988/TD)
A Night on Bare Mountain (arr. Stokowski)—Knussen (November 11, 1996/DG)
Pictures at an Exhibition (arr. Ravel)—Szell (October 30, 1963/E) / Maazel
    (October 20, 1978/T) / Dohnányi (February 5, 1989/TD)
Pictures at an Exhibition (arr. Stokowski)—Knussen (November 13, 1995)

NICOLAI, OTTO
The Merry Wives of Windsor overture—Sokoloff (May 1927)

ORFF, CARL
Carmina Burana—Judith Blegen, soprano; Kenneth Riegel, tenor; Peter Binder;
    Cleveland Orchestra Chorus and Boys Chorus; Michael Tilson Thomas
    (August 5/6, 1974/C)

PIERNÉ, GABRIEL
Cydalise and the Satyr: March of the Little Fauns—Sokoloff (May 14, 1928) /
    Lane; Cleveland Pops Orchestra (July 7, 1960/E)

PISTON, WALTER
The Incredible Flutist—Lane; Cleveland Pops Orchestra (August 21/22, 1958/E)

PORTER, COLE
Can Can: Can Can—Lane; Cleveland Pops Orchestra (July 7, 1960/E)

PROKOFIEV, SERGEI
Alexander Nevsky—Irina Arkhipova, contralto; Cleveland Orchestra Chorus;
    Chailly (March 18/20, 1983/D)
Cinderella—Ashkenazy (March 12/13/14, 1983/D)

Concerto No. 1 for Piano in D-flat major, Op. 10—Gary Graffman; Szell (March 25, 1966/C)

Concerto No. 3 for Piano in C major, Op. 26—Graffman; Szell (March 25, 1966/C)

Lieutentant Kijé suite—Szell (January 17/18, 1969/C)

Romeo and Juliet—Majeske, violin; David Zauder, cornet; Edward Ormond, viola d'amore; Maazel (June 4/5/6, 1973/D)

Romeo and Juliet suite—Yoel Levi (October 24, 1983/T)

Symphony No. 5 in B-flat major, Op. 100—Szell (October 24/31, 1959/E) / Maazel (October 3, 1977/C)

Symphony No. 6 in E-flat minor, Op. 111—Ashkenazy (May 2, 1993/D)

Symphony No. 7 in C-sharp minor, Op. 131—Ashkenazy (May 3, 1993/D)

RACHMANINOFF, SERGEI

Concerto No. 1 for Piano in F-sharp minor, Op. 1—Jean-Yves Thibaudet, piano; Ashkenazy (February 20, 1995/D)

Concerto No. 2 for Piano in C minor, Op. 18—Thibaudet; Ashkenazy (March 21, 1993/D)

Concerto No. 3 for Piano in D minor, Op. 30—Thibaudet; Ashkenazy (March 25, 1994/D)

Concerto No. 4 for Piano in G minor, Op. 40—Thibaudet; Ashkenazy (January 28, 1996/D)

Prelude in C-sharp minor, Op. 3, No. 2—Sokoloff (May 14, 1928)

Rhapsody on a Theme of Paganini, Op. 43—Fleisher; Szell (October 26, 1956/E) / Thibaudet; Ashkenazy (March 22, 1993/D)

Symphony No. 2 in E minor, Op. 27—Sokoloff (May 1928)

RAVEL, MAURICE

Alborado del gracioso—Rodzinski (February 22, 1942) / Boulez (July 21, 1969/C) / Dohnányi (May 26, 1991/TD)

Le tombeau de Couperin—Boulez (May 2, 1999/DG)

Concerto for Piano (Left-Hand) in D major—Philippe Entremont, piano; Boulez (November 20, 1970/C)

Concerto for Piano in G major—Krystian Zimerman, piano; Boulez (November 13, 1994/DG)

Daphnis et Chloé—Cleveland Orchestra Chorus; Maazel (July 15/16/17, 1974/D)

Daphnis et Chloé Suite No. 2—Rodzinski (December 29, 1941) / Szell (January 11/12, 1963/E) / Cleveland Orchestra Chorus; Boulez (April 3, 1970/C) / Dohnányi (May 26, 1991/TD)

La valse—Ashkenazy (March 18, 1990) / Dohnányi (May 26, 1991/D)

Ma mère l'oye suite—Ashkenazy (March 17, 1990/D)

Menuet antique—Boulez (May 2, 1999/DG)

Pavane pour une infante défunte—Szell (January 12, 1963/E) / Boulez (April 3, 1970/C) / Boulez (May 2, 1999/DG)

Rapsodie espagnole—Rodzinski (December 15, 1940; April 14, 1941) / Boulez (July 21, 1969/C) / Ashkenazy (March 17, 1990/D)

Shéhérazade—Anne Sofie von Otter, mezzo-soprano; Boulez (April 19, 1999)

Valses nobles et sentimentales—Ashkenazy (March 18, 1990/D) / Boulez

(November 14, 1994/DG)

RESPIGHI, OTTORINO
The Pines of Rome—Maazel (May 10/14, 1976/D)
Roman Festivals—Maazel (May 10, 1976/D)

RIEGGER, WALLINGFORD
Dance Rhythms—Lane; Cleveland Pops Orchestra (July 14, 1961/E)

RIMSKY-KORSAKOV, NIKOLAI
Capriccio espagnole, Op 34—Szell (February 28, 1958; March 1, 1958/E) /
    Maazel (October 22, 1979/D)
Le coq d'or suite—Maazel (October 22/23, 1979/D)
Le coq d'or: Introduction and Wedding March—Lane; Cleveland Pops Orchestra
    (July 7, 1960/E)
Russian Easter Overture—Maazel (October 23, 1979/D)
Sadko: Song of India—Sokoloff (May 1, 1927)
Scheherazade, Op. 35—Rodzinski (December 20, 1939) / Maazel (October 10,
    1977/D)
Symphony No. 2, Op. 9 ("Antar")—Leinsdorf (February 22, 1946)

RODGERS, RICHARD
The Boys from Syracuse: "Falling in Love with Love"—Lane; Cleveland Pops
    Orchestra (July 7, 1960/E)
Jumbo: "The Most Beautiful Girl in the World "- Lane; Cleveland Pops Orchestra
    (July 7, 1960/E)
The King and I: "March of the Siamese Children"—Lane; Cleveland Pops
    Orchestra (July 7, 1960/E)
Love Me Tonight: "Lover"—Lane; Cleveland Pops Orchestra (July 7, 1960/E)
Oklahoma!: "Oh, What a Beautiful Morning"—Lane; Cleveland Pops Orchestra
    (July 7, 1960/E)
On Your Toes: "Slaughter on Tenth Avenue"—Lane; Cleveland Pops Orchestra
    (July 7, 1960/E)
State Fair: "It Might As Well Be Spring"—Lane; Cleveland Pops Orchestra (July
    12/13, 1961/E)

ROME, HAROLD
Fanny: Selections—Lane; Cleveland Pops Orchestra (July 12/13, 1961/E)

ROSSINI, GIOACCHINO
La gazza ladra overture—Szell (March 15, 1958/E) / Szell (May 5, 1967/C) /
    Maazel (August 26, 1975/D)
L'italiana in Algeri overture—Szell (May 5, 1967/C)
La scala di seta overture—Szell (May 5, 1967/C)
Il turco in Italia overture—Szell (May 5, 1967/C)
Il viaggio a Reims overture—Szell (May 5, 1967/C)

RUGGLES, CARL
Men and Mountains—Dohnányi (January 23, 1994/D)
Sun-Treader—Dohnányi (January 23, 1994/D)

SAINT-SAËNS, CAMILLE
Concerto for Cello in A minor, Op. 33—Harrell; Neville Marriner (October 30, 1981/D)
Danse macabre, Op. 40—Sokoloff (May 1927; abridged)

SCHOENBERG, ARNOLD
Piano Concerto, Op. 42—Mitsuko Uchida, piano; Boulez (May 8, 2000/DG)
Five Pieces for Orchestra, Op. 16—Robert Craft (March 13, 1964/C) / Dohnányi (January 21, 1991/D)

SCHUBERT, FRANZ
Marche militaire, Op. 51, No. 1—Lane; Cleveland Pops Orchestra (July 8, 1960/E)
Mass in G minor, D. 167: Credo—Cleveland Orchestra Chorus; Shaw (September 26, 1961/RCA)
Rosamunde, Op. 26, D. 797: Overture, Entr'acte No. 3, Ballet in G major—Szell (January 7, 1967/C)
Rosamunde, Entr'acte No. 3, Ballet in G major—Leinsdorf (February 25, 1946)
Symphony No. 1 in D major, D. 82—Lane (October 28, 1966/C)
Symphony No. 8 in B minor, D. 759 ("Unfinished")—Sokoloff (May 1928) / Szell (November 26, 1955/E) / Szell (March 12, 1960/E) / Dohnányi (October 22, 1983/T)
Symphony No. 9 in C major, D. 944 ("The Great")—Szell (November 1, 1957/E) / Szell (April 27/28, 1970/A) / Dohnányi (February 10, 1985/T)

SCHUMAN, WILLIAM
New England Triptych: "Chester"—Maazel (January 11, 1976; live noncommercial release)
A Song of Orpheus—Leonard Rose, cello; Szell (January 11, 1964/C)

SCHUMANN, ROBERT
Concerto for Cello in A minor, Op. 129—Harrell; Marriner (October 31, 1981/D)
Concerto for Piano in A minor, Op. 54—Fleisher; Szell (January 10, 1960/E)
Concerto for Violin in D minor, Op. Posth.—Joshua Bell, violin; Dohnányi (October 17, 1994/D)
Kinderszenen, Op. 15: "Traumerei"—Sokoloff (October 1924)
Manfred overture—Szell (January 21, 1958/E)
Symphony No. 1 in B-flat major, Op. 38 ("Spring")—Leinsdorf (February 24/25, 1946) / Szell (October 24/25, 1958/E) / Dohnányi (November 2, 1987/D)
Symphony No. 2 in C major, Op. 61—Szell (November 28, 1952/C) / Szell (October 21/24, 1960/E) / Dohnányi (February 15, 1988/D)
Symphony No. 3 in E-flat major, Op. 97 ("Rhenish")—Szell (October 21, 1960/E) / Dohnányi (November 2, 1987/D)
Symphony No. 4 in D minor, Op. 120—Szell (November 26, 1947/C) / Szell;

Music Appreciation Orchestra (October 19/20/21, 1955/BMC) / Szell (March 22, 1960) / Dohnányi (February 15, 1988/D)

SCRIABIN, ALEXANDER
Poem of Ecstasy—Maazel (May 8, 1978/D)

SHEPHERD, ARTHUR
Horizon: "The Old Chisholm Trail"—Lane; Cleveland Pops Orchestra (July 14, 1961/E)

SHOSTAKOVICH, DMITRI
Symphony No. 1 in F major, Op. 10—Rodzinski (April 14, 1941)
Symphony No. 5 in D minor, Op. 47—Rodzinski (February 22, 1942) / Maazel (May 5, 1981/C)
Symphony No. 10 in E minor, Op. 93—Dohnányi (February 12, 1990/D)
Symphony No. 15 in A major, Op. 141—Kurt Sanderling (March 17/18, 1991/ER)

SIBELIUS, JEAN
Finlandia, Op. 26—Sokoloff (October 1924) / Rodzinski (December 20, 1939) / Levi (April 2, 1984/T)
Kuolema: "Valse triste"—Sokoloff (October 1924) / Sokoloff (May 1928)
Romance in C major, Op. 42—Lane; Cleveland Sinfonietta (August 12, 1963/E)
Symphony No. 2 in D major, Op. 43—Levi (April 2, 1984/T)
Symphony No. 5 in E-flat major, Op. 82—Rodzinski (December 28, 1941)

SMETANA, BEDRICH
The Bartered Bride: Excerpts—Dohnányi (June 6, 1993/D)
The Bartered Bride overture—Szell (March 15, 1958/E)
The Bartered Bride: Three Dances—Szell (August 2, 1962; January 4/5, 1963/E)
The Kiss overture—Dohnányi (October 16, 1994/D)
Libuse overture—Dohnányi (January 24, 1994/D)
My Country: "The Moldau"—Szell; Music Appreciation Orchestra (December 24, 1954/BMC) / Szell (January 4/5, 1963/E) / Dohnányi (January 24, 1994/D)
Quartet No. 1 in E minor (orch. Szell)—Szell (April 26, 1949/C)
The Two Widows overture—Dohnányi (January 24, 1994/D)
The Two Widows: Ballet Music—Dohnányi (October 16, 1994/D)

STILL, WILLIAM GRANT
Afro-American Symphony: Lento—Maazel (January 11, 1976; live noncommercial release)

STRAUSS, EDUARD
Bahn frei, Op. 45 (arr. Peter Bodge)—Leinsdorf (February 25, 1946)

STRAUSS, JOHANN I
Radetzky March, Op. 228—Leinsdorf (February 25, 1946)

STRAUSS, JOHANN II

Die Fledermaus overture—Szell (March 1, 1958/E)
On the Beautiful Blue Danube—Sokoloff (October 1924) / Szell (January 5, 1962)
Perpetuum mobile, Op. 257—Leinsdorf (February 25, 1946) / Szell (January 5, 1962/E)
Pizzicato Polka (with Josef Strauss)—Szell (January 5, 1962/E)
Tales from the Vienna Woods, Op. 325—Sokoloff (October 1924)
Thunder and Lightning Polka, Op. 324—Leinsdorf (February 25, 1946)
Voices of Spring, Op. 410—Szell (January 5, 1962/E)

STRAUSS, JOSEF

Delieren, Op. 212—Szell (January 5, 1962/E)
Music of the Spheres, Op. 235—Leinsdorf (February 25, 1946)
Village Swallows from Austria, Op. 164—Szell (January 5, 1962/E)

STRAUSS, RICHARD

Ein Alpensinfonie—Ashkenazy (May 1, 1988/D)
Also sprach Zarathustra—Ashkenazy (July 11/12, 1988/D)
Aus Italien, Op. 16—Ashkenazy (July 9/10, 1989/D)
Concerto No. 1 for Horn in E-flat major, Op. 11—Myron Bloom, horn; Szell (October 12, 1961/E)
Don Juan, Op. 20—Szell (March 29/30, 1957/E) / Maazel (May 9, 1979/C) / Ashkenazy (July 9, 1989/D)
Don Quixote, Op. 35—Pierre Fournier, cello; Abraham Skernick, viola, Szell (October 28, 28, 1960/E) / Harrell; Vernon; Ashkenazy (July 14, 1985/D)
Ein Heldenleben, Op. 40—Josef Fuchs, violin; Rodzinski (December 11, 1939; January 12, 1940; December 14, 1940) / Majeske; Maazel (January 10, 1977/C) / Majeske; Ashkenazy (July 8, 1984/D) / Majeske; Dohnányi (January 27, 1992/D)
Der Rosenkavalier: Waltzes, Op. 59—Rodzinski (December 26, 1940)
Salome: Dance of the Seven Veils—Rodzinski (February 22, 1942) / Ashkenazy (July 14, 1985/D)
Sinfonia domestica, Op. 53—Szell (January 10, 1964/C)
Till Eulenspiegels lustige Streiche, Op. 28—Rodzinski (December 26, 1940) / Szell (April 25, 1949/C) / Szell; Music Appreciation Orchestra (December 24, 1954/BMC) / Szell (March29/30,1957/E) / Maazel (May 9, 1979/C) / Ashkenazy (July 11, 1988/D) / Dohnányi (August 8, 1991/D)
Tod und Verklärung, Op. 24—Szell (March 29/30, 1957/E) / Maazel (May 1979/C) / Ashkenazy (July 10, 1989/D)

STRAVINSKY, IGOR

Le baiser de la fée—Stravinsky (December 11, 1955/C) / Knussen (November 19, 1995/DG)
Le chant du rossignol—Boulez (February 25, 1996/DG)
Faun and the Shepherdess—Knussen (November 20, 1995/DG)
L'histoire du soldat—Boulez (February 26, 1996/DG)
Jeu de cartes—Stravinsky (March 13, 1964/C)
Ode for Orchestra—Stravinsky (March 13, 1964/C) / Knussen (November 19,

1995/DG)
L'oiseau de feu suite (1949)—Szell; Music Appreciation Orchestra (October
    19/20/21, 1955/BMC) / Szell (January 22/23, 1961; March 3, 1961/E)
Petrouchka—Boulez (March 3, 1991/DG)
Pulcinella—Mary Simmons, soprano; Glenn Schnittke, tenor; Philip MacGregor,
    bass; Stravinsky (December 14, 1952/C)
Le roi des étoiles—Boulez; Cleveland Orchestra Chorus (March 3, 1996/DG)
Le sacre du printemps—Boulez (July 28, 1969/C) / Maazel (May 14, 1980/T) /
    Chailly (November 10, 1985/D) / Boulez (March 11, 1991/DG)
Scherzo fantastique—Boulez (November 14, 1994/DG)
Symphony in C—Stravinsky (December 14, 1952/C)

TARTINI, GIUSEPPE
Concerto for Violin in D minor, D. 45—Szigeti, violin; Szell; Columbia Symphony
    Orchestra (January 15, 1954/C)

TCHAIKOVSKY, PETER ILYICH
1812 Overture, Op. 49—Sokoloff (January 23, 1924; abridged) / Sokoloff (May
    1927; abridged) / Rodzinski (probably Ringwall)(April 14, 1941)
Capriccio italien, Op. 45—Szell (February 28, 1958/E)
Concerto No. 1 for Piano in B-flat minor, Op. 23—Graffman, piano; Szell
    (January 24/25, 1969; March 20, 1969/C)
Concerto for Violin in D major, Op. 35—Bell, violin; Ashkenazy (April 25,
    1988/D)
Eugene Onegin: Waltz—Lane; Cleveland Pops Orchestra (July 13, 1961)
Eugene Onegin: Polonaise—Maazel (January 17, 1977/C) / Dohnányi (October
    28, 1986/T)
Marche slav, Op. 31—Rodzinski (probably Ringwall)(December 26, 1940) / Lane;
    Cleveland Pops Orchestra (July 8, 1960/E)
The Nutcracker: Suite—Maazel (October 5, 1981/C)
The Nutcracker: "Waltz of the Snowflake," "Waltz of the Flowers"—Lane;
    Cleveland Pops Orchestra (July 13, 1961/E)
Romeo and Juliet—Rodzinski (December 26, 1940) / Maazel (May 5, 1981/C) /
    Chailly (April 8, 1984/D)
Serenade for Strings, Op. 48: Waltz—Lane; Cleveland Pops Orchestra (July 13,
    1961/E)
The Sleeping Beauty: Waltz—Sokoloff (May 3, 1927) / Lane; Cleveland Pops
    Orchestra (July 13, 1961/E)
Swan Lake: Waltz—Lane; Cleveland Pops Orchestra (July 13, 1961/E)
Symphony No. 4 in F minor, Op. 36—Maazel (May 14, 1979/C) / Maazel
    (October 5, 1981/C)
Symphony No. 5 in E minor, Op. 64—Rodzinski (December 20, 1939; January 8,
    1940) / Szell (October 23/24, 1959/E) / Maazel (October 10, 1980/C)
Symphony No. 6 in B minor, Op. 74 ("Pathétique")—Maazel (October 4, 1981/C)
    / Dohnányi (October 28, 1986/T)
Variations on a Rococo Theme, Op. 33—Harrell, cellist; Maazel (October 19,
    1979/C)

THOMSON, VIRGIL
Louisiana Story: Acadian Songs and Dances—Lane; Cleveland Pops Orchestra
(July 12/13, 1961/E)

TOMMASINI, VINCENZO
The Good-Humored Ladies (after Scarlatti)—Lane (April 3, 1970/C)

VAUGHAN WILLIAMS, RALPH
The Lark Ascending—Druian, violin; Lane; Cleveland Sinfonietta (August 11,
1963/E)

VERDI, GIUSEPPE
Don Carlos: "Ballo della Regina"—Maazel (July 15/16/17, 1974/D)
La forza del destino overture—Maazel (August 26, 1975/D)
Otello: "Ballabili"—Maazel (July 15/16/17, 1974/D)
I vespri siciliani: "Le quattro stagioni"—Maazel (July 15/16/17, 1974/D)

VILLA-LOBOS, HEITOR
Bachianas Brasileiras No. 2 (Little Train of the Capira)—Lane; Cleveland Pops
Orchestra (July 22/23, 1959/E)

WAGNER, RICHARD
Eine Faust Overture—Szell (December 10, 1965/C)
Der fliegende Holländer overture—Szell (December 10, 1965/C)
Götterdämmerung: "Siegfried's Rhine Journey"—Szell (November 2, 1956/E) /
Szell (October 7/11/12, 1968/C)
Götterdämmerung: "Siegfried's Funeral Music"—Szell (November 2, 1956/E) /
Szell (October 7/11/12, 1968/C)
Götterdämmerung: "Brünnhilde's Immolation"—Szell (November 2, 1956/E) /
Szell (October 77/11/12, 1968/C)
Lohengrin: Prelude to Act I—Szell (December 10, 1965/C)
Lohengrin: Prelude to Act III—Sokoloff (October 1924; May 1, 1927)
Lohengrin: Wedding March—Sokoloff (October 1924; May 1, 1927)
Die Meistersinger von Nürnberg: Prelude—Szell (January 26, 1962/E)
Rienzi overture—Szell (December 10, 1965/C)
Das Rheingold—Robert Hale; Hanna Schwarz; Nancy Gustafson; Eike Wilm
Schulte; Thomas Sunnegardh; Kim Begley; Peter Schreier; Franz-Josef
Kapellmann; Jan Hendrik Rootering; Walter Fink; Gabriele Fontana;
Ildiko Komlosi; Margareta Hintermeier; Dohnányi (December 6/7/8/9,
1993/D)
Das Rheingold: "Entrance of the Gods into Valhalla"—Szell (October 77/11/12,
1968/C)
Die Walküre—Poul Elming; Alessandra Marc; Alfred Muff; Robert Hale;
Gabriele Schnaut; Anja Silja; Karin Goltz; Ruth Falcon; Susan Marie
Pierson; Michele Crider; Penelope Walker; Katherine Ciesinski; Susan
Shafer; Sandra Walker; Dohnányi (November 9/10/11/12/13/14/15,
1992/D)
Die Walküre: "Ride of the Valkyries"—Szell (November 2, 1956/E) / Szell

(October 7/11/12, 1968/C)

Die Walküre: "Magic Fire Music"—Szell (November 1956/E) / Szell
   (October7/11/12, 1968/C)

Die Walküre: "Wotan's Farewell"—Szell (November 2, 1965/C)

Siegfried: "Forest Murmurs"—Szell (November 2, 1956/E) / Szell (October
   7/11/12, 1968/C)

Tannhäuser Overture—Szell (January 26, 1962/E)

Tristan und Isolde: Prelude and Liebestod—Szell (January 26, 1962/E)

WALTON, WILLIAM

Henry V: Two Pieces for Strings—Lane; Cleveland Pops Orchestra (July 12/13,
   1961/E)

Partita for Orchestra—Szell (January 21, 1959/E)

Symphony No. 2—Szell (February 24, 1961; March 3, 1961/E)

Variations on a Theme by Hindemith—Szell (October 9, 1964/C)

The Wise Virgins—Lane (April 3, 1970/C)

WARLOCK, PETER

Serenade for Strings—Lane; Cleveland Sinfonietta (August 12, 1963/E)

WEBER, CARL MARIA VON

Der Freischütz overture—Rodzinski (February 22, 1942)

Invitation to the Dance—Dohnányi (October 29, 1989/D)

Konzertstück in F minor, Op. 79—Casadesus, piano; Szell (January 20, 1952/C)

Oberon overture—Szell (January 4/5, 1963/E)

WEBERN, ANTON

Five Pieces for Orchestra—Dohnányi (October 6, 1991/D)

Passacaglia—Dohnányi (January 27, 1992/D)

Six Pieces for Orchestra—Dohnányi (May 4, 1992/D)

Symphony, Op. 21—Dohnányi (May 19, 1991/D)

Variations for Orchestra—Dohnányi (October 6, 1991/D)

WEINBERGER, JAROMIR

Under the Spreading Chestnut Tree—Boris Goldovsky, piano; Rodzinski (January
   9/10, 1940)

WIENIAWSKI, HENRI

Concerto for Violin No. 2 in D minor, Op. 22—Bell, violin; Ashkenazy (April 25,
   1988/D)

Cleveland Orchestra Premieres

WORLD PREMIERES

Year	Composer	Work (and soloists)	Conductor
1924	Moore, Douglas	Four Museum Pieces	Douglas Moore
	Shepherd, Arthur	Overture to a Drama	Arthur Shepherd
1926	Cooley, Carlton	Song and Dance for Viola and Orchestra (Carlton Cooley)	Nikolai Sokoloff
1930	Schillinger, Joseph	First Airphonic Suite for RCA Theremin and Orchestra (Leon Theremin)	Nikolai Sokoloff
1931	Loeffler, Charles Martin	*Evocation* for Orchestra	Nikolai Sokoloff
	Smith, David Stanley	Symphony No. 3	David Stanley Smith
1932	Marin, Marais	Five Old French Dances for Solo Viola (Carlton Cooley, arranger/soloist)	Nikolai Sokoloff
	Shepherd, Arthur	Choreographic Suite— Four Dance Episodes	Nikolai Sokoloff
1933	Loeffler, Charles Martin	*Beat! Beat! Drums!* (Adelbert Glee Club)	Nikolai Sokoloff
1934	Cooley, Carlton	*Caponsacchi*, Epic Poem for Orchestra	Artur Rodzinski
1935	Franck, César (arr. Arthur Loesser)	Organ Chorale No. 1 in E major	Artur Rodzinski
	Josten, Werner	Serenade for Orchestra	Artur Rodzinski
	Smith, David Stanley	*Tomorrow*, An Overture	Artur Rodzinski
1936	Lockwood, Norman	*Erie*, Symphonic Poem	Artur Rodzinski
	Piston, Walter	Prelude and Fugue for Orchestra	Artur Rodzinski
1937	Rubinstein, Beryl	Concerto for Piano and Orchestra (Beryl Rubinstein)	Artur Rodzinski
1939	Bloch, Ernest	Concerto for Violin and Orchestra (Joseph Szigeti)	Dimitri Mitropoulos
1940	Shepherd, Arthur	Symphony No. 2	Arthur Shepherd
1941	Harris, Roy	Folk-Song Symphony for Chorus and Orchestra (Cleveland Philharmonic Chorus)	Artur Rodzinski

1942	Kern, Jerome	Scenario for Orchestra on Themes from *Show Boat*	Artur Rodzinski
	Schuman, William	Symphony No. 4	Artur Rodzinski
1944	Bach, J. S.	Chorale Prelude, "Nun komm, der Heide"	Erich Leinsdorf
	Holden, David	Rhapsody, *Say Paw*	Erich Leinsdorf
	Lopatnikoff, Nikolai	Opus Sinfonicum	Erich Leinsdorf
	Martinů, Bohuslav	Symphony No. 2	Erich Leinsdorf
1945	Gould, Morton	Concerto for Orchestra	Vladimir Golschmann
	Still, William Grant	Poem for Orchestra	Rudolph Ringwall
1946	Brahms, Johannes	Two Chorale Preludes from the Eleven Chorale Preludes for Organ, Op. 22 (arr. Leinsdorf)	Erich Leinsdorf
1947	Copland, Aaron	*Letter from Home*	George Szell
	Hindemith, Paul	Concerto for Piano and Orchestra (Jesus Maria Sanroma)	George Szell
1948	Elwell, Herbert	Pastorale for Voice and Orchestra	George Szell
	Schnabel, Artur	Rhapsody for Orchestra	George Szell
	Toch, Ernest	*Hyperion*, A Dramatic Prelude	George Szell
1950	Bach, J. S.	Three Fugues from "The Art of the Fugue"	George Szell
	Dello Joio, Norman	Serenade for Orchestra	George Szell
1951	Dick, Marcel	Symphony	Dimitri Mitropoulos
1953	Martinů, Bohuslav	Rhapsody-Concerto for Viola and Orchestra (Jascha Veissi)	George Szell
	Shepherd, Arthur	Theme and Variations	George Szell
1954	Elwell, Herbert	*The Forever Young*, A Ritual for Soprano (Marie Kraft)	George Szell
1956	Turner, Charles	*Encounter*	George Szell
1957	Babin, Victor	Concerto No. 2 for Two Pianos and Orchestra (Vitya Vronsky and Victor Babins)	George Szell
	Dick, Marcel	Capriccio for Orchestra	Marcel Dick
	Rogers, Bernard	Portrait for Violin and Orchestra (Josef Gingold)	George Szell
1958	Blacher, Boris	*Music for Cleveland*	George Szell
	Creston, Paul	Toccata	George Szell
	Einem, Gottfried von	Ballade for Orchestra	George Szell
	Etler, Alvin	Concerto in One Movement	George Szell
	Hanson, Howard	*Mosaics*	George Szell
	Martinů, Bohuslav	*The Rock*	George Szell
	Mennin, Peter	Concerto for Piano and Orchestra (Eunice Podis)	George Szell
	Moevs, Robert	Symphony in Three Movements	George Szell

	Walton, William	Partita	George Szell
1959	Rochberg, George	Symphony No. 2	George Szell
1960	Meyerowitz, Jan	*Flemish Overture:Homage to Pieter Breughel*	Robert Shaw
	Whittaker, Howard	Two Murals for Orchestra	George Szell
1961	Blackwood, Easley	Symphony No. 2	George Szell
	Piston, Walter	Symphonic Prelude	George Szell
1962	Hanson, Howard	*Bold Island* Suite	George Szell
1963	Dick, Marcel	Adagio and Rondo	Marcel Dick
1964	Mennin, Peter	Symphony No. 7	George Szell
1965	Barber, Samuel	*Night Flight*	George Szell
	Dutilleux, Henri	*Cinq Métaboles*	George Szell
1966	Babbitt, Milton	*Relata*	Gunther Schuller
1968	Erb, Donald	*Christmasmusic*	Louis Lane
1969	Smith, Russell	Magnificat for Chorus, Soprano and Orchestra	Robert Shaw
1972	Erb, Donald	*The Seventh Trumpet*	Louis Lane
1974	Siegmeister, Elie	Symphony No. 4	Lorin Maazel
1975	Bamert, Matthias	*Once Upon an Orchestra*	James Judd
1976	Erb, Donald	Music for a Festive Occasion	Lorin Maazel
	Kurtz, Eugene	Three Songs from *Medea* (orchestrated version)	Lorin Maazel
	Premru, Raymond	Concerto for Orchestra	Lorin Maazel
	Walker, George	Dialogus for Cello and Orchestra (Stephen Geber)	Lorin Maazel
1977	Druckman, Jacob	*Chiaroscuro*	Lorin Maazel
	Harris, Donald	*On Variations*	Kenneth Jean
	Tal, Josef	Concerto No. 6 for Piano and Electronics (Joela Jones, piano)	Lorin Maazel
	Wuorinen, Charles	Tashi Concerto (Tashis)	Charles Wuorinen
1978	Humel, Gerhard	*Lepini*	Lorin Maazel
1979	Foss, Lukas	Quintets for Orchestra	Lukas Foss
1980	Bamert, Matthias	*Keepsake*	Matthias Bamert
1981	Gould, Morton	*Burchfield Gallery*	Lorin Maazel
1984	Miller, Donald	*Simple Gifts*	staff conductors
1985	Lang, David	*Eating Living Monkeys*	Christoph von Dohnányi
	Miller, Donald	*Kaleidoscope*	staff conductors

	Wuorinen, Charles	*Movers and Shakers*	Christoph von Dohnányi
1986	Miller, Donald	*Olympian Games*	staff conductors
1987	Miller, Donald	*Clap Hands* March	staff conductors
1988	Glass, Philip	*The Light*	Christoph von Dohnányi
	Trojahn, Manfred	Variations for Orchestra	Christoph von Dohnányi
1989	Eberhard, Dennis	*The Bells of Elsinore*	Christoph von Dohnányi
	Premru, Raymond	Symphony No. 2	Vladimir Ashkenazy
1990	Oliviero, James	Timpani Concerto (Paul Yancich)	Christoph von Dohnányi
1991	Osterfield, Paul	*Copyright 1990*	staff conductors
	Schnittke, Alfred	Concerto Grosso No. 5 (Gidon Kremer, violin; Alexander Slobodyanik, piano)	Christoph von Dohnányi
	Smith, Steven C.	*Shake, Rattle and Roll*	Jahja Ling
	Zwilich, Ellen Taaffe	Concerto for Oboe and Orchestra (John Mack)	Christoph von Dohnányi
1992	Rainsong, Lisa	*Straight Ahead* for Percussion	staff conductors
	Willi, Herbert	Concerto for Orchestra	Christoph von Dohnányi
1993	Conner, Jennifer	*Winter Hours Yesteryear*	staff conductors
	Demos, Nikitis J.	*The Little Engine*	staff conductors
	Shostakovich, Dmitri	Suite from *Hypothetically Murdered* (reconstructed from sketches and orchestrated by Gerard McBurney)	Leonard Slatkin
	Singleton, Alvin	*Durch Alles*	Jahja Ling
1994	Erb, Donald	*Evensong*	Christoph von Dohnányi
	Ryan, Jeffrey	*Ricochet*	staff conductors
	Taddie, Daniel	*Abacus*	staff conductors
1995	Paulus, Stephen	Concerto for String Quartet and Orchestra (Cleveland Quartets)	Christoph von Dohnányi
1996	Eberhard, Dennis	*Crooked River Oracle*	Christoph von Dohnányi
	Newman, Thomas	*Reach Forth Our Hands* (Debra Winger, narrator)	Jahja Ling
	Williams, John	Trumpet Concerto (Michael Sachs)	Christoph von Dohnányi
1997	Adams, John	*Century Rolls*—Concerto for Piano and Orchestra (Emanuel Ax)	Christoph von Dohnányi
	Carter, Elliott	Allegro scorrevole	Christoph von Dohnányi
1998	Schoenfield, Paul	Viola Concerto (Robert Vernon)	Christoph von Dohnányi
	Rathbun, Jeffrey	*Three Psalms of Jerusalem*	Leonard Slatkin
	Ives, Charles	Emerson Concerto (Alan Feinberg, piano)	Christoph von Dohnányi
1999	Rouse, Christopher	*Der gerettete Alberich* — Percussion Concerto	Christoph von Dohnányi

		(Evelyn Glennie)	
	Lindberg, Magnus	*Cantigas*	Christoph von Dohnányi
	Underhill, Nicholas	Concertante for Four Flutes	Christoph von Dohnányi
		(Joshua Smith, Martha Aarons,	
		John Rautenberg, Mary Kay Finks)	
2000	Birtwistle, Harrison	*Sonance Severance 2000*	Christoph von Dohnányi
	Rathbun, Jeffrey	*Motions for Cellos*	Christoph von Dohnányi
	Dalbavie, Marc-André	*Concertante il suono*	Pierre Boulez
	Thomas, Augusta Read	*Song in Sorrow*	Jahja Ling
		(Christine Brewer, Nanette Canfield,	
		Shari Pachinger, Stephanie Sikora,	
		Elaine Stockmeier, sopranos;	
		Laura Avdey, mezzo-soprano;	
		Elizabeth Stuart, alto;	
		Blossom Festival Chorus)	
	Horner, James	*A Forest Passage*	Jahja Ling

United States Premieres

1923	Casella, Alfredo	*Pupazetti* (Five Pieces for Marionettes)	Alfredo Casella
1924	Bridge, Frank	Suite, *The Sea*	Frank Bridge
1925	Enesco, Georges	Dance of the Theban Shepherds	Georges Enesco
1929	Schillinger, Joseph	March of the Orient	Nikolai Sokoloff
	Schubert, Franz	Symphony in E major, D. 729	Nikolai Sokoloff
		(orch. by John Francis Barnett)	
1930	Rivier, Jean	*Overture to a Don Quixote*	Nikolai Sokoloff
1931	Krein, Alexander	*The Rose and Cross*, Op. 26,	Nikolai Sokoloff
		Symphonic Fragments	
	Lazar, Filip	*The Ring*, Music for Orchestra No. 2	Nikolai Sokoloff
	Mosolov, Alexander	*The Foundry*	Nikolai Sokoloff
1934	Szymanowski, Karol	Symphonie Concertante	
		No. 4 for Piano	Artur Rodzinki
		(Severin Eisenberger)	
1935	Kassem, Thaddeus	Concerto for Voice and Orchestra	Artur Rodzinski
		(Eva Bandrowska)	
	Shostakovich, Dmitri	*Lady Macbeth of Mzensk*	Artur Rodzinski
		(complete opera)	
1936	Saminsky, Lazar	*Ausonia*, Italian Pages	Artur Rodzinski
	Shostakovich, Dmitri	Suite from *The Golden Age*	Artur Rodzinski
	Vaughan Williams, Ralph	Symphony No. 4	Artur Rodzinski
1937	Barber, Samuel	Symphony No. 1	Artur Rodzinski
	Szymanowski, Karol	*Harnasie*	Artur Rodzinski
		(Cleveland Philharmonic Chorus;	
		Marie Simmelink-Kraft, mezzo-soprano;	
		Edward Kane, tenor)	

1940	Walton, William	Concerto for Violin and Orchestra (Jascha Heifetz)	Artur Rodzinski
1943	Bartók, Béla	Violin Concerto No. 2 (Tossy Spivakovsky)	Artur Rodzinski
1949	Gal, Hans	*A Pickwickian Overture*	George Szell
1950	Poulenc, Francis	Sinfonietta	George Szell
1951	Jirak, Karel Boleslav	Symphonic Variations	Rudolph Ringwall
	Krenek, Ernst	Symphonic Elegy	Dimitri Mitropoulos
1954	Blacher, Boris	Variations for Orchestra on a Theme by Paganini, Op. 26	George Szell
	Bloch, Ernest	Sinfonia Breve	George Szell
1956	Andriessen, Hendrik	Symphonic Etude	Eduard van Beinem
1957	Donatoni, Franco	Concerto for Strings, Brass and Solo Timpani (Cloyd Duff, timpani)	George Szell
	Martinů, Bohuslav	*The Frescoes of Piero della Francesca*	George Szell
	Villa-Lobos, Heitor	Concerto No. 5 for Piano and Orchestra (Felicia Blumental)	George Szell
1959	Jolivet, André	Symphony de danses	George Szell
	Liebermann, Rolf	Geigy Festival Concerto for Side Drum and Orchestra (Robert Pangborn)	George Szell
	Lutoslawski, Witold	Concerto for Orchestra	Stanislaw Skrowaczewski
	Rodrigo, Joaquin	Concierto de Aranjuez (Rey de la Torre, guitar)	Robert Shaw
1960	Laajtha, Laszlo	Symphony No. 5	George Szell
	Skrowaczewski, Stanislaw	Symphony for Strings	Stanislaw Skrowaczewski
1961	Leeuw, Ton de	Mouvements retrogrades	George Szell
	Rogalski, Theodor	Three Rumanian Dances	Georges Georgescu
	Strauss, Johann II	New Pizzicato Polka	George Szell
	Walton, William	Symphony No. 2	George Szell
1962	Barraud, Henry	Rapsodie Cartesienne	George Szell
	Britten, Benjamin	*Cantata Academica— Carmen Basiliense*, Op. 62	George Szell
	Jolivet, André	*Les Amantes Magnifiques*	George Szell
	Kodaly, Zoltan	Symphony	George Szell
	Pascal, Claude	Cello Concerto (Andre Navarra)	George Szell
1963	Walton, William	Variations on a Theme by Hindemith	George Szell
1967	Chávez, Carlos	*Resonances*	George Szell
	Henze, Hans Werner	Quattro Poemi	Louis Lane
	Messiaen, Olivier	*Chronochromie*	Georges Prêtre
1968	Martin, Frank	Cello Concerto (Pierre Fournier)	George Szell

1970	Henze, Hans Werner	Compasses for Viola and 22 Players	Matthias Bamert
	Serebrier, Jose	Fantasia for String Orchestra	Louis Lane
1972	Parodi, Renato	*Capitoli*	Aldo Ceccato
1974	Beyer, Frank Michael	Rondeau	Lorin Maazel
	Bucht, Gunnar	Symphony No. 7	James DePreist
	Constant, Marius	*Candide* for Harpsichord and Orchestra (Elisabeth Chojnacka)	Matthias Bamert
	Taranu, Cornel	*Incantations*	Lawrence Foster
1975	Zimmermann, Bernd A.	*Stille und Umkehr*	Lorin Maazel
1976	Berio, Luciano	*Calmo* (Cathy Berberian, soprano)	Luciano Berio
	Blacher, Boris	Blues, Espagnola and Rumba Philharmonica for 12 Violoncelli Soli	Lorin Maazel
1977	Schurmann, Gerard	Variants for Small Orchestra	Lorin Maazel
1978	Kelterborn, Rudolf	Traummusik, Six Pieces for Small Orchestra	Matthias Bamert
1979	Kokkonen, Joonas	Symphony No. 4	Lorin Maazel
	Xenakis, Iannis	*Eridanos*	Lukas Foss
1980	Dutilleux, Henri	*Tout un monde lointain...* (Mstislav Rostropovich, cello)	Lorin Maazel
1981	Amy, Gilbert	Adagio and Stretto	Lorin Maazel
	Berio, Luciano	Coro (Cologne Radio Chorus)	Lorin Maazel
	Ginastera, Alberto	*Iubilum*, Symphonic Celebration, Op. 51	Yoel Levi
1985	Henze, Hans Werner	*I sentimenti di Carl Philipp Emanuel Bach*	Hans Werner Henze
	Henze, Hans Werner	Symphony No. 5	Hans Werner Henze
	Schnittke, Alfred	Violin Concerto No. 4 (Gidon Kremer)	Christoph von Dohnányi
1986	Cerha, Friedrich	Songs from *Baal* (Theo Adam, bass-baritone)	Friedrich Cerha
1987	Zemlinsky, Alexander	*Die Seejungfrau*	Christoph von Dohnányi
1989	Berio, Luciano	Formazioni	Luciano Berio
1990	Davies, Peter Maxwell	Strathclyde Concerto No. 2 (Ralph Kirshbaum, cello)	Christoph von Dohnányi
	Davies, Peter Maxwell	Symphony No. 3	Peter Maxwell Davies
1992	Holliger, Heinz	*Turm-Musik*	Heinz Holliger
	Ran, Shulamit	Concert Piece	Christoph von Dohnányi
1993	Copland, Aaron	*Grohg*	Oliver Knussen
	Messiaen, Olivier	*La ville d'en-haut*	Pierre Boulez

1991	Adams, John	Choruses from *The Death of Klinghoffer* (Cleveland Orchestra Chorus)	John Adams
1994	Birtwistle, Harrison	*Earth Dances*	Christoph von Dohnányi
1995	Knussen, Oliver	Horn Concerto (Barry Tuckwell)	Oliver Knussen
1999	Anderson, Julian	*Stations of the Sun*	Oliver Knussen

Index

Photograph numbers are indicated with a "P" (e.g., P123); photographs are arranged sequentially on non-numbered pages in three sections.

About the Author

DONALD ROSENBERG is the classical music critic for *The Plain Dealer* and vice president of the Music Critics Association of North America. He was formerly music and dance critic of the *Akron Beacon Journal* and *The Pittsburgh Press*. His writing has appeared in *Symphony Magazine, Opera News, Opera* (London), *Musical America,* and other publications. An accomplished French horn player, he has performed at the Aspen and Marlboro music festivals. He is a graduate of the Mannes College of Music (Bachelor of Music degree) and the Yale School of Music (Master of Music and Master of Musical Arts degrees). He was born in New York City and lives in Shaker Heights, Ohio.